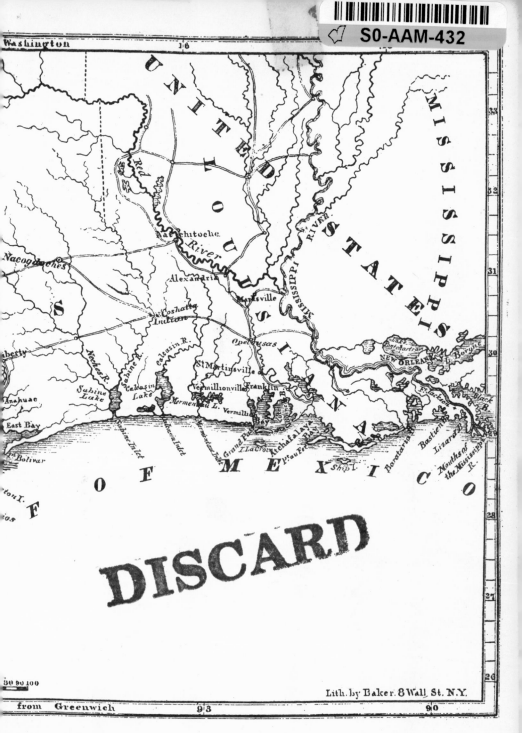

Lith. by Baker. 8 Wall. St. N.Y.

BOOKS BY HERBERT GAMBRELL

Anson Jones: The Last President of Texas
Mirabeau Buonaparte Lamar, Troubadour and Crusader
A Social and Political History of Texas (with L. W. Newton)

ANSON JONES

The Last President of Texas

ANSON JONES

The Last President of Texas

BY

HERBERT GAMBRELL

FOREWORD BY
WILLIAM RANSOM HOGAN

UNIVERSITY OF TEXAS PRESS · AUSTIN

SECOND EDITION

With Annotation and Enlarged Bibliography

For Virginia

CONTENTS

FOREWORD

In the spring and summer of 1845, as the tenth year of the independent existence of the Republic of Texas began, President Anson Jones, M.D., saw a long-nurtured plan materialize. He was able to present to the people of the border commonwealth a choice —annexation to the United States or full independence recognized at long last by Mexico and guaranteed by Great Britain and France. For four weary years—first as Secretary of State and then as President—he had labored and schemed for this moment. Logic dictated the correctness of his course. Texas had been rebuffed several times in its attempts to join the American Union. If annexation finally was to be achieved, why not use this alternative to secure the best possible terms?

But logic did not determine popular sentiment. Public meetings everywhere demanded annexation, immediate and unqualified. Frenzy for the move was whipped up by a swarm of official and unofficial agents of the United States. President Jones was flayed on every platform in Texas as a self-seeking tool of British intrigue, and serious attempts were made to remove him from office.

In insisting that the Republic of Texas maintain her international obligations to the end and that she enter the Union with dignity and on the most favorable terms, Doctor Jones achieved political oblivion and violent, unreasoning condemnation. During the next twelve years he became more and more isolated and depressed. Finally, after an accident left him with a withered arm and after a state legislature gave him not one vote in selecting two new United States senators, he committed suicide.

His widow soon arranged to publish a bulky manuscript which her husband had prepared, a manuscript that attempted to defend his course of action as Secretary of State and President, but instead revealed the writer as a man of twisted mind and warped recollections, in which his former colleague, Sam Houston, was always the villain.

The book written by Anson Jones (which by no means adequately pictured the Jones of pre-Annexation days), the legendary conception of Sam Houston as the only master of diplomacy in Texas (a view sedulously cultivated by several biographers of Houston), and an uncritical acceptance (by historians) of the anti-Jones bitterness of 1845 and 1846 as the correct view—all have served to stamp Anson Jones as the churlish little doctor whose brief period of glory went to his head. I am among those who have been guilty of these misconceptions. But I hereby hasten to recant.

On February 19, 1846, when President Jones delivered his valedictory address at the ceremony transforming his republic into a state, he expressed confidence that his fellow citizens would judge him rightly and that "history and posterity will do me no wrong." He was almost incorrect on both counts. But Herbert Gambrell now, more than a century later, has fixed Jones in his proper place in Texas and diplomatic history. He has done even more. He has written a book that is not only instructive but entertaining, a feat which heretofore I have believed virtually impossible—if the subject was Dr. Anson Jones. Between 1833 and 1846 the doctor's life was intertwined with most of the major events in Texas, and Gambrell illuminates all of them. After lively accounts of Stephen F. Austin's colonization activities, the development of the Texas Revolution, and the San Jacinto campaign, this volume launches into the most perceptive account of the diplomacy and politics of the Republic of Texas ever written. And the social history of the various capitals of the Republic is unforgettably etched into the background. All this, and Jones too.

When Anson Jones, M.D., drifted to Texas in 1833, he was following the path of least resistance. He had been a failure as a physician, a businessman, and a personality. But during the next twenty-six months he established himself as the leading physician in the Brazoria community in Texas and enjoyed the only period of tranquillity he was ever to know. He served in the Texas Army in 1836, first as a private and after San Jacinto as apothecary general, a glorified title that was equivalent to assistant surgeon general. After the Texas Revolution he entered politics by spearheading the opposition to the gigantic speculative scheme called the

Texas Rail Road, Navigation, and Banking Company, and was elected to the lower house of the Second Congress of the Republic. Here "Mr. Jones of B." took an intelligent interest in educational policy, became a master of legislative protocol, and began a serious study of foreign relations—a study that was to become his vocation. Jones next became minister to the United States in Washington, where he succeeded in developing contacts with the foreign ministers of Great Britain and France that greatly enhanced the interest of their governments in Texas. Before he returned to Brazoria he had been elected to the Senate of the Congress of the Republic, and—as every casual student of Texas history knows—he subsequently served as Secretary of State during Houston's second term in the Presidency and then as fourth President of the Republic.

The chief historical problem presented by the life of Anson Jones is to determine whether he was Sam Houston's pawn in the development of the foreign policy of angling simultaneously for annexation and recognition of independence. When Jones was running for President he wrote to one of his campaign managers: "If there be a community in our principles, I claim the rights of a *partner* [with Houston], not a mere *dependent beneficiary.*" Gambrell brilliantly demonstrates that, at least in foreign policy, the Jones claim of partnership was more than justified. Moreover, on at least one occasion Secretary of State Jones prevented President Houston from making a serious and almost irrevocable mistake, and later succeeded in gaining the Presidency in the face of a decided wavering of support from the outgoing Chief Executive.

The principal critical problems presented to the biographer of Anson Jones as an individual are to explain how a man who had failed in early life became a President and why he later committed suicide. Gambrell is manifestly successful in solving both problems, but just *how* he manages to maintain a notable level of reader interest is indeed puzzling. Some readers may be inclined to charge that he is a sort of literary alchemist, for he makes no effort to present the physician-diplomat-President as an exciting or lovable person. The explanation I favor, however, is that Mr. Gambrell of Dallas has something that Mr. Jones of Brazoria lacked. He has the most sprightly sense of humor I have encountered in the pages of a serious book. This is one of the qualities that make this the most readable and one of the three or four most important Texas historical works ever published. First-rate Texas history cannot be written without a sense of the ridiculous and a leaven of humor.

The foregoing is substantially what I wrote in the *Southwest Review* about Gambrell's *Anson Jones* a few months after the first edition was published in 1948. With the wisdom supposedly generated by advancing age, I have become disenchanted with most of my former favorable evaluations of books—but this one has had the opposite effect. As an exercise in self-criticism, therefore, I recently consulted the major reviews of the first edition. I do not know what J. Frank Dobie and Henry Nash Smith now think about *Anson Jones*, but in 1948 they equaled and in some respects exceeded my praise. In the *Saturday Review of Literature* Dobie wrote of the author's "power and skill and play of wit" that enabled him to develop history along with the unfolding of Jones' mind and character in a manner usually found only in "great plays and novels." "The achievement is high art," he concluded. In the *Herald-Tribune* Smith stated that "even when Mr. Gambrell is dealing with the pompous exchanges of diplomats and politicians, he writes with wisdom, a shrewd grasp of motives, and a quiet but pervasive humor." He added—and I bless him for his choice of words—that Gambrell's style has "deceptively easy paragraphs" that have "a quality that can be described only by the old-fashioned term elegance."

These authoritative evaluations serve to strengthen me in my conviction that Gambrell's *Anson Jones* combines the virtues (but not the less admirable qualities) of Eugene C. Barker's scholarly biography of Stephen F. Austin and of Marquis James' less accurate but engagingly written life of Houston. The University of Texas Press deserves nothing but approbation for reprinting *Anson Jones,* and for adding the citations of sources lacking in previous editions. The thoroughly researched and generously presented annotation and the enlarged and basically revised Bibliography add still more to the values which lovers of history will find in this new edition of a fully satisfying biography. I hope that the Press will keep it in print at least long enough for my grandchildren's grandchildren to purchase individual copies.

WILLIAM R. HOGAN

ANSON JONES
The Last President of Texas

PROLOGUE

LATE in October 1833, when Captain Jeremiah Brown's schooner *Sabine* dropped anchor at the mouth of the Brazos de Dios in the Mexican state of Coahuila y Texas, a disheveled and spiritless passenger took a long look at the coast of Texas.

Although the stretch of sandy beach was not without its attractions, the view held little charm for the newcomer. Around a flimsy structure that had once housed a Mexican garrison, stood on unsteady foundations a public house for strangers, four or five shanties for the permanent residents, two little stores. This was the port of Velasco, gateway to the Anglo-American settlements. It did not impress this citizen of Philadelphia, lately resident in New Orleans. The Brazos itself, always an unlovely stream—muddy, with low, raw banks, its mouth almost closed by a sand bar around which drifted flotsam and jetsam and wreckage—was just getting back into its banks after a devastating overflow. The immigrant's first glimpse of Texas did not reassure him.

Captain Brown's passenger was a man of undistinguished appearance, average in height and weight, with reddish hair and heavy-lidded hazel eyes. By his own confession, life had brought him only a succession of failures. Since leaving his New England home in 1816, he wrote:

I had struggled almost in vain against innumerable obstacles, and finally abandoning myself to a fate which it appeared I could not control or direct, I passively floated as it were upon the tide which bore me to Texas. . . . My sixteen years previous to 1833 had given me that *schooling* in the knowledge of the world at thirty-five, which men properly trained in early life generally have at *twenty-five*.

He had, however, sufficient knowledge of what he liked in this world to pass quick judgment on Brazoria, "the principal commercial town in this country" when he went twenty miles inland to view it. If he remained in Texas, Brazoria was to be his home: but a brief reconnaissance of the town, its environs, its prospects, and its inhabitants sufficed. He wanted no part of it: "I forthwith engaged my passage back to New Orleans on the return trip of the vessel." He had in his wallet just two dollars more than the price of a return passage; but at the moment it seemed to him better to starve in civilization than to earn a living in this miasmic wilderness.

But before he could get away his luck and the whole pattern of existence began to change. The *Sabine* sailed without him. Although he was a little slow in sensing it, he had arrived at his permanent home and was able eventually to convince himself that "somehow or other the destiny of Texas was interwoven with my own, that they were indissoluble, and that the one depended materially upon the other."

Within a dozen years this adventurer-in-spite-of-himself was to puzzle foreign ministers and diplomatists on two continents. He was to play a hand in a game for fabulous stakes, and there would be a time when statesmen at London and Paris and Washington watched him more closely than they did each other. It was a game that determined the course of American and, to a certain extent, world history.

Destiny had this role in store for Anson Jones, M.D., when he drifted into Texas in the fall of 1833.

I

THIRTEENTH CHILD

ANSON JONES'S early years were drab and bleak, like those of many another New Englander who grew up during the quarter century that included the War of 1812. His parents, Solomon and Sarah Strong Jones, were an honest and industrious couple who wore themselves out trying to wrest a living from the stubborn soil of western Massachusetts.

Anson, the thirteenth of their fourteen children, was born near Great Barrington on January 20, 1798, and his earliest recollections were of that "pleasant little village in Berkshire county, on the banks of the Housatonic . . . about five miles from the line of the State of New York, and ten from that of Connecticut." The town had been settled originally by the Dutch in 1730, and although by the end of the century almost all its inhabitants were farmer folk of English extraction, something of a Dutch flavor still remained. "Its politics," William Cullen Bryant noted when he located there in 1816, "are highly Federal."

But the youngest of the Jones boys was not brought up in the town and politics had little meaning for him while he lived in New England. His father was a tenant farmer and tanner who was driven by economic necessity to move his numerous family and small store of goods from one scrubby farm to another at frequent intervals. During the first eighteen years of Anson's life the family moved ten times within the limits of Berkshire County.

But for all that, there was good English blood in their veins, and the economic hardships among which Anson Jones was reared were of recent origin. His first American ancestor was William Jones, son of Colonel Sir John Jones and Catherine Cromwell, sister of the Protector, who ended his fifteen-year term as "Deputy Govr of New Haven & Connecticut" in 1698, exactly a century before Anson was born. Anson Jones could therefore, and did in his last years, trace his descent from Thomas Cromwell and John Hampden; and the Cromwell arms eventually were engraved on his table service. But Anson's father had been left an orphan at the age of seven and, coming to manhood in the disordered period of the Revolution without a nest egg, he failed to accumulate property or even a competence.

Anson learned his A B Cs in the country school taught by his sister Sarah; a little later he trudged five miles a day to a school at Egremont Plains; and, when he was ten or eleven, he "completed his English studies" under the tutelage of the Episcopal rector of Great Barrington, a brother of Bishop Griswold. When the second war with England began, Anson, then fourteen, was eager to help defend Boston against British redcoats, but his father, who had fought at Bunker Hill and had seen Burgoyne surrender at Saratoga, willed otherwise. He placed the youngster in Lenox Academy to begin the study of languages and mathematics while he himself joined other veterans of 1776 in the Silver Grays. A term at the academy completed Anson's formal schooling.

My father being very poor [he wrote], I was obliged to work and assist him in his business, and attend to my studies as I could find leisure and opportunity. . . . I studied with my book on the bench before me, while at work making harness, and obtained much of my education at "night schools," after working hard all day.

It was in a grim struggle for existence and for learning that this boy who was "fond of reading and study" but whose "constitution was very feeble and general health and strength delicate" passed the drab years of his New England boyhood. He was not fond of play and seldom had time for it; in spite of the large family of which he was a member, he somehow failed to learn that easy give-and-take which would have stood him in good stead in his struggle with the world.

The death of his mother and the consequent breakup of the home, together with a more acute realization of his father's poverty, precipitated Anson's first major crisis when he was eighteen. He must now choose a vocation and make his way in the world. But the decision of what he should do was made by his father and three older sisters, rather than by Anson himself—perhaps because he was the youngest boy and the most delicate member of the family, perhaps because he had already delayed too long in making up his own mind.

His brothers, practical and struggling men of business—Ira in Toronto and William in a saddlery shop at Utica—wanted Anson to learn a trade, and the boy was willing. While the family were debating the question of Anson's career, Solomon Jones one day took his son to inspect the plant of the Pittsfield *Sun*. It was Anson's first visit to a printing office, but he decided on the spot that he should become a printer. The trade did not require bodily strength and afforded endless opportunities for reading and study; yet "father failed for some reason to make any arrangement for the purpose."

The fact was that Anson's father and sisters, like the poor of all generations, had destined this youngest and puniest boy for a learned profession and had set their hearts on making a physician of him. "Notwithstanding I expressed my preference for this business," he said, "it was concluded that I should study medicine." But the decision was not hastily agreed to. The better part of a year passed between the death of his mother and Anson's final acquiescence, a step which "entailed years of unhappiness" upon him.

He had misgivings as to his fitness for the career that had been chosen for him. His father was poor and his solvent brothers still opposed the course he had agreed to take. He was physically weak, "shy and timid to a fault," without knowledge of the world, and "had no wealthy or efficient friends." Nor had his intellectual training been systematic or well rounded, although he had managed to acquire what he considered "a good English education and a tolerable acquaintance with Latin and Greek, and knew a little of mathematics." But the decision had been made, and, against his better judgment, Anson Jones at eighteen was dedicated to medicine. Of this decision, he declared a third of a century later, "If it were to make again I certainly should take a different course. Nor would I ever advise a youth, situated as I was, to make the choice I did, for, although some do succeed under such circumstances . . . success I should say, by my experience, is too dearly purchased."

In 1817 Anson Jones, shrinking from the very "idea of making an effort to obtain a profession" and almost certain that he could never succeed in medicine, left the rented homestead and glumly took the forty-mile road to the home of his sisters at Litchfield, Connecticut, to commence his professional studies.

The training of physicians by the apprentice system was the rule, for the day of medical colleges had hardly begun. Reading medicine under a practitioner (who had been trained in the same manner) consisted of helping the physician set bones and compound drugs, sweeping out his office, keeping his records, looking after his horses, and reading whatever his probably scant library afforded. If the neophyte was able to attend "medical lectures" for a month or two following his apprenticeship, so much the better; but ordinarily a certificate from his master and some sort of examination before the censors of the local medical society were sufficient to enable him to set up in practice for himself. Success under such a system depended upon the apprentice's self-assurance and his interest in the healing art. The timid soul was likely to make indifferent progress.

Young Anson Jones did poorly under the tutelage of his first preceptor, Dr. Daniel Sheldon of Litchfield. True, the doctor "put him through" Boerhaave and Van Swieten and gave him such clinical opportunities as he could; but at the end of the year Anson counted the time as lost. When, distressed over mounting debts, he determined to give up study temporarily and, for the first—but not the last—time "resort to teaching," Dr. Sheldon made no objection. In spite of young Jones's lack of enthusiasm for medicine, while he taught at nearby Goshen his conscience compelled him to continue reading such medical books as he could borrow.

William Jones, Anson's twenty-six-year-old brother who lived in Utica, after working three years as a saddler, had opened on slender capital a family grocery store at the lower end of Genesee Street. To this establishment Anson came at the end of his teaching engagement in Goshen, still bent on continuing the study of medicine. William was no more favorable to the idea than he had been two years earlier, but he allowed his younger brother to earn his board by clerking in the store and permitted him to read medicine under Dr. Amos G. Hull at odd moments.

At the end of his first year in Utica, Anson's debts drove him again to the schoolroom. He returned to find that his brother's business, never flourishing, could no longer afford the luxury of a clerk, and William's household budget did not allow for an extra plate at the table. Anson arranged to board, on credit, elsewhere when he returned to the office of Dr. Hull. It was a bad expedient as the sequel demonstrates. But now that he could devote undivided attention to study, young Jones's progress was satisfactory, and he won not only Hull's approval but his lifelong friendship and interest.

Jones was fortunate in his mentor; for, in addition to technical skill and wide practice, Dr. Hull had precisely those personal qualities that Jones lacked. Amos Gould Hull was a born doctor, son of a physician and nephew of another. The pattern of his life seemed almost to have been cut with a scalpel and his A B Cs learned from the *Handbook of Materia Medica*. In addition to the young men who studied in his office, he fitted two sons for the profession and married his daughter to a physician.

When Jones came to him Hull was at the height of his vigor and local fame, rounding out his fourth term as president of the Medical Society of the County of Oneida, riding a wide circuit, and supervising as many apprentices as he could. The local medical historian recorded:

As an operator he was daring and quick, if not remarkably expert; as a physician, kindly and attentive . . . profuse in the administration of drugs . . . a bustling man . . . kept three horses, and drove them without mercy; was prompt at a call, and officiously forward to get all he could of them. His pushing propensity showed itself in new and unheard of expedients . . . the sale of mineral waters . . . the practice of electricity and galvanism . . . the manufacture and sale of a hernial truss he invented. . . . Personally Dr. Hull was amiable and upright. . . . Rather short of stature, quick and impulsive in movement, neat in attire, he was withal a little vain of his appearance, and looked to it that the knee-buckles which confined his silk stockings were each day carefully polished.

Two years with such a master were enough to give a young man of Jones's stripe his bearings, as well as to induct him into some of the mysteries of the healing art.

At a meeting of the Oneida Medical Society on September 5, 1820, "Anson Jones, student of Dr. A. G. Hull, was examined and approved relating to his knowledge of physic and surgery," and received a holograph testimonial of his proficiency. In return, he handed the venerable president five dollars—two for the treasury of the society, one each for the three censors who had examined him. Now at last the timid young man had acquired a profession and received the courtesy title Doctor. In his hand he had a license to practice upon the ailing public for fees. Success seemed just ahead. His sisters were very proud; Anson was uncertain.

Armed with his license and a to-whom-it-may-concern letter signed by Dr. Hull, he went to Bainbridge, Chenango County, New York, rented half of a little office, and hung his new shingle alongside that of Lawyer William S. Stow, which had not been up long. He found a cheap secondhand pine desk in which to store his apothecary supplies and assembled an office chair from parts of two broken ones. There he sat, day after day, envying the magnificence of Stow's desk of walnut inlaid with tulipwood, and hoping that some of Stow's clients might need medical as well as legal advice. Jones thought that he failed in this first professional venture because "the ground was completely occupied by an old and experienced physician." Barely twenty-two, a stranger without social grace or money to spend, and still doubtful of his own professional skill, he could not reasonably have expected to succeed. While his debts mounted, he stuck it out for more than a year—praying privately, no doubt, for Providence to remove the older practitioner.

His schedule was not a crowded one, and for the first time in his life he had leisure and inclination to behave like a normal young American. At Bainbridge lived one of those fabulous characters of the post-Revolutionary era, whose house was the social center of the community and whose connection with large affairs brought to his board the great and near great of the region. This F. A. De Zeng, Esquire, as he then styled himself, had come to America in 1780 as captain of a company of King George's Hessians; but the war was almost over and De Zeng's heart was never in it. After peace he remained in the United States, married an American girl, and became a great landed proprietor as well as a promoter of internal improvements. Chancellor Livingston was his business partner and Governor Clinton his close friend.

Dr. Jones and Lawyer Stow were often in his home, less to hear the old gentleman talk of the great days when he was a baron of the Holy Roman Empire and gentleman-in-waiting to the landgrave of Hesse-Cassel, than to court his vivacious daughter, "a charming, polished young woman, the belle of the county." When the old baron chose Lawyer Stow to be his son-in-law, the young doctor decided that he had no reason, professional or personal, to linger longer at inhospitable Bainbridge.

The old practitioner was left in undisputed possession of the field when Dr. Jones renounced not only the town but his profession. He left his makeshift office furniture behind him and moved to Norwich to open a drugstore. Dr. Hull helped him obtain a line of credit in New York City, and he was soon launched as a businessman. Like his old preceptor, he might eventually build up a medical practice in connection with the store; meantime it would be a living. He was on the verge of getting even with the world, establishing himself personally and financially, when the importunate Hinman, landlord of his apprentice days, unable to reconcile Jones's apparent affluence with his professed inability to pay honest debts, ruined his prospects.

So soon as I got fairly under way my *friend* (?) Hinman sued and obtained judgment against me for my board (at Utica), and immediately took out an execution for debt and costs, amounting in all to some hundreds of dollars, I do not know how many. It was sufficient, however, to ruin me. . . . My stock of goods was seized by the sheriff, and . . . I disposed of them at much less than cost . . . to satisfy the execution in favor of J. E. Hinman; and immediately notified my creditors in New York of my situation, promising to pay every cent as soon as I might be able. Some mischievous persons, however, taking advantage of circumstances, had been to the trouble to circulate false reports of me in New York, and my creditors there refused to show me any lenity.

It was Mr. De Zeng, the old baron, who came to the rescue of the young man who had wanted to marry his daughter; he bought Jones's stock of drugs and enabled him to settle with Hinman.

At twenty-five Anson Jones had failed both as physician and as merchant. Perhaps his brothers were correct: perhaps he was not meant for success. There was no home to go back to. Solomon Jones, after living on the bounty of relatives pending the day when a grateful Congress would provide adequately for the veterans of

1776 and 1812, had died the year before. Anson was on his own.

He could not remain in Norwich, nor return to Bainbridge; and the debt judgments against him would have to be paid somehow.

When he was a student he had "resorted to teaching" to square his accounts; a ruined businessman now, he "resorted to medicine" for the same purpose. It required no cash capital, and his medical license was one of his few remaining assets. Harpers Ferry —perhaps because it was far away—would be his new home. To western Virginia he started, but Fate intervened at Philadelphia:

> I was arrested by one of my creditors and gave up my watch and the last dollar I had in the world but twenty, to satisfy his claim. Unable to prosecute my journey, and knowing that I had not a single friend at Harper's Ferry, I concluded to try my profession in the city of "Brotherly Love."

That was in 1823. Philadelphia was no longer the capital of the United States nor of the Commonwealth of Pennsylvania, but it was the second largest city of the nation, as well as the principal seaport. Its population and location, its growing reputation as a medical center, and the relatively small number of physicians then in practice there all marked Philadelphia as an ideal location for a young physician.

> In 1820 [wrote Dr. Frederick P. Henry] the city, with her 113,000 inhabitants, still spread along the Delaware river, Tenth and Eleventh streets being the western borderland, beyond which a physician's sign was rarely to be seen. Although some 25,000 people were added by 1825, there were only about a dozen more doctors than thirty years before . . . sixty-nine in all. . . . The profession in the few years before and after 1825 was less numerous in proportion to general population than at any time in the history of the city.

Jones was fortunate: his creditor's execution might have overtaken him at Trenton, or Bristol, or some other town already crowded with medical men. He had no option but to begin practice as soon as he had been relieved of his wallet and watch. Twenty dollars, even in 1823, could not last long.

He opened an office without delay; a new tin sign reading "Anson Jones, Physician and Surgeon" invited ailing Philadelphians into his combination office and living apartment. But somehow they failed to come. It was not that prospective patients suspected the deficiencies of his professional education, for there were many successful practitioners as poorly trained as he. The trouble was that they were unaware of his very existence. Here, as under other circumstances throughout his life, Jones's principal handicap was a certain reticence, the response of a timid and sensitive nature to the buffetings of an unsympathetic world, which made it difficult for him to form acquaintances. Without prepossessing personal appearance, grace of manner, or money, he had the habit of anticipating failure even while the issue remained in doubt. When patients failed to seek his waiting room he was not surprised; it was getting to be an old story:

I had made some acquaintances and friends. But after trying a few months I found I was not making expenses, and I then again had recourse to teaching for support.

But teaching, under such circumstances, soon palled on him; it was neither interesting nor lucrative. After six months in the schoolroom he received "an offer to go to South America, from Mr. Lowry, the American Consul for Laguayra," and in the autumn of 1824 he packed his bags and took passage in the brig *Coulter,* Venezuela-bound.

Venezuela was the cradle of South American independence, and Caracas, where Jones made his home, was the birthplace both of Francisco de Miranda, forerunner of the Latin-American revolutions, and Simón Bolívar, the liberator of South America. In April 1810 the Cabildo of Caracas had deposed the Spanish Captain General, and a year later the inhabitants of Venezuela proclaimed their independence from the mother country—the first such declaration in the Spanish colonial world.

For a decade the issue was undecided, until June 24, 1821, when Bolívar, with the aid of a British battalion, routed the Spaniards at Carabobo and assured Venezuela against reconquest. In other parts of the continent the struggle went on until the end of 1824. Venezuela, Colombia, and Ecuador, which owed their liberation to Bolívar, were united into Great Colombia until 1831, when Venezuela and Ecuador withdrew.

Into this Spanish province, recently transformed into an independent republic but still torn by internecine feuds, Anson Jones

came in the autumn of 1824. The United States had recently accorded the nation diplomatic recognition, although a consul had
been stationed there almost from the beginning of the wars of
independence and for some time there had been colonies of North
American fortune hunters in the cities of La Guayra and Caracas.
What young Dr. Jones, who had never until recently been more
than two hundred miles from his birthplace, thought of the situation and of the local mestizo chieftains, with their resplendent uni-
forms and bare feet, he did not say. He remained there two years,
attending strictly to his business, observing quietly, and refraining
from incautious comment. His immediate interest was not in politics or warfare, but in making a living and in saving money to pay
his debts.

Ironically this man, who had signally failed in the practice
of medicine in the second largest city of the United States,
met success in a country so healthful that "the medical class do
not obtain, because there is not so much need of them, the same
rewards as in countries where they are more necessary." Colonel
William Duane, another Philadelphian who visited Caracas not
long before Dr. Jones arrived, discovered only one young man
studying medicine at the university and only two native physicians in Great Colombia, "one of whom found, as he good na-
turedly said, that there was not enough sickness in Caracas to live
upon, and it became necessary that he should turn coffee planter."
The highest medical fee was four reals, or half a dollar, a visit.

Jones remained until June 1826, when he returned to Philadelphia on the *Coulter,* happy that he had "now succeeded in getting a few hundred dollars ahead." For the first time in his life he
had been in a human environment to which he knew himself to
be superior. In Caracas he had been a man of local importance,
whose services had been in demand and paid for in cash, and
whose opinions were deferred to.

The Anson Jones who returned to Philadelphia on the *Coulter*
had qualities and capacities lacking in the Anson Jones who had
come to Caracas two years before.

II

BROTHERLY LOVE IN PHILADELPHIA

B ACK in Philadelphia with his small store of Spanish gold
and a greater degree of self-confidence than he had before
known, he rented an office at 28 North Eighth Street, between Market and Filbert, and stocked it with drugs and medical
instruments—and samples of trusses. Dr. Hull had given him an
agency for his hernial appliances which would pay well if local
practitioners were disposed to recommend them.

Jones had once thought he knew as much about medicine as
he needed to know, but in Philadelphia, where the powerful medical alumni of the University of Pennsylvania dominated the profession, he found that men of his meager training were ranked
little above pharmacists and midwives. As he waited for patients,
and before he had spent all his savings, he "resolved to take a
course of lectures and *finish* my professional studies and gradu-
ate." Learning the theory of things he had been doing by rote
would satisfy his intellectual curiosity; a degree and a Latin
diploma would give him status.

Two years ago it had been rumored that young Dr. George
McClellan was planning a new medical school. McClellan had
asked the legislature for a charter; when it was refused, he organized a medical faculty and offered it to Jefferson College at
Canonsburg. There had been a report, as Jones was starting for
South America, that the offer had been accepted; but it was of
as little interest to him then as the news that Southern farmers
were moving into the Mexican province of Texas that year.

Now the new school was in full and spectacular operation. The
university had blocked a separate charter, but it could not forbid Jefferson College to establish a medical branch in Philadelphia. Dr. McClellan rented an old building at 518 Prune (now
Locust) Street for $550, called his faculty together, and assessed
the professors-designate $20 each to remodel it. The dilapidated

structure was near the Moravian burying ground, just around the corner from Independence Square and a short walk from Jones's new office. It had been a cotton factory, then the Tivoli Theater. It left much to be desired even after the professors had spent $120 on it. Students sat in opera chairs to watch McClellan operate in the first collegiate surgical clinics in the United States, and they went to the Green Room for their final examinations.

In March 1826 Jefferson Medical College had conferred its first degrees on a class of twenty "by writ of mandamus obtained from court." Physicians who were not members of its faculty were predicting that its existence would be brief; but Jones entered it rather than the university.

Among the students who enrolled at Jefferson in the winter of 1826–27, two were to achieve distinction, although neither sensed the potential greatness of the other. One was Samuel D. Gross, an earnest youth of twenty-one, already better trained than some of his professors, who was determined to master McClellan's surgical technique. He was to become famous on both sides of the Atlantic as a surgeon and teacher of surgeons. The other was Anson Jones, nearing thirty, a licensed practitioner these six years, bronzed under the genial South American sun, jingling a few dollars in his pocket, and, after school hours, sitting in his little office just around the corner.

The students found McClellan a fluent, provocative lecturer and spectacularly brilliant as an operator; but his diagnosis was often wrong and he lacked judgment and patience. With energy more amazing than Dr. Hull's, he administered the college, combated its enemies, taught and demonstrated surgery, and attended one of the largest private practices in the city.

Next in prominence was John Eberle, a short, dark-visaged man of German descent, whose lectures put the students to sleep, but whose books on materia medica and the practice of medicine became world-famous. The professor of chemistry was old Jacky Green, a simple-minded bachelor, not very deeply versed in science but agreeable and a gentleman. A worse man, Gross suspected but was not sure, might have occupied that chair. The obstetrician, the dullest lecturer Gross ever listened to, was retired at the end of the year for inefficiency. William P. C. Barton, in materia medica, was one of the distinguished scientists of his day. He had been a Navy surgeon, and his *Medical Botany of the United States* was a standard work. He was a brilliant teacher, except for a bitter temper which he directed at dull students and Nathaniel Chapman, professor of materia medica at the University of Pennsylvania. Benjamin Rush Rhees, a dapper, pompous little fellow, lectured on institutes of medicine and medical jurisprudence without ever sensing the importance of those subjects. Personally he was charming, but unfortunately for his reputation as a teacher, he took his lectures verbatim from books that some of his students had already read.

This was the faculty under whom Anson Jones *"finished* his professional studies and graduated," as characterized by one whose opinion on things medical and pedagogical was worth a good deal more than Jones's. Gross thought "they were perhaps, in the main, as competent instructors as any similar number of teachers in the schools of the country at that period." Jones knew they could help him fill in the gaps of his professional education, and he could well afford to pay their fees: anatomy, surgery, materia medica, and chemistry cost $14 each; theory and practice, institutes and medical jurisprudence, $12; and midwifery, $10. "So that," the regulation ran, "the whole amount paid by each student to the seven professors shall not exceed annually $90."

At the end of a single session Anson Jones presented himself in the Green Room of his alma mater, defended a thesis on ophthalmia, and in March 1827 received the coveted Latin parchment along with the other young men of the second graduating class of the institution—a class which "litigation and discord between two of the professors affected unfavorably."

Ten years after he began, at a cost of less than one hundred dollars, he had finished his medical education. True, he was the product of a college that had yet to win public favor and was still a butt of ridicule among the powerful alumni of the University of Pennsylvania, but he might succeed nevertheless, even in Philadelphia —if only he could get enough paying patients. Dr. Jones did not court intimacy with other practitioners or form a partnership. He sought to attract a clientele in the only way open to an ethical physician: the enlargement of his personal acquaintance. Another man might have joined a church; Dr. Jones took the fraternal route.

It was a new and delightful world, this formal, purposeful gregariousness that he found in Harmony Lodge No. 52, A.F. & A.M. The Masonic ritual, like that of the Episcopal Church, satisfied an aesthetic craving that the drabness of his life accentuated. He found he had capacity for grasping fraternal problems and suggesting solutions. Older members became accustomed to seconding the doctor's motions, and in 1830 they elected him Junior Warden, next year Senior Warden, and in 1832 Worshipful Master.

The sense of mastery Jones had gained in Venezuela carried him through medical college and into the complexities of lodgedom. It was as if he had spent his siesta time storing up the energies he was now releasing. The Dr. Jones that Bainbridge and Norwich and Philadelphia had known could not have projected himself into the role that he was playing in fraternal business.

He also joined the Odd Fellows, passed rapidly through the offices of Washington Lodge No. 2, and entered the Grand Lodge of Pennsylvania on March 23, 1829. Odd Fellowship was new in the United States and just being established in Philadelphia. It was nascent, plastic, expanding; it offered opportunities to help fix traditions, to set precedents that other men would follow.

Six days after he entered Grand Lodge, Jones organized Philadelphia Lodge No. 13. For it he drafted the constitution, by-laws, and rules that became "the model of the Order everywhere"; for it he procured a hall in Kensington which he managed as president of the trustees.

Four or five evenings a week he was in Grand Lodge; he served on practically every committee; he led the movement to erect the Grand Lodge Building in South Fifth Street, supervised its construction, officiated at its dedication, and was president of its trustees.

Noble Grand Jones was the man who could fill the place of any officer on short notice, who was sent on a "delicate mission" to Grand Sire Thomas Wildey, who drafted "all the forms necessary for all the different purposes of the Order," who designed and ceremonially awarded a medal to a brother "for the recovery of the degree books."

He became Grand Warden two months after he entered Grand Lodge; next year he was Deputy Grand Master, and in 1832 he defeated John Pearce to become Grand Master of all the Odd Fellows in the Commonwealth of Pennsylvania. "In every station I filled," he said, "I took a very active part—too much so for my personal interests."

The number of Pennsylvania Odd Fellows almost trebled between 1827 and 1829 and thereafter continued to increase rapidly. It was a middle-class, urban group, composed of tradesmen and mechanics with steady incomes and large families. A physician so devoted to the order should have profited professionally by the increase in the number of his brethren, but plainly Dr. Jones did not. It may be that Odd Fellows, when ill, preferred to be treated by a physician who was merely a physician and not a fraternal statesman.

The sense of mastery that had carried him to the pinnacle ebbed. His earlier sense of inadequacy returned only in part, but he developed an increasing tension—of which his preoccupation with the minutiae of fraternalism was doubtless a premonitory symptom—which was bad for his nerves and worse for his standing among the brethren.

Unrestrained by the traditions and formal procedures which governed his brother Masons, the enthusiastic Odd Fellows wrangled among themselves, and with their presiding officer, with Hibernian gusto. The life of a Grand Master was never an easy one, and to a man of Dr. Jones's temperament it was unbearably vexatious. New Englander that he was, he never doubted the validity of his own considered judgment. He had the physician's sense of the necessity of exact compliance with his prescription. To the creative exuberance of his brethren in this pioneer venture, he reacted with the irritation of a physician who feels that the patient has nothing to contribute to the cure but compliance. If they were not disposed to follow his directions, they would have to call in someone else.

He stuck it out for eight of the twelve months of his term; then on February 28, 1832, he announced that

in consequence of a conscientious difference of opinion with the Grand Lodge in regard to the propriety of measures recently adopted, he tendered his resignation from the office of Grand Master and as trustee of Fifth Street Hall, and as trustee of Kensington and as commissioner for the Grand Lodge loan.

The resignations were accepted and his expenses as Grand Master—two dollars—ordered paid. On July 23, 1832, he appeared for the last time in the Grand Lodge of Pennsylvania.

This man who could deal skillfully with an individual, sick or well, had not learned—would never learn—how to persuade groups of men. Occupational rigidity and the kind of arrogance that only the timid feel prevented his learning the art of persuasion.

Each year since his return from South America his income, including commissions as agent for Dr. Hull's trusses, had fallen a little behind his expenses. He resolved to leave not only Philadelphia but the profession of medicine as well. He resigned from his lodges, turned the truss agency over to the house of Parrish & Postill, closed his office, and looked southward for a career in business.

III

NADIR

A CERTAIN Thomas J. Spear, merchant of Philadelphia, was planning to extend his operations to New Orleans and he needed a partner with a credit rating. He invited Dr. Jones to become senior partner of a mercantile house, to be known as Jones & Spear, and resident manager in the Crescent City. The doctor,

never having as yet met with any satisfactory success in my profession, and, consequently, a good deal disgusted with it, too readily acceded to this proposal, and in October, 1832, sailed from New York in the ship *Alabama* for New Orleans.

Other Philadelphia physicians considered Jones's practice there a good one; his failure was not as complete as the loss of his brief enthusiasm for his profession. Dr. Hull, his old mentor who had also turned from medicine to business, hoped that Jones would establish himself in New York; but he was already committed to New Orleans. He supervised the loading of his merchandise on the *Alabama* and sailed south on October 10, 1832. The fifteenth day at sea the *Alabama* "lost five of her principal sails, together with her main top-gallant mast, and one seaman" and drifted for days—"from which cause alone," the management insisted, "her passage has been retarded." On November 9, twenty-nine days out of New York, she docked at New Orleans, her sixty passengers "all in good health and spirits." Dr. Jones, joined by the Reverend Joel Parker and six other passengers, presented Captain Robert Waterman a letter of thanks for his "courteous demeanor . . . great attention to duties . . . and decision evinced . . . under very trying circumstances." Anson Jones's name appeared for the first time in a New Orleans paper when the *Emporium* printed the testimonial letter.

While the *Alabama* floundered, the cholera epidemic, which

had already touched Philadelphia and New York, traveled along the routes of trade until it reached New Orleans the last week in October.

Early on the morning of October 25 a minister found two dying men lying on the levee, where they had been dumped from a steamboat during the night. A physician who chanced by in his gig pronounced them victims of the cholera and whipped up his horses, leaving them to be carted to Charity Hospital by some laborers who did not understand the English language. By noon both men were dead, and panic was spreading through the city. Families hurriedly put a few possessions into their carriages and rushed for the open country; others fought on the wharves like madmen for places on the river boats. Before night hysterical city folk were spreading the plague inland and up and across the river as fast as horses and boats could carry them.

Saint Louis Cathedral was crowded with women invoking the intervention of the Mother of God; the ten priests were not enough to administer extreme unction—they were dividing their time between the altar and the cemetery; the few men seen in the business district wore crape upon their arms. "All stores, banks, and places of business were closed. There were no means, no instruments for carrying on the ordinary affairs of business; for all the drays, carts, carriages, hand and common wheelbarrows, as well as hearses, were employed in the transportation of corpses."

During the night bodies were weighted with stone and thrown into the river. Many were buried without ceremony in house yards, gardens, vacant lots; others were "stacked like cordwood" in the cemeteries until trenches could be dug. The one Protestant minister—a Unitarian—stood for hours daily reading the burial office over corpses as they were placed in the ground.

When Dr. Jones selected New Orleans for his new home its population was more than fifty thousand; when he arrived there it was less than thirty thousand. Yellow fever had driven fifteen thousand away before the cholera arrived; then, within twelve days, six thousand more had died!

When the *Alabama* docked, Dr. Jones read in the *Louisiana Advertiser* that, although "scarcely a dray is seen moving through the streets . . . as confidence . . . is becoming, every day, more and more restored, the bustle and activity, to which we are accustomed, will shortly be resumed." The editor was cheered by the fact that for the first time in two weeks the sun was shining—and by the mortuary record of the day before: only fifty-seven interments by midafternoon. A white frost the next day convinced Dr. Halphen of the Medical Society that the epidemic had ceased in the city, although it had "broken out, with great violence, on several plantations." Benjamin Levy's *New Orleans Prices Current* gave its lay opinion that the yellow fever was "done with for this season." "Already," it observed, "people begin to wear cheerful countenances."

This was neither the time nor the place to launch a business venture, even if one had ample resources and an honest partner. Anson Jones had neither. Credit for the firm of Jones & Spear, commission merchants, had been obtained in the name of the senior partner. Spear turned out to be a grand rascal—"devoid of principle, and reckless of character and everything else." Jones soon parted company with him, but not in time to avoid suits for debt, or to salvage anything from the ruined business.

While Anson Jones, M.D., sat among the crates and kegs of his commission house, waiting for another failure to overtake him, medical history was being made in New Orleans. Three twenty-five-year-old physicians—Thomas Hunt from South Carolina, Warren Stone from Vermont, and John Harrison from the District of Columbia—made up their minds that New Orleans should become the medical center of the South and, with the courage of youth, began to make it that. They were establishing the (Tulane) Medical College of Louisiana and the clinics of Charity Hospital while Jones was trying to become a commission merchant. Nothing was likely to interest Dr. Jones less than permanent association with the healing profession except, perhaps, another partnership with Thomas J. Spear; but when his business failed he turned once more to medicine—as he earlier had "resorted to teaching."

At No. 40 Canal Street, across the way from the Dental Institute where prepaid, socialized dentistry was being experimented with, Dr. Jones hung up his Latin diploma and began waiting for patients. As luck would have it, New Orleans was phenomenally free of disease after the epidemics had done their work, but yellow fever could be counted upon for the summer months, and Dr. Jones stuck it out somehow until the sickly season came. It was

not such a bonanza for medical men as the autumn had been,
but he was succeeding as well as he "could reasonably expect"
when, he said:

I was myself attacked with the prevailing fever, and laid up sick
for several weeks. By the time I was well enough to attend to my
professional duties again the sickness had well-nigh subsided, and
I had not realized enough to support me until the next summer. I
had therefore to look elsewhere . . . for the means of making a
livelihood.

He took it philosophically; it was nothing new. . . .

But, at thirty-five, when most men are permanently settled and
on their way to financial security, Anson Jones's plight was desperate. He was discredited as a businessman—in debt, with suits still
pending against him—and was without much prospect for success
in the practice of his profession, even if he could manage to keep
alive until the next sickly season. He was a thousand miles from
anyone who might help him, in a city not yet accustomed to seeing
the United States flag atop the customhouse.

Considerations other than financial also counseled him to leave
that charming Latin city with its foreign customs and easy morals:

I found the pernicious habit of gambling, to which I always had
an inclination, was growing upon me there. Before going to New
Orleans, it is true, I had never indulged the inclination to any extent,
but there the constant temptation thrown in my way I found was
slowly overcoming my resolutions not to indulge this propensity.

Whilst in this place, also, partly from having frequently little else
to do and partly to overcome the feelings of disappointments I had
so often endured, and more particularly about this time, I also found
myself learning to imitate the fashionable practice of taking a
"julep" much oftener than was at all necessary.

Both of these practices I most cordially despised . . . felt anxious
to get away from the place and its associations.

The puritanism latent in him—that Cromwell blood in his
veins—was asserting itself. He must flee New Orleans not only to
make a living but to save his soul.

New Orleans had other visitors who liked juleps. At this juncture he made the acquaintance of two or three Texans, partic-

ularly Captain Jeremiah Brown, who commanded the *Sabine,* then in the Texas trade.

In 1833 every patriotic Texan was, ex officio, an evangelist for that New Canaan; Jerry Brown was one of the best. These Texans were in duty bound to prove that the northeast corner of the Mexican Republic was the ideal spot for a man in Dr. Jones's predicament. It was the land of opportunity. They knew (for they had just brought a cargo of buffalo hides from there) that Brazoria, never healthful, was in need of a physician. They also knew that every additional immigrant increased the demand for goods, and that the greater the demand for goods, the more the profit in the Texas trade. By all means the doctor must come with them to Texas.

From non-Texan sources Jones had already heard a good deal about Texas in New Orleans and had toyed with the idea of going there months before. B. S. Barclay, one of his Philadelphia confreres in Odd Fellowdom, had warned him to beware of "the unsettled *political* situation of the country." Texas, Jones had heard, was "a harbor for pirates and banditti." Banditti were not unknown in New Orleans, and he could even find a pirate or two in the local grogshops if he looked long enough.

Anson Jones was not, by nature, a pioneer; he had little in common with the people who were leaving the United States for Texas, attracted by cheap land and a chance to begin life again on a farm. But, his new friends countered, respectable men were coming into Texas nowadays to make fortunes and bringing their families with them. Professional men were coming—lawyers, many politicians, a few teachers, occasionally a minister of the Gospel; but there were not enough physicians. Texas was, and for a long time would remain, a frontier community, but that was an advantage. What should be more attractive to a medical man than the frontier where practitioners were few and a physician could name his own fee—and collect it?

Jones, remembering how he had tried for success and failed in New England, New York State, Philadelphia, and New Orleans, had no desire at the moment to try again the cities or older rural communities. Texas might be the place. At least he had an invitation, of sorts, to go there, when no other place was bidding

for his services. And if he did not get away from New Orleans and
its influences he would soon be unfit for any business.

He counted his assets and liabilities:

Cash on hand	$32	Liabilities, about $2,000
Medicines	50	(and increasing daily)

The fare to Texas on the *Sabine* was fifteen dollars if one slept
on deck. There was nothing to detain him in New Orleans, unless
he wanted to wait until February, when the suit of Samuel Lucas
vs. Jones & Spear would come to trial. In the course of a week he
could go to Texas, "take a look at the country and judge for
himself," as Captain Brown urged. Another fifteen dollars would
bring him back to New Orleans if he wanted to return. The
Sabine, with Jones aboard, cleared New Orleans for Brazoria
October 14, 1833.

To go to Texas was to follow the path of least resistance.

IV

MR. AUSTIN'S TEXAS

TWELVE YEARS earlier another young man of New England blood had left New Orleans for Texas to mold, by business acumen, amazing selflessness, and patience that amounted to genius, the economic and social forces of the Southwest and change the course of history. He was Stephen F. Austin,

twenty-seven years old; well educated for his day; experienced in public service and in business; patient; methodical; energetic; and fair-spoken; and acquainted from childhood with the characteristic social types that mingled on the southwestern border.

Texas had been a Spanish province for more than a hundred and twenty-five years before Austin came and was then in process of becoming a part of an independent Mexico; but, according to official report, it was still inhabited only by "the barbarians and wild beasts, with the exception of . . . San Antonio de Béxar and the Presidio of Bahía del Espiritu Santo [Goliad] . . . and they are but small." In 1820 perhaps as many as twenty-five hundred people of European blood were living in the vast arc between the Sabine River and the Rio Grande.

The transformation of this Mexican wilderness into a new Anglo-American frontier was initiated by Moses Austin, an aging and broken Connecticut Yankee. At fifty-nine he had worn himself out on the frontiers of Virginia and Missouri where, with imagination and industry, he had promoted one vast scheme after another to become a man of consequence and (on paper) of large estate. But by 1820 he was declaring that he was *"ruined . . . and to remain in a Country where I had enjoyed welth in a state of poverty, I could Not submit to."*

The Panic of 1819, following the lean years of the War of 1812, had wiped him out, as it had most western speculators and tens of thousands of farmers and small businessmen throughout the United States. The courts could hardly handle the volume of fore-closures, evictions, and debt suits; a good portion of every community was ready to be "on the move." Thomas Jefferson noted "unparalleled distress" in Virginia, where sudden contraction of currency was "producing an entire revolution in fortune." The situation was duplicated in almost every state.

The problem was acute but not unprecedented. The Americans, in their two centuries on this continent, had evolved a pattern for their individual rehabilitation in circumstances like these. The ruined man salvaged what he could and moved west with his wife and children and chattels to "take up government land" upon a promise to pay for it later. Largely by this process the frontiers had been populated until, in 1820, the westward movement stopped.

The public land of the United States was not filled up; far from it. But in 1820 the Congress, in its wisdom, reduced the price of land from $2.00 an acre (to be paid eventually with occupation meantime) to a cash payment of $1.25 in advance of settlement. That was a neat bargain for a fellow if he had $1.25—in which case he would probably stay where he was. The result might have been, but apparently was not, anticipated: the desire for new lands (on credit) skyrocketed, while the sale of land for cash plummeted. In 1820 four million acres less were sold than in 1819, and only 781,000 acres were patented during 1821. But for that new land policy, wrote one of Austin's colonists, "we had most of us never seen Texas."

Ruined and dejected though he was, Moses Austin was a promoter still, and here was a situation to challenge him. He knew as well as the next man the plight of the bankrupt entrepreneur and farmer; he knew better than others what could be done about it.

Twenty-two years before, when his son Stephen was five, he had become a subject of the King of Spain to launch his large, now ruined, enterprises in Upper Louisiana; and he would do it again in Texas—not exclusively, but chiefly, to rebuild his fortune in the little time that remained to him. He would open a legal gateway through the international boundary into Texas, and, as *empresario*, he would *give* the King's land to his fellows

in adversity. That would enable them to begin life anew, un-
harassed by creditors' executions. The King would profit from
the peopling of his wilderness, then valueless. Austin could earn
$18,000 in fees at once and patent for himself 100,000 acres,
which would increase in value as colonization progressed. This
Texas enterprise might ultimately be worth more than all he had
lost in Missouri.

Courage, hope, wisdom born of bitter experience, and Yankee
shrewdness guided the hand that threw the dice in this last great
gamble of a life of hectic speculation. These—and downright
luck—gave him what he sought: a contract to bring into Texas
three hundred families from the United States. Six months later,
after praying God to enable his son Stephen "to go on with the
business in the same way" he would have done, he died.

But Stephen F. Austin was incapable of doing anything "in the
same way" his plunging, tactless, humorless father would have
done. Perhaps because he had known his father so well and appreciated so thoroughly his finer traits, while observing periodically the devastating results of his less admirable ones, Stephen
had taken pains to become the antithesis of Moses Austin in all
save energy and integrity. Tactful, suave, easy-mannered, methodical, diplomatic, Stephen F. Austin—who never would have en-
terprised the Texas venture and who, if he could, might have
dissuaded his father from it—was to become the greatest colonial
proprietor since William Penn.

He dutifully assumed the responsibility, but he was not convinced of the ripeness of the enterprise or the magnitude of the
opportunity until he had explored Texas to select a site for the
colony, and read the letters of inquiry that swamped him on his
return. Then he knew that he could bring five times as many
people into Texas as his father had counted on. Missouri was "all
alive and nothing Spoken of but the province of Texas"; his
mother believed that "one third of the popolation will move [to
Texas] in the cours of another year"; his partner reported from
New Orleans: "There are hundreds on the way and thousands
ready to go."

The great news of free land in Texas—really free—was sweeping through the United States as rapidly as letters, newspapers,
and word of mouth could carry it. Apparently everybody who had

to move or wanted to move was looking toward Texas. Not until the days of the forty-niners was there anything like this "Texas fever."

The movement was slowed, but not stopped, when Mexico achieved independence. Austin's contract was with Spanish authorities. Would the new government, anti-Spanish and suspicious of all foreigners, approve the arrangement? Stephen F. Austin was confident that it would. He hurried to Mexico City to get the answer, thinking that he could comply with the legal formalities in a few days.

He arrived to find "the whole people and Country still Agitated in the revolutionary Convulsions—public Opinion Vacillating . . . Party spirit raging . . . the recently established Governm't almost sinking."

A Provisional Junta gave way to a Congress; Congress was displaced, then reassembled to preside over the obsequies of the Mexican Empire and to inaugurate a republic. Generalissimo Agustín de Iturbide, whose patriotic duplicity had united reactionaries and radicals to achieve independence, easily convinced himself that he could rule Mexico better than an imported prince and set himself up as the Emperor Agustín I. He remained upon his shaky homemade throne for seven troubled months. Then a rising under "a General Santana," as Austin understood the name, toppled him over. Austin coached new Mexican leaders in the elements of republican political science and discreetly steered them away from centralism, which he regarded as "the worst Gov't in the world . . . 100 tyrants instead of one."

He possessed his soul with patience and tried not to think what the delay was costing in Texas, as he waited, waited, waited, for the kaleidoscope of politics to come to rest long enough for him to finish his business and get back to his colony. At the end of a year his patient persistence got for him the legalization he had expected to obtain in two weeks.

That exasperating year completed Austin's training for his work in Texas. He had watched the fixing of the pattern that Mexican politics was to follow for years, and he had come to know personally the men at the capital who were to determine Texas affairs. His insight into the psychology and ideology of the new masters of Mexico enabled him to keep his frontier at peace with them for a decade.

Back home, fifteen months later than he had expected, Austin assumed almost complete powers of government, built his capital city San Felipe de Austin on the Brazos, and colonized four additional grants. The state of Coahuila y Texas gave contracts to two dozen other empresarios. Practically every inch of Texas was marked off on a map and assigned to someone who agreed to introduce a hundred or more families. If the agreements had been fulfilled Texas would have been thickly populated within a decade.

From the Sabine River to San Antonio de Béxar, and north to the Camino Real which connected San Antonio and Nacogdoches, the Anglo-Americans established their farms and ranches and little towns. It was the richest land in Texas, and the pioneers soon created there another frontier of the familiar American type, and a prosperous one.

By the time Anson Jones reached Brazoria in 1833, Austin alone had issued 1,055 land grants. With an optimism that would have warmed his father's heart, he was estimating the population of Texas (which was less than 30,000 two years yater) at 46,500 and describing the crop prospects, the industrial development, and the general prosperity in compelling terms. He informed the Mexican Government that among the Texans there were few who did not understand very well the importance of protecting their property and persons by means of a local government, well organized and well supported.

That his individualistic colonists and the unstable, tradition-bound Mexican Government did not approach the parting of the ways until colonization had been ten years in progress is a testimony to the paternal solicitude and vigilance of the great Empresario.

Slavery had been prohibited by decree in 1829; Austin got the decree set aside. On April 6, 1830, Mexico canceled colonization contracts, prohibited immigration from the United States, threw a ring of garrisons and customhouses around the Anglo-American settlements, and, in general, prepared to impress the colonists that they had obligations to perform, as well as opportunities to enjoy, in Texas. This was a new note, and it alarmed the Americanos who had learned from Mr. Jefferson that that government is best which governs least. They had not loved the tax collector in the United States and had never seen one in Texas.

Austin probably liked the turn of events less than anyone, but instead of blustering he convinced himself, then the Mexican Government, that the law could not possibly mean what it plainly said—and worked out a modus operandi that circumvented the immigration regulations. About the customhouses and the soldiers, he could do nothing except point out a little lamely that the troops could help fight Indians and that the men Mexico was sending into Texas would increase the market for Texas produce.

The truth is that the situation was rapidly getting beyond Austin's—anybody's—control. The pattern of political instability which Austin had watched a-forming in Mexico City during 1822–23 had become fixed: *plans, pronunciamentos,* and revolutions were daily rations below the Rio Grande.

Busy as they were ousting each other from the National Palace, the Mexican statesmen shared a common and recurrent nightmare: Texas was, somehow, about to be filched from Mexico by the Colossus of the North. Steps were intermittently taken, sometimes in top-lofty patriotism, sometimes in hysteria, to fix Mexican authority irrevocably in the region between the Rio Grande and the boundary of the United States.

The national pattern of disorder was reproduced, with variations, in the state of Coahuila y Texas, where factions in Coahuila shot it out over such issues as the validity of elections and the location of the capital. But in spite of the eagerness of a few leaders to involve the Anglo-Americans in Coahuila's quarrels, the colonists held aloof from that "perfect anarchy and confusion."

Within Texas, Austin's problem was complicated by hundreds of newcomers, some of them noisy politicians from the States who saw in Texas a likely field for their talents and knew or cared little else about it. To them Austin's almost superhuman feat of preventing an explosion of the combustibles that were smoldering on both sides of him looked very much like cowardice. The Empresario was "little better than a Mexican," and the sooner the Texans had done with his mealymouthed policy and harkened to new messiahs, the better off everybody would be. They had much to gain and little to lose by pouring oil on the embers Austin was trying to extinguish.

All new States, more or less, are infested [wrote one who certainly knew], by a class of noisy, second-rate men, who are always in favor of rash and extreme measures. But Texas was absolutely overrun by such men.

Austin saw his duty and was doing it—steering his "precious bark (the colony) through all the shoals and quicksands, regardless of the curses and ridicule of the passengers. *I* knew what I was about—they did not," he said without rancor.

Clashes between colonists and officialdom were not long delayed. To implement the law of April 6, 1830, Mexico sent a customs collector and a comandante—both former citizens of the United States—and troops to execute their orders. If the Mexicans had thought it tactful to send Americanos to enforce obnoxious new regulations, they reckoned neither on the character of the men selected for posts requiring supreme diplomatic talents, nor the temper of the Texans.

George Fisher, a Serb who had professed allegiance first to Turkey, then to the United States, and finally to Mexico, established the customhouse at Anahuac on Galveston Bay and ordered shipmasters to come to him there for clearances before moving their vessels from the mouth of the Brazos, where the colonists' shipping centered. No Texan saw anything in the order but Fisher's exaggerated notion of the importance of his job, except perhaps a calculated effort to inconvenience them. Defiance brought, reluctantly, the placing of a deputy collector at Brazoria, but Fisher's headquarters remained a hundred miles away from the principal port of entry.

Fisher was an obnoxious pettifogger, but the comandante was worse. This John Davis Bradburn, an arrogant Kentucky adventurer who was being rewarded for service in the Mexican revolution with a colonelcy and the Texas assignment, became the catalyst of the prelude to revolution. Officious and humorless, he began his administration by jailing the land commissioner, just arrived to issue long-delayed titles to settlers east of Austin's colonies; next he dissolved the ayuntamiento of nearby Liberty. Then he clamped martial law upon the coast country, impressed labor and supplies, encouraged slaves to run away, and declined to punish his soldiers for offenses against civilians.

The situation was full of dynamite, but irrepressible Texans could not resist making an oblique attack in frontier fashion. They would either bring this opinionated martinet to his senses or make a complete fool of him by practical jokes. A mysterious message was delivered one dark, stormy night by a tall stranger muffled in a big cloak, and anonymous letters addressed to "O.P.Q." were found in the laundry of the prisoners, hinting at impending attacks against his post. But the horseplay only further ruffled Señor Bradburn's official dignity without accomplishing either of the ends sought by the pranksters. The immediate result was to land several Texans—including William B. Travis, Patrick C. Jack, and Monroe Edwards—in the calabozo.

William H. Jack, Patrick's brother, infuriated and bent on teaching Bradburn a lesson, rallied volunteers at San Felipe, while John Austin (close friend but not a close relative of the Empresario) gathered ninety others at Brazoria.

In June 1832, 160 colonists, their guns primed and awaiting only the arrival of cannon from Brazoria to attack Bradburn, agreed upon the Turtle Bayou Resolutions. They had heard that Santa Anna was trying to oust President Bustamante, and they knew that Bradburn and Fisher represented Bustamante in Texas. Just in case, they declared their "deepest interest and solicitude" for the cause of "the highly talented and distinguished" Santa Anna, and "as *freemen* devoted to a correct interpretation and enforcement of the constitution and laws" pledged their "lives and fortunes in support of the same, and of the distinguished leader . . . so gallantly fighting in defense of civil liberty." They placed the document in safekeeping, for use when, as, and if. . . .

Before the cannon could come, Colonel Piedras arrived from Nacogdoches, released the prisoners, and promised pay for property impressed; Bradburn relinquished his command. The Anahuac garrison, like the Texans, declared for Santa Anna and sailed back to Mexico to help him.

But the little cannon of Brazoria, if they did not do service at Anahuac, precipitated bloodletting at the mouth of the Brazos. John Austin loaded the guns and a new lot of volunteers on a boat and started down the river. Colonel Ugartechea, comandante at

Velasco, had no intention of allowing armed rebels to pass his fort. The Texans of the Brazos bottoms had liked Ugartechea, but now they would as soon fight him and his men as Bradburn. After a three-day fight Ugartechea surrendered and his troops withdrew. One after another, the Mexican garrisons abandoned Texas—Anahuac, Velasco, then Nacogdoches and Tenoxtitlan—until by the end of the summer not a Mexican soldier remained in the colonies.

It was rebellion, successful rebellion; but the complications of Mexican politics and the adroit work of Stephen F. Austin, who was still of the opinion that his "standing motto—'Fidelity to Mexico'—ought to be on every man's mouth and repeated," were to make it appear, for a time, as something else. Texas affairs were more confused than they appeared. Substantial Texans deprecated the Anahuac and Velasco incidents, but they could not undo what had been done, and circumstances soon obliged them to defend acts they had opposed.

Austin himself was at Saltillo attending the legislature of Coahuila y Texas when the disturbances took place. When the *Santanista* Colonel Mexía overhauled a mail packet at Matamoros and learned of the commotion, he promptly arranged a truce in the civil war and embarked for Velasco with four hundred troops—and Stephen F. Austin—to save Texas for Mexico. Over and over Austin assured everybody who would listen to him: "There is no insurrection of the Colonists against the Constitution and Government, neither do they entertain ideas endangering even remotely the integrity of the territory." It worked. Mexía was willing on arrival to "assure the inhabitants that I will unite with them . . . and that the forces under my command will protect their adhesion to said *plan*" of Vera Cruz—Santa Anna's program for rescuing Mexico from Bustamante.

Colonel Mexía was saluted as his vessels reached the mouth of the Brazos by the same cannon that had driven Ugartechea away; he was the house guest of Mr. John Austin, who had led the attack on Velasco; honored at a "large, cheerful, and convivial" gathering at Brazoria where toast after toast to Santa Anna was drunk and carefully prepared addresses rang the changes on the loyalty of all Texans to Mexico and her next President. After basking a reasonable time in this congenial atmosphere, Mexía returned to less pleasant duties south of the Rio Grande, convinced that the Texans were *muy simpáticos* and as loyal as he to the Great Cause that he and General Santa Anna represented. In September came news that Mexico would not reopen the Texas customhouses.

The colonists had tasted success and found it good, but they could not leave their job half done, nor let well enough alone. The less cautious felt that the time had come to press for all they wanted. Exactly a month after Mexía had gone to assure his chief that the Texans were loyal, the ayuntamiento of San Felipe called upon the settlers to send delegates to a convention there on October 1, 1832. Fifty-eight came and elected as president Stephen F. Austin, of the Peace Party, rather than William H. Wharton, of the action group.

The convention first of all declared its abiding loyalty to Mexico and Mexico's Constitution. Then it asked, among other things, that the issuing of land titles and organizing of ayuntamientos east of Austin's colonies (interrupted by Bradburn) be resumed; that Texas be exempt from tariff duties on necessities for three more years; that customs officers in Texas be appointed by Texas alcaldes, rather than by the federal government. Especially did the Texans pray for repeal of the prohibition of Anglo-American immigration and for the admission of Texas as a Mexican state, separate from Coahuila.

In six days the delegates completed their work. The petitions were never formally presented, but the convention caused repercussions. Mexican San Antonio officially condemned it, as did the jefe político; the governor reminded the Texans that such a gathering was a "disturbance of good order," to say nothing of a violation of the tradition and laws of Mexico. Santa Anna, not yet President, frowned on it and thought he saw where the Texas affair might end unless measures were taken.

But there was no threat. The Texans, forgetting that the "right of the people peaceably to assemble and to petition the government for a redress of grievances" was a guarantee of the Constitution they had forsworn and not of the Constitution under which they were living, organized committees of safety and vigilance and prepared for a second convention. General Mier y Terán had warned the President of Mexico years before that these Americanos in Texas "travel with their political constitution in their pockets, demanding the privileges, authority, and offices which such a constitution guarantees." They recognized no geographical limitation on the truths Mr. Jefferson had declared self-evident.

The second convention met at San Felipe on April 1, 1833—the day that the Santa Anna regime was taking office in Mexico City. The pendulum had swung away from Austin and peace; William H. Wharton defeated him for the presidency of this convention. Three fourths of the delegates had not served in the 1832 body and, symptomatic of the times, a delegate from Nacogdoches was Sam Houston, who had hardly had time to complete his naturalization.

There was general agreement on objectives. Texas wanted the anti-immigration law repealed; she wanted separate statehood; and she wanted both without further quibbling. That there might be no delay, the convention, against Austin's advice, adopted a state constitution submitted by General Houston and instructed Mr. Austin to present it to President Santa Anna.

As Austin started for the capital, he knew that he was bearing what the Mexican Government might consider insolent petitions from a mutinous people, and he went with a heavier heart than he had had on his first trip to Mexico City a dozen years before, before his Texas was filled with loud-mouthed, impatient men who had no way of knowing what sweat and toil and tears it had cost to bring the region to a point where they would want to take control of its policies.

Santa Anna was playing a game of hide-and-seek, allowing the old liberal war horse, Vice-President Valentín Gómez Farías, to act as executive occasionally—always when there was ticklish business to be handled. Austin, his nerves a little brittle, had less than his usual patience with Mexican red tape. He told the Acting President that if the petition was not promptly granted the Texans might set up a state government without approval from the capital. Gómez Farías construed this as a threat and lectured Austin on his manners. For almost the only time in his life Austin found himself involved—and as the aggressor—in a quarrel.

In his anger, the idea struck him of having the Mexican element in Texas take the lead in organizing a state government, and he wrote the ayuntamiento of San Antonio urging that this be done without delay. Soon Austin and Gómez Farías repented their hot words and were friends again; and before Austin left Mexico City, December 10, President Santa Anna had agreed to practically everything the Texans asked, except separate statehood.

Delighted at how much he had accomplished after all seemed lost, the Empresario hurried to Saltillo to pay his respects to the new comandante general before reporting to his Texan constituents. But that letter he had written to San Antonio "in a moment of irritation and impatience" had gone from ayuntamiento to jefe político, from jefe político to Governor, from Governor to the President's office, where the experts pronounced it something close to treason and ordered the arrest of its author. The comandante general did his duty, and Austin was sent under guard to the prison in Mexico City that once had housed the Inquisition.

In Texas, for once, there was a period of political calm. Floods of unprecedented proportions destroyed crops and brought epidemics—cholera and malignant malaria—in their wake. Men were too busy garnering their scant crops, nursing their sick, and burying their dead to give much attention to anything else.

Into this Texas, during this unnatural political calm, came Anson Jones on October 20, 1833, with the

sole and exclusive object . . . to find a suitable field for the exercise of my profession, and to make myself useful in . . . pursuits altogether peaceful . . . in an hour when there appeared little expectation of war . . . little probability of it.

V

FIVE THOUSAND A YEAR

AS SUCH THINGS were then reckoned in Texas, Brazoria was pretty well established when Anson Jones arrived; it was already the commercial center of the province and, before the Big Cholera, had been a medical center of sorts, with a standing committee of four of the established physicians—Drs. Parrott, Phelps, Angier, and Cox (who also doubled as agent for well pumps)—appointed by the ayuntamiento to examine immigrants who proposed to practice surgery and physic.

John Austin, founder of the town, was a Connecticut Yankee who first visited Texas as a filibuster in 1819, later returned peaceably to become one of Stephen F. Austin's colonists. With Yankee acumen he acquired the most eligible town site on the Brazos River in 1829. The Empresario himself named John Austin's prospective metropolis. He called it Brazoria "for the single reason," he explained, "that I know of none like it in the world." Stephen F. Austin did not think well of the custom, already beginning, of naming Texas towns for towns in the United States. His own town was called San Felipe de Austin.

By March 1831, Brazoria had "about thirty houses, all of logs except three of brick and two or three framed, and several more were building." A half mile of forest had been cleared away from the west bank of the river, and squares of an eighth of a mile were selling at $20 to $140 each.

Some months before Dr. Jones came, Mrs. Mary Austin Holley, Texas's first publicity agent, sailed up the Brazos to Brazoria, "the third day from the mouth of the river, and the sixth from New Orleans." She recorded:

The whole male population, en masse, stood on the shore, the future quay, to welcome us. An arrival at Brazoria, is an event of some moment. The *port* was not crowded with shipping, nor would it be slander to allude to the *grass-grown* streets. We were safely moored among the tall masts (the only masts there) still flourishing in all their leafy honors. Not a *naked spar,* save ours, was to be seen. . . .

Too much must not be expected of Brazoria. . . . . One street stretches along the bank of the Brazos, and one parallel with it farther back, while other streets, with the trees still standing, are laid out to intersect these at right angles. . . . Its arrangements, as well as its wealth and greatness, are all prospective . . . it is but three years since the first tree was cut. . . . A stranger is more surprised to see brick stores and frame dwelling houses, than disposed to complain that he does not find more elegance and convenience. . . .

Everybody here is employed, and every house occupied. Some families, recently arrived, are obliged to *camp out.* . . . The place has . . . a busy and prosperous air . . . but has not yet advanced beyond the wants of first necessity. There is neither cabinet-maker, tailor, hatter, shoe-maker, nor any other mechanic, except carpenters . . . not even a blacksmith. . . .

Brazoria . . . contains from two to three hundred inhabitants . . . some families of education and refinement. . . .

But for all the energy that had been, and was being, expended to create an Anglo-American metropolis, there was one great obstacle to progress: the location was low and unpleasant, and the inhabitants were recurrent sufferers from fever and the ague. During the summer of 1833 the Brazos—which Mrs. Holley found "placid and beneficent in repose—mighty and terrible in wrath" —overflowed, destroying crops and greatly increasing the seasonal sickness; but it was the Asiatic cholera, which reached Texas for the first time that season, that decimated the settlements along the river. In April eleven of the twenty settlers at the mouth of the Brazos were stricken; seven died within a week. At Brazoria all but half-a-dozen families fled, but the toll was eighty deaths. The founder of the town, two of the physicians, the editor of the *Texas Gazette* (only newspaper in the colony), and the proprietress of the boardinghouse were among the dead.

When Dr. Jones reached Brazoria on November 1, 1833, the epidemic had spent its force, but the mark of death seemed still to be upon the place. Captain Brown had not been mistaken: there was a good opening for a physician at Brazoria—and for a mortician too. The population was hardly greater than in 1831

—about fifty families, most of them tending new-made graves in the little cemetery.

Anson Jones remembered New Orleans: his arrival in the wake of a cholera epidemic . . . his failure. He booked passage back to the United States.

But the *Sabine* remained in port a fortnight. Drs. C. G. Cox and J. S. Counsel had died during the epidemic, and families returning to Brazoria, still apprehensive, wanted doctors. The visiting physician, with his fifty dollars' worth of drugs, was "persuaded, through the earnest solicitations of Mr. J. A. Wharton and other citizens of the town and its vicinity . . . to give the place a fair trial." To be begged to stay anywhere was a new experience. Dr. Jones remained.

Unacquainted with the ways of the frontier, he watched with some astonishment the resiliency of the town. His new friend, Lawyer John A. Wharton, took over the editorial tripod, and his *Advocate of the People's Rights* was, within a month, chronicling the news, voicing the sentiments, and advertising the wares of Brazorians, as D. W. Anthony's *Gazette* had done before the Big Cholera.

William B. Travis was dividing his time between Brazoria and San Felipe, drawing bills of sale, wills, deeds, titles, handling probate matters (a brisk business late in 1833), and occasionally acting as special prosecutor, taking his fees, as Jones was to do, in land or anything he could get. A newcomer at the local bar was Godwin Brown Cotten, a former editor of the *Gazette*, who turned lawyer because he believed himself "as capable as many others who are now EXERCISING the profession."

There were other changes. Mrs. Jane Long, widow of the general, leased her tavern to M. W. Smith and published in the *Advertiser* of March 27, 1834, her "unfeigned thanks to the citizens of Brazoria and its vicinity for the very liberal patronage bestowed upon her during the two years of her keeping a public house." R. Stephenson was offering, at Howth and Williams's old stand, corn meal, flour, and old whisky "for cash or peltry," and H. B. Stratton advertised a stock of "new French, English and Italian goods, school books, histories, and miscellaneous books . . . also a very fine-toned piana Forte."

Jones's professional colleague, Dr. T. F. L. Parrott, administrator of Editor Anthony's modest estate, began the new year by marrying John Austin's widow. John A. Wharton handled the affairs of the late Dr. Cox, while William T. Austin looked after the complicated estate of his brother John.

Robert Mills, "Duke of Brazoria," and his brothers Andrew and David were getting control of the cotton trade and most of the commercial operations of the Brazos watershed. For years this firm was to dominate the economic life of the community and dispute with McKinney and Williams for leadership in Texas.

Brazorians were subscribing land and money to encourage Robert Wilson and William P. Harris "to bring a Steamboat to Texas for the purpose of running in its rivers, and to be and remain in Texas for the benefit of the Commerce of the Same." William P. Scott, later chief justice of the county, was establishing a local record for sartorial elegance and for heavy drinking. Henry Smith, first alcalde of the ayuntamiento, was completing his term, preparing to turn the empty treasury over to Edwin Waller with the understandable explanation that "the first dollar has yet to be received."

By Christmas the addition of "twenty excellent families" brought the population to about pre-cholera level and, if it was not yet a metropolis, Brazoria was at least functioning like an American frontier town. And its new man of medicine was imbibing some of its buoyant spirit as he attended the most lucrative practice he had ever had.

The country, too, was filling up with newcomers. Little log houses were dotting the clearings between the plantations of the earlier settlers, and wagonloads of immigrant farmers were passing through the town almost every day. Most of them were young men, some of them with young wives; others were widowers. A few widows with half-grown children, already inured to frontier life in the United States, came along with the immigrant trains, hoping that life would be kinder to them than in the place where they had buried their husbands.

Mrs. Sarah Pevehouse Smith reached Brazoria County with a group of immigrants in January 1834. With her came her fourteen-year-old gray-eyed daughter Mary and her four other Arkansas-born children. Her husband, a Virginian, had died, and after that her small farm near Little Rock seemed less attractive each time she heard tales of the fertile, free land of the Brazos Valley. In the fall of 1833 she disposed of her holdings, loaded her goods and implements and children into her wagon, and joined a Texas-bound caravan. Three months later she recounted to her new neighbors near Brazoria an odyssey that was notable even in a day of hard travel.

These Arkansas immigrants had reached the Sabine River about the middle of November, worn out from travel through heavy rain and unseasonable cold. Across the river lay their New Canaan—the land of second chance—but the Sabine was not to be forded. The rains that drenched the immigrants had swollen the river, and there was neither bridge nor ferry.

While women and children shivered around flickering campfires the men chopped down wild mulberry trees and tied the green limbs into a crude but serviceable raft on which the twenty families with all their belongings ferried perilously into Mexican Texas to begin their trek anew. From the Sabine crossing to Brazoria was less than three hundred miles, but the party had no guide and there were no roads. On New Year's Day they were still en route, but before the end of January they were encamped on the sites of their new homes and were catching the expansive atmosphere of the new province.

Early onset of the sickly season in the spring of 1834 kept Dr. Jones riding his forty-mile circuit night and day until September, when he was stricken with bilious remittent fever while attending a case at the Phillips plantation on the Bernard. He managed to reach home, turned his practice over to his apprentice, James N. Berryman, and lay abed two months. He made his will and resigned himself to die.

When he recovered, Dr. Jones determined to lead an existence more compatible with the demands of his health and more in keeping with the status he now had in the community. He rented and furnished a house and, in the fall, brought his unmarried sister Mary from New York to make a home for him.

Anson Jones had cast his lot permanently among an agricultural people, but he was no farmer, although he had spent his youth upon a barren New England farm—a succession of them —and he was never to become a planter in Brazoria County. But

the lush plantations along the Brazos and the Bernard and Chocolate Bayou represented a way of life that appealed to him.

It was the Old South over again, these broad acres tilled by
slave labor; plantation houses that seemed luxurious in the raw
country; cotton and sugar marketed by the Mills brothers, or
McKinney and Williams, or the great commission houses of New
Orleans; plantation masters who wore suits imported from New
York, hunted with hounds, entertained on a scale that Jones had
never before observed at close range, and pursued politics as an
avocation.

Jones would become one of them when he could afford it, but
for the present he was only a physician with his residence in town,
devoting himself "exclusively and earnestly" to his profession, receiving good fees in good lands or chattel or mortgages and, very
occasionally, in Mexican or United States coin.

The habits of Southern hospitality he acquired late. In Brazoria,
where frugality had been made respectable by her New England
founder, the doctor's carefulness in money matters marked him
as thrifty, not parsimonious. He enjoyed the prodigal hospitality
of the plantations as a guest from whom return of the compliment
was not expected. He learned the manners, without incurring the
expense, of gracious living.

Jones's genuine unconcern about politics set him apart from
other immigrants. He instinctively avoided political argument.
Among his patients were leaders of the War Party, prominent ad-
herents of the Peace Party, and many who, like himself, were little
interested in public affairs. With politically minded acquaintances
Jones's role was one that he had learned as a neophyte physician:
he listened attentively, nodded gravely, said nothing. No remark
of his offended a listener's political opinions or became a topic of
controversy during his early years in Brazoria; but subconsciously
he was storing away information that later was to be useful.

His attitude was instinctive, a compound of common sense and
innate caution. Politics was not his game. His primary concern
was winning friends and influencing them to call professionally
on Dr. Jones. In Philadelphia he had learned, too late, that sick
people prefer a physician whose preoccupation is medicine. His
professional success was remarkable.

By the end of the year he felt himself, for the first time in his life, firmly established—with a practice worth five thousand dollars a year and the expectation of becoming "as wealthy as any man in Texas . . . from the practice of medicine . . . and the investment of its proceeds."

He could look back upon his fourteen months' residence in Texas as the one period of his life during which he had allowed no external factor to deflect him from the course he had set for himself. He was a practitioner of medicine and a tutor of medical apprentices. His interest in everything else was desultory.

Brazoria had been tranquil enough when Jones settled there, but as the months passed the political temperature of the doctor's little world steadily mounted. Stephen F. Austin was still a prisoner in Mexico. For a time both factions in Texas—the Peace men, temporarily without leadership, the War Party led by the Wharton brothers—were disposed to give more thought to repairing the devastation of inundation and cholera than to political grievances. The ayuntamiento was strongly anti-Mexican, but it declined to fall in with Austin's suggestion that Texans organize a state government without authority from the capital. Even William H. Wharton signed the printed warning January 1, 1834, that the course recommended by Austin would mean war. He urged Texans to wait a year or two before pressing for separate statehood.

Juan N. Almonte visited Brazoria and other Brazos River towns in July to see if there was foundation for Vice-President Farías's suspicion that the colonists were ready to disavow their Mexican allegiance. The Texans, he reported to the government, had been misunderstood at the capital; he believed that Texas would remain quiet if Mexico could attain a degree of political stability.

William H. Wharton, leader of the "war dogs," had been at his Eagle Island plantation since the adjournment of the convention of 1833, more secluded from the public eye, he thought, than was Austin in his Mexican prison. "I have confined myself exclusively to the pursuit of agriculture, and have not been ten miles from home," he wrote in November.

But the younger Wharton, John A., lived in no such isolation. His law office at Brazoria was a busy place, but he had willingly assumed the editorship of *The Advocate of the People's Rights* when he became convinced that the Texas press was "muzzled, devoted to the interest of a few and not accessible to all"—that is, devoted to the interests of Stephen F. Austin and the Peace Party. The Empresario's friends believed that the *Advocate* began publication primarily to attack Austin and his policies.

"The Austins: May their bones burn in hell!" was John A. Wharton's contribution to the toasts proposed at a political dinner.

The Austins were a numerous clan. Along the Brazos were two families of them: one headed by the absent Stephen F., who lived at San Felipe; the other by William T. Austin, whose late brother had founded the town of Brazoria. The families were distantly related, if related at all, but they were of the same political faith.

William T. Austin, a peaceable and unassuming citizen, felt obligated to defend the honor of all the Austin clan and sent his challenge to Wharton. He then engaged the expert services of his neighbor, W. D. C. Hall, who had been a friend of Lafitte, to teach him marksmanship. When the antagonists met on the field of honor, the inexpert Austin managed to disable Wharton's right arm before the lawyer-editor could bring his gun into play.

John A. Wharton was Dr. Jones's oldest friend in Texas; it was he who had induced the doctor to remain at Brazoria. Although he did not share the lawyer's opinion of the Austins, Jones must have felt keenly for his friend as he watched the shattered arm slowly mend. It was the first time that anyone close to Dr. Jones had been involved in an affair of honor, but within two months the code duello was to alter his immediate future. James N. Berryman, his former apprentice, whom Jones had dubbed Doctor and taken into partnership, was killed in a duel with R. A. Stevenson.

At Brazoria on November 8, 1834, an election was held to determine whether a new Texas convention should assemble at Béxar on the fifteenth. This time the occasion was a schism in the state of Coahuila y Texas, and Juan N. Seguin, who, with other San Antonio Mexicans, had opposed the previous conventions, took the lead in advocating this one. His strange bedfellow in this enterprise was Henry Smith, jefe político of the Department of the Brazos, outspoken foe of all things and ideas Mexican. Austin's friends opposed the Béxar convention on the double ground that it would jeopardize the Empresario's safety in Mexico and would be counted a victory for Austin's political enemies at home, particularly Henry Smith. Sixteen Brazorians voted for the convention, fifty-seven against it. William H. Wharton did not vote. But John A. Wharton headed the list of sixteen who wanted action, and the Duke of Brazoria was also among them. Dr. Jones was not among the seventy-three citizens who went to the polls.

As little concerned with politics as Dr. Jones were farmers of the community, like John Woodruff, who seldom came into town to hear the latest rumors. Woodruff was a widower whose clearing and cabin were not far from the Widow Smith's new home. He admired the Arkansas woman's spunk in coming to Texas alone and the workmanlike way in which she had set up her establishment with no man to help her. Management of the Smith household was in the capable hands of young Mary, who became an efficient housewife before she was grown, while her mother did a man's work on the farm.

The Smiths, for their part, were not unaware of the Woodruffs —Mr. Woodruff and his six children—and how difficult it was for a man, without a wife's help, to rear a family in this new country. Community of interest resulted in a merger of households. On October 18, 1835, Mrs. Smith and Woodruff made bond to be married by a priest if ever one appeared, and became Mr. and Mrs. Woodruff. Mary, then sixteen, continued to be the governess of the eleven assorted Woodruff and Smith children, to whom four subsequently were added.

The medical fraternity in Brazoria had increased in numbers, if not in strength, by the year 1835. Cards of Drs. Thomas J. Bernard, Thomas R. Erwin, Arthur Applewhite and John Y. Wallace appeared in the *Republican*. Drs. Applewhite and Harris declined to be examined for license and a lively newspaper controversy in which Jones took no part ensued. Population was growing in even greater proportion than the medical fraternity, and insanitation and the miasma of the Brazos made work for the doctors.

Dr. Jones had established his clientele before the newcomers arrived, and "was this year again eminently successful in business." He always alluded to his profession as "business." The practice of medicine was a means of making a living, and more than once he had quit it. The medical aspects of his practice did not intrigue him—only the financial return it brought, or failed to bring, him. He was a competent physician who practiced medicine for the same reason that another man might be a printer or a merchant.

He had learned the hard way to value financial independence and he was methodically attaining it. It cost him little to live, and he collected what was owed him. During 1835 he filed thirty-six suits in the Primary Court at Brazoria; only three involved more than fifty dollars. John A. Wharton, or the firm Jack and Wharton, represented him in court.

Seasonal illnesses, scarlet fever, and a localized smallpox epidemic in the spring of 1835 kept him constantly riding his wide circuit, but circumstances were beginning to make him, in spite of himself, "an anxious observer of the political horizon of my adopted country."

VI

AN ANXIOUS OBSERVER

REVOLUTION was inexorably getting under way in Texas, although some of the principal actors were tardy in discovering—or admitting—it. This revolution was no design of a single master. It was the unplanned combination of concepts and aims of a large number of zealous workmen unskilled in such things, whose unsynchronized activities introduced infinite variation in the design and whose mutual distrust generated almost continuous strife among them.

It was a time of frenzied activity on the part of the few, apathy on the part of the many. The isolation in which farms, ranches, even towns, stood from one another; the lack of roads and facilities for communication; the inevitable distortion of such fragmentary news as passed from community to community; the unpredictable behavior of men under great and opposing stresses, and the individualism that was the keynote of the Texan character—all made confusion inevitable.

To Dr. Jones it was "quite apparent" that war with Mexico could not be avoided, but he had become so habituated to his middle-of-the-road position that, he recalled,

I . . . counselled forbearance, and the maintenance of peace as long as the one was proper or the other possible. I . . . was not one of those who early this year secured the appellation of "war-dogs". . . . I resisted all applications to take part in premature proceedings of rashness.

Proceedings of rashness, however, did not wait upon the doctor's participation. Mexico began the year 1835 by re-establishing customhouses among the Texans. Captain Antonio Tenorio was put in charge at Anahuac, and a deputy collector was stationed at Brazoria. Once more there was friction, once more the Texans played practical jokes on Mexican soldiers, and again Mexican soldiers lodged Texans in their calabozo. It was the seriocomic play of three years ago over again. Anahuac was again the scene, but the leading roles were played now by Tenorio and Gonzales, Andrew Briscoe and William B. Travis, instead of Bradburn and Fisher, William H. Jack and John Austin.

President Santa Anna, systematically stamping out opposition to his centralized regime, had already detailed his brother-in-law, General Martín Perfecto de Cós, to crush the federalist state government of Coahuila y Texas and keep an eye on the mercurial Texans from the *Comandancia General de las Provincias Internas* below the Rio Grande.

Citizens of Austin's capital, San Felipe, three days' journey up the river from Brazoria, learned with great apprehension of the goings on in Coahuila and of Cós's determination to bring the Texans into line. Leaders of the War Party there seized General Cós's courier, read to turbulent mass meetings the comandante's intercepted instructions to his subalterns in Texas, and applauded Lawyer William B. Travis as he and forty volunteers galloped toward Anahuac to release the imprisoned Texans.

Travis received Tenorio's surrender without a struggle on June 30, and the volunteers, flushed with victory, returned home to discover that sentiment had reversed itself and that mass meetings were now condemning their action. Even San Felipe disavowed them, and War Party leaders were busy writing General Cós assurances of the loyalty of all Texans to Mexico. But the comandante was not as gullible as the Texans thought: he demanded, as proof of loyalty, not effusive letters, but the handing over to him, for military trial, five of the Texan leaders, including Travis and Samuel M. Williams, Austin's partner.

Then sentiment veered the other way along the Brazos.

Committees of safety and correspondence had already sprung into existence, as they had in the British colonies two generations earlier, and Texan counterparts of Patrick Henry and Samuel Adams began preparing the public mind for organized resistance. The comandante general moved headquarters from Matamoros to San Antonio de Béxar, the better to enforce the New Order among the Texans.

By late summer cautious Dr. Jones was willing to take his first step in revolutionary politics by signing, along with leaders of the

War Party and miscellaneous Brazorians, "a paper written and circulated by . . . John A. Wharton" recommending the convening of delegates "instructed so that no party may rule, and that the people be fairly represented." They made two copies of it. The Wharton brothers headed one list of the 140 signatures, with Dr. Jones the eighteenth, just above Dr. Branch T. Archer. Jones signed the other copy third, preceded only by William H. Wharton and the Duke of Brazoria. Young Ira Jones also signed. He had come from New York to become his cousin Anson's apprentice in the spring and was now his partner.

"This document," Dr. Jones explained, "did not appear to embrace any *war* measure. There was a great division in the minds of the people. . . . I thought we were too few to divide, and, therefore, wished to bring about union and concert of thought and action."

But the doctor's old friend Ammon Underwood believed that the convention movement, at Columbia at least, was a stratagem of the War Party, "conducted with much intreague and deception knowing that a majority of the people were opposed to that measure for many pertinent reasons." He was referring to a mass meeting held at Columbia six days after Dr. Jones signed the Brazoria document. The Columbians demanded a convention to secure "peace if it is to be obtained on constitutional terms, and to prepare for war—if war be inevitable."

The proposal for another convention was immediately suspect because it originated with the War Party. The Peace Party was numerous enough to defeat it—if it could find a spokesman.

Stephen F. Austin, titular leader of the Peace men, returned from his detention in Mexico after the convention had been suggested but before the election of delegates. He found a changed and chaotic Texas, and Texans thought they discerned in him a changed man. Leaders of the War Party, as well as old friends, hailed him "as the only physician that could correct the disorganized system and restore a healthy action to the body corporate," and towns vied for the honor of being the first to hear him speak. His own town, San Felipe, once warlike, was now headquarters for the Peace Party. Brazoria was dominated by the Whartons, Dr. Archer, and other War men.

Austin accepted the invitation of Brazorians who desired to

"express their approval of his public services and their respect for his private virtues"; but he and they knew that this September 8 meeting was to be no symposium on the past services of the Empresario. It was to offer a forum for Austin's program for the immediate future. He had spent his first night at home walking the beach, "his mind oppressed with the gravity of the situation, forecasting the troubles ahead of Texas." Solitary thought, rather than conferences with men anxious to become leaders, showed him the direction in which he should move and carry Texas with him. Never, perhaps, did a man hold the destiny of a people, and half a continent, more completely in his own hands than did Austin when he met with the Brazorians on September 8, 1835.

"Pursuant to the arrangements, the company seated themselves to a dinner at Messrs. Fitchett and Gill's, gotten up in the best style," the *Texas Republican* of September 19 reported. They listened to interminable toasts in the Jacksonian tradition, then settled back to hear the Empresario.

To the delight of the War Party, Austin made it unmistakably clear that he, for one, was done with half measures. He declared:

If any acts of imprudence have been committed by individuals, they evidently resulted from the revolutionary state of the whole nation, the imprudent and censurable conduct of the state authorities, and the total want of a local government in Texas. It is, indeed, a source of surprise and creditable congratulation, that so few acts of this description have occurred. . . . Texas certainly did not originate the revolution, neither have the people, as a people, participated in it. The consciences and hands of the Texians are free from censure, and clean. . . .

As a citizen of Texas, I have a right to an opinion on so important a matter—I have no other right, and pretend to no other. . . .

I see but one way, and that is by a general consultation of the people by means of delegates elected for that purpose, with full powers . . . to adopt such measures as the tranquility and salvation of the country may require. . . .

With these explanatory remarks I will give as a toast—*The constitutional rights and the security and peace of Texas—they ought to be maintained; and, jeopardized as they now are, they demand a general consultation of the people.*

Cousin Henry Austin wrote two days later: "the only thing I did not like was the 7$ a head for the ball and supper and $30 more for a decent suit of clothes. . . . There were sixty covers and . . . the table was three times filled by men alone. . . . You never saw such enthusiasm."

In Austin's audience sat visitors from other municipalities as well as the solvent citizens of Brazoria. Dr. Jones, like a good many others, had never before seen the Empresario, but he had seen in Texas the evidences of his wisdom and patience. The tone of his talk, as well as the soundness of his reasoning, appealed to a man of Jones's temperament. One month before, the doctor had participated for the first time in the public affairs of Texas when he signed, a little hesitantly, Mr. Wharton's petition. The words of the prudent Austin now focused his attention on politics.

Three weeks after the Brazoria dinner, at Gonzales on the Guadalupe, came the "Lexington of the Texan Revolution." Texans, defending a cannon labeled "Come and Take It," sent a Mexican force scurrying back to San Antonio de Béxar. The citizens' army at Gonzales, organized on ultra-democratic and individualistic lines, elected Stephen F. Austin their commander, after sectional and personal animosities had almost dissolved it; and for forty days and forty nights the Empresario was General Austin. He led his oddly assorted troops to Béxar to evict Cós, symbol of Mexican authority in Texas.

Ira Jones, who had scarcely had time to become acclimated in Texas, felt the urge to join in the fight, as did many other young Texans, and he set out for Béxar with his cousin's blessing and letters of introduction to Old Ben Milam, who was to die gloriously in the storming of the place. The war was coming very close to the Jones household, and the doctor was beginning to be anxious for the safety of his spinster sister who kept his house.

Military commotion delayed the convening of the delegates at San Felipe until November 3, General Austin's birthday. Of the ninety-eight men elected, only fifty-eight appeared to sit in this Consultation of the Chosen Delegates of All Texas in General Convention Assembled. The war had been in progress a month; the Consultation would decide what the Texans were fighting for.

Dr. Branch T. Archer of Brazoria, a Virginian reputed to be the most accomplished swearer in the Brazos country, was elected president. Texas, he declared in his keynote speech, was not battling alone for her rights and liberties but was "laying the corner-

stone of liberty in the great Mexican republic." R. M. Williamson
and John A. Wharton—William Wharton was at Béxar with the
army—argued realistically for a frank declaration of independence, which won fifteen votes; but Don Carlos Barrett and Sam
Houston were able to convince thirty-three delegates that a more
ambiguous statement, affirming the right, but not the fact, of independence, would serve better.

Dr. Jones had not been a candidate for membership in the Consultation, but he took time to look in on its deliberations and to
see how the Brazoria delegates—Wharton, Henry Smith, Edwin
Waller, and John S. D. Byrom—were acquitting themselves.

On the way to San Felipe he encountered the Reverend José
María Alpuché e Infante,

a Mexican of some distinction, and a friend of Zavala's, who . . .
disaffected with his own government . . . had come to Texas to
take part in opposition to it. He represented to me that he could be
of service, if he could get to San Felipe and have an interview with
Zavala, but could not ride horseback. . . . I . . . learned there
was a buggy in town belonging to Col. W. B. Travis of San Felipe
. . . had my horse tackled to it, and with the Padre started . . .
over roads literally covered with water, or knee-deep in mud. The
first day we lost our road, got benighted. . . . The next day we went
to Cole's; here we were detained by stormy weather more than a
week.

Close association taught Dr. Jones several things about his
fifty-year-old traveling companion. Alpuché had been a curate in
Tabasco, a senator in the Mexican Congress, and was a brother
Mason. He was, in fact, the founder of one branch of Masonry
in Mexico—as Jones was to be in Texas. But his ecclesiastical,
fraternal, and political careers had been stormy ones, for he was
a type of the restless spirits thrown up by revolution—"a sort of
Danton, without his brains."

Before they reached San Felipe, Dr. Jones was convinced that
his guest "was, in the first place, a *coward,* and in the second
place, *untrustworthy.* . . . it would have been unfortunate for
Texas if his advice had been followed; and that it was not followed, was probably owing to me, in a great measure"—and in
greater measure, of course, to the rains that delayed their arrival
at the Consultation. For his part, Padre Alpuché later had some-

thing to say of the Texans. He told Santa Anna—so a friend reported to Austin from Mexico—that he had "found Such a Set
of Villians and Rasculs that he could not Stay there . . . that he
was in all the Secrets of the Rebbles of Texus." "Cant his damd
Scalp be Taken of?" the reporter asked Austin.

When Dr. Jones and the visiting statesman at last reached San
Felipe, the Consultation had almost finished its work. The doctor
did not approve of the personnel or the tone of the gathering:

> There appeared to me a plenty of recklessness and selfishness, but
> little dignity or patriotism. . . . I was introduced to Bowie—he was
> dead drunk; to Houston—his appearance was . . . that of a broken-
> down sot and debauchee. The first night after my arrival, I was kept
> awake nearly all night by a drunken carouse . . . Dr. Archer and
> Gen. Houston . . . to judge from the noise . . . the whole burden
> of the conversation . . . abuse and denunciation of . . . Stephen
> F. Austin. . . .
> I remained but two or three days. . . .

The Brazoria doctor who, so far in Texas, had been conspicuous chiefly for his inconspicuousness and for his reluctance to par-
ticipate in political discussion, became bolder at San Felipe, as he
later recalled it. All this talk of fighting for the principles of a
constitution that was as dead as Hector and re-establishing liberty
in the great Mexican republic struck him as not only silly but dishonest. And he said as much:

> I took occasion . . . publicly to express my opinions of what I
> saw and heard, until my friend, Col. John A. Wharton . . . assured
> me my life was in danger . . . and advised me, that . . . it was
> not the disposition of some parties to allow the utterance of
> them. . . .
> Perhaps my feelings carried me too far, but . . . History will not
> be able to say much in favor of that "Consultation". . . . I returned
> to Brazoria, satisfied that we were in a bad scrape.

When he returned from the Consultation the physician had met
and, in a manner, had taken the measure of many of the politicians
and the head of every government Texas was to have for ten
years. His neighbor, Henry Smith, was elected Governor soon
after Jones left San Felipe. David G. Burnet, then a judge under

Mexican commission, was to become ad interim President within four months. Sam Houston, elected major general by the Consultation, was to be first and third President of the republic. Mirabeau B. Lamar, second President, was not at San Felipe, but he had visited Brazoria just before the Consultation met. Anson Jones probably would have predicted, in November 1835, no such distinction as any of them attained, and if any of them divined in the self-appointed critic of the Consultation the person of a future statesman, they recorded no hint of it.

In retrospect, Dr. Jones believed that during this period, and later, he had no thought of a political career. It had been a long time since he had sat in, or even watched, meetings that reminded him of the great days when he was Grand Master of Pennsylvania Odd Fellows. Now that the memory of the unhappy phases of that activity had grown dim, leaving only the recollection of having participated in clashes of opinion and having been at the center of things, Jones was, without analyzing his motives, directing himself toward a participation in affairs of moment.

On March 1, 1835, he had revived his interest in fraternalism when he met with his Masonic friends, John A. Wharton, Asa Brigham, Dr. James Æ. Phelps, and Alexander Russell at the John Austin place near Brazoria. It was the first such gathering of Texan Masons since 1828, and the five brothers agreed to apply to the Grand Lodge of Louisiana for a charter—tactfully suggesting that their lodge bear the name of the current Louisiana Grand Master. Apparently it did not occur to any of these Texans to request a charter from the Grand Lodge of Mexico, as Austin and some associates had tried to do seven years earlier. Their natural affinity was to the Masonry and to the other institutions of their mother country, and they knew that the tenuous political ties with Mexico were already dissolving.

Before the dispensation arrived, naming Anson Jones as first Worshipful Master, the doctor was embarked upon an enterprise of more importance.

I took steps to aid in calling a public meeting of the citizens of the municipality or county of Brazoria, at Columbia. There was a large attendance. I drew up, offered, and advocated, as chairman of the committee, resolutions in favor of a "Declaration of Independence from Mexico" and calling a Convention of the people of Texas on the first Monday in March, 1836, to make the Declaration, and to frame a Constitution. . . .

These recommendations were advocated by myself, J. Collins-worth, and B. C. Franklin, and opposed by W. J. Russell. Fearing to trust the vote, I proposed . . . the resolutions be signed by those who approved them, and go to the country as the expression of the individuals whose names should be appended. . . . We succeeded in getting about twenty or thirty names from among those who were present; but . . . nearly everybody signed before they were pub-lished. . . .

The people of the country were at first startled by the boldness of the Columbia Resolutions, but . . . by the 2d of March following, there were but few in the country who did not acquiesce in the propriety of the course proposed in those resolutions.

Later, when other men had forgotten those resolutions and their author, Dr. Jones's recollection was sharpened. Fifteen years afterward he was sure that in offering those resolutions he

took the first efficient step for the *independence* of Texas. . . . I had kept aloof and taken no part in bringing about or accelerating the public difficulties, but now they were upon us, I had no disposi-tion to shrink from duty or responsibility. The crisis had come. . . .

The resolutions were published on Christmas Day. Two days later Holland Lodge at Brazoria held its first session, with Wor-shipful Master Anson Jones in the chair.

In Philadelphia, Jones had been impelled toward fraternalism by loneliness and dearth of patients. In Texas, Masonic and polit-ical activities at first were a relaxation from the exacting demands of his profession. While Ira was with the Texan army at Béxar, the entire "business" of Drs. Jones and Jones—"more pressing than ordinary"—fell to the senior partner alone while he was be-ginning his participation in public affairs.

On New Year's Day, 1836, the three Brazoria Joneses held their last reunion. Mary was to return to New York in February, Ira was soon to die after serving on two fronts in the Texan war, and the doctor himself was to devote the greater part of the year to military activity. Never again was Anson Jones to live the tran-quil life he had come to love during his first twenty-six months in Texas.

Another, more hectic, career was about to begin.

VII

1 8 3 6

THERE was no mistaking the portents of things," Dr. Jones said, "when the year 1836 dawned upon Texas. Santa Anna and the Mexican people were thoroughly aroused . . . evidence of an early and formidable invasion came with every breeze from the west."

From San Felipe de Austin, a little to the north of Brazoria, came news even more discouraging, but no worse than the doctor expected. The Consultation had created, in November, a state of Texas, theoretically a member of the Mexican federal union which Santa Anna had dissolved by decree a year before the Consultation assembled. Even in time of peace, well-disposed men could hardly have administered a government under the arrangement the Consultation ordained. During that hectic winter choleric gentlemen with conflicting aims distrustfully shared ill-defined and co-ordinate powers.

After they had established a postal system, authorized a little navy, and filled the civil list, the Governor and council fell to examining the patriotism and good faith of each other. Governor Henry Smith, by January 10, was declaring to the council:

You . . . seem determined . . . to destroy the very institutions which you are pledged and sworn to support. . . . You . . . Mexican like, are ready to sacrifice your country at the shrine of plunder. . . . I am now tired of watching scoundrels abroad and scoundrels at home. . . . I am now prepared to drop the curtain. . . . A convention has been called which will afford a sovereign remedy to the vile machinations of a caucussing, intriguing, and corrupt council. . . . your body will stand adjourned until the first of March. . . .

The council did not adjourn. Instead, after registering

astonishment that this community could have been so miserably deceived in selecting for the high office of governor, a man whose language and conduct prove his early habits of association to have been vulgar and depraved, and his present disposition that of a disorganizer and a tyrant,

it declared Henry Smith removed from office and cited him to trial. Then the council empowered the marshal of Texas to commandeer "the power of the country, all officers of the civil and military, and all the citizens of the country" to take from Smith the records of his office. But the marshal could find only three men willing to aid him. Mr. Smith retained the papers and continued to receive mail addressed to the Governor. Proclamations and broadsides issued by both parties to the quarrel kept the printer at San Felipe busy.

If Jones found nothing to comfort him in the turn of civil affairs, he found the military situation even more disquieting. Daily the situation of Texas was becoming more ominous. President Santa Anna, vowing to avenge the eviction of Cós from San Antonio de Béxar in December 1835, and to redress the "perfidy, ingratitude, and the restless spirit of the colonists," was in personal command of an expeditionary force of six thousand moving toward Texas.

North of the Rio Grande there was an incredible mixture of panic, cross-purposes, and complacency. Such Texan troops as remained under arms were divided in their objectives and recognized no single authority, military or civil.

A hundred almost destitute volunteers remained at San Antonio after twice that number had left for home against explicit orders from their commander. General Houston had ordered the Alamo demolished and its military stores transferred to Gonzales, but the volunteers did not recognize Houston's authority. Colonel William B. Travis, of the regulars, had only thirty men to show for two weeks' desperate recruiting work. "The people are cold and indifferent," he reported; "they have lost confidence in their own government and officers. . . . Volunteers can no longer be relied upon."

At San Patricio on the Nueces, Frank W. Johnson and James Grant, with about a hundred volunteers, were planning to take Matamoros, below the Rio Grande. James W. Fannin was at Goliad with less than five hundred, planning to join them.

Houston, a commander in chief without an army or the means

of getting one, was on furlough, visiting the eastern frontier, making treaties with the Indians, and doing what he could to checkmate the Matamoros expedition.

A moderately equipped army, led by a general who combined in his own person the functions of commander in chief and dictator of all Mexico should have been able to make short work of the unruly and disorganized Texans.

From passers-by Dr. Jones and the other Brazorians heard disquieting rumors of the advance of the Mexicans. By the end of February, General José Urrea had brought nearly a thousand of his soldiers through Matamoros to San Patricio and had wiped out Johnson's volunteers while the Texans were still searching for horses and mules on which to ride triumphantly into Mexico. Then Urrea's division deployed to track down Grant and Fannin.

At the Alamo there was confusion and the courage of desperation. Travis was writing: "We are illy prepared . . . we have no more than one hundred and fifty men . . . very disorganized. . . . For God's sake and the sake of our country, send us reinforcements." The volunteers, commanded by James Bowie, had dwindled to two small companies, but they were still disposed to question the authority of the regulars headed by Travis.

On February 1, Dr. Jones presided over Brazoria's polling place while his neighbors solemnly selected delegates "clothed with ample, unlimited, or plenary powers" to represent them in the Convention of the People of Texas at Washington-on-the-Brazos. The Governor and council had issued the election writs before their quarrels had paralyzed the provisional government.

Dr. Jones received five complimentary votes. He believed that he would have been one of the four Brazoria delegates, had he not "declined all requests to become a candidate," but he was then only "solicitous to give a right direction to affairs, and perfectly willing to let whoever wished have the carrying of them into execution."

Asa Brigham, James Collinsworth, Edwin Waller, and John S. D. Byrom were elected representatives of the Brazoria municipality. The votes of forty-seven recruits from New Orleans, who had been in Texas less than five days, helped to elect them.

During the month between the election and the opening of the convention, public sentiment everywhere veered unmistakably to independence, and there was no division of opinion on that question at Brazoria. Waller and Byrom, who had represented Brazoria in the Consultation that refused to decree separation from Mexico, received smaller votes than Brigham and Collinsworth, who had never before participated in a public assembly in Texas. Neither of the Whartons was a candidate; both were already in government service. William was commissioner to the United States; John, adjutant general of the Texas Army.

After the election, the tempo of life at Brazoria was accelerated; the normal routine was lost. Dr. Jones packed his sister Mary off to New York, closed his house, and, while looking after his remaining patients, began methodically "to prepare for the storm." The Masonic lodge struggled on until he, as Worshipful Master, presided over its last meeting at Brazoria. Jones wrote:

I well recollect the night and the fact that Bro. [James W.] Fannin, who one month after became so celebrated for his misfortunes and those of his unfortunate party at Goliad, acted as Senior Deacon. It seemed indeed that the gloom which prevailed in the Lodge that night was a foreboding of its and their unhappy fate, which was so soon to overtake both.

Santa Anna's armies converged on San Antonio de Béxar on February 24. Travis, still "determined to sustain it as long as there is a man left," made a desperate, heroic, but strategically futile stand against overwhelming odds. The siege lasted ten days; it ended when the last Texan there was killed. The massacre at the Alamo was the answer to the hope that Mexico would wage civilized warfare. Never was there more selfless heroism; never more complete catastrophe.

Four days after Santa Anna began the siege of the Alamo, on March 2, delegates to the convention, shivering in a drafty gunshop at Washington-on-the-Brazos, declared Texas independent. Then, harassed by rumors that the Mexicans were close upon their meeting place, they hurriedly put together a constitution, selected officers to administer their Republic for the duration of the war, and adjourned.

The only travelers who passed through Brazoria westward or northward were recruits fresh from the United States, trying to find some part of the Texas Army. One by one houses were being closed and Brazorians were "taking the Sabine chute"—moving as fast as they could toward the United States boundary. The news was that the convention had elected Sam Houston commander in chief, with authority over all land forces, two days after independence was declared; but he did not leave Washington until Travis's final appeal from the Alamo reached the convention on March 6.

At Gonzales, General Houston found 374 untrained men, poorly armed and unprovisioned. That was the Texas Army on March 11, 1836. Houston organized them into a single regiment with General Edward Burleson as their colonel, regretted that he could not teach them "the first principles of the drill," then dispatched his orders to the volunteers at Goliad, now indisputably subject to his control. No one could now deride him, as Henry Millard had done two weeks earlier: "I understand Genl. H. has made one recruit and commenced a regular Drill. (hurrah for the army.)"

While Houston was making his farewell speech at Washington-on-the-Brazos on Sunday, March 6, the Alamo had fallen, but he did not learn of it until the night of the eleventh. He promptly pronounced the story false and arrested the Mexicans who brought the news; actually he believed the report. It was confirmed two evenings later, when Mrs. Dickenson arrived from San Antonio and told the story in all its tragic detail—and added that General Ramirez y Sesma was on his way to exterminate all armed Texans. Before sunup next day Gonzales had been evacuated and burned, and the Texas Army was heading for the Colorado River. The frenzied Gonzaleans—thirty-two of their men had answered Travis's appeal just in time to die in the Alamo—were fleeing eastward, spreading panic as they went.

The Runaway Scrape had begun.

The storm for which Dr. Jones had been preparing had come. "An invaded, unarmed, unprovided country, without an army to oppose invaders and without money to raise one," was confusedly bestirring itself. Brazorians in increasing numbers joined the Runaways. Anson Jones confided his business and professional interests to his cousin Ira, appeared before the Land Board to claim a headright on March 16, and three days later set out with Adjutant General Wharton, Dr. J. Æ. Phelps, and other neighbors to find Houston's army. Dr. Jones had enlisted for the duration as a private in Captain Robert J. Calder's infantry company.

The Brazorians found the army on March 24 at Beason's Ferry on the Colorado (near present Columbus), where it had been camping five days. General Sesma, with 725 men, was two miles north, awaiting reinforcements. The motley army under Houston's command now mustered more than 1,200—some said 1,800; nobody knew exactly—and the general was writing, the day Dr. Jones arrived: "On the Colorado I make my stand." The next day John Sharp was carrying Houston's message back to Brazoria: "Our Army will never leave the Colorado, but go on westward."

Next day the general ordered his army eastward.

He never explained his change of plan, but he observed the demoralization that it caused. By the time he reached the Brazos more than half of his men had quit him, and volunteers on their way to the army faced about to flee eastward with their families. The Runaway Scrape was in full swing, and Texas, as President Burnet said, was a moving mass of fugitives. The convention at Washington had asserted Texan independence, given the Republic a constitution, and inaugurated an ad interim government headed by David G. Burnet and Lorenzo de Zavala; but that did not reassure Texans as, with the stories of the Alamo and Goliad fresh in their minds, they learned that their army was moving away from, not toward, the enemy.

The last day of March the unruly remnants of the Texas Army reached Groce's Retreat on the Brazos. The heavy mud and driving rain through which they had marched, the example of Captains Mosely Baker and Wyly Martin, who refused to follow Houston farther, and the growing suspicion that the general intended to retreat until he reached United States soil fanned embers of mutiny which had smoldered for weeks. While the unhappy Texans lay in the muddy, miasmatic bottoms, Alexander Somervell and others polled them on deposing Houston. J. H. Kuykendall believed the whole army "favored such a course, and would take it, should it become necessary. . . . Gen'l. Houston could not have been ignorant of what was in agitation."

The general's answer was stricter discipline and reorganization of his force, now again about 1,200 men. Sidney Sherman, who had joined the army at Gonzales, was made colonel of a new regiment, and other promotions were announced. A court-martial, with Private Anson Jones as judge advocate, considered cases of insubordination and sentenced one soldier to be shot.

The hole Army was marched out to the ground [Robert Hancock Hunter remembered], the grave was dug & a coffin was there, & the Army was formed in a half circle, a round grave. The man was blindfolded, & made to kneel on the [ground] by the coffin, & there [were] 12 men to shoot him, the officer gave command. He said present arms, take ame. Just at that moment, Colonel Hockley was coming in a lope from camp, holloing, halt, halt, halt, & the oficer said order arms. Colonel Hockley rode up and said Lieutenant here is repreave.

The disciplinary effect of the gesture was negligible, however, because the soldiers considered the condemned man "a hardened villain" who probably deserved to die. Houston's real problems were not made by such men but by average citizen-soldiers who honestly believed themselves better strategists than their general.

Civilians were moving eastward more rapidly even than the Texas Army. Rumors of Mexican vengeance disturbed every household, and when a division of the Mexican Army camped in Brazoria County within six miles of John Woodruff's farm, the Smith-Woodruff entourage joined the Runaways. Mr. Woodruff was as brave as the next fellow, but he knew that no one man could defend a family of a dozen. Young Mary Smith said:

We went down the Brazos to Lynch's landing; crowds of women and children joining us on the way, with all sorts of home made vehicles, none of which, however, were comfortable. We had the only covered cart and the only steel mill in the company, and that mill was going from day light until dark when we camped. Most of the carts were made with wheels sawn from large trunks of trees, holes were bored in the center for the axle trees and the wheels were guiltless of tires. Some carts had bottoms of solid rawhide with up-right poles on the sides and back, woven in and out with rawhide strips. Others had bottoms woven of ropes and rawhide strips.

We camped two weeks in pouring rain and then the sufferings of those without shelter were terrible. Some had only sleds, such as were used on the plantations for hauling water, and upon them they hastily piled a few necessary things—and the babies. Many women and children walked. Oxen drew the vehicles, only a favored few could afford horses to ride, and carriages were unknown.

All along the route evidences of alarm and hasty flight were visible. In one place an open trunk from which some articles had been hastily snatched; in another a looking glass hung on a tree, showed where some toilette had been rudely interrupted.

Occasionally the Runaways came within sight of the army.

On reaching the Brazos Bottom [soldiers found the] . . . road was filled with carts and wagons loaded with women and children . . . other women . . . walking, some of them barefoot, some carrying their smaller children in their arms or on their backs, their other children following barefooted; and other women . . . with but one shoe, having lost the other in the mud; some of the wagons were broken down, and others were bogged in the deep mud. Taken all in all, the sight was the most painful by far, that I ever witnessed [Dr. Nicholas D. Labadie said]. But the cries of the women were still more distressing . . . raising their hands to heaven, and declaring they had lost their all, and knew not where to go; expressing their preference to die on the road rather than be killed by the Mexicans or Indians, and imploring with upraised hands, the blessings of God on our arms, and encouraging us to be of stout heart. . . .

However much the plight of the Runaways may have moved a man of medicine, some of Private Jones's fellow soldiers were impressed principally by the opportunities for profit that the situation presented. Colonel Millard, president of the army's court-martial, wrote his business partner from the camp west of the Brazos, April 7:

Attend to the Land business and b[u]y all you can . . . now is the favorable time when the country is in such a panic about the war being brought into the middle districts. Tell Glasscock to pursue his purchases and fear not the fate of Texas—we shall certainly prevent the enemy from crossing the Brasos.

While the army sweltered in the Brazos swamp, drinking stagnant water from the old bed of the river, an epidemic of dysentery broke out and "nearly every tenth man" had measles. Tardily a Medical Corps was organized, manned by the doctors who had enlisted in the line, plus a few others recruited for the purpose. Private Jones,

at the very earnest solicitations of Col. Sherman, and many . . . former patients in the army . . . consented to take the post of surgeon to the 2nd Regiment. . . . I made it a condition of accepting that I should be permitted to resign so soon as the necessity of my acceptance of the place should cease; and that, in the mean time, I should be permitted to hold "my rank" as a private in the line.

The surgeon general was Alexander W. Ewing, a twenty-seven-year-old Irishman, who had studied medicine at Edinburgh and came to Austin's colony by way of Pennsylvania. Young Drs. William F. H. Davidson and John P. T. Fitzhugh, from Nacogdoches, looked after the health of the First Regiment of Volunteers. Surgeon Jones's assistant in the Second Regiment was Dr. Shields Booker of Brazoria. Dr. Phelps of Brazoria, who had come with Jones to the army, was appointed civilian hospital surgeon. Dr. Bomar and Dr. Nicholas Labadie were assigned to the First Regiment. The medicine chest, they discovered, was "in great confusion."

President Burnet, reflecting the sentiment of Cabinet and people, ordered Thomas J. Rusk, Secretary of War, to join the army and "compel it to take a position before the enemy"—authorized him, in fact, to assume command himself, if necessary. To Houston the President wrote:

Sir: The enemy are laughing you to scorn. You must fight them. You must retreat no farther. The country expects you to fight. The salvation of the country depends on your doing so.

Rusk reported the army "in fine spirits, ready and anxious to measure arms with the enemy," when he arrived. After conference he agreed with Houston that it should move farther east— to the other side of the Brazos. By the thirteenth the men were in their new camp.

While the move was in progress General Houston entertained in his tent John J. Linn, a civilian from Victoria, and plied him for political and military advice.

He presented to me an outline of his "Fabian policy," and stated his belief that the Mexican dictator would meet with a defeat as crushing and disastrous to his unholy cause as that which befell the great Napoleon in Russia, could he once be seduced sufficiently far east. . . . I dissented very respectfully from his views . . . believing that the army . . . would prove itself more than a match for the "ragged Indians" of the "Napoleon of the west" any time. . . . I urged the peculiar desirableness of the Brazos [where the army then was] upon which to make the trial of strength and valor. . . . The general said that he had given this point much consideration. . . .

Private Jones was another consulted on policy by Major General Houston. They met at a dinner party at the Groce plantation house on April 15.

He asked me, after supper, privately, what I thought of the prospects. I told him that . . . if the retreating policy were continued much longer, he would be pretty much alone.

When Houston told Jones he had just discovered a "traitor" in his staff, the doctor immediately guessed, correctly, that he was one James H. Perry, "a good looking gentleman, plausible in his manner, unembarrassed by diffidence," whom the general had appointed an aide because he was a West Pointer. Houston had intercepted, read, and showed to Rusk a letter from Perry to the Secretary of the Navy which "contained some comments upon the movement of the army, and the conduct of General Houston which seemed to be offensive to him." The young man had written, the general later explained, that Houston *"did not drink ardent spirits, but eat opium to great excess."* Jones understood Houston to say that Perry was endeavoring to have the general removed from command of the army so that Perry could have the place.

I told him I had no confidence in Perry, and thought him a reckless fool, but that he (Houston) might depend upon it, there was a deep and growing dissatisfaction in the camp, and that Perry's conduct was but an index of that feeling.

He seemed thoughtful and irresolute; said he hoped yet to get a bloodless victory; and the conversation dropped, with an expression of an earnest hope on my part, that the next move he made would be *towards* the enemy.

Pretty straight talk for a private to give a commander in chief, but Private Jones was also a regimental surgeon, a judge advocate general, and an assistant to the adjutant general of this army.

When the army resumed its march, still eastward, it had received from Cincinnati two beautiful new iron cannon—the Twin Sisters—and from Georgia, Editor Mirabeau B. Lamar, who had returned to fight for Texan independence. In the makeshift camp east of Groce's plantation were the fieldpieces that cinched Texas independence a week later and the three men the Texans were to elect as their rulers during the ten years that Texas maintained her independence: Major General Houston, Private Lamar, Private Jones.

Private Jones was overtaken on the march by Captain John M. Allen, who handed him a parcel from New Orleans. In it was the charter from the Grand Lodge of Louisiana for Holland Lodge No. 36 at Brazoria—which had already held its final session. As Jones read the parchment he was, in imagination for the moment, again Worshipful Master of his lodge, wondering if he or any of his brethren would survive to meet again upon the compass and part upon the square. But there was no time for speculation. Into the saddlebags went the charter, and on toward San Jacinto went Private Jones.

Whether by Houston's orders, as he insisted, or against his wishes, as Jones believed, the army took the road to Harrisburg instead of the one toward the United States. Before noon, April 18, the men had pitched camp opposite the smoking ruins of Harrisburg and were resting, when Houston learned that General Santa Anna was at the San Jacinto River, less than a day's march to the east. The captured Mexican courier's saddlebags, Labadie noticed, had "belonged to Travis . . . had his name upon them."

Next morning General Houston wrote out a formal, official statement of intentions, addressed it to the Secretary of War, and delivered it in person to him. It was meant to silence his enemies, if he himself should not live to attend to that important matter; and, lest Rusk and the letter also be lost, he addressed a copy to his friend Henry Raguet of Nacogdoches, for the record:

This morning we are in preparation to meet Santa Anna. . . . We go to conquer. It is wisdom growing out of necessity. . . . Every consideration enforces it. No previous occasion would justify it. . . .

We will use our best efforts . . . the odds are greatly against us,
. . . My country will do justice to those who serve her.

Then he and Secretary Rusk addressed the soldiers. "The army
will cross, and we will meet the enemy," Houston announced, calling upon cowards to fall out. His remarks ended with a battle
cry: "Remember the Alamo! Remember La Bahia!"

The troops echoed the cry, as if to rehearse it.

More than a hundred Texan soldiers were disabled from
measles and diarrhea. These, with all the wagons and baggage,
Houston left near Harrisburg under guard. Dr. Jones was read
out in general orders to help Hospital Surgeon Phelps attend
them.

As he watched his comrades move for the first time *toward* the
enemy, Private Jones made a quick decision. He would do his
duty, but he would disobey the order:

I . . . attended to my daily routine, handed over my sick to the
hospital surgeon, and joined the army . . . about sundown. and
proceeded with it to Lynchburg.

Having come this far as a private of infantry, and having been
at some pains to retain that status, Jones did not intend to permit
medical chores, such as he had done as a civilian, to interfere with
the duties of his combat rank. Besides, his good friend Dr. Phelps
had lived in the Brazos bottoms long enough to be something of a
specialist in measles and diarrhea.

The army marched until two o'clock next morning, caught an
hour's uneasy sleep, then started again. At six they halted for a
hurried breakfast. One of the surgeons wrote:

Our guns were stacked, and three cows that happened to be near
by, were shot down and immediately large numbers started off for
wood to kindle fires. The surgeons' mess was the third fire kindled.
A pot of brackish water with a handful of half-pounded coffee
thrown in was ready to boil, when Dr. Booker came up with a dozen
eggs, which were at once put in the pot of coffee to boil.

At this moment the spies were coming up in a gallop, and the
word was given: "To arms, to your arms!" The eggs were taken out,
and each one drinks his small share of the hot boiling coffee the best
way he could; but when the eggs were found to contain chickens, I

surrendered my share to others, who finding them well cooked, swallowed them quickly, when each seized his rifle and hastened to his post, leaving some fifty fires just kindled.

Midmorning of the twentieth, near Lynch's Ferry, the Texans saw Santa Anna's advance guard approaching and fell back half a mile to a live-oak grove on the plain of San Jacinto. Across the prairie in front of them filed the Mexicans who had just burned the town of New Washington on Galveston Bay. They camped near the south edge of the prairie, lunched, and then, instead of taking their siestas as good Mexicans would have done, they began throwing grapeshot from Santa Anna's six-pounder toward the Texans. The Twin Sisters answered with broken horseshoes, and the Mexican fieldpiece, from protecting timber, continued to reply.

The diversion of the day came about four o'clock in the afternoon when Sidney Sherman, with Houston's reluctant permission, called for volunteers to capture the Mexican cannon. Sherman, colonel of the Second Regiment, had the only military uniform and the only flag in camp, and many in the Texas Army—including Sherman himself—thought he would make a better commander in chief than Houston. Perhaps this enterprise was, as Houston's enemies believed, a ruse to draw the commander in chief into battle.

Sixty-eight Texans found horses and volunteered to go with Colonel Sherman, and off they galloped toward the Mexican cannon. Major Lysander Wells, one of Sherman's men, heard:

"Whiz! whiz! came a shower of grape from their confounded piece of artillery. . . . At the same time four companies of infantry came filing out from near the cannon. . . . we drove their cavalry nearly back to their cannon; when their trumpet sounded *no quarter!* . . . But, finding ourselves exposed to the incessant fire of an unequal number of cavalry, their artillery, and two hundred infantry, and *our own infantry not having come up* to engage theirs . . . we were at length obliged, reluctantly, to retire. . . . Two days after, I was informed, by a Mexican soldier, that Santa Anna, in person, commanded the field-piece throughout the skirmish.

Secretary Rusk, Privates Lamar and Lane, and a few other Texans did not retire—Lane because his horse had fallen, Rusk because his path was blocked by Mexican cavalrymen, and Lamar because he expected General Houston to send support. As a lancer bore down upon Lane, Lamar swept over to save the life of his comrade; then he saw the Texan Secretary of War surrounded by mounted Mexicans. Digging spurs into his mount, Lamar wheeled into the circle and knocked down one of the Mexican horses to make a gap through which Rusk escaped. An involuntary shout of admiration went up from the Mexicans at Lamar's exhibition of daring horsemanship, and the punctilious Lamar took a moment to acknowledge it with a bow before he returned with Rusk to the Texan camp.

Behind the Texan line, Labadie of the Medical Corps, rifle in one hand, rope in the other, was helping pull forward one of the Twin Sisters—just in case Houston should decide to support Sherman with heavy artillery. The general shouted an order to the surgeon, but it was only to divert him from military to medical duties. Devereaux J. Woodlief, one of Sherman's raiders, had stopped a Mexican bullet with his hip. They had hardly lifted Woodlief from his saddle to the grass, "resting his head upon a large knot the best we could," when young Olwyn Trask was brought in, his thigh shattered.

Surgeon General Ewing, Surgeon Jones of the Second Regiment, and Labadie examined the wounded—these two privates and Lieutenant Colonel James C. Neill, who had been disabled by a random shot earlier in the day. The Medical Corps commandeered Vice-President Zavala's place across the bayou—the only house in sight—for a field hospital and had their patients taken there.

There was little rest in the Texan camp on the night of April 20. Little knots of excited men relived the first skirmish with the enemy and recriminated Houston for not following up the raid— or at least sending in support, as Sherman and his friends swore he had promised to do. The Texan soldiers were subsisting on excitement; no mess had been established, and they had only the scraps of food they carried in their pockets. Everywhere there was voluble uncertainty as to what their general would do, now that Santa Anna was in front of him.

"Your camp that night . . . was one of uproar and confusion," one of his captains reminded Houston. "Officers and men were seen grouped together discussing the practicability of doing anything." When the night guard was doubled, however, sheer exhaustion quieted the men for a few hours, but by daybreak they were at it again "and all were of the same mind. . . . 'Let us attack the enemy and give them h-ll at once,' " Labadie understood them to say.

Breakfast was hardly over . . . when . . . Deaf Smith, passed . . . remarking: "A hot time is preparing for us—the enemy is increasing." . . . Houston declared it was only a sham, and no reinforcement. Yet many became clamorous, and murmurs were heard. . . . "The delays of our commander are continually adding strength to the enemy, and diminishing our own; yesterday, they had 500; today they have 1500, and tomorrow they will have 6000. Today we *must* fight, or never" [Labadie quoted the men, exercising an obvious editorial restraint].

About ten that morning, Col. Wharton [adjutant general of the army] visited every mess in camp, and slapping his hands together, he spoke loud and quick: "Boys, there is no other word today but fight, fight! Now is the time!" . . . Over one-half the men paraded, expecting orders, but, up to noon, nothing could be decided . . . finally, Houston said to Wharton: "Fight and be damned!"

This was enough. Wharton again went among the men . . . telling them . . . that it was now decided. . . . Many of the companies had been standing for over four hours, expecting orders to march each moment, and their patience was well-nigh exhausted.

It was past three o'clock when all arrangements were finally concluded. The music struck up a lively air as we bid good-by to our camp.

As the lines were forming, with much clatter and bustle, surgeons compared notes and discovered that the matter of assigning specific stations to the Medical Corps had escaped the attention of the general and his staff. None of the doctors had ever before been in battle—or in an army—and there was no time now for anyone to tell them what was customary. They decided "to follow the line, and fight with our arms as circumstances might direct." Labadie fell in with Sherman's regiment, of which Private Jones was surgeon, just as the first shot was fired.

The Texans advanced to find, as Labadie remarked with a trace of understatement, "the enemy somewhat unprepared for us at that hour." Santa Anna was asleep in his tent, and most of his men were also taking siestas. The wakeful ones were leading

horses to water or lolling about camp. They might have been in
the patio of their own barracks a thousand miles from Texas, for
all the caution they exhibited. It took little more time for the
Texas Army, its fife and drum playing the unmartial but popular
"Come to the Bower," to penetrate the Mexican lines than it
would have taken a man to walk the distance between the two
camps. The enemy tried to rally, individual soldiers who could
find guns fired a few shots, then the contest became a foot race.
Robert Hunter said with awe:

They did not git to fire there cannon but 3 times. Our men shot
them down as fast as they could git to the gun. Our men took there
gun loded, turned it on them & shot them with there own gun, &
they give up.

The battle itself—it was, technically, hardly that—lasted the
eighteen minutes required for the Texans to gain complete possession of the field and the munitions and baggage of Santa
Anna's army. General Houston ordered a halt, some of the soldiers said, but the Secretary of War had informally but loudly
countermanded it. Labadie heard Rusk shouting at the top of his
voice: "If we stop we are cut to pieces. Don't stop—go ahead—
give them hell!"
Almost immediately the Texans were in the middle of the camp
from which soldiers of the dictator were fleeing.

General Houston gave orders not to kill any more but to take
prisners. Capt Easlen said Boys take prisners, you know how to take
prisners, take them with the but of your guns, club them, & said
remember the Alamo remember Laberde, & club guns, right & left,
& nocked there brains out. The Mexicans would fall down on there
knees & say me no Alamo me no Laberde.

There was no time to reload the clumsy rifles, but the butts
made good clubs and the long barrels gave leverage. The sudden
release of the pent-up rancor of old Texans—some of whose
grudges antedated the general's arrival in Texas—and *Blutlust*
generated by the primitive intoxication of bashing skulls put most
of the 905 individuals in the Texas Army beyond any commander's control, until they quit the slaughter from physical and spiritual exhaustion. With more truth than he probably intended,
Houston later said to these citizen-soldiers: "You have . . .

borne yourselves in the onset and conflict of battle in a manner unknown in the annals of warfare."

When the Mexican camp had been overrun, Secretary Rusk and one of the surgeons found Houston on a little bay pony, his left leg dripping blood from the pommel of the saddle. The commander in chief

faces his horse about, and orders the drum to beat a retreat. But the men, paying no attention to the order, shouted . . . over the glorious victory, and it was difficult to hear anything. Gen. Houston then orders the drum to stop . . . [and] cries out, as loud as he could raise his voice:

"Parade, men, parade!"

But the shouts and the halloing were too long and loud; and Houston, seeing he could not restore order, cries at the top of his voice:

"Gentlemen! gentlemen! gentlemen! (a momentary stillness ensues) Gentlemen! I applaud your bravery, but damn your manners. . . ."

Col. Wharton come up to us, and speaks to Houston in a low voice, pointing in various directions, as if showing what he thought should be done, when Houston turning and looking him full in the face, says:

"Col. Wharton, you have commanded long enough; damn you, go about your business!"

Private Jones stumbled on two folio books on the battleground and stooped to pick them up. They were too large to put into his saddlebags alongside the charter of Holland Lodge, but they were such important-looking Spanish manuscripts that he was careful to preserve them. When he found time to examine them he discovered that they were Colonel Juan N. Almonte's "Private Journal of the Texan Campaign" and his general order book. If he had had the leisure, he could have read the day-by-day account of Almonte's progress from February 1 to April 16. He already knew Almonte's story from that date. But Private Jones had no impulse then to become a historian.

The wounded were taken across the bay to Gen. Zavala's house . . . nineteen in all badly wounded, thirteen of whom were lying on the floor. . . .

Prisoners were being brought in to the guard-house every hour. . . . The number of officers, ranking from a lieutenant to a general, was . . . fifty, and the number of wounded prisoners was 280 privates.

None of the Medical Corps examined them or considered attending wounded Mexicans a part of the duty of a surgeon in the Texas Army. For three days the prisoners were without medical care. Dr. Ewing, Dr. Jones, Dr. Bomar, and Colonel Hockley agreed that Dr. Labadie, who had once been Bradburn's post surgeon at Anahuac and therefore knew how to practice medicine in the Spanish language, was just the man to look after them; but Bradburn had bilked Labadie and he vowed never to attend another Mexican soldier unless his fee was guaranteed. General Houston finally, in the presence of other surgeons, promised Labadie three hundred dollars. "I faithfully discharged that duty, but have never received the first cent of the promised compensation," Labadie lamented a quarter of a century later.

The Texan wounded fared little better than the Mexicans. Labadie wrote:

Although there were some twenty-three of our men lying wounded on the floor of the hospital . . . for three days none of them had their wounds dressed a second time, except four or five who had been attended by their regular surgeon.

Dr. Anson Jones, who was attending on Dr. Mott[ley], desired my presence. . . . Poor Mott, I can never forget him. . . . As I entered the little room where he lay, he cast on me one of those looks of deep distress. . . . "Doctor, I am a gone case." Alas, what could I say? Dr. Jones was by him, doing all that could be done. . . . He was shot through the abdomen, and . . . mortification was now taking place. . . . "My friend," said I, "your time is come; God alone can help you, for we can not." "Must I die?" . . . He . . . died that night. . . .

The Mexican commander in chief was apprehended in flight by Texans who did not immediately suspect his identity. Major Lorenzo de Zavala, Jr.—who had brought along his French valet when he joined the army of these Texans—was strolling with Secretary Rusk when the ex-Napoleon of the West was returned to the battlefield. Rusk observed:

Santa Anna recognized young Zavala at once, and advanced to meet him . . . uttering many expressions of kindness, such as are customary among Mexicans. . . .

"Oh my *friend,* my *friend,* the son of my *early* friend," with which, and other exclamations in the same strain, he embraced young Zavala, with high indications of apparent feeling, and, I think, *dropping a tear.*

Young Zavala returned his greeting with that deference which would have been due to his former rank and power; but . . . his look seemed to wither Santa Anna . . . staring him full in the face, he replied immediately, with great modesty, and something of a subdued tone,

"It *has* been so, Sir."

Robert Hunter, who watched the scene, wrote:

You could not have heard it thunder, for the shouts from the prisoners, exclaiming, vive, vive, vive, Sant Anna. . . . The men took Sant Anna down to General Houston, & Sant Anna asked in Spanish if there was any one present that could speak Spanish, & Moses Austin Bryant, & a little man by the [name of] Baker, responded, & Sant Anna asked for Almonta. Baker went up to the gard and cald for Almonta, & he got up & answered to his name. When Almonta got there, it looked like the hole Army had geathered there. General Houston ordered Sant Annas tent to be put up . . . in a bout 10 or 12 feet of Houston's tent. There was a large tree had bloed up by the roots. Houstons tent was on one side of the log, & Sant Anna tent was on other of log. I & Merdith Tunget, stud by that log & garded Sant Anna, it come our lot to gard him several times.

The Mexican President was eager to arrange for his own release, but General Houston declined to consider that until after Santa Anna dispatched cease and desist orders to the commanders of the various Mexican corps in Texas. The Mexican dictator wrote with Castilian nicety to Filisola:

The small divisions under my immediate command, having had yesterday evening an unfortunate encounter . . . an armistice has been agreed upon with General Houston, until some negotiations are arranged, by which the war is to cease forever. . . .

Much remained to be done at San Jacinto, but Houston's wound disabled him. It was four days before he was able to dictate his official report of the battle. Disposition of the spoils of the enemy was quickly made, but the Mexican dead remained unburied. Pending decision as to who should dig the graves, the

Texas Army moved its camp a few miles from the site of the victory.

The land that the Battle was fought on was the property of a widow woman Mrs Mc Cormac an irish woman. She came to camp to see General Houston. She wanted to know if he was agoing to take them ded Mexicans of[f] my Leg [League]. They hant me the longes day I live. Houston told [her] no. He wanted Sant Anna to bury them, & he would not. Sant Anna said that it was not a Battle, he cald it a massacre. Plage gon him what did he call the Alamo and Laberde [Hunter wanted to know].

The wounded Texans slowly recovered or died on the floor of Zavala's house. The inadequate medicine chest had long ago been emptied and all Zavala's linens converted into surgical dressings. A surgeon, in desperation, was systematically searching for sheets, bandage rags, tallow—anything that could be used in the hospital—in the huge pile of plunder taken from the Mexican camp, when the heap exploded. A youngster, toying with the Mexican pistols, had touched a trigger. A ball grazed the chin and lodged in the left arm of the inspector general of the Texas Army as he sat writing the official inventory of the plunder: twenty boxes of good Mexican cartridges exploded in the heap. Robert Hunter, who was standing nearby, said:

It was for a few minutes, like a little battle. . . . We thought that Col. Ugawtechea & General Fillasola, General Wool had come up from Richmond & had attacked us. . . . There is one [thing] about it, I know we were pritty badly scared.

The Smith-Woodruff family and other Brazoria refugees heard the sounds of the battle at their camp on Clear Creek, eight miles away. They had rushed to the San Jacinto River, found Santa Anna's men camped just where they had intended to cross, and had turned south to wait under the trees for developments.

When Mr. Woodruff heard, on the twentieth, that a battle was to be fought he was so certain of its outcome that he immediately got his numerous family ready to return home.

While Dr. Jones was at San Jacinto, his Brazoria neighbors— Mary Smith among them—were listening to the din of musketry and the shrieks of the men. While he attended the wounded, the

Runaways were moving slowly toward their log houses on the Brazos.

General Houston must have grinned when he read the instructions from the Texan Government, dispatched from Galveston Island five days after he had defeated Santa Anna:

If you consider it inexpedient to risk an engagement with the enemy and consider a retreat inevitable from the position you now occupy, you are hereby ordered to march with the Army under your command to the nearest and most convenient point to this Island. . . .

He wrote no reply. He could wait until the news caught up with the President and Cabinet. Then, perhaps, they would come to him, not he to them.

By May 5, all of the government—except David Thomas, Attorney General and Acting Secretary of War, who had died of blood poisoning at Galveston—had reached San Jacinto and had begun to take charge of the civil and military situation.

The general's wounds grew worse from neglect, and the surgeon general prescribed an operation in New Orleans. Rusk resigned the Secretaryship of War to take command of the army, and Mirabeau B. Lamar succeeded to his cabinet post. James Collinsworth of Brazoria had already taken Samuel P. Carson's place as Secretary of State, and Peter W. Grayson of Matagorda was the new Attorney General.

Private Jones handed over the health of the Second Regiment to his cousin Ira and became assistant surgeon general and medical purveyor to the army. President Burnet confirmed the appointment but changed the title to apothecary general, and the new staff officer accompanied Generals Houston and Santa Anna down the Bayou to Galveston Island.

There Apothecary General Jones wrapped the journal and order book of Almonte in stout paper, addressed the package to the New York *Herald*, and handed it to the captain of a vessel bound for New Orleans. Mr. Bennett of the *Herald* had the journal translated and published it serially beginning June 22.

Apothecary General Jones went with the presidential party to Velasco and waited until the treasury could find a hundred dollars for an official journey to New Orleans. Before the end of

May, Anson Jones was again in the wholesale market of New Orleans, not as a merchant seeking customers, but as a buyer, authorized to outfit at public expense the Medical Corps of the army of a sovereign, if as yet unrecognized, nation—and with money enough back home to settle all the judgments against the defunct firm of Jones & Spear.

He arrived too late for the fanfare and festivities attending the first news of the Texan victory and the arrival of General Houston, but not too late to visit Captain Jeremiah Brown of the *Invincible,* Texas Navy, held to $10,000 bail for the capture of the American brig *Pocket.* Captain Brown had intercepted her en route to Mexico with a cargo of war material.

This was the Jerry Brown who, less than three years ago, had persuaded Jones that there might be a place for him in Texas.

VIII

BRAZORIA

THE Brazoria to which Apothecary General Jones returned in midsummer of 1836 had suffered from the war, but there was no such devastation as the town had just experienced when he first saw it almost three years earlier. Neither flood nor epidemic, but only a division of the Mexican Army and a few bands of Texan volunteers from the United States had visited it during Dr. Jones's absence. A good many of the Brazorians had fled in March—some to fight the Mexicans, others to join the Runaways—but the town was not left uninhabited. It was a sort of quartermaster depot for the Texas Army.

While General Santa Anna pursued the Texan Government and army eastward, General Urrea scoured the coast between the Colorado and the Brazos. On April 22, as Santa Anna was writing of his "unfortunate encounter" at San Jacinto, the division commanded by Urrea marched into Brazoria.

Many English, American, and German colonists awaited me at this place with their families [General Urrea wrote in his *Diary*]. . . . They expressed satisfaction with the treatment accorded them, which was no other than that which should be accorded to peaceful and industrious citizens who had refused to take up arms against their adopted country at the instigation of the rebels . . . and as proof of their gratitude, they gave me information that was very important for our war operations, offering to contribute to its termination by persuading those colonists who had taken up arms to lay them down. They felt confident that they would, as soon as they were assured that their lives and property would be respected. . . . Many advantages could have been secured from the good disposition of the colonists of Brazoria, and I had intended to avail myself of it. . . . I was assured at Brazoria that Houston did not have more than seven or eight hundred men. . . . Men were not lacking, of those who had served under him, who now offered to lead me to that formidable Houston. . . . Many goods, liquors, and food supplies were found in Brazoria also, which according to the colonists themselves, belonged to the enemy. They voluntarily offered to gather these supplies and take them to three points I designated for their deposit and safe keeping.

But the Brazos River towns kept their supplies. Major E. Morehouse and his battalion of New Yorkers saw to that. They had landed at Velasco on March 5 and started to join Fannin, but news of that commander's defeat diverted them toward Houston's camp on the Colorado. A courier from the general turned them back to Columbia, "where or near it [it] was supposed that the army would make a decided stand." A second order sent them to Brazoria, ten miles southeast. When men direct from the army headquarters reported that Houston was still retreating—was probably beyond the Trinity River by then—Morehouse made up his mind that there should be a battle on the Brazos, even if the Texan side were represented only by his New Yorkers. He ordered his battalion—less than a hundred men and boys—to attack General Cós's division at Fort Bend.

"Citizens . . . held out the idea that it was a slaughter pen & I was too desperate a man . . . but all the volunteers . . . were in readiness," Morehouse said. Before he could strike, however, he "hea[r]d the sound of the enemies Bugle . . . Genl Cos was on his march . . . to reinforce Genl Santa Ana." Soon Morehouse got from

sundry prisoners . . . the first intelligence of a battle having been fought and won by the Texians. . . . Having been so unfortunate as not to have participated in the first & great battle, concluded to give battle to Genls Urrea, Sizma & Filisolia who had possession of Columbia & Brazoria. . . . A few hours before my arrival the enemy had Evacuated Columbia, leaving a guard for the purposes of destroying the public & private stores, when my advancd guard fired upon them & fortunately saved the Town &c.

Had I been but a few hours Earlier [the major lamented] I might have captured some 15 of the Mexican principal officers. . . .

Dr. Jones had confided his affairs at Brazoria in March to Cousin Ira, and from the field had sent him additional instructions at every opportunity. On March 30 he wrote:

Should it become necessary to evacuate Brazoria, I wish you to make the best disposition possible of my property there, my writing

desk, papers, and trunk particularly, so that their ultimate safety
may be insured. Dr. Parrott . . . will be able to advise you. . . .
I requested Mr. Pleasant D. McNeel . . . to consult you in regard
to the negress Sally. Mr. Andrews must either give her up or give a
receipt for $600, or $15 per month for hire, on account of the estate
of John Graham. I depend upon you to attend to my interests below
the same as I should do if there myself. . . .

But Ira had left Brazoria for the army before the Mexicans arrived and he was still with the Second Regiment when the apothecary general returned to Brazoria from New Orleans. Anson Jones
reverted to inactive status but retained his rank until May 10,
1837. In October, Surgeon General Ewing begged him to come
to Columbia to help straighten out the medical records of the
army. "There are many complaints against the department," Dr.
Ewing wrote. "I endeavored to rectify them with the Old Man
[Houston]; your presence is required here very much." But Dr.
Jones was too busy gathering together his scattered possessions
and repairing his property, damaged by neglect and military use,
to give much attention to Ewing's difficulties. He was "too much
used to complaints from volunteers to be much troubled about
them"; and as for the Old Man, Jones thought he "had better
get sober, and attend to affairs he knows something about."

Gradually Brazorians who had been with the army or had
"taken the Sabine chute" returned, and every boat brought a
crowd of new citizens from the United States. It was months before anything like normalcy was restored. Brazoria was never
again to recapture its pre-revolutionary character that had given
Anson Jones his first feeling of oneness with a community, as well
as his first sense of spiritual and material success.

Beyond the precincts of the town things had changed too.
Urrea's army, and unidentified rascals who followed it, had taken
most of the portable property from farmhouses abandoned by the
Runaways. When the Smith-Woodruff family reached their home
it was desolate and bare, and they found it more difficult to reestablish themselves than it had been to start from scratch two
years earlier. The confusion caused by strangers who disembarked
on the Brazos searching for cheap lands, meantime picking up a
living somehow, contrasted vividly with the peaceful isolation of
their farms before the war.

If they must live in an atmosphere of agitation, the Woodruffs concluded, it would be better to move into town, where confusion had its compensations. But they did not choose Brazoria, whose days of greatness had already passed; nor Columbia, temporary capital of the Republic. They had heard of the new city of Houston that the shrewd Allen brothers were building about twenty miles from San Jacinto battlefield. They decided to abandon farming and grow up with the metropolis on Buffalo Bayou. There would be opportunities for Mr. Woodruff, and there there would be advantages for the children that Brazoria could never offer. To Houston they went, camping as they had done in Brazoria County, until their house could be built.

Not only along the Brazos River, but throughout Texas the aftermath of revolution was as confused and unhappy as the San Jacinto campaign itself. Runaways returned to find their houses robbed, their fences burned, their crops overgrown with weeds. Strangers swarmed everywhere, bent upon land speculation and other get-rich-quick schemes. The spirit of gambling, always apparent in Texas, was rampant.

Old Texans in the army returned home as soon as possible, but their places were filled several times over by newcomers attracted by the disorder—men who started from the United States "to fight for their rights" before they learned of San Jacinto, and others who, having heard the news, kept coming toward Texas.

The Texas Army, now numbering about 2,500 men—most of whom had arrived since April 21—moved to Victoria, then to Coleto, near Goliad, the site of the massacre of Fannin's men. It was left pretty much to its own devices.

I am now several Weeks without having received any communication from the Government [complained Brigadier General Rusk on June 1]. I have enquired as to the supplies, munitions and reinforcements which might be expected and . . . have not received . . . the slightest information. . . .

We are here in an old delapidated Town, with many unpleasant associations, and have not one days provisions. . . .

At the mouth of the Brazos the government of President Burnet was leading a troubled, precarious existence. Its official guest was General Antonio López de Santa Anna, who had signed peace

treaties on May 14 and was awaiting transportation home to be-
stir himself for their ratification. Richard Bache, a grandson of
Benjamin Franklin, guarded Santa Anna's shanty—more to protect him from the Texans than to prevent his escape. The army
and some of the Cabinet deplored the treaties and demanded
Santa Anna's head. President Burnet detailed Vice-President
Zavala and the Secretary of the Treasury to escort him to Mexico
aboard the Texas Navy schooner *Invincible;* but before the vessel
could sail, a boatload of volunteers from the United States landed
and took charge of the situation, while citizens and civil authorities looked on helplessly. They fetched the Mexican dictator
ashore and announced that he was remaining in Texas. Captain
Jeremiah Brown had made bail in New Orleans and was again
commanding the *Invincible* in the service of his adopted country.
He sent word to President Burnet that his vessel would not leave
port against the wishes of these recruits—who had not yet discovered the location of their camp or the name of its commanding
officer.

The captive Mexican President was taken to Quintana and
then to Orozimbo, Dr. J. Æ. Phelps's Brazoria County plantation. Here he remained while his future became a major political
issue.

There were rumors of a new Mexican invasion. Texans remembered apprehensively the Runaway Scrape and asked about
the army. Major General Houston, still technically commander
in chief, was on sick leave, and Brigadier General Rusk was in
actual command. Before the end of June, President Burnet commissioned Mirabeau B. Lamar as major general and sent him to
take charge of the unruly army. The officers—then the men—
with democratic disregard of protocol, voted to reject the commander appointed by the President and Cabinet. The army gave
its allegiance first to Thomas Jefferson Green of North Carolina,
then to Felix Huston, recently arrived from Mississippi.

The Truth is [Private P. H. Bell thought] the President and his
Cabinet have incurred such a mass of odium that [should] they now
send one of the Old Patriarchs here on the most sacred mission he
would be viewed with suspicion. . . . And I believe that 'tis sus-
ceptible of demonstration that God in his wisdom & perfection could
not please the dissatisfied spirits of this Army.

Civil affairs were equally chaotic. "My God," T. F. McKinney was exclaiming, "what a burlesque on government." Not a Cabinet officer elected by the convention remained with President Burnet, and that peripatetic executive, whose industry and patience were phenomenal, was beginning to long for a less harrowing existence than had been his since March 17. He was blamed for whatever was done—or left undone—and no one had time or inclination to consider the difficulty with which he managed to preserve at least a semblance of constitutional forms. Even in his official family there was criticism, dissension.

Secretary of State Collinsworth, for example, left the Cabinet on May 13 because, he declared, Burnet was conferring "the highest offices in your gift . . . upon persons who had never been in the country except temporarily upon speculations." He himself, as he reminded the President, had been in Texas about fifteen months and therefore spoke as an old settler.

While independence was being achieved at San Jacinto, Vice-President Zavala was threatening, enigmatically, to resign "for reasons which I will explain to Congress & the Nation." He reconsidered, however, and agreed to escort Santa Anna back to Mexico as official representative of the new Republic of Texas. But when the volunteers hustled him and the Mexican general off the *Invincible* on June 3, in defiance of the President's orders, he asked to be excused from further connection with the Burnet administration. It was obvious to him that "the present Government of Texas has lost the moral confidence of the People." Illness prevented his participation in public affairs until he gave up the office on October 21, to die soon thereafter.

On July 23 President Burnet scheduled the first general election of the new nation for the first Monday in September. The Constitution adopted May 17 was to be ratified by the citizens—if a copy of it could be found in time. The manuscript had been taken to Tennessee, where it was printed in a Nashville newspaper. From this it was reprinted in a Cincinnati paper. The *Telegraph and Texas Register* reprinted the Cincinnati reprint on August 3, and Texans at last had an opportunity to study the charter of liberty under which they had been living, theoretically, since May. Voters were also asked to express their preference as to annexation to the United States.

Public attention, however, was not focused on ratification of the Constitution or upon approval of annexation—there was no real opposition to either. The important questions were who would be chosen President, Vice-President, senators, and congressmen.

Henry Smith of Brazoria, long-time voice of the anti-Mexican faction, sought the presidency as a vindication of his management of affairs as Provisional Governor in 1835. Stephen F. Austin was, strangely enough, the candidate of the leaders of the old War Party. Not realizing the extent to which the Texan electorate of 1836 was composed of men who neither knew nor cared to know that without the Empresario's work there could have been no Republic of Texas, Austin sought, almost instinctively, to continue in the service of his people and yearned—not very hopefully—for vindication.

The obvious candidate was the wounded hero of the perhaps unfinished war of independence, whom men had already dubbed Old Sam Jacinto. The general refused to evince any interest in politics, but a "large mass meeting" at San Augustine on August 15 started the Houston boom. Five days later six hundred persons at Columbia demanded his candidacy. He managed to maintain his silence until eleven days before election, then bowed to *vox populi* with the eloquently simple declaration: "The crisis requires it." But, he piously hoped, "Duty . . . will not always require this sacrifice of my repose and quiet."

Although there was no formal canvass by the presidential candidates, the campaign generated tremendous heat. Lieutenant Colonel Henry Millard wrote from the army headquarters August 2:

I have just returned from Valesco where I have been . . . on a mission from the army to the Government—whom I found Imbicile Inactive and Incapable . . . a complete disorgani[z]ation of every department. . . . I left them fully employed in devising ways and means of perpetuating their power that and speculation being their employment for the Last 2 Months primary object is now to Elevate Stephen F. Austin to the presidency and no stone will be Left unturned by them to effect their object that they may again come into power under his patronage. Genl. Austin is with them hand and

Glove, and their ostensible object in my opinion is to throw us back under the Mexican Dynasty.

The Mexicans are again collecting their forces at Matamores and I presume will be upon us in Oct or Nov [Millard wrote twenty days later] . . . the Great Majority of this army will not keep the field under Austin *should* he be Elected of this you may rest assured.

General Houston, too, "was firmly impressed with a belief that, if either of the gentlemen [Austin or Smith] should be elected, it would be next to impossible to organize and sustain a government." He was confident of his own ability to "form an administration which would triumph over all the difficulties attendant upon the onset of the constitutional government of Texas."

When the votes were counted, Houston had 5,119; Smith, who had withdrawn, received 743, and Austin, who declined to withdraw although defeat was certain, had 587.

"The body Politic," one of Dr. Jones's Brazoria neighbors commented, "is unlike Every other machine that Ever Existed. other machines may be thrown out of order by some accident but this is only right by accident."

Anson Jones was engulfed, as all Texans were, by the bitter political discussions which tapped the deepest, as well as the most recent, prejudices. He gathered together his scattered possessions and prepared again to practice medicine.

IX

A MAMMOTH SCHEME

D R. JONES took no part in the acrimonious political contest of 1836 and never disclosed for whom he voted. While the campaign was in progress he was visiting old friends and patients along the Brazos and San Bernard rivers.

At William H. Wharton's Eagle Island plantation, ten miles from Brazoria, a violent attack of dysentery kept him abed more than two months. It was no time to be ill, but if one had to be sick Mrs. Wharton's hospitable home was the ideal place for convalescence. It had long been the doctor's favorite visiting place. This famous establishment

was a story and a half with two long galleries and a large hall, also an office and several rooms in the yard. . . . In planning the home, Wm. H. Wharton sent to Europe for a landscape gardener to beautify the yard and lake that was near the residence. . . . In summer the gentle gulf breeze and wide expanse of lawn and the landscape[d] garden on the lake made it an ideal place. . . . Mr. and Mrs. Wharton were ideal hosts, being well educated and in possession of a fine library, and income sufficient to entertain on a lavish scale. They had negroes who did nothing but hunt, and whose duty it was to keep the table supplied with game, which was always abundant.

Before Dr. Jones returned from Eagle Island to Brazoria his cousin Ira had come back from the army and, after a brief illness, had died. His house had been broken open and everything valuable stolen—even the saddles and bridles—and his desk had been robbed of all his money.

Two lawyers had "squatted" in one room of my office [he said] and I was unable to get them out for several weeks; when I succeeded it produced a "challenge" from my friend the Chief Justice J. Collinsworth, which I accepted, to fight with pistols at ten steps. It was, however, settled, his object having been to "bluff," which, when he found out it would not succeed, he got his friend T. F. McKinney to get him out of the scrape.

At nearby Columbia the statesmen of the first constitutional regime of Texas had set to work on October 3. Both of the Whartons represented the Brazorians in the First Congress—William in the Senate, John in the House, along with Dr. Branch T. Archer. The houses of Congress deliberated in insubstantial frame buildings that looked suspiciously like barns and were furnished with improvised benches and rickety tables. At night congressmen who could find no better accommodations rolled up in their blankets under the trees. This temporary capital resembled an encampment more than a seat of government.

Two weeks after the Congress assembled, the ad interim President and Vice-President sent in their resignations and Sam Houston and Mirabeau B. Lamar were inaugurated at impromptu ceremonies at four o'clock that afternoon.

Columbia was ten miles from Brazoria, on the circuit Dr. Jones had ridden professionally for three years and which he was beginning to ride again. Two of his San Jacinto companions sat in the Senate, and ten others were representatives. Jones's neighbor, Dr. Archer, whom he did not admire, was scheduled to become Speaker of the House, but when he tardily arrived with his credentials as a member, he found that Ira Ingram of Matagorda had already been elected Speaker.

Never before had Anson Jones watched at such close range the legislative and executive processes, and never before had he been so aware of the keenness of his own political judgments. He found himself studying proposed legislation as carefully as men who sat in Congress and he began to listen attentively to "solicitations from various *friends* (?), from various motives, to become a candidate for member of Congress from Brazoria."

Anson Jones, M.D., had come a long way psychologically since he had taken his first timid step in Texan politics eighteen months before. He was now not only cogitating on the state of the nation in the privacy of his office and as he rode between the plantations of his patients; he was discussing public questions so earnestly on the street corners of the capital that other men were thinking of him as a potential statesman.

The *Telegraph and Texas Register,* published by the Bordens
at the capital, added the doctor's name to the candidates to succeed Senator Collinsworth when that Brazorian resigned to become Chief Justice of the Republic. Willis A. Faris, Dr. E. Harris,
David G. Burnet, and William G. Hill were already in the race.
Dr. Jones, a little startled by this unauthorized listing of his name,
immediately wrote the editors to explain that

the announcement was induced through a misunderstanding of some
remarks made by me on the subject of the pending election. . . .
However grateful I might be, under other circumstances, for the
suffrages of my fellow citizens . . . I am not now a candidate for
them.

It was all very pleasant, but the doctor was still trying honestly
to believe that he wanted nothing more from life in Texas than
success in his medical business. He might be willing someday to
serve his country in the Congress, but in February 1837, he
"never had an intention of opposing any of the gentlemen now before the public." No man in Brazoria was more widely known—or
at the moment less popular—than ex-President Burnet; Hill, who
was elected, was one of the oldest settlers in the county and a
veteran of the Béxar campaign. Faris, who had attended the convention of 1836 as an unofficial secretary, was Clerk of the House
of Representatives; and certainly Dr. Jones did not want to oppose his medical colleague, Dr. Harris.

Anson Jones had never been a candidate for office, but he knew
that a late entry into a five-cornered race for a short term was not
the way to make a political debut.

With that perverse suggestibility that characterizes the solitary
man, Dr. Jones's withdrawal from a race he had never actually
entered committed him to politics. He reviewed more closely the
deliberations of the first session of Congress and put mental question marks by some of the acts—especially the charter it had
granted to the Texas Rail Road, Navigation, and Banking Company.

That corporation was a Napoleonic concept. Its promoters had
fought for Texan liberty, but they had not come to Texas exclusively for that purpose—nor to meditate idly upon the economic
possibilities of an inchoate nation. They were empire builders in

the British sense, and they had their plans ready for the First Congress to approve.

Their legislative agents were members of the Congress, and both were Brazorians: Archer in the House, Collinsworth in the Senate. Fellow incorporators included Thomas Jefferson Green, M.C., Béxar; Augustus C. Allen, founder of the new city of Houston and brother of John K. Allen, M.C., Nacogdoches; Mosely Baker, M.C., Austin County; A. C. Horton, senator from Matagorda, and Thomas F. McKinney, merchant-banker and financier of the revolution. In the early stages Stephen F. Austin and J. Pinckney Henderson had given their blessing to the enterprise; Austin withdrew from it on his deathbed.

Congressman Green (who had to be denied a seat in the Senate of the next Congress because he was not yet a citizen of Texas) presented on Friday, December 9, the petition of Congressman Archer and Senator Collinsworth. Three legislative days later the committee to which it was referred reported that it had "carefully considered the same, and recommended its passage" with a minor amendment. Mr. Allen of Nacogdoches, brother of one of the incorporators, moved concurrence "and the question being taken was carried."

Mr. Fisher of Matagorda and Mr. White, who had risen from overseer of a Brazoria plantation to become congressman from Jackson, pushed the legislation through, with the aid of Mr. Allen. Except for an effort of Speaker Ingram of Matagorda to increase the bonus on earnings (which was voted down 10 to 16), there was no debate. Rules were suspended and the charter was approved instanter, with only five dissenting votes.

The Clerk was instructed to hurry over to the Senate with the good news, but the Senate calendar was so crowded that senatorial approval of the charter had to wait almost twenty-four hours. Then, on the afternoon of December 14, "the rules being suspended the Bill was read and passed its third and final reading" without a record vote. Two days later President Houston signed it and its senatorial sponsor left Congress to become Chief Justice of the Supreme Court of the Republic.

Promoters never had smoother sailing before a legislative body or encountered greater difficulties after they thought they were ready to set their enterprise in operation. Dr. Jones decided that

it was time for disinterested men to enter the councils of the nation
to counteract the alliance between speculators and government
that the Texas Rail Road, Navigation, and Banking Company
charter typified. His friends urged him to run for Congress, and
he agreed to make the race.

It would be difficult [Jones thought] to analyze the arguments and
feelings by which I was actuated in consenting. I had "fought, bled,
and died" for the country in the first place, and this had increased
my desire to see it prosperous and successful. Habit had accustomed
me to reflect more and more upon public matters. The First Congress of Texas had committed the most woful blunders, and there
had been much reckless and interested legislation. . . . 1st, the
Texas R.R., N., and B. Co. . . . 2d, the location of Houston as
the seat of government; and 3d, the sale of Galveston Island. These
three acts constituted a perfect "selling out" of Texas to a few
individuals, or, at least, of everything that was available in 1836.
. . . Houston and Galveston were *pretty respectable* speculations
by members of a legislature; but the other was a grabbing up of
everything that was left.

The Texas Rail Road, Navigation, and Banking charter, one
of the shrewdest of the promoters declared after analyzing it, gave
the corporation powers more liberal "than any other in my recollection." The authorized capital was five million dollars—ten
million if the company desired. Its network of railways and canals
was to connect the Sabine with the Rio Grande, and the company
was to have the right of eminent domain on public lands within a
mile of its routes. It was not only the first railroad corporation
chartered by Texas, but the first one west of the Mississippi River;
and Congress had not been disposed to weigh the proposal in
apothecary's scales.

But transportation was only one of the objects of the promoters.
Their primary interest was banking—the kind of banking done by
the Bank of England and the late Bank of the United States.

Upon payment of $25,000 in gold or silver to the Treasury of
the Republic, the company might open its central bank, with a
specie capital of a million dollars, and begin to issue its currency.
Branches might be established as the business grew. There was no
bank in all Texas, and Congress had not yet authorized the Treas-

ury to emit Republic of Texas currency—possibly never would have if this bank had functioned as planned.

There were to be 50,000 shares of stock. The bank was to pay to the public treasury 1 per cent of its dividends; it could not charge more than 10 per cent discount, and its currency was to be in amounts of $5 or more. The Republic was also to receive 2½ per cent of profits from transportation, and in time of war troops and military supplies were to be transported free of charge. The life of the charter was forty-nine years, renewable upon payment to the Republic of $500,000.

In the United States, President Jackson's seven-year war on the second Bank of the United States had just ended, with the expiration of the institution's charter. He had mobilized the distrust that little men have always felt toward great financial establishments to destroy the bank. The issue was not yet dead in the United States. It could easily be stirred in Texas.

Not many Texans understood the intricacies of banking. Instinctively they feared institutions that fed on mortgages and mysteriously made their paper money valuable—or worthless. The haste and unanimity with which the charter had been pushed through Congress, and the financial stake of congressmen and senators in the scheme—rumor also included the President— were grounds for vague suspicion. But it was a jubilant letter Congressman Green wrote Congressman Archer the day after Christmas that made the Texas Rail Road, Navigation, and Banking charter a political football.

The privilege [Green rhapsodized] of discounting thirty millions of paper at ten per cent. per annum upon its ten millions capital stock; its *unrestricted* privilege to deal in bills of exchange; its *unrestricted* authority over the establishment of tolls, fees and charges of the works; the privilege of taking, at the minimum government price, all the lands within half a mile of such works; its full and ample power to buy and sell all species of property . . . the right that foreign stockholders have to hold real estate in Texas not otherwise allowed to them, together with its *ninety-eight* years' duration of charter, are privileges . . . *beyond arithmetical calculation.* . . .

But suppose you were to invest one million dollars at present in . . . the best lands in the country . . . at an average of fifty cents per acre; in less than two years, if the emigration continues as it has

since the commencement of the revolution (and we have a right to
expect its tenfold increase), such an investment will have increased
not less than one thousand per cent.

But . . . it will not be necessary for you to do more than survey
the road [from Copano Bay to San Antonio], before *millions* of
property may be sold upon it, &c. . . .

It is at the option of your corporation to commence *any* public
work at pleasure, and to prosecute the same *free of any legislative
restrictions or penalty.*

Opposition to the corporation began before subscription books
were opened in Texas. The *Telegraph and Texas Register,* principal newspaper of the Republic, which had followed the government to Houston, pronounced the Texas Rail Road, Navigation,
and Banking a monopoly in violation of the Constitution, and
served notice on July 29, 1837, that

we shall oppose this corporation to the utmost extremity, and . . .
shall incessantly labor to accomplish its destruction.

Let those HONEST legislators exult to behold ONE MILLION OF
DOLLARS [the editor had heard that the money was in hand], all
accurately counted, and neatly arranged in high and shining piles; &
. . . stifle if they can, the bitter, bitter reflection, that this golden
fruit of speculative legislation, like the forbidden fruit of Eden, is to
entail an hereditary curse upon their posterity; that it is to choke up
every channel of enterprise throughout our land; control our currency; paralyze our commerce, destroy every germ of internal improvement, and, finally, compel every class of our citizens to bow
down and do homage at the feet of a foreign, monied, aristocracy!

In Brazoria County the spearhead of the anti-Texas Rail Road,
Navigation, and Banking movement was Dr. Anson Jones, and
his organ was the Matagorda *Bulletin,* Brazoria being at the moment without a newspaper. When Jones "chanced to see" T. J.
Green's letter to Dr. Archer—indiscreetly circulated to stimulate
stock subscriptions—he wrote a trial balloon to the editor at
Matagorda on August 14, in which he pointed with pride to the
uprightness of Texans outside of Congress and viewed with alarm
the monster Congress had created to enslave them. He signed the
letter "Franklin."

Before that letter could be published, the Houston *Telegraph* of
August 19 had announced Dr. Jones's candidacy for Congress.

In the next issue it printed a demand that the Brazoria candidates "declare their sentiments on the rail road, navigation, and banking company."

Competition was keen for Brazoria's two seats in the House of the Second Congress. Congressman Archer, president of the Texas Rail Road, Navigation, and Banking Company, did not seek re-election, but Congressman John A. Wharton, who had failed to register a vote against the charter, announced. Mathew C. Patton, William J. Russell, Patrick C. Jack, and Anson Jones also entered the race. Wharton was the doctor's oldest friend in Texas, a hero of San Jacinto, and dean of the Brazoria bar. He was too busy trying to rescue his brother William from the Mexicans at Mata-moros to campaign. Patton was a county-seat merchant. Russell had commanded the schooner *Brazoria* in the battle of Velasco and served in the Béxar campaign, but the doctor had not yet forgiven his opposition to the Jones Resolutions for independence back in 1835. Jack had been jailed with Travis at Anahuac, served in both conventions and in the Béxar campaign, then became junior partner of Wharton & Jack, the law firm that handled the doctor's litigation.

The Matagorda *Bulletin* of August 23 carried the letter written by Dr. Jones but signed with the name of the Father of American Thrift.

When I first read this charter [he wrote], I rose from its perusal with astonishment . . . but . . . I did not realize the extent of the evil . . . until I chanced a few days since, by accident, to see a letter from Gen. T. J. Green [from which he quotes the most damning parts]. . . .

The famous East India Company, with its forty millions of subjects, sinks into a pigmy, in comparison with this mammoth scheme of wealth. . . .

This paltry sum [the $25,000 bonus] will scarcely buy the slaves on a single cotton plantation, much less a *whole nation of freemen!* and is, comparatively, less than the miserable mess of pottage for which Esau sold his birthright. It is but a poor bait, and does not begin to cover the hook. . . .

Fellow-citizens! this institution . . . will destroy, in ten thousand ways, *the liberties of your country.* And was it . . . to endow this splendid foreign aristocracy . . . that you have suffered so many years of toil and privation . . . that you have so freely poured out your blood and treasure in the establishment of your independence? Was it for this you fought and bled at Velasco [Brazoria County], at Goliad, at Conception, at San Antonio, and at San Jacinto? . . .

Let your consciences answer these questions, and let the response be given at the polls . . . September 4th, when you will be called upon to choose between the advocates and the opposers of this institution.

Anson (Franklin) Jones was elected.

X

THE CITY OF HOUSTON

THE crowded, raucous new "city" in which the Second Congress met was the seventh capital the Texans had had in their fourteen months of independence. The First Congress had found accommodations at the sixth capital inadequate and the Columbians little disposed to do anything about it. The Congress promptly designated a new seat of government and moved to it as soon as it could.

Fifteen places had vied for the honor, but none of them got it. The congressmen preferred a city that existed only in the imagination of its promoters, the enterprising Augustus and John Allen, brothers, who had prenatally christened their speculation in honor of the President of the Republic.

The Allens had tried unsuccessfully to buy the site of Harrisburg; then, with vision born of promotional necessity, they discovered in a new tract on Buffalo Bayou eight miles away advantages which were certain to make it "beyond all doubt, the great commercial emporium of Texas." It was a part of the estate of the late John Austin, founder of Brazoria; they bought it for $5,000 from Dr. T. F. L. Parrott, who married Austin's widow. The city began when

Augustus C. Allen mapped out on the crown of his stovepipe hat (and later upon paper) streets, squares, etc., and then with a knife that he wore in his girdle, blazed out the pathway of Main Street.

Settlers began hustling toward the new city even before the sale of lots began. Newcomers, bent upon getting their businesses into operation before the government arrived, were on the ground early, and old Texans, like the Woodruffs of Brazoria County, were there also. When Mr. and Mrs. Woodruff, with their dozen children, reached the site of the future commercial emporium not a house had been built. They camped on their lot near the cemetery while their home was under construction.

Among the settlers, speculators and adventurers, representatives of many nationalities and men of the most diversified tastes, interests and pursuits . . . John K. Allen moved with the ease and grace of a born leader and diplomat . . . a man of youthful appearance, slight build, dressed with the most scrupulous care, of cordial but confident air, wending his way from place to place about the town, ever ready to dilate on the rising glories of the "great commercial emporium" and producing from the green bag which he always carried well filled with titles, papers, deeds to lots, which he would present to any actual settler on condition that he made the necessary improvements.

At the end of March a tourist waded from Harrisburg through mud and water ankle-deep, looking for the new city. He found that it

consisted of a one-story frame, two hundred feet or more in length, which had just been raised, intended by the enterprising proprietors for stores and public offices; several rough log cabins, two of which were occupied as taverns; a few linen tents which were used for groceries [saloons]; together with three or four shanties made of poles set in the ground, and covered and weather-boarded with rough split shingles. All, however, was bustle and animation . . . I might say that there was concentrated all the energy and enterprise of Texas . . .

Persons came pouring in until . . . a floating population had collected of some four or five hundred people . . . which gave the city the appearance [but surely not the air] of a Methodist campground. . . .

It appeared to be the business of the great mass of people, to collect around these centers of vice [groceries] and hold their drunken orgies, without seeming to know that the sabbath was made for more serious purposes, and the night for rest. Drinking was reduced to a system, and had its own laws and regulations. . . . Texians being entirely a military people, not only fought, but drank, in platoons. Gambling too was carried on to such a disgusting extent at all times. . . .

In a new country among a population of six or seven hundred persons, where but one-half were engaged in any regular business (and there was not more than this proportion in Houston, unless drinking and gambling may be considered such), riots of all kinds were to be expected. . . .

I do not think I would be authorized to state that there were those in Houston, who made duelling an occupation; but I feel at liberty to say that there were some who seemed to think that there was no better way to employ their time than to lecture upon the principles of honor, to lay down the laws of the pistol, and to let no occasion pass to encourage others to fight.

Z. N. Morrell, a backwoods preacher, drove his eight-ox team one hundred and sixty miles to lay in supplies at this new emporium. Late Saturday afternoon he swam his oxen across the bayou to the city of tents, where he found "plenty of 'John Barley Corn' and cigars" and some of the supplies he wanted. Sunday morning

after changing the garb of the wagoner for one similar to that worn in the city [he said], I went in search of a place to preach. Upon inquiry I was informed that there never had been a sermon preached in the place. . . . Soon seats were prepared in a cool shade. . . . The sermon was preached to an attentive, intelligent audience.

Two months later there were three resident clergymen (all of whom were also physicians) but no church organization, although plans were under way to build "the first temple dedicated to the dramatic muse in Texas."

"Woodruff's near the old grave yard" became a stopping place in the new city. John Woodruff had evidently concluded that a man who sat at table daily with a family of twelve might as well add a few paying guests. One of them, the Reverend W. Y. Allen, a young Presbyterian missionary, noted in his diary: "Mr. W. is a Baptist brother, and I boarded with him for some time, he charging me only half price."

On May 2 the *Telegraph and Texas Register* temporarily surmounted all obstacles to issue its first Houston edition. It had taken ten days for the vessel carrying the type cases and press to reach Lynchburg from Columbia. There new troubles began; the editor reported:

A great part of the ensuing day was spent in groping at the rapid rate of one or two miles an hour, to the very crown of the "head of navigation of Buffalo Bayou" at the City of Houston. . . . We immediately proceeded in search of the "nearly finished building in-

tended for our press," our search was fruitless. We succeeded in
renting a shanty, which although like the capitol of this place,
"without a roof, and without a floor; without windows and without
a door," is the only convenient building obtainable during this session of *congress*.

N.B. Our troubles have not yet ended. The shanty is falling about
our ears, and driven the workmen outside for safety, the devil alone
looks smiling on the mischief.

When it rained, the roof of the shanty let in enough water to
make the floor a bog. After another shanty with a better roof had
been occupied, the paper ordered from New Orleans failed to
arrive; then there was no ink. "Want of this black article has
kept our subscribers in the dark for the past week," the edition
of June 20 explained.

But scarce as paper and ink were, the *Telegraph* found space
to answer aspersions that were being made against the character
of Texans in general and Houstonians in particular. They, the
editor insisted,

are neither heathens, infidels, renegades, anthropophagi, but simply
what the Yankee term Americans, and what the Americans and
Europeans term Yankees; similar in language, manners, and customs to the citizens of all the new states of the union, and, if differing
in any respect, solely in this, that from the peculiar circumstances
in which they have been placed, they embrace more of the enterprising and adventurous. . . . We feel confident that no people
of the present day are more characterized for a regard for all the
social virtues.

This champion of Texan virtue was Francis Moore, Jr., a
Massachusetts physician who had been a Texan almost two years.

In statue [wrote a member of the Houston police force] he is a
long slabsided, knock-kneed, six footer, and . . . sports but one
arm. . . . During the intolerably hot weather . . . the same Kentucky jeans pants, the same pair of stitchdowns, the same long and
flowing green robe, and the same redoubtable ancient drab beaver,
adorned the tall and disproportioned outward man . . . but of the
materials that adorned the inner man, I cannot so well define.

On the day that Moore was writing his defense of his fellow
citizens, John J. Audubon jotted down his impressions of the new
city:

Houses half-finished, and most of them without roofs, tents, and a liberty pole [used in the April 21 celebration], with the capitol, were all exhibited to our view at once. We approached the President's mansion . . . wading through the water above our ankles . . . the ante-chamber . . . muddy and filthy, a large fire . . . a small table covered with papers . . . camp-beds, trunks . . . strewn about the room. . . .

While waiting for the President we amused ourselves by walking to the capitol, which was yet without a roof, and the floor, benches, and tables of both houses of Congress were as saturated with water as our clothes had been in the morning.

The Woodruffs' new house, while crowded and uncomfortable, at least had a roof, and its occupants were busy. Mr. Woodruff was acquainting himself with the community. Mrs. Woodruff was nursing her youngest child. Mary Smith—eighteen years old now—continued as general manager of the crowded household. But she found time to watch the novel sight of a city springing up about her almost overnight and to become a part of the decorous social life of the permanent residents, who looked with some apprehension upon the goings on along Main Street and about the capitol.

The riffraff that swarmed the tented city had no part in the lives of the country-bred Smith-Woodruff children, but in this bachelor city—the feminine population was estimated at forty— there were steady young men who intended to establish themselves as solid citizens and were looking for wives to help them do it.

Mary Smith had reached a marriageable age. All her life had been spent in rural Arkansas and Texas, and she had been brought up to know that a woman could do as much useful work as a man. She had early learned habits of industry and self-reliance. Her air was one of quiet competency and modest distinction.

Her features are clearly defined, her dark eyes bright and steady, expressing at once sincerity and vivacity, her mouth and chin evince firmness tempered with sweetness. Her voice . . . soft and her enunciation peculiarly distinct. There is nothing vague, or vacillating in appearance, manner, or character, about her.

One of the eligible Houstonians was Hugh McCrory, a twenty-seven-year-old Kentuckian who had come to Texas as one of Felix Huston's volunteers. He arrived too late to fight the Mexicans, and when he was furloughed he came to the capital to grow rich with the town. He bought lots near the center of Houston, helped James Wright establish the firm of Wright & McCrory, and began to look about him for a wife.

He found Mary Smith. To them the county clerk made out the first marriage license issued at Houston, and the Reverend H. Mathews, a visiting Methodist, pronounced them man and wife on July 23, 1837.

Mr. and Mrs. McCrory lived with the Woodruffs, but they were buying supplies of crockery, tableware, Dutch oven, pot-hooks, and other household gear for a home of their own. Hugh already owned a lot; when they could hire a carpenter they would build.

Hugh's business was prosperous. People liked him, and his neighbors selected him alderman from his ward, to serve on the first governing body of the new capital. Mary was very proud of her popular, steady husband; and conscious, too, of the rise in her own fortunes. Four years ago she had been a barefoot immigrant girl on a little Brazoria farm. Then she had moved to the city—not a city, but the city—capital of a nation and its future commercial emporium. At her stepfather's house she listened, as she passed platters of buffalo meat and fluffy biscuits, to the conversation of men who believed they could make Houston the largest, richest place in Texas. Her own husband was one of those men—not a promoter, but a solid man of affairs, and a colleague of Editor Moore in the City Council. What plans for their future Mr. and Mrs. Alderman McCrory could make!

Twenty-six days after their wedding Hugh became a municipal official. Twenty-six days after that—on September 13—he died. They buried him in City Cemetery.

In the nearby Woodruff home Mary resumed her role of general manager of the large and growing family of Woodruffs. She was wearing the widow's weeds her mother had laid aside two years before.

Congressman Anson Jones of Brazoria arrived in Houston twelve days after Alderman McCrory's death. He took a room at Woodruff's.

XI

MR. JONES OF B.

D R. JONES and Mr. Jack took their places as Brazoria's representatives in the called session of the Second Congress on September 25, 1837. Captain Russell followed them to the city of Houston and contested Jack's election until the committee on privileges and elections ruled that Jack, not Russell, was entitled to the place. The chairman of that committee was Anson Jones.

In Brazoria and in other counties, elections had turned on the Texas Rail Road, Navigation, and Banking charter, and the doctor entered Congress pledged to rid the Republic of the incubus. He was not long in perceiving, however, that the atmosphere of the House was different from that of the hustings, and that rules of procedure had not been devised to expedite mandates such as his. He could not achieve his object instanter.

By temperament and from occupational habitude, Jones had abundantly the capacities and traits that other members of Congress—indeed, most of the statesmen of the Republic—lacked. By nature he was a methodical, reasonable man. As schoolmaster he had developed an almost spinsterish insistence upon having all things done decently and in order; then he became a physician, habituated to diagnosing ills before trying to cure them. He was no swashbuckler, and slap-dash performance he abhorred. Not because he set out to be, but because his nature made it inevitable, he became the indispensable man of the Second Congress.

In that Congress Anson Jones laid, without intending to do so, the foundation for the career that was to absorb his thought and energy for a decade. All the time he honestly believed that he would quit politics at the end of his one-year term, but circumstances which he neither directed nor fully understood were enmeshing him in the affairs of the Republic. Service in the House began as a temporary diversion from his "business." In 1837, as earlier—and later—he believed the country was in "a bad scrape" and his impulse was to do something to right matters. But it was not a job to be done quickly. As he delved into one phase of governmental activity it led him inevitably into another and another, until at last he was hardly able to remember the days when his only concerns had been the comparatively simple ones of a county-seat physician.

He was on hand at the hour appointed for convening the session, although most of his colleagues did not appear until next day. It was he who moved the reading of the proclamation that called them together. He and Congressman Menefee counted the ballots for Speaker, declared the Honorable Joseph Rowe, M.D., elected, and escorted him to the unpainted podium. He was chairman for the House of the committee to inform His Excellency the President that the Congress was ready to receive him.

The appearance of President Houston before the lawmakers of Texas was no casual affair. The First Congress, whatever its omissions in other matters, had established a protocol which made men wonder whether the Texans, by living on Latin soil, were not losing their republican simplicity. John Adams himself would have approved the pomp and circumstance of the official journey of the Texan executive from one side of that pine building to the other:

The Senate . . . entered the hall, preceded by their sergeant-at-arms; the President *pro tem.* took his seat on the right hand of the Speaker, and presided jointly with him.

The Senators were provided with seats in front of the chair, and the officers of the two Houses associated in their several duties at their respective stations.

At twelve o'clock, His Excellency the President entered the hall, accompanied by the heads of the several departments, and other officers of the government . . . preceded by the joint committee of the two Houses. The President was received by the members of the two Houses standing uncovered, and was conducted to a seat between the President *pro tem.* of the Senate, and the Speaker of the House.

The heads of the departments . . . and the other attendants of His Excellency were accommodated with seats on the right hand of the chair.

The members having resumed their seats, after a short pause, His Excellency rose, and read [his message]. . . .

His Excellency, having concluded, retired from the hall, conducted and accompanied as on his entrance.

During Dr. Jones's service in the House, when His Excellency the President or a distinguished foreigner visited Congress, Jones was usually on the arrangements committee. Ceremonial etiquette, witnessed in Venezuela and practiced in lodge halls, was being put to effective use in the city of Houston. As ceremonial master of the House, Anson Jones devised the table of precedence for the reception of non-members within the bar of the chamber. First came His Excellency the President, followed by the Vice-President, senators, Cabinet officers, the Chief Justice, commanders in chief of Army and Navy, and foreign diplomatic agents with their suites. Next in precedence were ex-Presidents and Vice-Presidents of the United States, then former executives of Texas; next, former members of the United States Congress, ex-Cabinet officers, ex-governors of states and territories; and finally "such distinguished strangers as the Honorable Speaker or a majority of the House may at any time invite [and, as a happy afterthought], also, all Editors of newspapers within the Republic of Texas."

In the serious business of the House, Mr. Jones of B.—as his name stands in the record to distinguish him from his colleague and "adopted cousin," Oliver Jones of Austin County—was a willing and intelligent worker on the floor and in committee.

Throughout the session, adjournment was usually taken "on motion of Mr. Jones of B.," and when *pro forma* motions were to be made, the Speaker automatically looked toward that gentleman's desk.

For a beginner in politics, the Gentleman from Brazoria drew good committee assignments; but the truth is that most of his colleagues were as inexperienced as he in legislative business. None of them had served in legislatures in the States, although a few had sat in the ayuntamientos and hectic pre-independence assemblies of Texas. Seniority created no problem: only seven had been re-elected from the First Congress.

Mr. Jones of B. became chairman of the committee on privileges and elections; a little later, of the ways and means committee; and finally, of the committee on foreign relations. He was also a member of the committee on the state of the Republic and the finance committee, and he drew the schoolmasterish duties of examining enrolled bills and reporting unfinished business.

Special assignments—on select committees to consider repeal of the Texas Rail Road, Navigation, and Banking charter, to reward Béxar and San Jacinto veterans, to revise the land system, to fund the national debt, to select a permanent capital site, to digest the report of the Secretary of the Treasury, to consider a national system of education, to revise the tariff, to amend the judiciary law, to consider claims, to charter railroads—left him little time to sit of evenings in Mrs. John Woodruff's parlor.

Repeal of the Texas Rail Road, Navigation, and Banking Company charter was the first business on the tapis, although the President had not called the session for that purpose. The honor of introducing the repeal bill fell to William W. Gant of Washington, one of the five who voted against the charter in the First Congress. Jones was chairman of the special committee to which the Gant bill was referred. His committeemen were Jack of Brazoria, Gazley of Harrisburg, Rusk of Nacogdoches, and Thompson, who (with Speaker Rowe) represented San Augustine. All of them were lawyers; Gazley was a physician and merchant as well.

Jones, whose previous study of the law had been restricted to the sections on debtor and creditor, learned in committee that the problem was not so simple as it had seemed to him and his constituents. The Jones committee handled the repeal bill like a hot potato—first asking leave to return it because the stockholders were asking a modification of the charter and, when it came up for third reading, shunting it to the judiciary committee over the protest of Mr. Gant.

The Gentleman from Brazoria was in a most unhappy situation. He had become convinced that it would be as unconstitutional for the Second Congress to repeal the charter as it had been for the First Congress to grant it. His New England conscience would not permit him to take the easy route of voting for Mr. Gant's bill, but he knew that his vote against it would require explanation at home. For the benefit of his conscience and his constituents, he addressed the House on the legal aspect of the problem. The remedy, he declared, lay not in the Congress, but in the Supreme Court. Two unconstitutional acts could accomplish nothing. The interpretation of the law and the Constitution was the function of the Court.

"I want to see the company tried and executed, not murdered!" thundered Mr. Jones of B.

The corporation did not "take root and fasten itself upon the country," as Jones once feared it would. A decade and a half later, without re-examining the facts, the doctor convinced himself that "what Jackson did for the United States in the destruction of the United States Bank . . . I did for Texas. . . . No voice but mine was raised against the institution. 'Alone I did it,' and its friends have so declared. . . .'" The truth is that the death of the bank was due in very small part to him, or to the Second Congress, or to the Supreme Court, whose Chief Justice was a promoter of the company, or, in fact, to anyone in the Republic of Texas.

Panic began in the United States in May of 1837 and continued until 1843. The promoters had expected to get $1,025,000 specie for bank capital and bonus, as well as most of the stock subscriptions, from a handful of capitalists in the United States. Two months after banks there suspended specie payment, which drove coin into hiding, the incorporators of the Texas Rail Road, Navigation, and Banking Company discovered a mutuality of interest between the Republic and the company, which made it—as they euphemistically announced—"desirable that the actual citizens of Texas should be stockholders." Houstonians subscribed $86,000 and promised to take more; but most Texans, like their kinsmen in the United States, were busier seeking tomorrow's grocery money than long-term investments. Their paper money was worthless, and there had never been enough coin in Texas to lift trade much above the barter level.

Despite the panic, the directors of the corporation believed they saw a way to salvage those privileges beyond arithmetical calculation—and to solve the Texas money crisis as well. The bank could print beautiful currency, if only it could save its charter. The $25,000 bonus was to be paid in hard money—which was not to be had as the date of forfeiture neared. But Congress had ordered that promissory notes of the Texas Government be accepted "as Cash for all dues owing or coming to the government."

Promissory notes were plentiful and sometimes as cheap as fifteen cents on the dollar. A little before dead line, President Archer of the company tendered old Henry Smith, Secretary of the Treasury, $25,000 of his star money and called his attention to the act of Congress which made it equivalent to cash.

Here was a nice question of law.

Were "cash" and "specie" synonymous terms, and was payment of a bonus in order to obtain a privilege the same thing as payment of taxes or custom duties? General Green declared that "no lawyer in Texas, or out of it, who is honest, will hesitate to say the tender was legal." But the lawyer whose opinion counted promptly said that it was not. He was the Honorable John Birdsall, Attorney General and soon to be Chief Justice. "I am quite clear," he wrote in an official opinion, "that the Government is fully justified in requiring a literal compliance on the part of the bank, with the provisions of its charter." He held that the bonus was not a *due* to the government in the sense that Congress contemplated, for should the company decide to forego the privilege, nothing would be owed the government. The opinion, by broad inference, suggested that Texas currency would be a flimsy foundation upon which to erect a bank of issue.

No specie, no charter.

On June 5, 1838, Secretary Smith returned the star money and gave the promoters a statement that tender of the bonus had been made in Texas currency before the expiration date of the charter. Later one of them contended that the law was complied with and "therefore all the rights under the charter were vested in the company," but no effort was made to open the bank or to test in court the validity of the contention.

When Anson Jones left Congress, the Texas Rail Road, Navigation, and Banking Company was dead. The doctor had led a wild-goose crusade, and his inconvenient conscience prevented his casting the vote that would have helped to substantiate the later claim that he alone slew the dragon. But the dragon was dead, that was the important thing. He had hated it as much as any man and had let his public know it. As a physician, he knew that a person—natural or artificial—was not the less dead because malnutrition, instead of external wounds, stopped the heart.

Study of this banking scheme, coupled with awareness of the plight of Texas currency, directed Jones's attention to public finance. Long before he came to Texas he had dabbled in it to the extent of writing on the general subject for Poulson's *Advertiser* in Philadelphia. In Congress the validity and stability of fiscal operations of government became a matter of genuine and immediate concern to him. Panic in the United States had precipitated a crisis which was making it increasingly difficult for the Texans to achieve the implied objective of their revolutionary finance: the operation of a solvent government without specie and without redeemable currency.

A few weeks after Dr. Jones became a congressman a mass meeting at Houston considered this problem. Jones wrote the declaration of policy that was adopted.

"Treasury drafts," he declared, "if issued within the range of actual resources, will be safe, valid, secure and convenient." He then pointed out that banks in the United States had suspended specie payment, and that the circulation of their notes in Texas was a fraud not to be encouraged. The only way out for Texans was to accept no currency except that issued by the Republic of Texas. Papers throughout the Republic published Congressman Jones's formula for curing the most worrisome economic ill of the body politic.

Thus identified as an authority on public finance, Jones was soon digesting the reports of the Secretary of the Treasury for less acute members of the House, examining the business routine of the auditorial and other offices, and advocating that a five-million-dollar loan be sought in London and Paris, as well as in Washington. He moved to tax all bank stocks, devised a scheme of change notes, and made many suggestions regarding a revision of the tariff, including a thirty-per-cent reduction on medicines. He opposed an effort to put cotton goods on the free list. Finally, on motion of Mr. Jones of A., Mr. Jones of B. was added to the finance committee.

Before Anson Jones became a member of the House, he had appeared before Congress as a petitioner for medical legislation. He had drafted, got the Brazoria County commissioners to sign, and presented, through Senator William G. Hill, the first request for governmental regulation of the practice of healing arts in the Republic of Texas.

In June 1837 the doctor had warned the First Congress prompt action was required to protect the Texans from

Individuals assuming to be Physicians who . . . have neither graduated or been licensed. . . . However feeble and inefficient the aids of Science and Skill may be . . ., Ignorance and Quackery are undeniably injurious.

He urged the creation of a Medical Society or a Board of Medical Censors, and he wanted the Congress to pass a bill regulating fees "and all other matters relating to the Medical Profession."

For the convenience of the Congress, the medical lobbyist wrote out a bill that would have created a Medical Board consisting of Anson Jones, Brazoria; R. H. Wynne, Matagorda; Robert Peebles, Austin County; James B. Miller, Washington; R. A. Irion, Nacogdoches; W. M. Sheppard and W. W. Hall, Harrisburg. It required all medical practitioners to obtain from a member of the board a temporary certificate (fee $10), and from the whole board a permanent license (fee $50). Graduates of medical colleges were required to exhibit their diplomas to the board, but they were exempt from the fees. Fine for violation of the act was to be $500 for each offense—half to go to the informant. Unlicensed practitioners could not "by Law collect any debt accruing therefor." The bill did not specifically require the board to examine candidates for knowledge of medicine and surgery.

Senator Horton of Matagorda, with the aid of Senator Everitt, a physician from Jasper, pushed the Jones bill through the upper house; but it died on the table of the representatives.

The First Congress adjourned without regulating medical practice, after airing the problem. Then the newspapers took the matter up. The *Telegraph and Texas Register,* as usual when crusading was to be done, led the movement. On June 24 the *Telegraph* declared:

These pseudo M.D. or Drs. are . . . more dangerous than the hostile Indians, and not considerably less numerous. Certainly more brave men have fallen under their hands than the rifles of the Caddos, Wacos, Towaccanies and Comanches ever reached. We had rather at any time see a company of armed Mexicans in battle array, than a squad of these grave gentry, parading with their Pandora boxes in the shape of pill bags. . . . Some of these impostors have acquired the honorable title of doctor merely by the simple process of emigration; and, distinguished by the vast fund of medical knowledge acquired in a livery stable, cook shop, or tan vat, they decide upon the morbid state of the human system . . . with all the confidence of a Broussais or a Silliman. . . .

[A scoundrel] some weeks since, was flourishing as a second Aesculapius in one of the villages of the Brazos, who a few months previous was a shoemaker in Tennessee! Failing in the wholesale business of soles, he concluded to emigrate, and give the devil his due by disposing of souls at the lowest price, charging only a meal's victuals for a dose of medicine! . . .

PRESCRIPTION

Establish in each county of Texas a medical society, composed of regular graduates of medical colleges of the United States and Europe, for the purpose of examining and licensing all person duly qualified to practice medicine.

Being ourselves bound by peculiar ties to the genuine sons of Aesculapius [the editor was Francis Moore, Jr., M.D.], we assure them that our columns shall ever be open to receive the proceedings of any medical association and the *list of physicians regularly licensed to practice medicine.*

The Senate of the Second Congress repassed the medical bill but provided that the censors be elected by Congress. Jones, instead of introducing his own bill, waited until the Senate measure reached the House. Then, by three amendments, he reworded it into some semblance of what he wanted, moved suspension of the rules, and got it approved by a vote of 17 to 9. The Senate promptly concurred and on December 18, after Jones and another congressman had invited the senators into the House chamber, Congress elected by ballot eleven medical gentlemen to regularize the practice of the healing arts in Texas.

Only one of those elected had been named in the original Jones bill—R. A. Irion, former senator from Nacogdoches, now President Houston's Secretary of State. The medical scholar of the group was Ashbel Smith, whose political and medical careers were to be curiously interwoven with Jones's. The others were Isaac Jones, Red River; Asa Hoxey, Washington; George W. Hill,

Milam; J. McNeil Stewart, Brazoria; Albert M. Levy, Matagorda, Jackson, and Victoria; Thomas Anderson, Mina and Gonzales; Joel Jackson, Austin and Colorado; J. B. P. January, San Patricio; and H. Bissell, Béxar.

The Gentleman from Brazoria seems to have been the only congressman who had been graduated from an institution of higher learning. His alma mater was the new medical college he attended for a few months in Philadelphia; but his title, Doctor, and the way he had of quoting Latin and French aphorisms were enough to make Jones a sort of congressional authority on educational proposals.

No state-supported school existed in Texas. The Declaration of Independence berated Mexico for failure to establish public education, and the Constitution made it a duty of Congress to provide schools as soon as possible. The First Congress had not considered the matter; in the Second an effort was made to begin the educational establishment at the top. Congressman Douglass of Nacogdoches moved the incorporation of the University of Texas, but when it came to a vote, Jones voted with the two-to-one majority to postpone action. Jones had never attended a university, but he knew that one could not be created by congressional fiat in a country that had neglected to provide an elementary school. The children of Texas—like the dozen or so at his boardinghouse who were being taught their A B Cs by their older sister Mary—might someday need a university, but in 1837 they needed the most elementary of primary schools.

Jones of Brazoria recommended "means for the establishment of a general and uniform system of education, under the control and direction of Congress," and meantime sought to dedicate public lands for the ultimate endowment of a university at the permanent seat of government. His recommendation was approved by the House and an initial apportionment of ten thousand acres of land agreed upon, but Mr. Jones of A., to the disgust of Mr. Jones of B., got the proposal referred to the judiciary committee. There it remained when the Second Congress adjourned sine die. "Branch was Chr & I scolded him about it," Jones noted in his diary. "W. H. Wharton has promised me to bring the matter up again next session."

For the present, Mary McCrory would continue as schoolmistress of the Woodruff establishment.

XII

GUIDE, PHILOSOPHER, FRIEND

CONGRESSMAN JONES, during the winter of 1837–38, was acted on by stimuli that impelled him subconsciously to chart a new course. Since the breakup of his little home at Brazoria before the revolution, he had not known the serenity of spirit and the creature comforts that come to a man in his own house. He missed the quiet cottage that his sister Mary had made home for him at Brazoria, even more than he missed the genteel hospitality of the Brazos and San Bernard plantation houses that acclimated him socially to Texas. For a year and a half—through the discomforts of war and the disorders of its aftermath—he had been without a home base, living in a world of men.

In the crowded household of the Woodruffs at Houston it was something, even as a paying guest, to know again a clean room, good food, and an ordered existence, and to have comforts provided by a comely young woman of eighteen—even if her eyes were sad.

Woodruff's became to him an oasis in this raucous, bachelor city.

It was not that city life, as such, was distasteful to him. As far as limited funds allowed, he had found enjoyment in staid Philadelphia and in exotic New Orleans. But this boom town of Houston seemed to have all the vices of a city without the compensating urban virtues and amenities that come with age and orderly development. Here Jones found on every hand the temptations he had fled New Orleans to escape. He was older now by four years and conscious that he was a personage of professional and political importance. More than most men, Jones needed human companionship and warm personal attachments, but a deference to his new status as statesman combined with a residual timidity to deny him the pastimes of unattached males in this city of strangers.

Committee work filled many, but not all, of his evenings. He had energies for which there was no outlet. In his lonely Philadelphia days he had found companionship in lodgedom; there assiduity born of tedium had brought him leadership among the Odd Fellows and the Masons.

There was no lodge of any fraternity in Houston, but there was a remedy for that. That charter from the Masonic Grand Lodge of Louisiana that had gone through the battle of San Jacinto with Anson Jones was still among his papers. When he got back to Brazoria after the war the fifteen members of his Holland Lodge had scattered and several of them were dead. He did not try to reconvene the lodge there. How better could a lonesome statesman employ his leisure than in founding the first permanent lodge of Free Masons in the capital of his nation? It would give the congressman the sort of relaxation he enjoyed most: it was pastime with a distinctly purposeful flavor.

In Houston he found George Brown of Brazoria, who had been an officer of Holland Lodge. Together they looked about the crowded city for other Masons. When they found ten, Worshipful Master Jones opened Holland Lodge in due and ancient form and ceremony on the evening of November 8, 1837, in the Senate chamber. Then, doubling as deputy of the Grand Master of Louisiana, he formally installed the lodge.

But it was no longer necessary for Jones to take the initiative in joining a group or establishing an organization; his status now was such that he was automatically included in the plans of others. On December 5, 1837, he was elected an officer of the Philosophical Society of Texas. At the call of Vice-President Mirabeau B. Lamar, who had heard of Franklin's American Philosophical Society and had attended a meeting of a Franklin Society in Alabama on his way to Texas two years before, "a number of gentlemen from different parts of the republic, formed themselves into an association . . . purely scientific and literary in its character." Its function was to be the diffusion of knowledge; its immediate purpose was the "collection and diffusion of correct information regarding the moral and social conditions of our country."

General Lamar was elected president of the society. Congressman Jones was a vice-president, as were Surgeon General Ashbel
Smith, Secretary of State Irion, Speaker Joseph Rowe of the
House (all physicians), and David S. Kaufman, a Nacogdoches
lawyer. Former President Burnet and W. Fairfax Gray, clerk of
the Supreme Court, were secretaries, and Attorney General Birdsall was librarian.

The twenty-six charter members constituted a large portion of
the professional and political talent of Texas. The learned callings
were all represented, and in about the proportion one might guess:
fourteen lawyers, four physicians, one clergyman. Four of the
founders were farmers; two were professional soldiers. One—
A. C. Allen—was a man of business. They elected him treasurer.

These founders called upon

intelligent and patriotic citizens to furnish to the rising generation
the means of instruction within our own borders, where our children
. . . may be indoctrinated in sound principles and imbibe with their
education respect for their country's laws, love of her soil and venera-
tion for her institutions.

We have endeavored to respond to this call by the formation of
this society, with the hope that if not to us, to our sons and successors
it may be given to make the star, the single star of the west as
resplendent for all the acts that adorn civilized life as it is now
glorious in military renown.

Texas has her captains, let her have her wise men!

Of more immediate urgency, most Texans thought that winter,
was the land problem. Not only pre-revolutionary colonists who
had failed to get all they wanted, but soldiers lured to Texas by
promises of landed estates, and old-time speculators from the
United States who saw in Texas a richer field for their talents
than even the old Southwest had provided—all these were clamor-
ing for a chance at the gigantic public domain, which, the Texans
claimed, extended through New Mexico and Colorado into Wyo-
ming.

No public land had been legally distributed in Texas since
1835, and last-moment grants of the legislature of Coahuila y
Texas, so fraudulent as to make even some of the beneficiaries
blush, had been invalidated by the Constitution of the Republic.

Yielding to pressure from all sides, the First Congress had ordered
(over President Houston's veto) that the General Land Office
should begin operation in 1837.

That law, Congressman Jones thought, "vested . . . certain
rights and privileges which made it incumbent upon the next
legislature to pass the land law of 1838, which, objectionable
though it may have been, was the best, under the circumstances,
which could have been passed." President Houston did not agree
with Jones's reasoning and vetoed the bill. Again Congress overrode the veto, with only two dissenting votes in the House, none
in the Senate. Jones declared:

> I defy any man . . . to draw up a bill which Anglo-Saxon land-
> stealers cannot take advantage of, without violating the rights which
> had inured to citizens of Texas under former legislation by Mexico,
> Coahuila, and Texas herself. The Mexican colonization system . . .
> was not well adapted to prevent the frauds of Anglo-Saxon cupidity
> and Anglo-Saxon ingenuity. The fault, therefore, is in the system
> which public faith required us to carry out, and not in the "law" by
> which it is done. . . . The President in his veto pointed out the evils
> of the bill, as the [Jones] committee had done which reported it, but
> failed to point out any remedy, or propose any plan by which the
> public faith could be preserved. Everybody of ordinary sagacity knew
> there would be frauds committed the moment a land office was
> opened in Texas. It took no prophet to tell us that; it would have
> taken *all* the prophets and apostles to boot to have told us how
> frauds were to be prevented. . . . The greatest fault after all that
> can be found in this bill is, that it did not stop "perjury". . . .

A complication in the land matter was the bounty promises
made during the revolution. Young as Texas was, she had a first-
class veteran problem on her hands when the Second Congress
assembled, and the veterans were demanding land. By modern
standards there was no expert veteran lobby, but there were
enough veterans in Congress itself to assure consideration of the
claims of those who had risked life and limb for their adopted
country.

Unfortunately for the maximum effectiveness of veteranism,
many of the congressmen, like Jones, were old settlers too. Their
claims as such took precedence in their thinking over the demands
of men who came to Texas only to fight.

The called session was only two weeks old when Kelsey H. Douglass of Nacogdoches offered a bill for the benefit of the veterans. Jones got it referred to a special committee of which he was chairman. Branch wanted to reward each veteran with 960 acres; Jones opposed it. Grant moved 640; Jones voted against it. Then Jones suggested 320 acres for each three months' service. Rusk then tried to get the same amount for everybody who reached Texas before April 18, 1838 (double the amount for heads of families and widows), but Jones retorted that the matter before Congress was rewarding veterans, not immigrants.

The veteran land bill squeaked through by a majority of one, with Jones opposing it vigorously. As soon as it had passed he sat down and wrote "solemnly to protest against the passage of this bill, and I confidently appeal to my God, my country, and posterity, for the correctness of my course." Veterans had been placed on a par with old settlers in locating their lands, and this, Mr. Jones of B. declared, was not only in direct violation of the Constitution and two acts of Congress, but "at variance with the plainest principles of common justice." Other provisions, too, were "a most palpable and direct violation of the solemn pledge of this government," in the opinion of the Gentleman from Brazoria.

Not only soldiers who had reverted to civilian status but soldiers still under arms engaged the attention of the Second Congress, His Excellency the President, and the chairman of the House committee on privileges and elections.

Neither the empty treasury nor the safety of the Republic permitted such an army as Texas then had, composed principally of non-residents and commanded by a military adventurer who was himself not a citizen of Texas. Recruits continued to arrive from the United States, but it was clear to the government that its primary problem was not to augment the military establishment but to get rid of the men already on the rolls—or, at least, to bring them under civil control.

When Colonel Albert Sidney Johnston, armed with a commission signed by President Houston and the Secretary of War, arrived in camp in January 1837 to relieve Brigadier General Felix Huston of the command, the old commander in chief disabled the new in a duel. Dr. Anson Jones and Surgeon General A.

Ewing hurried to the camp to examine Johnston's wound. Huston retained control of his defiant troops until May, when he came to the capital to urge Congress to order him to lead his army into Mexico. While Congress dallied with the suggestion, and Old Long Shanks, as the soldiers called Huston, was busy lobbying, His Excellency the President saw an opportunity that he knew how to use.

Sam Houston sent his Secretary of War secretly to the army to furlough all but six hundred of Huston's men and to assign the remainder to widely separated posts, where they might be of conceivable use against Indians. "Texas," the President assured the furloughed soldiers of the Republic with inadvertent irony, "has never forgotten that you are her adopted sons." When Old Long Shanks discovered that his army had dissolved, Texas lost much of its charm for him. He returned to the United States and settled down to the practice of law.

Even so, there remained enough soldiers on the muster rolls at the time of the September elections in 1837 to create a nice problem for Congress, particularly for Jones's committee on privileges and elections. Were regularly enrolled soldiers, whether in camp or on furlough, possessed of the privileges of suffrage? Many of them had voted in the second national election, and Mr. Jones of B. raised the question by introducing a resolution which declared that no regularly enlisted soldier (whether on active or inactive duty) was entitled to vote. The House adopted the Jones resolution, and application of the rule brought interesting results.

In Mina, for example, L. C. Cunningham had received sixty-seven votes and Jesse Billingsly only sixty, but Billingsly was seated because thirteen of his opponent's constituents were Rangers. The seat of Fielding Jones of Victoria was challenged by J. J. Linn, although the name of "Mr. Jones of V." had already been added to the House roll. Mr. Jones of B. found that Linn, who received eighteen votes from civilians, had a majority of legal votes. Fielding Jones had fifty-four soldier votes, but only twelve civilians voted for him.

Not every man legally elected was eligible to membership in the House. Mr. Jones of B. reported that a Mr. Walker unquestionably had received "a majority of the legal votes of the county of Refugio, but . . . he has not the requisite qualifications for

citizenship . . . and is consequently ineligible to a seat in this
House."

Such problems suggested the desirability of defining more clearly
eligibility for officeholding in this land of strangers where, the
editor of the *Telegraph and Texas Register* declared:

> Crowds of enterprising emigrants are arriving on every vessel and
> so numerous have our citizens become that we confidently believe
> [the city of] Houston alone could, in the case of a second invasion,
> furnish an army of able bodied men, nearly equal to that now en-
> camped on the banks of the La Baca.

The Congress wrestled with the problem and, at Congressman
Jones's suggestion, stiffened the requirements for political prefer-
ment. No man could thereafter hope to hold a political office until
he had spent at least 180 days in the Republic. Old Texans—
those who had lived in Texas a couple of years or more—were
protecting their priorities.

While these and other matters of state were before Congress,
young Mary McCrory, herself the widow of a veteran, heard the
statesmen who boarded at Woodruff's discuss the problems at
table. As Texas congressmen went, Dr. Jones was a reticent man.
His was still the conversational technique he had learned in medical consultations—he listened to the opinions of others before he
tried to bend them by argument to his own notions. Perhaps for
that very reason his colleagues listened with respect when the
Gentleman from Brazoria spoke his mind. More than men who
had wives and daughters at home, Congressman Jones subconsciously felt the stimulus that a feminine auditor gives to conversation. It is likely that some of the best phrases he used in debates
in the House were coined at Woodruff's dinner table—addressed
ostensibly to, say, Congressman Burleson, with Mary McCrory
listening as she served the table.

Dr. Jones was not a stranger to Mary when he came to live at
Woodruff's. She had heard of him—as who hadn't?—in Brazoria
when she was a little girl. His good horses, clean linen, his air of
quiet dignity, the fact that he was a professional man gave him
a premier status in the eyes of a country girl.

Now she saw him every day, heard him gravely discuss problems of state, and read his name in almost every issue of the

Telegraph. He was very kind and considerate; he was tactful. Not only reticence but gentle manners distinguished him among these boarders. He was not a frontiersman; he treated ladies with a finesse that contrasted vividly with the hearty but clumsy courtesy of the country-bred. As a man of medicine he had become a practical psychologist; Mary was not the first grief-stricken young woman he had known—but she was the most attractive. He knew how to demonstrate his sympathy and convey the increasing admiration he was beginning to feel without opening anew the wounds in her heart.

It was a pleasure to her to do little kindnesses for the Brazoria doctor—replacing a lost button on his broadcloth coat, mending a frayed cuff. For that he was grateful; it would be pleasant on a more permanent basis.

There was increasing awareness between them, but Mary's year of mourning had months to go. He would not rush the matter. He would remain at Houston, at Woodruff's, until summer. He could wait—he was used to waiting.

At Jones's call, representatives of the three Louisiana-chartered lodges in Texas met in the Senate chamber on December 20, 1837, to found, upon Jones's motion, the Masonic Grand Lodge of the Republic of Texas. Congressman Jones was at the secretary's desk; Brother Sam Houston was chairman. Congressmen Rusk and Douglass, Senator Burton, Charles S. Taylor, a signer of the Declaration, and Judge Adolphus Sterne were there representing Milam Lodge at Nacogdoches. James H. Winchell (who was expelled from Holland Lodge next day for un-Masonic conduct) sat as proxy for the brethren of McFarlane Lodge, San Augustine.

The motion to establish the Grand Lodge of Texas was put and carried. Anson Jones was then unanimously elected first Most Worshipful Grand Master of the Republic of Texas.

Getting the Grand Lodge into operation demanded time and patience and precisely the sort of talents that the first Grand Master possessed. Eight times in a single month he presided over sessions, and in the intervals he conducted a heavy fraternal correspondence; all this in addition to his duties as congressman from Brazoria and Worshipful Master of Holland Lodge.

The climax of his career as first Grand Master came a week

before the Congress adjourned. The Grand Lodge, "preceded by the Grand Tyler and directed by the Grand Marshal," made an official visitation to Holland Lodge "and were received with the Grand honors according to the ancient usages and customs of the Craft."

After the formal welcome was concluded Grand Master Jones read from manuscript a carefully prepared address. He proudly announced that nearly two hundred Masons had already been affiliated in Texas; he reviewed the history of Holland Lodge from its inception and declared:

It has the high honor now of numbering among its members men who are alike an ornament to society and to Masonry; men who gallantly sustained the cause of human liberty on our fields of glory and in the councils of the nation, and more especially ONE who, like our immortal Brother George Washington, has ever been first in war, first in peace, and first in the hearts of his countrymen! . . .

It did no harm to pay a compliment to Sam Houston.

After the Grand Visitation in May was over and Congress adjourned, Anson Jones did not meet with his Masonic brethren for more than a year.

When spring came Mary McCrory put aside her widow's weeds, and the sadness almost disappeared from her expressive eyes. She was a radiant, handsome young woman; sensible, too.

When Congress adjourned he had Mary's promise and Mrs. Woodruff's blessing. They were to be married in June.

XIII

ANNEXATION?

FOREIGN RELATIONS became the avocation of Mr. Jones of B. during his term in Congress; it was to become his vocation.

To most Texans of 1836 foreign relations had meant merely getting Texas into the United States, which they thought could be done almost overnight. Even before he took his place in the Second Congress, Anson Jones had become convinced that it was not to be easy.

Stephen F. Austin and Wharton and Archer of Brazoria had left Texas at the end of 1835 and had been in the United States as Texan commissioners four months when independence was declared. After that event, George C. Childress, author of the Declaration, and Secretary of State Carson—recently a member of the United States Congress from North Carolina—rushed off to join them in such haste that they neglected to bring along diplomatic authority to negotiate for annexation, or even officially to ask for recognition of independence. "If we had had those powers," Austin had written from Washington April 6, "Texas would have been, by this time [two weeks before San Jacinto], recognized, if not admitted into this Union."

Five weeks after the battle, Collinsworth of Brazoria and Peter W. Grayson, equipped with credentials that to Texan eyes appeared ample, were started toward Washington to supersede the commissioners. Both had been members of President Burnet's itinerant Cabinet—Collinsworth, a San Jacinto veteran, had been Secretary of State more than a month; Grayson was rounding out three weeks in the Attorney General's post. As participants, they could testify to events of March 2, April 21, May 14, and transactions of the Texan Government thereafter.

When they reached Washington, just after Congress adjourned and as President Jackson was preparing to leave for the Hermitage, the Texas question was in every newspaper and on everybody's tongue, but no responsible officer of government would discuss it with the Texans.

The President, after Henry Clay's committee on foreign relations had recommended recognition if the new Republic had a *de facto* government, had parried by sending Henry M. Morfit to study at close range "the civil, military and political conditions of Texas." Pending report, the man in the White House would not talk.

Secretary of State Forsyth's conversation was even more exasperating than the President's silence. There was, he pointed out, no imprint of the Great Seal of the Republic of Texas on their commissions. That, of course, made it out of the question for him officially even to receive the gentlemen. The commissioners hesitated to explain that their government had stupidly placed other matters ahead of the important one of providing itself with a great seal. Collinsworth trailed Jackson to Nashville, hoping that Old Hickory would unbosom himself on the prospects, but he learned nothing.

While Commissioners Collinsworth and Grayson waited in the United States, President Burnet's government in Texas committed a grave diplomatic blunder. It conducted a plebiscite on annexation during the first national election. Texans were jubilant when it was announced that only ninety-one men in the whole Republic opposed entering the Union; but soon they learned from Washington that diplomacy was not to be conducted at polling places and that the referendum had "greatly embarrassed" negotiations.

When the Houston administration took charge of Texan affairs, William H. Wharton of Brazoria was drafted from the Senate to go once more to Washington. He was expected to consummate annexation before Jackson left the presidency in March 1837; and—just in case annexation should be delayed—he was instructed to spend his spare moments in "full and free conversations with the British, French and other foreign ministers." Memucan Hunt went along to aid him, and Fairfax Catlett "to take charge of, and safely keep, in a neat and regular manner, all documents, papers and records."

This was the fourth Texas mission that had arrived in Washington within a year. Clerks at the Department of State must have marveled that there were so many diplomats among the thirty thousand Texans.

Wharton got to the capital before Christmas and called at once on Secretary Forsyth. "The most that I could get out of him," the Texan reported, was that Jackson would soon speak on the subject of Texas, and that Forsyth wished Texas would get its first recognition somewhere else. When Jackson finally spoke, he did not recommend immediate recognition.

Convinced that already vocal opposition to annexation was about to defeat even recognition, Wharton first got the President's confidential promise—they were both Tennesseans—that he would grant recognition if Congress asked him to, then organized an informal but effective Texas bloc in House and Senate. He "answered a thousand interrogatories" and, over the pen name "Jefferson," wrote pamphlets and newspaper articles to combat the abolitionist anti-annexation petitions that were (to the delight of ex-President Adams, now a member of the House) piling up on committee tables.

Jackson thought Congress should act; congressmen thought the President should tell them officially to act. There the matter was deadlocked when General Antonio López de Santa Anna, escorted by two Texas colonels, arrived in Washington January 17, 1837.

Wharton had a bad moment when Santa Anna suggested that Mexico might relinquish Texas directly to the United States upon payment of a quit claim. That would have been annexation with a vengeance. It would have left the government of the Republic high and dry, while its territory became public lands of the United States. He felt a little easier when Jackson promised him he "would *perish* before he would be guilty of any injustice to Texas, or attempt to bind her against her consent," and when he recalled that Santa Anna was no longer President of Mexico and, in fact, had at the moment no influence there.

When the ex-Napoleon of the West at last left for Mexico aboard the United States Navy frigate *Pioneer,* Wharton reported the situation "in *statu quo,* I might say *ante bellum.*" But behind the scenes things were moving. Not only did the foreign relations committee re-request the recognition of Texas; it asked an appropriation for a diplomatic representative to the court of President Houston in the city of the same name. The money was promptly voted and President Jackson, ready to leave the White House, paused for a last official act:

On Friday night last, at near 12 o'clock [Wharton wrote on Sunday to his government], he consummated the recognition. . . . He also sent for Genl Hunt and myself and requested the pleasure of a glass of wine, and stated that Mr. Forsyth would see us officially on Monday. . . . [I shall] write at large after this interview with Mr. Forsyth.

The old general had ended his administration by nominating Alcée La Branche of Louisiana for the Texas mission, but Wharton never wrote at large of his official reception by the Secretary of State. The interview never took place.

At the Department of State quibbling over the credentials of the Texan Legation continued. Convinced that they could no longer remain unreceived in Washington "without injury to Texas, and some sacrifice of dignity on their own part," both Texan ministers departed—Wharton toward the Republic of Texas, Hunt to try, unsuccessfully, to float a loan for his country in Mississippi. They left their Secretary of Legation, Fairfax Catlett, as Chargé; but when he exhibited his credentials to the Secretary of State, Catlett reported:

He told me that he could not formally receive me as such inasmuch as Messrs Wharton and Hunt had not been regularly accredited, and my commission as Secretary of Legation rested upon a Texian Minister first being formally received and accredited by this Government.

Wharton, hastening home to report "the views, embarrassments, and probable policy" of the new Van Buren administration, boarded the Texan man of war *Independence* at New Orleans April 10.

As the schooner neared Velasco most of the populace of the port gathered on the beach, with the Secretary of the Navy, to welcome the returning diplomat. Wharton could almost see his Eagle Island plantation from the deck. If he looked in the other direction he could see the *Libertador* and the *Vencedor del Alamo,* commanded by Commodore López in person, bearing down on the clumsy, slow-moving *Independence,* whose crew of thirty-one included "six seamen, the balance not knowing one part of the ship from the other."

After a four-hour skirmish the Texan vessel struck colors. When Commodore López took charge of the prisoners, the disgusted skipper of the *Independence* tossed his sword overboard rather than hand it to the Mexican commodore. William H. Wharton, with the crew and other passengers, was lodged in the adobe *calabozo* at Matamoros, comforted by the Reverend Michael Muldoon, former pastor of Austin's colony, as he awaited rescue.

Capture of its leading citizen within hailing distance of his home created excitement enough in Brazoria County. Mrs. Wharton, Dr. Branch T. Archer, and John A. Wharton worked frantically to get him back. While John undertook to get action from the Texan government, Mrs. Wharton and Dr. Archer started on horseback to Washington to interest the United States. Near the Louisiana line Mrs. Wharton's horse fell and the distraught lady returned to Eagle Island on a stretcher. As soon as her broken leg had been splinted she booked passage to the United States on an oyster boat and was aboard it when she was handed a note from her husband. He was doing as well as a Texan could be expected to do in a Mexican jail, and he believed that Mexico would be willing to exchange him and his fellow captives for some of the soldiers taken at San Jacinto and still detained at Liberty. By inference, he did not think an appeal to Washington necessary.

The exchange of prisoners was a project after the heart of John A. Wharton, and he took it in hand. He rented the schooner *Orleans* for four thousand dollars and in July entered the mouth of the Rio Grande under a flag of truce with thirty Mexican prisoners to exchange. The vessel was blown aground and two men drowned, while Mexican officials argued whether to permit the Texans to land.

When at last John Wharton came ashore he learned that William, weeks before, had walked unchallenged out of prison, dressed in the garb of a priest—lent him by Padre Muldoon. The Texas Navy officers had also escaped with the aid of a lieutenant in the Mexican service who hankered for a commission from the Republic of Texas.

News of recognition by the United States reached Texas long before Minister Wharton could make a personal report of how he had brought it about and tell of the prospects for annexation. When he returned from Matamoros the Texans knew that recognition, under all the circumstances, had not solved, only further complicated, their national problems. William Fairfax Gray wrote March 21:

Rode to Columbia to inquire into the truth of a rumor that has reached us, that the United States has acknowledged the independence of Texas. Found it true. . . . Does not give much satisfaction to the President and Cabinet of Texas. All persons are disappointed. Their hopes have been so highly raised of a speedy annexation . . . that they can't at once be reconciled to the new state of things presented by recognition [without annexation]. Texas independent, and compelled to fight her own battles and pay her own debts, will necessarily impose heavy burthens on her citizens. Direct and all sorts of taxes. . . . Lands are not considered so valuable now as they were a few days ago; and the squabbles . . . that will take place here among the leaders! The prospect before us is anything but cheering.

All this had happened before Dr. Jones became a congressman. The Republic of Texas, it was clear, would have to set her house in order for a protracted season of independence. That involved replacing makeshift legislation of the First Congress with sturdier stuff, as well as defining a foreign policy which ignored the possibility of ultimate annexation.

When General Hunt returned to the Texan Legation in Washington, quibbling over credentials had ceased and President Van Buren, knowing that he could not forever postpone facing the Texas question, officially received the Texan Minister at high noon on July 6. Hunt ventured the pious hope "that nearer relations than those of harmonious diplomatic intercourse will ere long exist," and the shrewd New Yorker whom Jackson had placed in the presidency replied "with great dignity, and much at length"; but he got no nearer commitment upon annexation than a polite echo of the sentiments of Hunt's formal address. The Texan reported that he was "really more embarrassed by the plain republican simplicity" of the White House "than he could possibly have been" by the pomp of "the oldest monarchy in the world"—or even (he might have added) by the ceremonial protocol of his own government at muddy Houston.

Now officially received and accredited, Minister Hunt set to work in earnest to achieve "the great and paramount object— Annexation." General John T. Mason, whose "experience and long personal acquaintance with many of the politicians of the U.States" equipped him to give "important aid," and Attorney General P. W. Grayson were assigned by President Houston to help him with the lobbying. Delay in the Texas matter, however, had become a habit in the State Department. Three weeks passed after Hunt's reception before Secretary Forsyth signed a letter of credence for Alcée La Branche, Chargé d'Affaires to Texas, and it was autumn before that diplomat reached his post of duty.

It was no part of Hunt's plan to permit the coolness of Secretary Forsyth to discourage him. He helped that uncomfortable gentleman solve the problem of what to do with his spare time by handing him, on August 4, "a communication of twenty odd pages in length . . . upon the subject of annexing Texas."

Although the Texan Minister, in his modesty, disclaimed having presented "all the inducements to the union of the two republics," he overlooked nothing in the fields of history, economics, or national pride that would have strengthened his case.

He waited hopefully twenty-one days for the official answer. When it came, the first paragraph told him the story, but there were many more pages. Forsyth informed Hunt on August 25:

In giving to the undersigned instructions to present, in reply, a prompt and decisive indication of the course it has been deemed necessary to adopt the President indulges the confident expectation that no unfriendly spirit towards the government or the people of Texas will or can be imputed to the United States. . . .

The United States are bound to Mexico by a treaty of amity and commerce . . . [and] might justly be suspected of a disregard of the friendly purposes of the compact, if the overture of General Hunt were to be even reserved for future consideration. . . .

The inducements mentioned . . . powerful and weighty certainly as they are . . . are light when opposed in the scale of reason to treaty obligations and respect for . . . integrity of character. . . .

If the answer which the undersigned has been directed to give . . . should unfortunately . . . induce an attempt to extend commercial relations elsewhere, upon terms prejudicial to the United States, this government will be consoled by a consciousness of the rectitude of its intentions, and a certainty that although the hazard of transient losses may be incurred by a rigid adherence to just principles, no lasting prosperity can be secured when they are disregarded.

Irritated by the unctuous tone of this communication, no less than by the obvious fact that Forsyth's eye was less on sacrosanct obligations to Mexico than upon the growing opposition among Van Buren supporters to the extension of slave territory, Hunt penned the Secretary of State a rejoinder, the incivility of which is atoned for by the note of realism it injected into the discussion.

Mr. Forsyth's government, the Texan Minister reminded him, tried to buy this selfsame Texas from Mexico long before Spain acknowledged Mexican independence, and the venerable Jackson, whose policies Van Buren said he intended to follow, had even publicly offered the governorship of Texas to a citizen of North Carolina, Hunt's home state. There was, he continued, as little prospect

of the recovery of Texas by Mexico at this time as there was of the reconquest of Mexico by Spain at the time that General Jackson believed the charge d'affaires (Mr. Butler) of this government had succeeded in negotiating the acquisition of Texas. . . . Mexico was then as much at war with Spain as Texas now is with Mexico—and it is believed that as friendly treaty and commercial relations existed between Spain and the United States at that time as are now maintained between the United States and Mexico. . . .

Texas has generously offered to merge her national sovereignty in a domestic one, and to become a constituent part of this great confederacy. The refusal of this government to accept the overture must forever screen her from the imputation of wilfully injuring the great interests of the United States, should such a result accrue from any commercial or other regulation which she may find it necessary or expedient to enter into with foreign nations. . . .

The efforts . . . to open a commercial intercourse with Great Britain and France, it is believed will succeed. . . .

More letters were exchanged, but there was no weakening on the part of Forsyth or Van Buren before the Second Congress of Texas assembled at Houston in September 1837. Grayson, the auxiliary Texan Minister, soon convinced himself that although "the most prominent men of both sides of politics here are heartily in favor of annexation . . . the determination is to give the question the go-by . . . until weightier matters can be adjusted— touching the future ascendancy of . . . the Loco focos and Whigs"; and Hunt eventually concluded "it would be derogatory to ourselves to insist upon it any longer."

In Texas, Congressman Jones was starting his legislative career by inquiring into the expediency of increasing the navy for use against Mexico and otherwise evincing an interest in the permanency of the Republic.

When Chargé Alcée La Branche tardily arrived at the capital, Jones escorted him to a seat of honor in the House of Representatives and the same day proposed a resolution to clarify the annexation issue:

Whereas, It appears from the public papers of the United States, that a portion of the citizens of that country are of opinion, that Texas seeks annexation to the United States of the North at the expense of their Union; therefore, be it resolved that this house disclaims such a doctrine, and expressly declares, that no such intention, or wish, exists on the part of the people of this government.

The resolution was tabled, but Mr. La Branche must have taken note of it and of another motion offered by Mr. Jones of B. ten days later:

Resolved, that the President of this Republic be respectfully requested to reduce the representation of Texas, at the City of Washington, to that of a Charge d'Affaires.

There was no point in Texas's maintaining a minister plenipotentiary at the capital of a nation that accredited to her only a chargé. Before the Christmas recess Jones was voting with the majority to recall the Texan Minister from Washington—and the Texan Consul from New York, for good measure.

Redefinition of the Texan attitude toward annexation was the major topic in both houses during the last session of the Second Congress, which began April 9, 1838. In the Senate, Dr. Everitt's foreign relations committee promptly prescribed that the proposal of annexation be "unconditionally withdrawn"; but, although only two senators spoke against it, the resolution was tabled.

"Indignant at the position we occupied, and satisfied it was impolitic and unwise in every respect to occupy it longer," the Brazoria physician who now served the House as chairman of its foreign relations committee proposed even more drastic surgery than the medical man in the Senate had suggested.

Two days after Texas celebrated the second anniversary of the battle of San Jacinto, Mr. Jones of B. arose in his place and in his individual capacity asked the adoption of a joint resolution calculated to remove all doubts.

Whereas [Jones read from his manuscript], the citizens of the Republic of Texas . . . in the year 1836, expressed an almost unanimous desire to become annexed to the United States of North America . . . which proposition . . . has been distinctly and unconditionally refused by that government, and for reasons which it is impossible for time or circumstances to invalidate or alter;

And whereas, it is believed that Texas, having interests at variance with those of a large portion of the United States, and having also demonstrated her ability for self-government, and for successfully resisting the efforts of her embecile enemy to subjugate her, and now trusting, as a wise policy dictates, to her own strength and resources, no longer desires such annexation; and whereas, it is a fact, that pending this hopeless negotiation, the recognition of the independence of Texas by England and other powers, so essential to our welfare, is delayed or prevented—

Therefore, Be it resolved by the senate and house of representatives of the republic of Texas in congress assembled, That his Excellency the President be authorized and required, so soon as he may think proper, to instruct our minister resident at Washington, respectfully to inform the government of the United States of North America, that the government of Texas withdraw the proposition for the annexation of Texas to the said United States.

By one vote, with several members absent, the Jones resolution was defeated. Could the discretion allowed His Excellency the President have lost votes for the measure? Next day Mr. Rusk explored that possibility by amending the Jones resolution to require the executive "immediately" to withdraw the annexation proposal. The roll call showed that, although some of the absentees had returned, two representatives who had voted for the Jones resolution were absent, and the amended resolution was defeated by the identical vote of 13 to 14.

Anson Jones had placed his sentiments (as of April 1838) on record, even if Congress would not.

This resolution of April 23 was a sort of valedictory by a statesman untroubled by the specter of a campaign for re-election. Politics, even foreign relations, had begun to interest the gentleman from Brazoria less and less. As a solvent citizen of Texas he, of course, wished his country well; but he had made up his mind to leave its political salvation to others.

Mary Smith McCrory was his fiancée, and Brazoria was beckoning—not the county electorate, but a neat white cottage in town, with a broad fireplace and books and eventually children —an office in the yard, patients and friends coming and going, and good horses in the stables for country calls or an evening drive.

It would be more lucrative and satisfying, and infinitely simpler, to practice medicine than to continue as a volunteer physician to the body politic. There were too many of these volunteer political doctors. They could never agree upon a diagnosis—or upon a prescription.

As soon as the Second Congress adjourned sine die on May 24, ex-Congressman Jones hurried to Brazoria with a light heart. He was about to begin to live his own life, unrestricted by political or financial worries.

Little Brazoria was no city, certainly, and probably never would be; but there was a peaceful, contented atmosphere that warmed the doctor. Old acquaintances he saw on the streets made him glad that he had been directed to Brazoria by inscrutable destiny five years earlier, and that he had deliberately determined to remain a Brazorian even now, when he could achieve success anywhere in the Republic.

He threw off the mood of his recent avocation by polishing his instruments, dusting his bottles, and making lists of supplies to be ordered from Houston or New Orleans. He told people on the street that in a few days he would resume his practice. To particular friends he confided the secret: the doctor's house, which he was busily and clumsily setting in order, would be presided over by Mary—not the Mary Jones they had known in 1835, but a new Mary, who would be Mrs. Anson Jones.

The doctor's pleasant occupations and reveries were interrupted by General Houston's courier, who handed him a letter addressed to the Honorable Anson Jones. It was marked confidential and sealed with the wafer of the Executive Department.

I have resolved [His Excellency's bold script informed the excongressman] to appoint you the agent from this Government, for the purpose of procuring a navy in the United States. . . . In the whole matter there is nothing connected with the politics of the day. God keep me clear of the heat of the natural as well as the political season!
When I see you, I will explain some things, harmless and . . . amusing. . . . Meantime let me know if the situation will be agreeable to you. It will meet with the approbation of all the members of the cabinet.

The doctor left his professional shingle dangling in Brazoria and returned reluctantly to the capital. He found that the President had changed his mind as to the mission but not as to the destination. A new minister plenipotentiary was needed. General Hunt, tired of Washington and its ways, had resigned. His colleague, Peter W. Grayson, who was planning to succeed Houston as President, had just declined the honorable exile, as this diplomatic post had sometimes been called.
Would Dr. Jones undertake the Washington assignment?
The doctor said no, then—after some hesitation—maybe.

I told him [Jones said] . . . that although I had come to Houston agreeably to his request, it was to decline the appointment tendered. He then urged and insisted on my taking the office of Minister, said he did not know any one else he could get whom he could trust, and appealed to my patriotism [and vanity?] to induce me to consent—asked if I could start on the 8th July. I partly engaged that I would. This was on the 22d June. . . . I did not see him again previous to my leaving Texas—having been taken sick the next day & continued so untill the 9th July when I visited Irion [the physician who was Houston's Secretary of State] . . . I had daily conversations with him whilst I remained in Houston which was untill the 15th July. . . .
[George B.] McK[instry, Chief Justice and political factotum of Brazoria] called to see me while I was sick, appeared anxious I should decline the mission to the U.S. & run for Senator. I wrote H[ouston] the day he left & expressed my reasons for not wishing to do so. . . .

Mr. La Branche called to see me twice and assisted in bleeding me, was very kind and attentive.

Anson Jones's acceptance was doubtful in his own mind, but not in Houston's. The President had his commission and letter of credence made out on June 25 and left them for the Secretary of State to deliver. Perhaps he knew his man. Many times before he had seen a tyro in politics behave like an old fire horse.

Dr. Irion's preoccupation was fixing the international boundary between the United States of the North and the sovereign Republic of Texas, but Dr. Jones was primarily interested in clearing up every ambiguity in Washington as to annexation. He stipulated that he "be permitted to withdraw the proposition, which was agreed upon."

Almost before Dr. Jones realized what he was doing he had committed himself to a chore that was to change not only his immediate plans but his whole life. The marriage would have to be postponed: patriotic duty took precedence over personal desires. Mary consented—or was it she who suggested postponement? In any event, she promised the doctor to wait.

As soon as he was able to ride horseback Dr. Jones placed his diplomatic credentials in his saddlebags and returned to Brazoria to take his oath as Minister before his neighbor, Chief Justice W. P. Scott, and to arrange his affairs for a year's absence.

His illness, the new perspective that appointment to the diplomatic corps gave him—maybe a vaguely understood resentment at having consented to rearrange his personal plans and postpone his marriage—made the town he had loved and planned to live in the remainder of his life pall on him in three days. He wrote in his diary:

Tired of the place and its dullness, everything seems changed. Resolved never to make it my home for another day. Went in the evening to Mr Wharton'. Spent two days as I always do at his house *pleasantly.* . . .
22 Sunday. Embarked on the Steam boat Columbia   crossed the Bar in a small boat after dark   sea sick.

Another Texan diplomat in that constantly changing procession of foreign representatives was on his way abroad with a mission to perform.

XIV

THE THREAD

MINISTER JONES left Texas in a dejected mood. He was leaving behind him all his earthly possessions—and Mary McCrory. The three-day passage of the *Columbia* from Velasco to New Orleans was rough, and he was seasick. There was a fire alarm and the arrogant ignorance of steamboat engineers and the helplessness of *"poor dumb* passengers" irritated him.

Even New Orleans held no charm for him. He was

struck with the dull appearance & the small number of vessels. . . . On touching the wharf the Boat was crowded with News Collectors busy taking notes. I had hoped to have got on to Washington without any notice, but the papers found me out and published what they knew.

The Collector of the Port or the one acting as such, showed he was a genuine Republican by treating me with the utmost rudeness and indifference. Had difficulty & Delay in getting a permit to land one trunk;—and a small bundle he would not permit me to land without sending it to the C[ustom] H[ouse] for inspection so I abandoned it & he at my request scratched it off the Baggage entry which I had made. . . .

It was not the sort of treatment a Minister Plenipotentiary of the sovereign Republic of Texas expected to receive. "So poorly stood Texas. . . . The Collector knew I was her accredited Minister."

When he learned at his New Orleans hotel of the suicide of two of his predecessors at the Washington post, his gloom deepened:

I shall be surprised at no ones committing suicide after hearing of Col. Grayson's doing so. It is the first time in my life that any one in the circle of my immediate acquaintance has done such an act & it has shocked me more than the Death of a Dozen others would have

done in the usual course. I believe party abuse has been the cause
acting upon some predisposition to morbid melancholy. Collinsworth's drowning himself was a thing in course I had expected it as
I knew him to be deranged & when excited by liquor almost *mad*.

In all the annals of suicide perhaps no parallel to these cases can
be found. Two years ago they were both in this House and on their
way to Washington together as Commissioners on the part of Texas
to procure *recognition* & at the time of their death both candidates
for the highest office in the Republic. both committed suicide about
the same time & at the distance of 2000 miles from each other. both
at the time holding high & responsible offices in the Republic of
Texas. Grayson's loss is a . . . national calamity.

It meant, among other things, that the next President of Texas
would be Mirabeau Buonaparte Lamar, former major general of
the Texas Army, who was no friend of Anson Jones. He had been
one of a committee that publicly urged Thomas J. Rusk to become
a candidate. When Rusk declined, several of these committeemen
urged Lamar to make the race, but Jones was not among them.
President Houston's Minister to the United States started up the
Mississippi River on the steamer *Buckeye* on July 30, knowing
that his mission would end as soon after Lamar's inauguration in
December as the new President could fill the place with a supporter. But Minister Jones's major purpose could be accomplished
before then.

Twenty-four days he spent on uncomfortable river boats, stage-
coaches, and trains. Travel through a terrain he had never before
visited diverted him from the despondency in which he had begun
his journey, and he found a certain pleasure in jotting down his
observations on the topography and flora and human fauna along
the route.

He ascended the Mississippi, then the Ohio.

We have several passengers on Board from Ioway [August 8], full
of the glories of the young kingdom. Amused myself with the Bur-
lington I.T. paper full of frothy patriotism, the future greatness of
Ioway, Stump speeches & announcements of candidates. . . . Notwithstanding all which they cannot get a respectable man to accept
the *high* office of Governor. Poor Uncle Sam the "greatest, Meanest"
of Republics. . . .

[August 9] fell into a perfect Hoozier Crowd. God deliver me in

future from such a demi savage race. I would sooner travel among
Choctaws. Texas, at least what I have seen of it, is half a century
in advance of this western country in civilization & refinement. . . .

A Hoozier undertook to *root* me out of my bed last night, but I
succeeded in driving him off by speaking some English, a language
he did not understand. . . . A party of *gentlemen* gamblers from
St. Louis in spite of hot weather, crowded cabins, & presence of
women (I had like to have written ladies) have been busy at their
"vocation" ever since we came on Board. . . .

One fellow on board undertook to draw a comparison between
Ioway & Texas—the man is a fool, for there is no comparison
between them.

At Louisville Jones stopped off to attend the theater, call on
local bankers, and spend a night at the Galt House. Unless

driven by necessity I think I will not again travel up or down the
Ohio at low water. Still I have been amused, instructed, and gratified
by the trip. The novelty has more than counterbalanced all the unpleasant circumstances. . . .

Mr. Wiggington of the Louisville Bank, whom Jones particularly wanted to see, was out when he called, but Mr. Thruston,
the cashier, received him "with great civility." Before Jones had
had his dinner at the Galt House, Wiggington returned his call
and persuaded him to prolong his stay one day "to attend a party
at his house to be given on my account."

These hospitable Louisville bankers had been friends of Grayson; they were as shocked as Jones at his suicide. Mr. Thruston
did not believe the rumor that an unhappy love affair had been
the cause; he agreed with Jones that it was "party abuse." Mr.
Thruston was an expert judge of broken hearts; his young sister
Jeannette had cracked many—they were painful but not fatal.

It was a pleasant evening. "Mr. Budd, a Roman Catholic Gent.
formerly a little anti-Texas," was less so after meeting Minister
Jones, and "Mr. Brand, a very intelligent gentleman . . . concluded to go there next fall." It was good to be considered an
oracle—and to be treated as a member of the diplomatic corps
should be treated. He promised to pay his respects to Thruston's
father when he reached Washington—and to Miss Jeannette.

He continued to Cincinnati by boat, then transferred to a
miserable coach for the trip to Wheeling, which carried him

through Springfield and Columbus. When he reached the capital of Ohio on August 16, he wrote:

Mediocrity in everything appears to be characteristic of the Buckeye State; every where I have seen nothing like intellectual refinement. Most of the females were barefooted & appear to be mere household drudges. Such a State can never make a figure except for the pounds of pork or the number of Brooms it can make. Columbus now contains about 5000 Inhabitants. Supped at a small place late at night 20 Ms from Columbus. Daughters & Wife to wait on the table as every where else in Ohio. I would about as soon Starve.

On arrival at Baltimore, August 22, the Texan Minister Plenipotentiary's trunks, all his money, letters, and credentials were misplaced. He retrieved them after a frenzied search of two hours, then solaced himself at the "Museum performance in the Saloon. Saw Miss Wells show her person to a large audience of *Women* & Men & went home completely disgusted with the concern."

By supper time the next day he was at last in Washington. The prospect of his official debut made him "feel like a School boy just before examination & wish the *'ceremonial'* was well over." He took quarters at Mr. Gadsby's National Hotel, tried to find the staff of his Legation, and rested from his travels.

Gadsby's was not, however, to be the permanent location of the Legation of the Republic of Texas during Jones's tour of duty, for this new Minister was no Memucan Hunt. In asking the Texas Senate to confirm Hunt's appointment, President Houston had pointed out: "From the state of our finances it is very desirable that the Minister should be a Gentleman of fortune, and one whose own means for the present should be expended in his support. Mr. Hunt thus far has made no requisition on this Government for means of support." The Senate confirmed Hunt instanter. The condition of Texan finances had not improved—and Jones was not a gentleman of fortune.

As soon as he had made his first official calls he would seek a boardinghouse—preferably one where politicians lived—to save money and to build good will for Texas among fellow boarders, while he kept an ear open for unofficial information. For a few days he lived in a style befitting the diplomatic representative of a great nation. He would not admit, at the start, that his government and he were pinching pennies.

Fairfax Catlett and Sandy Harris, his Legation staff, were not to be found in Washington, so the new Minister himself wrote the Secretary of State to announce his arrival, then settled down to read the files of his Legation.

From the letter book he learned that President Houston on May 19 had instructed his Washington representative:

> Should the present session of the Congress of the United States adjourn without having acted definitively on the proposition for the annexation of this Republic to that of the U. States, you are hereby instructed, by direction of the President, to withdraw immediately thereafter the proposition aforesaid.

That was precisely what Jones's own resolutions of April 23 would have required the President to do, but the Texan Congress had been too timid to demand it. No wonder Houston's Secretary of State had assented so readily to Jones's insistence that he be permitted to withdraw the annexation proposal. How like Old Sam Jacinto to let his new envoy discover these instructions after he got to Washington, instead of giving him the satisfaction of knowing from the start that he had adopted what Jones advocated.

The Minister read the ensuing correspondence to see what, if anything, had been done pursuant to the President's instructions.

Jones's predecessor, General Hunt, had resigned and left Washington before the May 19 instructions arrived. Fairfax Catlett was uncertain as to the duty of an acting chargé. He "was entirely satisfied that a *literal* execution of them was impracticable there being . . . no proposition, as coming from Texas, still pending before this Government, and therefore, none to be withdrawn." Catlett reminded his government that General Hunt's optimistic proposal of August 4, 1837, "was rejected absolutely and unconditionally, and not even reserved for future consideration. . . . In what manner then," the puzzled Chargé had asked Secretary Irion, "can a proposition be withdrawn, which is not even admitted to exist?" Nothing was before the government of the United States but "petitions and memorials of their own citizens and the Resolutions of their own State Legislatures. The [only] question . . . was . . . whether they themselves would make a *new* proposition in their own part to Texas," he explained a little tediously.

Catlett, knowing the posture of matters at Washington and afflicted with a logical mind, had missed the point of the instructions. Jones, who had thought up the idea, must have smiled at the bewilderment of the Chargé. He knew that there was no proposition pending at Washington; he had known it when he introduced his resolutions in April. The lines to be spoken at the Department of State in Washington were a bit of play acting; the audience was not the Secretary of State, nor even the President of the United States. The audience was in London and Paris and Brussels. It was the gesture of locking a door that had been slammed in one's face, so that it could not be reopened at will from the other side.

For ten days Minister Jones studied the accumulated correspondence at the Legation and, for relaxation, read the pamphlets and essays on the Texas question that had been pouring out since 1836. There were pamphlets on Texas—most of them anti-annexationist—on every newsstand, and J. Q. Adams's anti-Texas tirade in the House was still evoking impassioned communications in the newspapers, although Congress had adjourned six weeks before.

Jones read Channing's Letter to Henry Clay and pronounced it "the most grave piece of hypocritical Humbug & falsehood I have ever seen," and the published rejoinders to it "too mild." Even H. S. Legare's Texas speech and Morfit's report on Texas contained "a good deal of Sophistry." A reading of the current screeds and a brief reconnaissance of the Texas question at Washington strengthened the conclusion he had reached when he was only a Texas congressman:

Annexation [he concluded on August 26 as he waited for the President of the United States to become officially aware of his existence] is at an end & for the present Texas *can* if she *will* get on without it. *If the next administration pursues a proper course* not many in Texas will wish for it. How *glorious* will Texas be Standing alone, and relying upon her own strength. . . . [He added on October 2:] we remain a "Spunky little independent Republic" with all our blushing honors thick upon us.

On August 27—his Legation staff still absent—he got A. McCurdy to sign letters to the Washington papers announcing "that

Mr. Anson Jones, Minister Plenipotentiary from the republic of Texas is at Gadsby's" and asking that his presence be noticed in the press; but he was a little irked by the "rather equivocal terms" in which the *Intelligencer* heralded his "advent." The *People* declared his appointment "was a reward for supporting the [Houston] administration"; that drew a three-line rejoinder in the Minister's diary:

The journals will show that I never supported the *administration*. My votes will uniformly be found opposed to every [four letter word obliterated, and this interlined:] measure I did not approve. I only supported the country & its President, opposing error & extravagance.

That day Mr. J. Elliot, who, like Minister Jones, had once been in Venezuela, called, as he did on all diplomatists new to Washington, with a copy of his *Diplomatic Code*. It was an interesting two-volume work, containing the text of treaties to which the United States was party. For years it had been standard equipment for diplomatic representatives of foreign powers, not because they needed to study the text or to curry favor with Mr. Elliot by buying his compilation, although he was an editor of some importance. The real value of the work lay in its Appendix, which was a sort of rule book of American diplomatic procedures, forms, and etiquette. With Elliot's *Code* at hand, the greenest diplomat could commit no great errors. Jones made good use of it.

On Wednesday, in response to "a very polite note," he called on Mrs. Eliza Page. The lady was not at home, but Minister Jones "was received by her daughter, with whom," he wrote and later deleted, "I half fell in love." It was not for that that he had come to Washington. Next day he wrote *"M. McCrory."*

He was restless. There was, he recalled, a friendly gesture he had not yet made. He must pay his respects to Judge Buckner Thruston, father of the amiable young banker who had made his visit to Louisville so pleasant. Mr. Elliot's *Code* colored even his private social calls. He left cards at the judge's door on his first visit—punctiliously including a second card for the judge's daughter, who, he judged from what her brother said, had so many cards that even one from a minister plenipotentiary and envoy extraordinary would make no great impression.

He went on to the Library of Congress, which he found "a
very splendid concern . . . evidence of what the powers & industry of man has accomplished." But it was no use; Jones was
already "tired of this routine of visits & anxious to be at work."

He could not officially join the diplomatic corps until he had
shaken the hand of the still-absent President of the United States;
he sought relief from tedium in a brief excursion.

First he went to Philadelphia in a train "full of Episcop Clergymen going to attend the triennial Convention."

Put up at Mrs. Yokes cor 7th & Chestnut. The first person I recognized was Dr. George McClelland. After I crossed Broad Street coming into town from the west every thing seemed natural. I could
hardly recognize that I had been absent at all. It seemed like a
dream.

If Philadelphia had not changed during Jones's absence, Jones
had. What memories must have come back to him as he looked
once more at those familiar cobblestones and dingy buildings of
the City of Brotherly Love, which he first had seen nearly two
decades before. Here, on his way to Harpers Ferry in 1823, he
had been arrested for debt, relieved of his wallet and his watch.
Unable to proceed, here he had unsuccessfully practiced medicine,
then fled to Venezuela. Here, on his return, he had completed his
professional education, become Worshipful Master of Masons
and Grand Master of Odd Fellows—and failed again in medicine. Only six years before he had left Philadelphia in disgust.

As the Minister Plenipotentiary of the sovereign Republic of
Texas, with head erect, walked the familiar streets of the city of
his humiliations, he must have had an impulse to shout: "I am
Anson Jones. You thought, if you knew me at all, that I was a
failure. You were wrong. Look at me. I have helped create a
nation. I am a member of its diplomatic corps, engaged in mo-
mentous negotiations that your grandchildren and their grandchildren will hear of. I am Anson Jones."

But Jones, being Jones, shouted nothing. He probably enjoyed
the astonishment of Dr. McClellan, founder of his alma mater,
at the role that his former pupil was now playing; and he did
not permit "Mr. Lawrence, his brother & Mr. Evans" to remain
in ignorance of his current status when he met them on the street

and took them to the theater. After a two-day round of visits with old friends and lodge brothers he was off to New York for a hectic week with relatives and official and volunteer agents of Texas. There he saw George Bancroft, Jacksonian historian of American democracy, visited the theaters and museums, and looked up a few friends of his less prosperous days.

In Philadelphia again, he called at the Bank of the United States, an institution with which he had had no dealings during his residence in that city. Now he was there to see about borrowing five million dollars. With Messrs. Williams and Burnley, Texas agents, the Minister gravely canvassed with Mr. Nicholas Biddle, president of the bank, the prospects for the Texas loan.

On another evening, for old times' sake, he met with the trustees of the Fifth Street Odd Fellows Hall. Less than a decade ago he had been president of the board, weighted with responsibilities that then seemed very grave, and commissioner to float a loan for the Grand Lodge, to boot. All that was not as far away as it seemed to him. It was among these Odd Fellows that he had learned his first lessons in corporate finance, practical politics, diplomacy.

How good that diplomatic training had been, he would soon learn at Washington. His watch was in his pocket, and this time there was no creditor between him and his destination.

He had hoped to remain Mr. Gadsby's guest until his formal presentation, but after waiting a month without learning when that important event would take place, he found cheaper quarters. On September 26 he "visited the Dep of State with Mr. C. wrote my first Despatch to Dr. Irion—Removed from Gadsby's to Mrs. Pitman on 3rd St. in the evening." Here he soothed an aching tooth with laudanum, meditated upon the desirability of the expansion of Texas to the "Bay of St. Francisco" and the Californias, and came to the conclusion that old J. Q. Adams had been "acting a double [he first wrote it quintuple] part. He has lost Texas to the U.S. & is trying to hide his blame for the loss in smoke."

Not until October 2 did President Van Buren return to the White House and appoint a day for the ceremonial reception of this latest of the envoys from the Texans—cautiously requesting in advance a copy of his "intended address." Minister Jones, who

had learned among the Odd Fellows and the Masons the art of
felicitous expression of stereotyped sentiments, had written out his
"short & non *Commital"* remarks more than a month before. He
sent a copy of them over to the Department of State without
delay.

Apparently not so nervous and self-conscious as he had been
on his arrival in Washington, Jones spent the evening preceding
his formal presentation at "Euka." Before two o'clock the next
afternoon a hired hack took him and Aaron Vail, Acting Secretary of State, to the Executive Mansion.

In "the small room immediately east and adjoining the large
circular room" they fidgeted two or three minutes; then the moment came:

The President entered alone. I advanced to meet him when the usual
civilities were exchanged. I then took from the table within my reach
the Letter of Credence which I had laid down there [he had almost
lost that precious letter once; he was taking no chance on misplacing
it now] and holding it in my hand made a complimentary address

to the crafty little man who had already made it perfectly plain
that Texas would never enter the Union through his efforts. This
was not what Minister Jones had traveled twenty-five hundred
miles to say to the President; this was merely a formal preliminary that had to be got out of the way before he could "be at
work." As if he were addressing a room full of people, Minister
Jones told the President:

In delivering this I have it especially in charge to assure your
Excellency of the continued friendly feelings of the Government and
people of Texas towards the Government and People of the United
States, and to express their sincere and ardent wishes for your own
future happiness and prosperity, and that of the country over which
you preside.

For my own part, I consider myself most fortunate, Sir, in having
the distinguished honor of appearing before the Chief Magistrate of
this great, free and happy nation, as the Diplomatic Representative
of my adopted country; and it will ever be my greatest happiness, as
it is my imperative duty in the discharge of my official functions, to
promote, by every means in my power, the friendly relations now so
happily existing between Texas and the United States, and the
reciprocal interests of the two Governments.

No dynamite in that, certainly; nor in the President's reply:

It gives me much pleasure, Sir, to receive you as the accredited representative of the Republic of Texas, and I reciprocate very cordially the assurances of good will. . . .

The carefully rehearsed Address to the Republican Throne had been delivered, and the Occupant, noticing no deviation from the manuscript submitted in advance, spoke the hundred words which, freely translated, meant: "I am officially aware of your existence." Then, for a quarter of an hour, the President became a host with a guest in his house:

He then advanced & again offered me his hand [the Texan wrote that evening in his diary]. Said he was glad to see me and invited me to a Seat. He made enquiries, of me about myself, asked me if I was not from North Carolina or intimated as if he was under that impression. [Hunt, Jones's predecessor, and General Henderson, European agent, were both North Carolinians.] I remained about 10 minutes, When the conversation stopping, I rose—the President rose and again shook hands, & saying he should be happy to again see me—bade me good morning. Accompanied by the actg Secretary I left the room. On the front steps the Secty took leave, saying I would always find him at the Dept & that he would be happy to do anything for me in his power. So ended the ceremony of presentation.

At last fully accredited, although "hardly yet initiated into the 1st degree of dip. life," Minister Jones was optimistic: "I have got hold of the thread, however & think I can follow the windings."

His first official letter was a notification to "A. Vail, Esquire, etc, etc, etc.," that Texas was ready to exchange ratifications of the boundary agreement signed by his predecessor and Mr. Forsyth in April. Then, as Mr. Elliot's *Diplomatic Code* instructed him to do, he "called with Cards" upon as many members of the Cabinet and of the *corps diplomatique* as a man could in one afternoon. The engraved cards of the Minister of the Republic of Texas, with a corner turned down to show that they were left by that gentleman in person, were deposited at the residences of the Attorney General, Mr. Felix Grundy of Tennessee; the Secretary of State, Mr. John Forsyth of Georgia; the Secretary of the Treasury, Mr. Levi Woodbury of New Hampshire; the Secretary of the

Navy, Mr. James K. Paulding of New York; and the Secretary of War, Mr. Joel R. Poinsett of South Carolina—who, like the Texan Minister, was a physician and had lived in Latin America.

Messrs. Pontois, Krehmer, Tacon, Martini, and Fox of the diplomatic corps also received cards of the Texan Minister that afternoon, which probably impressed none of them at the moment. Some of them were to become well acquainted with Mr. Jones and his mission before the next spring. That evening at his boardinghouse the weary Texan Minister received General Alvear and his son Emilio, from Buenos Aires, and Mr. M. Edwards of Brazoria County, Texas, who was later to become internationally famous as a forger.

The next day was Columbus Day, although it was not yet so designated on the calendars. For Anson Jones it was a sort of second independence day for his adopted country. That morning he spent carefully polishing the most important letter he had ever written. It had to be brief; it must say neither too much nor too little. Its tone must be neither arrogant nor obsequious, but firm. It would be published in the capitals of Europe.

Minister Jones did not have the pleasure of presenting that letter personally to Mr. Secretary Forsyth, whose unctuous rejection of annexation on August 25, 1837, had made it necessary. The head of the State Department was still vacationing in Georgia, and the letter went to his chief clerk, who was looking after routine business during the absence of his chief. The matter, Jones and his government thought, was too urgent to await the Secretary's return to Washington.

At high noon on October 12 the Texan Plenipotentiary was at the Department of State, exchanging ratifications of the boundary agreement and reminding Mr. Vail a little sharply of "the strong desire of the Government of Texas to have this question settled by running the line" without further delay. A sovereign nation needed clearly defined and marked boundaries with its neighbors. The sooner this United States-Texas line was established, the clearer it would be to people in both countries—and in Europe— that the new Republic was a separate entity.

After Minister Jones departed from the State Department with a certified copy of the boundary agreement in his pocket, Chief Clerk A. Vail read:

Sir: Since the date of Mr. Forsyth's correspondence with General Hunt on the subject of the proposition to annex Texas to the United States, although that proposition was considered by this Government as finally disposed of, Texas has, nevertheless, continued to be generally regarded by the people of both countries as in the attitude of an applicant for admission into this Union.

In order to prevent future misunderstanding upon this subject, and believing that an explicit avowal of its present policy, in reference to this measure, would conduce mutually to the interest of both countries, the Government of Texas has directed the undersigned respectfully, but unconditionally, to withdraw the proposition above mentioned.

The undersigned, minister plenipotentiary of the republic of Texas, therefore, in accordance with his instructions, has the honor to announce to the Secretary of State of the United States the formal and absolute withdrawal of the proposition for the annexation of Texas to the United States.

The undersigned embraces this occasion to tender to Mr. Vail renewed assurances of his distinguished consideration.

ANSON JONES

The next day Mr. Vail "had the honor . . . to state that Mr. Jones's note had been laid before the President."

That job was done.

It remained, however, to publicize the fact—not in Washington or in Texas, but in Europe. Jones at once reported to his government and by the same mail wrote "in duplicate" to General J. Pinckney Henderson, the thirty-year-old North Carolinian who for more than a year had been the roving ambassador of the Republic of Texas to western Europe. Henderson's primary assignment was to procure recognition from England and France. Although he had such prestige as attached to the title brigadier general of the Texas Army, native good sense, legal acumen, tact, and familiarity with Texan affairs gained through seven months in President Houston's Cabinet, Henderson had not yet been received in his diplomatic capacity at any European capital.

Britain's Foreign Minister, Lord Palmerston, professed to be unconvinced that Mexico would permit Texas to retain her independence; but three months in England convinced Henderson that Queen Victoria's ministers were really more concerned over the legal status of slavery in Texas and the possibility of annexation to the United States than the specter of Mexican reconquest. The issue was further confused at London by a Mexican proposal to compensate British holders of Mexican bonds with grants of land in Texas. The best the Texan could get from Palmerston was a peculiar left-handed trade agreement which—whatever it did to Texan pride—opened the ports of each country to the commerce of the other.

Palmerston sensed that the Texas trade might be valuable to England. If Texas was indeed still Mexican territory, he reasoned, it was amply protected by England's existing trade treaties with Mexico. There was the slight irregularity of clearance papers which would be issued to Texan vessels by a government that England and Mexico did not officially know, but British port masters "would shut their eyes to the circumstance." As Palmerston explained it to Henderson:

a Texian Ship would be admissible into the Ports of Great Britain as a Mexican Ship according to the stipulations of the Mexican Treaty, notwithstanding that the Documents issued for the use of such ship would bear upon their face that they were the avowed acts of a Govt. in Texas, assuming the style of a republic independent of Mexico.

President Houston phrased it more felicitously for Texan publication:

Our vessels and goods under the national Flag and with Texian papers, are to be admitted . . . in the same manner as the vessels and goods of Mexico, under the scope and stipulations of the treaty with that Government.

By the spring of 1838, Henderson had gone to Paris, where there was no anti-slavery agitation and no bloc of Mexican bondholders to lobby against the recognition of Texas. France, in fact, was at the moment beginning a war to collect $600,000 owed Frenchmen by Mexico. Diplomacy had failed to collect the claims, and when Henderson arrived in Paris the French Navy was beginning its blockade of the Mexican ports. This episode—"the Pastry War"—might through Texan skill be turned into an advantage; without careful management it might block negotiations. General Henderson would know how to use the information that Minister Jones could now give him. The harassed Texan ambassador-at-large to western Europe had written to "His Excellency Mr. Jones" at Washington as soon as he heard of his appointment:

Allow me to congratulate you upon your appointment to the distinguished station you hold, which I do most cordially, as a countryman, if not as a friend and acquaintance. How far I have a right to claim either of the latter, I am at a loss to know, as I have only been informed by our Government and through the newspapers that "Dr. Jones is appointed Minister to the United States," and inasmuch as I know two Dr. Jones' in Texas personally, and have heard of one other. But however that may be, allow me to congratulate you. . . .

The Secretary of State instructed me to say to the French and English Governments that he had *instructed you* to withdraw the proposition for the annexation of Texas to the United States. It will be better if I can say you *have* withdrawn it. Please inform me on the subject. . . . In great haste.

His Excellency Mr. Jones did not need this reminder. He had, in fact, sent Agent Henderson the information he wanted two weeks before he received the request for it.

"It will remove one obstacle in the way of the recognition," Henderson wrote Jones on receiving his letter.

The Washington Legation's correspondence with Texas was not heavy. During nine months as Minister, Jones sent six despatches to his government, all in impeccable form and consecutively numbered, with many enclosures. Secretary of State Irion wrote to him three times but assigned no new negotiations.

Dr. Irion's final—and longest—communication was written two weeks before the end of the Houston administration. "The withdrawal of the proposition for the annexation of Texas to the United States," the Secretary reported, "has given general satisfaction, and will have a most favorable effect on our negotiations in Europe." The Pastry War, he hoped, would insure French recognition of Texas; probably "France will keep the enemy occupied untill our own vessels will be afloat." The five vessels of war under construction for Texas in Baltimore

will enable us to command the Gulf, shut up the enemie's vessels in their ports, and ruin their commerce. . . . Harrassments of this kind will soon force them to acknowledge our independence. The acquisition of such a fleet will have a most happy tendency in securing the permanent and uninterrupted prosperity of the country, by inspiring confidence abroad, thereby increasing emigration to Texas, and promoting our negotiations in Europe.

Europe. Europe held the key to the immediate future of the Republic of Texas. Jones understood that even better than Irion, and he was temporarily in a better position to help those negotiations than any other citizen of Texas. The "thread" he had got hold of was a long one; it ran not only among the foreign legations of Washington City but to the capitals of Europe. Minister Jones prepared to "follow the windings."

XV

JEANNETTE

THE lonesome bachelor Minister of Texas was spending many of his evenings at the pleasant home of Buckner Thruston, father of the cashier of the Louisville Bank. Judge Thruston had left the United States Senate thirty years before to accept a federal judgeship which he still was holding. He was a sound Democrat, a repository of useful information, and a good chess player. He was also the father of Miss Jeannette Thruston, a belle of the capital. As the Minister and the judge moved queens and bishops and pawns across the chessboard and talked of men and measures, Miss Jeannette was busy with her own affairs.

On the last day of November, as he sat with the judge, he caught a glimpse of "The Miss Jene" of whom he had heard so much, and for whom he had left a card three months ago. "She is somewhat pale—but her elegance of mind and manners & sweet voice, tact, wit and sense make her, altho not decidedly pretty, vastly interesting." Minister Jones would not cease to play chess with the judge because Miss Jeannette interrupted their game— and his chain of thought. Evenings at Thruston's were more pleasant than the official dinners he had to attend.

Minister Jones was creating no excitement in Washington society; his only social engagements were the dull and formal receptions to which members of the diplomatic corps were invited in the order of their rank and seniority.

Thrice he dined with the President, and once with each Cabinet officer. The éclat of his first dinner at the White House was marred by a too-early arrival—"found Mr. Van Buren alone, being the first who arrived"—and embarrassment at the contrast between his nondescript dinner clothes and the resplendent coats of the Old World diplomats. He was reassured when he noticed that the Mexican and Argentine ministers, as well as the President himself, were "in plain black suits like myself."

At Secretary Forsyth's dinner for the diplomatic corps "most of the foreign Ministers were there," but Jones "did not mind them much. . . . Did not feel very well nor leave in time. . . ."

At Secretary Woodbury's he dined with President Van Buren, the diplomatic corps, and two members of the House: Speaker James K. Polk and John Quincy Adams, who had re-entered public life, it seemed to Jones, to animadvert upon Texas. "Poor Adams," he wrote in his diary that evening, "has lived too long for his own fame or the good of his country."

He knew that the European diplomats he was meeting at these stiff and formal gatherings could be useful to him and to Texas, even if the statesmen of the United States were showing little interest in his Republic. Without instructions from his government, Minister Jones had evolved a plan of diplomatic action. M. Pontois, Louis Philippe's urbane Minister, and Mr. Fox, who, with more hauteur than Mr. Jones thought becoming even in an Englishman, looked after Her Britannic Majesty's American interests, were the diplomatic colleagues he wanted to concentrate upon. His plan was to make it clear in London and Paris that the products of Texas were indispensable to British and French national economy. He was already in communication with General Henderson on that subject.

As a first step toward starting this campagn of his own invention, Minister Jones became a student of economics. He visited the Library of Congress again and again, not idly to admire that "very splendid concern" but to read on subjects pretty far removed from medicine, or even diplomacy in its narrow sense. He recognized that community of economic interest was the firmest basis for cordial relations of one nation with another. He knew that Texas had resources that could become indispensable to Europe.

An article in McCulloch's *Dictionary of Commerce* focused his attention on cotton.

Texas was the newest Cotton Kingdom and might become the greatest. As the old Southwest became progressively unproductive, cotton planters were trekking into the rich bottoms of the Brazos and the Colorado with their slaves and implements, to begin "mining" the best cotton lands of the continent. For five years in Texas Jones had been watching this development. In Washington he grasped its significance.

Texas cotton could be marketed more profitably in England than in the United States, now that Henderson had completed the trade agreement. Might not the still-fluid tariff policy of the Republic make possible a community of economic interest with England that would go far toward assuring not only prosperity but the continued independence of Texas? The more Jones thought on the matter, the surer he was that he had hit upon a key to the heart of the nation of shopkeepers. "If England does not take the 'blind Staggers,' " he concluded, "she cannot much longer remain indifferent. . . ."

The problem was how to titillate Downing Street with the prospect.

The Queen's representative in Washington, H. S. Fox, was an odd creature locally spoken of as the "spectre minister" because of his unsociability and his weird personal appearance. An observer of Washington society said:

Fox is an old bachelor, who dines at twelve o'clock at night, and breakfasts at one the next day. . . . He is a solitaire, who, though he does not forget all, is "by all forgot." His few servants threaten to leave him, as they do not like leading the life of an owl:—sleep all day and work all night.

When Jones saw his British colleague—infrequently—at official dinners, their seats were too far apart for conversation. Her Majesty's Minister sat above the salt, Sam Houston's among the lesser fry. Mr. Fox never called with cards (or otherwise) at the Texan's boardinghouse, and Mr. Jones never had opportunity to verify the local legend that the whole British Legation "smelt of sheep" because only mutton was served at Mr. Fox's table.

Lord Palmerston was unlikely to learn about the importance of Texas to the Empire from Mr. Fox. Jones found other ways of getting information to London.

European representatives of the United States occasionally visited Washington and were entertained with the diplomatic corps. They could be useful to Texas when they returned to their posts of duty, and Minister Jones managed, in one way or another, to impress some of them with a few well-chosen facts regarding the future role of his spunky little independent Republic. One in particular became, under Jones's coaching, a sort of unofficial Texan agent.

About a month after the Texan Minister "respectfully but unconditionally" declared that his Republic no longer desired annexation, the Chevalier De Norin, Minister of Sweden, called at Mrs. Pitman's boardinghouse to see Mr. Jones. With him was a Mr. Christopher Hughes. Jones had called with cards on the Chevalier and later had visited him—more because of his personal agreeability than from any notion that Scandinavia might affect the future of Texas.

His companion Hughes was the American Chargé to Sweden and Norway, currently visiting in Washington. He was a career diplomat whose wit and social grace had won for him a place in the inner circles of European diplomacy more important than his rank and assignment might suggest. He had served his country abroad for more than two decades. He understood European psychology, and he knew the right people in London and Paris.

To Minister Jones's descantation on the Republic of Texas, its present status and potential greatness, Mr. Hughes listened with more than a polite interest and asked questions that elicited data not included in the stereotyped exposition. As they talked, an idea formed in the mind of the Texan Minister, and the same idea occurred to Mr. Hughes: Might not this worldly-wise, discreet American who knew his way about the European chancelleries do missionary work for Texas on his way across Europe to Stockholm? Equipped with data by Minister Jones, he could—entirely unofficially, of course—do what no Texan agent could even have opportunity to do. Mr. Hughes was distinctly interested.

The two diplomats became fast friends—one, new at the game, filled with evangelical zeal, the other steeped with knowledge of how things are accomplished in diplomacy. When Mr. Hughes sailed for Europe in April he knew as much about Texas as the Washington representative of the Republic could teach him in a few months. Minister Jones went to New York to see his friend aboard the *Siddons* and handed him a bulky manuscript to read en route:

The good sense of those who direct the councils of France and England must, sooner or later, convince them of the importance of

Texas in a commercial point of view . . . and . . . if they properly appreciated her present and prospective advantages and resources, no delay would occur in making that recognition.

You, my dear sir, have it in your power, in the course of your connection and friendly intercourse with many of the leading men of both of those countries, to give correct information in regard to these matters, and to disabuse Texas of many unfounded slanders, and consequent prejudices, which the press of this country unfortunately have given currency to. This I need not ask you to do, as you have already promised it in advance, and I only make these suggestions to recall the matter to your recollection on your arrival among your friends in Europe.

With the note was a memorandum on Texas potentialities which recapitulated much that Mr. Hughes already knew. Minister Jones's spunky little Republic, he reminded his friend, "has now sustained herself as a separate and independent nation, *de facto* and *de jure,* for more than *three,* and has been virtually separated from Mexico for more than *four* years. She can *never be resubjugated.* . . ." Nor, he implied but did not say, annexed to the United States. Then followed an economic prophecy:

Texas contains upwards of two hundred millions of acres of good land, much of it equal to any in the world. She has at least one hundred millions of acres of *cotton* land and is capable . . . of producing enough of that *great staple* for the supply and consumption of the world. She has more cotton lands than all the Southern States together.

She has, at least, fifty millions of natural pasture lands. . . .

Beef and wool can be raised cheaper and easier than in any part of the United States, and these must, in a few years, become immense staple products of the country, second only in importance and value to her *cottons!* . . . Texas will add the article of sugar to her staple productions, and export immense amounts of it within the next twenty-five years.

To say nothing, therefore, of the other natural resources of Texas, her mines, her mild and salubrious climate, &c., it cannot, I think, be denied by anyone, that she will shortly become an object of interest to European nations, who must perceive, upon a little consideration of the matter, how vastly important and beneficial her progress is, and *may become,* to their great *commercial* and *manufacturing* interests. Particularly does this appear to me to be true as it regards Great Britain and France.

Mr. Hughes paused in London to write unofficially to his old friend, Lord Palmerston:

. . . I venture to enclose Mr. Jones' memorandum, and to recommend it to your consideration, and to that of Lord Melbourne. The subject is really one of *great* and *growing* interest, and I don't see why *Johnathan* has not a right to nurse and dandle *John's* grandson. More *in the family way* I will not say.

Mr. Jones is an exceedingly gentlemanlike, modest, and estimable man, and commands the respect and esteem of everyone in the United States. . . . I made his acquaintance last winter at Washington, and formed quite a favorable opinion of him. I should think he *may* be the man sent here when you *may* take the view of the Texas question in London, that has, you know, long since been taken of it in Washington.

The Foreign Minister read the Jones memorandum, dispatched it to his Prime Minister, and confided to Hughes: "The subject . . . is important, but not without some difficulties."

Armed with letters of introduction from Palmerston to Lord Granville in Paris and Lord William Russell in Berlin, Hughes then proceeded, still unofficially, to the Continent.

In Paris he joined forces with General Henderson and with M. Pontois, French Minister to Washington, home on leave. Pontois, Henderson reported to Jones, "told me he had seen you frequently and conversed with you on Texan affairs. I am glad to find him so favorably disposed toward Texas. He informed me . . . that he told his Majesty that France must recognize Texas without further delay."

Minister Jones's industry in Washington, unspectacular and barren of obvious results, was bearing fruit in Europe.

He had made an advocate of Texas of M. Pontois and had equipped Mr. Hughes to aid and abet General Henderson in Paris. That zealous Texan, handicapped by ignorance of the French language and the subtleties of diplomatic negotiation, needed expert assistance. Training at the bar had equipped him to argue powerfully, point by point, for his cause; but when his arguments were all made, there still was needed a touch of finesse which only an experienced diplomat could give.

The fact is [Hughes wrote Jones], it was my accidental presence at Paris and my personal standing with several of the most powerful and influential French diplomats (who happened to be at home, old colleagues of mine), and my success *through them* in gaining the confidence of Marshal Soult. It was to *these* causes that we owed our success; and I conscientiously believe . . . that if I had not taken up the subject *as* I did, and *when* I did, Texas would *still* be unrecognized by France. If I were to name the European to whom you are most indebted for the success, I should name the Marquis de Rumigny, now French ambassador at Madrid, with whom I have been on brotherly terms for twenty-four years—the most able of the French diplomatists, and the most cherished and confided in by the King. . . .

Rumigny and Hughes alternated as Henderson's interpreter at the Foreign Office, bringing to bear their knowledge of diplomatic art as they translated the Texan's phrases. Before the end of September, General Henderson was writing jubilantly to Jones: "On the day before yesterday I completed the negotiation by signing a treaty with Marshal Soult, and on the same evening I was presented to the king as minister of Texas."

As he waited to know of the good effect his missionary work in Washington was having in Europe, Minister Jones knew little of what was going on in Texas beyond what he read in the Washington newspapers. Except for a routine notification that Lamar had been inaugurated—written sixteen days after the event—and a brief note the new Secretary of State, Barnard E. Bee, scribbled him January 31, 1839, "in much haste and merely to give you the current information," he heard nothing from the new officialdom of his Republic.

His recall from Washington was only a question of time, for the new President of Texas had too many friends hungry for political plums to allow the nation's top—in fact, only—diplomatic post to remain long in possession of an anti-Lamar man. Happily, however, Minister Jones and the new head of his government saw eye to eye on the all-important question of Texan diplomacy. Both considered annexation a dead issue. Lamar declared in his inaugural address:

I have never been able myself to perceive the policy of the desired connexion, or discover in it any advantage either civil, political or commercial which could possibly result to Texas. . . . the step once taken would produce a lasting regret, and ultimately prove as disastrous to our liberties and hopes, as the triumphant sword of the enemy.

Minister Jones did not share President Lamar's feeling that annexation would be a disaster; he only knew that annexation would be impossible unless American sentiment changed. He had set forces in motion that might change it.

The arrival of young Moses Austin Bryan from Texas to be his Secretary of Legation gave him the most direct news from home he had received in a long time and increased his social activities. Together they attended a brilliant semi-official party at the Georgetown home of General John P. Van Ness, mayor of the District and uncle of a Texas congressman. Bryan wrote his parents:

We sat down to dinner at 6 o'clock P.M. (a fashionable hour to dine in these parts) and rose from the table about 9, and then went to a dancing party in Georgetown where I saw more beauty and fashion than is common—— At 1 we left the party in Georgetown enjoying themselves, and on our way home stopped at the Theatre, to see how the military ball came on—— There I saw *two hundred and fifty* ladies and Gentlemen dancing at once—some sixty cotillions, which you know was a sight to me [in Texas ladies—and gentlemen who could dance cotillions—were scarce]—at 2 we left the ball and came to our boarding house and glad enough to get to bed.

Jones, older and more accustomed to city life, wrote: "Dined at Gen Van Ness went to Mrs. Carter's (Georgetown) with Mr. Lenneys & Mr. Bryan, staid until after midnight, went from thence to the Theatre, to a Military & Civil Ball."

Official and semi-official invitations came often enough, but the private residents of the District concentrated their attention upon the more spectacular members of the diplomatic corps, leaving representatives of lesser nations pretty much alone. After three months in the capital Minister Jones ruminated on this subject and wrote in his diary:

From the Citizens of this Republican city I have recd no attention, probably because I have not sported 75¢ worth of gold lace.

With those who did sport gold lace—the European ministers— Jones did well enough. Perhaps the unexpected procurement of an unofficial Texan agent through his friendship with the Swedish

Minister had suggested to him that he should neglect no individual whose home base was in Europe. France, Austria, Belgium, Holland, Spain, Russia, even Sardinia, had opportunities of learning of the Republic of Texas from the reports of ministers and attachés of legations with whom Minister Jones conversed whenever he could make an opportunity. Baron de Mareschal of Austria and some of the others had difficulty in remembering that Minister Jones represented a foreign power until they perceived his objectives.

Evenings at Judge Thruston's were becoming a routine with Minister Jones. He was a lonely man, a victim of vaguely defined unhappiness. His fortieth birthday was approaching, and—especially after he chanced to meet up with a Mr. Throop, a friend he had not seen since 1822 who was now the father of six children— he was conscious "that I am not a *'very young chap'* myself."

On December 15 he "visited Miss Thruston. Spent the evening at Chess with Judge Thruston, was much annoyed by *pups*." A man couldn't concentrate on the chessboard with a house full of silly young men dancing attendance on a pretty girl. Politics was a chess game he could play without irresponsible youngsters looking over his shoulder and chattering about nothings.

American statesmen and politicians of both parties came to know the Texan Minister during the second session of the Twenty-Fifth Congress. Every evening he sat at dinner with "Some 10 or 12 members of Congress from the North, at Mrs. Pittman's, an excellent boarding house." Among them were James Buchanan, Democratic senator from Pennsylvania, who was to be Secretary of State in the Polk administration; John W. Allen, a Whig congressman from Ohio; Samuel Prentiss, Whig senator from Vermont, and Samuel Birdsall, a newly elected Democratic congressman from New York. Through these and other acquaintances the Texan Minister met Calhoun and Clay and Webster, as well as their satellites from North and South. When time hung heavy he whiled away an afternoon or evening in the diplomatic gallery of House or Senate, and he took more than a spectator's interest in legislation before the Congress.

Tuesd. 8th [January 1839] Called in the morning on Col. Preston [senator from South Carolina], got him to agree to move for taking off the duty on Cotton. . . .

Wednesd. 9th. Made visits got the Bound[ary] Bill through the Senate. . . .

Tuesday 19th [February] in the morning with Mr Yell of Arkansas & drew up a Resolution which he promised to offer in the House calling on the Prest for information in relation to frontier Indians &c. &c.

Like all good Americans who could find an excuse for doing so, Jones called on Dolly Madison. The widow of the fourth President, now past seventy but looking twenty years younger, "moved like a queen in her crowded rooms, dressed in black, with a turban she had been accustomed to wear at the White House"—a visible symbol of the happier days of Washington society when Gentlemen from Virginia set the tone of the place.

Madame Calderon de la Barca, vivacious Scottish wife of the Spanish Minister, soon to be transferred from Washington to the city of Mexico; Madame Iturbide, daughter-in-law of the former Mexican Emperor Agustín; other celebrities of the capital, and all the museums and theaters were visited by the lonesome Texan.

Before Christmas "Miss Thruston" was sometimes "Jeannette" in the Minister's diary. Ceremonial calls kept him away from the judge's on New Year's Day, but January 2 he "went with Miss Guest to the House heard Mr. Clay, after dinner walked with Miss Thruston. Thursday 3d called on Miss T. found her in Tears. Spent morning there. . . ."

By March 12, after two consecutive evenings at Judge Thruston's, he recorded a deliberate judgment: "Miss T. is the best informed Lady in this Metropolis, & the most agreeable."

Nathaniel Amory, who arrived after Jones had left Washington —and Jeannette—forever, thought he understood the situation. He wrote his uncle:

The Lady I most admire is . . . Miss Jenette Thruston a Celebrated Belle of Washington for manners and mind and for having rendered many swains miserable by refusal, among others our Texas Doc Jones, who if he had as much discernment in "affaires de Coeur" as politicks, would never have incurred the certainty of refusal where so total a want of sympathy existed. . . .

XVI

MR. LAMAR'S TEXAS

THE new administration in Texas, which took office December 10, 1838, was a new administration indeed. The new President, Mirabeau Buonaparte Lamar, had arrived in Texas in 1836 just in time to become a hero of San Jacinto. He had served briefly as Secretary of War and more briefly as major general of the army before he was elected Vice-President in the first national election. He succeeded to the executive office, without Sam Houston's blessing, in the second.

Lamar proposed a new order in the foreign, as well as the domestic, affairs of the Republic. He presented the broad outlines of his program for Greater Texas in his inaugural address, then set about, with great industry but not always with tact, to lay foundations for a nation that could remain forever independent.

Into his official family he brought men who shared the vision and were willing to work toward actualizing it. Of Houston's Cabinet, he retained only Postmaster General Robert Barr, an inoffensive civilian and an Old Texian—he had been in Texas more than five years. His humdrum duties did not include the making or execution of new policies. The Attorney General was John C. Watrous, another civilian, recently arrived from Mississippi. Texan courtesy granted to these sole civilians in a cabinet otherwise populated exclusively by military gentlemen the title "General," derived from the portfolios they held. All of Lamar's other secretaries had first seen Texas in the year 1836, after the battle of San Jacinto; each of them bore a military title as bona fide as that of the President himself.

The State Department was given to Barnard E. Bee, a South Carolinian and a Texas colonel. He had served in the Burnet, then the Houston, Cabinet until he was appointed to accompany General Santa Anna to the United States. His friends were already telling him that he should succeed Lamar in the presidency at the next election.

His colleague in the War Office was General Albert Sidney Johnston, a second lieutenant in the United States Army four years before. Richard G. Dunlap, protégé of Andrew Jackson, was appointed to the Treasury. He, too, was a general—a brigadier of the East Tennessee militia. Memucan Hunt, Secretary of the Navy, had been a militia general in North Carolina and more recently had negotiated for annexation in Washington.

There was an atmosphere of impetuosity about these vigorous young men. They had no patience with the crafty caution of the Houston regime. They believed it possible to mold the future to their liking, both within Texas and in the capitals of the world; and with such wisdom as they possessed, they set about it.

The first and most important objective was to get from Mexico a prompt and categorical acknowledgment of the fact of Texan independence. President Lamar preferred to do it through peaceable negotiation, but he was willing to fight again if Mexico insisted. That matter settled, the Republic of Texas could plan a future limited only by the capacity of her statesmen, he believed.

With a boldness of which no diplomat would have been capable, Lamar determined to send an envoy directly to Antonio López de Santa Anna, who once again was ruling Mexico. For this difficult mission the President chose his Secretary of State. After all, Bee knew the Mexican President pretty intimately: he had escorted him from his Texas prison to the District of Columbia less than two years before; he had even lent him money!

When Bee was ready to start toward Mexico in February, the President could give consideration to maneuvering aid at Washington for the negotiations with Santa Anna.

Anson Jones was still Minister there, and so far as Lamar knew, he was not averse to remaining. He had neither asked for reappointment nor forwarded his resignation; he had only pointed out that the government had failed to provide him "any assistance in the duties of this Legation" since the departure of Catlett in October. After waiting three months, Jones asked "Mr. Sandy Harris formerly attached to the Legation in the capacity of Secretary to Gen. Hunt . . . to discharge the duties of the Secretary of Legation untill the one promised shall arrive."

It was not clear to Lamar what need for a legation staff a minister might have whose government had assigned no duties, but in January the President sent Moses Austin Bryan to Washington to keep Minister Jones company. Young Mr. Bryan was not only a veteran of San Jacinto but a nephew of the great empresario. The appointment was a public compliment to the Austin clan, rather than an effort to accommodate Anson Jones.

It was never a part of Lamar's plan to entrust the Washington end of negotiations with Mexico to Jones—or even to inform him as to what was contemplated. The matter of persuading the United States to mediate between Texas and Mexico was intricate, and only a Cabinet officer who had helped to evolve the complex plan could execute it. The Secretary of State himself was the President's first choice, but after word of his preference had leaked out he changed his mind and sent Bee to Mexico. General Dunlap of the Treasury was designated to succeed Minister Jones at Washington.

The choice was made in February, but on the eve of departure Dunlap discovered that an employee of the Treasury under the previous administration had helped himself to negotiable bonds "and gambled them off." He tarried to bring the rascal to an accounting. It was May before he reached Washington, carrying in his pocket a letter for the Honorable Anson Jones.

Meantime, Minister Jones, convinced that he was to be displaced but uninformed as to when or by whom, began to give more thought to the new order in his Republic than to the events at the capital of the United States.

President Lamar was proposing a National Bank for Texas. Anson Jones, who in the Texas Congress had regarded himself as an authority on fiscal matters, read the scheme with critical interest, but without edification.

Saturday, February 9th. Called with Mr. Bryan on the President, afterwards on Col. Preston & Gov. Butler & Judge Thruston. All agree with me upon the impracticability of Gen. L's Bank in Texas.

Six weeks later "Mr. Teackle's memoirs on Banks fell into my hands—draws my attention to the subject of paper money." For two days he "staid at home and read," making some rough calculations. Then, after studying a *History of Banks,* an *Essay on*

Banks, and Gouge's *Short History of Paper Money and Banking,*
he spent a day writing a "plan of a Bank" which he believed contained more knowledge of the subject, if less rhetoric, than President Lamar's. But he did not forward it to His Excellency. He
had already, as diplomatically as he could, asked "the determination of the President in regard to myself." Pending a reply to that
inquiry, the plan of the bank—and a good many other plans—
would remain in his own letter file.

While he waited he read the proceedings of the trial of Sam
Houston before the House of Representatives in 1832 for an assault on Stanberry, wrote five lines of comment, then carefully
obliterated them. Next he reread the speeches in Congress on the
independence of Texas by Benton of Missouri, Walker of Mississippi, Preston of South Carolina, Huntsman of Tennessee, and
Bynum of North Carolina.

But what he wanted was not data on the early history of his
Republic; he wanted a letter from its present rulers.

April 8. No intelligence from the [word obliterated] Cabinet at
home, each and all of whom appear to be exclusively engaged in the
promotion of their own petty personal interests and advancement.
Everything else [including Jones!] seems neglected.

April 9. A foolish project appears to be on foot to send a minister
(Col Bee) to Mexico, a shallow proceeding which will probably
result in no good.

April 10. It will take about one year for the present Admn of
Texas to demonstrate its weakness & its corruption. Every honest &
tried friend to the country has been removed out of the way to give
place to a few newly imported knaves who intend to reap the profits
of others toil and sufferings.

April 12. No General Dunlap has come to hand. I do not understand the shuffling at home, evidently "something is rotten in the
State."

From forebodings of disasters that lay ahead of his Republic,
Minister Jones turned his thoughts to the man whom the Texans
had chosen by an almost unanimous vote to direct the public
policies. He had observed Lamar at intervals for four years—first
as an immigrant seeking land at Brazoria, then as the fellow private in the army who became a colonel as the battle started. More
recently he had watched him preside over the Texas Senate. Jones

had done what he could to discourage his presidential aspirations in the summer of 1838.

It is strong evidence of the poverty of worth or talent in a country when such a man as Lamar is selected for the head [he wrote April 13, 1839]. He is a very weak man and governed by petty passions which he cannot control and by prejudices which are the result of ignorance. Obstinacy he possesses, and what his friends call *honesty* though it is a very equivocal kind. The situation of the diplomatic Representative of such a Gov^t as Texas is above all others the most irksome and disagreeable. . . . I will hold no other office untill a change, and a radical one, is produced, as nothing but disgrace can come from a connexion with the present parties.

These were Anson Jones's private meditations as he waited, waited.

A trip to New York to see Mr. Christopher Hughes off for Europe interrupted, temporarily, these ruminations upon what Lamar and his cohorts were about to do to Texas.

James Treat called on Jones at the Astor House, "had a long conversation with him on the subject of a treaty with Mexico. Went with him to the American to see Gen: Mason," another friend of Texas—and of the Texan five-million-dollar loan. This Mr. Treat was determined to negotiate peace between Mexico and Texas on his *"own Hook"* if Texas would not commission him a secret agent.

The first of May, Minister Jones was in Baltimore to visit the yards where the vessels were being built for the Texas Navy, and wondering if the *Viper* would be ready in time to carry him home. He was visiting with Captain John G. Tod, T.N., when General Dunlap "came to hand."

The Minister of Texas and the Minister-designate greeted each other stiffly, inspected the Texas men-of-war together, and rode the same train into Washington Saturday evening. On arrival, Dunlap went to his hotel; Jones walked thoughtfully to his boardinghouse.

Sunday, Minister Jones followed his customary schedule: "attended church at Mr. Owens [Episcopal], evening at Judge Th's." At his room he found a letter that General Dunlap had left for him.

It was dated March 14. He received it May 5.

The Hon: Anson Jones,
    SIR, The President having appointed the Hon: Richard G. Dun-
lap Minister Plenipotentiary of the Government of Texas, near that
of the United States, I am directed to request you to turn over to that
Gentleman, all the books, papers, seals and archives of the Texian
Legation at Washington, and to say that as your services will no
longer be required near that Government, you will return home at
such time as may be convenient to you.
    I have the honor to be very respectfully Your Obdt Servt
                                            JAMES WEBB [Rubric]

That was not a letter of recall; it was a letter of dismissal.
Jones's reply reached Minister Dunlap early Monday morning:

Hon. R. G. Dunlap, &c., &c.,
    SIR: . . . Having more than two months since understood that
a person was appointed to supersede me as Minister to this Government, and not having then received, as I expected, a *letter of recall*
to be presented to the President of the United States on my taking
leave of this Government, finally I wrote about seven weeks ago to
the Secretary of State at home, requesting that if a letter had not
been sent as above, that it might be immediately done. As none, however, has been forwarded me either through you or the ordinary con-
veyances, I presume it has been the intention of the Government to
withhold it. This, independent of personal considerations, I very
much regret, as a contrary course would have been in accordance
with propriety and the usages of friendly nations, respectful to this
Government, and is due to the character and dignity of Texas. . . .
    I shall be happy to have an interview with you as requested, on
subjects connected with my late mission to this Government, and will
be at home to-day at 12 o'clock for this purpose, if it will suit your
convenience to call at that hour.
    I remain, with great regard, your most obedient servant,
                                            ANSON JONES

General Dunlap called, received the papers of the Legation,
and tarried for a long interview with the outgoing Minister; but
so busy was he in setting in motion the complicated negotiations
in Washington with the Secretary of State and the Mexican Embassy for the mediation of the United States in the matter of
Texan independence that it was more than a week before he

found time to relay to the Texan Secretary of State the lecture on diplomatic etiquette that Jones had given him on May 6:

You will please forward to the President of the United States [Dunlap wrote his friend Webb] a letter of recall of Doct Jones this will answer, altho the same ceremony is observed in taking leave where the two Governments are on good terms, that are observed in the presentation of a Minister. I send you Wheatons elements of international law which has a code of etiquet for the diplomatic corps.

Jones, of course, had mastered Elliot's *Code;* but Wheaton was equally authoritative. Poor Judge Webb had been plumped from his law office into the State Department in the midst of such frenzied plan-making that he had had no time to learn diplomatic formulas, even if he had had copies of both Wheaton and Elliot available.

S. A. Roberts, Dunlap's Secretary of Legation, wrote President Lamar three days after Dunlap's arrival of Jones's feeling regarding the letter and that Dunlap had explained that it was attributable to oversight or ignorance.

I think he is satisfied, & if Judge Webb will call on him on his arrival & make the amends honorable which I think he ought to do, I believe he may be *made a friend of.* He speaks highly of your state papers, approves the general course of your measures, etc but says he does not *know you*—that he has often *tried* to form an acquaintance (*an intimate* one I mean), but that you have never met his advances in the spirit in which they were made. . . . I give you all this for what it is worth.

Anson Jones, a private citizen now but entitled to government transportation home, spent his last morning in Washington "at Judge T's," then went to Baltimore, where he methodically inventoried his diplomatic wardrobe of nine coats, fourteen pantaloons, seven vests, one dozen shirts, three dozen collars, five black stocks, three pairs of boots, one of bootees, one of pumps, one of slippers, one morning wrapper, two hats, and "Stockings, Gloves, Hdkffs &c. &c innumerable," and spent a tedious two weeks "waiting for the *Viper.*"

Baron de Mareschal, Minister of Austria, came over to cheer him up; Count de Baillet took him to the races at Kendall Course;

and he visited and revisited the theaters and museums. On May 18 came a letter from Jeannette, and he "spent the evening philosophizing upon the degradation of human nature." On May 22 he "dispatched a letter of seven pages to J." Three days later he was on his way to Texas.

"Doct Jones . . . is a different man here, from what he was in Texas," Moses Austin Bryan reported.

XVII

LIKE CERTAIN FEVERS

ON JUNE 21, 1839, the Honorable Anson Jones made a triumphal entry into the principal port of the Republic of Texas aboard the *Viper*. This new schooner of the Texas Navy belonged to "one of the most beautiful squadrons in the world of its size"; as for the *Viper* herself, General James Hamilton declared she could be compared "in symmetry to nothing else than a beautiful woman." On this maiden voyage she carried five sailors and six passengers. Ex-Minister Jones's traveling companions included Moses Austin Bryan and Samuel M. Williams.

Williams, junior partner of McKinney & Williams, "the Barings of Texas," had supervised the construction for the Texas Navy of what General James Hamilton of South Carolina pronounced "positively . . . the handsomest & most promising vessels I have ever seen in my life."

Young Mr. Bryan had been recalled as Secretary of Legation in Washington to make a place for the son of a Lamar officeholder. To the Brazoria *Courier's* complaint that it was a shabby way to treat a man who had had the appointment "literally forced on him" by Lamar, the Houston *Morning Star* rejoined: "You are 'not a little astonished,' eh, Mr. Courier? Well then, all we can say is that you are wonderfully behind the times. You should not be astonished at anything of that kind, now-a-days." Two weeks later the *Star* said that it was not a case of allowing the new Minister to select his Secretary of Legation, for "Gen'l Dunlap was too grateful for an opportunity to figure at Washington to stickle about the prerogative. . . ." Lamar gave Bryan's place to Samuel A. Roberts, son of his old friend, Dr. Willis Roberts, Collector of the Port of Galveston.

The Anson Jones who was returning to Texas "a different man . . . from what he was" a year before when he last saw Galveston found that Galveston, too, had changed. The population had

grown to nearly three thousand. Vessels from the States and from
Europe—sometimes thirty in a single day—were unloading cargoes and immigrants at McKinney & Williams's wharf and sailing
away with their holds full of Texas cotton, which Jones thought
"the best possible negotiator for the Government of England."
The two hotels were filled to capacity, and three more were being
built. Store buildings and dwellings were going up at a miraculous
rate. "The timber of a frame-house, containing 20,000 dollars'
worth of goods," Galvestonians were telling visitors, "had been
growing in the State of Maine ninety days before."

Jones had left Washington resolved to hold no public office,
"untill a change, and a radical one, is produced" in the Texan administration. On his twenty-five-day voyage he read Mr. Bancroft's *History of the United States,* a work replete with instances
of the way in which Providence utilizes frail men to further great
causes, and full of implications for a man in Jones's state of mind.

Providence was, in fact, busy in Brazoria while he was ending
his diplomatic career and journeying homeward. At the Galveston
wharf they told him that the Brazorians had elected him senator.

John A. Wharton, the doctor's oldest friend in Texas, had died
in December; his brother William, who had been Jones's political
mentor, died the following March. *"Could not one suffice!"* the
doctor, deeply moved, exclaimed. William had been senator from
Brazoria, a leader of congressional opposition to Lamar; his
friends thought Anson Jones his logical successor.

The President and his advisers immediately cast about for a
man "whose abilities and qualifications . . . principles, and his
future course" would bolster the administration. They selected
William T. Austin, who had once injured John Wharton in a
duel; and they urged the President to call the election "before the
probable opponent Anson Jones can return or have been long returned from the United States." Lamar obliged them, but a combination of anti-Lamar, pro-Wharton, pro-Jones sentiment gave
the office to the diplomat President Lamar had dismissed.

When the Brazorians told him what they had done and why,
his first impulse was to decline; but the more he cogitated on how
that man in the White House had tried to defeat him, the more
he was inclined to give in to "the overpersuasion of many worthy
citizens" to put himself "in constant contact with an administra-

tion which was gradually sucking the life-blood of the country away."

The reception of Anson Jones at Galveston—unprecedented in the brief diplomatic annals of the Republic—was more than an expression of approval of his services abroad; it was in a sense the curtain raiser for a political revolt against President Lamar.

Dr. Jones would announce his decision on the Senate post on a suitable occasion; meantime he was busily occupied accepting the homage due an elder statesman of the three-year-old Republic. He called at the navy yard to receive an ambassadorial salute of fifteen guns—which probably was not ordered by the President or his Secretary of the Navy. He "partook afterwards of a collation at the Mayor's," along with bemedaled Commodore Ribaud, an unofficial representative of the King of the French. Then he received a delegation of frock-coated gentlemen who requested the diplomat to give Galveston the privilege of organizing a testimonial dinner in his honor. He told them he would consider it.

Anson Jones—ex-Minister, senator-elect—was, for him, in a jubilant mood for a few days.

Visited all my friends on the Island. Went in the evening to the Station in the Beach and took Supper and a Bath there. Accepted invitation to dine with citizens of Galveston.

This was all very pleasant, but Diplomatist Jones had duties to perform. A man who had lectured the administration on its violation of protocol must himself commit no breach of etiquette. The city of Houston lay fifty miles up Buffalo Bayou. There were the officials upon whom he must call formally to terminate his ambassadorial career. There, too, he had left Mary McCrory—with promises and plans made before he knew the universe contained Jeannette. How to terminate a diplomatic connection was something a man could be certain about. Mr. Elliot's *Code* told him exactly what he should do. At least he knew authoritatively how to handle one part of the business that called him to Houston.

Dutifully he traveled nine hours up the bayou. His formal calls on the Secretary of State (Vice-President Burnet was at the moment holding that post) and other officials of the Lamar administration made him once more, *de facto* and *de jure,* a private citizen.

He did not find Mary McCrory. The Woodruffs, they told him, had moved to Austin.

There were always the Masons. He went around to Holland Lodge. "Joined in a celebration of the day [John the Baptist's] with the Masons. Presided as G. M." Whatever remarks he made in the lodge hall were not the ones he had rehearsed on his way up the bayou; but at least there was someone to listen to them.

Five days later Dr. Jones "dined with the Citizens of Galveston."

With becoming modesty and prolixity Citizen Jones thanked his hosts for their approbation; reminded them that his talents had always been dedicated to public service in times of trouble and danger; "but situations of high responsibility, while I distrusted my own powers too much to *seek,* yet . . . I have never felt at liberty to *decline.*"

He could not, of course, share with them any diplomatic secret. "The respect due to the Government and its officers"—even such a government as General Lamar's—required that these important data be communicated by the head of the nation, when, as, and if he "deemed advisable and proper." Jones confided to his friends:

I am happy, however, to know . . . that I have . . . given entire satisfaction. . . . For giving this assurance, I have the highest and best authority—the Presidents of the two Republics themselves!

All that a diplomat could do for his country Jones implied he had done. But diplomacy, he gravely admonished his fellow citizens, could never save the Republic. Only Texans resident in Texas, and exercising the responsibilities of citizenship day in and day out, could cure the ills that made the survival of their Republic problematical. "Our final success or failure . . . must depend altogether upon our selves—our prudence and exertions."

We are yet, fellow-citizens, surrounded by many and serious difficulties. . . . The best talent of the country should . . . be put in requisition . . . the credit of the country . . . appears every hour sinking still lower. . . .

Texas . . . inhabited *now* by an intelligent and enterprising people . . . will take her stand as the second great successful experiment in representative, free government. . . . And . . . there exists entire confidence among the most intelligent men in the United States, and, so far as I have means of knowing, in Europe, in the final successful issue of our struggle, and that we have before us the almost certain prospect of a long and brilliant career as a free, independent nation. Let us not disappoint these hopes, nor betray this flattering confidence.

He confessed he had returned to Texas determined "to retire for a while from public life," only to discover that his patriotic neighbors willed otherwise. He would enter the Senate in November,

believing that Texas needs my services, and that of all her old friends, now more than ever she did. . . . In the discharge of these duties [he promised] I shall . . . "nothing extenuate, or set down aught in malice."

The peroration of the senator-elect's remarks was a toast to his shaky Republic:

Texas! her cause is that of Justice, of Rational Liberty, and Constitutional Law. May they soon be permanently established from the Sabine to the Rio Grande and from the Gulf of Mexico to the Pacific Ocean; and may no strife exist among her citizens, except that noble and glorious strife of—Who shall best promote this great object.

At that democratic table Jones sat above the salt, and there was no gold lace among those Texan banqueters to divert the spotlight from him.

Before he visited his constituents in Brazoria the returning statesman went to Houston to celebrate the Fourth of July and to make a formal call on the Honorable Alcée La Branche, Chargé in Texas of the government near which he had recently served. For old time's sake he attended a meeting of the Masonic Grand Lodge—which lacked a quorum—but he shrewdly "declined a dinner at Beauchamps Springs, & escaped the row there."

At Brazoria the new senator "visited every body" and on July 20 "dined with all the Citizens of Brazoria Co. had a very pleasant party"—so pleasant, in fact, that he kept to his bed for a week following it.

This "welcome-home" dinner for the county's most prominent citizen, the *Courier* reported,

was perhaps the largest and most respectable ever assembled in the County of Brazoria, under similar circumstances. The sturdy yeomanry of the neighborhood—those honest old settlers who, like their worthy guest, had borne the heat and burden of a day that tried men's souls in the darkest period of our history—with other highly respected gentlemen from different parts of the country, were those who had surrounded the festal board. The party was respectively addressed by Dr. Jones, Mr. Austin Bryan, and the Hon. E. L. Holmes . . . amid deafening shouts of acclamation.

Brazoria County may well be proud of her proscribed sons.

As soon as he could travel again Senator Jones was at Eagle Island plantation to pay his respects to the widow of Senator William H. Wharton. The great plantation house, where he had so often been a guest, seemed desolate without the booming voices and infectious laughter of its late master and his brother John—the man who had persuaded Jones to cast his lot with these Texans. With more emotion than Jones usually permitted himself, he wrote in his diary at Eagle Island:

The loss of my friends was brought home to my mind & feelings with great force.

Mrs. W. gave me Mr. W.'s report on the Tariff. The quieting Land Titles, remodelling the Constitution & abolition of the Tariff were favorite schemes of Mr. W.—& I promised Mrs. W. to carry them out if on reflection I approved them.

Everything he heard and saw in Texas corroborated his forebodings as to whither Lamar was leading the Republic.

The folly of Lamar is in nothing more apparent than his threats of *offensive* war against Mexico.

Texas is overwhelmed with Army & Navy officers—there are enough for Russia & poor Texas is without means to support them many weeks longer.

Borrowing may serve to protract the crisis a while, but it must come with a tremendous crash e'er long.

Gen. Lamar may mean well. I am not disposed to impugn his intentions—he has fine belles lettres talents & is an elegant writer. But his mind is altogether of a dreamy, poetic order. A Sort of political Troubadour & Crusader, wholly unfit by habit or education for the active duties & the every day realities of his present station. Texas is too small for a man of such wild visionary "vaulting ambition."

The Republic of Texas was spending during 1839 more than a million and a half dollars; its revenues were less than two hundred thousand. Texas currency was just reaching a new low of sixteen cents on the dollar, and no one who could get McKinney & Williams's crisp new bills, worth one hundred cents on the dollar, or New Orleans exchange, was accepting government paper.

For weeks before the Texans elected representatives to their Fourth Congress on September 2, there was considerable stirring throughout the Republic. Lack of organized parties made it difficult to correlate opposition to the administration; but, as Dr. Branch T. Archer was pointing out to his friend the President, "The suffering condition, and heavy complaints of our . . . fellow-citizens [are] all charged as you know (whether right or wrong), to Executive neglect, or indifference. . . ." "I hear every day that you are losing your popularity," Memucan Hunt assured the President from New Orleans; "almost every one coming from Texas says so."

As the congressional election neared, anti-administration sentiment crystallized around a few great names and hosts of lesser ones. Sam Houston was a candidate from San Augustine. General J. Pinckney Henderson in Europe, offended at learning from his successor that Lamar had replaced him as European agent, offered to serve from Harrisburg. Anson Jones had already been elected to the Senate from Brazoria to complete Wharton's term.

Local leaders in other counties—offended at the President or objectively convinced that the Lamar policies were wrong, sometimes both—offered their services in the House. In some sections Lamar's friends were devoted to the cause and did what they could to elect Lamar men to Congress; but, as General Thomas Jefferson Green warned the President two weeks before the election,

It must be perfectly plain, that the time has arrived when you and your administration require vindication by responsible names. The within [encomium and invitation to speak at Velasco] I think will be the first effort that way. . . . I am no politician if the reaction does not commence with this letter and your *coming home* to see your old friends here would be most favorable.

Green, Archer, William T. Austin, John Sharp, L. H. McNeel, Ambrose Crane, G. M. Stone, Edwin Waller, and J. C. Hoskins signed the eulogy, which declared that "no man could have done better and few indeed as well—for which you are entitled to the gratitude of your country and the homage of posterity."

Green wanted the President to come to Brazoria County and defend his administration at Velasco, "where the citizens have unanimously been with you at all times," to help elect Lamar partisans to Congress. But the President did not come, and the reaction did not commence.

The Brazorians elected William H. Jack, brother of Jones's colleague in the Second Congress, and John W. Harris, law partner of the late John A. Wharton. Senator Jones made it a point to vote in that election.

Genl L's friends dont work as they ought [lamented a devoted partisan after the election]. Why on earth, when truth, justice, patriotism & talent too are all in his favor why I ask are there not more able and lucid articles in the papers—— He seems to me to drag the whole load without even a friendly "god speed ye" to encourage him—— It's well for him he has so much constitutional fir[m]ness. . . .

But the President's constitutional firmness did not assure him a comfortable working majority in the Fourth Congress. Only ten of the congressmen elected with Lamar in 1838 were returned to the Fourth Congress. Thirty newly elected men were to control the House, and there were four new senators. It might be possible, Senator Jones reflected after the election, to "roll back the tide of reckless and adverse legislation." It was worth his while to try. His friends in Brazoria had promised he would serve two years, and his conscience required him to do it.

As a statesman pledged to reform, he listened attentively to grievances of citizens as he traveled through Brazoria, Harrisburg, and Galveston counties; but the purpose of the tour was non-political. Dr. Jones was investing his considerable accumulated capital in choice lands and city lots.

Jones found that Houston had become a thriving city during the year he had been away, but that its citizens were much perturbed by the decision of the Third Congress to move the capital to Austin. There were more than 2,000 residents in Houston—1,620 men, 453 women—and five steamboats were plying every day between that city and the port of Galveston. Senator Jones shared the local sentiment against moving the government from this place where, the *Morning Star* boasted, there

now are hundreds of buildings, neat and comfortable, large stores well filled with the conveniences and many of the luxuries of life, fine hotels offering accommodations for a hundred boarders, and two theatres in successful operation

—but he made no investments in Houston real estate.

The *Morning Star* considered removal "among the *possibilities,* but most certainly not among the *probabilities,*" and believed that the congressmen who voted to establish the new capital "were not in the full exercise of their reasoning faculties."

In April, His Excellency the President had sent Edwin Waller of Brazoria County to create a capital city on the upper Colorado, in the Indian country, more than two hundred miles from the coast. Waller was determined that the new town should be ready to receive the President and his Cabinet in October and the Fourth Congress a month later. On June 2 he reported to Lamar: "The public buildings *shall* be in readiness for the next Congress. I have two 16 foot square rooms up now. . . ." Unwelcome confirmation of Waller's prediction was given Houstonians two months later by the *Telegraph:*

Twenty or thirty buildings have already been completed [an Austin correspondent wrote, adding gratuitously] and they are better buildings than were built during the first year in Houston. . . . The buildings will be ready . . . previous to the time prescribed by law.

After pointing out that the prevailing opinion at Houston was that the new Congress would be wise enough to *"assemble* there and adjourn to this place," the *Morning Star* bowed to the inevitable. The August 13 issue announced:

In about twenty days . . . the officers of the government and the public archives will be on their "winding way" to the new city of Austin.

Well, we have one consolation left, and that is, that we have done everything we could to prevent it. . . .

One day while oxcarts were creaking out of the old capital with the archives and paraphernalia of government, a citizen of the new capital rode into Houston looking for Senator Jones. John Woodruff had ridden two hundred miles to deliver a letter from Mary McCrory. He found him on Monday. Thursday Jones "wrote to Jeannette."

Friday he began a six-day meditation upon the wrong-headedness of Lamar.

The administration is operating like certain fevers upon the constitution bringing the patient to the extremest point of exhaustion possible & then leaving him either to die or recover. This is the only way Gen. Lamar can do with the country.

A visit to the Masonic lodge and the new race track at Galveston and "a letter from Christopher Hughes at London with a copy of one from Visct Lord Palmerston" refreshed his spirits. He was ready to move on to Austin, but an epidemic of "Yellow Fever, alias cold plague," detained him in Houston.

He arranged and rearranged his papers, saw Mrs. Hubbard in *The Blind Boy* at the theater, bought more lands, and puttered about for nearly three weeks. On October 20 he started "in Company of Col. H. D. McLeod *& Teddy O. Rourke* for the Metropolis," stopping on the way to visit Leonard Groce, Mrs. Wharton's brother, at his plantation. After an eleven-day journey he was "at Austin, mid every discomfort & privation."

XVIII

THE CITY OF AUSTIN

MARY McCRORY was experiencing discomforts and privations at Austin that were unrelated to the physical inconveniences of a raw community. She knew a new Texan capital could, would, become a civilized place in a few months; she had seen that happen in Houston. Other outcomes were not so certain. She had written a letter and sent it two hundred miles, two hundred miles that her fiancé seemed in no hurry to traverse.

She had known a succession of losses. Hugh McCrory had died almost before their life together had begun. Her marriage to Dr. Jones had been postponed soon after their engagement was announced.

When the Third Congress had met at Houston during the winter of 1838–39, another statesman sat in Jones's place at Woodruff's and Mary found little to interest her in the political talk at the dinner table. As boarders discussed the plan to build a new capital city far up the Colorado River, Mr. Woodruff began making plans to move his family there.

Earlier that year President Lamar had hunted buffalo between Waller and Shoal creeks on the upper Colorado River. Elated at killing the largest bison he had ever seen, His Excellency climbed to the top of one of the hills, gazed with poetic imagination about him, and exclaimed: "This should be the seat of future Empire!" In May surveyors began marking out a checkerboard of streets and lots while Edwin Waller collected logs and carpenters to build shelter for the government. Despite the fact that he believed "every engine of falsehood has been called into requisition to prevent its occupation for governmental purposes" and the work was "liable every moment to be interrupted by the hostile Indians," Waller got the job done in five months.

Life in the capital was crude and hard, but President Lamar

refused to believe that stout Texans would "repine at the sacrifice of a few personal comforts which the good of the nation may require of them." As in Houston two years before, settlers were pouring in to get themselves established before the government arrived—and hoping that this capital of Texas would be the permanent one.

In June, John Woodruff brought his wife and assorted children and stepchildren to Austin. They arrived while Mr. Waller was completing his first two cabins. Indians were already beginning to pay nocturnal visits to the men whose industry was breaking the stillness of their hunting grounds. In October the Woodruffs were still camping, keeping alive on buffalo meat. A stranger on his way to visit them encountered "men just setting off to bury the bones of thirteen men recently murdered by Indians . . . great excitement. . . . Guards were posted around the town. . . ."

As the day for the opening of the Congress neared, the number of strangers in town greatly increased, as did activity along Congress Avenue, the broad central boulevard that ran from Capitol Hill to the Colorado River. Men who had been in New Orleans thought "the Avenue" was wider than Canal Street. After a rain it was much more difficult to cross.

Seat of Empire Hill was left vacant until Texas could afford to build a capitol befitting her future greatness. Below it, on the west side of the Avenue, Mr. Waller had built a sprawling house for the use of Congress and a smaller one for His Excellency's office. On a hill east of the Avenue—higher than Capitol Hill but less centrally located—stood the two-story executive mansion. Its front and back porticoes, clapboard walls, and white paint made it, the *Telegraph* declared, "almost a palace contrasted with the houses of the frontier hamlet." The steepness of the hill gave it a splendid isolation—and made a hard pull for the President's $2,300 carriage. The legislators who had business with His Excellency were to find that hill even more wearisome than did the President's horses.

Sturdy little cabins for the government departments, "fitted up in a neat and commodious style," faced each other along Congress Avenue. In wet weather clerks traveled between offices on horseback, and wheeled vehicles carried fence rails to lift them out of the bogs and hog wallows.

During October, after forty ox wagons had unloaded their cargoes of papers and furniture, the government of Texas began functioning again. President Lamar reported that the officials resumed their duties in their new quarters "with very little inconvenience to themselves, and no derangement of the public business beyond its tempor[ar]y suspension."

With furniture and fittings borrowed from lodges, individuals, and executive departments, the halls of Congress were made habitable. The Hall of Representatives had "portraits of Washington & Austin—16 ink stands, 5 Candlesticks, 10 sand boxes, 3 benches, 1 large table and stand for the speaker, some old chairs." The Senate chamber was more simply furnished: "7 benches, 2 tables, 1 Table and Stand for Speaker, 3 good chairs."

Anson Jones reached Austin the last day of October 1839—"no room nor bed to be had for love or money." Major S. Whiting had printed Volume I, Number I, of his Austin *City Gazette* the day before. In it the Senator from Brazoria read:

It is difficult to give a full and just description of this spot with its surrounding scenery. If Rome was celebrated in song for "Seven Hills," Austin may well boast of her "thousand mounds" covered with bowers equal in splendor to the Arcadian groves

—which was true enough; but a statesman couldn't sleep on a mound or eat scenery. Edwin Waller, fellow Brazorian who had tried to defeat Jones's candidacy, finally rented him a room at his house.

Officially Jones had come to represent Brazoria County in the Senate of the Fourth Congress; unofficially he was there to invest in choice lots and become as much of a permanent resident as the city had during its troubled early years.

No policy could possibly have been more unwise than the removal of the seat of Govt to Austin, & corrupt means were used to place it there. But [he philosophized] now that so much money has been expended I shall be for its remaining at that place.

Money indeed had been spent to transform this square mile of Indian country into a site for white habitation—money that Senator Jones thought was needed for other purposes. Drayage, by oxcart, on the archives alone had cost $21,223.41.

Establishing the capital beyond the fringes of settlement was a Lamaresque gesture, and Senator Jones thought ill of it—but not ill enough to blind himself to the opportunities it offered a man with a sense of land values and cash in his pocket.

The first auction of city lots had been held before he arrived, but as soon as he reached the city he began buying, with the expert advice of his host Judge Waller. Before the winter was over twenty choice lots representing an investment of about eight thousand dollars were recorded in the name of Anson Jones.

"Attended sales of town lots. Saw Mary," the statesman wrote in his diary November 1. It was not the reunion either of them had looked forward to when he had left for the United States.

Austinians were still talking about the fanfare with which President Lamar had been escorted into his new capital on October 17. "Such of the citizens as were able to procure horses" paraded two miles out to greet him, and

as General Lamar passed down between the two lines, the Orator of the day, supported by the Marshalls, and followed by the Standard Bearer, moved up and met his Excellency. . . . His Excellency the President replied in a short but pithy and appropriate speech; and after the cheering had somewhat subsided, the company was again put in motion. . . .

As soon as his Excellency crossed the city line, a salute of twenty-one guns was fired from a six-pounder. . . . On reaching Mr. Bullock's hotel . . . a large concourse of citizens who had been unable, for want of horses or harness, to join the cavalcade, stood ready to tender every mark of respect in their power. . . .

Inside Mr. Bullock's crowded dining hall the official dinner lasted five hours. To the twelve scheduled toasts and their responses, guests added twenty-five volunteer expressions of sentiments. The President of the Republic stood in the unpainted tavern surrounded by new log shacks and lifted his glass to the future glories of his new capital:

By the touch of his [Waller's] industry, there has sprung up, like the work of magic, a beautiful city, whose glory is destined, in a few years, to overshadow the ancient magnificence of Mexico,

His Excellency said with conviction.

The Reverend W. Y. Allen, in that same beautiful city, "supped on Buffalo meat, and hot coffee in a tin cup, with Bro. Woodruff, at his camp." With him supped the Woodruff children and step-children, including Mary McCrory. At Houston, Mr. Allen had been a fellow boarder with Jones at Woodruff's.

Anti-Lamar men at Austin—citizens and congressmen—resolved to make Sam Houston's entry into the city a demonstration appropriate to the Hero of San Jacinto and an ex- (and possibly a future) President. Senator Jones was "engaged to address Gen. H. on his arrival." The general represented "the East" (San Augustine); the senator from Brazoria was from "the West," as things were reckoned in the Republic of Texas. The Trinity River was the dividing line between the sections.

The day that the Fourth Congress convened, Senator Jones, escorted by a cavalcade marshaled by three colonels, rode to meet the Hero of San Jacinto three miles from the capital. There he delivered the "warm and eloquent greeting" that he had spent Sunday composing and listened to the general's "brief but impressive" reply. The speeches were duly reported in the Austin *City Gazette* and reprinted in the Brazoria *Courier*.

The third evening of the Fourth Congress, "many citizens of the Republic . . . desirous of testifying their respect for General Sam Houston, and their gratitude for his services," requisitioned Jones to preside over the dinner. The former Minister to Washington could be depended upon to manage the affair with éclat.

President Lamar had been banqueted at Bullock's; but this

dinner was handsomely served up by Mr. Hall, and about two hundred persons sat down to the table, which was prepared for a much larger number. . . .

One of the absentees was Mr. Lamar; the weather was very bad.

The first toast—to the United States—brought "three cheers"; the second, to General Houston, "3 times 3"; the third, to the President of the Republic, evoked none.

The diners drank to "Freedom of opinion and liberty of speech" and to currency "based upon agriculture and commerce, and sustained by industry and economy." Then

General Houston responded . . . in one of the most eloquent speeches we [the local editor] ever remembered to have heard; and impressed us with a more favorable opinion of his powerful intellect and generous devotion to his country, than we before entertained. Many passages of his speech were strikingly brilliant. At the close of which, he offered the following sentiment:

"Texas:—If true to herself, she can be false to no one!"

As Old Sam Jacinto took his seat John B. McLeod raised his glass to the toastmaster:

Hon. Anson Jones:—The gentleman and the soldier, the legislator and the diplomatist; he has been tried and approved by the people!

Dr. Jones responded. . . . "Redemption to our currency; not by loans, but by industry, economy, and wiser legislation."

The Speaker of the House toasted "Retrenchment and Reform"; the congressman from Matagorda prescribed "lasting infamy and disgrace" for "every legislator who shall shrink from the duty of exposing and defeating" the plunderers of the public domain; and Dr. R. F. Brenham opined that "the price of Liberty is eternal vigilance."

Near the end of the evening, A. C. Hyde, a Brazorian and one of the toastmaster's companions on the *Viper,* arose to declare a sentiment:

Anson Jones:—He deserves to be Vice-President. With such men as Sam Houston and Anson Jones at our head, Texas will have nothing to fear.

It was the thirty-fifth of forty-three toasts. The forty-first was by David Harry, who wanted General Houston to be the next President—without committing himself on the vice-presidency.

There was no hurry about deciding that. The election would not be held until 1841; this was 1839.

XIX

SOME COURTLY LANGUAGE

Thursday, November 21st, 1839. At Austin—I was inquired of by an influential friend of the Presidents to know on what terms I would be his friend.

My reply was "Bid him disband his legions   submit his conduct to the general censure, & stand the judgment of a Texian Senate & Cato is his friend."

WHEN Dr. Jones edited his diary for publication he substituted "I" for "Cato." Perhaps he suspected that the Texans could not identify Cato; maybe he recollected that his acting of the role of the Censor was a little spotty.

Mirabeau B. Lamar kept his legions—and this Texan Cato never became his friend. There was no open warfare, no intention on the part of the senator from Brazoria to be a mere obstructionist—only a profound and deepening distrust of the capacity and judgment of the President and his advisers.

In conversation with the President & his Cabinet [when the Fourth Congress was a month old] I expressed the opinion that our *Scale* of operations was too large:—that this was a great fault, thinking & acting as a great nation, when we were but a first-rate *County* . . . & that we were about to realize the fable of the frog & the Ox—& burst. I was *hooted* at . . . "nous verrons."

On the principle that any executive, even Lamar, should be humored in the matter of appointments, Senator Jones voted more often to approve than to reject the President's nominees, although several of the appointees were distasteful to him.

On the confirmation of General Richard G. Dunlap, the man who superseded him in Washington, Senator Jones declined to record a vote—but he stayed in the Senate chamber to watch eight of his twelve colleagues vote to retire the general to private life. When the President nominated Barnard E. Bee to take Dunlap's place (with the rank of Chargé), the vote to confirm was unanimous, although Jones considered Bee "a very weak man."

Anson Jones's vote assured confirmation of two members of Lamar's Cabinet—the senator's host, Edwin Waller, as Postmaster General, and Louis P. Cooke as Secretary of the Navy. Both of them were Brazorians; Cooke had succeeded Jones in the House of the Third Congress. Much as Jones deplored James Webb's ignorance of diplomatic etiquette, he made no objection to the unanimous confirmation of him as Attorney General; he knew that a man might be a very good lawyer without knowing all the rules in the Appendix of Mr. Elliot's *Diplomatic Code.*

The Secretaryship of State gave His Excellency the President great perplexity—not uncertainty as to foreign policies, but as to which of his supporters should have the honor of signing the letters that implemented them.

During the year following the departure of Barnard E. Bee on his Mexican mission, after less than two months as Secretary of State, Lamar was unable, as he explained to the senators, "to fill said vacancy with entire satisfaction to myself." Politicians and citizens began to wonder, as month after month passed, if the President intended to leave the premier post of his Cabinet unfilled the remainder of his term.

James Webb, Vice-President Burnet, Judge Webb again, Nathaniel Amory, then the Vice-President once more signed communications as Acting Secretary during 1839. Actually, Lamar was keeping the place open, hoping to placate General Henderson with it—if that gentleman ever got home. By 1839 Henderson was as experienced a diplomat as the Republic had: he had been Houston's Secretary of State, and three years in Paris and London had made him a sort of career diplomat. Henderson, however, was honeymooning after his marriage to Frances Cox in Paris, and no one knew when he would return to Texas. Meantime criticism of Vice-President Burnet's plural officeholding became so insistent that Burnet quit the State Department on January 20, 1840.

Lamar then nominated Abner S. Lipscomb to be Secretary of State, and the senators unanimously confirmed the appointment. Secretary Lipscomb remained in the office about four months— one of the longer tenures of this administration, during which headship of the State Department changed thirteen times. The senators recognized, of course, that Lamar was actually his own Secretary of State; in the opinion of at least one of them it made no great difference who bore the title.

Anson Jones, the only Texas senator with an hour's experience in diplomacy, was chairman of the committee on foreign relations. His colleagues were Stephen H. Everitt, M.D., of Jasper (who had been chairman of the committee in previous Congresses) and Francis Moore, Jr., M.D., editor of the Houston *Telegraph and Texas Register*—an all-medical cast.

As the session got under way and Chairman Jones examined more closely President Lamar's vigorous, if somewhat desperate, foreign policy, he modified some opinions he had formed in Washington. There, as he heard at second and third hand of the apparently quixotic and unrelated schemes that Lamar and his friends were laying, Jones had been certain that no good could come of any of them. Now in the Senate, theoretically if not actually sharing responsibility with the President for foreign policies, he was not so sure.

Among so many plans there must be a few sensible ones; and Jones recognized that, no matter how much Lamar's policies diverged from a true course, there was no constitutional way to reverse the direction of foreign affairs until the end of the President's term—two years off. Some of the less objectionable schemes of the administration should perhaps be given a fair trial. If they failed, the onus would rest upon Lamar. If they succeeded, the country would profit.

Senator Jones's first report on foreign relations urged his colleagues to give the President a free rein in one matter that he had once pronounced "a foolish project . . . a shallow proceeding which will probably result in no good." The President informed the Senate in secret session, December 12, 1839, that he had sent a secret agent to negotiate peace with Mexico, authorized to pay five million dollars if necessary. So secret was the whole business that His Excellency declined to reveal his agent's name "even to the honorable congress," but he did communicate the instructions governing the mission.

Privately, if not officially, Chairman Jones knew that the agent was James Treat; before leaving the United States Jones had

had "a long conversation with him on the subject of a treaty with Mexico."

This secret message was "on motion of Mr. Jones of Ba. referred to the Committee on Foreign relations." Six days later he and W. Lawrence of the House committee reported their "most intire gratification" that "the anxious deliberations of the Executive" had resulted in a plan "marked by forecast, discretion and wisdom."

The plan was to offer Mexico five million dollars for a clear title to the land between the Nueces and Rio Grande—claimed by Texas since 1836, but never a part of Mexican or Spanish Texas—plus unequivocal acknowledgment of Texan independence, plus an advantageous trade treaty.

Chairman Jones thriftily pointed out that war to obtain peace would cost more in two years than five million, "to say nothing of the loss of human life" and the economic and social dislocation that war would entail. On the other hand, if peace were assured, Texas property values would increase "at least fourfold" within five years.

Texas, he believed, could count upon the active aid "of a power not less distinguished for the magnanimity of her policy than the extent of her resources" in this negotiation. Lord Palmerston—Christopher Hughes's British friend Palmerston—had hinted as much in Parliament and confirmed it in a conversation with General James Hamilton, who had just returned to Texas from London.

There was a beautiful Hamiltonian scheme. Mexico had defaulted on bonds owned by Britishers to the amount of about five million dollars, and she was now offering to exchange the worthless bonds for grants of lands in Texas, which Mexico and England still regarded as legally a part of Mexico. If that arrangement were made, England would have additional reason to refuse to recognize the independence of Texas, and she would not encourage Mexico to acknowledge it. Why not agree that Texas would redeem those worthless Mexican bonds by paying the proceeds of the loan directly to the British bondholders? That would create powerful British backing for peace between Texas and Mexico and relieve Mexico of a burdensome debt which she had no prospect of paying. The scheme was complicated, but it might work.

Joint resolutions passed on Jones's recommendation expressed "entire approbation [with] the present policy of the Executive for establishing relations of peace with Mexico"; empowered him to appoint a commissioner to effect it; authorized borrowing at six per cent the sum required, and stipulated that Great Britain was to be asked to guarantee the faithful performance of the treaty. Chairman Jones also stipulated that General James Hamilton, Texan agent for western Europe, was to be given a copy of the report signed by him and Mr. Lawrence.

While the resolutions were pending, Senator Jones "spent the evening with Gen Houston   Gen Hamilton   Mr. Labrans and others. Gen H. proposed a correspondence which I accepted and agreed to an arrangement with him in which some English Gentlemen are concerned."

In January 1840 a wagon train of carpets, tapestries, carved and gilded furniture, paintings, books, fine wines, and bric-a-brac from Paris and New Orleans was creaking toward Austin from Houston, consigned to Count Alphonse de Saligny, Chargé of the King of the French. They were to make habitable the first European legation in the Republic of Texas and give a touch of Old World charm to the frontier capital. Dr. Jones had known this Frenchman in Washington, and he wanted to do everything he could for him in Texas. He introduced him officially to the Senate in February. In August, Saligny bought one of Jones's Austin lots for bona fide money. (The count had thriftily used counterfeit currency to pay his teamsters.)

In the routine business of the Senate, Jones played the role he had played in the House of the Second Congress, except that for obvious reasons he was not chosen to escort the President when he visited the Congress. Originally assigned to the committees on foreign relations, public lands, and education, Jones was later added to those on finance, post offices, and roads, and became chairman of the judiciary committee. Day after day he raised points of order, moved to refer matters to committees, moved for secret sessions, moved to open the doors, moved to have reports printed, moved adjournment. Vice-President Burnet ap-

pointed him to almost as many special committees as Speaker
Rowe had in 1838–39.

Seldom did he allow his dislike for Lamar to flare in debate,
but when a senator characterized a resolution demanding information from the President "indecorous and disrespectful . . .
unworthy of a gentleman or senator," Jones of Brazoria solemnly
asked

if the honorable gentleman from Nacogdoches would do the senate
the favor, to submit some code of refinement and etiquette, by which
they can address His Excellency the President of the Republic of
Texas:—sir, shall we do it in the grand oriental style? In French,
Italian, Hebrew, or Spanish? Or will he invent some new and courtly
language in which we shall salute his royal ears? Sir, if His Excellency is too dignified to listen to common language, he had better not
preside over the destiny of this nation!

Occasionally Senator Jones was as resolute as a Lamar partisan
in defending presidential prerogatives. A senator complained that
he could never find the President or his secretary when he had
official business with His Excellency and proposed that the Senate
prescribe the hours which Lamar's secretary should spend in the
President's office. Oliver Jones supported the proposal, convinced
that the slipshod manner in which the executive office was being
managed had resulted in

deceptive management . . . even fraud in some bills; some had been
lost—some altered and others disposed of in other ways. . . . Mr.
Jones said he had frequently gone to the Executive office, and as
often gone "up the hill," but could never be honored with a sight
of His Excellency. It is universally known, said Mr. J., that he is but
seldom to be found at home; and if his Excellency and his Excellency's Secretary are too dignified to condescend to hold official intercourse with committees of Congress, he thought it high time to quit
business and go home.

Mr. Jones of B. did not agree with Cousin Oliver as to the
remedy for the situation. The Senate, he thought, had no jurisdiction over the comings and goings of His Excellency's office
help; and he "doubted not but that the President if properly
called on, would give every satisfaction, and enable the com-

mittee to know when and where to find him." Mr. Jones of B. "trusted the resolution would be rejected," but he declined to vote upon it.

The basic weakness of the Republic of Texas was its finances. During the fiscal year 1839–40 the Treasury had received $458,919.86 in Texas money (worth $92,000 specie)—about one third of it from the sale of Austin city lots—and had put in circulation audited drafts and certificates "nearly ten times as much as the gross revenue."

By 1840, despite (perhaps because of) the multitude of stratagems the Republic had devised "to meet the various tastes and fancies of those with whom it had dealings, or wished to have dealings," the problem had become extremely complicated.

Did a man wish to lend money to it? He had the choice [Gouge explained] of four loans: namely, the one hundred thousand dollar loan act, and the million dollar loan act of the Provisional Government (both of which remained unrepealed) ; and the million and the five million loan acts of the Republic.

Was the Republic indebted to him? He received an audited draft. This he might keep if he chose, or pay it in for land-dues. Did not this satisfy him? He could exchange his audited draft for treasury notes, which were receivable for all public dues. Was not this satisfactory? Then he could receive in exchange for it treasury bonds bearing eight per cent interest. If he chose to keep them, the interest would be constantly accumulating; and if he should have immediate use for them, they were receivable everywhere in public payments. Did not even this satisfy him? Then he could fund his draft in ten per cent stock, the interest on which was payable semiannually "in gold and silver."

The plight of Texas seemed almost hopeless to the senator from Brazoria. As a member of the finance committee, he tried to teach his colleagues the rudiments of sound finance, but they were not apt pupils. It was not that they were stupid; he thought they lacked the *"honesty* and *patriotism"* to face the facts.

Anson Jones found himself slipping back into the groove of earlier experience. Fraternalism had helped him find himself and had given him training that carried him far politically. In Texas Masonry he had started at the top—head of both his local lodge and the Grand Lodge. As he acclimated himself once more to

Texas and Texas politics, he instinctively turned to Masonry. He was not now seeking a training ground or even an instrumentality; he was obeying the impulse to have part in an enterprise he had helped to start.

The Masonic Grand Lodge, like other institutions that ministered to, or depended upon, the personnel of government, had followed the capital from Houston to Austin; and Anson Jones was on hand for the first "Special Grand Convocation" there December 8. Brother Branch T. Archer, who was rounding out his year as Grand Master, magnanimously appointed Brother Jones Senior Grand Warden pro tem.

The following Sunday, Congressman Samuel M. Williams of Galveston succeeded to the Grand Mastership, although Archer was willing to serve another term. Grand Secretary George Fisher and Grand Treasurer Thomas G. Western were re-elected. Adolphus Sterne of Nacogdoches succeeded Anthony Butler as Senior Grand Warden; Alexander Russell took the place of C. Dart as Junior Grand Warden. That afternoon they were installed and "proclaimed by the Grand Marshall *pro tem* as such"; and the meeting "was closed in ample form, at 5 o'clock P.M., in peace and harmony."

Jones's Masonic activity was henceforth to be a sort of barometer of his mood. During his first year at Austin he seldom missed a meeting of the Grand Lodge and served on innumerable committees; thereafter he was often absent. He had personal preoccupations, and some of the despair he was beginning to feel for the future of Texas he perhaps unconsciously applied to the future of the Grand Lodge. True, Lamar was not a member, but many of his mercurial advisers were.

Senator Jones's interest in public affairs was perceptibly waning. He said it was because this "crazy administration have nearly ruined the country"; but that was not the sole, or even the principal, reason. True, his matter-of-fact, puritanical spirit was jarred at the way Lamar's friends were trying to make Texans forget each grandiose failure by projecting another scheme more appealing to the imagination, while all the time the value of currency was sinking, the revenue dwindling, and no scheme that an economist could approve emanated from the Cabinet. It was also true that Congress, having become accustomed to spending lavishly money that did not exist, continued to make appropriations on the basis of estimates double or treble the probable revenues.

All of this unquestionably irked methodical Senator Jones, but the principal reason for his growing distaste for Texan politics was that his attention was focused elsewhere.

As the forty-three days of the Fourth Congress passed, Senator Jones found himself giving more thought to his own immediate future than to unsolved problems of his nation. He had discovered that there was little one man could do to right the ship of state. At first he was willing to "waste my strength in unavailing and hopeless efforts"; then he decided "to let the vessel drift" and devote his energy to things that promised more success. His senatorial pay was $215 for the session, and he was paying $75 a month for table board. He would seek economic security and provide for his personal happiness.

This new town of Austin, he concluded, soon "must be a place of some importance; its situation & the many natural beauties it possesses insures this event."

It was already beginning to look like a city, despite gibes of Houston newspapers still incensed over the moving of the capital, despite vocal hostility of "eastern" congressmen—notably Mr. Houston of San Augustine—in spite, even, of Indian raids. Four-yoke ox teams brought in great loads of fine fat buffalo and venison from the Brazos for Austin dinner tables, and other teams were hauling in corn and potatoes.

The blazed trails to Austin, however, were new and muddy, and the services of supply occasionally failed. On Christmas Day the *Gazette* broke a two-week silence to explain the paper shortage:

We have five wagons at present, loaded with paper, materials, and another press on their way; a part of them have been already twenty-seven days out of Houston.

The helpful *Morning Star* reported for the enjoyment of Houstonians who had not "followed the government":

By letter received from Austin, we learn that *mattresses* are particularly in demand, and that there is not one to be obtained at any price. The good people of that city have got tired of sleeping upon blankets and would like an immediate and plentiful supply of beds.

Candles are selling at $9 per pound—an excellent reason why the people want beds, as nobody can afford to sit up long after dark; and hard floors, with only a blanket or two, are not so very agreeable these long winter nights.

On January 15, 1840, an unofficial census showed that Austin's population at the end of six months was 856. The 711 white citizens included 550 grown men, 61 ladies, 100 children; there were 145 blacks to wait on them. The city had thirty-five mechanics, nine stores, nine groceries, six faro banks, two printing offices, two tailor shops, two silversmiths, six inns, four lawyers, six physicians, and "only about 20 gamblers," recorded the census taker, who was chaplain of the Senate. Of the 856 souls in Austin, only seventy-two were church members, he added.

A month earlier the Houston *Telegraph* had estimated Austin's population as "three or four hundred, mostly visitors."

Without, for the present, changing his legal residence—he had been pledged to serve still another year in the Senate—Jones "abandoned all idea of resuming practice in Brazoria" and decided to become a practitioner in Austin, where medical men were almost as scarce as they had been in Brazoria seven years before.

The bachelor Republic was becoming tamer, what with Thomas J. Rusk and Sam Houston addressing Sunday-school meetings and some statesmen getting married almost every month. J. Pinckney Henderson brought to Austin the bride he had married in France and introduced Senator Jones to her at church, just six days after Jones's forty-second "birthday passed without any celebration." A married man would have had some notice taken of his birthday!

At Mrs. Eberle's hotel, where the senator from Brazoria began boarding in January, he was watching and abetting romance. Mrs. Rebecca Greenleaf Westover McIntyre of San Patricio was a guest there, while waiting for the Republic to pay her for oxen and carts lost in 1836. She had come to Texas in 1834, lost her first husband in the Goliad massacre, her second by drowning, and now she needed expert aid to get her claim adjusted.

Both of the Senators Jones—Anson of Brazoria, Oliver of Austin County—became "earnestly interested" in the plight of this comely, forty-year-old widow. They pushed through the Senate the joint resolution awarding her $1,100. With that Cousin Anson rested, but Cousin Oliver, one of the elder bachelors of the Republic, did not. "With his usual decision of character, he determined at the moment of introduction . . . 'There is a woman that I would marry!' "

Exactly two weeks after the lady's claim had been adjusted the senator from Brazoria "assisted at the wedding of the Hon. Oliver Jones & Mrs. McIntyre. Gen Rusk officiating as Judge on the occasion."

Henderson was married; Cousin Oliver was married; gossip said that Lamar himself would soon be married. Celibacy in the once-bachelor Republic was becoming conspicuous.

On February 5 Jones wrote in his diary: "Senate adjourned . . . Freedom and liberty . . . once again restored. *'Aucun J' respire.'* " Dr. Jones—he was beginning once more to think of himself as a physician—spent two days "bidding farewell &c. to the various members."

When they were gone, he took Mary McCrory riding.

Until the second Monday of next November the Doctor would have no public responsibilities. He had done his duty for Texas until the Fifth Congress should convene. He was sure that His Excellency was too glad to be rid of congressional heckling to call an extra session.

Mr. Jones of B. became Anson Jones, M.D., and placed a sign to that effect on the house lately occupied by the secretary of the Senate. That night Mr. Tod shot Lieutenant Crary; presumably Dr. Jones got his first Austin patient.

One Saturday Dr. Jones "spent the morning at Mrs. Bullock's. Mary was there." Two weeks later he "spent the day with Mary," then he spent a week doing something that he recorded, then tore out of his diary. At the end of that week, on March 12, he "commenced Boarding at Mr Woodruff's."

The next day was Friday the thirteenth. Jones

woke up at night with the alarm of "Indians." The suburbs of the town were plundered of all the Horses and Ward & Hedley killed & scalped—heard the cries of the latter while under the hands of the Indians.

Nine days later

news came in from San Antonio of the destruction of the Com-
manches who came in for the purpose of celebrating a Treaty and of
the Death of Eight of our most valuable citizens [in the Council
House fight] whose lives appear to have been most wantonly sacri-
ficed. San Anna was whipped with only seven killed!

Thereafter Austin had "constant alarms of Indians and Mexicans" and "heavy & constant rains," but Dr. Jones pushed ahead
with the cottage he was building. April 27 he "made preparations
to move from the Office on Congress Avenue—The Carpenter
finished my house on Pecan Street which has cost a little over
twenty three hundred dollars Texas money exclusive of the Lot
on which it stands."

Dr. Jones was happy as he dared to be. There was enough
"business" to keep him occupied, although sickness was not so
prevalent as it had been in Brazoria and Houston. He was buying
more lots and leagues and labores and lending money for good
interest. There was a pleasant rumor that he would be the next
Vice-President of Texas.

It was spring—and the Valley of the Colorado was very beautiful. Anson Jones was discovering again what a pleasant, comfortable companion Mary McCrory was. When he wanted to see
Mary he did not have to spend the evening playing chess with Mr.
Woodruff.

They resumed their plan-making where diplomacy had interrupted it in 1838. Mary had been assembling her trousseau for
nearly three years, but as the day of the wedding neared she found
that she needed additional finery not to be had in any of the
nine stores of Austin. An oxcart fetched what she needed from
Houston.

Mary's trousseau was complete. The doctor's house was ready
for occupancy; his public duties temporarily finished. When the
county clerk began issuing marriage licenses in Austin on May 7,
every reason for delay had disappeared. Dr. Jones went to the log
courthouse on Saturday, May 16, bought the second marriage
license issued in Travis County, made an appointment with Chief
Justice Smith—whose election he had opposed—for the next day,
and promised him a fifty-dollar fee.

The *Texas Sentinel* of May 23, 1840, chronicled the culmination of romance:

MARRIED.—In this city, on Sunday morning last, by Judge J. W. Smith, Hon. ANSON JONES, of Brazoria, to MRS. MARY McCRORY of this city.

The complete story of the doctor's marriage, as told by him, is among the masterpieces of laconic writing. After he and Mary had lived happily together for ten years, he wrote in his memoirs:

At this period [during the Second Congress] I became engaged to be married to my present wife, Mrs. Mary McCrory. The marriage was fixed for the last of the month [June]; in the meantime I again made a visit to Brazoria on private business. . . . In consequence of accepting [in June] this appointment [Minister to the United States], the marriage arrangement was postponed until I should return from Washington city, which . . . was understood would be in the course of one year. . . . Having abandoned all idea of resuming practice in Brazoria . . . I, at the close of the session of Congress [February 1840] commenced building myself a house on Pecan Street. On the 17th of May I was married, and spent the summer principally in making improvements on my place, or in doing nothing. . . .

These were his diary jottings for the three weeks that included his wedding day:

Wed. [May] 13th. Thursd. 14th   Frid 15 At Austin   Sat 16th Do. Sunday Morng May 17th. Married. Monday 18th. wrote disclaimer denying the authorship of "Juvenus" & other pieces. Tues. 19th   Wed. 20th   Thursd. 21st   Fri 22d   Sat 23d   Sun 24th Mond 25th at Austin   Tuesd. 26th   Wed 27   Thursd 28   Fri 29 Sat 30th   Sund 31 At Austin and housekeeping at my residence on Pecan St. Monday June 1st. At a loss what to be doing—consequently doing nothing. . . .

XX

NOT BY MY VOTE . . .

THE senator from Brazoria and Mrs. Jones became a part of the decorous social life of Austin, which the doctor found pleasant and professionally profitable. For several months he relaxed and enjoyed the sensation of living as a private citizen.

A child was on the way.

A man with a wife and child dependent upon him must have an estate. Not that Dr. Jones had ever lost sight of his goal of becoming "as wealthy as any man in Texas"; thrift was a part of his nature. He had a certain expertness in private, as well as public, finance. But as the year 1840 passed, this matter of achieving economic security subtly changed from a thing desirable to something imperative. The route to it did not lie through office-holding.

As his friend George K. Teulon of the Austin *City Gazette* pointed out that fall, day laborers were better paid in Texas than the civil servants of the Republic.

Congress will soon convene, and the pay of its members will not purchase their food. The members cannot long live upon patriotism; and many of them have nothing else but that and their pay to live upon.

Dr. Jones was more fortunate than some of his colleagues. In addition to patriotism and a senatorial stipend, he had his lands and lots, the interest on loans, and an income from medical practice—which would be larger if he did not have to attend the Senate every day and sit up half the nights in committee meetings.

He was getting his estate in order. In November he cleared up the last of those New Orleans debts by deeding two ten-acre lots in Galveston to Samuel Lucas "in full pay^mt. of his Claim"—the suit against Jones & Spear for $445.72 that had driven the

doctor to Texas in 1833. How long ago and far away that seemed.
Later that month he "wrote to Sister Almira, offered her & her
Children 1,000 acres of Land if she removed to Texas." From
hopeless debtor to landed proprietor, dispensing estates with generosity—that was the economic saga of Jones's first seven years
in Texas.

In September he left his comfortable Austin cottage to spend
eight weeks handshaking among his Brazoria constituents, but
his heart was not in politics. He wrote Mary on October 14:

I am much disposed to fix myself here in future and to leave the
noise and clamor of politics entirely. I regret, indeed, that I ever
entered their arena at all.

The sort of things that politicians should delight in irked him.
The town of Brazoria itself jarred him, so much had it (and he)
changed since 1838.

Sat. 17th   Wasted at McNeel's in yielding to a wish on their part
to have the reputation of associating with me at the cheap rate of
giving me something to eat.
Sun. 18th   Disgusted with them & their relative Mills   left &
returned to Brazoria. . . . Mon 19th   Brazoria, although wealthy
is on the score of the more magnanimous virtues every way to be
contemned.

Two days after he returned to his cottage in Austin from his
legal home in Brazoria he "rather mechanically" took his seat
in the Senate of the Fifth Congress "with Knaves & fools," intent
only upon "making a close of my services to the public and
returning to the practice of my profession. . . ."

At the Texas White House, atop its steep hill, the thought-
fulness of a Galveston admirer of His Excellency the President
had replenished the cellar before Congress convened. James Love
shipped Lamar two barrels of whisky,

one as good as was ever tasted at 1.50 the other good at 40.cts. the
first you may give your friends, the other to those who profess to be
so but are not, and by all means to those who want office, short
rations is best for them.

Dr. Jones drank from neither barrel.

He was convinced that "little can or will be done for Texas

this Session, or while the present party are in existence." He
tested that opinion when he proposed "to repeal all the laws authorizing the issue of promissory Notes of the Government." One
senator joined him in voting for his resolution; everybody else
seemed content with the Lamar system of public finance. A month
later Jones confided to his diary: "If it were not for appearing to
yield too easily to adverse circumstances, I would resign my seat
in the Senate to-day."

The Brazorian was a little glad when

the President obtained leave of absence, the Vice President vacated
the chair of the Senate to assume the executive functions, and I
was chosen by one majority to fill his place [over Harvey Kendrick
of Matagorda, a fairly consistent supporter of administration poli-
cies]. Deciding questions of order suited me, gave me employment,
and filled up time which otherwise would have hung very unpleas-
antly on my hands; for, in the proceedings of a Congress, when the
government was rushing downward with hourly increasing velocity,
I, of course, could feel neither interest nor pleasure. It was at best
only "locking the stable door after the horse was stolen."

As senators debated, Mr. Jones of B. sat passively in the chair,
taking little part in molding legislation. His attitude could not
have been more impartial if he had actually been the Vice-
President, instead of a senator with a constituency. He had ceased
to hope; he had almost ceased to care what was done.

He took some pleasure in the unanimity with which the Senate
ratified treaties with Great Britain and the Netherlands and a
project for a treaty with Belgium; but privately he was wondering
if this shaky Republic would survive long enough to reap any advantages.

Acting President Burnet reported failure of negotiations with
Mexico and counseled Congress:

If the sword must decide the controversy, let the decision be
prompt and final. . . . Texas proper is bounded by the Rio Grande
—Texas, as defined by the sword, may comprehend the Sierra
Madre. Let the sword do its proper work.

Senator Jones was presiding over the Senate when a joint committee brought in a report on that recommendation. He did not
speak on the question, but he appreciated the cool sense of the

gentlemen who replied to oratory with a recitation of unpleasant
facts:

> Your committee are fully aware that it is a fact well known and
> long established that money is the sinews of war. . . . That we have
> neither money at home nor credit . . . abroad is an undeniable fact,
> how humiliating soever may be the acknowledgment. How, then,
> are we to sustain an army in the field? . . . For defensive measures,
> your committee know not. . . .
> Your committee are of opinion that it would be much easier to
> sustain an army beyond the Rio Grande than within our own ter-
> ritory; that there the war would be made to support the war. . . .

Tempting as the prospect of plundering Mexico was to some,
the Congress contented itself with disbanding the regular army,
laying up the navy, and reducing appropriations by two thirds.
It would not even approve President Lamar's proposal to occupy
the portion of New Mexico claimed by Texas since 1836. That
was a project to tempt adventurous Texans who would have preferred to march directly against the Halls of Montezuma.

But to His Excellency it was infinitely more than that. Ancient
Santa Fé was the place where caravans from northern Mexico
met wagon trains from Saint Louis, to exchange annually goods
worth twenty millions. If Santa Fé were—as all good Texans
believed—Texan territory, the President wanted the Texan flag
to wave over the Governor's palace and over the customhouse.
He saw a Texas revenue collector there doing better business than
the one at Galveston—receiving dues in gold and silver.

Legislators saw it as a mere conquest-and-glory scheme. They
declined to sanction the venture, but it did not occur to the solons
that they needed specifically to prohibit it. Senator Jones thought
the Fifth Congress had made its attitude clear enough.

His own distrust of the administration extended now even to
opposing some executive nominations. He helped reject Congressman William Menefee for the Secretaryship of the Treasury but
made no objections to John G. Chalmers, whom the Acting
President nominated for that post. Chalmers was a physician—a
ranchman and a merchant, too; he had arrived in Texas too
recently to have earned political enemies.

When Burnet asked the Senate to confirm Thomas William

Ward as commissioner of the General Land Office, the vote was 7 to 6—with the Senator from Brazoria voting aye. He liked that interesting Irishman who had come to Texas to fight in 1835 and lost a leg at Béxar.

Jones also voted with the majority to confirm Burnet's nomination of George W. Terrell as Secretary of State, sensing perhaps that Terrell would refuse to identify himself with the Lamar administration. "The day was," Congressman Sam Houston lamented, "when it was reputable to hold a place in the Cabinet. Those days are gone by, and days must pass ere we shall see those times again."

But Jones could not bring himself to vote for Branch T. Archer as Secretary of War, even though he was a fellow Brazorian and a fellow physician. The senator still had several scores against that gentleman, including the Texas Rail Road, Navigation, and Banking matter. His vote was not needed.

After Archer was confirmed (9 to 5) Major General Felix Huston called upon the senator from Brazoria to deliver a note from the new Secretary of War, inviting Jones to a duel. The senator had recently bought a thirty-dollar pair of holster pistols, but he was no more disposed to use them on Archer than he had been to shoot it out with Chief Justice Collinsworth in 1836. He replied on December 9:

> You complain of no *personal wrong* or *injury* which I have done you nor ask of me any redress. I can therefore only regard your note as intended to make a gratuitous, wanton, and unprovoked attack upon me, and more in the character of a malignant assassin seeking life than that of an honorable gentleman demanding satisfaction for any grievance.
>
> The charge in your note that I am a plunderer of public property is as false as it is contemptible—facts well known to yourself. You may perhaps be the defender of public property, but you will recollect it was not by my vote, and I sincerely regret that the defense of my country's interest has not fallen into better and abler hands. . . .

Colonel Barry Gillespie delivered the letter. The Secretary of War did not pursue the correspondence.

It was a month for exchanging challenges—and declinations— in Austin. Vice-President Burnet declared language used in the House by General Houston "personal and offensive" and demanded satisfaction, which the congressman from San Augustine declined to give him. The leaders of the anti-administration faction knew better ways to deal with members of the Lamar party.

Despite the personal feuds among the politicians, which the approach of the date for the national election accentuated, a semblance of official dignity and decorum was maintained during the congressional season. Acting President Burnet gave his first levee at the White House in January, and to it he invited the citizens of Austin as well as government officials. The Austin *City Gazette* was "pleased to see men of all parties attending, thus paying that respect which is due to the first officer of the Republic."

During the closing days of the Fifth Congress the retiring senator from Brazoria was bargaining with the retiring representative from Houston County, the Honorable Greenberry Horras Harrison. Mr. Harrison had married the widow of Jones's old friend George B. McKinstry, late Chief Justice of Brazoria. Their wedding had taken place in the White House on January 14, and despite his dislike of the official occupant of that mansion, Senator Jones had climbed the high hill to witness the ceremony. The Gentleman from Houston was remaining in Austin to publish *The Weekly Texian,* and his bride liked the cottage on Pecan Street which the Joneses intended to vacate as soon as their child was born. On February 2 the bargain was made: The Harrisons swapped the Joneses lands valued at $23,536 for the house (which had cost $2,300) and some of the senator's Austin lots. Even allowing for the depreciation of Texan currency and the general inflation, the doctor lost nothing on that deal.

Ten days later he added four dollars to his senatorial pay and mileage and bought a nine-hundred-dollar carriage—not so fine as His Excellency's dazzling equipage, but better adapted to the rough and muddy roads between Travis County and Brazoria. In his spare time the doctor was arranging his papers, packing household goods, methodically preparing to vacate the house on Pecan Street as soon as Mary could travel. He kept Mrs. Woodruff, Mrs. Harrison, and a hired Negro girl busy the day long, preparing for the two big events. The doctor knew all a man could know about the mysteries of childbirth and prided himself on his stoicism, but he found himself unaccountably nervous as he awaited the delivery of this child. He had been practicing obstetrics twenty-one years before he understood why prospective fathers behave as they do.

On February 25 he went downtown. The time was near, but he needed exercise and there were things he must attend to. He called at the blacksmith's to have the carriage readied for the long trip to Brazoria, bought twenty dollars' worth of "Cigars &c," paid thirty dollars for a ticket to a military ball and nine dollars for a quart of fine brandy. Next day he wrote in his diary:

26th About a quarter past One in the morning my Son Saml Houston was born, persons present Mrs. Eliza Faris, Mrs. Ann C. Harrison, Mrs. Woodruff & myself. In the evening of the same day a Ball was given to my friend Col. Wm. G. Cooke of the 1st Infantry.

A month later he put Mary and Sam Houston Jones in the new carriage and started for Brazoria. Behind him lay the new capital where "unsatisfactorily and unprofitably enough" he had sat out Senator Wharton's term in the Fourth and Fifth Congresses.

Anybody was welcome to that seat in the next Congress. Timothy Pilsbury got it.

Mr. Jones of B. was once more Anson Jones, M.D.

XXI

FAREWELL TO POLITICS

WHEN Anson Jones left Austin in the spring of 1841 he closed the door of politics behind him, but he did not lock it. On other occasions he had left office with gestures of renunciation. This time he made no public statement. He simply planned his future without regard to the results of the summer elections. *Vox populi* might call him from retirement. He did not count upon it—but the virus of politics was in his blood. He had not yet found a vaccine that gave him immunity.

Ever since the election of Lamar, Jones had at intervals given thought to which Texan could—if the Republic managed to survive Lamar's term—

remove the rubbish & wreck & begin to build anew from the foundation—if happily we shall have means. We may patch up the shaking concern for a year or two [he had thought in December 1839] but it is a discouraging and a thankless task.

The obvious man, people were saying, was Sam Houston. Jones had thought so, too, before he returned from Washington, but he was not so sure as he watched the performance of the Hero of San Jacinto in the Fourth and Fifth Congresses. Houston was leading the anti-administration bloc in the House of Representatives, apparently

only intent upon making Lamar's administration as odious as possible. . . . He is willing the government should be a failure [Jones wrote on New Year's Day, 1840] in order that he may have it to say there is no one but *"Old Sam"* that the people can depend upon, & that he is the only man that can successfully administer the Govt of Texas. Lamar is certainly no statesman, & he and his friends are ruining the country & going to the Devil as fast as Gen. Houston can possibly wish—— This he sees and chuckles at. . . . He is skillful to destroy his enemy. . . .

Vice-President Burnet had undeniable claims to the succession. As wartime executive, his services on the civilian front had been as notable as Houston's on the battlefield; and since 1838 his multiple assignments—president of the Senate, Acting Secretary of State, Acting President—had given him unrivaled insight into current executive problems. But he was handicapped by his close association with Lamar, whose political star was declining, as well as by his own personality traits.

David G. Burnet is a good honest man enough [Jones thought] has patriotism & means well enough, & has decided talent. But he lacks tact and judgment; & is always too much under the influence of his prejudices which are very powerful—he has every kind of sense but common sense, & consequently will never do for a Statesman.

Then there was always Thomas Jefferson Rusk, who had demonstrated his abilities in many fields—law, military command, Cabinet post—and had some of the frontier glamour that appealed to the Texans. Rusk declined the vice-presidency in 1836 because he was too young to hold the office. In 1838 he refused nomination for the presidency. Anson Jones, with some private doubts as to Rusk's fitness for any position requiring steadiness, had urged him to make the race. Now he was Chief Justice of the Supreme Court, which was holding its first session in a little "house belonging to Maj. A. Brigham, in the lower part of the city." Jones was sure that Rusk had "neither the learning, the application nor the character to do credit to the place" and before the next presidential election "will probably *'blow out.'* " Later Jones conceded that the Chief Justice "has more talent than I have given him credit for," but he feared "it is all for Demagogueism, cunning & treachery." It turned out that Rusk wanted neither the presidency nor the chief justiceship. He resigned after presiding over one brief term of the Court and refused to consider the presidency.

Old Governor Henry Smith, whose policies as provisional executive in 1835 had been partially vindicated by subsequent events, and whose fiscal ability had been demonstrated as Houston's Secretary of the Treasury, could "hardly succeed" as presidential candidate, Jones thought, but he might get in as Vice-President.

Talk that Anson Jones himself would be a candidate for the vice-presidency had begun in November 1839, when he presided over the dinner that launched Houston as a candidate for the presidency. The *Brazos Courier* the following February suggested a ticket headed by Houston and Jones. The Austin *Sentinel* promptly declared it "too early yet to agitate this exciting question" and a little later heard from Brazoria that it was likely that "neither the paper nor county would support either of them." Lawyer H. P. Brewster, editor of the *Brazos Courier,* had become a Lamar zealot and was doing "no small good lately to the administration party by his conduct of the Brazoria press; and has most effectually killed off Dr. Anson's Vice-Presidential asperations," General Green reported to Lamar. The Austin *City Gazette,* edited by Jones's friend, G. K. Teulon, enthusiastically seconded the Houston-Jones ticket

as guaranteeing to the world that the citizens of this republic are determined to support those men and those men only who are in favor of an economical government and retrenchment, at the coming election.

Texans had much to do in the year and a half before election besides speculate upon who would succeed Mr. Lamar and Mr. Burnet. For about a year the newspapers printed little gossip on that subject. Behind the scenes, however, the politicians were busy. Friends of the President were undertaking to create a permanent party to assure a continuation of the Lamar policies. His opponents were less busy. Most of them seemed to feel that time was on their side; they believed in "giving Lamar rope."

Political gossip that came to the President from over the Republic was full of optimism. Thomas G. Gordon reported from Houston:

Genl. Green and myself have electioneered with the people on our route to know their feelings towards your administration of their affairs—— I have not heard *one man* on the way speak but with satisfaction of the general course you have taken, and upon enquiry *here* find that all *honest* & good citizens approve of you and your measures, and none but gamblers, loafers and office seekers are Houston's friends. I am assured that not "ten good citizens here waited on Houston," who is here now and has been for some weeks. . . . It is all humbug to talk about Houston's popularity in the *East*.

From Galveston James Love wrote:

to judge from appearances I would say that the ranorous hostility heretofore existing against you is on the decline. . . . It is impossible that he [Sam Houston] can live, he is a bloated mass of corruption. And shou[ld] he live I cannot believe th[at] we are destined to that scourge.

There was actually no probability—only hope among his enemies—that Houston would die. His health was robust and his habits were undergoing a thorough and semi-permanent renovation. About the time that Anson Jones was marrying Mary Mc-Crory in Austin, General Houston was in Alabama marrying Margaret Lea. For the following half year "the Great Ex" was concerned exclusively with his domestic affairs and with the transformation of his personal habits under Mrs. Houston's supervision. Not since his arrival in Texas had the general been so silent upon public questions or apparently so unconcerned as to the fate of the Republic. He wrote only one political letter between May and December that year. Like a great bear, Houston was hibernating until intuition told him it was time to emerge.

Dr. Jones, too, had tried to avoid thinking of politics, but he found it difficult. Until March 1841 he lived in the capital, where politicians swarmed, and he read the newspapers. The Austinians delighted to banquet political and military heroes, and Dr. Jones was their favorite toastmaster. Some weeks he presided over two dinners; some weeks there were none; but whenever the doctor presided, he managed affairs with skill and to the satisfaction of everyone.

Although men of all shades of opinion were present [the *Gazette* said of the General Burleson banquet in 1840], not a single toast was offered calculated in the slightest degree to wound the feelings of even the most sensitive.

Toastmaster Jones himself set the pattern. His toast was to

Our Mother and Our Grand Mother—The United States and England: The former can show her kindness by keeping her Indians at home, the latter by acknowledging our independence; Justice demands that both should be done.

A putative candidate did well to confine himself to issues which would not be decided by Texan voters. None of these fifteen-dollar-plate banquets had been ostensibly political, and it had done the doctor no harm to figure in the public prints, whether his vocation was to be medicine or politics, or both.

The ill luck which dogged President Lamar's policies had beset also the efforts to form a permanent Lamar party, according to capital gossip, as Jones was leaving Austin.

General Lamar has returned & taken the helm of government into his own hands [Henry Millard wrote from Austin, March 16, 1841]. Him and Burnet are at outs, Lamar has declared himself in favor of Sam Houston for next president, in fact that appears to be the order of the day, you would be surprised to see all the heads of departments, Beaureaus & clerks who were so strong for Burnet . . . all advocating the Election of Sam Houston. Even they say to old Doct. Archer & Mayfield. Burnet is completely done, he could not now in the western counties be elected fiddler Genl to the old chief.

H. J. Jewett thought that the rupture between the two executive officers "never will be healed. Burnet treated Lamar ungenerously and by his conduct has completely alienated Gen Lamar's friends from him." Texans, James Love philosophized, "must have some one to abuse, at present they seem to have fallen on Burnet."

That had been the talk at the capital when Anson Jones packed his goods to move to Brazoria. The muddlement of Texan politics made 1841 a good time to bow himself out of the picture for good. On the other hand, he was shrewd enough to know that this very muddlement offered better opportunities to a politically ambitious man than placid times. All things considered, Brazoria County was a better place than Austin from which to observe developments. It would be easier there to avoid conversations on dangerous political topics; and, if he should after all determine to have no further part in politics, Brazoria was the place for him to practice medicine.

The Jones family reached Brazoria County on April 11. Mrs.

Jones and little Sam visited at Columbia with Mrs. Josiah Bell while the doctor went to see former patients and old political associates along the Brazos and San Bernard. He spent three days in the town of Brazoria, a day with John W. Cloud on Oyster Creek, and a day with Judge Waller. Then he went, with Senator W. H. Daingerfield of Béxar, to Houston and Galveston for a week. The doctor needed medical supplies for his new office— and political leaders on the coast wanted to confer with him. He was keeping both possibilities—medical business and politics— open.

At the end of April he was back in Columbia, willing to make the race for the vice-presidency. "He informed me on yesterday," Henry Smith wrote F. R. Lubbock from Brazoria on May 1, "that he would be a candidate." Smith and Jones had often discussed the vice-presidency during the sessions of the Fifth Congress, and Smith had agreed months before that he would not run if Jones did.

A week later the courthouse in Brazoria rang with oratory. Chief Justice William P. Scott presided over the mass meeting and John W. Cloud reviewed, with appropriate superlatives, Dr. Jones's public career in Texas and hailed him as the people's choice for Vice-President. He was the best-fitted man in Texas for the place.

Moreover, sir, he is the intimate personal and staunch political friend of General HOUSTON. . . . he, himself has declared that it is his wish, should he run for office, that the name of ANSON JONES should be coupled with his own. . . . The Hon. ANSON JONES is prominently deserving of his country's suffrages, from his own intrinsic talents, from his correct affections; and from being Gen HOUSTON's choice!

Jones's old enemy, William J. Russell, seconded the nomination, and a committee of five informed the doctor of the desires of his fellow Brazorians.

Two days after the Brazoria meeting a similar rally of Fort Bend County citizens at Richmond nominated Edward Burleson for the vice-presidency. At San Felipe, Cousin Oliver Jones presided over a "large concourse of people" who heard Anson Jones extolled by William H. Jack and, with three dissenting votes, called upon him to accept the nomination. Memucan Hunt and William Menefee also entered the race.

For its support of Anson Jones, the Austin *City Gazette* said on May 26, 1841, "comment or apology to our readers we deem altogether uncalled for and unnecessary." The vice-presidency was of prime importance.

We must remember, fellow-citizens [Editor Teulon continued], that in electing a Vice President you sometimes elect a President; in proof of this, it can hardly be necessary for us to refer to recent events [the death of President Harrison, April 4] in the United States.

As Dr. Jones waited to see how the vice-presidential boom would develop, he settled down to medicine and surgery. After visiting with such old political friends as Colonel William G. Hill and Dr. Phelps, he rented Shierburn's store building in Columbia for twelve dollars a month and opened his office.

He was "constantly engaged in Practice" for more than two months, but the postal service of the Republic, poor as it was, brought him enough mail to prevent complete concentration upon his "business." G. K. Teulon of Austin, volunteer public relations director of the Jones campaign, was insisting that the doctor tell him what his plans were. James Burke wrote from Montgomery and Houston urging that the doctor go on a campaign tour, as General Hunt was doing. J. Pinckney Henderson wanted Jones to visit eastern Texas to allay the reports industriously circulated that he opposed the interests of that section. There were "a hundred or more" letters "from men of all parties" urging Jones to tour the Republic. Vice-presidential candidacy was more complicated and burdensome than the doctor had anticipated.

At the capital, the President of the Republic, rid of the Congress that would not sanction his Santa Fé expedition, was making a last, very great, gamble. Atop his high hill in Austin he was writing resounding proclamations to welcome mestizo New Mexicans into the fellowship of Nordic Texas. Hugh McLeod, in a little cabin on Congress Avenue, was planning the route, and from all parts of the Republic—even from the United States— volunteers were coming to march to New Mexico.

The President, never a legalist or a financier, counted confidently upon the success of his march on Santa Fé. When it succeeded, most of the economic problems of Texas would disappear —and its success would atone for the earlier misfortunes of his administration. He never anticipated failure.

Everything here is alive with the Santa Fé expedition [A. C. Hyde wrote Jones from the capital May 27], which will . . . cost the Government about half a million. Things are getting on worse than ever in the departments, they are paying no attention to any of the acts of Congress. It is an awful state of things that our Government should be in the hands of such men. . . .

Ex-Senator Jones agreed. He thought it a "despotic exercise of executive power, which no *monarch* would have dared venture upon in these times"; Congress had, "in effect, positively inhibited" it. He recorded for posterity that he had voted against it every time it was before the Senate—and awaited news of the debacle. It could, he felt, be only "a chase of silly hopes and fears, begun in folly, closed in tears."

At the end of July, Jones decided that his original impulse to retire from politics was the correct one, and he wrote his chief supporters in Houston of his decision to withdraw. Promptly came the answers:

I was present with the persons in consultation [wrote W. H. H. Johnston] and can say I never saw persons more zealous in any cause than they appeared to be in yours. . . . I am authorized to say to you for Col. Fisher, that anything he can do towards forwarding your election in a pecuniary point of view, will be done with pleasure; (and you know he is not slow). I advise you to come over by all means and see them; I am confident you will not regret it. . . .

Thomas G. Western, F. R. Lubbock, I. N. Moreland, George Fisher, and Dr. A. Ewing sent a full report of the Jones caucus by the same courier. They did not intend to allow the doctor to quit the race, and they considered his suggestion that the Jones supporters compromise with the friends of Burleson or Hunt about as sensible as recommending an "amalgamation . . . of oil and vinegar." They wrote him August 7:

We find no reasonable excuse for your position . . . and much less for that part relating to pecuniary means; for "where there's a *will* there's a *way*." Your doctrine of not making an electioneering tour through the country is not *tenable*, at least at *present* in Texas.

. . . The position Texas now occupies is that of a people, free, un-shackled, and untrammelled, by the influence of any clans; but it is nevertheless *absolutely* necessary for a candidate to make a tour, especially in the populated and commercial points, inasmuch as the population is a transient one; and much as you may be known in your own and other counties, yet the present population of this city, in its great majority, does not know you (personally).

. . . come without delay to this place. . . . The press—personal services, industry and labor, and pecuniary means . . . all will be necessary to be called into requisition. . . . Your presence will unite all, and a united, strong pull, will carry the point without fail. You *must* arise from your lethargy . . . we deprecate, in common with you, *"Talia augilia* and *defensores istos,"* yet the *time* and circumstances require it.

A week later Jones was in Houston explaining his position to his friends:

The sacrifice is too great. I do not wish the office; I have not the means to spare; and if I had, I am opposed *"toto coelo"* to such a course [electioneering]. Propriety, therefore, requires me to decline.

Anson Jones, M.D., returned to his improvised office in Shier-burn's store building, took lodgings for his family and servant at Mr. Ammon Underwood's, and devoted himself exclusively to his patients.

By fall I had succeeded in establishing a business about as extensive as I could attend to. But my office-holding had impoverished me, and embarrassed my affairs just at a time when the wants and expenses of a family were beginning to be felt.

While the doctor "was beginning to emerge from these difficulties," he watched with singular detachment the acrimonious presidential contest between Burnet and Houston. Both loved a political fight and neither was squeamish about his tactics. Immigrants recently from the States said the campaign surpassed in bitterness the "hard cider" campaign of 1840. It was great fun for the Texans, whose opportunities for amusement were limited. Few of them agreed with the editor of the Houston *Morning Star,* who sighed, two weeks before election day:

We should be heartily glad when this political canvas is over. For we are tired of the eternal din of politics, politics, politics. Now politics won't make our bread or take it away.

The result was never really in doubt; the election was a sort of referendum on two questions: Is Texas more prosperous now than when Lamar became President? Is Sam Houston a great man? The voters answered the first question "No," and the second "Yes," two to one.

The vice-presidential canvass was less exciting, but the vote was closer. The *Texas Sentinel* thought "the friends of Dr. Jones will generally cast their votes for Burleson," and it was the *Morning Star's* "humble opinion since Dr. Jones has resigned, that the country is not going to suffer much whoever is elected." Memucan Hunt tried to visit every county to ask for votes. "I never saw a man more zealously engaged in a cause," James Webb declared, "did his life depend upon success, he could not use greater exerti[on]s to obtain it." Edward Burleson refused, like Jones, to make a speaking tour. He wrote from Bastrop:

Were my pecuniary ability ample, and my time unemployed, both by domestic labor, and almost weekly defense of the frontiers against the merciless savage, I am principled against any individual electioneering for so high an office.

The voters preferred the frontier hero to the man who appeared so eager for the position. Burleson carried thirty of the thirty-six counties. He received 6,141 votes; Hunt, 4,336.

During the election campaign, and for two months thereafter, Anson Jones, M.D., attended to his business in Brazoria County with the singleness of devotion he had not felt since 1836. It was good to be a country doctor—and profitable, too.

XXII

WITHOUT MONEY, WITHOUT CREDIT . . .

THE election of 1841 marked the end of an era in Texas. The tally sheet of Lamar's three years of great plans, great activity, great spending—and great calamities—was so thick with debits and credits that it would be years before the Texans could strike a true balance. Of one thing, however, two thirds of them were certain in 1841: The Republic needed a leader who could determine policies by studying the immediate situation as closely as he did the ultimate goals. They thought the new President could do it—and so did he. "Our country can recover itself, and, with the blessing of God, its regeneration is certain. . . . It is the voice of the people, it will be done. . . . I will lay my shoulder to the wheel," Houston announced November 25, as he traveled toward Austin to assume what he considered a receivership of a bankrupt enterprise.

The day before he wrote a single letter. It was addressed to Dr. Anson Jones.

When I came here I was about to send over for you . . . I then heard you would be . . . at Austin. Now, all this preface is to ask you if you will be so good as to accept the station of Secretary of State. . . . I will assure you that you will find worthy associates in the cabinet. . . . you were always embraced in the plan. Don't say you are "poor." I am—all are so! The officers shall have salaries, and in good money. It can be done—and shall be done! ! . . . when we meet I will amuse you, by laying open a world of wonders, *some of them at least amusing.*

The Brazoria County physician was not at nome to receive the letter. He had gone to Austin the last day of October to straighten out some titles at the General Land Office. On the way he stopped at Burleigh, the home of Oliver Jones, to prescribe for "Cousin Rebecca," who was ailing. He found Cousin Oliver, now a retired senator, more interested in the bricks he was making to finish his house than in politics. At General Burleson's Bastrop home

I had liked to have stumbled upon a wedding Trip [he wrote]. Mary B. was made Mrs. Wayne Barton the evening previous, & I had the pleasure of receiving (after a tedious day's ride of 40 miles) a cup of excellent coffee from the hands of the Bride, as well as a hearty welcome from the Vice Pres' elect.

He found Austin "dull enough." Cabinet officers of the old regime were leaving; Burnet was packed to return to his farm, and Lamar was

very busy in riding all over and about town a little black galloping poney which is his sole employment & constant amusement. He appears very content and satisfied with the way the country is ruined. The balance however have long faces. . . .

Every thing & every body appears to be waiting the *"moving of the waters"* by Old Sam [he reported to Mary on November 19]. Congress are doing little except prying into the different offices to find the *leaks* by which the money has all run out—& contriving the means to stop some of them—a little on the old principle of "after the Horse is stolen, locking the barn door."

The ball to General Burleson is . . . Monday next. I expect to attend. . . . Harrison is selling so much *finery* that you would think such a thing as *"Retrenchment"* had never been discovered.

The citizens of Austin and the politicians were "in a buzz making preparations to 'Hail the Chief,' " as Dr. Jones attended to his business and prepared to return to Brazoria County. Then, on the last day of November, the letter which the President-elect had written six days before overtook him—a week before Houston arrived.

The Secretaryship of State tantalized him, but he was unde-cided. He had a living to make and his medical practice was lucrative. "I have concluded upon nothing definite," he wrote his wife after a week of uncertainty. The next day the President-elect and his retinue galloped into the city Lamar had built and Houston never learned to love. After appropriate addresses to the delega-tions that rode out to greet him Sam Houston was "escorted to Mrs. Eberle's and joined a most boisterous (and we might well say ravenous) crowd in a collation . . . it was all rush and confusion [wrote a guest at the hotel] and thereby I lost my dinner."

Jones found the general that day

in excellent health & spirits. He was well received, by the citizens of this town & a large party of ladies & gentlemen collected at Mrs. Eberly's this evening, & are now amusing themselves & him with music & dancing. . . . I have given no promise as yet to accept a place in the Cabinet. . . .

Kenneth L. Anderson of San Augustine, Speaker of the House, promised Jones he would accept the Treasury Department if Jones would take the foreign office. "His persuasions, more than any other man's induced me to accept," the doctor said. There were of course conferences with Houston himself, during which the doctor caught some of the President-elect's missionary zeal for the reconstruction of Texas.

I was solicited, urged, *implored,* and finally persuaded. . . . I was assured I should have worthy associates in the cabinet, &c., &c., &c., &c., and promised as a *sine qua non* to acceptance that I should have a paramount control.

On inauguration day Dr. Jones wrote his wife that he had

consented to accept the Office of Secretary of State, temporarily, & subject to such arrangements as I may make in my private business. Col. Hockley is appointed Sec⁷ of War & Navy—K. L. Anderson (the Speaker) is to be Sec⁷ of the Treasury, & Judge Terrill Att⁷ General—Major Brigham, Treasurer—G. Borden Collector at Galveston. No other appointments are certainly fixed upon and known— I take charge of the State Dep⁺ to-morrow—& make my appointments. . . . You must not scold me for staying so long in Austin. . . . I will escape at the first possible moment.

At noon on Monday, December 13, 1841, the reform and retrenchment regime was inducted before a crowd of about a thousand citizens

in the rear of the Capitol, where a covered platform had been erected for the ceremonies of the inauguration; back and above which, were flags of the battalions taken at San Jacinto, and in the center the portrait of Austin. An awning had been stretched over head, and chairs were ranged around for the members of the Senate and House, and the ladies.

Into the enclosure which made the Capitol look like a frontier fort marched the three generals—Lamar, Houston, Burleson—escorted by committees of the two houses of Congress and preceded by the Travis Guards. Three years before, Houston had attended Lamar's inauguration, dressed in a costume of George Washington's time, to deliver an unscheduled valedictory which exhausted the audience before his successor had a chance to speak. This time the outgoing President was attired in a broadcloth suit of current style and he declined to speak.

General Houston

appeared on the stage in a linsey-wooley hunting shirt, and pantaloons, and an old wide brimmed white fur hat. I thought in this Gen. Houston demonstrated more vanity than if he had appeared in an ordinary cloth suit [Josiah Gregg thought]. He knew it would be much remarked, and thought it would be popular no doubt, with the body of the people. Gen. Burleson also appeared and was sworn in in his fancy Indian leathered hunting shirt—probably more for the purpose of being in unison with the president than for vanity—though Burleson was a *hunter* of the plainest raising and education. . . .

When the Travis Guards had "filed off before the platform" and "the Hon. R. E. B. Baylor had addressed the throne of Grace in a pathetic and appropriate prayer," Mr. Speaker Anderson rose to administer the oath to the new President.

At the very instant the oath was taken, the firing of artillery commenced at the arsenal. A telegraphic arrangement had been made, so that there was scarcely a divisible space of time between the oath and the booming of the first gun. The effect was very fine, the arrangement not being generally understood.

The startled audience then settled back to listen to the President deliver his inaugural address, which the *Telegraph* declared "brief and very interesting." A stranger, who had never before heard Houston speak, was more impressed by its length and impromptu nature than by its content or delivery:

He did not demonstrate that extemporaneous eloquence, which I had expected to see and hear; indeed I could but pronounce the manner of his address rather dry and monotonous. A part of the substance did well enough; but he certainly would have done better not to have been his own eulogist—I should say he dwelt too much and unbecomingly on the merits of his former services and administration: of which the people generally do not speak nearly so favorably as he himself.

For more than a week after his inauguration His Excellency delayed communicating his appointments to the Senate. Some of Houston's friends had asked Secretary Jones

as a particular favor to them, and as a duty you owe your country . . . use your personal and political influence with the General to have *sober, honest,* and *practical* men in his cabinet. . . . The country expects . . . an economical cabinet . . . men of energy, of business habits—men who will curtail every possible expense in their departments. Now you have as much, if not more influence over him than any other man . . . use it to persuade Houston to two things: 1st. Against the exclusive appointment of Eastern men, as this would make the West jealous; and 2nd . . . the appointment of steady, energetic men. Let him do this, and his cabinet will possess the confidence of the whole people, and he will become more popular than ever. . . . All Houston's friends . . . are straining every nerve to effect a reconciliation between the two generals (Houston and Lamar). No obstacles will be thrown in the way by Lamar, and I wish I could gain your valuable assistance with the other.

Reconciliation between the incoming and the outgoing Presidents, given the personalities of the two generals and the exigencies of the political situation, was neither probably nor necessarily desirable. Jones strained no nerve to bring it about. But the selection of the three men (Congress had reduced the portfolios from six to four) who would sit with him in the Cabinet was important to the country and to him personally.

Houston constructed the Cabinet around Jones. He had been watching Jones evolve from a timid country doctor into a man of affairs since 1836—at San Jacinto, in Congress, as Minister to the United States, in the Texan Senate. The future of this Republic depended upon the skill with which external factors were manipulated. He knew how to use the doctor's firsthand knowledge of the intricacies of diplomacy and his analytical, cautious mind. Such qualities as Jones lacked, Houston believed he himself had in abundance.

The attenuated military and naval establishment was handed over to impetuous George Washington Hockley, who had been the President's devoted friend and partisan for twenty years. They had first met in Washington City when the Old Chief was a young congressman and Hockley a clerk in the War Department. Hockley followed him to Tennessee, then to Texas. At San Jacinto he was his military man Friday. Now he was again cast in that role with the title Secretary of War and Marine. That was one appointment on which the President did not seek the advice of his Secretary of State.

Nor did he need his help in choosing the Attorney General. George Whitfield Terrell had held that post when Houston was Governor of Tennessee a dozen years earlier, and he was available again. While Houston had been living with the Cherokees, Terrell was losing his fortune in Mississippi. Then, tardily, he had come to Texas to begin again. Lamar had given him a district attorneyship, but to Houston's delight Terrell had declined to become Secretary of State under that administration. Terrell was a shrewd political adviser and a good lawyer. He would be useful in the Cabinet.

Three of the four places in the Cabinet were filled before Congress adjourned. There was talk that the Senate would not confirm them. General Alexander Somervell thought on December 22 that "A. Jones as Sec. of State, and Hockley as Sec. of War will rub through the Senate with difficulty; indeed I am not sure but that H. will stick by the way." He was mistaken. On Christmas Eve the nomination of Jones was unanimously confirmed, and Hockley and Terrell were also approved, with only K. H. Muse of Nacogdoches voting in the negative.

Expediency counseled delay in filling the Treasury post until Speaker Anderson in the House and William Henry Daingerfield in the Senate had done what they could to get through administration measures. Both expected the appointment, and Houston was not the man to disappoint either of them until the work was done. Mr. E. Lawrence Stickney, who wrote a good hand, signed papers as Acting Secretary. Mr. Secretary Jones looked after public relations and lobbying for the Treasury until Congress adjourned and Daingerfield moved from the deserted Senate chamber to the Treasury office, where there was plenty of work but no money. The Honorable Mr. Anderson mounted his horse to return to his San Augustine farm—consoled a little later by a district attorneyship.

The new Secretary of the Treasury was a courtly, astute Virginian, whose sartorial elegance was one of the wonders of the frontier capital. Like Terrell, he had come to Texas in 1837 and had begun his political career under Lamar. He had been Jones's colleague in the Senate and a leader of the Jones-for-Vice-President boom last summer. He probably was the only politician in Texas who managed to retain, concurrently, the friendship of Lamar and Houston. Jones had preferred Speaker Anderson for this post, but he could find no objection to Mr. Daingerfield.

It was an excellent Cabinet. If it was not one of all the talents, it at least contained a wide variety of them. With each of the four men the President had had, as things were then reckoned in Texas, a long and intimate acquaintance. They were competent, agreeable, steady men, and each was able to serve His Excellency in the broad field of practical politics beyond the duties of the office assigned him.

Only Secretary Hockley—as became a war minister in time of alarums and excursions—had a dash of frontier glamour; the others atoned for deficiencies in flamboyance by workmanlike attitudes toward the problems at hand. The President's grand manner, and Hockley's, gave the regime the atmosphere Texans expected.

Edward Burleson presided awkwardly over the Senate, deciding points of order by the rule of common sense more often than by Jefferson's *Manual,* and casting his vice-presidential vote against the administration more often than for it. He seldom visited the executive offices. He was not, in fact, a member of the administration party. The President and the Secretary of State had little respect for Ned Burleson's political acumen, and they soon were to have less. He remained a frontiersman, hunting down Indians and Mexicans when opportunity offered, and speaking his mind with a candor that impaired his political usefulness.

Secretary Jones made his home in Austin with Major Asa Brigham, the Brazorian who had been Treasurer of the Republic since 1836, when Jones and Robert Mills signed his $50,000 bond. He had come originally as a guest when he thought he would soon return to his medical office in Columbia. He remained as a roomer after he accepted a place in the Cabinet.

Mrs. Jones and Sam Houston Jones ("the young Secretary of State," his father now called him) remained in Brazoria County. There were no suitable accommodations for them at the capital, and Dr. Jones thought his tenure of the State Department would be temporary. When it was certain that he would retain the post, there was talk that the capital would be moved. All things considered, it seemed best not to bring his little family to Austin. "It affords me a good excuse," he wrote Mary in January, "for taking *leave of absence* for a while, & I want to get away from here so bad that I am scarcely in a good humor any part of the time."

Living conditions in Austin were still primitive. Three days after Jones took office Indians broke into Major Brigham's stables and stole all the horses. Two of them belonged to John W. Cloud, a Brazorian, who had to borrow Dr. Jones's horse to get home.

Everything was too expensive for a man whose salary was $1,500, Texas money. Sugar, worth $25 a barrel at Houston, sold for $40 in Austin; flour, $20 at Austin, was $10 a barrel at Houston; and table board was twice as high at the capital. In general, the Houston *Morning Star* reported, prices were "from seventy-five to one hundred per cent. above the Houston cost of every item which is waggoned to Austin."

But facilities, if not the means, for gracious living were increasing. The White House atop President Hill was now rivaled in magnificence by the Legation the French Chargé had built on the lot Anson Jones sold him.

Our old friend Mr. Saligny [he wrote Mary] has his house finished & furnished in almost regal magnificence. I was over it with his Steward yesterday. The new furniture is Parisian & beautiful, the colors are orange, damask & gold.

The Chargé himself was absent, vowing never to visit the Texas capital again until a new administration had apologized to him for the indignities he had suffered under Lamar's. The Austin *City Gazette* had explained the matter last September.

The difficulties were in the first instance altogether of a private and personal character between M. de Saligny and Mr. Bullock, and were lamented by the friends of both parties; the difficulties were increased by the killing of Mr. B.'s pigs by one of M. de S.'s servants, whereupon Mr. B. assaulted the servant, and the minister made his complaint to the government. The district attorney, under the instruction of the government, had Mr. Bullock arrested to answer for said assault, and the District Court not being in session at the time, Mr. B. was bound in heavy recognizances to appear before said court to answer the charge. Thus that matter stands until the next session of the court in November next. As might naturally be expected, this occurrence still further embittered the feelings of both parties to such an extent that, in April last, Mr. Bullock, who keeps a public hotel in this city, meeting M. de Saligny on his premises, ordered him off. M. de Saligny immediately made a second complaint, and insisted on the immediate punishment of Mr. Bullock; on this, Mr. B. was again handed over to the judiciary, and bound over, as in the former case, to answer the charge at the term of the District Court. A long and warm discussion took place between the French minister and the Texan Secretary of State [Mayfield]; and the whole matter has been referred to the French Government. . . .

In conclusion, we would remark that M. de Saligny . . . is brother-in-law of M. Humann, the Minister of Finance of France. . . . The connection thus existing between M. de Saligny and a member of the French Cabinet accounts for all the obstacles thrown by that government in the way of Messrs. Lafitte & Co.'s fulfilment of their contract for the Texan loan.

The difficulty was no evidence of British intrigue, as some Texan editors liked to believe; it was a simple matter of the aggression of Mr. Bullock's pigs. They invaded M. Saligny's stables to eat corn, and they were killed by M. Saligny's vigilant manservant. Mr. Bullock thrashed the servant, under the Texan theory that a man who would lay hands on a neighbor's pig or horse was a public menace. M. Saligny, operating under the effete Napoleonic Code, which holds that pigs are only pigs, when they are not nuisances, was indignant; and he took steps, at Austin and at Paris, which to him seemed proper.

Texans abandoned their factional quarrels to stand behind the rights of Mr. Bullock's pigs. Those pigs, William M. Gouge believed, saved the Republic of Texas just as surely as the cackling of geese once saved Rome; for

If the loan had been obtained, it would have been used in establishing a national bank, by which every dollar would have been made to look like ten. The result would have been that the debt of Texas, instead of being twelve millions, would have been twenty-five, thirty, perhaps forty millions. The most intelligent Texans agree in opinion that this would have been the result. All honor, then, to Mr. Bullock and his pigs; and this heretofore much despised animal must be regarded hereafter as possessed of classic interest. If his figure, carved in marble, should be placed over the entrance of the treasury of Texas, it would serve as a memento to future ages of his having been the salvation of the Republic, and teach Mr. Branch Tanner Archer's "thousands and millions, born and unborn," that the humblest of agents may be instrumental in producing consequences of the utmost importance.

Without the five-million-dollar loan Texas would have to look to her own impoverished citizens to supply the means for operating her government. She was entering an era of retrenchment.

Economy was the slogan of the new President, and it was also the watchword of the Sixth Congress, which had been in session a month and a half when Houston succeeded Lamar. Three fourths of the representatives were new, and almost half of the senators. In the upper house the veteran Senators Greer, Moore, and Barnett sat on the finance committee. The House finance committee, headed by Tod Robinson of Brazoria, was reinforced by a standing committee on retrenchment, whose chairman was "Fiery Jones of Gonzales," a lawyer-editor recently come from Georgia. Both of them were serving a first term, and they considered themselves watchdogs of the empty Treasury.

Lamar's Secretary of the Treasury, Dr. John G. Chalmers, had reported disbursements for the past year $1,176,288.72; receipts, $442,606.67—all except $4,776 in inconvertible Texas paper. The amount of the public debt was a matter of conjecture. Excluding what was owed for the navy and floating debts, the amount of which "cannot be ascertained," it was $5,782,788.91. Including them, Chalmers guessed, the total might be about $7,-300,000; others guessed it was more.

The money of the Republic was never more plentiful. More than four and a third millions of paper dollars were in circulation. It passed in trade at "no more than fifteen to twenty cents" on the dollar, but it was still being received by the government at face value.

The vital importance of a change in its character must strike the most careless observer [Secretary Chalmers had pointed out] . . . the continuation of the present policy for a much longer time will result in the inevitable dissolution of the Government.

On November 22 the committee on retrenchment made its first report.

Whatever may have been the causes [Fiery Jones of Gonzales announced, after examining the Treasury records] . . . we now exhibit to the world, too obviously not to be seen by others, and too painful and mortifying not to be felt by ourselves, the spectacle of a *bankrupt Government, and an impoverished people.* . . .

The farce which we have been playing, of attempting to sustain a government on the scale of an empire, can no longer amuse the world or profit ourselves.

The committee proposed to abolish "every office not absolutely necessary," to reduce all salaries, and provide for efficient collection of revenues. Specifically it wanted to abolish seven offices, including that of Attorney General; reduce the number of clerks and assistants in every office; reduce the President's salary from $10,000 to $4,000, the Vice-President's to $1,000, Cabinet officers' to $1,200, minor officials to $700, $600, or $500 a year. In the end, the President was given $5,000, Cabinet members $1,500, and the Attorney Generalship was not abolished but the salary was reduced to $1,000.

Before Houston delivered his first message to Congress, a bill to repeal the laws authorizing that five-million-dollar loan Jones had discussed with Mr. Biddle in Philadelphia and to recall the loan commissioners had been introduced. The new President told Congress on December 20:

It seems that we have arrived at a crisis in our national progress, which is neither cheering for the present nor flattering for the future. . . . Notwithstanding my unremitting exertions since my inauguration, to make myself acquainted with the true condition of the government, I have not been able to derive . . . clear and satisfactory information. . . .

There is not a dollar in its Treasury—the nation is involved from ten to fifteen millions. . . . Business connected with some of the important branches of the different departments, has remained unsettled and unascertained for the last three years. . . . We are not only without money but without credit; and for want of punctuality, without character. . . .

The President asked Congress to suspend even promises to pay until it could hope "to redeem in good faith such as it ought to redeem." He suggested that direct taxes be reduced by one half and that only gold, silver, or "paper of unquestionable character" be accepted in payment of government dues. The previously authorized currencies should be outlawed and $350,000 in new paper, secured by a million acres of Cherokee lands and issued in increments of less than $50,000 a month, should be authorized. In lieu of the five-million-dollar loan which Texan agents had been trying to peddle since 1837, President Houston suggested realistically that the Republic mortgage public lands for $300,000 ready cash.

The next day Jones wrote Mary:

Everything goes on here very well, so far. The Old Hero keeps perfectly cool & sober, & has sent a Message to Congress, replete with practical good sense, & one which has given very general satisfaction.

Affairs of state were in a more prosperous condition than the scant wardrobe he had brought to Austin for a brief visit nearly two months before. Even in this country where the President sometimes wore a blanket and the Vice-President a hunting shirt, it was expected that the Secretary of State maintain urban standards of dress.

. . . bring me some *clothes* [he begged his wife], as I am getting out "at elbow" a good deal . . . a Coat, & some socks (woolen) with a pair of drawers, &c.

Mr. Secretary Jones, in the absence of a Secretary of the Treasury, was the administration's financial expert. A financial oracle of the Second Congress, he had helped defeat a promissory-note scheme—which, however, the next Congress enacted while he was abroad; and, as Jones noted with melancholy satisfaction, "all the evils . . . I predicted, came to pass soon thereafter." For two years in the Senate he had been vigorously opposing one after another of Lamar's financial recommendations. Now he was called upon to propose a positive line action for this bankrupt

Republic. To the Cabinet council two weeks after he became a member of the administration he diagnosed the situation and prescribed an unpleasant but effective cure for Texas.

She has impending a floating, promiscuous debt of, say six millions, and a funded one of two and a half. Her *annual* income will not suffice to pay the *interest* on the latter alone, if it were all directed to that object. . . .

But *one course* presents itself. The public debt must be postponed for the present, and the revenues collected in gold and silver. The expenses of the Government *must* be reduced to a sum within the probable amount of these revenues. . . .

The navy should be put in ordinary; and no troops kept in commission except a few Rangers on the Frontiers.

The Indians should be conciliated by every means in our power. It is much cheaper and more humane to *purchase* their friendship than to fight them. . . .

By a steady, uniform, firm, undeviating adherence to this policy for two or three years, Texas may and will recover from her present utter prostration. It is the stern law of necessity which requires it, and she must yield to it, or perish!

She cannot afford to raise another crop of "Heroes."

In the meantime, Texas must adopt some plan for the ultimate, just payment of her public debt. . . . But for the present she has to consider the question of "to be or not to be" alone! and exclusively!

The Sixth Congress had already ordered wholesale retrenchment, calculated to leave on the pay roll only "offices of labor instead of pleasure." The salary budget that year dropped from $173,506 to $32,800. Then congressmen considered the new President's proposals, with Secretary Jones acting as liaison officer between the legislative and executive departments. But the new men who controlled that Congress were unwilling to follow slavishly the advice of the President or his Secretary of State.

The proposed loan of $300,000 for immediate expenses was rejected, on the ground—perhaps well founded—that nobody would lend Texas that much money. Instead of the $350,000 exchequer bills Houston wanted, Congress authorized only $200,-000 and ordered them canceled as they came back into the Treasury. The Congress furthermore directed a joint committee to take from the Secretary of the Treasury "each and every character of the liabilities of the Government, except exchequer bills, on file, or cancelled, or in blanks, in said department (which is not private property) . . . and the same set fire to, burn up, and wholly destroy," and thereafter to repeat the ceremony on the first day of every month.

"Retrenchment," Jones remarked, "was the watch-word . . . and rigidly was it enforced, as the pockets of all government officers attested." Playfully he wrote to his frugal wife while Congress was doing its work:

Col. Hill has done me the favor to show me Mrs. Hill's letter in which she informed of your *extravagance,* &c. &c. You must stop it, because I wish to *dash* a little myself—& I cannot afford it unless my wife is *very* economical & in the late storm of *retrenchment,* I lost $2,000 per annum.

Exodus of Lamar appointees had deprived the Texan capital of a considerable portion of its population, and wholesale reductions in the government personnel during the winter further relieved congestion along Congress Avenue and made possible a reassignment of the public buildings.

In the cabin vacated by Lamar's Adjutant General, Mr. Secretary Jones installed the archives and personnel—three clerks—of the Department of State

with a determination to snatch the country from the verge of destruction upon which she was tottering, and to save her if possible, notwithstanding the almost insurmountable difficulties. . . .

XXIII

SECRETARY OF STATE

Hon. Anson Jones Secy of State
  SIR: On entering upon the duties of this Bureau I find the business of the office greatly in the rear. . . . The office being intierly destitute of Mail bags, locks and keys—it is necessary that a supply should be immediately furnished.
  Respectfully Your Obet Servt. A. C. HYDE Clerk P.O. Bureau.

THE Secretary of State was learning on January 6, 1842, the status of a department of government for which the retrenchment Congress had made him responsible. He had appointed Mr. Hyde, a Brazorian recently postmaster at Austin, to look after the mails. He asked Congress to give Hyde what he needed, but the mail that interested him that winter was not handled by his Post Office Bureau. It was diplomatic correspondence, transmitted in locked, leather pouches by special messengers from Washington City, London, Paris.

After some hesitation he retained Joseph Waples as chief clerk of the Department of State, despite the fact that he had been employed during the Lamar administration—maybe because of it. Mr. Waples was a tight-lipped bachelor from Delaware with a capacity for order and detail that Jones appreciated. He had personally packed the archives and brought them to Austin. He would know where to find the papers the new Secretary wanted to review. And he would know how to pack them again.

During the long winter evenings as he waited for Congress to adjourn, Secretary Jones thumbed the papers in his departmental archives to refresh his memory on details of five years of Texan diplomacy.

These archives made it clear how much his own activities as Minister to the United States had improved the posture of the Republic. At Washington he had terminated talk of annexation and thereafter had spent more time with ministers from Europe

than with the American Secretary of State. On the credit side
of the balance sheet, the new Secretary could place recognition
by France, tentative recognition by Great Britain (both of which
he had helped bring about), recognition by the Netherlands, and
the possibility of early recognition by Belgium—if one could believe reports of incurably optimistic Commissioner James Hamilton.

As far as vellum documents with great seals could make it, his
spunky little Republic was a nation among the nations. But the
other side of the international balance sheet was

anything but favorable—no treaty of amity with the United States—
England hesitating about ratifying the one made with her—France
estranged and about assuming a hostile attitude. . . .

These things were in the records that Mr. Waples dug out of
the files. Another factor, not yet of record, was developing during
that year—and it was to modify every plan the methodical Secretary was making.

Mexico—tumultuous, unstable, volatile Mexico—held the key
to the future of Texas—for more reasons than the statesmen in
the Halls of Montezuma knew. Not once since the revolution had
the cloud of Mexico lifted from the horizon of Texan affairs.
Lamar's Santa Fé expedition made it darker than usual the
winter Jones began formulating policies.

As weeks, then months, passed and no news came, apprehension grew that this last great scheme of Lamar had failed, as
others had failed before it. The day Jones became Secretary of
State he heard a rumor that the Mexicans had captured all the
expeditioners. Thereafter the rumor came oftener and oftener.

For two weeks the new (Houston) Congress debated impeach-
ing Lamar, his Vice-President, and his Secretary of the Treasury.
Powerful men—Speaker Anderson, Isaac Van Zandt, George T.
Woods—demanded it; but by a majority of twelve the House
declined to arraign the poet-President who, even his enemies were
beginning to feel, had had more than a just portion of ill fortune.

At the end of the year 1841 the Texan Secretary of State knew
the expedition was lost, although official report was still lacking.

The Santa Fe expedition has failed and all the poor fellows engaged in it have either perished or been led into hopeless mexican

captivity [he wrote Mary, January 3, 1842]. It has thrown a perceptible gloom over our city for several days past. How strange are the changes & vicissitudes of a few months or days. I now occupy the room a short time since used by H. McLeod, the Commander of that ill-starred and *foolish* enterprise. It is now the office of the Secretary of State. In this room the expedition was principally planned. . . . Now ask for all that crowd, of fools & knaves & flatterers of power who basked in the smiles of executive influence—& where are they! Gone and scattered forever—— Some are dead, others doomed to hopeless misery . . . in the Mines of Mexico, the rest powerless weak—accused & despised, & wishing themselves with the others.

    —"And like the baseless fabric of a vision," have "Left not a wreck behind!" or rather nothing but a wreck.

That wreck was upon the official doorstep of Anson Jones.

Two weeks later he read the details in a letter from Señor Manuel Alvarez, United States Consul at Santa Fé. Other Texans read it too; and a wave of infuriated hysteria swept through the Republic. Congress rose to the occasion by ordering the boundaries of Texas moved westward to the Pacific Ocean and southward to the Tropic of Cancer—an addition of about two million Mexicans and half a billion acres to Big Texas, which then had perhaps 50,000 inhabitants.

With regard to the right of Texas to extend her boundaries so as to include any portion of Mexico [exulted a congressman] . . . there can be no two opinions. . . . That it is good policy . . . not the shadow of a doubt. . . .

Let us . . . extend our jurisdiction to the Pacific, and submit the question to the high arbitrament of heaven.

Whatever heaven thought of this fiat annexing half of Mexico, President Houston branded it a "legislative jest" and vetoed it. He believed in the Manifest Destiny of the Nordics as ardently as any congressman, but he was a realist. Texas was bankrupt, her handful of citizens unable to control the territory she already claimed. It would "appear curious to nations in amity with us," he lectured Congress, "that a people destitute of means to meet their most pressing wants . . . should assume . . . to govern a country possessing a population more than thirty to one"—and in area larger than the United States of the North then was.

"Legislative Humbug!" shouted the *Telegraph* when Congress overrode the veto, then adjourned. "We think," commented Editor Moore, who was one of the senators, "the two governments may now turn to each other with the self-complacency of two boys that have been playing tag, and say—*'now we are even.'*"

In this crisis a citizen who signed himself "A" came forward with a suggestion. Texans were grumbling that M. B. Lamar had dispatched the expedition on his own responsibility, and they thought M. B. Lamar, somehow, should be made to pay for it. Congress refused to impeach him, and there was no way to make him reimburse the Treasury—or the families of the captives. Congressman Harrison's *Weekly Texian* on January 26, 1842, printed A's proposal: Swap M. B. Lamar to Mexico for the Santa Fé prisoners!

President Houston probably thought less of the Santa Fé expedition and of M. B. Lamar than did A, but he put on a grave face when he read the suggestion and remarked to Secretary Jones and Memucan Hunt that Lamar would certainly duel with A if he could identify him.

"If he wants a fight," retorted General Hunt, "I am his man."

At Galveston, ex-President Lamar read that issue of the *Texian*. He concluded that A was Anson Jones, polished his pistols, and decided that it was

doubly important that the audacious offender should not be permitted to go unpunished. . . . I cannot allow him to escape from his responsibility to me. . . . call upon Mr. Anson Jones [he instructed James Webb] . . . Accept no equivocation or explination . . . require of him a categorical reply. . . .

Had the production eminated from the Editor of the Texian or from any irresponsible scoundrel like him, it might be suffered to pass unnoticed . . . but coming . . . from one of the highest of our public functionaries & bearing the aspect of a govmt measure, the people at large are as much interested in the matter as myself. . . . The malignant spirit which pervades the piece, as well as the flagicios & diabolical proposition which it contains, calls aloud for redress at my hands. . . .

Unaware of the ex-President's anger, Secretary Jones remained at the capital, attending to public business and formulating tentative plans. The diplomatic situation he had mastered; the muddled domestic problems were clear to him. President Houston encouraged him to consider himself the administration's strategist. It assured expert counsel in foreign and, to an extent, in domestic affairs. At the outset of the administration Jones believed he was in paramount control, and he was as assiduous as the President himself in formulating broad policies and maneuvers. He believed he

originated, as well as controlled and managed, the foreign policy of the country for three years. Gen. Houston had had very little to do with it. . . . I occasionally consulted with him, and after explaining the course I proposed to pursue in regard to our foreign relations, and obtaining his consent thereto, I proceeded to execute my plans. . . .

His plans were shaped with realism and had the impress of urgency. It was as if his Republic stood marooned on an island of quicksand in the middle of a narrow but swollen and rising river. Her footings were uncertain and endangered by the waters. Safety lay on the granite banks of the stream, where broad highways stretched in opposite directions to the limitless future. To the east the road was annexation; it crossed the Sabine and ended at the Potomac. To the west the road was secure independence, recognized by Mexico and all the world. It ran straight toward the Pacific, with branch roads northwest through the Rockies and southward into northern Mexico. Texas would have to place herself upon one of those roads before the floodwaters of bankruptcy, insubordination, and reconquest overwhelmed her.

With a practicality that was of a piece with his whole nature, Jones designed and began to construct two bridges, one to the east, one to the west. Either would serve Texas—if it were completed in time. To Mr. Secretary Jones that winter it was not a question of which road was better, but which road could be reached.

The Secretary's first move was to call home Lamar's agents abroad and fill their places with men in the confidence of the new administration who understood, so far as anyone could that winter, the new foreign policy of the Republic.

To Barnard E. Bee, Mr. Secretary Jones wrote on December 27, 1841, dismissing him from the service with a reprimand:

I am also directed by the President respectfully to inform you that he views your long absence from Washington as a desertion of your Post, injurious to the interests of this Government and disrespectful to that of the United States.

Then, with his mind fixed on Paris or London or Mexico, he wrote a formal letter of recall for Bee addressed to the "Minister of Foreign Affairs of the United States." A vigilant clerk in the Legation at Washington corrected the inadvertence before it was presented to Secretary of State Webster. Mr. Secretary Jones was following the spirit, if not the text, of Elliot's *Diplomatic Code*.

Bee had gone to Washington to negotiate a trade treaty, but the treaty was never drafted—perhaps because the Texan Minister was spending more time at Charleston and New Orleans than at the capital. When Bee was recalled, trade between Texas and the United States was still governed, to the disgust and inconvenience of shippers, by a Mexican treaty with the United States which had expired in 1841, leaving the trade unprotected.

To Washington went Major James Reily, a former Texas congressman who had a Hibernian gift for diplomacy and a wife who was Henry Clay's niece. On January 26, 1842, Secretary Jones "instructed Reily in reference to Treaty, Indians—& annexation." The new Texan representative near the government of the United States was to conclude without delay that trade agreement that Lamar's Chargé had failed for two years to negotiate, to exhort the United States to keep her Indians out of Texas, and—cautiously, noncommittally—to ascertain if the United States might be interested in inviting Texas into the Union. Reily would be discreet and suave; Jones counted on nothing immediately regarding annexation. Jones was unlatching that door that had been slammed in Texas's face—he did not open it, but Reily was to whisper to the United States that the door was no longer locked.

A snarl in the diplomatic thread that connected Texas with France was threatening difficulties out of all proportion to its actual significance. Those seriocomic difficulties of Count Alphonse de Saligny with a Texan pig, innkeeper, editor, and Lamar's administration, which had amused Citizen Jones when

he read of them in the papers last fall, he found officially "be-
queathed to me by the Administration of Gen. Lamar—indeed,
a few such troubles constitute about all they had left to bequeath,"
he added.

Saligny had withdrawn from his legation at the capital, first
to Galveston, then to New Orleans. He was now demanding official apology from the Republic of Texas for the indignities he
had suffered; if the apology was not forthcoming, he would order
a French squadron to Galveston to present an ultimatum.

Secretary Jones was fond of that effervescent Frenchman,
whom he had known since his Washington days. He was willing
to do much for him as a friend, but what he could do as a responsible spokesman of the Republic was quite another matter. He
could not write to an offended diplomat things he would say in
private conversation, or even on the stump in Texas. He would,
in fact, write nothing to Saligny. The Chargé had made his difficulties an official matter between governments; the Secretary
would handle the matter through his own Chargé in Paris, but
he would permit Saligny to read the letter.

Though accidental circumstances may have placed individuals in
public stations who have been mistaken in giving proper expression
to national feelings and sentiments [he wrote January 20] . . . the
present administration would not be doing justice to these sentiments
if it failed to disclaim . . . the abusive language of which in moments of unfortunate excitement M. De Saligny was the object.

Major Reily was instructed to stop in New Orleans to show the
letter to Saligny.

More pressing than negotiations with the United States or the
settlement of the Saligny affair was the termination of the services
of General James Hamilton.

That ubiquitous South Carolinian, whom Jones had often encountered in Texas and in the United States, had dedicated his
talents to the Republic at the start of the revolution. Now in his
middle fifties, he had had several spectacular careers, the latest
as Lamar's commissioner seeking five million dollars wherever it
might be found.

Lawyer, planter, industrialist, banker, speculator, Hamilton
had served South Carolina as congressman, nullification Gover-

nor, and general of her army to defy the United States; his motto was, "He who dallies is a dastard." In 1835 he had become a sort of honorary Texan. He declined command of the revolutionary army to serve Texas in other capacities. Since 1838 he had been the roving financial and diplomatic agent of the Republic, concocting schemes in the capitals of western Europe, each more dazzling and presented with greater enthusiasm than the one before it. Now he was on his way to Texas to report to the new President and receive new instructions from the Secretary of State. While he was en route, the retrenchment Congress repealed the loan act after declaring more in sorrow than in anger:

> For six long years the prospect of this loan has gone before us as a cloud by day and a pillar of fire by night. . . . It has induced us to do things we ought not to do, and leave undone the things we ought to have done. . . . The pending of this negotiation has been a curse;—its success would be a greater curse still. . . .

Soon Hamilton would be in Jones's office—resourceful, tireless, hot-tempered General Hamilton, who had fought fourteen duels and wounded every adversary. On January 26 the Secretary wrote him, lumping Hamilton's many official titles into an all-inclusive *"Minister Plenipotentiary etc. etc.":*

> The Laws authorizing a Loan to be negotiated for five Millions of Dollars having been repealed . . . and your functions as Commissioner having in consequence transpired . . . His Excellency the President has directed me to inform you that he will at an early date appoint a successor to discharge the various diplomatic functions, in Europe, which were devolved upon you by his predecessor. . . . As diplomatic relations have not been established with any of the courts to which you were accredited it has not been deemed necessary to send you formal letters of recall for presentation on taking leave of them finally.
> I have the honor to be with the highest respect Your Obt Svt
> ANSON JONES

A week later Hamilton sat in Jones's office, explaining with his usual fluency his final, greatest project. He had negotiated the arrangement that would change the course of Texas history! It was no mere five-million-dollar loan; it was for seven million, and it involved a scheme to people Texas with thrifty Belgians. With him was Captain Victor Pirson, fresh from the Belgian Legation in Constantinople, to select lands for the colonies. Texas would borrow seven million dollars at six per cent for twenty years, secure it by taxes and customs and public lands. The King of the Belgians would underwrite it in exchange for the deposit in his treasury of the first three and a half millions until the last half of the loan had been repaid. Meantime, Belgians would colonize Texas; Belgian merchant ships would supply Texas; in short, little Belgium would become the godmother of big Texas!

The President and the Secretary of State listened impassively to the vehement presentation of this ultimate in Hamiltonian financial schemes and passed the papers to Congress without recommendation. The Senate declined to act on the proposal, and the ex-commissioner departed for South Carolina, his two-hundred-thousand-dollar expense account unpaid. Captain Pirson lingered awhile among these Texans who needed money badly, but not that badly.

General Hamilton's European mission left Secretary Jones's department a legacy of British treaties—as yet unratified by England. In November 1840, Hamilton had got Palmerston to sign two treaties much desired by Texas: a trade convention (to replace the makeshift arrangement Henderson had made) and an agreement that England would try to induce Mexico to recognize the independence of Texas and be rewarded, if she succeeded, by the assumption by Texas of a million pounds of Mexican national debt. To the two treaties Hamilton wanted, Palmerston added a third which Hamilton did not want but had to accept: an anti-slave-trade agreement.

Hamilton's bearer of dispatches was a Londoner who, like all Britishers, disapproved of slavery; he seemed to the general an inappropriate person to explain to the Texas Government how and why he "had been obliged" to sign that slave treaty. The first two treaties reached Texas in time to be ratified by the Fifth (Lamar) Congress. The slave treaty, delayed until Hamilton could find a suitable messenger, arrived after Congress adjourned and was in Secretary Jones's files. Without Texan approval of it, Palmerston would not ratify the other two.

The solution, the Secretary saw, was ratification of the slave treaty before the Sixth Congress adjourned. When the Senate as-

sented on January 22, 1842, the way was at last clear for Texas to
begin large-scale diplomatic operations in western Europe. That
was essential to the success of plans he was making.

On the Continent one lonesome, destitute Chargé—a holdover
from the mission of 1837—represented the interests of Texas.
When Henderson came home he left his Legation secretary,
George S. McIntosh, as Acting Chargé until the Lamar administration made other arrangements. Two years passed; then, ten
days before Lamar's term ended, McIntosh was confirmed as
Chargé and Lamar's Secretary of State (who did not know his
first name) wrote him: "This appointment would have been
made long before this—but hitherto it has been wholly impossible
to pay your outfit. Nor is it even now certain that this can be
done." It turned out that McIntosh got neither outfit nor salary.
He remained uncomfortably in Paris, protected by his diplomatic
status from his creditors.

Before his credentials could reach him his successor had been
chosen and confirmed by the same Texan Senate that had approved his appointment two months earlier. Secretary Jones did
what he could for Mr. McIntosh: he sent, with his recall, scrip
for 9,600 acres of Texas land, which he hoped would satisfy the
creditors.

The new Chargé to the Court of Saint-Cloud was Ashbel
Smith, M.D., close friend of the President and long-time medical
colleague of the Secretary of State. He had studied a year in Paris
and knew his way about London, spoke French like a Parisian,
and was a shrewd negotiator. In every way Dr. Smith was the
ideal man for the European mission.

It was unnecessary for Dr. Jones to write Dr. Smith detailed
instructions regarding his mission. For days he had been in conference with the President and the Secretary of State; he knew
what was to be done and how to do it. They relied on his "zeal,
judgment and discretion." "So soon as you can," Jones told him
February 5, "leave for Paris. . . ."

XXIV

MR. HOUSTON'S TEXAS

CONGRESS have broke & We are all glad," wrote Hyde of
the Post Office Bureau February 9, "times are getting
back to the old strain." It had been, T. B. Huling thought,
"one of the damndest Congress Ever was in the republic . . . has
done more harm than Good to Texas   a great Pitie there should
be an other for four years to come."

Whether Congress had been good or bad for the country, its
adjournment gave Secretary Jones an opportunity to visit his wife
and son, whom he had not seen since October. To encourage him
to remain in the Cabinet, His Excellency, who was himself planning to get away from the capital as soon as he could, gave him
leave "to absent yourself from Austin until such time as you can
arrange your private affairs." The Supreme Court adjourned, too,
leaving two thirds of its docket untouched; and one by one the
heads of executive departments departed, until only Secretary
Hockley of War and Marine was left in Austin "as the 'Government.'"

Mr. Secretary Jones appointed Chief Clerk Waples Acting Secretary and on February 10 started for Burleigh, Cousin Oliver's
plantation on the Brazos, where Mary and young Sam had been
waiting for him two weeks. As he jogged along the road he cogitated upon his long-neglected business. "The salary of Secretary
of State, when reduced to par funds," he had already discovered,
"would not more than pay a negro's hire"—and he already had
two black servants on his personal pay roll. Maybe he could collect delinquent medical fees while he was on leave and sell some
of his land. Maybe he could find a young physician to carry on
his practice with such help as he could give by mail and during
vacations, for a share of the fees and the prestige the doctor's
name would bring him. His land trading he could look after at
the seat of government.

All along the road he heard the rumor that had already reached him in Austin, that Mexico was sending an army into Texas. General Mariano Arista at Monterrey was calling the inhabitants of the "Department of Texas" back to their Mexican allegiance— and, in phrases that might have been composed in 1835—promising immunity to those who submitted and destruction to those who persisted in rebellion. Some San Antonio Mexicans had already joined Arista, and his army was momentarily expected to begin the Texan reconquest by seizing the Alamo city as a base of operations. If San Antonio fell, Jones suspected that new capital that Lamar had built eighty-five miles away would be the next target.

At Cousin Oliver's a courier from Austin overtook him with a letter from his faithful Waples, whom he had left expertly packing the papers of the department for another move.

All business in the department has been suspended for the week past [he reported] except placing the archives in security, which was done by burying them under the Post-Office Bureau. . . . We only buried the records and uncopied letters and papers, thinking if the place was taken they (the Mexicans) would suppose by finding so many papers and documents in their arranged situation in the various offices, that they had got all the *archives* of the Government, and would not likely look for any thing hidden. . . . General Burleson is about to start for . . . Bexar, determined, as the ball is in motion, to keep it rolling to some purpose.

The Secretary on leave found no time to attend to private business. At Burleigh he joined Mary and the baby; but before they could start for Brazoria the President called him to the city of Houston, where he was trying to assemble his scattered advisers. As in 1836, Texas's strongest defense would have to be the stupidity of the enemy. The retrenchment Congress had disbanded the army; only untrained and infuriated volunteers, undirected by the government, stood between the Texans and whatever force Santa Anna was sending into Texas.

A secondary line of defense, not available in 1836, was diplomacy. With skillful management this crisis might be the means of settling, once and for all, Mexican claims to Texas. The new Secretary of State explored that possibility.

His Excellency was grim when Jones joined him at Houston, not far from San Jacinto; and the Secretary of State was in little better humor. On them was falling the onus of Lamar's Santa Fé expedition. Together they started to Galveston to inspect the inadequate defenses of the island. News from Mexico, the United States, and Europe would reach them there a day earlier than at Houston, and diplomatic dispatches could be posted to New Orleans without delay.

Secretary Jones's first caller there was General Albert Sidney Johnston, former Secretary of War, who called to present a peremptory note signed "M. B. Lamar." The ex-President demanded to know

whether you were the author of a certain communication signed A., which appeared in the *Weekly Texian* of the 26th ult., or whether you had any agency in advising, or any connection whatever with said publication. . . . I must demand a prompt reply, and an unequivocal answer.

Jones read it, scowled, and bowed the General out. Lamar had no right to make that demand. Jones was too busy to duel, or even match phrases, with a man whose political significance was at the moment nil—too busy with the aftermath of Lamar's Santa Fé expedition. By the code duello as practiced in this Republic, he might have returned the note without an answer, but he did not. He reached for his pen and, with economy of words, referred Lamar to his former Secretary of the Navy, Memucan Hunt, "for any or all information you require." As to the merit of A's suggestion that the ex-President be traded to the Mexicans, Secretary Jones made no comment.

That disposed of, Secretary Jones could begin building the diplomatic bridges he had planned during the winter. This Mexican threat was a colossal absurdity, but it was very real. Mexico had not recognized the independence of Texas, but the great powers of the world had: the United States in 1837, France in 1839, England in 1840. Mexico was a sort of perverse mortgage holder whose claims had been extinguished but who still declined to sign a release and was threatening to repossess the property. By shrewd diplomacy Texas might hope to mobilize civilized opinion to force Mexico to surrender her claims.

There was another string to this bow. Europe was overpopulated, and thrifty British, Belgian, French, Dutch, and German farmers were looking for new homes across the Atlantic. Colonies of Europeans between the Rio Grande and the Texan settlements would develop the country—and serve as a buffer against Mexican attacks. Mexican invasion would ally with Texas the homelands of the imperiled immigrants. Colonization and diplomatic interposition were the matters uppermost in Secretary Jones's mind that March, while President Houston and Secretary Hockley were immersed in military business.

When Ashbel Smith met him at Galveston, ready to sail for France, Secretary Jones informed him of an additional assignment. He would proceed without delay to London as first Chargé of Texas to the Court of St. James's, exchange ratifications of the three English-Texas treaties, and ask Her Majesty's government for "prompt" and "efficient" interposition between Mexico and Texas, as provided in one of them.

He would also assist the English, French, Belgian, and German empresarios "to bring population and Money to Texas from the Storehouses of Europe." The French colonizer, Henri Castro, Jones commissioned Texan Consul General at Paris. William Kennedy, who had published last year a two-volume work in England that was already stimulating trade and immigration, was returning to London as Texan Consul General with a contract to colonize Englishmen in Texas. He had asked Jones to exchange with him a *"viva voce adieu,"* which the Secretary did —it was a good chance to send messages to Lord Aberdeen, new Minister of Foreign Affairs. Captain Victor Pirson was also sailing for Europe with an option on a huge tract for the settlement of Belgians. In Germany, Prince Solms Braunfels was forming his German colonization company.

Joseph Eve, Chargé of the United States, conferred with Jones at Galveston; but Count Alphonse de Saligny, representative of the King of the French, was still absent. He had not been mollified by the mere reading of the letter Jones had written to Paris last January; he demanded a copy of it and an invitation from the Secretary of State to return to his post. In the crisis Jones gave in and on March 2 wrote directly to Saligny and asked Dr. Smith to hand the letter to him personally, with appropriate flourishes.

It is the desire of His Excellency, the President [he wrote], that the unfortunate difficulties existing between Texas and France should be immediately arranged to the satisfaction of both parties. The regard and sympathy . . . for France . . . is sincere and ardent as well as his desire to reestablish and perpetuate those friendly relations. . . .

For the more speedy attainment of this important object, His Excellency, has instructed me to say that he would be most happy to see you again at your post, near this Government. I avail myself of the occasion offered in making this communication to renew to you the assurances of my distinguished consideration.

Given a little time—time for Smith to get to London and Paris, time for empresarios to send colonists to Texas, time for English and French ministers to arrive with whom Jones could negotiate verbally—he believed he could construct a strong bridge to independence.

When the Secretary of State had finished with Smith and Pirson and Kennedy, he took time to buy chinaware for the home he hoped soon to establish, jewelry for Mary, toys for Sam, pantaloons and a cap for himself. If the crisis proved as serious as the Galvestonians feared, imports would soon be cut off. He needed to buy what he wanted now.

It was true, that rumor of invasion that Mexican women had been circulating for weeks. Texas Rangers and volunteers—to the number of 107 men—hurried to Béxar. On March 6—sixth anniversary of the fall of the Alamo—Colonel Carrasco galloped into San Antonio to demand surrender in the name of General Vasquez. The defenders of San Antonio considered the suggestion. Fifty-three of them were willing to fight it out with Vasquez's fourteen hundred men; fifty-four voted to leave the place to the Mexicans, and it was so ordered. They lighted slow fuses in the powder kegs in Twohig's store and evacuated the town.

Another runaway scrape was beginning. The Guadalupe Valley was deserted from Seguin to Cuero; and as the settlers fled, two thousand angry Texans hurried toward San Antonio with their rifles.

His Excellency the President had been brushing up on military literature. Dr. Cornelius McAnelly had lent him a copy of the *Anabasis,* and he scanned it as he listened to rumors of invasion and wondered if he would have once more to take the field. Quite a man, that fellow Xenophon, the President thought—"worth the notice of Napoleon, or of Jackson"—or of Houston himself.

It was March 10 when Mr. Secretary Jones returned to the city of Houston, "where every thing was *booh!* Mexicans & war——" The President had remained at Galveston to issue war orders. The Collector of Customs would immediately send to Houston "such arms as you have . . . excepting three hundred guns . . . for the use of Galveston." Colonel Alden A. M. Jackson would please to place "the fort at the east end of the Island . . . in an efficient state of defense, in case of a descent of the enemy by sea." Secretary Hockley would at once move all the public archives from Austin to Houston, and Brigadier General A. Somervell would join the volunteers at Béxar, "take command of the same, and . . . maintain the strictest discipline. . . . Prudence and confidence will be of more importance than enthusiasm. . . ."

Brigadier General E. Morehouse at Houston was to "hold troops in readiness to march at a moment's warning." The Texan Consul at New Orleans would recruit only volunteers who could supply their own guns, ammunition, and clothing for six months. To the citizens of Texas the President published his assurance that no private property would be impressed—unless necessary.

To his Secretary of State he wrote:

DEAR JONES,—The moment the New York sails I will be off for Houston. I hope to see you there. I pray of you leave me news, if you leave before my arrival. You will hear that I am busy. God bless you. Thine ever

HOUSTON.

But His Excellency was not too busy to assure Daingerfield, his Secretary of the Treasury, who was in New Orleans,

I do *not* require of you to come home post. . . . I hope, my dear fellow, you will succeed to the perfection of your wishes & hopes with the fair and lovely Mary. Daingerfield, she would make a noble matron, and I do . . . pray that you may have the pleasure— aye, the felicity of *matronizing* her Ladyship, or her *young lady-ship! ! !* . . . .

Do pray be easy about matters here. . . . Tho' Congress left me manacled, I will maintain my oath and my prerogative. . . .

Next day he wrote again to his Secretary of State:

DEAR JONES,—If any news arrives about the enemy, no matter what *lies,* I wish no order given for the troops to turn out, until I can act on the facts.

Every report will be sent in to excite the public mind. *Heroes must be made to the west,* and there are so many pretenders that the United States cannot furnish supplies of glory.

General E. Morehouse's troops were ordered to Béxar, to report to General A. Somervell, who, the President thought, was in command there. To Secretary Daingerfield, who was still lingering uncertainly at New Orleans, he assigned an additional chore:

Jones, Hockley & Miller are with me. I can get on. . . . I wish you to have announced in the papers that all persons acting as agents from Texas in the United States, not *under your orders* from the President *will not be recognized.* . . . Heretofore great impositions have been practiced and I wish no more. *Do crush imposters.* Do the best you can—I know you will! ! ! . . . .

P.S. I wish I had some good stationery war paper, &c. &c.

When Brigadier Somervell of the militia rode into camp near Béxar to take charge of the situation he was told that the volunteers had already elected Vice-President Burleson their commander. There arose a jurisdictional dispute. Would the elected commander give way to the one appointed by the chief executive? He would not—at least not for two weeks. When at last General Burleson agreed to retire, Somervell declined to command these men who did not want him. It made no immediate difference. The Mexicans had retired from San Antonio and Refugio and Goliad toward the Rio Grande, after loading on their wagons and pack mules all portable property. The "reconquest" had been only a raid.

Mr. Secretary Jones wrote in his diary at Houston, "War ended," bought a new pair of saddlebags, and started for Burleigh. Copies of the proclamation inviting the Texans back to their Mexican allegiance had been scattered by Vasquez's troops as they marched toward San Antonio. President Houston read his copy at Galveston while he was writing his war orders. "I have received General Arista's proclamation," he told Somervell dryly, "and if he should come on I should be glad to make his personal acquaintance."

On the heels of Arista's proclamation came published copies of Santa Anna's reply to the forthright proposal of James Hamilton and Barnard Bee (Lamar men, both) to pay him five million, plus a two-hundred-thousand-dollar bribe, for recognition of Texan independence. The matter properly belonged to the Department of State, but Jones was not at his post. His Excellency replied:

> Your communications . . . would have met a more ready attention had it not been for a marauding incursion made by a Mexican force upon the defenseless town of San Antonio. . . . Apprehending that the force had some other character than bandits and plunderers, commanded as it was by regular officers, it produced a momentary excitement and claimed the attention of the Executive; but as the bandits have withdrawn, characterizing their retreat by pillage and plunder, as has been usual with Mexicans, I am left at leisure. . . .

That leisure enabled His Excellency to review in five thousand words the story of the colonization of Texas by freemen, the tyrannies that brought on the revolution, the magnanimity Houston himself had shown Santa Anna, and Santa Anna's subsequent perfidy. And now, the Hero of San Jacinto concluded:

> You touchingly invite Texas to "cover herself anew with the Mexican flag." . . . You have threatened to plant your banner on the banks of the Sabine. Is this done to intimidate us? . . . it will amuse those conversant with the history of your last campaign. . . . believe me, Sir, ere the banner of Mexico shall triumphantly float upon the banks of the Sabine, the Texian standard of the single star, borne by the Anglo-Saxon race, shall display its bright folds in Liberty's triumph, on the isthmus of Darien.
>
> With the most appropriate considerations, I have the honor to present you my salutations.
>
> SAM HOUSTON.

At Burleigh, Cousin Anson and Cousin Oliver pondered what the Old Chief had written and published in the papers, and the Secretary of State noted in his diary: "New War commenced."

The President, back in Houston, was indeed harassed and brittle.

If the people will fly in the face of the laws and constitution [he declared] it is to be deplored. . . . all the officers of the government will repair to this point—and should any refuse to come, their offices will be considered vacant and accordingly filled.

You may be assured I will not falter. . . . I am the sole judge of the emergency which may require the removal of the offices. The time has come; and if the offices are here I will create the officers. . . .

His Excellency had given Owen O'Brien a roving commission to round up his scattered Cabinet. Mr. O'Brien had called first at Burleigh and exhibited the executive summons:

Sir, You will proceed forthwith . . . to Oliver Jones, Esquire's, on the Brazos. You will show this to Doctor Anson Jones, and request that he will come to me as soon as possible. You will then proceed on to where you may find Col. George W. Hockley, Secretary of War, and W. D. Miller, Esq., my Private Secretary, and let them know that I desire them to come to me.—If Col. Hockley is usefully employed in the army, and he should think . . . his presence necessary there, he may remain until I can learn more of our situation.

No express has been received from any of the forces; nor does the Executive know what is to be depended upon. Rumors are arriving hourly and daily, but no authentic facts. . . .

At Houston mail awaited Secretary Jones. From the army camp near Béxar, General Somervell reported:

I arrived here on the 17th. . . . The men and officers refused to obey. . . . Burleson was selected without opposition. I have no doubt political intrigue has been at work, with the view to block out the next President. It is a rough concern, and no glory that can be won in the field will ever polish it. . . . The hobby on which they ride is, invasion of Mexico, to give peace and happiness to poor suffering Texas, and thereby achieve immortal glory for themselves.

From the capital of the United States, Texan Chargé Reily wrote him: "I would rather die than to remain here. . . . You can see from my official letter that nothing can be done here in the way of any negotiations for Texas."

A physician whose own baby was at the colicky age, Jones perhaps understood these symptoms of the body politic. He filed the letters and started writing in the makeshift State Department office he had rented from Major Thomas G. Western. "Sat. 26th Issued proclamation of blockade of Mexican Coast from Tobasco to Brasos Santiago." Then he added a note to a letter the President had scratched off to ask Daingerfield to accept donations for the Texan cause. Poor Daingerfield; he was yet in New Orleans, Miss Mary still uncourted.

We are now in for the whole affair with Mexico [Jones wrote him]. The President and the people are unitedly determined to prosecute the war with energy. . . .

Let all who wish, join the Standard . . . now is the proper time for them to come, or to contribute. . . .

Five days later, after the President had left town, Jones again wrote Daingerfield:

The storm and excitement . . . has pretty much subsided and settled down into a cool but resolute determination to march against the enemy with the purpose of extorting by force of arms a recognition of our independence, and not to lay them down until this has been accomplished.

No troops have yet been ordered out by the President. . . . I hope to God the President will act with promptness and energy and follow up the *Manifesto* by *deeds*. . . . I want to see in the course of six weeks Matamoros, Tampico, and Vera Cruz—in our power and a formidable Army in the valley of the Rio Grande. . . . Then, I think, we may *negotiate* and settle the matter in short order.

That was what Jones wanted done, but his instinctive caution asserted itself. Could Texas do it, without money, with her own volunteers insubordinate, and with adventurers flocking in from the United States, lured by the hope of plunder? The business would be too risky.

To Ashbel Smith he wrote, "War with Mexico is now pressing upon us," and it was rumored that England was backing Santa Anna. Jones was unwilling to believe it, but he wanted Smith to lose no time in ascertaining the facts.

Should the President convoke Congress? Jones thought not. "I can not trust their wisdom in our present attitude. . . . I do not wish bad matters made worse," Houston decided.

Secretary Jones instructed Waples to hurry to Houston with the seals of state, of war and marine, and the clerks of the departments; then he started for Columbia, hoping to attend to some of his neglected business while he waited their arrival.

At San Antonio the ardor of the volunteers and of their elected commander cooled. The President wrote Daingerfield ironically of "the prudence, wisdom & subordination of Neddy, good Neddy Burleson." Good old Neddy had, indeed, sent his men home on April 2, then sat himself down to compose a letter to the public, which the President fortunately did not see until three weeks later.

Disbanding of the refractory, unpredictable volunteers at Béxar was the first good news Houston had received in months; it called for thanksgiving. The next Sunday he attended divine services— "the first time I was in church for the last three years (except 3 times)," he remarked. Monday, refreshed and optimistic, he wrote to enlist good old Neddy's aid in a matter which, he said reprovingly, "your absence at Bexar has prevented my addressing you." A highly personal communication from one John Welsh, dated "Webbers Purrary," suggested that he should appeal to Burleson's sense of civic responsibility.

Sir Old Sam [Welsh wrote His Excellency] We did heart that you was goin to move the seat of government and the publick papers and that you swore you would do it, and then when you come to Austin and found out the boys would not let you do it you sed you never was goin to move it. Now Sam you told a dam lie for you did promise the people in Houston that you would move it, and I heard a man say that you told Hockley not to bring all his servants becase you would all go back soon. But the truth is that you are afeard you Dam old drunk Cherokee We dont thank you becase we would shot you and every dam waggoner that you could start with the papers   you cant do it and we ax you no odds. Travis and Bastrop Fayette Gonzales can bring 1000 Men out and Ned Burleson and Lewis P. Cook have promised that you shant budge with the papers I heard them myself and you know Burleson and Cook can make you squat you dam blackgard indian drunk Now old fellow if you want to try Ned Burlesons spunk just try to move these papers, and old Ned will serve you just as he did your Cherokee brother when he took the Hat what you give to your Daddy Bowles You shall hear more from me when I am ready.

The archives of the nation were still at Austin, despite orders for their removal to Houston. Irate citizens were holding to those papers "like death to dead negro," Major S. Whiting wrote Lamar, "& are determined they shall not be taken from here 'till ordered by a higher power than Sam Houston." If that was not an "insurrectory attitude," Houston knew not what insurrection could be. He addressed Burleson on April 11, not as General, as was his usual custom, but as Vice-President of Texas, and called upon him

as the second officer known to the Constitution to put down all insurrectory acts and conduct and to sustain the Executive . . . confident that you will not fail to maintain the oath which we have solemnly taken to support the constitution and the laws. . . .

I feel bound to urge your influence and authority in preventing the interposition of any impediment to the removal of the archives to this place in obedience to the orders of the Executive. I regard the archives of the Senate [he added as a happy afterthought], in cases of emergency, as under your care; and, of course, under your control until they reach the point of safety which may have been designated.

The Secretary of State was still visiting along the Brazos River. When he arrived at Burleigh, Cousin Oliver gave him a note Waples had left there for him four days before. Waples had the Great Seal and the seal of state in his saddlebags and was hurrying toward Houston as rapidly as "roads very bad and heavy" permitted. "I left Mr. Hall in charge of the office, with everything securely boxed up," the faithful clerk reported.

In the placid atmosphere of the Brazos plantation country the Secretary of State reconsidered the invasion of Mexico, which had seemed so desirable when he was among the war dogs of the coast. If it could be done it might solve the problems of Texas; but, he concluded, the Republic had neither the money nor the men, nor the leadership to assure success, and failure would ruin Texas.

But the President had not changed his mind: he was about to mobilize the militia for a "general movement against Mexico." "The President," Jones concluded when he heard that, "must certainly be running 'mad,'" and began wondering if he ought to remain longer in the Cabinet. He wrote Waples to let him know if "anything of particular moment occurs" and to send weekly reports of departmental business, but not to expect him at the office for some time. He had business to attend to—and, in his current frame of mind, he could not be much help to His Excellency.

In the April 20 issue of the *Telegraph,* Houston and Jones and all Texas read Vice-President Burleson's appraisal of the administration's military policy:

Fellow Citizens of Texas:—It has been truly said, that the greatest reward which a patriot can enjoy, is the approbation of his fellowmen. To this, I feel, in my heart, I am entitled. . . .

I feel no hesitancy in believing that if my orders had permitted me to cross the Rio Grande . . . by this time . . . we would have . . . an honorable peace. But President Houston says that "120 days will be necessary before we can make a move. . . ."

The only course left me was to disband the remaining troops. . . . That the volunteer army refused obedience to the appointment of the commander by the President is no fault of mine. . . . they called me to that . . . station . . . without my solicitation or wish. . . . there was no "constitutional" objection to my responding to the call. . . . if any ask why it is that the Vice President is in the field? my answer is that I love my country more than I fear the executive's displeasure. . . .

I still believe . . . the campaign should have been made. . . .

Another interested reader of the Vice-President's blast was Count Alphonse de Saligny, belatedly returning to his post in response to Jones's assurances that all was now well. The French Chargé attended a San Jacinto Day reception and reported to Paris:

Hardly had I entered the room where General Houston was, with Col. Hockley, Judge Terrell and his *Etat-Major,* when he came to me and, taking me by the hands, said with effusion . . . "Henceforth the 21st of April will be doubly dear to me."

The President outdid himself in apologies for the indignities the Chargé had suffered under Lamar and in expressions of gratitude for His Majesty's magnanimity in sending Saligny back. He himself, he assured the count, might not have been so forgiving.

The Secretary of State was absent from this touching scene. He was laboring over the ledgers of his medical business, posting books and making out statements. He could delay no longer arranging his affairs. What he did not collect promptly might never be collected if the President persisted in warlike plans. For three weeks he remained with patients and former patients at Columbia. The weekly reports and papers he had instructed Waples to send had not been delivered. He knew little more of the transactions of the government than the patients who visited his office. He was determined to remain away from his political duties as long as possible; he might never resume them.

President Houston commuted between Galveston and Houston, administering all departments of government personally. "I have never felt the influence of circumstances more than at the present moment," he wrote. "Every hour is big with events, pressing and important. . . . I am literally worn down by continued labor." But he did not revoke Jones's leave of absence.

The Houston *Morning Star* on May 17 reported all Cabinet officers except Dr. Jones were in town; that day the Secretary of State rode in from Columbia to take his place in council and attend to his accumulated correspondence as well as he could without his archives and form books. If he had memorized all the forms in his copy of Elliot's *Code*—now buried under a log cabin two hundred miles away—it would have saved him embarrassment. The routine documents he signed were "some what unusual in form as there were none of the usual blanks," but he knew well enough how to draft the proclamation calling a special session of Congress at Houston on June 27, which the President insisted upon issuing against his advice. Jones countersigned it reluctantly on May 24.

When his desk was cleared of current business he was off for New Orleans. President Houston had discovered that the retrenchment Congress, in its haste to wipe clean the slate of financial commitments, had overlooked an act of 1839 authorizing a loan of a million dollars, and his Attorney General assured him that he could act under its authority. To his Secretary of State he entrusted the mission and gave him passage to New Orleans at government expense.

You will proceed forthwith to the United States [His Excellency ordered Jones on June 10] . . . be governed by your letter of instructions . . . with the privilege of making such changes in the negotiation as you may deem expedient. You will receive for your services the compensation allowed by said law.

That was good news to a man whose board bill was more than his official salary. If he succeeded—and collected his ten-thousand-dollar commission—his immediate financial problems would be solved.

Tuesday, June 14, in New Orleans he "Consummated contract with Alexandre Bourgeois d'Orvanne & Embarked . . . for Galveston." Four days later he was back in Houston, reporting to the President that M. Bourgeois promised to lend Texas one million dollars. Would that make war against Mexico feasible? The city of Houston, like New Orleans, was full of war talk, and the Texas Congress would assemble in two weeks to give it legal sanction. Still a little uncertain as to what Texas ought to do, the Secretary of State renewed his leave of absence and started for Columbia, thinking deeply upon the state of the nation as he rode. When he arrived he wrote in his diary a sentiment soon to be shouted in the halls of Congress:

We must fight with Mexico   Another San Jacinto on the Rio Grande will secure to Texas nationality   Independence   The Anglo Saxons once preccipated beyond the Rio Grande no one can predict their limits, or their point of stop   If Mexico Is wise she will invoke with us the interference of the United States France and England to mediate.

For a month his headquarters were Shierburn's store building in Columbia, the facilities of which were enriched by a stock of medicines he brought from New Orleans. G. K. Teulon, friend of his Austin days, who was now with Minister Ashbel Smith in London, reported:

The government here have purposely been humbugging the pair of us, until they have teased me of all my money and patience, so that sundry small presents laid in for some of my friends have disappeared to stay the cravings of an outraged belly, or, in plain English, have been sold to pay board. . . . I have no faith in the ministry; they are evidently biased in favor of the yellow bellies. . . .

The one encouraging note from London was that the Masonic Grand Lodge of Texas had been recognized by the Grand Lodge of England which, Teulon pointed out, "holds no communication with any of the Grand Lodges of the United States."

Toward the end of June congressmen and volunteer advisers

converged on the city of Houston, where they found the hotels full, prices exorbitant, and Houstonians little interested in the comfort or convenience of statesmen. The old capitol building was now a hotel, and the proprietor declined to turn out paying guests to accommodate the penniless government.

Administrative offices were scattered about town in whatever rooms could be had on a promise to try to pay. The Congress accepted the hospitality of fraternal and religious organizations. The Senate convened June 27 in Masonic Hall, Keasler's Arcade, then with fine impartiality moved to the Hall of the Odd Fellows. The House deliberated in the new Presbyterian church. There the President delivered his war message on June 29. It was no stereotyped greeting of hope and cheer, nor was it designed to conciliate the gentlemen who listened to it.

The difficulties which now engulfed the Republic, His Excellency began, he had anticipated and pointed out to them at Austin last winter, "but the honorable Congress did not accord in his suggestions, and the precautionary measures were not adopted." The President had done what he could with the limited power the Congress had left to him; it was now for the people's representatives to say what should be done. So far as he was concerned, the President declared with beautiful ambiguity, he considered it "now quite time to adopt and pursue such a course of policy as will secure to us peace and the recognition of our independence."

Wynns of Harris promptly offered a "Joint Resolution declaring it the policy of Texas to carry on an offensive war with Mexico," and on the Fourth of July, Mr. Isaac Van Zandt of the committee on military affairs declared:

We are no longer the controller of our own movements, but are called without notice, order, or discipline to the field, whenever it shall suit them to attack our frontier. . . .

Under this melancholy state of things the majority of the committee, sincerely believe and they would submit it to the House of Representatives, as the deep, deep conviction of their minds that the only course left us IS AN APPEAL TO ARMS, AND TO THE GOD OF BATTLES. . . .

When Texas had repaid Mexico in full for the horrors and ravages Texans had endured, there would be peace. Could Texas

afford war? Certainly. Foreign capitalists were already eager for
her public domain; let the President sell or mortgage "millions
of acres," without making any "cold and sordid calculation"
whether that would be "incompatible with the genius of our institutions." Then let the President open subscription booths
throughout the Republic "to receive the contributions of individual liberality." Texans would oppose to Santa Anna's "chain-
gang legions . . . the brave warriors of our young Republic, sustained . . . by voluntary munificence." The funds needed, he
assured the House, were "not so large."

That was fortunate. Secretary Daingerfield, who was begging
loans and contributions in the United States, was reporting that
he could borrow nothing, but free-will offerings amounted to
"$927.44 & 10 Barrells Beef."

Dr. Jones read in the *Morning Star* an account of the oratory
that followed Mr. Van Zandt's report.

The speech of Mr. [Fiery] Jones of Gonzales in favor of the
measure, was worthy of the days of "76," and was received, with
rapturous applause by all parties. Messrs. Mayfield, Wynns, Cooke
and Van Zandt have also nobly sustained the measure. The opponents of the bill have not yet made any direct attact upon it. . . .

The House authorized the President to command the army in
person, after rejecting Mr. Cooke's proposal to insert "provided
he be the choice of the assembled troops." The President reported
that the resignation of Felix Huston as major general of the militia
"has been tendered; but, in consequence of the unsettled state of
his accounts, with the Department, it was not accepted," whereupon a joint resolution was introduced "requiring the President
to accept the resignation of Gen. Felix Huston &c."; then the
office was declared vacant. Texas was too busy to contend again
with Old Long Shanks. On the twelfth the war bill was passed,
21 to 14.

That disposed of, Mr. Fiery Jones of Gonzales wanted a committee "particularly to send for and exercise all Englishmen,
Frenchmen, Dutchmen, and Belgians, who are in the country,
and are suspected of having money, to ascertain if any propositions have been made to them by the President for negociating a
loan."

The Galveston *Civilian* reported that on July 18

Mr. Mayfield introduced a resolution calling upon the Secretary of the Treasury for further information relating to the [Jones-Bourgeois] one million Loan, and availed himself of the opportunity as he generally does on almost all occasions to make a great many remarks not particulary complimentary to the Executive, and in my humble opinion entirely irrelevant and uncalled for, and I really think the house were pleased when the gentleman from Washington, Mr. Williamson, took the matter in hand, to the astonishment of many, as he has been opposed to the President, and in his peculiar manner handled Mr. Mayfield, to use a common phrase, without gloves, much to the amusement of all within hearing. . . .

The war Bill has not yet been acted upon by the Executive, and if I am allowed to prophesy, it will be vetoed, and if so it will elevate Gen. Houston so far above all his enemies that hence forward he will be invulnerable to the shafts so lavishly aimed at him.—His refusal to accept the almost unlimited powers vested in him . . . will evince his superior strength of mind in refusing what his enemies have so loudly declared was his only object and desire—the complete control of the purse and sword. . . .

The *Civilian* continued in a prophetic mood. The matter under consideration July 20 was the seat of government.

I should not be surprised at any action that may be taken on the matter, as all will depend upon the humour of the House, and I presume the state of the atmosphere. There never was a greater misnomer applied to any set of men congregated together for any purpose, than the name of deliberative body applied to the House of Representatives of Texas, for in my humble estimation, they do not deliberate on any thing. . . . As the question now stands, there is before the House two Bills, one censoring Gen. Houston for attempting the removal of the archives and declaring Austin to be as safe a place as any other for the archives, and another declaring it unsafe and requiring the immediate removal of all the Government offices to Washington; and I should not be at all surprised if both of them passed.

In the Senate business was conducted with more decorum—and more pointed criticism of the President. The war bill was passed, but Senators Jack, Moore, Webb, and Greer filed strong protests against features of it. Senator Colquhoun of Béxar was less wordy: "I object to . . . authorizing the President to take command of the Army in person—because of his inefficiency and inability to command an Army. . . ." Earlier this gentleman had declared enigmatically, "The Senate is not the proper place to decide on the private character of the President."

In the midst of parliamentary wrangles the President sent for Mr. Waples. "He desires me," Waples wrote Jones, "to request you to repair to this place as early as practicable, as business of importance requires your presence. What that business is he did not communicate. . . ."

Secretary Jones did not come. He had, in fact, about decided never to return to the Cabinet. Two weeks later Waples wrote him more urgently: "The President is much harrassed and perplexed. If I could be permitted to have any influence with you, I would very much desire you would not resign, at all events, without visiting this place, for I know your presence here would have a desirable influence at this time. . . ."

The President himself wrote the same day, the snappishness of his temper reflecting in his bluntness. The Secretary of State was no longer Dear Doctor, or Dear Jones; he was Dear Sir, and there was no complimentary closing:

I have been much embarrassed in consequence of your absence during the session of Congress now near its adjournment. Many subjects with which you have had connection have been brought upon the tapis, and your presence would have relieved me from reflections which have been ventured against me. At one time I have heard that you were ill, at another that you were not. Is it in your power to make me a visit? Your doing so would afford me much gratification. Do so if you can, and if not, please apprise me what I am to expect or calculate upon. Please present me with my compliments to your lady.

The tone of His Excellency's message told Jones that he had better have a talk with him. Maybe he ought to leave the Cabinet; but if he should leave, he preferred to resign rather than be dismissed. He started at once. On the way he became violently ill and remained eighteen days at Colonel William T. Austin's.

His Excellency waited as long as he could, then vetoed the bill he had called the Congress together to enact. He could fight no war with ten million acres of vacant land; it required cash. Item by item, he argued that the bill not only failed to meet the emergency but laid a precedent for a dictatorship. "I can never sanction," His Excellency declared, "the adoption of a principle at war with the convictions of my mind, the practice of my life, and the liberties of my fellow men."

Congressmen listened, ordered a thousand copies of the veto message printed, but they did not override the veto. The next day they adjourned and started for their homes to explain as best they could the lame ending of the session.

While the Secretary of State lay abed at Colonel Austin's, that "useless and pernicious" session the President had called "to make capital for himself" ended in a quarrel "by which the country has been injured and disgraced." He was a little glad not to witness the closing scenes. "As the President 'has made his bed, so he must lie,' " he wrote.

His opinion as to a proper policy toward Mexico had changed often during the three months that he was not in daily touch with the President and as he considered various circumstances and contingencies. At first he opposed war *"toto coelo"* and suggested that the President kill enthusiasm for it by asking Congress for a heavy war tax. Later he thought Congress should not be called together, even to enact the war tax. War, or at least a warlike gesture, he then thought, was inevitable and maybe desirable: it might put Mexico in a humor to grant recognition. But when the President began readying the militia Jones had concluded the idea of carrying war into Mexico was the most absurd scheme since the Crusades. The Old Chief, he believed, was intoxicated with the phrases he had written Santa Anna and felt obliged "to *attempt* to carry out his *brags."* When His Excellency declined to approve the war that Congress wanted, Jones saw nothing ahead but irregular, uncontrolled, freebooting expeditions against Mexico— which would create all the problems but could achieve none of the results of straightforward warfare.

Adjournment of the war session eased the tension. His Excellency wrote his absent Secretary of State another Dear Sir letter, but he subscribed himself "Truly thy friend":

That you were unwell I knew, but until yesterday, I was not apprised of your extreme illness. I was glad to hear you were "able to shave"—these shaving times.

You no doubt have all the particulars of Congress. "It got through," as some of the members said, while others, in my opinion, thought they had only got their "foot into it." They are gone, and no war, nolens volens, but as much as can be had of the willing kind. . . . Had I sanctioned the war bill . . . I would have been in a state of constant vexation, and threats of revolution would have been constant . . . for my country's sake and for the credit of those who have been so anxious, I sincerely hope there will be volunteers enough to answer the design of a visit to the Rio Grande. We will see. . . .

In the expectation of seeing you here I did not send you letters. . . . Major Reiley . . . sent his resignation, which I, of course, accepted. The Major thinks his case a hard one. His mind appears to have fallen into a queer snarl about money matters; he cannot understand them, with all that we have done. In his place I have sent Mr. Van Zandt to Washington. He will be prudent, and will not "jump high" enough to endanger his safety. Don't attempt to come, until you can do so without danger of a relapse. Since Congress rose, all things appear to wear smoothly, and I hope we will get on, after a fashion. The chances now are rather in our favor. Though, as Fullenvyder said, it "will be a d——d dight squeese."

I pray you to commend me with best wishes to Madam, and kiss for me your auburn-pated urchin [Sam Houston Jones]. . . . When you can in safety come, I will be very happy to see you.

So Major Reily would leave Washington. Jones understood better than Houston Reily's queer snarl about money matters. The Republic of Texas still owed part of his own stipend for that same post in 1838! As for Reily's successor, Jones thought "Van Zandt is well enough—*very* well."

When at last he was able to travel he rode with Colonel Austin to Houston for a single day. Van Zandt's instructions had already been written, and he had started for Washington without giving the Secretary of State an opportunity to brief him on his mission. Instead of the customary credentials, the new Minister carried only a piece of paper stamped with the Great Seal and signed by the Acting Secretary.

The books and papers of the Department being in Austin, we are at a loss for the form of a letter of credence [Waples explained], therefore I sign a blank sheet which you will have filled in the usual form (which you will be enabled to find in Washington) . . . perhaps a copy of Mr. Reily's credence is on record there. You will also please forward a form for full power to this Department, in order that one may be furnished you.

Waples certainly should have brought Elliot's *Code,* along with the seals in his saddlebags instead of burying it at Austin.

The President was willing enough to extend Jones's leave of absence until he could regain his strength and finish his business in Brazoria County, but before he could do either, another attack of fever confined him for ten days. While he languished at Columbia, Hockley became angry with the Old Chief and left the Cabinet. Daingerfield was still in the States. Only Attorney General Terrell remained with the President. "Occasional jars will test the solidity of a building," Houston wrote philosophically when Hockley quit him, "and Heaven knows that my poor Wigwam 'gets several.' "

Mr. Secretary Jones's department had been getting some jars, too, during his absence. Archibald Hyde, whom he had made head of the Post Office Bureau, encountered executive displeasure and left government service. The President concluded that he "has done no duty properly, & made contracts contrary to law . . . ." And, he lamented to Waples, "those who are stupid and lazy, are sometimes malignant & vicious." He detailed his own private secretary, Miller, "to take charge of the Bureau of the General Post Office, as its head and perform the duties pertaining thereto according to law"; five weeks later he appointed John Hall "Chief and Assistant Clerk thereof."

Some of the concerns of the Department of State, however, were more prosperous than the Post Office Bureau while Secretary Jones was absent. At Washington City, Major Reily had climaxed an otherwise uneventful diplomatic career by negotiating with Secretary Webster the commercial treaty Texas had sought since 1836.

I was here alone [he wrote Jones August 3] unaided, unexperienced, the representative of a young Government, destitute of political weight and whose commercial importance had not developed itself, and forced to enter upon the discussion of points and topics in which Texas felt the most vital interest, with some of the loftiest and most powerful intellects of the United States; under such circumstances [he modestly admitted] the . . . treaty was concluded.

The text of the treaty went to the bottom of the ocean when the steamship *Merchant* sank, and it was months after Reily returned to Texas before an official copy of it came before the Texas Government. It was a good treaty—if it could ever be ratified by the Senates of the two powers.

While the Secretary of State lay ill of a fever at Columbia, Captain Charles Elliot, R.N., arrived in Texas as the first British Chargé and Consul General. His commission was a year old when he reached Galveston August 28, 1842. Lord Aberdeen had declined to send a diplomatic representative to Texas until he had on his desk the Texan ratification of those three treaties Hamilton had negotiated in 1840. When Ashbel Smith brought the ratifications and presented his credentials as Texan Chargé at London, England was willing to send across her representative. Attorney General Terrell—the only Cabinet officer at Houston—did the honors for the State Department and presented the captain to His Excellency the President.

Judge Joseph Eve, Chargé of the United States, was in Texas; Saligny had returned to Texas; now Her Britannic Majesty's Chargé was here. The personnel of the *corps diplomatique* accredited to the Republic of Texas was at last complete. The Secretary of State could negotiate in his own office—if he ever returned to it.

At San Antonio de Béxar, the Honorable Anderson Hutchinson wrote in his diary: "Monday Sept 5, 1842 Opened the District Court of Bexar No invasion expected." There had been a rumor that Santa Anna was sending 1,500, maybe 3,000, men to San Antonio; but the worst anybody expected was a party of marauders. The case before the court was that of Shields Booker *vs.* the City of San Antonio. Dr. Booker, formerly of Brazoria and Dr. Jones's assistant surgeon at San Jacinto, was suing for a fifty-pesos fee that Mayor Juan N. Seguin had promised him. His attorney was Samuel A. Maverick, a signer of the Declaration of Independence and congressman-elect. The testimony, which was in Spanish, ran on and on.

The whole day of the 10th . . . passed . . . strengthening the general belief that the rumor was either a hoax or the character of the force advancing misrepresented [said Congressman William E. (Fiery) Jones of Gonzales, who was in San Antonio that day].

At day light on the morning of the 11th Sept. we were aroused from our slumbers by the firing of a piece of cannon almost in the edge of town, succeeded immediately by the sound of martial music & the tramp of a body of men——A dense fog obscured them from actual observation until they had advanced into the public square when they were immediately fired upon by our party, who amounted to about fifty in number—the fire was soon returned by the Mexicans. . . . This lasted a few minutes when the fog disappearing discovered to us that we were surrounded on all sides by bodies of regular troops. . . .

The uniformed Mexicans disarmed the defenders of San Antonio and put them under guard, then marched into the courthouse. Judge Hutchinson, the whole personnel of his court, every lawyer in town except one, two congressmen-elect, and a former lieutenant governor were taken prisoners; and the case of Booker *vs.* the City of San Antonio was never finished.

Once more volunteers flocked toward San Antonio; once more the President detailed General Somervell to command "all troops who may submit to your orders." This time Vice-President Burleson remained away from the bivouac. There was fighting along Salado Creek, but a week after the Mexicans entered San Antonio they evacuated the place with fifty-three prisoners and what plunder they could carry, trailed for thirty or forty miles by a posse under Old Paint Caldwell. Again there was panic in the west.

General Somervell led his Texan volunteers toward the Rio Grande. There they plundered the Mexican town of Laredo on December 9. Somervell apologized handsomely to the alcalde, returned what he could of the loot, and sent two hundred of his men home. Ten days later he ordered his men toward Gonzales. Half of them obeyed; the others elected William S. Fisher to command them and proceeded across the Rio Grande toward Mier, where on Christmas Day they won a brilliant tactical victory—and were taken prisoners by General Ampudia. To the Santa Fé and "courthouse" prisoners from San Antonio were added the Mier prisoners at the Castle of Perote.

While Mexicans raided Texas and Texans were retaliating, Mr. Secretary Jones was busy along the Brazos and the San Bernard. On Friday, September 23, he "brought Mrs. Jones   Sam & Svt. home   rec^d an Express Dispatch from the President"—another Dear Sir letter, without chitchat or complimentary salutation.

During your absence, business has greatly accumulated in the Department of State. There is much of high importance that should be attended to immediately. Not a single member of my cabinet is present, and events are thickening and pressing upon me.

I regret that you have not been with me since your health was sufficiently restored. . . . The assistance of my Cabinet will be for the future not only desirable, but indispensable to the administration of public business.

My health is so bad that I have to employ an amanuensis.

The Secretary on leave endorsed the letter: "I have done everything necessary in the Department of State, though a good deal absent from Houston during the summer. The claims of my family I cannot wholly pretermit. . . . I *have been obliged* to do something for a support aside from office."

Six days later he started for Houston, where he thought his office was located. "On the way," he said, "I learned the President, in a pet at that place, had packed up and gone to Washington on the Brazos. . . ." Dr. Jones "returned to Columbia having given over the trip to Houston & left Mrs: Jones   Sam & Sv^t at Dr. Phelps's."

He would remain, he announced, "until the government took a notion to light."

XXV

WASHINGTON-ON-THE-BRAZOS

IN OCTOBER 1842, the carriage and wagons of the President of the Republic of Texas lumbered into the sleepy town of Washington-on-the-Brazos, seventy miles northwest of Houston, a hundred miles east of Austin. His Excellency, a little mud-spattered and bedraggled, entered his new capital astride "a fine large pacing mule, which he called Bruin." It was his third seat of government in ten months—and the tenth Texas had had in the six troubled years of its existence.

The road from Houston—so little traveled that His Excellency often lost the trail—was along the east bank of the Brazos, until it reached the ferry at the foot of Washington's Main Street. Not until the river was crossed and the traveler ascended the first of two steep bluffs did the town come into view, the unpainted houses nestled in a post-oak grove.

A visitor pronounced Washington a few months before President Houston arrived "a fine Place, but," he added, "all the fine Stores and dwelling Houses most all deserted." There was not a house there more than seven years old, but everything "looked old and weatherbeaten," and there was a decrepit air about the place —except during racing season.

For six years the Washingtonians had been living meagerly, hoping that Providence would again bring them prosperity, as it had done once before. In 1836, when the town was new and its citizens enterprising, it had been host to the Independence Convention, which on March 2 declared Texas a nation, then, harassed by rumors of the advance of Santa Anna's army, threw together parts of a constitution, inaugurated an ad interim government, and left pell-mell to protect their families, or join the army.

After San Jacinto, Washingtonians drifted back, but the glory of their town had departed with the government. Gunsmith Byars organized a Baptist church, while his neighbor, Mr. John W.

Hall, an original proprietor of the town, laid out a race track and began to breed quarter horses. A visiting clergyman in 1840 found there a "remarkable devotion" to the racecourse.

While promoters of the post-independence towns of Texas—Galveston, Houston, Richmond, San Luis—were busy publicizing their town sites, Washingtonians sat in their post-oak grove and hoped some immigrants would come their way. They thought that grateful Texans should make the birthplace of independence the Philadelphia of Texas, but they bought no advertising space to exhort them. Too late they learned that Texas towns were built by promotional skill and by printer's ink, not patriotic sentiment.

This place [George W. Bonnell reported] is more celebrated for its good society and the hospitality of its inhabitants than for their enterprise; and the natural advantages which it possesses, have been neglected, and they have received all their goods through Houston, thus aiding to build up a rival town at the expense of their own prosperity.

Even the county seat was moved away. Little remained at Washington to attract visitors but Mr. Hall's racecourse, the faro banks along Main Street, and the saloons of John Rumsey and B. M. Hatfield, who "sold alone for cash, consequently did not command the trade that was given to his rival." The highly respectable resident population of 250 watched with impotent disapproval the doings of the hundred or so "gamblers, horse racers and sports," who had most of the money. The moral situation had been markedly, if temporarily, improved during the summer of 1841, when the Reverend W. M. Tryon and the Honorable and Reverend R. E. B. Baylor held a protracted meeting in Independence Hall. "Over half of the town joined the church," a resident reported, "which had a good effect on the inhabitants thereof."

To this sleepy village, its birthplace, the widely traveled, almost exhausted Texas Government returned in the fall of 1842.

Several considerations had prompted the President to leave the city that bore his name. It was still a boom town, its inhabitants intent on business to the exclusion of everything else, and there was a housing shortage. Houstonians were willing to have the government remain there but saw no reason to give it quarters when men were waiting, money in hand, to rent the rooms it occupied. There was no appropriation for office rent, and a good many Texans thought President Houston should move back to the log office the Republic provided for him in Austin. A newspaper predicted October 2 that the President would be "unable to get the legislative branches of the government together unless he should again locate them upon the frontier, or summon the members to some point in the Brazos valley."

The British Chargé thought correctly that His Excellency was

driven away by some of those springs of local politics, feuds and jealousies, which run into such long streams of talk and knavishness, on this side of the Atlantic, and are so insignificant and unintelligible every where else . . . [to] Washington on the Brazos, where there are 12 or 13 Wooden shanties, and to which place there are no means of getting except in an ox train, or a Bât horse. . . .

Unable to remain at Houston and unwilling to return to Austin, the President decided that Washington was the constitutional capital, and it was his duty to transport his government there. Washingtonians offered to provide quarters, and on September 10 His Excellency requested them to send six wagons for the governmental paraphernalia at Houston.

Washington's one hotel was soon overflowing, and every home of more than two rooms had boarders. Judge John Lockwood, chairman of the citizens who invited the government to Washington, entertained the President, his family, his private secretary, and the Acting Secretary of War. The judge's young son found the Hero of San Jacinto fascinating:

I remember him sitting near the edge of the gallery chewing tobacco, and invariably when he went to spit he would turn and spit on the floor; but his conversation was so entertaining, his wit and humor so captivating to the large crowd which he invariably drew around him that this peculiarity was not noticed by anyone save my mother.

The President was expecting not only congressmen to meet him at Washington, but the Indian chiefs; and he desired the diplomatic corps—which persisted in remaining at Galveston—to witness both spectacles. The British Chargé hesitated to leave the cramped but relatively safe room he shared at the island with Judge Eve, the American Chargé, and four strangers.

The President writes me [he reported to London] . . . that He finds things at Washington rather raw and as He has been accustomed to the elaborate comforts and luxuries of an Indian Wigwam, I presume He must be living in a commodious excavation.

Washington lost its lethargy as government clerks and small boys helped the village carpenter make habitable buildings that had been vacant for years. To His Excellency went the most commodious office structure in the place—a one-room log law office with a fireplace, furnished with one couch, one table, one chair.

Across the street, in easy walking distance, a clapboard edifice that had been a carpenter shop—"roomy enough to transact all the business of the then young republic"—was made ready for the Secretary of State, who remained in Brazoria County while Mr. Waples unpacked the current files of the department. Pending the arrival of Mr. Secretary Jones, diplomatic documents were drafted there and taken down Main Street to the cabin where George W. Terrell signed them, a little self-consciously, "Atty Genl. and Acting Secretary of State." He was repaying Secretary Jones for past courtesies by attending to urgent business for him; "the pompous addenda to my name," he explained, "is a mere whim of the 'Old Chief.' "

One month after the President reached Washington "after sundry bothers and mishaps," Secretary of State Jones arrived in company with Count Joseph de Boos-Waldeck and Count Victor Leininger Westerburg, who were reconnoitering the Republic for German colonization. He had put his medical practice in charge of Dr. D. C. Gilmore and left Mary and Sam at Dr. Phelps's plantation. The next few months would decide whether he should rejoin them permanently as a retired statesman and full-time practitioner in Brazoria County or bring them to a new plantation house near Washington, remain with the government, and plan to succeed the Old Chief in 1844.

The President, without consulting him, had asked Congress to meet three weeks earlier than the law required, and on November 14 congressmen began straggling into town in no good humor. Every morning for a week Mr. Secretary Jones sat in the Speaker's chair in Independence Hall, pronounced "no quorum," and tried it again next day.

In the loft above Major Hatfield's saloon the Senate did no better. Vice-President Burleson's arrival was delayed four days, and even then it seemed probable that most of the senators would not answer the President's summons.

Mr. Secretary Jones drafted for His Excellency a proclamation reciting that, "from reasons unknown to him, a quorum has not been formed," then proceeded to "direct and require" Congress to assemble December 5 at Washington, "then and there to deliberate." The papers reported that one western congressman had gone to Austin, where he was walking every morning to the capitol, declaring "no quorum," and repeating the performance next day. Most of the absentees went to no such trouble: they simply remained at home.

On November 24 a bare majority of the House answered roll call, elected their Speaker (Nicholas H. Darnell defeated Jones's old friend G. W. Hill, M.D., by four votes), ordered "chairs, tables &c. for the use of the members," and heard a motion to adjourn and meet at Austin on December 5.

The afternoon the House organized, Mr. Secretary Jones exchanged his brief case for an instrument bag and started for Brazoria County. While the House wrangled and the Senate waited for a quorum to begin its arguments, he "Made out accounts for 1841 & 1842 for Medical Services & posted Books," and rode the circuit of his patients with Dr. Gilmore. After three weeks he returned to matters of state.

Congress had got off to a bad start. It did not receive His Excellency's message until December 1; the upper house still lacked a quorum, but senators agreed to listen to the discourse "as individuals."

Since the commencement of legislation in Texas [the President lectured them] . . . we find the proceedings of Congress . . . characterized by . . . selfishness and partiality. . . . Its decline, since the year 1838 . . . has been regular and more rapid than perhaps that of any other country. . . .

The chimera of a splendid government administered upon a magnificent scale, has passed off and left us all the realities of depression, national calamity, and destitution. . . .

The frontier difficulties were due to a "want of discipline and order" and activities of "individuals not functionaries of the government"—and to the refusal of the previous Congress to approve the President's plans for a frontier defense.

This Republic, its President declared, was "an anomaly in the history of nations": it was trying to exist without a currency, without adequate revenues, without means of communication. It had suddenly changed from "unrestricted and unlimited extravagance . . . to a state of things, where we are without means, without appropriations and without disbursements. . . ." The President had told the Sixth Congress how to solve these problems, but Congress had not solved them.

His "most fervent desire" was that the "patriotism and wisdom" of the Seventh Congress would improve the country's "present depressed condition," His Excellency assured these men who had come together reluctantly, some of them defiantly.

There were not enough Houston partisans to enact the President's program, nor enough anti-administration men to prevent their consideration. Mr. Cazneau, whose home was in Austin, tested the strength of his bloc the day after the President's message. He moved that Congress adjourn, to meet on December 5 at Austin, "the time and place designated by law." When that motion lost by only three votes, twelve congressmen voted to adjourn until March, "then organize and proceed, forthwith, to the West, and join the Army in the expedition over the Rio Grande . . . the President of the Republic . . . to command the expedition." Other congressmen wanted to assemble at Nacogdoches, Galveston, San Felipe—anywhere except the place the President had asked them to meet.

After disposing of these proposals, no quorum was mustered in the House for days; but when Mr. Secretary Jones returned legislative proposals were plentiful. Warren of Brazoria wanted "to quiet marriages in the Republic of Texas" by statute; the retrenchment committee was suggesting further reductions in appropriations; Jesse Grimes was proposing to confiscate estates of "traitors and enemies of the Republic"; and there was a statesmanlike proposal before the House to save half the expense of the postal system by restricting mail delivery to county seats—or three fourths of the cost by making deliveries along a single route from San Antonio to Fort English.

It had been November 30 when the Senate at last got a quorum and held it long enough to elect clerks and invite the Reverend Mr. Tryon to pray for the Senate, gratis, when convenient. Senator Webb (Lamar's friend Webb, who lived at Austin) wanted the Senate to adjourn sine die; when that was defeated, 4 to 6, he resigned. Then there had been no quorum until December 9, when Senator Jones (Cousin Oliver) appeared and the Senate moved temporarily from Hatfield's to "a room at Mr. Norwood's."

Five days later, when William H. Jack, frail, brilliant senator from Brazoria, took his seat, the anti-administration bloc had a leader, and obstructionist tactics gave way to a positive program. Senator Jack began by suggesting reductions in the pay roll and the repeal of the Houston-sponsored exchequer system.

Dr. Jones returned to his office December 15, read his accumulated mail, listened to reports of the doings of the Congress, and became once more a statesman. He spent the night with the President, all the next day in Cabinet council—Daingerfield had returned from the United States, so the Cabinet, like the Senate, now had a quorum—and the third day he "Dined with a large party at Gen. Houston's." From all appearances, this Congress would be a difficult one, but at least Jack of Brazoria was leading the opposition in a more statesmanlike manner than Pilsbury had done in the last Congress.

Jack was introducing a steady stream of proposals: abolish the Secretaryships of the Treasury and of War and Marine—"mere sinecures"—and let Mr. Secretary Jones look after national defense along with the foreign relations and post office; abolish all foreign missions, to save money and curtail executive patronage— doubly desirable "if the sword and the purse are united," as Jack thought Houston wanted them to be. He proposed inquiry into almost every transaction of the President's office and kept His Excellency and his secretary busy explaining what had or had not been done—and why. Jack declined to vote for the 1843 appropriation bill because it was too lavish; his economy suggestions had not been written into it.

In the House a proposal to abolish all duties on imports and finance the government by a four-dollar poll tax was lost by a tie vote. Portis was proposing a bill "to protect innocence and prevent fraud." Dial got through one "to establish a Sabbath, or day of rest, throughout the Republic of Texas," after Caldwell tried to substitute Friday for Sunday.

Texans generally probably needed a day of rest, but a reporter for the Houston *Morning Star,* who "had the curiosity to visit Congress," found the lawmakers in a thoroughly relaxed condition.

I went first to the House of Representatives. . . . The Speaker was sitting listlessly in his chair and before him were a few members, some sitting, some standing, and some leaning against the posts, apparently waiting for a quorum. The Door Keeper was sitting on a log outside the house.

Finding little here to interest me, I proceeded to the Senate . . . where I found the President looking at the Senators, and the Senators looking at him. The Senate I learned, was waiting for the House to progress with business, and the House, I suppose, often waits for the Senate, and in the meantime certain members steal away occasionally and *"Consult the book of prophesies,"* alias, a pack of cards.

Thus our Legislators *labor* for their country.

As Secretary Jones listened every day to the President's diatribes against Congress and individual members of it, and to congressional maledictions against His Excellency, he became increasingly critical of the Old Chief. This Congress was certainly abusing the congressional privilege of being captious and dilatory, but Jones thought the fault lay more with the President than with the legislators. He was apparently determined not to agree with the people's representatives on anything, and more consistently and effectively than Jones had ever seen him do it, he was nettling the congressmen. There had been times when that game had amused Jones, but not now.

On his recent trip he found the people were getting tired of wrangles at the capital, and some were saying that Dr. Jones would make a better President than Houston. The election was nearly two years off, but it was a Texan custom to begin choosing the next President as soon as the current one was inaugurated. Some of Houston's friends were saying that Jones could achieve the Old Chief's objectives better than the Old Chief himself was doing. As snarls developed, Jones found himself remembering that and deciding what he would do—if he were President.

The representatives declined to buy furniture for the President's house in Washington; declined to order the archives brought to Washington; declined to change the time and place of meeting of the Supreme Court; declined, in fact, to do many of the things senators wanted done and most of the things the President recommended.

Sidney Sherman, Houston's enemy since San Jacinto, expressed "regret that the Chief Magistrate should so far forget the dignity of his station as to attempt to defame a coordinate branch of the Government. . . . The House will reject with proper indignation a charge against their integrity." His Excellency had had the temerity to suggest that certain documents he was sending be read to the House before being sent to a committee (Sherman's committee) "to slumber until the close of the session."

The partners of Jones and Gilmore did not fare well that legislative season. Dr. Jones was trying to get Congress to order payment of an old claim of his, which Jack pronounced just but which the senators declined to approve. All Dr. Gilmore wanted was a divorce from his wife Charlotte, but even that was refused.

The Senate, after bickering over it, approved a modification suggested by the President in the commercial treaty with the United States that Reily had negotiated, which was yet unratified by the other government; confirmed Congressman George W. Hill, M.D., as Secretary of War and Marine; thanked the Reverend Mr. Tryon for his unpaid services as chaplain, and omitted the customary vote of appreciation to the Vice-President.

The House rejected administration bill after administration bill and suggested that some of them be considered by Congress in the year 1855. On the last day of the session it listened to an excoriation of the President by Messrs. Cazneau and Caldwell (from the county in which Austin is situated and the adjoining one where Vice-President Burleson lived) and failed by only one vote to tender "the thanks of the country" to the Austinians who defied with artillery the men the President sent to move the archives.

Congress overrode His Excellency's veto of the frontier defense bill, elected Thomas J. Rusk major general of militia with full authority to call out the troops at his discretion and to pay them, and secretly authorized the sale of the Texas Navy, which was too expensive for the Republic to keep afloat and too difficult for the President to control.

Then with thanks to the citizens of Washington "for their usual bland and polite conduct toward the members," but none to the President, the lawmakers ended their labors January 16.

That Congress, like all the Congresses of Houston's second term, was "a campaign by the majority against Sam Houston"— or so it seemed to the President. Three of his opponents in the House, he declared, "were debarred a seat *by the constitution,* and one of the senate—but they were not questioned." To the British Chargé, His Excellency confided:

The recent Congress manifested a disposition to destroy the country rather than fail in my destruction. My good fortune did not desert me, and the country, I am happy to say to you, is in a more prosperous state, than it was this time last year. . . . My measures were rejected and none substituted in their place, but every possible impediment attempted to be thrown in my way. If I did not succeed, they failed to produce the hindrances which they attempted.

It seemed to Mr. Secretary Jones that the "opposition have got a little 'Rope' & appear very much disposed to 'hang themselves' with it." The President, the Secretary of State, congressmen— everybody—were a little relieved when the session ended before that was done.

During the congressional season Anson Jones was giving anxious, if inconclusive, thought to his own future course. At the very time that he needed money most, his non-medical income had dropped almost ninety per cent—from $15,931.79 in 1840 to $1,758.25 during 1842. He had ended the least prosperous year he had known in Texas with liquid assets of $615 (exchequers), a child on his knee, and another on the way.

His mind was divided. Could he afford longer to hold this office that did not even pay his board bill? Was the title he wore, and the opportunity it gave to help determine the destiny of Texas, worth what it was costing him? He wondered but did not try to decide at once.

He and the President were once more on fairly good terms, and Dr. Gilmore was keeping his medical office open in Brazoria

County. As long as he could ride occasionally into Columbia and make the rounds of the plantations, he could have his cake and eat it too. He could also open a medical office at Washington, where there were not enough physicians to care for the increased population. . . .

His life would have been simpler if he could have made a clear-cut choice between politics and medicine, but life in Texas that winter was not simple—for Anson Jones or anybody else.

XXVI

ARMISTICE

THE diplomatic plans Secretary Jones had made last winter and had begun to implement during the spring were almost at a standstill. Mr. Van Zandt arrived at Washington City on December 7 and "was recd and treated with great civility by Mr. Webster." An interview of three quarters of an hour convinced him that nothing could be done for Texas so long as Daniel Webster charted the foreign policies of the Tyler administration. The godlike Webster made it clear that the Reily commercial treaty would not be ratified; that the United States would not mediate between Mexico and Texas; that Texas might as well prepare for another invasion by Santa Anna, "nothing would prevent it." Among the friends of Texas, in and out of the government, Van Zandt found "the greatest difference of opinion in regard to the policy Texas should pursue," but agreement that "emigration of a substantial character" could not be expected "untill our difficulties are settled." In Congress old John Quincy Adams had "again gotten up the abolition excitement," which boded no good for any Texas negotiations. President Tyler and some of the Cabinet still wanted annexation, but they could not trust the Senate to ratify it.

From Ashbel Smith in Europe, Secretary Jones learned that France was willing to join England and the United States in a tripartite mediation between Mexico and Texas, but Lord Aberdeen declined to give "France and the United States any pretext for putting their hands in Mexican affairs." England would help Texas, Smith was sure, but in her own way, and alone.

The time had come to double Texan diplomatic representation in Europe. Smith would need to stay close to London and Paris to nurse along British interest and keep an eye on France. On January 20, Secretary Jones commissioned his Cabinet colleague, Daingerfield, Chargé to the Netherlands, Belgium, and the Hanse

towns of Germany. He instructed him to proceed "with convenient speed" to New Orleans to have new paper money engraved
for Texas, next to Washington City to learn the latest from Van
Zandt, then to London or Paris to acquaint Chargé Smith with
the current posture of Texan affairs, and finally to The Hague.

The new Chargé was the first man officially dubbed knight in
this democratic Republic. If Napoleon could create his Legion of
Honor and Iturbide his Order of Guadalupe, Sam Houston ought
to be able to give gentlemen ribands to stick in their coats. There
was nothing in the Constitution against it. "I surely have the right
to start an order," Houston declared, "and then to create some
reward for the worthy, as we have no cash, to encourage Gentlemen in preserving order."

Sir William Henry Daingerfield was deputized by the President
to salute

Colonel Ashbel Smith, and announce to him, that *he,* as well as
yourself, is a Knight of the order of San Jacinto, and the Ensign of
the order, is a Green Ribbon, in the left breast, or Button hole of the
coat opposite the heart. . . . If you wish . . . wear the Ribbon as
part of the uniform, and if it is Green, then wear a blue or Red
Ribbon.

At least two of his nation's diplomats would not have to appear
at court in unadorned black, as Jones had done at Mr. Van
Buren's; but His Excellency presented no riband to his Secretary
of State. When knighthood flowered unexpectedly in Texas, Jones
was at Mr. Woodruff's on Mill Creek, getting Mary and Sam
ready to bring to Washington County. He was tired of "camping"; the discomforts of the makeshift capital would be more
endurable if he had the companionship of his wife and the "young
Secretary of State."

His return was delayed by a flood on the Brazos, the worst
since 1833. The ferries were lashed to treetops until the current
slowed and the driftwood passed. On the last day of January the
ferryman at Washington ventured across with a boatload of statesmen who had been water-bound at the capital a week; and with
him Mr. Secretary Jones

returned to Washington with family & took boarding for them at
Mr. Farquhar's three miles from Washington. The Brazos River is
three feet above its highest bank and rising.

Settling temporarily in the country had a double advantage. He was inaccessible to those he did not want to see, and he had opportunity to study closely the operations of Mr. Farquhar's prosperous plantation. For a decade Dr. Jones had planned some-day to become a plantation master, with an establishment as com-fortable and profitable as Dr. Phelps's Orozimbo, if not as elegant as Wharton's Eagle Island in Brazoria County. His judgment told him that Brazoria had passed its crest; Washington County was the coming agricultural region. He was dickering with young Moses Bryan Austin, his former secretary, for a quarter league not far from Mr. Farquhar's.

Room and board were $75 a month—$15 or $25 more than the exchequers Jones received as head of the Cabinet were worth, but only half what accommodations in town would have cost. At Farquhar's he was master of his own time. He could study farm-ing, get reacquainted with his family, and confer and correspond in privacy on the matter of the next presidency. Waples looked after routine business in the office, and one of Jones's slaves, who was porter of the Department of State, rode out for the Secretary when he was needed in town. Official business was dull that season and would remain dull until he learned the effect, in the United States and in Europe, of the new policy he had outlined for Van Zandt.

The Republic of Texas, he wrote the Chargé near Mr. Tyler's government on February 10, would never again ask for annexa-tion; but if the United States should "take some step in the matter of so decided a character as would open wide the door of negotiation . . . you will be authorized to make a treaty. . . ." Sentiment in Texas was currently "very unanimous" for annexa-tion, but if the United States desired Texas she must act promptly.

While the Secretary of State was wondering if Mr. Van Zandt would be able to maneuver Mr. Webster into a decided step, the President of Texas was dreaming, as Lamar had done, of the riches of New Mexico. On February 16, Colonel Jacob Snively, Inspector General on Houston's staff, was authorized to intercept a caravan loaded with $150,000 worth of goods as it crossed Texas soil en route to Santa Fé—and give the Texas Treasury half the spoils. This privateering expedition by land was the Houstonian version of a Santa Fé expedition. Like his predecessor, he waited hopefully for news from the west.

Attacks on the administration and the countercharges by Houston partisans, including the President himself, shifted that winter and spring from the halls of Congress to the public prints. His Excellency believed "the Jacobins of France were not more rabid . . . than . . . disorganizers of Texas." The papers published little but political diatribes. Nobody in Texas was much perturbed by these fulminations; Texans knew how to evalute them. But republication in the United States created the idea that Texas was a land of "demagogical madness and diabolical insubordination." These "outrageous and abominable slanders . . . uttered at home and sent here abroad," kept Mr. Van Zandt in a state of nervous excitement. They produced, he and Daingerfield wrote Jones, "entire want of confidence in the stability of our institutions"—and had defeated ratification of the long-sought trade treaty. "Time, the knife, or rope, will cure the evil," the President philosophized; but for the present he combated it only with words—which invited further controversy.

Secretary Jones was discreetly silent on controversial topics and a little irritated by the "petty warfare" the President was carrying on. His own communications to the press were state papers—excerpts from Van Zandt's dispatches—published to demonstrate that annexation was not to be as easy as the Texans, in their ignorance, supposed; and that their own political bickerings might defeat it. When Van Zandt complained that publication of dispatches, with the names of his informants "standing out in bold relief," would make it impossible for him to get confidential information, Secretary Jones replied tartly that he would have to assume, as Jones himself did when at that post, that *"the Secretary of State knew his business."*

Mr. Van Zandt was doing exactly what Secretary Jones wanted him to do at Washington—hinting to statesmen, "to alarm them to some extent," that Texas was seeking connections with Europe, and dwelling on British interest in Texas to the President, which "aroused him considerably." Jones had concluded that he would no longer "maintain an attitude of supplication towards the United States, but will try a different course. We have begged long enough—too long, indeed." His plan was to open up alternatives. Van Zandt was talking of British connections to make the United States want annexation; Smith in London was harping on annexation to induce England to procure acknowledgment of Texan independence from Mexico.

Mrs. Jones and the baby came into town to spend a week with Mrs. Houston. They were getting to be friends. However much Mary Jones disapproved the naming of her first child for the President, she found Margaret Houston a pleasant companion. They had a good deal in common, besides the occupational colleagueship of their husbands; both were "in the condition ladies like to be in who love their lords and masters." While the ladies knitted and talked, Mr. Secretary Jones made a trip to San Felipe.

When he returned he found Captain Charles Elliot, R.N., in town. This gentleman had been British Chargé in Texas since August, but his earlier visits to the seat of government had coincided with Secretary Jones's absences. The captain was a rangy, weather-beaten, blue-eyed man who wore a flopping white hat and smoked an enormous pipe. He looked more like a plainsman than a sailor—or a diplomatist. He had been in the Queen's Navy since he was fourteen, but for more than a decade he had been in administrative, quasi-diplomatic posts. In Guiana he had been Protector of Slaves; in China, the plenipotentiary who precipitated the Opium War. Now, as penance for his sins, he was in Texas.

From Daingerfield, who had talked with the captain at Galveston, Jones heard that this "frank, bold, honest-hearted Englishman" believed Mexico would recognize Texas in six months and that he scented dark mystery in Daingerfield's going to Europe by way of Washington, D.C. " 'Hit him agen' on the subject of *annexation*," Daingerfield counseled; ". . . *that is the spot* between wind and water with him." That was unnecessary advice.

Soon after Captain Elliot reached Washington-on-the-Brazos, James W. Robinson arrived there with a message from President Antonio López de Santa Anna. Lawyer Robinson, former Lieutenant Governor of Texas, San Jacinto soldier, former judge, had unluckily been in San Antonio the day the Mexicans interrupted court there last September; since then he had been a guest of the Mexican Government.

In the Castle of Perote he had meditated upon two great problems: how to compose the differences between Mexico and Texas, and how to get James W. Robinson out of the *calabozo*. On January 9, the first anniversary of General Arista's invitation to the *Tejanos* to return to their Mexican allegiance, Robinson wrote Santa Anna a letter full of artless guile. The Texans, he assured El Presidente, were weary of war, anxious for peace—willing, in fact, to reunite with Mexico under certain conditions, which Robinson would be glad to explain. He was behaving like Santa Anna after the battle of San Jacinto—promising what he thought would move his hosts to send him home. Santa Anna understood, but he also saw in the proposal an opportunity to "do something about Texas," which would bolster his declining prestige in Mexico. After an interview with the Texan at Magno del Clavo, he gave him a letter and sent him on his way. When Robinson landed in Texas he published the gist of Santa Anna's peace proposition, then proceeded to Washington-on-the-Brazos.

The terms were brief and simple. The Texans had only to acknowledge allegiance to Mexico to be forgiven all their political crimes and misdemeanors and become once more contented citizens of *la patria*. Texas thereafter would be, technically, a department of the centralized Mexican Republic, but actually she would be autonomous. The central government would handle her foreign relations, but the Texans would make all their own laws, and no Mexican troops would ever molest them.

I was with General Houston [Elliot reported] when Mr. Robinson arrived at Washington. The President placed in my hand the original paper General Santa Anna had delivered to Mr. Robinson. . . . I did not detect that that Gentleman had more to communicate to General Houston than had already been made known to him through the medium of his Newspaper.

His Excellency remarked to Elliot that although this proposition "came to him in a strange and informal manner indeed," it evinced a peaceful disposition which he reciprocated. He would send commissioners to parley, but "an armistice would be indispensably necessary"—he wanted the British Minister to make that clear to Santa Anna.

To Judge Eve, Chargé of the United States, President Houston professed that he saw behind this business the hand of England,

and maybe France: "Some of the powers have touched him in a tender part and this I regard as *wincing.*" But, he added with greater frankness than he evinced to Elliot, "it is a curious piece of workmanship, and will do very well to file away as a curiosity for after times, and that is about as much use as can be well made of it."

Houston wrote no official reply. Santa Anna's letter, he pointed out, was

without character or comeliness . . . neither addressed to Sam Houston, the President, or to the people of Texas . . . as much applicable to the moon as to Texas. But I certainly will not gratify those who are ruining the country, to know what I even think of it, or that I think of it at all.

He did, however, dictate a letter for Robinson to sign—a long, crafty exposition of how Texas had changed since Santa Anna last visited it. The Texans were united and prosperous, not torn by factions as he and El Presidente had supposed; and there were treaties with foreign powers, which complicated negotiations. As for General Houston, he "could not ascertain what his purposes were—if he had any," but he believed if Santa Anna should release all Texan prisoners and proclaim an armistice it would have "a good effect."

If Santa Anna took that bait, Texas would have peace, temporarily at least.

Within Texas were two disturbing elements: anti-Houston politicians, and Indians. One of these the President knew how to conciliate: he called the chiefs of the red men to confer with him at Washington-on-the-Brazos. Negotiations were to be made, but not by the Department of State; the President personally conducted the Indian relations of this Republic. By executive order, Attorney General Terrell was riding the frontier, presenting plugs of tobacco and shawls to the head chiefs, to be distributed by them to lesser chiefs "so as to build up and establish their own influence; and thereby render it available to Texas," and telling them, in the name of the Great White Father:

If the chiefs come to see me, I have a pipe preparing in which we are to smoke of peace, and I will send to Houston and Galveston and buy suitable presents for them. . . .

Great preparations were being made for the reception of the chiefs. A Philadelphia lapidary, who was visiting the Texan capital to exhibit an Alamo monument he had just completed, was commissioned to design and carve a "large council pipe for Indian purposes," and Stephen Z. Hoyle was buying five hundred dollars' worth of presents, ranging from flashy beads and butcher knives to shrouding, from the white merchants and from Jim Second Eye and Red Horse.

In a shady grove near town, Luis Sanchez, Jesse Chisholm, and other Indian agents issued rations of beef and corn to the chiefs and their squaws and designated places for their tents as they arrived early in April. One brave had brought two squaws; with perfect impartiality "he caused his wives to stretch each one tent, directly opposite the other, with just passing room between them." The bucks lay on buffalo robes smoking pipes that looked like (and were) tomahawks, while the squaws did the work; but the luxurious idleness and the visits of curious townsmen made them restless. They wanted to get on with the council.

The camp was on the road to Secretary Jones's home, but he did not visit it. All Texan officials remained away until the President's sense of the dramatic and knowledge of Indian psychology told him it was time for the official visitation.

On Monday the President and his staff mounted horses in front of the executive office and, after instructions by the President on the protocol of powwow, galloped toward the camp.

There had been no warning of the visit, and there was consternation in camp until the Indians saw that the leader of the advancing column was their host, the President of the Republic. When the procession reached the campgrounds the horses were slowed to a canter and the riders circumscribed the camp, their eyes fixed straight ahead, as if passing in review. The chiefs hurriedly formed an aisle through the middle of the tents down which the official party walked. His Excellency ceremonially greeted each chief, then embraced him Indian-fashion—"which is done by placing one arm over and one arm under, as is done by boys when engaged in wrestling; this is accompanied by an energetic squeeze."

Then the Texan chiefs and the Texan officials seated themselves in a huge circle around the stone calumet Mr. Nangle had carved. At a signal from the President it was filled with sumac and tobacco, lighted, and the long stem handed to His Excellency. With the solemnity of a bishop celebrating pontifical High Mass, he lifted his eyes to heaven and exhaled the smoke. Then the stem went to the eldest chief, and on around the circle until each red man and white had smoked it with "prayers to that Power which upholds nations and rules their destinies, that our troubles might come to an end." When the stem had made the circuit His Excellency rose, looked first to heaven, then at his brethren seated at his feet. For a moment he stood silently, like a granite monolith.

Magnificent in physique, superbly caparisoned, instinctively dramatic in gesture and expression, he began a talk. The words were English, but he spoke them with a moving Indian cadence and inflection that conveyed meaning even before Luis Sanchez translated them. He knew the channel to the Indian mind: he was establishing a personal, primitive immediacy of relationship. He was counseling his red brothers to make war on no one, not even Mexicans or each other; and "judging from their grunts and other demonstrations" they agreed.

Secretary Jones's reasonable mind had long counseled peace with the Indians as more humane and cheaper than coercion. Now he sat stiffly among the savages and heard the President make that policy seem reasonable and attractive to them. For the moment he was lost in admiration of Houston's technique and, in spite of himself, a little under the spell of his primitive diplomacy. Two days later Jones again "Attended Council. Bintah, Jose Maria Hadda, bah, A-Ca-quass & James St. Louis spoke on behalf of their respective tribes." They promised to be good.

After the chiefs departed with their squaws and presents, the Secretary of State and the President considered negotiations with white men—which required the sort of discretion, subtlety, and acuity that Jones possessed. The President asked him to go to Galveston to confer personally with the diplomatic corps "in reference to the many subjects of moment now before your Department, connected with our foreign relations."

He made a leisurely two-week journey by way of Columbia, Orozimbo, and the home of his colleague, Hill, Secretary of War and Marine. There was much to attend to. He needed to check

medical accounts with Dr. Gilmore, discuss his presidential prospects with certain gentlemen, close the deal for Bryan's quarter
league near Washington, and buy slaves for himself and his
mother-in-law.

On May 6 he was at Tremont House in Galveston, where for
six days he entertained the diplomatic corps—Eve of the United
States, Elliot of England, Cramayel (Saligny's temporary substitute) of France—with wine, cigars, and such information as he
thought discreet to share.

At Galveston unofficial news from abroad was "every way
unfavorable," and official dispatches he received there no better.
An English warship brought word that Mexico had quelled the
rebellion in Yucatán—which meant that Santa Anna would have
troops to send into Texas. The Texas Navy, in defiance of the
President's orders, was in Mexican waters, instead of Galveston
Navy Yard. The Mier prisoners had escaped, been recaptured,
"and *every tenth man shot.* . . . News from Dr. Smith . . .
quite unfavorable. . . . Van Zandt has written . . . nothing
encouraging. . . ."

Van Zandt had, in fact, relayed to Secretary Jones sage advice
from Secretary Webster:

SIR; your affairs assume so many different *phases* that it is impossible one day to tell what will be the appearance on the next. If
your Government would take the advice of its friends, to remain at
home, unite among yourselves, confine your soldiers to your own territory, and to the defense of your own soil, supress insubordination,
prevent marauding parties upon the frontier and consolidate your
energies, then Sir, we might be able to do something effective.

As for annexation, there was no immediate prospect, although
Van Zandt believed Tyler was "trying to fix things up . . .
stopping to spit on his hands in order to get a better hold." "If,"
the Chargé prophesied, "the Captain succeeds in getting a full
crew on board who will be ready to obey orders . . . I think he
will give a broadside that will tell for the lone star."

Key place in the new crew was the Secretaryship of State,
which Webster vacated (to Tyler's delight but not at his request)
in May. Abel P. Upshur's succession to the post seemed to friends
of Texas providential. There was no more vigorous advocate of

annexation in the country, and few abler strategists. Nothing now would be left undone by the Tyler Cabinet to bring Texas into the Union.

On June 3, William S. Murphy arrived at Galveston with his commission as Chargé of the United States near the government of Texas to succeed Joseph Eve, the urbane Kentucky jurist who had served since 1841. Murphy listened two days to political gossip and reported to his government that President Houston was completely under British influence and opposed to annexation. The reports this fuss-budgety, Anglophobic Ohio militia general sent to the United States did more to quicken interest in Texas than any propaganda Jones himself could have devised.

A week after his arrival, General Murphy saw Her Britannic Majesty's sloop *Scylla* arrive with dispatches for Captain Elliot, and he saw Elliot the same day send a messenger to Washington-on-the-Brazos. Something, obviously, was afoot. He must watch Elliot and Houston and Jones closely.

The message the British Chargé sent Secretary Jones was Santa Anna's agreement to proclaim an armistice and treat with Texan commissioners. Elliot and his French colleague, Cramayel, thought "an honorable and desired peace" might result from the negotiations.

Neither Jones nor the President shared that optimistic hope, but they knew how to use the offer to further the alternative possibilities of annexation or independence. It could be made to appear that Texas was about to receive Mexican recognition under British auspices. If anything could crystallize annexation sentiment in the United States, the specter of a British satellite on her southwestern border would do it.

The proclamation Jones drafted June 15 adroitly stated the facts: Mexico had proposed negotiations with Texas through Her Britannic Majesty's Chargé in Mexico; Texas was accepting them through the British Chargé in Texas; and those Britishers would handle all further communications regarding the matter. Not stated was the fact that Mexico was proposing autonomy, not independence, to Texas and that nobody in the Texas Government expected more to come of negotiations than a lull in Mexican forays.

The *Scylla* remained in Galveston Harbor until Captain Elliot's messenger returned from the capital, then started for Vera Cruz. The same day the papers published the Texan armistice proclamation. To General Murphy it was further proof of British dominance in this Republic. Even before he could present his credentials he suspected that Texas had embraced a proposal that made annexation unacceptable.

Two days later Secretary Jones formally received Chargé Murphy in his office; but beyond the diplomatic civilities, of which Jones was master, he had little to say.

What steps are in progress [Murphy reported to his government], I know not, nor can I know until they shall develop themselves to the world. England may at this time be setting on foot a negotiation of vast consequence . . . in all probability such is the case.

Jones had promptly forwarded Van Zandt all his correspondence with Elliot touching the armistice, but he professed great reluctance to let Murphy see it. It did no harm—might do a great deal of good—to keep the general, and his government, on the anxious seat. On July 6 Jones wrote Van Zandt to speak no more of annexation at Washington City,

The United States having taken no definite action in this matter, and there now being an increased prospect of an adjustment of our difficulties with Mexico . . .

It is believed that the settlement of our difficulties with Mexico . . . will very much simplify the question of the annexation of Texas to the United States, and if after this event Texas should continue to desire this annexation, a treaty for the purpose would be more likely to succeed. . . .

It being therefore the policy of this Government to occupy itself for the present exclusively with the subject of an adjustment . . . with Mexico, the instructions given you on the tenth day of February [to angle for annexation] . . . are hereby suspended. . . .

XXVII

AN UNCERTAIN DIE

I WOULD soberly ask what the d——l are we to do? I shall suspend any opinion on that subject until I see you! . . . I have a thousand things to say to you when we meet." General E. Morehouse was writing Secretary Jones from Houston, June 25, on the presidential election, which was still fifteen months off.

The general was troubled by talk that former President Lamar would enter the race, but that gentleman had no intention of running. He wanted James Webb, who had been his Attorney General and who was now a senator, to enter the lists; but Webb refused. Vice-President Burleson, people said, was almost certain to be a candidate. Whether he was to be a Houston or a Lamar man he had not decided.

As in all previous Texas elections, everybody was waiting to see what Thomas J. Rusk would do.

Houston is tottering on his throne, but if he can by any means, bring to his aid the popularity & influence of Rusk [Webb lamented to Lamar], he is safe. He may go on . . . & set the Constitution, laws, & every thing else at defiance, & laugh at those who oppose his high-handed lawlessness.

Houston was ineligible to succeed himself. Most of his friends and many of his opponents regarded Mr. Secretary Jones his political heir apparent. He was the only Cabinet officer considered. Hockley was not presidential timber, Daingerfield had gone to Europe, Terrell was in poor health. Jones avoided committing himself on the succession, and the President was elaborately silent on that subject.

Finally Moses Johnson, M.D., of nearby Independence asked

the Old Chief questions Dr. Jones would never have asked. In July he reported to the Secretary of State:

> . . . I think he would be glad to see you succeed him, for he thinks you the greatest man in Texas, or nearly so. He told me he had rather have you for Secretary of State than Daniel Webster.

Interesting, Jones thought, and true, maybe.

If Jones should decide to become a candidate, he wanted a friendlier press than Houston or the administration had. He could count on the opposition of the anti-administration organs, and there were not enough other newspapers in the Republic greatly to influence public opinion.

The city of Houston was the key place. The *Telegraph* there was the most widely read and the best-edited paper in Texas, and its editor, Dr. Francis Moore, Jr., was violently anti-Houston—and anti-Jones. When Jones heard that John N. O. Smith was starting a rival publication he promptly offered him his blessing; before long he was a silent partner. It was named *The Citizen* (later *The Democrat*) and was dedicated to "a firm and unwavering support of the principles and policies of the present administration." The first number was issued in July 1843.

During that year the crops had been good and immigration was again flowing into the Republic. Public agitation of political issues might appear to a stranger highly personal and acrimonious; but the Reverend Caleb S. Ives, who had been an Episcopal missioner at Matagorda five years, believed the Republic was experiencing

> great external moral renovation, which is still in progress . . . is beyond anything of the kind I have ever before witnessed. Many of the dissolute character have gone; the community is more orderly, sober, and industrious, and more ready to support law and order.

The 175 men who had gone with Colonel Snively to capture that rich Santa Fé caravan at last were heard from. They had organized at the end of April, unanimously declined to share the booty with the government. For their sins, instead of capturing the wagon train, they themselves were captured and disarmed by Captain Philip St. George Cooke and 300 United States dragoons on what the Texans claimed was the soil of their Republic. Another bubble had burst; another wreck of Santa Fé on the doorstep of Mr. Secretary Jones.

The presidential succession was being discussed wherever two or more Texans were gathered together. Next to his law partner Rusk, General Henderson preferred Jones; but he warned the Secretary of State, "We could not concentrate a majority of Houston's friends upon you." Only Judge Ochiltree, of all Jones's East Texas friends, believed that summer he could be elected.

At Nacogdoches Jones sentiment was stronger, but his Cabinet colleague, Terrell, was afraid that if Judge John Hemphill and Vice-President Burleson also entered the race Jones would be defeated. W. D. Miller, the President's private secretary, advised Jones to make the round of the county barbecues during the congressional election that summer, "mingling with the people . . . extending your acquaintance," as Hemphill was doing. The Texas voters, Miller reminded him, "always like to see as well as hear the object of public attention."

Judge R. M. Williamson, a critic of Houston but an ardent Jones man, reported that prospects were "truly flattering"— everybody in Montgomery County, which cast the heaviest vote in the Republic, was for Jones.

More significant was a note from the President, who was "mingling with the sovereigns" at the big barbecue at Crockett:

. . . Henderson . . . is mistaken . . . your claims . . . I regard as equal to any man's for the station. Maintain your position unmoved. . . . Henderson is honest and noble, but he is not a good calculator. . . .

You can weather the storm. . . . I can see no reason why my friends cannot rally upon you. . . .

But Jones was not yet a candidate. Native caution made him hesitate until he was sure the Texans—the right Texans—wanted him; and honesty compelled him to admit that there were others whose chances were better. Four men, he concluded, would be stronger candidates: General Henderson, General Rusk, Judge Abner S. Lipscomb, and Kenneth L. Anderson—all lawyers of nationwide reputation. If any of them ran, he would not. As opportunity offered, he was asking each of them if he would make the race.

It was not that he lacked ambition; it was that he had reached a point in his personal evolution when he was so certain of his capacities that he no longer felt the need of demonstrating, even to himself, that he had them. He had come a long way since the time when he considered it important whether he was to be a lodge official or an officeholder—even President. That he could fill the office he knew; but he would neither seek it nor decline it if it came his way. Time, he felt, was on his side. If he should be mistaken, he could do very well without office.

"It has been excessively dull here since the President and the Cabinet left," he playfully wrote Miller in August; "and we of the State Department having nothing else to do all turned in and got sick. . . . The hot weather and the fever nearly killed politicks."

He was spending most of his time at the Farquhar plantation. Mary's time was very near, and she was more nervous than she had been before Sam's birth. The Secretary of State was more a midwife and nurse in late August and early September than a statesman. He was finding young Sam H. Jones—"Captain Sam" to the President—an entertaining companion; he was finding a joy in teaching that redheaded youngster that he never had felt in the classroom or with an apprentice. Mrs. Woodruff, Mary's mother, came to help him on the first of September.

Mon. 4th [he noted in his diary] General Election throughout the Republic. Wrote Sundry despatches to Capt. Elliot. Gen. Houston Started to the Trinity with his family. Between 10 & 11 O'clock P.M. had a second Son born.

Tues. 5th At home.

Wed. 6th Went to town—in the evening had an attack of the 'grippe."

Thurs^d 7th Sick at home—Wrote O. Jones, Rachael, Dr. Gilnore, &c.

On the twelfth the Secretary of State wrote Her Britannic Majesty's Chargé d'Affaires:

The fact is simply this: On the 4th inst. (being the day of general election) my good lady, having, as I suppose, great respect for the day, presented me with a second son, and we cannot agree upon a name for him. Mrs. J., on the birth of our first, wished to call him after his father; but I . . . contrary to her wishes, called him after our much-abused friend "Sam Houston". . . . she has not yet recovered from her pique. To satisfy her, I offered to let her name this second one, and was vain enough to think she would call him "Anson"; . . . she absolutely and positively refused . . . and the child, without some remedy can be found, will have no name. On Sunday we held a conference . . . when it was proposed to call the boy "Charles Elliot." Your simple assent, now . . . will settle this difficulty. . . . there is no gentleman than yourself living, for whose good qualities, both of head and heart, both his parents entertain a more profound respect. . . .

The British diplomat countered with a compromise: "The cognomina 'Anson' and 'Elliot' are both becoming and of good augury." Let the newest Jones heir be called " 'Anson Elliot Jones,' or at the pleasure of the fair contracting lady, 'Elliot Anson Jones'. . . ." Dr. Jones overruled the captain's suggestion but filed the letter away for Charles Elliot Jones to read when he grew up.

The most important item on the Secretary's official agenda was coaching the commissioners who were to negotiate the armistice with Mexico. Colonel Hockley, former Secretary of War and Marine, and Samuel M. Williams, junior partner of McKinney & Williams, had been chosen for this task, but the details were left for the Secretaries of State and of War and Marine to work out. "Do as you and Dr. Hill think best in the premises. The whole matter will not be concluded during my term, and 'as you make your bed, so must you lie in it,' " Houston wrote Jones from East Texas.

There was a slight disagreement between the Texans and the Mexicans as to what political entity the Texan commissioners were to represent. Were they agents of a sovereign republic, or merely spokesmen for a recalcitrant Mexican province?

Sat. 22d   Col⁸ Williams & Hockley Commissioners to Mexico arrived in Washington. Sund. 24th   Gen Houston returned from Trinity—Dr J B Miller [new Secretary of the Treasury] came home with me and staid the night.

Secretaries Jones and Hill authorized Hockley and Williams only to arrange an armistice when they met with the Mexican commissioners at Sabinas in the state of Tamaulipas. That armistice was to continue during negotiations with Mexico for a permanent peace, to be conducted later by other commissioners at Mexico City. Their verbal instructions, not part of the written record, were to prolong discussions as long as possible.

A few evenings later Vice-President Burleson was Mr. Secretary Jones's house guest. Each believed he would be the next President of Texas; they found other and more fruitful topics of conversation than the coming campaign.

On October 6, Jones received two important communications. The first was an order from the President to proceed to Galveston to arrange with Viscount Cramayel for a line of Royal Steam Packets between Texas and France and to interview the English and American ministers. The diplomatic corps accredited to Texas still insisted on living in the seaport, much to the inconvenience of the State Department. Jones would visit them as soon as he could, but the other letter of October 6 demanded attention first. It was from Dr. Moses Johnson:

> Friend Jones,—We propose to hold a meeting . . . before you go below, and send the proceedings to the *Planter* not saying much about your being a Houston man. . . .
> I must see you before we act. I don't want to forget the Old Chief, but would like bringing in as much of the opposition as possible.

Dr. Jones visited Dr. Johnson at Independence, then started for the coast. It was a slow journey which took him through the Brazos Valley settlements to Brazoria County, where he tarried nine days, medical business and politics both being brisk.

> 29th arrvd at Galveston at 10 ½ O'Clock A.M.—attended Church at Rev^d Mr. Eaton   Capt Elliot & family were there. . . . Spent the afternoon with Gen. Murphy at Shaw's,—the eveng with M. de Cramayel & arranged the terms of the conventions about the Royal Line of Packets, touching at Galveston,—Mon 30th at Galveston wrote to Count Cramayel spent the evening at Captn Elliot's & called on Mr. Kennedy with Gen. Houston   Tuesd. 31st Attended to Sundry private matters of business. . . .
> Nov 1st 1843   Wed. Started for Houston. . . .

On this trip Mr. Secretary Jones purchased a suit, hat, gloves, and other haberdashery suitable for a statesman; a printing press for Mr. Smith's *Citizen;* M. A. Bryan's quarter league near Washington; a Colt pistol; a thousand-dollar slave, the boy William; and supplies for his medical office. Thus equipped to become a presidential candidate, a molder of public opinion, a planter, or a private practitioner of medicine, he returned to Washington-on-the-Brazos. There he found an accumulation of important mail.

Old James Burke of Brazoria was asking him questions he could not answer categorically:

Are you a candidate for the Presidency? If so, do you run on the strength of Houston's popularity, or upon your own merits? In other words, are you the Administration candidate? My personal predelictions [are] in your favor. . . . But I could not consent to vote for any one for the Presidency who depended on the popularity of Sam. Houston and the fame of San Jacinto to carry them into office. . . . *You* . . . have substantial merits which would constitute a far more legitimate claim upon the people, and would be a much surer passport to public favor. . . . I do not think it would be necessary for you to denounce the administration, or even to attempt to conceal your warm friendship for Gen. Houston; but I do not think you should permit your name to run as the *nominee and special favorite* and candidate of the administration. . . . I do not think that popularity is transferrable in Texas as in the United States.

From Commodore John G. Tod, Texas Navy, who was visiting in Washington City:

. . . I found every thing connected with Texas of vital interest. . . . I conversed freely with Mr. Van Zandt . . . the President and Secretary of State. . . . Texas, Annexation, English and Mexican affairs . . . were the sole object of our conversation. . . .

In talking about our next President for Texas I have always mentioned Anson Jones; and wherever he is known, I have been gratified to find that the event would be received with joy, and hailed as an omen of prosperous days for Texas.

I was very sorry to find the subject of annexation suspended by us. . . . I consider our prospects at present more flattering for accomplishing the object than they have ever been, or probably may be again.

The wires are working, gradually manufacturing public opinion. . . .

If we get our independence recognized by Mexico, and settle our difficulties with the Indians, I do not know that annexation would be considered of so much importance; but it would relieve us from great trouble and responsibility . . . small nation as we are. . . .

That was unofficial news from the United States.

Before he could answer his mail, into his office on November 11 walked Charles H. Raymond, secretary of the Texan Legation at Washington City. He was bearer of a bulky, sealed communication from Minister Van Zandt—too important and urgent to be trusted to the erratic mail service of Mr. Secretary Jones's Post Office Bureau.

Minister Van Zandt, since July, had been pursuing a policy which had brought results: he not only never discussed annexation, he avoided even the consideration of its possibility—which was a difficult role for him to sustain.

In every interview [Van Zandt had reported to Jones a month before], Mr. Upshur . . . invariably mentioned the question, and dwelt . . . at some length; in fact, the announcement to him that my instructions were suspended, seems to have fired him anew in regard to it. He has frequently inquired whether there has been a change in the views of the Texian Administration. . . . I have always replied . . . my instructions were suspended. . . . Mr. Upshur frequently remarked with much earnestness of manner, that he hoped Texas would not change her former policy . . . that he was actively engaged under the instructions of the President, in preparing the minds of the people for it, and in learning the views of Senators . . . and so soon as they conceived it safe, they would renew the proposition on their part.

And now, under date of October 16, Van Zandt was reporting the result of that game of coyness and enclosing a letter from Secretary Upshur which, he thought,

places that question at once in a tangible shape, it comes to the point and presents the *issue:* Are we ready to negotiate a treaty of annexation, or not?

. . . I have thought it my duty to dispatch this communication by a special messenger. . . . Having no means to employ a special agent for this purpose . . . Mr. Raymond Secretary of the Legation, at my request . . . has consented to take charge of this dispatch and depart for Texas immediately. To him I must refer you for information. . . .

Mexico was nibbling at one of the baits Texas had thrown out, and the southwestern border would be quiet as long as Texan commissioners could contrive ways to prolong their parley with Santa Anna's men. Now the United States was swimming toward another bait that had been long in the water; so long, in fact, that Jones was reeling it in. At any time for six years she could have had the bait; now it would be harder to catch than gentlemen at Washington City—the Texan Chargé included—suspected.

Van Zandt was, for him, importunate. He was in "a most humiliating position—not a stiver in my pocket, and fearful to borrow lest I never shall be able to pay," just when the spotlight was turning toward him and the negotiations Texas had prayed for since 1836. "I hope," he urged Jones, "you will accept annexation; 'twill be the best move we can make. . . ."

If only Mr. Secretary Jones could have coached the Minister to the United States before he went to Washington City, he might have explained some matters of strategy that he could not put in writing. Not all of the negotiations of Texas centered on the Potomac, and there were possibilities and probabilities not yet fully explored of which he was unaware. The answer to Upshur's invitation—and to Van Zandt's urgings—was No, but he would not send it until the President returned to the capital.

Secretary Jones could not yet explain the complexities to Van Zandt, but he endorsed his letter:

Mr. Van Zandt does not understand my position. I am as willing for annexation as he is, but I do not believe it can be effected in the manner now proposed, and am unwilling to risk every thing on a single throw of an uncertain die.

In his understandable pride in the results he had got from the men on whom he was working, the Chargé had overlooked the most important factor in the situation. Secretary Jones was looking beyond the President and the Secretary of State to the United States Senate, without whose approval the treaty would not be worth the paper it was written on. He knew from firsthand experience that a Secretary of State could not always control a

Senate. Until he was assured that two thirds of the senators of the United States would vote for the treaty, Jones did not intend to let it be negotiated. Rejection would mean a loss of Texan prestige—and Texas had none to lose.

While Mr. Raymond was bringing Van Zandt's dispatch to Jones, the President was speaking at the Presbyterian Church in Huntsville.

I question very much, my friends [he said] whether England would have us if she could get us. To my mind it is clear that England does not *care* about the abolition of slavery. . . . She knows very well that a slave population will develope the resources of a new country in one-eighth of the time it would take by free labor. . . .

England don't want you, in my opinion, gentlemen! She has a great many mischievous & unruly subjects to govern already; and if she had Texas in addition, she would be glad to get rid of us.

Two days later His Excellency spoke at the old capital in Houston, recounting the difficulties of his administration and the hopeful nature of recent news:

I have this day received new evidences from France, England, and the United States. What evidences had we a year ago? Then we encountered nothing but indifference, apathy, coldness and neglect. Now it is far different. Each of the nations is striving to rival and outstrip the others in conferring benefits upon us. Texas is surely advancing to that goal she has so long been struggling to attain. . . .

While the President was addressing the Houstonians his Secretary of State was reading the most interesting mail he had received in many years. It was from Dr. Moses Johnson, who "most earnestly" hoped Dr. Jones would yield to the demands of his friends.

Washington County citizens had gathered under the management of Dr. Johnson at Independence on October 28 to nominate candidates for the presidency and vice-presidency. The meeting had been conducted with all the protocol of Texan mass meetings—with a chairman, a secretary, a committee on resolutions, a committee on correspondence, and addresses by five orators, "who all eloquently alluded to the distinguished talents, patriotism, and great moral worth, both as a public and private citizen, of Dr. Jones." Then a committee was appointed, "re-

tired, and after a brief absence returned" with resolutions which
reviewed Jones's ten years of service to Texas, pointed out that
he was "intimately acquainted with the history and present condition of the Government" and "fully qualified to foster and protect the growing interests of our common country," and declared
him the most suitable person for the next presidency of the Republic. Without preliminary oratory the Honorable Kenneth L.
Anderson of San Augustine was nominated for the vice-presidency.

A week later came a letter from San Augustine, signed by
O. M. Roberts and four other East Texans, tardily telling "Mr.
Anson Jones" what he already knew, that he had been nominated
for the presidency "by a large and respectable meeting of the citizens of this county, lately holden," and adding:

> You will much oblige your fellow-citizens in the East by accepting
> this nomination. . . . Their selection is made with a view to their
> own interests, and to the dearest interests of the whole country. . . .
> Their support . . . will be warm and energetic. And your success
> will crown their hopes with another bright prospect of their country's
> safety.

It made Mr. Houston's Secretary of State happy to think that
his nomination "was the spontaneous act of the *people of Texas,*
and without any agency on my own part. Party had nothing to
do with it. . . ."

The presidential campaign of 1844 had begun. The *National
Vindicator,* published in Washington by Mr. Thomas (Ramrod) Johnson—"the unflinching defender of the character and
true interests of Texas by whomsoever she may be assailed," subscriptions payable in "Beef, Pork, Corn, young Cattle, or seed
Cotton"—became a Jones organ. When its pro-Jones articles and
editorials were copied by other newspapers the fun began. One
article traced the doctor's career from the time he migrated from
Louisiana to Texas. That writer

> ought to have gone farther back ["Archer" said in the Houston
> *Morning Star,* ignoring fact in pursuit of analogy], and given his
> history from the time he migrated from his *native* village, among the
> black hills of Herkimer County in New York, where several political
> peddlers commenced their career. Dr. Jones, I am informed is a

countryman of Martin Van Buren, but perhaps . . . the *writer* wishes to create the impression that he is a son of the chivalrous South. Shame to the man who is ashamed of his birth place. . . . If his political career in Texas had been characterized by any brilliant or useful public act, his foibles *might* be overlooked; but unfortunately like one of his countrymen he depends on political juggling and other than merit for success. The language that venerable Hugh L. White applied to Van Buren is peculiarly applicable to him:

"He is nothing but a mere tuft of political mistletoe having no root of his own, adhering to and supported by the limb of a distant trunk altogether, and must as infallibly perish whenever that trunk ceases to nourish him as the tuft on yonder oak, whenever the oak shall have decayed and fallen."

Ten days later the *Star* informed the voters—most of whom had arrived in Texas since San Jacinto—that Anson Jones was not a hero of that battle but "was actually on the opposite side of the river when the battle was fought." The Galveston *News*, of which M. B. Lamar was godfather, further examined the allegation that "this knight of the pestle was '*present at the battle of San Jacinto*'":

If the writer means by this to insinuate that the Doctor was actually in the battle or in any wise participated in its dangers, he is quite mistaken. When the preparation for the battle was going on, he crossed the Buffalo Bayou. . . . We do not mean to say that he absented himself to avoid the approaching conflict. O, no, the Doctor is quite too brave for that; he was only discharging the obligations of his office, which . . . did not require him to inflict wounds but to heal them. . . . this being altogether in accord with his natural disposition, he felt it incumbent upon him not to place himself in a situation where a fatal accident might deprive the army of his professional services. This is a laudable prudence and entitles him to as high a praise of heroism as any who mingled in the battle.

M. P. Norton, a down-East Yankee lawyer from the state of Maine who had been in Texas only a year, took over the direction of Jones's public relations at the end of 1843. After organizing a Montgomery County Jones boom, he started "with family and *plunder*" toward Houston to open a law office, serve as postmaster, and keep an eye on *The Citizen*. Norton was something of a political expert; he quickly translated what he had learned in Maine into Texan terms and placed it at the service of Dr. Jones.

"The Old Dragon, family & Co. leave this morning for Washington," General Morehouse wrote Jones from Houston on November 25. He was referring to His Excellency the President, who was heading back to his office to get matters in hand before the Congress assembled, bringing with him a new presidential costume. His political stock was rising. Former enemies were grudgingly admitting that the Old Chief was managing pretty well to muddle through difficulties that would have ruined a less versatile politician. Some of them were crediting it to good luck, others to the Secretary of State.

For nearly a month Jones had studied Upshur's invitation to Texas to make a treaty of annexation. Van Zandt was eager for instructions, but delay would do no harm. Texas had waited long enough for that overture; the United States could wait a month.

Members of the Eighth Congress began drifting into Washington-on-the-Brazos the first of December to interrupt the orderly schedule of the Secretary of State's meditations. Thirty-four of the legislators were planters or farmers; only twelve were lawyers. Maybe the President could get on with this Congress, the last of his administration, better than the ones before it.

After the House, with Secretary Jones presiding, had elected Richardson A. Scurry Speaker, and the Senate had re-elected John A. Greer president pro tem, and a special committee had arranged to "have the floor propped," His Excellency the President, with that new

garment made of fine Broadcloth, in the style of a Mexican blanket, lined with yellow satin, with gold lace all round it . . . fixed on him in his own peculiar style, which made him appear to the best advantage

strode into the hall of the Representatives to deliver his message to Congress. With him walked the Secretary of State, whose new black broadcloth suit did not catch the reporter's eye.

His Excellency was in fine fettle that afternoon—"looking better than I ever saw him in my life," an old friend said—and his manner was cordial and gracious. Half these senators and all but six of the representatives were new men. He would not antagonize them—not at the start.

It affords me pleasure [he began] . . . to felicitate you upon the present promising aspect of our affairs. Abroad, we are at peace with all the world—at home, plenty fills the land. . . . I confidently rely upon your intelligence and patriotic coöperation. I rejoice that you have it in your power to aid the Executive. . . .

Then he reminded them that when he took office Texas was without currency, without credit, even without mails; Mexico was harassing her, Indians were hostile, and the citizens despondent. Foreign governments regarded the Republic with apathy. Immigration had almost stopped, which "deprived us of many a strong arm for the sword or the plough"; and the inflow of capital had ceased.

After two years of Houston's rule the great powers of the earth were interested in Texas. Her Britannic Majesty's government had interposed between Texas and Mexico, an armistice had been arranged, and the Texans imprisoned in Mexico released. His Majesty the King of the French was establishing a line of royal steamships direct to Texas. A Texan chargé had been sent to Holland, Belgium, and the Hanse towns, further to stimulate Texan trade with the continent of Europe, and the Chargé at Paris was negotiating with Spain for trade between Texas and Cuba.

That was the situation: England doing all she could to bring peace between Texas and Mexico; France starting direct steam-packet service; Dutch and German vessels crowding Galveston Harbor; soon there might be lucrative trade with Cuba. And what was the United States doing? Nothing; according to the President's message, less than nothing. She had neglected since 1842 to ratify a commercial treaty with Texas; she had arrested on Texas soil an expedition sent out by the President of the Republic. The implication was inescapable: the real friends of Texas were across the Atlantic.

But His Excellency did not mention the latest development. He did not say that the Secretary of State had already signed a rejection of an invitation to consider annexation. Four days later

Jones "Dispatched Mr Raymond, Sec. of Legation to U.S." with it.

The interposition of foreign friendly governments, by which an Armistice has been established between Texas and Mexico, and the prospect of a permanent peace . . . has been extended . . . chiefly with a view that . . . Texas . . . should continue to exist, as a separate and independent nation [he explained to Van Zandt]. The great object and desire of Texas, . . . the establishment of a permanent and satisfactory peace with her enemy, . . . appears now on the eve of being realized. . . . it would not be politic to abandon the expectations which now exist . . . for the very uncertain prospect of annexation. . . .

This government . . . deems it most proper and most advantageous to the interests of this country, to decline the proposition for concluding a treaty . . . [but] whenever the Congress or Senate of the United States shall throw wide open the door to annexation by a resolution authorizing the President of that Country to propose a treaty . . . the proposition will be . . . promptly responded to. . . .

The present determination of the President on this subject does not proceed from any change in his views . . . but from a change in the relations of this country with other powers.

The key to the door to annexation Anson Jones retained in his own pocket, where he had placed it in 1838. He intended to keep it there until he knew with greater certainty what the United States Senate would do—and what lay across the Atlantic—and across the Rio Grande.

Mr. Raymond had hardly left town before the Senate rushed through a resolution asking the President

to recall the said special messenger and delay his departure, until the matters communicated through him, shall have been made known to the Congress, and such action shall be had thereon, as shall be deemed advisable.

The vote was 6 to 6; Vice-President Burleson voted aye.

His Excellency read the resolution and bristled. Then, in three thousand plain English words, he shared his thoughts—but not the desired information—with the senators. The "comity of intercourse" with which the session had begun had ended.

That resolution was an "outrage" which could not be explained by "a want of intelligence"; it was "intended to reflect directly upon the Executive and to countenance and endorse the multiplied slanders and defamatory 'reports' which have been busily circulated through the medium of factious demagogues and incendiary presses." The President had already communicated "all the intelligence he conceived necessary and proper"; he would continue to withhold "such information as, if made public, might operate to the prejudice of the country."

He did, however, tell the senators that

a proposition has never been made by this government to any other affecting our nationality, since the year 1836. . . . If every syllable of the international correspondence . . . were exhibited naked to the world, the Executive is confident it could not fail in securing the approval of the people to the ability, industry and integrity of the gentleman who is at the head of the Department through which such correspondence is conducted. . . . The Senate are the constitutional advisers of the President; but they are not to dictate to him what correspondence to hold or what policy to pursue. . . .

The President was

irresistably drawn to the conclusion that his opportunities for forming correct opinions are at least equal to those who are occasionally engaged for a few weeks in the business of legislation. . . .

This Congress, like its predecessor, had killed a week waiting for a quorum. In the Senate there was a bloc of six senators, led by Jack of Brazoria, that could be counted on to embarrass the administration. Jack was asking almost every day for the President to submit a detailed report on expenditures, on correspondence with foreign powers, on the Snively expedition; and, as usual, was proposing to reduce appropriations and abolish offices filled by executive appointment. James Webb was on his feet almost as often for the same purpose.

In the House, Mr. Cazneau was back to represent the anti-Houston westerners. Thomas J. Green, recently a Mier prisoner, was there to speak for anti-Houstonites generally; he occupied the place Jones had once held from Brazoria. Mr. Fiery Jones of Gonzales was also back and chairman of the House foreign relations committee. Of less importance but of interest to Jones was young James B. P. January, M.D., who was making

his legislative debut with certain notions regarding the practice
of medicine in the Republic. There was a move on to repeal the
Medical Censor Act Jones had helped pass in the Second Congress, to declare that a physician's fee during a last illness was
not a preferred claim against the estate of the man he failed to
cure, and to establish an Association of Physicians of the Republic of Texas. Dr. January did not see eye to eye with Dr.
Jones on these reforms, nor did the other four physicians in that
Congress.

While the President and the Congress were settling into the
usual snarl, the Secretary of State was closing a contract with
the widow of General James R. Cook to rent her plantation,
which adjoined the land he had bought from M. A. Bryan. Come
the first of the year, he would begin on a modest scale the life
of a planter. That was a more appropriate occupation than medicine for a presidential candidate in an agrarian republic, and it
could be profitable. In fact, he could combine both businesses
neatly, as his Cabinet colleagues, Hill and Miller, were doing,
and as most of the physicians of Brazoria County long had done.

The presidential canvass in the newspapers was warming up.
The Houston *Morning Star* continued to point out the shortcomings of Dr. Jones: he had killed no Mexicans at San Jacinto; he
had accomplished nothing as Minister to the United States; he
had not been re-elected to the Senate; he had had no part in
arranging the Mexican armistice; had not even made treaties
with the Indians. Judge Terrell had negotiated with the savages,
while

Dr. Jones was snugly esconsed in his office at Washington, and engaged in the more profitable business of *practicing medicine.* If he
has pocketed the fees of his patients and his salary as Secretary of
State, he should consider this a sufficient recompence without asking
for the gratitude of the Nation.

From Brazoria old Peter McGreal reported:

It is admitted by those who will oppose your election—and I regret
to say that there are some of them in Brazoria—that you . . . will
be supported by all, or nearly all, of Gen. Houston's friends. . . .
. . . Gen. Burleson . . . from his ignorance and want of capacity
. . . would be but an automaton in the hands of designing, unprin-

cipled, and dishonest politicians of the country, and, Heaven knows, we are afflicted with more than a fair proportion of that class. . . .

General Henderson now believed "all things are working well for you" in East Texas. Norton was in Houston:

My great anxiety is to get charge of the paper, as something must surely be done to revive the hopes of our friends; but I cannot do it until I get the Post-office arranged. I am to have Campbell's office adjoining the printing-office.

Three days later he was urging Jones to send him documents to set the record straight on matters "which have been grossly misrepresented in the 'Telegraph.' We must have a regular correspondent at Washington. . . . Efforts are unremitting here, as at Washington, to induce the belief that the President and Cabinet are opposed to annexation. . . . Do not fail to let me be informed on every thing important. . . ."

President Tyler's third annual message to the United States Congress reached Texas late in December. While it contained no hint of Upshur's proposal to negotiate for annexation, there was a long section on the futility of Mexico's hope of regaining Texas which alarmed Norton.

I am afraid [he wrote Jones on December 27] Tyler's message will produce an unfavorable influence over our Mexican negotiations, and yet it seems to me that it should be responded to in our press in the kindest [manner]. If we . . . could change the probable movement there for annexation, to such strong measures on the part of the United States as would secure our independence, or rather *enforce* it, I should feel much hope. . . . The three great parties there might unite on such a measure . . . and thereby avoid the dangers they might encounter in favoring or opposing annexation. Reily says if he can raise money enough he will go there immediately, and he thinks he can effect it. He proposes to go on his own account, if he can get money enough from Government for former services to pay his way.

"I think with you," Jones replied at once, ". . . & should like much if Reily could go on to Washington to act upon your suggestion. . . ." If the United States would force Mexico to recognize Texas, then Texas could consider calmly what she wanted ultimately to do.

In the Texan Congress anti-administration men were busy. Ogden had introduced a joint resolution to accept annexation before it was negotiated; Cazneau wanted to know why Secretary Jones had not announced the result of the election for major general of militia. When Lewis proposed that the editor of the *Vindicator* be allowed a seat to report proceedings, "candles, paper &c. to be furnished," Cazneau claimed the same privilege for the reporter of the anti-administration *Telegraph*. A compromise to establish a press gallery for all reporters was voted down, 32 to 4.

Mr. Lott, aged twenty-three, opined that His Excellency was aping and consorting with royalty; he proposed that the President furnish the House of Representatives

immediately and without delay a copy of the letter to the King of the Netherlands, in relation to the marriage of his daughter; his answer thereto; also his correspondence with foreign powers now in treaty with this Republic on the birth of his son Sam.

Mr. Cazneau approved the resolution but desired to insert after the word Sam "also his wife and children in the Cherokee nation."

Anson Jones spent the last evening of the year 1843 in the library of General Cook's plantation, to which he had moved two days after Christmas. He was casting up his accounts—financial and political—as he usually did at the end of a year. During 1843 he had received from non-medical sources $5,318.03, and his medical office at Brazoria was doing well. He had invested $3,665—more than twice the amount of his salary as Secretary of State—in "Negroes & Land &c."

His political balance sheet was more complicated. To his diary that night he confided thoughts and apprehensions that neither his supporters nor his opponents suspected:

Monday 31st. The close . . . of the 2^d year of my term as Secty of State.—Affairs in the main have been managed agreeably to my wishes & advice. . . . Gen. H. & myself are drifting away from each other hourly—He has not kept faith with me in relation to Cabinet appointments. . . . Appointments are now made to these offices without consultation with me & this is a breach of the *implied* understanding. . . . I think it was "so nominated in the bond." But I

have a vitally important object to accomplish . . . Annexation to
the U.S. or ultimate peace & independence. . . . I have resolved
not to be diverted. . . . I may have to play the part of "Curtius"
& if so am prepared & willing to make a sacrifice like his. . . . I
am also content to let Gen: Houston be the "Caesar"—for it is only
by yielding to his vanity & ambition that we can get on together . . .
the successful issue of the important measures now pending require
that we should co-operate. . . . His *position* as President puts in his
power to do great harm, & the condition of public affairs are becoming too critical to sustain any violent jar or shock. . . .

I am not at liberty nor would it be proper for me publicly to
oppose any of his acts or any part of his policy. . . . There are but
two courses I can take, either to resign, or to hold my peace. . . .
Were the country out of her difficulties I should not hold office an
hour under Gen Houston—indeed I should never have taken office.
. . . If I resign all is lost for which I have so long labored, if I hold
on I must do a violence to my sense of what is right. . . . I must in
the language of Scripture, "do evil that good may come" . . . appear as his Coadjutor in measures which I disapprove "toto
coelo". . . .

XXVIII

THE ABSORBING QUESTION

D R. JONES knew that Texan legislators that winter, like their constituents, were afflicted with "annexation fever." It made them nervous, irritable, suspicious. The silence of the President and the Secretary of State on the subject invited apprehension and criticism, but diplomacy was an executive function not to be shared with Congress until matters were further along. Mr. Secretary Jones could not tell Congress, but he was sure

. . . the most we can hope for is *Independence*. The President nor his Cabinet, nor myself are *not* opposed to annexation & have never by word or act in any way opposed it. The effort to induce a contrary belief is *malicious*. But *Independence* is we think the only *feasible* result—& will answer the purpose very well. . . . A letter however has been signed by most of the members of Congress, certifying . . . nine tenths of the people of Texas are in favor of the [annexation] measure. . . .

There were more ways to play this annexation game than those gentlemen suspected. Neither they nor their constituents would have a chance to decide the question until many more moves had been made in Washington on the Potomac, Mexico, London, and Paris. Even then Jones was placing an unsigned resolution in the diplomatic pouch for some Texas-minded member to introduce in the Congress of the United States. It might change the situation.

In a series of whereases, it reviewed the whole unsavory course of Mexican history, declared her President "a monster" whose government "ought no longer to be tolerated by civilized nations," and called, in the name of the people of the United States, upon President Tyler to break relations "with this scourge to humanity, this disgrace to civilization."

To the newspaper in Houston that was advocating Jones for the presidency of Texas went a copy of these resolutions—"unofficial entirely & very *ultra*"—with Jones's explanation that

the object . . . is to *alarm* Santa Anna. . . . say . . . "that you understand such a preamble & Resolutions were to be submitted to the Congress of the U. S. & that they *ought* to be passed &c., &c."

I send you also herewith all the correspondence between Texas & Great Britain on the subject of *Slavery* which you are at liberty to publish . . . & say it was in accordance with instructions from me. It will quiet all the noise about *"Bobolition."*

Getting his plantation established afforded Mr. Secretary Jones some relief from great emotional conflicts that winter. He was premier of the Cabinet, committed to see intricate negotiations to a conclusion. He and the President had once agreed upon ultimate objectives, but as negotiations Jones had been nursing along came near fruition, he was no longer certain that they wanted the same thing. Each of them was instinctively ambiguous in his dealings with other men; during that winter each became increasingly ambiguous with the other. The President wrote more and more diplomatic communications with his own quill and his Secretary of State wondered if the President could avoid getting his lines of intrigue confused.

The presence of Congress was a complication. The House, like the Senate, suspected the purposes of the President and the Secretary of State on the United States annexation overture and demanded the documents in the case. To the House resolution, the President replied on January 1:

This call for information is so general, that it would necessarily embrace a transcript of nearly the entire correspondence of the Department of State. The labor . . . would be impracticable within the probable duration of the present session of Congress.

. . . if they desire information on the subject of our foreign correspondence, the Honorable Speaker of the House, accompanied by the chairman and members of the Committee on Foreign Relations, will be received at the State Department, at any time when the Head of that Department has leisure, and they can obtain all the information they desire upon any and every subject. . . .

Mr. Kendrick moved to print a thousand copies of His Excellency's refusal to share diplomatic secrets with the representatives of the people. That lost, but some thoughtful congressman furnished a copy of it, which was marked secret, to Dr. Moore, who printed it in the *Telegraph* ten days later. When the House delegation called on Jones he convinced them nothing treasonable was afoot in his department.

Before Congress met, Jones had hoped the old quarrel over the removal of the capital might not be renewed. He believed the President's insistence upon keeping the government at Washington against the wishes of a majority of the legislators was a mistake—not because Washington was a poor location, but because it provoked an embroilment at a time when harmony was needed. "Knowing this he has ceased to counsel with me upon it," Jones noted.

When he heard His Excellency declare in his annual message that the Mexican and Indian menace had disappeared, he knew the fight was on again. If Mexicans and Indians no longer threatened, how could Austin be thought unsafe? Westerners pushed through a bill ordering the executive to return there, and Houston, without Cabinet advice, promptly vetoed it. Austin, he now declared, was still unsafe; the present thirty-thousand-dollar government pay roll could not support enough population to make Austin tenable; and finally he was of the opinion that Austin was not, had never been, legally the seat of government. If the people wished it there, let Congress order an election. So far as Sam Houston was concerned, the capital would remain on the Brazos until the sovereign voters ordered it to the Colorado.

While Congress was sitting, Norton sent Jones an article from the Houston *Democrat* (new name of the *Citizen*) quibbling over annexation which, he thought, "takes about the right ground," and warned him he would "see every effort used to enforce the opinion that the government are opposed to annexation, and even to assistance from the United States." Jones read the article and instructed Norton: "I beg of you to cease your fire . . . opposition to it will do *serious injury*—to us." Neither the Secretary of State nor his organ could afford to appear critical of annexation at this juncture.

Captain Elliot, sojourning in New Orleans, wrote Jones:

Well-informed persons in this country laugh at the idea of annexation, and when you remind them that, in that case, the agitation of the subject is cruel, . . . they laugh again. . . . The good effect, or otherwise, upon Gen. Houston's negotiations [with Mexico] for the pacification of Texas, is not a consideration at all. But I see good reason to hope that those negotiations will reach a happy conclusion.

Jones's old New York friend, Lot Clark, reported to him unofficially that "the sober judgment of seven-eighths of the country is, that our territory is already too large and unwieldy for a free government. At any rate, I feel *quite sure* it will never be made larger. . . ."

At Washington City, Secretary Upshur counted the noses of senators and believed an annexation treaty would be ratified by *"a clear constitutional majority of two-thirds."* This he communicated to Chargé Murphy and suggested that he warn Texas to beware of Britain—"the lamb can make no contract with the wolf, which will protect him from being devoured."

At the Texan Legation, Van Zandt had spent an anxious week after he received Jones's rejection of the annexation overture. He believed additional data he was sending would change Secretary Jones's mind, and he was withholding from Secretary Upshur the communication of December 13 until he heard further from Texas. He wrote Jones on January 20.

That same day at Washington-on-the-Brazos the President of Texas drafted a communication to his Congress. For three exasperating weeks he had been contending with a hostile majority, abetted by Chargé Murphy, determined to force his hand on annexation. Elliot and Saligny, who might have negatived that game, were absent. Already the Texan congressmen had signed and forwarded to Washington City that declaration that nine tenths of the Texans were eager for annexation. They had spoiled the plans to frighten the United States into a ratification of the treaty. Convinced now that Congress would take the annexation matter out of his hands—maybe impeach him—if he did not act, His Excellency wrote his secret message on the "important and absorbing question" on January 20. He declared "he should have felt himself delinquent," if he had failed to do so.

Annexation would soon be agitated in the United States Congress, he pointed out. If the Texas Congress wished the executive to explore the matter at Washington City, it would immediately provide for an auxiliary minister. Houston expressed no opinion as to the desirability or probability of annexation, and he cautioned the Honorable Congress to maintain the utmost secrecy "as to the true motives of our policy."

The failure of the annexation effort would "diminish our claims to the confidence of other nations," create distrust in Texan stability and suspicion that at the first opportunity the Republic would cease to be a nation. These dangers might be minimized if the United States would sign with Texas an alliance against Mexico, he hinted.

Action [he concluded] must now be taken by the United States, and we must watch and meet their disposition toward us. If we evince too much anxiety it will be regarded as importunity, and the voice of supplication seldom commands in such cases, great respect.

The next day David S. Kaufman, chairman of the Senate committee on foreign relations which was composed of "ardent friends of the great and desirable object," recommended "compliance with His Excellency's request . . . fully convinced that if we are annexed to the United States at all, it can only be done by means of a treaty between the two Governments."

The House was not only willing to send a Texan negotiator to Washington but proposed to proceed with legislative acceptance of annexation. Not until the last day of Congress were the details of the joint resolution, authorizing the additional agent and appropriating five thousand dollars for the mission, agreed upon.

While Congress debated in secret, the Secretary of State was conferring with the President. He had sent Mr. Raymond back to Washington six weeks before to tell Mr. Van Zandt that he could not negotiate upon that subject until the United States Congress had "thrown wide the door." The communication was secret—as secret as anything could be in Texas—but everybody knew what he had done, and nearly everyone disapproved it. The administration had almost overplayed that British-interest angle. Texans were saying that Jones and Houston were more completely under the control of Her Britannic Majesty than of the electorate of Texas.

Secretary Jones authorized Van Zandt on January 27 to begin preliminary discussion of annexation terms as soon as he believed that "the door will be opened" and promised him he would receive full power to conclude a treaty when Texas had evidence that the United States Senate would ratify it. Van Zandt might also sound the United States on an alliance against Mexico.

General Murphy, Chargé of the United States in Texas, knew little of what was afoot, for both his own and the Texan government neglected to tell him secrets. To him President Houston wrote February 3:

(Strictly confidential) . . . Your clear and comprehensive views in relation to Texas . . . are not less statesmanlike than important. . . . The subject of annexation has been one of deep interest here, and in which I partake largely of the feeling which a patriot should entertain. . . . whatever they might be.

The United States must annex Texas—Texas cannot annex herself to the U. S. . . . . As yet, the U. States have adopted no course that could encourage a confident hope. . . . I am sure I cannot be suspected of interposing any impediment to the ascertainment of our position in regard to the U. States.

When we meet, I will have much to say to you. . . . But until I shall enjoy this pleasure . . . I have to request of you, under the most confidential injunctions, to communicate to your Government a desire on the part of this, that . . . they would order to the Gulf by the first or fifth of March next, at least five vessels of war . . . subject to your orders. . . . I need not suggest to you the influence which the unexpected appearance of a portion of the naval force of your Government would have. . . .

Congress adjourned February 5. That day the House rejected a Senate bill "for the promotion and general diffusion of Medical Knowledge," which provided that an Association of Physicians of the Republic of Texas should be organized in March, and that the Secretary of State should determine who would be charter members. Once established, this association would, under its own rules, regulations, and schedules of fees, confer "degrees, diplomas and Honors . . . grant licenses to all applicants, qualified to practice Medicine . . . and do all other acts and things necessary for the promotion of its objects. . . ."

January of Jackson read the report that killed the bill. His principal objection was that the Honorable Anson Jones, M.D., was Secretary of State; the Honorable J. B. P. January, M.D., did not propose "to leave it to the discretion of that *distinguished* individual to decide upon the merits of applicants." Instead of being an effort to "promote and diffuse medical knowledge," Dr. January had "no hesitancy in pronouncing the bill is an attempt to legislate into professional eminence a few unmeritorious individuals."

That disposed of, Means of East Texas proposed a vote of confidence in the President, but Caldwell of West Texas promptly moved to table it. The Indian-affairs committee reported non-concurrence in the President's Indian policy; the foreign-relations committee declared the President's refusal to share with the House diplomatic correspondence "a gross and unwarranted insult" based upon "dangerous political doctrine," which created a suspicion of "a dark misterious and tortuous train of Machivellian diplomacy." The committee returned that message to His Excellency for "further consideration and revision." Hogg of Nacogdoches wanted three hundred copies of the letter and report printed for public use. The House voted thanks to Speaker Scurry but declined to thank "the citizens of Washington for their polite conduct."

In the Senate that day Greer reviewed the allegations of bribery, corruption, treason, and abolitionism that were being circulated against the President, the falsity of which was indicated by the fact that during the eight weeks of Congress no move had been made to impeach him. "Sam Houston," he declared, "is entitled to the admiration of the nation and the support of the Senate." The westerners tried to table that declaration, but it carried, 8 to 4. Then, with fine impartiality, the senators expressed appreciation of Vice-President Burleson, declared themselves "entirely satisfied with the manner in which the duties of chaplain have been performed," and started home.

J. Pinckney Henderson would be the auxiliary Minister of Texas to negotiate annexation. Secretary Jones thought him uniquely fitted for the post. He had negotiated for Texas at Paris and London; he was an annexationist—and he was a shrewd lawyer who knew how to protect the interests of his client. The President wrote him posthaste, February 10, that as

the Secretary of State has rode out of town, I avail myself of the chance to say to you, *by all means come directly to Washington* . . . on your way to Washington City. . . . The lions are all stirred up, and the menagerie is quite full. . . . Matters appear about ripe, if they will only advance. . . .

In Brazoria County there was a rumor that annexation was almost certain. Colonel Morgan L. Smith wrote Jones:

Many believe it; the prospect has excited general joy throughout B—— county. An impression is entertained that Gen. Houston is not friendly to the measure, and that Congress will do nothing. A general mass meeting is spoken of in that event, with the intention to recommend all the other counties to hold such meetings, and have a Convention, &c.

Shades of 1835! Brazoria, cradle of the revolution, was about to take matters into her hands again, with Morgan Smith trying to play the role of Anson Jones!

This Col. Smith [Jones endorsed this note] was a brawling New York politician, broke, and came to Texas . . . to embarrass the Government by demagogueism and noise. God help annexation. . . . "Save me from my friends," it would say, if it could *talk! ! !*

Captain Elliot, still in New Orleans, wrote Jones on February 10 that he judged annexation "entirely out of the question," but

I was concerned, indeed, to see that some movements had been made in your Congress in another sense. . . . But I am very sure the President will never lend them the least countenance. . . .

With Elliot's letter came one from Ammon Underwood, Jones's confidential friend and former landlord at Columbia:

While I write our town is illuminated by burning of tar barrels, &c, and loud festival shoutings and rejoicings at the now certain prospect of annexation. Your name is cried aloud as Governor Jones instead of President. . . . I had much rather give my vote for you for Governor. . . .

"We are not 'out of the woods' yet, by a long way," was Jones's sage comment.

From Galveston, Irish Charles Power wrote Jones on February 12:

> We have no news here except such as has been spread by that silly old man, Murphy. . . . I do not think there is so much desire for annexation. . . . Far better were it for Mexico to have us, weak and imbecile, as her neighbor, than . . . to allow a power like the United States [to] say—Texas, enter the Union.
>
> The Presidential chair is not canvassed here at all. . . . Burleson seems to be the man most spoken of. You may rely on one thing, that Galveston is about as ultra as any other portion of the republic, and were Houston to achieve the independence, annexation with even bounds, and every desire of this incongruous population, he would not have a friend, hardly, down here. . . . Hence, I say, defend me from the position of Chief Magistrate under such circumstances.

In the office of the Houston *Democrat* there was no enthusiasm for annexation and great uncertainty. "I am actually puzzled," J. N. O. Smith, the publisher for whom Jones had bought a press, wrote his patron. "Some advise me to continue the publication of articles showing the disadvantages of the measure, while others contend that their effect is to induce the belief that the President and yourself are opposed to it. This latter opinion I shall take an early occasion to present in its true light."

Jones asked him to let annexation alone, and instead begin "Publication of correspondence with British Government on Empresario Claims." Those documents would demonstrate that the Secretary of State was resisting, as a Texan should, British efforts to get control of any part of Texas.

Norton, who was managing Jones's interests there, was having trouble with Publisher Smith.

> Who wrote the two editorials which have placed the paper in an attitude hostile to the measure I do not know. Smith says they are *confidential*, and I began to suspect they came from Washington. One thing I do know—if the course is persisted in we do much to injure the influence of the paper with the people. . . . Smith must be *strongly* advised by you to admit nothing as editorial without consulting me, and then I will be responsible for all.

All of which Jones hopefully interpreted as meaning "they will quit piping against annexation, as I have repeatedly requested."

John Manson of the *Democrat* staff was a difficult problem. He had begun a series of bitter articles analyzing the shortcomings of the Eighth Congress; now he projected a work on annexation.

It has suddenly assumed [he wrote Jones] a position which . . . is really alarming, from the inconsiderate favor with which the insidious subject is received by the unthinking, many-headed populace. . . . I have determined to lay the matter before the public in a pamphlet form [because publication in] . . . the *Democrat*, might implicate you, and be prejudicial in the coming election. . . . We have enemies enough to contend with, without making more.

The book . . . will only extend to some twenty pages; and if we can raise funds enough—about $25, to publish it by subscription— the thing shall be done. . . . What say you; will you or any of your friends subscribe—please say so in your next.

I have entertained you (I hope) with this desultory scrawl; because I am of opinion that the principal ought to have a knowledge of those who pull the wires.

Jones offered up a silent prayer for protection from his wire-pulling friends and persuaded Mr. Manson to leave annexation to the Department of State.

Jones was launched as a presidential candidate, and he did not intend to withdraw; but the increasing complexities of the situation he would have to face before election—and after—made him wonder why he had ever entered politics. When Hockley wrote him from Mexico "you go into it with your eyes open . . . nobody can know better than yourself how unthankful an office it is," Jones searched his soul, then endorsed Hockley's note:

This is very true. . . . And I have no expectation that the presidential chair will be any thing else than one of thorns . . . my only object in consenting to take it is, to consummate a policy which has already cost me great labor and great sacrifices. . . .

From complexities of candidacy and diplomacy the new Jones plantation three miles from town was a refuge. Two Negroes of his own and four others hired from neighbors were getting it in order, under the supervision of Mr. J. Campbell, who "came to live with me & brought his horse" in January, and was building the Jones plantation house "& two log Cabins for 200 acres of Land $200 in cash and $100 in Stock at Market prices." This new plantation was to be christened Barrington, in honor of the doctor's birthplace in Massachusetts. But all was not well in the slave quarters.

I must beg your attention to a little matter of private business [Jones wrote Norton]. I own a negro man "William" who is here & his wife "Esther" belongs to Judge Andrews and is at Houston. The man is very anxious to have his wife here, & I will thank you to enquire & let me know if Mr. Andrews will sell or hire her, & if so what would be his terms.

He was operating on a large and, for him, an expensive scale. He called in loans and budgeted his expenditures carefully. He noted one prospective economy hopefully and naïvely in his journal: "Wed. Jan. 24th   Mrs. J. says she will not want another dress untill next fall." A line drawn through the entry indicates that this happy illusion was temporary.

General Murphy arrived at Washington-on-the-Brazos so alarmed at evidences of British machinations against annexation that he was willing to promise Jones that the United States would concentrate forces on the border and in the Gulf. News of annexation negotiations, Jones knew, would terminate the armistice mission of Williams and Hockley in Mexico and perhaps bring another Mexican invasion of Texas. Murphy's promise of protection made it safe to open the negotiations at Washington City.

Henderson could now proceed to join Van Zandt. A search of the Treasury safe turned up two hundred dollars in specie, which was handed to the auxiliary Minister along with instructions to the custom collector at Galveston to find him eight hundred dollars more. When Henderson and Miller, the President's secretary who had been appointed secretary of the auxiliary legation, started toward the Potomac, the President and the Secretary of State had time for other matters of statecraft. The President re-read his recent letters from General Jackson.

You know, my dear General, that I have been, & still am your friend [Old Hickory said in one]. . . . You never could have become the dupe to England, and all the gold of Santana . . . could not seduce you from a just sense of duty & patriotism. . . .

[And in the other:] My dear Genl I tell you in sincerity & friendship, if you will achieve this annexation your name & fame will be enrolled amongst the greatest chieftains of the age. . . . Now is the time to act & that with promptness & secrecy. . . . Let the threats of Great Britain and Mexico then be hurled at us,—if war the[y] wish our fleet and army will freely fight them. . . .

The old man had been Houston's patron saint, his "Venerated Friend." Feeble with age and infirmities, he was hoping to see annexation completed before he died. Houston wrote him February 16:

. . . So far as I am concerned, or my hearty cooperation required, I am determined upon immediate annexation to the United States. It is not the result of feeling, nor can I believe that the measure would be as advantageous to Texas if she had permanent peace, as it is indispensably necessary to the United States. . . . Texas might remain at peace for a half century . . . [then] she would have sufficient means and ample capacity to subjugate Mexico. . . . But notwithstanding I . . . unreservedly cooperate in the contemplated measure . . . it is wisdom growing out of necessity, and not an abandonment of principle. . . . A special Minister, together with our resident Chargé, has been appointed . . . to consummate the work of annexation. . . . Now, my venerated friend . . . Texas is presented to the United States, as a bride adorned for her espousal. . . . Were she now to be spurned . . . she would seek some other friend . . . she could not ponder long.

While the Old Chief was writing that still Older Chief, the Texan Secretary of State was explaining the recent turn of events to Postmaster Norton at Houston. What with his "farming & gardening & improving a place" and his "public duties," Mr. Secretary Jones had been neglecting private correspondence. He let Norton know how matters stood as of February 17:

There has been a large [Jones] meeting here to-day—every thing went off pleasantly and unanimously—quite a contrast to the "Burleson" fuss or *farce* of the previous week. . . .

Capt Jno. G. Tod (formerly of the Navy), arrived here this morning with despatches from the City of Washington for me & Gen.

Murphy—All about annexation which appears likely to take place —I have not thought so untill within a week past, but now believe it next to certain. . . . If it can be effected I think the safety & welfare of the country will be best assured. I have no desire but to see Texas prosperous & happy. If I should wish to hold any office in a State Gov^t it would be that of Senator in Congress—but it is too soon to "count chickens" yet as they are not hatched and the eggs may all be *addled*.

The demonstrations of opposition [to annexation] . . . in some of the papers may not be amiss. . . . By not appearing over anxious for annexation we perhaps strengthen the chances for such an event, at all events we place ourselves in an attitude to obtain a fairer bargain than if we were to induce the adverse party to believe we were unitedly solicitous on the subject. In a mere party point of view, however, I think it . . . impolitic for the "Democrat" to keep up its opposition. . . .

A rumor is busily circulated & I have often heard it that Gen. H. and myself are opposed [to annexation]. . . . I say . . . that the administration has been laboring for the last year . . . to effect either *independence* or *annexation,* that one or the other of these is sure now to happen soon, that either will answer very well, & that for whichever is obtained the present administration will be entitled to equal credit. . . . I would not be so foolish as to labor to effect what I did not *wish* to effect. . . .

This question will I think be determined one way or other in the next 60 days. In the mean time I would say to my friends "Stand to your posts"—it will be time enough to cease the contest when "our flag is struck". . . .

From all parts of Eastern Northern & Middle Texas I have the most favorable accounts—& even at the West there are some favorable demonstrations. The Battle however (if fought at all) will have to be fought principally in the hot months of July & August. Untill then it will I think be best to *"be asy"* or if not *"asy"* as *"asy as you can"* as the paddy has it. I rely much on *you* and the *"Democrat"*. . . .

I hope you will write me by every opportunity. . . . Be as candid as you please—— The frankness of a friend can never offend. . . . A Barbecue is to come off at Independence next Saturday. . . . Gens. Houston & Murphy (the Lions of the day) are invited & have promised to attend—— All the world are to be there—except

Your friend

JONES [Rubric]

Norton promised

an *armed neutrality* on that matter [the presidency] for sixty days; and I trust, if annexation shall fail, as I fear it may, that our candidate will be able to furnish evidence that it was not owing to any want of friendship to the measure, on his part, or of exertions to effect it.

The Houston *Morning Star,* pledged to no neutrality, pursued its steady anti-Jones course.

GREAT PUBLIC MEETING [it reported February 27]. A few months since a public meeting was held in Washington County at the residence of Capt. Coles, and resolution adopted nominating Anson Jones for the Presidency. The few papers under the patronage of the Doctor announced this as a *great* public meeting. But it was soon made known that only *twelve* persons attended the meeting, and that Dr. Johnson who *presided,* was the former *partner* of Dr. Jones in business at Austin! This . . . being a complete *faux pas,* an attempt was recently made to convene another to bolster up the hopeless claims of the Doctor. A public meeting for this purpose was lately held at Washington, at which we learn at least ten persons attended, exclusive of those in the employment of the Government. And resolutions were adopted highly complimenting the *"fine native intellect* of the Doctor". . . .

Next day the *Telegraph* assured Texans that

our country is not so destitute of able and independent men as to render it necessary to elect a chief magistrate who is so embecile that he will be required to be kept in leading strings by his predecessor.

For the encouragement of the Texans the *Western Advocate* pointed out that there would be six, maybe eight, presidential candidates. Dr. Jones, General Burleson, Judge Hemphill, Judge Lipscomb, and Robert (Honest Bob) Wilson were already in the field, and General Rusk and General Johnston were "spoken of as likely." But the *Northern Standard* rightly guessed that the contest would be between Jones and Burleson. Where, the *Standard* wanted to know, was Anson Jones when Burleson and Hemphill were hurrying to the defense of San Antonio?

If we are not greviously in error, he was practicing medicine in Brazoria and at the same time drawing his pay as Secretary of State.

. . . [He has] never yet done one thing . . . to entitle him to the gratitude or support of the people. . . . Has he rendered the country high service? No! . . . Is he brilliant in capacity? No! What claims has he then upon the people? Only this, that a few loud mouthed partisans . . . strive to make discord perpetual . . . and have chosen to carry out their scheme and give it cohesion, *this man* . . . they think the wily Secretary may be run in, upon the soldier reputation of his patron. We think not. . . .

As the Texans—and Jones—wondered whether there would be another President of Texas, Jones wrote "Messors J. Pinckney Henderson and Isaac Van Zandt Esquires" to negotiate under instructions written by Stephen F. Austin on November 18, 1836, when annexation was first sought, and those written by Anson Jones on January 27 and February 15 of the current year of grace. They would stipulate for "the ultimate creation of at least four States" on Texas soil, and for the United States to take over the vessels and debts of the Texas Navy. As for the limits of Texas, they were to insist upon the boundaries specified by the act of the Texas Congress in 1836.

At Washington City things were moving rapidly. Minister Van Zandt, not knowing that a new colleague and new instructions were on the way, began drafting the treaty upon which his heart was set. He and Secretary Upshur, he wrote Jones,

For some days . . . engaged in discussing the terms . . . and had agreed upon all the main points. . . . I had given to him for examination an outline of the points which would be required to be included; and he had submitted to me a similar draft, in his own handwriting, embracing his views, which corresponded fully with my own in every main particular. . . .

On February 28 there was a trip down the Potomac.

In great haste, I write you [Van Zandt scribbled to Jones] to inform you of a most awful calamity which occurred today on board the war steamer Princeton, which was making a pleasure excursion down the river, with the President and Cabinet, the diplomatic corps, a number of members of Congress, and an immense crowd of ladies on board.

In firing for the third time one of the large 225-pounder guns of the Princeton, it burst, killing dead Mr. Upshur, Secretary of State,

Mr. Gilmer, Secretary of the Navy, Com. Kennan, Mr. Maxcy, Charge d'Affaires to Belgium, and Mr. Gardiner. . . . I was on board, and not far from the gun, when it exploded. Capt. Stockton had nearly all his hair burned off, and Col. Benton was very much stunned. Others are said to be missing; but the confusion was so great that it is difficult to speak with certainty. . . . The occurance will have, I fear, an unfavorable influence on our affairs here. Texas has lost two of her best friends. . . .

XXIX

SECRET, DARK AND DILIGENT

THE President of the United States sat, pale and shaken, at breakfast on February 29, 1844. He had narrowly escaped death in the *Princeton* disaster which had taken the lives of two of his Cabinet and several other warm friends; their bodies were on their way to the White House. Before he could consider what he should do, or even finish his breakfast, Congressman Wise of Virginia was with him, urging that he make John C. Calhoun Secretary of State. The President refused. The two men rose, shook hands stiffly, and told each other they were parting for the last time.

After nearly a week of anxious calculations—he was trying to reconstruct his Cabinet with eyes squinted toward the presidential election in November as well as the Texas treaty—Tyler relented on March 6, offered the place to Calhoun and, without waiting for his reply, sent the nomination to the Senate, where it was immediately confirmed. Ten days later Calhoun accepted, but not until March 30 did he enter on his duties. Thirty precious days lost to Texas, after Van Zandt had everything arranged.

As the Texan Chargé waited impatiently for instructions that would authorize him to sign the treaty, he read in a Baltimore paper

that Genl Henderson had been appointed a *special minister and Plen. and En. Exy.* to conclude a treaty of annexation with other particulars of an alleged secret act of Congress etc. . . . Why all these matters should be . . . heralded throughout this country by the newspapers and yet I receive no information [he wrote Jones] . . . is most remarkable.

It was not only most remarkable, it was most injurious, "a matter of infinite regret." The "whole opposition" was aroused and "daily pour forth the vials of its wrath." Texas must act quickly, but Van Zandt's hands were tied. He already had everything ready for Henderson "whenever he comes," and could not move without him. If he delayed much longer the efforts "to lay the treaty over" would succeed, he wrote March 25. The Chargé was unhappy about many things—the failure to receive instructions promptly, the leak in secret information, the fact that his government had not trusted him to conclude this business which he had handled skillfully to the point of completion. He must sit idly by while anti-Texas sentiment crystallized, waiting for a coadjutor he did not need.

When General Henderson tardily arrived at the end of March, he found his business was so well known that there was no point in concealing it, American congressmen being, he found, "as good hands, generally, to keep secrets as our own." Everybody in Congress wanted to delay the annexation question until after the presidential election.

I have said to all [he reported to Jones] that this is the *third* time that Texas has urged the measure . . . that it cannot be postponed. . . . Texas . . . must now seek safety . . . by annexation, alliance, or other engagements . . . that any delay at this time on the part of the United States will be fatal. . . .

Friend Van Zandt and myself agree perfectly on all points. We avoid all distinctions of party, and treat it, and ask them to treat it, exclusively as a national matter, although we see who our real friends are. . . .

John C. Calhoun had been committed to the Texas cause— and to annexation—since 1836. It was for this reason that he had been urged for the Secretaryship of State and that Tyler, who on other grounds would not have wanted him, appointed him.

He found the Texan negotiators waiting for him—and he found reports from General Murphy full of apprehension that Houston, his Cabinet, all his confidential friends were secretly opposed to annexation. "The number of British agents, crowding Galveston and Houston would astonish you. Secret, dark and diligent in something or other, which men known or suspected to be friendly to annexation cannot find out."

General Duff Green, Tyler's confidential agent in London and the father of Calhoun's daughter-in-law, had already reported his version of what Britain was up to: "The British government will guarantee the payment of the interest on a loan upon condition that the Texian government will abolish slavery."

To the new Secretary of State, whose life was dedicated to the proposition that slavery was the cornerstone of the American Union, that meant that Texas must be annexed to protect the "peculiar institution," if for no other reason. There was nothing for Calhoun to do but to get a treaty on paper and signed as soon as possible, and hope that somehow it would be ratified. He went to work with Messrs. Henderson and Van Zandt, and on April 12 the Texans wrote "hastily" but fully to Secretary Jones the circumstances of the drafting of the treaty. Before their letter could reach Texas the treaty would be before the United States Senate. It was not, the envoys wrote,

such an one as we expected to make or had a right to wish. But . . . the best we could frame with the prospect of its ratification. . . . The only inquiry with us was: What will the Senate of the United States agree to? and not, What can we get from the Executive of the United States? . . .

Before they agreed to sign, the Texans extracted from President Tyler a promise that, should the treaty be rejected by the Senate, he would immediately ask Congress for "a law annexing Texas as a state. . . . And it is confidently believed . . . such a law can be passed."

Too late to guide their dealings with strait-laced Secretary Calhoun, the weary plenipotentiaries of Texas received additional advice from President Houston—written four days after they signed the treaty:

It is the first duty of Statesmen and patriots to insure the liberty and well being of their country. This is now our attitude, and every honest man in Texas will justify and approve that policy, which will place us in a situation where our liberties are secured, whether it be by annexation, or the establishment of our Independence. France and England will act effectively, if we do not permit ourselves to be trifled with, and duped by the United States. But of this subject, as your situation may soon call your attention you will be the best Judges.

A Diplomatic agent may eat and sleep enough for health, and may drink generously with the Diplomatic agents of other countries, provided, he can induce them to take two glasses to his one. Men are fond to be thought knowing, as well as wise, and when listened to with attention, frequently impart knowledge, at the wine table, which they would not dream of in the forenoon of the day. You can instruct yourselves much by the course intimated.

April 22, 1844, the day after the eighth anniversary of San Jacinto, the Texas treaty went to the United States Senate. For ten days Tyler had been busy preparing a message placing the Texas matter on a broad national basis, and his Secretary of State was selecting documents to prove annexation necessary for the perpetuation of slavery. "I have placed the Texian question on that issue," he declared. "I am resolved to keep it there, be the consequence what it may." The consequence was not long in developing; diplomacy gave way to politics: the question was who should be the next President of the United States, not what should become of Texas.

The national conventions of both American parties met before the treaty was voted upon, and Texas was one of the pawns in the coming election. By coincidence, Henry Clay, who was certain of the Whig nomination, and Martin Van Buren, who had been endorsed by Democratic conventions in twenty-four of twenty-six states, declared on the same day against immediate annexation. The President himself was hoping, if he could not get the Democratic nomination, to head a new "Tyler and Texas" party. It was, old John Quincy Adams said, "John Tyler's last trump card for a popular whirlwind."

As official Texas awaited news from the Potomac, the Secretary of State busied himself more and more with his plantation while the President remained in the executive offices. The personal relations between them were not uncordial, but they were strained. Mr. Secretary Jones increasingly distrusted His Excellency and resented the personal hand he was taking in diplomatic negotiations. Houston, believing that a President should do whatever he wanted to do in his own government, had no qualms about personally assuming the functions of any Cabinet officer and was oblivious to Jones's resentment. He was, however, beginning to wonder whether Jones was the man to succeed him.

After the manner of politicians, neither hinted to the other

what was uppermost in his own mind. Each was playing a waiting game, and there were innumerable contingencies to be considered. That the situation would change before election time
was clear, but neither could foresee in the spring what the next
six months would bring, for himself or for Texas.

The presidential campaign was limping along. Pro-Jones articles in the *Vindicator* and the *Democrat* were reprinted in other
papers, even the opposition press; but they lacked effectiveness
and sparkle.

As a politician, Dr. Jones has been a firm and consistent supporter
of the present administration [the Harrison *Times* reported]. In fact
much of the success that has resulted from the policy pursued is to be
attributed to his untiring efforts in the Diplomatic relations of our
Country. The negotiations with the foreign powers that brought
about the interference and mediation with Mexico, and ultimately
the Armistice, were the works of Anson Jones, and to his skill in managing our foreign relations may no doubt be attributed the present
prosperous condition of the country.

Jones himself was such a passive candidate that Norton could
not

decide whether you are so certain of annexation as to lose all interest
in other matters, or whether you feel too sure of success in the coming elections to look much after them. It is certain your enemies are
making untiring efforts in all parts of the country, and that their
efforts should be met. . . .
Is there any thing you wish urged particularly on public attention
at this time?

Jones replied at once, on March 26. Mrs. Jones and the baby
were sick; he was unwell, and had been

so much at the desk & confined writing that I am *sick* at the sight
of a sheet of paper. It is true *annexation* like Moses's rod has swallowed up all else—I am not so certain of its success however—but I
do assure you that nothing will be omitted which can properly be
done to ensure its accomplishment. . . . We are now in so far that
we cannot if we would, go back. But if annexation should not take
place I *do* feel pretty "sure of success in the coming elections."

If annexation fail by Treaty, I think if we can reach the object by
a law of the U. S. Congress, we should agree to it that way. But this

is too far off to determine upon now. Let us hear from our agents at Washington, & let the Congress of the U. States first act. It will be time enough for us then.

Norton read the optimistic letter of his candidate for President, conferred with Major Reily, then wrote President Houston that his and Jones's "leading friends do not promise much unity of action in regard to the approaching political canvass" and requested a confidential conference.

The President passed the letter on to Secretary Jones, who scented "treason in camp." A letter he had just received indicated the nature and extent of the treason.

I can no longer disguise from you [Norton said] that there is a settled determination among many of your leading friends in all parts of the country . . . to have a new candidate in the field for President,—either Hemphill, Henderson or Rusk. . . .

Even your friend [J. W. "Smoky"] Henderson told me yesterday that he thought Hemphill would command more votes than any other candidate. . . . Letters . . . from Eastern Texas . . . strongly recommend running one of the candidates named. If circumstances would allow it, I should . . . say many things which I do not wish to put on paper.

I wish you would write by next mail, if only to acknowledge the receipt of this, as I do not like to have such communications afloat. . . .

By return mail Norton received his reply:

My nomination . . . has been by a general concert of our friends throughout all parts of the country. If a change is made it must be by the same general concert. I am willing to support any honest & capable man. . . . I have only to say to you beware of Traitors & I will also quote from very good authority the simple remark "That fear admited into public councils betrays like Treason" . . . .

I do not mean to be understood that I am indifferent *to the honor* of being elected to the office of Pres^t. What I meant to say was that I knew the cares & troubles which the office brought with it—that I had not sought the nomination . . . that I had yielded to the wishes of my political friends, rather than my own, in consenting to be a Candidate. I personally *solicited* Gen. Henderson, Gen. Rusk & Judge Lipscomb successively to suffer their names to be run, and it was perfectly understood by my friends that if Judge Hemphill or

K. L. Anderson Esq. should be fixed upon that I would not oppose. In fact Col. Anderson after Gen. Henderson would have been my first choice. But it was decided otherwise, & whether for good or ill —for success or defeat—it is now in my humble opinion too late in the day for a change. . . .

President Houston and his family departed for the coast, not primarily but incidentally in response to Norton's urgency. His Excellency wanted to get news from the United States as soon as it came from the ships and keep in personal touch with the diplomatic corps at Galveston. General Murphy was troubled lest his promise of American protection for Texas had been disavowed by his government. What the United States needed, Dr. Jones thought, was "another *scare*. One or two doses of *English* calomel and *French* quinine . . . and the case will be pretty well out of danger."

After a "full and satisfactory conversation" with Murphy, the President wrote Jones that, from Henderson's instructions not to negotiate without an assurance of protection for Texas, Tyler's government would

readily see that the game is to be a two-handed one. If the United States should interpose any difficulty . . . it would be an easy matter to say, "Gen. Henderson, your mission is terminated." . . . Already the subject of annexation has caused the failure of our negotiations with Mexico. I have seen Hockley and Williams. . . . I think the subject of the [Norton] letter which I bore here will be at rest for the future. All was *smoke,* as I believed. . . .

Norton believed that day Jones could carry the county, maybe also the city of Houston, and he added:

I never did suppose you particularly ambitious, but I did suppose that the office of President would be to you, or any other man, a matter of more interest than you seem to consider it in your letter.

That day, too, the Houston *Morning Star* reported:

Some of the most influential citizens of San Augustine and of the whole East . . . have no idea of accepting any stilted representative of the present administration. . . . Dr. Jones is very well in his way, but we do not admire the way, and we must be permitted to say that there is in his case, a total absence of claim upon the people of the country. He has never done them any service but what has been *paid* for, and the payment was an extinguishment of future claim.

There are some who object to General Burleson as not being sufficiently qualified, and it is in fact the only tangible objection that can be made, and to a certain extent we admit its justness. But then his opponent . . . is so inferior as to put comparison out of view.

The next day the President moved on to Galveston to reassure Captain Elliot, who had been in New Orleans for months observing "the present agitation of Texian affairs" in the United States and now desired to know Houston's intentions. To the British Foreign Office the Chargé reported the President's conversation in "General Houston's language as nearly as my memory serves me." He had yielded reluctantly to pressure of the Texan Chargé at Washington, the United States Government, and "persons of great weight in that Country to whom he is warmly attached" to negotiate for annexation; but he still preferred independence. He had instructed Henderson not to negotiate unless the United States agreed

to place at the disposal of the Government of Texas, a Column of 1000 infantry, and 600 or 700 heavy Cavalry . . . a Naval force equal to that of Mexico . . . also . . . distinctly guarantee to Texas the acknowledgment of it's Independence by Mexico, if . . . annexation failed. . . . Instructions to General Henderson are precise and imperative upon the refusal to open negotiations till the required written guarantees of the Government of the United States are duly furnished.

The Britisher asked Houston to terminate annexation negotiations until negotiations with Mexico were completed. But, he reported,

General Houston would not take this step. . . . Neither do I imagine that he has ever entertained much confidence in the success of the Scheme of annexation, or certainly any personal wish to postpone the Independence of the Country to such a solution. . . .

At Sabinas below the Rio Grande, Colonels Hockley and Williams had conversed with Señores Landeras and Jaunequi, Mexican commissioners, for nearly four months. They were playing for time and trying to avoid any political commitments; but when the Mexicans heard that annexation was about to be negotiated at Washington City, polite conversation ended. On February 15, 1844, the commissioners hurriedly signed a paper which referred to Texas as a department of Mexico, and the Texans, "scarcely feeling safe," hurried home.

Hockley, who returned by way of Galveston to Washington-on-the-Brazos, reported to the Secretary of State that "Elliot has gone off miffed, and I don't wonder at it; that error must be reformed." Hockley was a good man but too ardent an opponent of annexation. Jones retorted:

I cannot help Capt. Elliot's being "miffed," nor can I admit there has been error in consenting to treat for annexation. We must take care of ourselves. The British Government is too slow for their own interests.

The President at Houston was reading diplomatic dispatches as they reached the post office, answering them, then sending them on to Mr. Secretary Jones with a synopsis of what he had already written and mailed to the agents in the United States. He had told them, he wrote Jones on April 14:

If annexation is not effected at the present session of Congress, or if a treaty should fail, and the action of Congress be ineffectual, and they refuse to form an alliance with us, to call upon the English and French Ministers [to the United States] and ascertain the prospect of those Governments giving us a guarantee against further molestation from Mexico, and an indefinite truce. We cannot be trifled with in the present crisis of our affairs.

I saw Capt Elliot and so far arranged matters that I hope we shall suffer no serious detriment, at the same time I did not commit myself or nation. . . .

"That silly old man Murphy," United States Chargé, still convinced that much skulduggery was afoot but unable to discover exactly what it was, decided to apply directly to the sources of information. To the Texan Secretary of State he wrote that he heard that England or France, maybe both, had protested against annexation negotiations, and "Mr. Jones is well aware that I would be very glad to have copies of these protests . . . under any injunction of confidential privacy he deems proper. . . ." How Jones wished that he had received such protests—they would have insured annexation! He did not reply to General Murphy's request, but he wrote on the back of it:

Our American Minister partakes of the common feeling in the United States, *jealousy* and fear of *England,* to say nothing of France. He ought to have more sense. . . .

Pending an answer from Jones, Murphy set off up the bayou to see the President. "I fear he is in a bother," the President wrote his Secretary of State, "and will not know how to get on smoothly with his matters." He never had, never did.

Jones's campaign manager, M. P. Norton, and the President were in frequent, if not continuous, consultation at Houston. On April 18, Mr. Secretary Jones "Gathered from my Garden, Peas, Irish Potatoes & Beets," then rode into town to read the latest news from the coast. There was a letter from Norton:

I do not wish to bring forward a single article in relation to the Presidency until this matter of annexation shall be settled. . . . The President is disposed to carry out, on his part, as I think very fairly, all such measures as may be likely to help forward the business of annexation . . . and leave us. And this course will help us in the election, if the measure fail. I intend the *Democrat* shall be the last paper that abandons it—get back, at least, if I can, what was lost by its early opposition. But when we do give it up, we must give it up *forever*—if England take such course as will sustain us.

Can you not persuade him [the President], when all hope of annexation . . . shall have failed, to withdraw Van Zandt, as well as Henderson, from the United States? It will certainly place us on better grounds with Great Britain. . . .

The obvious artlessness of that suggestion was not lost on Jones. "Gen. Houston," he commented, "despairing of annexation, is thinking of entangling alliances with European powers, and through the writer of this, wishes to commit me on the subject." That portion of Norton's letter remained unanswered. Jones was convinced now that Houston was officiously interfering with diplomacy "with a view to ultimately defeating annexation"; and he suspected he wanted to sabotage the Jones candidacy. The President, so he wrote Jones, was heartily weary of waiting for good news from Washington and "curious to know what move we will next have to make on the chessboard"; he asked Jones to write him "such a letter as you would not care to see published." Jones wrote him nothing.

On the night of April 28 a diplomatic pouch addressed to the Texan Secretary of State, which had left Washington City on April 12, reached the Houston post office. It contained the annexation treaty and the commissioners' explanation of it. Norton handed it to the President, who read the contents, then reached for his quill. First he wrote to Messrs. Henderson and Van Zandt, who, with much difficulty and some violation of instructions, had made this treaty between Texas and the United States:

It does not embrace the guarantee as fully as was contemplated. If annexation should fail . . . we are without any security. . . . 'Tis well enough, we cannot go back and therefore we must march forward with decisive steps. . . .

If the present measure of annexation should fail entirely . . . it is the last effort at Annexation that Texas will ever make. . . .

This dispatch is written because several days would elapse before an Express could reach Washington and return. . . . As the business is important, I do not care about official formality. The substance is what I am now after, and for that reason I write.

Then to Secretary Jones at Washington-on-the-Brazos he wrote:

I send you the treaty; you will read it. It had as well been made in Texas, though I presume it will do very well. All we had to do was to dispose ourselves decently, and in order.

I regret that the impetuosity was so great on the part of our agents as not to require some security . . . against . . . a failure of annexation. . . . It was regarded in the instructions from your department as a sine qua non to entering upon negotiations. You will see that Mr. Calhoun has jockeyed . . . he has clearly outwitted them. . . .

I would be truly gratified if you were here to meet emergencies. . . .

Come down if you can, if but for a few days. I may have to remain here for a month. Write and inform me.

Mr. Secretary Jones, "from a bed of sickness and extreme prostration of strength . . . fever attended with excessive depression of spirits &c. &c.," read the report of the ministers and the treaty.

To Norton he wrote: "The *Treaty* I suppose we must take, and like honest Sancho 'not look a gift horse in the mouth.' "

For his own record he wrote:

It had been better that our commissioners, both at Sabinas and Washington City, had not exceeded the limits of their instructions. No *final* result in relation to the destiny of Texas was immediately anticipated from either negotiation; consequently it would better have subserved the honor, interests, and the ultimate decision of the questions of independence or annexation, if the commissioners in each instance had exhibited less intemperate zeal in bringing their respective negotiations to a close, *outside* of their powers. The fact that the negotiations were on foot in Mexico and in the United States answered every purpose in reciprocally exciting the zealous rivalry of opposing nations, which was the object aimed at by me; and the sacrifice made in each case was injudicious, unnecessary, hurtful. . . .

To W. D. Miller, secretary of the "secret" legation, he wrote next day:

The negotiation of the Treaty has taken people here by surprise. . . . They do not wait to know the terms of the agreement but "go it Blind" in rejoicing.

I do not partake very strongly with you in your fears about its ratification by the Senate of the U.S. . . . . But "nous verrons."

. . . Assurances from England or France for guaranteeing our independence at this moment . . . would favor the ratification of the treaty. They will hold off until the matter is decided, & if annexation fail, they will come in with their good offices fast enough. It will be a very easy matter to "swap" an assurance of maintaining our national unity as a separate & distinct nation in all future time, for a guarantee to us by England & France from molestations by Mexico. . . .

All eyes are now strained towards the U. S. . . . . In a few weeks they may all be turned to England & France. I am satisfied we will do very well in either event.

From Washington City Henderson wrote Jones: "We are in a tight place. Both parties are laboring to make capital out of the Question." Secretary Raymond of the Legation was employing his leisure in writing political articles for the Texas press. "I cannot better promote my country's interest than in advocating your elevation," he wrote Jones.

President Houston, still in close conference with Norton, wrote Jones on May 8:

> If the treaty is not ratified between Texas and the United States, I will require the negotiations to be transferred to Texas. You and myself can manage them tolerably well! ! !

With that letter came one from Norton:

> . . . I cannot write you what I could say on the subject if I could see you. . . . If I were myself in your place . . . I could not be pursuaded to hold on as a candidate. . . . Gen. Houston has come, I think reluctantly, into my view of a change of candidate. . . . Should you . . . conclude to go out of the canvass, Gen. Houston suggested . . . every thing in relation to any change remain a secret until announced . . . for ever, if we get annexed. . . .

Things were becoming clearer. Jones listed *"traitors* discovered—viz . . . H[ousto]n. smoky H[enderso]n. and R[eil]y," consulted his memory, and added:

> Twelve months ago I earnestly sought . . . to decline being a candidate . . . hesitated . . . six months . . . then told them that, should they think best, I should withdraw at any time—I should be willing to do so; but in the present critical posture of public affairs . . . I do *not* think *my friends* wish me to resign the candidature, or that they deem such a course best for the country. . . . I will not yield to traitors.

Those vague, dark apprehensions that General Murphy had long entertained and shared with the government of the United States were intensified by letters from President Houston, who took the time to sketch for him in many pages the bright future that lay before Texas as an independent nation—and the peril that such an arrangement might be to the United States. His Excellency also wrote the commissioners at Washington City:

> Since I have had time to reflect . . . I begin to entertain some apprehension that our Senate may not be disposed to ratify it. . . . The U. S. will realize everything from the Treaty while Texas will derive very little. . . . Keep the Govt. here advised by every mail of all passing events. Always sleep with one eye open. Do the best you can.

Norton, watching the President, was growing increasingly apprehensive and discouraged. To Jones he wrote May 16:

> . . . it is of the utmost importance that you should be here. Gen. Houston . . . is about to take some strong measures, and has probably recalled Henderson; and if there were ever a time when he needed the aid of his friends, it is now. He expected, without any doubt, to meet you here . . . will be greatly disappointed. . . . So far as I can learn, the election is *given up* by our friends throughout the Republic. I have not heard a man intimate the belief that we could succeed for the last two months.

"Judge Norton," Jones reflected, "is perfectly honest, faithful, and honorable himself, and, naturally enough, thinks every body else so; but he is timid, wavering, and nervous. . . . I can and shall be elected. . . ."

He would not go to Houston, but he would send to confer with the President and Norton his

> particular friend *Dr. Moses Johnson* of Independence [who] . . . is entirely in my confidence in political matters, a well wisher to the cause and the country. . . . He is apprised of my views on the subject & will communicate them to you. . . . Confer with him freely & with entire unreserve . . . in mutual confidence.

Before Dr. Johnson arrived the President had given instructions to the commissioners to the United States. Texas was no longer to be

> a bone of contention, to be worried and gnawed by . . . conflicting politicians. . . .
>
> We must . . . regard ourselves as a nation *to remain forever separate*. . . . Texas, alone, can be well sustained . . . can now command interests which will require no such sacrifice. We must act. . . . Gen. Henderson's remaining there longer would be unnecessary. . . .
>
> The locality of our seat of government is such that the Executive has had to substitute himself in correspondence for the Secretary of State, and dispense with the services of that valuable officer, for the sake of despatch. . . .
>
> . . . this government, relying upon the pledges given by that Government will confidently expect that no molestation to Texas by Mexico will be permitted or the aids already ordered withdrawn, without the consent of this government.

The desires of the people of Texas, with my love of repose (this far I am selfish) had determined me in favor of annexation. My judgment . . . has never fully ratified the course. . . .

Separately Houston wrote Henderson:

There is some little talk about the Presidential election, but our people are not quite so loud as they were in 1841. I hope we will not have to inaugurate another; but if we should, I pray God he may be an honest man with capacities sufficient to discharge the duties of his station. . . .

Then to the Secretary of State His Excellency wrote a note and sent it by Dr. Johnson:

DEAR JONES,—This will reach you before I can. Don't say anything about the *matter alluded to,* until I can see you! I was surprised at your letter. . . . What I do with my friends is done face to face, and not by halves. I am a *little mortified.* If a man cannot be open with his friends, to whom will he be honest? . . . I want to see you!

Salute your lady for me, and be assured of my constant regard and good faith. . . . Thine truly, SAM HOUSTON.

The doctor was not convinced; he believed the President was still *"Crawfishing* about, trying to defeat my election." He read the other letter Johnson had brought him. It was from Norton:

Yesterday morning Gen. Houston . . . showed me your letter, and it was finally determined to act on your suggestion, and take measures for a change of candidates [the doctor interlined: I made no "suggestions" authorizing a *clique at Houston* to take any such measures] . . . had letters written to Stuart of the *Civilian,* and Lewis, and Chas. B. Stewart of Montgomery, notifying them of the fact; and in the evening Dr. Johnson arrived. . . . I have succeeded in getting back my letters, and . . . the matter is to rest as it is until Gen. Houston reaches Washington. . . .

Dr. Johnson has entirely different views on the subject of the election from any other man I have seen. He says that in Washington, and some other counties, you would even beat Gen. Houston. I think he is deceived. . . .

To Jones this was "detail of the treason of Gen. Houston, J. W. Henderson, and James Reily."

From Washington City, W. D. Miller was reporting to Jones confidentially that

annexation cannot take place . . . most remote of probabilities. . . . As to the provisions of the treaty itself, I have not heard a whisper of objection. . . . The opposition is upon the general and naked question of Annexation. . . . To effect it by act of Congress is yet more difficult and uncertain. . . .

In this state of things the gov^t and people of Texas will have to decide deliberately and calmly what to do. North of this place we have but very little sympathy. . . . They would rejoice if our country should be lost and our gov^t overturned. . . . They will neither help us themselves nor permit any other people or power to do so. . . .

Also confidentially, and more authoritatively, came inside information from Senator George Evans of Maine, one of the ablest of the Whigs. Jones had known him at Washington City in 1838, when Evans was already a veteran congressman. During the annexation negotiations Jones had been sending him data that might help the Texan cause if whispered about by a non-Texan.

. . . I stated 3 or 4 times in conversation with gentlemen the substance of them, but without the slightest intimation of *names*. The[y] may have caught an idea or two. . . .

The Senate yesterday removed the injunction of secrecy from all the [annexation] documents—*a very unusual step*—but so strong is the condemnation of the Administration. . . . I told you before, that the Adm^n was too weak to carry any thing. In reference to this matter, it is admitted on all hands, to have been most bunglingly—miserably—suicidally managed. The grounds upon which it is made to stand are such, that no northern senator can safely vote for it however inclined to annexation. . . . There was no fear or jealousy of Engl^d at the bottom of it. It *was designed purely* & solely *to make Tyler Pres't* once more. . . . It seems to me the best condition for Texas is to be a free, separate republic. . . . You must struggle on with your embarrassment some time, but a few years is nothing in the life of a nation. . . .

Not all Texans thought highly of the treaty or of annexation. Colonel Jacob Snively, one-time Texan Secretary of War and recently commander of an unfortunate freebooting expedition, wrote from Washington-on-the-Brazos on May 20:

I hope we never will be an integral part of that imbecile government. There is too much corruption in the U. States; it would be utterly impossible to unite such a virtuous republic as this to such an unprincipled country as Uncle Sam's. Did you ever see such a treaty as has been made by our Commissioners at Washington?

General Murphy, convinced now "the treaty will be ratified" despite British intrigue and other sinister influences, wrote Jones a United States fleet was arriving at Galveston, "where she will remain under my orders. . . . All these ships are guarding the Texan Coast under and in pursuance of the arrangement between us," he reminded the Secretary of State.

God save the mark [Jones exclaimed at this protection which had arrived before it was needed]—protecting and guarding us against whom, Mexico! A common Texas "dug-out" with half a dozen men, could do that. It is either fear of England and France, or some ulterior object, not yet apparent which has brought all this array of armed ships upon our coast. . . . I have never believed the Senate would ratify the treaty of annexation, but the measure will be accomplished notwithstanding. The storm is up, and nothing but the alliance will now allay it. Mr. Murphy, his Government, and his "people" are too well frightened for any other result to happen, if the game is played right by Texas.

XXX

WARY AS FOXES

IF TEXAS was to play the game right that would bring her into the Union, Jones must deal the cards. Of that Jones was certain—and it was important that others should share his certainty. To the wavering Norton he wrote on May 26:

I think you have been very much decieved by some designing persons but have to thank you for your candor. . . . [I] insist upon no friend of mine going along with me further than he thinks proper, and for the best interests of the country. I can do very well without office, and if defeated shall only be a common loser. . . .

Three months only remain untill the election comes off. . . . Would it be safe to break up the encampment, and without order or organization retreat, in the face of the enemy? Would not defeat under such circumstances be certain? . . .

You must have caught some infection from the opposition when you talk to me about my running "upon another man's popularity" and tell me that "popularity is not transferable" &c. I thought I was the representative of certain principles,—principles which I have for two years steadfastly, constantly uniformly consistently (but how ably I leave others to say) advocated and defended, & upon the *popularity* of which I depend for support. If perchance I shall gain some friends, from my previous connexion with Gen. Houston, will you please look around this country and tell me how many malignant active bitter vindictive personal & political enemies I have made for myself by that connexion—— Then strike the balance and see how the account stands, if you please. . . . If there be a community in our principles, I claim the rights of a *partner,* not a mere *dependent beneficiary.* I beg you will learn to understand me— better than you appear to do. Or if you insist upon my depending upon his *popularity* do me the sheer justice also to state that I am potently opposed by his *unpopularity.* . . .

I shewed Gen. Houston your letter. . . . He read it all over, but appeared not the least shaken in his opinion, nor did he shew the

least disposition to change the views which he had all along given me
to understand he entertained on the subject. . . .

I have *never been beaten* in my life for any office,—nor do I ever
intend to be. . . .

In northeast Texas the *Northern Standard's* first choice was
Hemphill; eventually it supported Burleson. The *Telegraph* at
Houston regularly reprinted its anti-Jones squibs and added a
few of its own devising. The *Telegraph* held that

the school in which Gen. Burleson has been raised—the battle field
and the legislative hall—is much better calculated to make a Statesman, than the Apothecaries' Library or Physician's Practice.

"I think there is but little doubt of Dr. Jones's election," Henry
F. Gillette wrote Ashbel Smith in Europe from Houston on June
4; "and yet I fear the contest will be close. We are doing all in
our power for him. . . ."

The *Democrat,* now that Norton understood Jones was in the
race to win, resumed the campaign with aid from the doctor—
lists of hundreds of men "to whom an occasional number of the
paper might be sent with advantage," and assurances that in
supporting Jones

the *Democrat* is not alone. The *Vindicator* now circulates about 900
copies . . . into every "nook and corner" where the *Telegraph* can
be found. Besides there is the *Red Lander* . . . with a circulation
much larger than that of the *Telegraph,* the *News,* and the *Intelligencer* put together. There is also the *Harrison Times.* . . .

The news from every quarter is . . . most favorable. . . . *I am
not deceived.* . . .

It is true there are a few men of the opposition who make themselves busy in saying that Burleson will be elected—two to one, three
to one, four to one, and some six to one. But they are appointed and
commissioned to do this, and no more. I know one in particular who
has taken his stand at a certain corner, and repeats over an assertion
like this, to every one that passes, parrot like. . . .

I say once more to you—I am a candidate, and shall continue to
be so, and that, whether I get a vote or not . . .

The future of Texas, he believed, hung on a continuation of
the Jones policies of angling simultaneously for independence

and annexation. The opposition promised vaguely to do something else.

He knew Burleson, who had never given a thought to diplomacy, could neither grasp the intricacies of the situation it had taken Jones eight years to master nor devise diplomatic strategy. He distrusted, even more than he did the forthright Burleson, the men who would be his advisers. For Jones to quit the race now would not be merely abandoning a leaking ship which he knew how to bring safely into port; it would be handing over the helm to a man whose heart might be pure but who had never before been aboard a ship. Withdrawal would mean the inevitable failure of all the plans he had envisioned for Texas. He would remain in that race, come what might.

John Manson of the *Democrat* was coming to life again and writing the doctor with more sense than usual. Never, he warned,

undervalue a cunning and unscrupulous enemy. . . . If they *mine,* we must countermine, for if it was possible that there were any chance of Texas being again cursed by the rule of the Lamar faction, I would sooner see her annexed to the United States, Mexico, or the Devil. . . .

. . . I have engaged to furnish one or more articles every week for the *Democrat,* either as leaders, or communications, offensive and defensive, until the election is over. . . .

. . . pay us a visit here . . . it would strengthen your friends and weaken your enemies. There has been a report, originating with some who call themselves your friends, of your withdrawing from the contest. . . . Your presence down here would put that at rest for ever.

The doctor did not visit Houston. Mr. Manson would have to understand that

it is against all my principles, feelings, and practices, to go about electioneering. . . . The Presidency . . . is an office neither to be sought nor declined. This is a question the people must decide for themselves. I have counselled with my friends, when requested. . . . I . . . consider it my duty to repel attacks made upon my character as a man, and my acts as a public officer; but beyond these I shall not go. . . . I am compelled to remain at my post, and administer the public affairs. Further than this, the policy I am now pursuing with the United States, England, France, Mexico, and other powers

. . . is not ripe for an exposure to the world. A prudent and discreet policy requires I should keep silent for the present, which I could not do were I to go among the people electioneering. The Opposition must necessarily have the advantage of this circumstance.

President Houston, whatever his personal preferences had once been, wrote from East Texas, where he was feeling the pulse of the populace:

MY DEAR JONES . . . I hope you have received no worse news than what I have to send you.

A gentleman passed here yesterday from San Augustine . . . who states that he did not see but one man in a travel of three weeks (except one), but what would vote for yourself and K. L. Anderson, and that *one* was Judge Scurry, and he said he "had promised Burleson, and wished you elected!"

The gentleman stated that you would get nearly all the votes in San Augustine, Nacogdoches, and the counties around them; and in the Red River region . . . at least two-thirds of the votes. In . . . Montgomery I did not hear of one man that would vote for Burleson. . . .

You will now go on with all your skill and appliances, and you know what *licks,* and where to give and how to give them. . . .

News almost as good came from the city of Houston, where J. W. (Smoky) Henderson was running for Congress:

Some cause, I know not *what,* has marked a powerful revolution in your favor. . . . I shall make the Presidential election a strong point in the canvass. . . . I was in favor of [Pinckney] Henderson . . . then . . . Hemphill . . . but as the issue is now made and the time is come . . . to work, I have taken my stand and I start the canvass as your friend. I believe you will get 500 votes in this county; the whole vote will be 750 or 800.

To this John Green, Esq., added that nobody was now "reckless enough" to bet against Jones's election. Jones identified both as members of the Houston clique that had tried to get him out of the race; now, "finding I would be elected with or without their support, concluded to *take their stand* for me. . . ."

There were even Jones supporters in Austin, traditional opponent of everything and everybody associated with the administration which had moved the capital. Postmaster H. G. Catlett wrote Jones on June 23 of the

increased flattering prospects of your triumph . . . over moboc-racy, misrule, reckless speculation, and air-castle building. . . . When the election shall be over, and unprincipled demagogues, des-peradoes, and disorganizers are laid low, and the people have time for sober reflection, your day will come indeed. . . . I predict that you will leave the Presidential chair with more universal popularity amongst the *people* than either of the other ex-Presidents have done.

Even Major Reily, once counted by Jones among the "trai-tors," fell into line. He wrote Norton from Washington-on-the-Brazos, where he was sitting in a "damnable Court Martial . . . perfectly gorged with *Militia Military glory":*

The party lines are being strictly drawn. It is to be a contest of principle. . . . I now begin to feel anxious & shall stand by my old *friends* & exert whatever little influence I may have in defeating those who would ruin the present policy. Old Sam must be active. I think if Chalmers, Jeff Green et al can be induced to put forth a circular in behalf of Burleson the victory [for Jones] will be won.

Chalmers, Jeff Green, et al., did not issue their circular. Gen-eral Green was too busy with his private projects to take much part in politics this summer. He was not even seeking re-election as congressman from Brazoria.

Since April 22, when J. Q. Adams wrote in his diary: "The treaty for the annexation of Texas to this Union was this day sent in to the Senate; and with it went the freedom of the human race," statesmen on two continents and citizens of two nations had awaited the verdict of that body. Andrew Jackson had warned the senators that "Houston and the people of Texas are now united in favor of annexation—the next President may not be so. British influence may reach him."

Senator Benton of Missouri, who considered himself the oldest friend of Texas and the original annexation man, led the opposi-tion to ratification of the treaty. The present movement, he said, was sponsored by speculators in Texas lands and bonds, and led by John Tyler in order to get himself into the presidential race of 1844 as the "Texas candidate anointed with gunpowder."

Debate had begun on May 16 and concluded on June 8. The

forty senators the late Secretary Upshur had counted upon to ratify the treaty had dwindled to sixteen (fifteen Democrats, one Mississippi Whig); the opposition had grown from an anticipated dozen to thirty-five (which included seven Democrats). When the vote was announced J. Q. Adams gave thanks for this "special interposition of Almighty God" which delivered the United States from a "conspiracy comparable to that of Lucius Sergius Catilina." Most observers attributed it to other causes, but the result was unmistakable: Texas could not be annexed by treaty.

Early in July all Texas knew that annexation had failed. Official notification of the fact was communicated by General Murphy in a note that ranks among the gems of diplomatic correspondence: "The treaty is rejected, and so is my nomination: the tail went with the hide!"

By July the Texans also knew that Santa Anna was again making threatening gestures in their direction. The armistice had expired May 1, and on June 19 he decreed a resumption of hostilities. The alternatives Jones had worked for had temporarily failed simultaneously, but there were ways to revive them.

To His Excellency, still lingering among the East Texans, Mr. Secretary Jones sent the latest diplomatic dispatches from the United States and from Europe. The kaleidoscope was changing rapidly—and so were some of His Excellency's plans for the future of the Republic. He wrote Jones on July 8 to suggest that Ashbel Smith ascertain from England and France

what they propose to do in our behalf. . . . We are not in a situation to make any pledges until we know absolutely what they propose to do. We will try hereafter and keep the jockey word when we have got it (What boot will you give us?). . . . Mr. Van Zandt . . . announces . . . his resignation. . . . You will accept it in the most courteous terms. . . .

Until I arrive no appointment will be made to supply the place of Van Zandt . . . our Minister's leaving Washington City will have a favorable influence on the general concerns of Texas. We shall have to be as sharp-sighted as lynxes, and wary as foxes, for we are not yet out of the woods. . . .

I wish you to ascertain of the legation at Washington, whether the different legations of the several Governments were waited upon, and whether it was ascertained if they would act conjointly . . . in bringing about pacification between Texas and Mexico. . . .

I will now drop into politics. . . . I have heard of but two men in the country who would positively vote against yourself and Anderson. . . . So far as I can hear or learn, your and Anderson's prospects are excellent. . . .

P.S. . . . address the British authorities at Mexico . . . (if you should think well of the plan) to inquire of Santa Anna if he considers . . . the armistice . . . at an end . . . if he meditates another invasion of Texas. . . .

Jones's intuition told him the President was about to take the wrong road. "Going over to France and England in a hurry," he endorsed the President's letter; and later added, "I did not let him. . . . Gen. Houston was calling my attention one way, while the *game* was running another;—but did not succeed."

He wrote Norton:

Our friends in the U. States are still sanguine that annexation will yet take place and that before the expiration of the next twelve months. Among very many of our people I learn there is a strong disposition to hold on to the policy. Henderson will be with us soon and on his arrival I shall be able to form a definite opinion on this subject. For the present I hope you will not take grounds *against* annexation. Untill something better . . . offers . . . hold on to that. . . .

It was prudent to mark time on the annexation question, but not on the presidential succession. Five gentlemen from the counties of Washington, Brazoria, and Montgomery met at the capital on July 12, organized the Central Jones Committee, and issued an address to the people of Texas. Mr. Ramrod Johnson's *Vindicator* printed as an extra the four columns of campaign thunder which ended with this exhortation, which expediently ignored the rift that was widening between the candidate and the President:

SAM HOUSTON was the *President*—ANSON JONES the *Secretary of State*. Together they counselled—together they planned—together they labored, and the present prosperity of Texas is the result of their united wisdom. . . . We look to Anson Jones as our destined President. . . .

Who is better qualified to obtain these important objects [trade

treaties, peace treaty, etc.] than Anson Jones . . . understanding
thoroughly and committed heart and soul to the policy of Houston?
Or is it his antagonist, Edward Burleson, knowing *little* and claiming
to know *little,* save of war and Indian battle? . . .

We present [Jones] . . . as a worthy candidate—*just,—generous,
—patriotic,—high minded; a statesman understanding our position
and our wants; and able and willing to consummate the grand and
elevated aims of Sam Houston. . . .*

If Jones thought too few of his friends were bestirring themselves in his behalf, poor General Burleson was finding over-
zealous partisans an embarrassment. He was, as Jones put it,
"travelling for his *health*" among the voters. Every politician
who disliked Jones, or Houston, or long-established policies of
the Republic attached himself to the border hero, who knew not
how to accept proffered help without appearing to agree with
every helper. The *Red Lander* conceded that Burleson was, indeed, "the Marion of Texas," and recommended that he follow
the example of the "Swamp Fox" of the American Revolution
and rest on his military laurels instead of losing them in politics.
Border warfare was not a presidential function. The *Red Lander*
reported that Burleson had already chosen his Cabinet, and that
it included Mosely Baker and David G. Burnet.

The *Democrat,* on June 5, warned voters that Burleson was
controlled by the men who had dominated Lamar's administration and that he was supported only by malcontents. The general
hotly denied the charge and announced what Jones called
"Burleson's new creed."

"I have been misconceived or wilfully misrepresented," Burleson informed the *Democrat.* He would not order the government
back to Austin; he would "be controlled by the voice of the nation" in that and all other matters. He would not immediately
invade Mexico, but only "repel invasion, and with promptness
chastise the invaders." He would not even change Houston's Indian policy; he would only strengthen it by guarding more
closely against "bad Indians." He would not inaugurate a
Lamaresque "expenditure of the public money"; he was a frugal
man and his administration would be an economical one. He
was, in fact, above all partisanship; he was for sound policies by
whomever suggested. Oblivious of the conflicting and contradic-

tory orders that "the people" could be depended upon to shout, Burleson promised to do precisely what "the people" wanted. Burleson, late in the campaign, was endorsing every policy that Jones thought he had helped initiate and had been pursuing three years.

Jones read the letter and wondered who could have written it.

It is mournful [he wrote Norton] to think that a candidate for the Presidency could stoop so very low. The object is to play for the East & North—but it will not answer. . . . Burleson's letter . . . meets with no favor here from any party. Some of his friends are open and loud in denouncing it & its (reputed) Author.

For Jones's benefit the *Vindicator* rehearsed the Texas Rail Road, Navigation, and Banking scheme of 1836,

which was detected and prevented by the intelligence and firmness of Gen. Houston and the Hon. Anson Jones. . . . Among the "associates" who originally formed this company, we believe the only ones now living and in the country are Messrs. Thomas F. McKinney, T. J. Green, A. C. Allen, and Mosely Baker.

We believe that neither of these gentlemen has been, since August, 1836, the political supporter of Dr. Jones. . . .

There was the crowd of speculators, the *Vindicator* implied, that would control Burleson.

To a large segment of the electors of Texas the real question was not the diplomatic skill of Anson Jones or the personal heroism of Edward Burleson. It was: What does Sam Houston think? Both candidates were claiming his personal friendship. Jones was his political heir apparent; Burleson was now approving his policies. The Old Chief was "indisposed to mingle in politics"; he said nothing for publication until a month before the election. Then at the request of some Houston citizens he read for the first time Burleson's "new creed."

I was not displeased [he wrote] upon the perusal of his letter to ascertain that he entertained for me a high personal regard. Circumstances however have not thrown us much together. I always found him associated with men opposed to me personally and politically. . . .

During the last session of Congress I had the pleasure of meeting him but twice & then in the streets. He did not visit me. . . .

On almost every question affecting the policy of the present administration, which required the casting vote of the vice President, he gave it *against* the Executive.

During these events I never permitted myself to use an unkind expression towards him because I did not attribute his actions to himself, so much as I did to the influence of those with whom he associated.

In the Spring of 1842, after the Mexicans had retired from Bexar, he delivered an address . . . in which he cast many reflections upon the Executive. . . .

You further wish to know, gentlemen, whether I consider Dr. Anson Jones liable to the imputations cast upon him . . . and whether I am opposed to his election.

I am not opposed to his election. If I have not been a noisy advocate for his success, it has not been because I did not confide in him. I had confidence in him in the army of 1836 at San Jacinto. As Executive, I appointed him Minister to the U. S. in 1838, I knew him in the Senate for two sessions at Austin. When I was elected President . . . I selected him as the first officer of my cabinet. Since then I have been intimately associated with him. He has concurred in my policy and with distinguished ability he has conducted the foreign relations of the govt. and I have confidence that if the choice of the people should devolve the duties of President upon him, he would consult the true interests of the country, and that he would endeavor to carry out the policy which he might conceive would best promote its honor and prosperity. . . .

Burleson's declaration in favor of Houston policies was the signal for a drive to bring sincere Lamar partisans into the Jones camp, on the plea that they and the country would fare better under a straightforward Houstonite than under a man whose declarations varied with the winds of a political canvass. Major James Reily, once a Lamar man, then a Houston man, recently a lukewarm Jones man, took this matter in hand as he stayed at the capital "about 70 days on this damnable Court Martial" trying Commodore Moore of the Texas Navy.

Never was my patience so completely wearied out [he wrote Lamar's friend Starr on August 5]. Job certainly was a patient man & sorely tempted, but if the devil had detailed Job on a General Naval Court Martial composed of Military officers, with such a President—such a Judge Advocate & such a counsel for accused as

I have been on, Job would have cursed God & died. Enough however of this Horse Marine Court——

. . . Waples I think is on an electioneering tour. He is bitter against my candidate Anson Jones. I cannot support Burleson . . . his recent letter . . . shews that he is in the hands of men that write & dictate his sentiments to him & will dictate the course he must pursue if elected. . . . I confess myself more anxious in this Presidential contest than any one before. I dread to see the men in power that Burleson will have around him if elected. Caznau—McLeod—Jeff Green—Archer—Chalmers—et al. . . . Not one opposition leader has quit or denounced Burleson, strong & decided a Houston man as he declares himself in his letter, although several nonexpectants, have quit. . . . I consider Jones' election certain.

From Fort Bend County, home of ex-President Lamar, came word to the *Vindicator* that

Gen. B. has many warm friends in this county who esteem him too highly to assist in elevating him to an office which he is incapable of filling. They do not wish his reputation as a border warrior and patriot tarnished by an attempt to discharge the duties of that high and responsible office.

From the county named for Lamar came this letter:

I have just been informed that Gen. B. is on his way to this district. We hail this as a favorable omen for Anson Jones, for so certain as he makes a few *stump speeches* and mingles with the people they will readily conclude . . . that the former is well qualified and the latter is entirely destitute of qualifications. . . .

The *Vindicator* pointed out that it was passing strange that the man who three years before considered electioneering beneath the dignity of a candidate for the Vice-Presidency was "at this very day going the rounds and in his own person actually soliciting votes for a *still higher* office."

Candidate Jones was declining all invitations to visit with the voters.

Were I to make a tour through the country, I should either be compelled to neglect official matters or resign [he explained to a constituent in Harrison County]. The latter would, indeed, be very easy, but in the present crisis of our negotiations . . . a desertion of my post. I am not yet without hopes of annexation; and as I have had a great deal to do in this matter, I have some pride in wishing to go through with it. The charge that I am "inimical to further negotiations with the United States for the re-annexation of our country to that" is wholly without foundation in fact, and a base slander.

While Burleson went from barbecue to barbecue, making a speech here that sounded like Houston, one there that sounded like Lamar, but always delivering his message—by whomever written—with the ineptness of Burleson himself, the doctor was dividing his time between the plantation and his office in town— and, Burleson men charged, practicing a little medicine too.

General T. A. Howard, new Chargé of the United States, arrived at the capital early in August, his enthusiasm "much tempered by the chastening circumstances," he told Secretary Jones, of the deaths in rapid succession of his predecessor, General Murphy, and of the United States Consul General and acting Chargé, Colonel Green. Mr. Secretary Jones, in the absence of the President, formally received him and his letter of credence. The Secretary's reply was reminiscent of the one he himself had listened to from the lips of President Van Buren in 1838. The Chargé's "friendly sentiments and kind wishes" were "highly appreciated and fully reciprocated" by Jones, who would take pleasure in co-operating in "preserving the good understanding which now so happily exists between the two countries and in drawing still closer the ties which should unite them. . . ."

General Howard was an old Tennessee friend and partisan of Houston—it was for that reason that Tyler had sent him to Texas—but he was not disposed to stretch his instructions on that account. When Jones notified him promptly that Mexico was threatening to renew hostilities and asked the protection General Murphy had promised, Howard replied that protection had been promised only during the pendency of the treaty, not after its rejection. Jones himself had extracted that promise, and he knew well enough that

The reason why the request for *protection* was made of Mr. Murphy, was, I had no idea the treaty of annexation proposed by Mr. Tyler would, or could, be ratified by the Senate of the United States. I therefore wished Texas should not be left in a worse situation, after the failure of the treaty, than she was before its negotiation; for by it we ran the risk of offending not only Mexico, but England, France, and other European Governments, our friends. Gen. T. A. Howard's "hair splitting" answer

was no answer at all. Jones instructed the Texan Legation at Washington City to make clear to President Tyler and Secretary Calhoun that if they wanted annexation ultimately to succeed, they had better make good Murphy's promise.

That attended to, the Secretary of State returned to his plantation and "commenced taking fodder." From this bucolic occupation he was summoned to town to attend the new American Chargé, who died on August 18. A week later Jones wrote Norton of "the distress occasioned by the death of Gen. Howard, the hurry of arranging his affairs, and the duty of writing to his family—between all of which I had not time to write scarcely any one else." The New Orleans *Bee* commented lugubriously: "Gen. Howard is the fourth diplomatic agent of this country who has died in Texas within a short period." Eve, Murphy, Green, now Howard. Was there a jinx on the Texas mission?

With Congress not in session, the Supreme Court adjourned, the President and most of the Cabinet away, Washington-on-the-Brazos lapsed back into its pre-1842 lethargy as the hot days came on. Political gossip was the principal commodity exchanged there and throughout the Republic; and as election day neared, the exchange was brisker. New rumors were being minted daily by supporters of both presidential candidates; most of them dealt with the character and probity of the rivals, a few with prognostications of policy.

Already we hear it whispered [the *Vindicator* warned] . . . that Jones is opposed to Houston and annexation. . . . The next rumor we expect to hear . . . will be that of Mexican invasion, in order to throw the whole country into confusion and call the people from their homes, and raise a tremendous excitement, just for the occasion. The leaders of the Red Back and Glory party are up to all such tricks. . . .

And so the presidential campaign, which the New Orleans *Bee* thought "rages almost as fiercely in Texas as among the people of the United States," worked toward its climax. The per-

sonal issues simmered down to one of intellectual capacity. The
East Texas *Red Lander* preferred a literate President:

we do not assent that he must be a *book worm,* but we do say . . .
he must have a cultivated intellect improved by a general and critical
knowledge of civic and political history, together with a knowledge
of the arts and sciences to render him useful to the station to which
he is called.

The La Grange *Intelligencer* rejoined for westerners that Andrew Jackson, an uneducated soldier, defeated the Harvard-
bred John Quincy Adams. "In the contest now going on in our
little Republic for the Presidency, between the brave and wise
old border hero, Burleson, and the educated Apothecary General Jones," the *Intelligencer* found some similarity to the contest
between Jackson and Adams. Burleson, already dubbed the
"Marion of Texas," was about to become—without Houston's
or Jackson's approval—"The Old Hickory of Texas."

The most serious charge against Jones appeared in the *Northern Standard* two weeks before election day—in time to be reprinted in almost every county, but too late for effective reply.

Dr. Jones' organ has long been speaking in disparaging terms of the
Government of the United States. . . . HE HAS ALL ALONG BEEN
OPPOSED TO ANNEXATION. . . . he does not consider that an allegiance with the United States can be as much to our advantage as
one with England—that the Government of the former . . . has too
many antagonistic interests to conciliate before it would dare extend
an official hand to raise us if we were down or to sustain us if we
were falling.

Does Anson Jones believe the people of this country so base and
mean spirited as to feel a pride in helping to swell the wealth and
overgrown power of England? Yet this is the ambition and this is
the policy of Anson Jones. . . . While our friends in the United
States are making the most active exertions . . . Anson Jones is at
the same time prosecuting negotiations with England which will give
her a monopoly of our commerce and will forever exclude us from
the Union.

That picture of Jones as the tool of England cost him many votes
among these people, some of whom had fought in the War of
1812 and whose fathers had fought Britain in 1776.

On September 2, 1844, the Texans recorded their choice, and during the next ten days the Chief Justices of the thirty-six counties sent the results to the Secretary of State. In his drafty office Anson Jones tallied the returns.

Washington County, where he had lived since 1842, gave him a majority of almost two to one. In Bastrop, Burleson's home county, he got 16 votes to the general's 260. Every voter in Refugio County—five—voted for Burleson, as did the 195 Gonzaleans and the 66 San Patricians who voted in that election. In Travis County (Austin) the vote was 7 for Jones, 144 for Burleson. The doctor lost Harris County by 16 votes, and Brazoria went against him 74 to 242; but in Montgomery County, which polled 1,007 votes, 907 of them were for Jones.

The general had carried the solid but sparsely settled west; the doctor had carried the solid east, where most of the people lived. When he had counted nearly 10,000 votes the result was beyond doubt.

Before any other Texan, Anson Jones knew that he would be the next President.

XXXI

INTERLUDE

FROM immigrant to President in a decade. . . .

The President-elect remembered that October day in 1833 when he drifted into Texas, penniless, intent only upon making a new start, ambitious only to pay off his debts, resolved only to avoid involvements of every kind. Texas then had been a raw frontier—perhaps 20,000 English-speaking people thinly scattered along the Gulf coast and the broad watercourses. Those Texans, like Jones, were concerned only with primitive necessities as they labored to rehabilitate themselves and to make Texas a habitable province of Mexico. That province had been good to Dr. Jones. It had given him financial security, self-confidence, status—which was all he had wanted then.

As the years passed, a new Texas—and a new Anson Jones—evolved. The Mexican province grew restive, rebelled, asserted her independence, and won it on the battlefield. For eight years she had been laboring to justify the role of nationality she had assumed. At every step Jones had aided: revolutionary soldier, legislator, diplomat, senator, Cabinet officer in charge of foreign relations. Not since 1836 had he been a private citizen concerned only with his own affairs.

His own destiny had become inextricably intertwined with that of Texas. Years ago he had drawn a Texan star in his diary. On its five points he lettered three five-letter words: T-e-x-a-s, A-n-s-o-n, J-o-n-e-s; opposite his name he wrote "President." Now he was First Citizen of this nation he had helped to create.

The Republic of Texas had given him all that he wanted, more than he had hoped to have. Financial security had grown into comparative affluence; he owed no man a penny and he had land in half a dozen counties. He was a planter, a slave master, building a plantation home that would soon be the White House of the Republic. He had an excellent wife, two bright boys, and a third child was on the way. To his status as a man of medicine had been added status as a statesman. No man had served Texas longer or more competently than he; none was better fitted to see her through the next three years; men said that of him—and he believed them.

The Texas of which Anson Jones would be President bore as little resemblances to the Texas he had first known as did Mr. Secretary Jones to the bankrupt commission merchant of 1833. Only the major outlines and gross dimensions were the same.

A hundred thousand people had come to Texas since his arrival; the 20,000 had increased to 125,000. Cities stood where Jones had seen unbroken sod, and towns dotted the open country as well as the riverbanks. Brick and clapboard houses were replacing log cabins in the towns and on the farms, houses furnished with imported goods from the States and from Europe. Along the frontier, settlers from the States, Britain, France, Germany were establishing themselves, and more were coming. At Galveston ships of a dozen nations docked with luxury goods and necessities and sailed away with Texas cotton, tobacco, sugar.

He and Texas had developed together. He had helped the Republic pass through the disorders and distempers of infancy and childhood into a stormy adolescence. Now she was strong, vigorous, promising; but under the stress of half-understood emotions she was impulsive and headstrong. She needed a guardian who understood her and her milieu; one who could guide her into right decisions. He had asked for that guardianship, and it had been granted him. His duties would begin next December.

The three months between election and inauguration gave him opportunity to contemplate the past and plan for the future, with a minimum of interruption from the present. Government business was dull that season.

President Houston was much absent—ill of "violent attacks of chill and fever" in the East Texas swamps, then attending barbecues and dinners in his honor throughout the Republic. Vice-President Burleson was sulking in his tent near Bastrop, "in no very good humor with the gentlemen who brought him out" or with the President-elect. Secretary Miller of the Treasury and Secretary Hill of War and Marine had returned to their medical offices, and Ebenezer Allen, successor to Terrell as Attorney General, had no official duties he could not perform at his own law office in Houston. The Secretary of State did whatever was necessary in the various offices but spent most of his time at his plantation.

His mail was heavy. Old friends and men he had never heard of were offering congratulations and advice. Mr. Thomas (Ramrod) Johnson of the *Vindicator* wrote from La Grange, in a western county that voted for Burleson:

The impression here is, that you will be led in leading-strings by Sam. Houston. This I know to be false . . . that your whole movements will be emphatically your own, I am as sure as that you are elected President.

. . . The people here, now under defeat, will expect nothing at your hands . . . [you should prove] they are mistaken. This will at once . . . insure a liberal support to your administration. . . .

Let there be no rejoicing or gratulation—success is glory enough without crowing about it.

Old Dr. J. Æ. Phelps of Brazoria reported:

Your political enemies in this county are mum. Those who say anything, say they would have supported your election had they not been thoroughly convinced that you were, positively, politically, and personally, opposed to annexation. Others, who are opposed to the present Administration, say there will be no hopes for anything good under yours; and some who were violent, now say they will *tolerate* all your good executive acts. The whole, however, are excruciatingly disappointed. *So mote it be.*

Colonel James Morgan of New Washington predicted that Jones would "not meet with that hostility from any quarter which your friends at one time anticipated."

His Highness Charles, Prince of Solms, apprehensive of the effect of annexation on his colonization projects, begged in Teutonic English of the President-elect

a slight notice whether the probability is for the independence of our beautiful Texas; whether we may flatter ourselves with the hope of a man with enlightened views, like you, dear Dr. Jones, at the head of the Government, or whether Texas should fall into the condition of a territory of the United States.

That was one question dear Dr. Jones declined to answer. There was another, from John P. Willis, a plain farmer of La Grange, one of Jones's forty-seven supporters in that county:

. . . should annexation not take place, or peace with Mexico . . . carry war into the enemy's country, and offer the conquered country to the victors. . . . a war of aggression would be the true policy. . . . The whole West would sustain you . . . and nothing could or would redound so much to your popularity. . . . money and men can be procured to any amount.

J. Harvey Winchell, the original Jones-for-President man— he had toasted the doctor as a future President of Texas in November 1837—wrote him how to "immortalize yourself by a single act." Winchell had lived in Mexico since 1840, "sometimes teaching, sometimes fighting, and other times practicing medicine; noting everything." If the doctor wanted "the name of Anson Jones to descend to posterity in the highest niche of fame," he would at once send discreet commissioners quietly to Santa Anna, who would gladly sign a treaty with Texas. Winchell was sure immediate peace with Mexico would "be far more beneficial to all interested than the procrastinated question of annexation;" "peace may be had, almost on our own terms, if the affair is managed discreetly." So sure was he that Jones would follow good advice that he was traveling through Texas, "teaching the folks to speak the Castilian language, preparatory to the opening trade with our neighbors—now our enemies—the other side of the Rio Grande."

Such conflicting advice from his constituents demonstrated that, while his election to the presidency was a vindication of him as a man and as a public official, he had been elected without a platform. He was committed only to continue the "sound policies" of the Houston administration, but neither he nor the electorate had made a tabulated list of them. The *Morning Star* had been certain that "without the sanction of Sam Houston he would not get a tenth of the vote in the country," but the doctor was convinced that "I probably lost more than I gained by my association with him." He was determined not to be "kept in leading strings by Sam Houston," as the opposition charged he would be. He had been elected President and he would be the actual as well as the titular head of the nation. He would follow his own judgment as problems presented themselves.

There had been no clear-cut division on the annexation question, and Jones had been supported by annexationists and anti-annexationists. Annexation was at a standstill until the citizens of the United States decided whether their new President would be James K. Polk, who wanted Texas, or Henry Clay, who did not. They would decide the first Tuesday in November, and Jones would know the result about the time the new Texan Congress met to inaugurate him as President.

As he waited, he received from Chargé Smith in London a proposal which could make the decision of the United States of no importance to Texas. Lord Aberdeen had learned that the annexation treaty had failed, and he was proposing for England and France,

if Texas desired to remain independent, to settle the whole matter by a Diplomatick Act . . . guaranteeing the separate independence of Texas, etc., etc. . . .

. . . Such an act [Smith pointed out] would . . . give to the European Governments . . . a perfect right to forbid, for all time to come, the annexation of Texas to the United States, as also even the peaceful incorporation of any part of Mexico . . . with Texas. . . .

It was, Smith thought, worthy of "gravest consideration." He had dispelled the extreme dissatisfaction France and England had felt at Texan negotiations for annexation.

It was pleasant to know that England was willing now to exert herself for the Republic. Jones could remember when no Old World power considered Texas worth serious attention. That thread of Texan advantage that he and Christopher Hughes had unwound toward Europe was now almost untangled by two years of Dr. Smith's expert diplomatic ministration; almost, but not quite.

This "Diplomatick Act" was a straw in a favorable wind, but Texas need not clutch at straws. The price—becoming a sort of European protectorate—was too high for Texas to pay for guaranteed independence. There might be better propositions for her to consider after the United States election. If not, Texas had a newly elected President who was capable of shaping this favorable British disposition into a more acceptable—and advantageous—proposal.

The President Texas still had rode into the capital at the end of September, his nerves brittle, quivering with a sort of palsy from the ague and the quinine he took for it. Mr. Secretary Jones read him the proposal for the "Diplomatick Act." With amazement and anxiety, he listened to instructions to accept it at once, without delay. It was a momentary opinion, Dr. Jones was sure, of a man who was obviously unwell; but unhappily it was the opinion of the man who was still chief executive of the Republic. Could he persuade him against this catastrophic ending of years of negotiations, convince him that this was no time for dramatic gestures or impulsive action? To Jones's delight, the President did not insist.

In a few days Houston would be gone to an Indian powwow. If he could be kept from bungling matters until he was safely out of the way—off with his red brothers who would give him a soothing and harmless audience for dramatic gestures . . .

He turned back to his desk with relief as Houston rode off to visit the Indians. On it lay an order signed in the bold script of the President:

Let our Representative (Dr. Smith or Col. Daingerfield) be instructed to complete the *proposed* arrangement for the settlement of our Mexican difficulties as soon as possible—giving the necessary pledges, as suggested in the late dispatch of Dr. Smith on this subject. . . .

The Secretary dug from his files a letter the President had written him from East Texas on July 8—two weeks after Ashbel Smith had listened to Aberdeen's proposal—looking toward the same arrangement. He laid it beside His Excellency's order and concluded that the Aberdeen proposal had been "arranged perhaps between Gen. H. and Capt. Elliot, or Mr. Saligny, secretly," and not a word said to him! He had never been less sure that he understood the Old Chief—or that the Old Chief really understood himself—than at that moment.

He was sure that was not the way. Independence on unfavorable terms must not be accepted. The interest that had produced

the offer must be kept alive, nursed, shaped to a better form—
and meantime the alternative solution of Texas's dilemma, annexation to the United States, must be cultivated.

Alternatives had come to be a sort of obsession with Jones.
For thirty-five years of his life he had never had an alternative.
If a course he embarked upon failed—it always did—he had
nothing to fall back upon. Never, until he came to Texas, did
he have a choice as to what he should do. Here he had always
contrived to have a secondary line of action in mind if the primary one should fail. While he practiced medicine he pursued
land trading. When he went into politics he did not relinquish
medicine. As Secretary of State, he continued both. Now he was
President-elect, but a junior partner kept his medical office open,
and he was setting himself up as a planter.

So it was in charting the diplomacy of Texas. From the first
he had aimed at getting a choice: annexation or independence.
He had never pursued one without prodding the other. Just as
he never let himself get into a position from which there was no
possible—and tolerable—retreat, he wanted to shape things for
the Republic so that Texas might always have an alternative.
To a degree Houston was an alternative-seeker, but for other
reasons. Houston's career had been a series of triumphs and ca-
tastrophes—from each of which he rose dramatically, phoenix-
like. His was the alternative-seeking of the Indian; it was not
caution that grew out of failures that seared the soul and shook
the ego. It was Houston's nature to burn bridges. It was Jones's
to make sure he had two bridges open, then to withdraw from
the one he decided not to cross, without lighting flares or sending up rockets.

At the end of four days he knew what he must do. Deliberately
he wrote across the back of the President's note and signed his
name with rubric:

The within order cannot be obeyed for it would either defeat
Annexation altogether, or lead to a War between Europe & America.
Besides it would directly complicate our relations & entangle us
with France & England—produce disturbances & revolution at home
& probably render it very difficult if not impossible for me to administer the government of Texas successfully—— Gen. Houston
has furnished no explanations of his motives for this course of policy.

If they be to defeat annexation—produce a War, or break down my administration (about to commence) I cannot favor any of the objects & can conceive of no other.
Sep^t 28th 1844

Jones sent instructions to Dr. Smith to close his mission in Europe without further discussion of the "Diplomatick Act," and to proceed forthwith to Washington-on-the-Brazos for conference. The Secretary of State and the President talked of other matters on His Excellency's infrequent visits to the capital.

In the lull before his inauguration the President-elect began to plan for his administration. Major Reily would return to Washington City as Texan Chargé; General George W. Terrell would succeed Ashbel Smith in England, France, and Spain; Colonel Daingerfield would continue to look after the rest of western Europe. All had been appointed by President Houston at the suggestion of Secretary Jones. They understood Jones's policies and could be trusted to carry them out in the various courts. If the new Senate confirmed them Jones would make no new nominations. Barnard E. Bee thought that if Jones should send General Houston to London "he would be delighted . . . and make a wonderful impression there"; but the President-elect preferred Terrell. "I should like to oblige Gen. Houston," he said, "but cannot trust him so far from home."

The personnel of his diplomatic corps he considered complete, and his Cabinet was no great problem. Allen would remain as Attorney General. Jones had not known him long, but he was competent and discreet. Dr. Hill promised to remain as Secretary of War and Marine. Dr. Miller was leaving government service at the end of the Houston administration, and the Secretaryship of the Treasury would go to Judge W. B. Ochiltree of Nacogdoches. Ashbel Smith would take the State Department when he returned from Europe. Better than any other Texan, Dr. Smith could effect the policies Jones had been formulating and was now about to have an opportunity to implement. Moses Johnson, M.D., would be Treasurer of the Republic. The minor officers and clerks would remain undisturbed. The salaries were so small that sinecure hunters did not seek those places.

At Galveston at the end of September there arrived for the first, but not the last, time in Texas that versatile journalist,

promoter, and diplomat-on-special-mission, General Duff Green.
It was he who had discovered the British "plot" to free the slaves
of Texas, which Calhoun considered the imperative reason for
annexation. Now he dashed into Texas, exhibited a commission
as United States Consul, wrote Secretary Jones that he apprehended a Mexican bombardment of Galveston, commandeered
the U.S.S. *Woodbury* which Acting Consul Stewart Newell was
holding to transmit diplomatic dispatches, and was off to Vera
Cruz as special Minister to Mexico, promising Jones on his return to "have much to say to you on matters and things." Newell,
outraged by Green's conduct, also wrote to give his friend Jones

some idea of his future by his present course. . . . I fear he has
arrived with such views of personal interest as may meet a severer
disappointment than he anticipated . . . the short, but rapid course
pursued, left him no time to practice that courtesy due as a gentleman if not an officer.

There was a man, Jones sensed, to keep an eye on.
General Terrell picked up some interesting political gossip at
Galveston as he was about to embark for Europe. He wrote
Secretary Jones on November 12:

I have ascertained . . . there is an organization going on among
the Opposition members to play the same game on you that was
played on old Sam, to wit: to pass another retrenchment bill before
your inauguration. Their principal object is to cut down your salary
as President . . . be on the lookout. . . .
Major Donelson, the new Chargé from the United States, is here.
We spent a very agreeable evening together—discussed annexation,
and all the other exciting topics of the day. You will find him a very
agreeable and intelligent *gentleman;* one with whose plain, unpre-
tending bearing you will be much pleased.

Andrew Jackson Donelson, godson of Old Hickory, had been
on Texas soil two days. President Tyler had sent him posthaste,
as soon as he heard of General Howard's death, to see to it that
Texas remained in a receptive mood. British Consul Kennedy
pronounced him "well adapted to promote the main object of
his Mission among the people of Texas. His solicitude for 'Annexation' is . . . lively. . . ."

Perturbed by his conversation with Chargé Terrell, who made no secret of his opposition to annexation, and by what he heard of the coolness of Houston and Jones toward it, Donelson proceeded to Washington-on-the-Brazos. When he presented his credentials to Mr. Secretary Jones (who in ten days would be President) he was greeted with the enigmatic statement that if the hope "of a common destiny" which the Texans "have sometimes indulged" should fail, he trusted that "the most friendly relations" would continue to exist between the two nations. Then President Houston pointedly reminded him that the Texans "have sent their ministers to the very doors of your Senate house, and asked for admission, more than once thereat"; but annexation had failed—through no fault of Texas.

Neither of these gentlemen, Donelson reported to Washington City, was opposed to annexation at the moment; but "Every day's delay is adding strength . . . to British influence. . . . Delay will increase the difficulties already in our way, if it does not make them insurmountable."

Donelson's apprehensions would have been even greater if he had known that at that moment the British Chargé at Mexico City was listening to terms of Texan independence acceptable to the Mexican Government:

Mexico will yield the Territory which is now occupied by the so-called Republic of Texas, that is from the Rio Colorado to the Sabina. . . .

Mexico . . . demands . . . guarantee of England and France united, that under no pretext whatever shall the Texans ever pass the Boundaries marked out. The same nations shall also guarantee to Mexico the Californias, New Mexico and the other points . . . bordering on the U. States. . . . If the U. States carry into effect the annexation of Texas . . . England and France will assist Mexico in the contest which may be thereby brought on. . . .

At New Orleans Terrell conferred with Count Alphonse de Saligny, who was on his way back to Texas. France, Terrell reported to Jones, was now

ready to give the guarantee spoken of by Dr. Smith, *provided* Texas will pledge herself to hold no further negotiations on the subject of annexation. . . . Mr. Saligny said to me, *in private conversation,* what he would not say to the Secretary of State, viz.: that his Government looked upon itself as having been *very uncandidly* dealt with by ours, and will be very cautious in interfering further in our behalf.

It is my candid opinion . . . that annexation will never take place. . . . How long are we to follow this *ignis fatuus,* this Will-o'-the-wisp conjured up by the distempered brain of wild and reckless speculators? . . . Had we better not, Jackson-like, take the responsibility at once—give the guarantee, and make a finish of it? Texas, free, independent, prosperous and happy, will ratify the act; and annexation, as it should, will slumber forever in the *'tomb of the Capulets'.* . . .

It is really amusing . . . to stand in a crowd here and hear the politicians talk of Texas. Sam. Houston is a traitor—his Cabinet no better—and as for the President-elect, he is bought in advance by British gold. . . .

After his talk with Saligny, Minister Terrell recalled that Jones had given him no authority to execute the proposed "Diplomatick Act" when he reached London and Paris. He remembered, too, that he had heard at Galveston that the new Senate might reject his nomination. "Look to this, Miller," he wrote President Houston's private secretary, whose chores as liaison man between the President-elect and officeholders and office seekers were heavier than his official duties; "I would not be rejected for a good deal."

In the United States the presidential campaign warmed. President Tyler had withdrawn from the contest—if indeed he may be said ever to have entered it—on the plea of Andrew Jackson. His staying in might divide the votes of friends of Texas. Henry Clay, who in April had pronounced talk of annexation "perfectly idle and ridiculous, if not dishonorable," climbed part way back on the fence as the campaign warmed. James K. Polk, the Democratic nominee, entertained "no doubts as to the power or the expediency" of bringing Texas into the Union, and his party demanded "the reannexation of Texas at the earliest practicable period." The campaign was fought on that issue.

The popular vote in November was close; Polk and the Democrats—and Texas—received a plurality of less than 40,000, but they had an electoral vote of 170 to 105.

The people of the United States at last had spoken: they

wanted annexation. The people of Texas had spoken repeatedly: they wanted annexation. Lord Aberdeen in London and M. Guizot in Paris, watching events with increasing apprehension, also spoke—softly, diplomatically: annexation must not take place. In Mexico there were rumblings that if annexation took place, there would be war.

XXXII

THE PRESIDENT

IN DECEMBER 1844, as Texan congressmen were gathering at Washington-on-the-Brazos, the Congress of the United States reassembled on the Potomac. It was a lame-duck session to attend to odds and ends until the new President should be inaugurated March 4, but President Tyler had no intention of letting the Texas question sleep those three months. Had not, he reasoned, annexation been presented "nakedly" in the November elections, and had not the people "decisively" approved it? "It is the will of both the people and the States," he told Congress on December 3, "that Texas shall be annexed to the Union promptly and immediately." He hoped to get that part of Mr. Polk's work done before March 4.

Senators and representatives began reviving old plans for bringing Texas into the Union and inventing new ones. Texas was almost as vital a subject of discussion that winter as it had been during the presidential campaign—more vital than it had ever been in Congress—and Major Andrew Jackson Donelson was already among the Texans to see that they accepted whatever invitation Tyler could coax from the Congress of the United States.

In the Valley of Mexico, too, there was a new administration that December. The constitutional dictatorship under which Antonio López de Santa Anna thought he might rule forever had fallen: he had neglected to reward the men who helped him gain supreme power. Two days after Tyler asked the United States Congress to annex Texas, four days before Anson Jones became President of Texas, General Santa Anna was a prisoner of the new regime. "My situation is worse," he complained, "than when I was a prisoner of war among the Texan soldiers of fortune." He was confined for a time in the Castle of Perote, from which the Texans had been liberated; then he was banished "forever" from Mexico. José Joaquín Herrera sat uneasily in the presidential palace, timidly trying to please three irreconcilable factions in revolution-torn Mexico.

Across the Atlantic there were changes that month in Her Britannic Majesty's Foreign Office on the Thames. That granitelike Scot, the Earl of Aberdeen, still in charge of policy, had decided to take a new tack on the Texas matter. For almost a year he had hoped to block annexation by getting France to join England in coaxing from Mexico a recognition of Texan independence. The "Diplomatick Act" he had suggested to Ashbel Smith had been rejected by the man who was now President of Texas, and news from Washington City, Paris, Mexico, and Texas had convinced him that England should let Texas matters drift. On December 31 he ordered "a passive course, or rather a course of observation." But the mails were slow; Her Majesty's representatives in Texas and Mexico did not receive these new instructions for months.

The Ninth Congress of the Republic, which most Texans (including its members) hoped would be the last, assembled December 2, 1844. Half the senators and all the representatives had been chosen in the election that gave Dr. Jones the presidency and returned General Burleson to his "colt-breaking."

The issues in that campaign, except for the inevitable local struggles of the "outs" against the "ins," were not sharply defined. Houstonism, pivotal issue in eight previous elections, was a little blurred in 1844, but the presidential contest was too uncertain for many congressmen to attach themselves firmly to either candidate. It was safer to pronounce for or against general policies.

Annexation was no issue. Texans, emotionally if not technically, had been committed to it since 1836; the congressmen and senators they elected in 1844 were of a mind to expedite it. No Texas politician then was publicly opposing it, but a good many men of substance were privately urging the President-elect against it.

At ten o'clock on the morning of December 2, Anson Jones climbed the unpainted stairs outside Major Hatfield's saloon and took his place in the Speaker's chair in the room above. He was there as Secretary of State to organize the House of Representatives, as required by law. As he did his legal duty he took the measure of these men with whom, as President of the Republic, he would have to get along.

For the first time in three years a quorum was present the first day. Thirty of them were new men with little or no legislative experience, many of them strangers to one another and to the President-elect. They would control the House. Brazoria's two representatives were not Jones men. They had settled there after Jones had moved away, and that county had voted for Burleson three-to-one. Tod Robinson, a North Carolinian and an anti-administration man in the Sixth and Seventh Congresses, had been replaced by General Green in the Eighth, but now he was back. His colleague was Stephen W. Perkins, a thirty-five-year-old planter from Kentucky, who had lived in Brazoria four years. The President-elect could count on nothing from either of them; and the ten men who had been re-elected from the Eighth Congress were not Jones partisans.

When Mr. Secretary Jones declared a quorum present, freshman Congressman Dugald MacFarlane, of MacFarlane's Castle, Matagorda, stood in his place and in thick Scottish accents nominated the Honorable John M. Lewis, a Montgomery County farmer and a legislator of one term's experience, for Speaker of the House. William Menefee of San Felipe, who had been in political eclipse since the Lamar Congresses, was now back to represent Colorado County; he countered with the nomination of the Honorable George Sutherland of Jackson County, who had not served in the House since he sat in the Second Congress with Menefee and Jones in 1838. Mr. Lewis, elected on the first ballot by a majority of one, pointedly reminded the sixteen colleagues who had voted for him and the fifteen who had not that he was "a decided partisan"; he intended "to dispense stern justice to every member."

The "practical men" of the House, Congressman John S. (Rip) Ford thought, included Robert M. (Three-Legged Willie) Williamson of Washington, the Patrick Henry of Texas and a senator last year; William R. Scurry, "the dirty-shirt orator of Red River"; Smoky Henderson of the city of Houston, surveyor, lawyer, man of the people; the "subtle and astute" General Cazneau of the city of Austin, who marshaled the clans of the west; General Hugh McLeod of Galveston, late commander of the Santa Fé expedition, archfoe of Houstonism, "readiest speaker in the ranks of the opposition"; and scholarly, legalistic, anti-Jones Tod Robinson of Brazoria.

Across the street from Hatfield's, in Mr. W. W. Massie's store building, senators were assembling with John A. Greer in the chair. General Burleson's term as president of the Senate had only a week to run; he did not interrupt his stock farming to organize the Senate for his successor to preside over—or to watch Dr. Jones take the presidential oath.

Brazoria's senator was sixty-four-year-old Timothy Pilsbury—they called him Old Ayes and Noes in double token of his physiognomy and the frequency with which he had demanded roll call in the House of the Fifth Congress and as Jones's successor in the Senate of the Sixth. He had been Chief Justice of Brazoria since 1842, and Jones had thought he ought to remain there; but in the summer of 1844 he sponsored an anti-Jones circular and announced for the Senate. Jones instructed his editor in Houston "to lash the drunken worthless traitor *'Pilsbury,'* " but here he was, occupying the senatorial seat William H. Jack had vacated by death, urging the Reverend Orceneth Fisher for salaried chaplain against the Reverend William M. Tryon, who had prayed gratis for the last Senate, and about to become chairman of the finance committee.

Young, urbane, Pennsylvania-born David S. Kaufman, ardent annexationist and stanch friend of President Jones, was there from East Texas. The Old Guard was represented by Uncle Jesse Grimes, who had been a Texan since 1826, and Isaac Parker, who came in 1833; both were counted as elder statesmen—sensible, matter-of-fact farmers, not likely to be swept off their feet by political squalls. A new senator was James K. McCreary, M.D., of San Felipe, who was neither a professional nor a political crony of the President.

President Houston's message to Congress on December 5 was a brief and—considering the opportunities the occasion offered —conciliatory document, which showed how much three years of Houstonian guidance had benefited the Republic.

England and France, he reported, still friendly despite annexation agitation, were working for the prosperity of an independent Texas without expectation of any special advantage. "They will not ask it—they do not expect it—we would not yield it."

As for the United States, she still declined to ratify a commercial treaty with the Republic, and Houston was unable to predict whether one would ever be ratified. Mexico had remained on her side of the Rio Grande since 1842. The armistice had failed, but all but one of the Texan prisoners in Mexico had been released.

The Indians were peaceable, and "the finances of the country are in the most healthy and prosperous condition." There was a balance of $5,948.91 in the Treasury.

At long last the regime of Sam Houston was approaching its end, and a new President—a civilian, a diplomatist, a methodical and careful analyst—was ready to take charge of this Republic that for eight years had been ruled by major generals.

The President-elect, suspicious of Houston's attitude toward the alternatives Texas was about to face and his attitude toward him and the administration about to begin, had avoided open rupture with Houston. They had been long associated, and it was impossible to distinguish sharply between Houston policies and Jones policies. They had differed more on technique than on ultimate objectives. Both were men of great consistency. Houston's first and last loyalty was to himself and to whatever attitude he assumed on an issue. Jones, undramatic and cautious, was governed by circumstances rather than a desire to maintain an attitude. He disliked quarrels, thought it more important to carry a point than to defy the opposition, and preferred diplomacy to name-calling.

The outgoing and incoming executives were often together as the time neared for the baton to pass from the one to the other, but they spoke little of policies and future plans. Houston was too shrewd to coach the man who believed he had been in paramount control of policies three years; Jones felt no need of Houstonian counsel. He only wanted the Old Chief to make a graceful final bow and leave the future of Texas to him. They arranged details, dined together; each sent regards to the other's wife and children—and wondered what the other was thinking.

On that polite and distant note the regime of Sam Houston came to an end and the administration of Anson Jones began.

Congress canvassed the election returns the State Department had compiled, declared Anson Jones elected President by a majority of 1,389 and Kenneth L. Anderson Vice-President without opposition, sent committees to notify them of the fact, and appointed other committees to arrange for the inauguration.

On December 9 the President-elect and the Vice-President-elect marched together to the rough wooden platform in front of Independence Hall. Behind them came His Excellency the President, followed by his Cabinet and the chaplain of the House of Representatives. Before them sat the representatives and the senators and "a numerous and respectable assemblage of free citizens." There was no military company, not even a cannon, to lend pomp to the ceremonies; it was the simple transaction of public business, a transfer of authority from a military hero to a civilian.

Houston spoke first:

I proudly confess that to the people I owe whatever of good I may have achieved. . . . collisions have existed between the Executive and the Legislature. Both were tenacious . . . both may have erred. . . . I take with me no animosities. . . . I leave the country tranquil. . . .

Let her legislation proceed upon the supposition that we are to be and remain an independent people. If Texas goes begging again . . . she will only degrade herself. . . . If the United States shall open the door, and ask her to come in . . . you will then have other conductors, better than myself. . . . But let us be as we are until that opportunity is presented, and then let us go in, if at all, united in one phalanx. . . .

If we remain an independent nation, our territory will be extensive —unlimited. The Pacific alone will bound . . . our empire. . . . We have our destiny in our own hands. . . .

Then the Honorable Anson Jones took the oath of office, kissed the Bible, and advanced to the lectern, a crisp manuscript in his hand.

I approach the discharge of the duties [he began] . . . with a profound sense of the importance of the trust . . . and a sincere distrust of my own abilities. . . .

When I turn my eye upon the distinguished individual who has this day for the second time, vacated the Presidential chair . . . when I recur to the decided feelings of approbation with which my other distinguished predecessor entered upon his official duties, and recollect the difficulties and embarrassments with which they were at all times surrounded . . . and then . . . find myself preferred . . . to an individual enjoying in an eminent degree, the confidence of his fellow-citizens, I am indeed admonished . . . to regard the success likely to attend my efforts, with unfeigned distrust and apprehension. I can only throw myself freely and frankly upon the co-ordinate branches of government, for that aid and support which I have no doubt, will be promptly accorded to such measures as are best calculated to promote the general welfare. . . .

Very decent, very gracefully put, thought his hearers; but what of the policies of this new President? Houston had plainly counseled continued independence. Would Jones stay in the Old Man's "leading strings" or would he champion annexation? All the world knew that Mr. Tyler was trying to bring Texas into the Union "promptly and immediately." For all the Texans knew, the Congress of the United States was at that moment "opening wide the door." They wanted to know what the new President would do about annexation.

President Jones, looking much like a schoolmaster as he stood at the lectern, his auburn head silhouetted against a leaden sky, read on without gestures or oratorical inflections.

"It belongs not to the present occasion to discuss . . . policy," he read. What, they wondered, would be an appropriate occasion for declaration of policy if this was not? "It is however due to the frankness which I intend shall ever attach to my conduct of executive functions, to state briefly in advance the objects which I conceive of importance to the welfare of the country. . . ." That was more like it; soon they would know what President Jones intended to do about the absorbing question. The audience listened more attentively.

He declared himself for "the maintenance of the public credit . . . preservation of the national faith . . . reduction of expenses . . . entire abolishment of paper money . . . protection and encouragement to our agricultural and manufacturing interests . . . schools . . . institutions for the moral and religious culture . . . peace with Mexico . . . desirable immigration . . . introduction of capital . . . just relations with our red brethren . . . a penitentiary system . . . bridges . . . roads

. . . navigation . . . commercial relations with foreign powers
. . . no entangling alliances . . . settlement of land disputes
. . ."

At last, turning to the representatives and senators, he declared: "A brave, patriotic and struggling people have confided
their most important interests to our care and keeping. It will
be . . . my constant desire . . . to co-operate with you in every
thing. . . ." Then with his eyes turned to the heavens, he asked
Providence to watch over Texas, and the inaugural address was
finished.

Not a mention of annexation, no hint of his own attitude; only
a plea for sensible legislation, some of which was long overdue.
Spectators and congressmen, then the newspapers, buzzed. The
President continued to say nothing on the absorbing question.
"I had the right to be silent," he asserted, "and the grave keeps
not its counsels more safely than I did mine."

That evening, in the Hall of the Representatives above Hatfield's, he was honor guest at the inaugural ball. "The attendance
of prominent men and beautiful women was very large, and the
ball-room was densely packed." A good time was had by all,
except the President and a "rather large, very attractive, very
popular" young lady who was sitting out an intermission with
young James K. Holland. When the music started, Holland said,
"we sprang up to take our places, but I observed that she was pull-
ing back; and on looking around I saw she was sinking through
the floor into the saloon below. I had just time to catch her by
one arm. Gen. Chambers lent his assistance, and together we
drew her up." The carpenters had neglected to nail down the
boards that covered the stair well when they moved the steps
outside the building.

President Jones attended the ball as a matter of duty, but he
was not in a festive mood. The gravity of the oath he had taken
that morning weighed upon him, and as he had watched the
faces of legislators and citizens he had begun to wonder if he,
anybody, could induce them to be patient enough to wait for
alternatives—or to weigh them calmly when they came. Dignified and detached, he stood stiffly greeting the revelers for a time,
then rode back to the plantation to be with Mary. She was very
near confinement.

The new Congress had been in session a week, and already it was considering most of the bills that had been debated for years: bills to reduce the number of Cabinet officers from four to two, to dispense with all foreign legations, to reduce salaries, to adopt free trade, to provide a separate Supreme Court, to fix the location of the seat of government. On that ancient problem there were the usual suggestions to move everything to Washington, to move everything back to Austin, to refer the question to the people. Mr. Smoky Henderson offered a compromise: make the city of Houston the capital until the first census. There was no chance of it, but it did him no harm in his home district.

Judge Ochiltree, the new Secretary of the Treasury, had suspected the "complexion" of this Congress would be wrong as soon as he learned who had been elected. "Our people," he complained to Jones, "have been lamentably wanting in calling out their candidates for a full expression of their political tenets." After watching the legislators in operation two weeks, he was sure the westerners had organized "to destroy the party in power." One scheme was to pass all relief bills proposed. If the President vetoed them, he made enemies; if he approved, there must be a flood of paper money. "This sort of honeyfugling," the President countered by veto after veto, which did not add to the harmony of that session.

Two weeks after his inauguration the President sent the House his message, which was read, then sent over to the Senate, "there being but one copy of it."

The turbulence which characterizes the infancy of nations, His Excellency said, was about over in Texas. Thousands of immigrants had come to Texas in the last few months, more were on the way, and schools and churches were being established everywhere. Wise legislation would complete the foundations for unprecedented prosperity.

The time had come to abandon paper money, to reduce expenditures, and to tax lightly but collect all taxes assessed. Texas was not yet ready for complete free trade, but she should seek reciprocal tariff agreements abroad for the benefit of her cotton and other agricultural products. As for the seat of government, the President thought the people should decide by vote where it should be for the next twenty years. He asked no appropriation for army or navy; rangers could protect the frontier. If Congress would by legislation iron out the kinks in the land system, provide a penal code, and a lighthouse at Galveston, little else would be needed in the way of legislation that year.

The President's legislative program squinted neither toward annexation nor continued independence; it was aimed solely at problems that had long been unsolved and must be solved in either event.

Senator Pilsbury of the finance committee construed the President's economy talk literally: he proposed to cut 1845 appropriations almost in half, leaving Jones only $83,953 with which to conduct the government. That reduction, the Senator from Brazoria declared, would not

impair the respectability of our infant association or deprive the Executive of the power of fulfilling the high duties for which he has been selected by a "confiding people."

Instead of referring the seat of government question to the people, Congress instructed the executive and heads of departments to return to Austin. Jones promptly vetoed that bill but promised to regard it an advisory opinion and asked for $5,000 to rehabilitate government buildings at Austin in case he should deem it expedient to move there.

A new note in congressional proceedings was solicitude for the clergy and the tools of their profession. Two winters ago neither house had had a chaplain; last winter local ministers prayed for the representatives of the people without pay; this winter each house had its salaried chaplain. That was not all. This Congress voted to excuse all ministers from jury service and from working on the public roads. Some were proposing even to exempt them from military duty and from paying taxes on "one saddlebag and one watch"; others wanted to admit theological books duty-free.

After the clergy had been taken care of an effort was made to do something for lay Texans who liked books, but the House would not hear of it. Twice finance committeemen wrestled with a proposal to put all books on the free list. First they pointed out that essential books—Bibles, Testaments, primary-school books —were already admitted without duty, and they saw no reason why professional men and "gentlemen of literary leisure who have no other means of disposing of their time" should not pay the taxes, since it obviously did not prevent their buying what they wanted to read. A week later they presented a disquisition on popular literature. Most books, they declared,

pamper a vicious and depraved literary taste. . . . the good books already amongst us are but little studied. . . .

If three-fourths of the light literature which now cumbers our library shelves and bookstores, were to share the fate of the Alexandrian Library, the cause of public learning and public morals would suffer no material damage.

The bill was indefinitely postponed and the report tabled.

These statesmen, however, believed in book-learning so strongly that they and their predecessors chartered nineteen schools—seven of them "universities"—in nine years. Only one has survived under its original name, Baylor University, whose charter President Jones approved on February 1, 1845, just before Congress adjourned.

His Excellency the President was still silent on annexation. Let Texas do nothing until the United States acts, he counseled; then let Texas calmly consider what she should do. He heard from Washington City that the joint resolution on annexation was certain to pass. That was interesting, if true. A few months ago the same source was assuring him the annexation treaty would be ratified. "Going it blind" for the treaty that failed had injured the prestige of Texas. If President Jones could manage it, Texas this time would sit by silently until the United States had finally and irrevocably committed herself.

This noncommittal attitude would enable the President to rebuild the alternative of assured independence that had collapsed with the failure of armistice negotiations with Mexico and Jones's own refusal to sanction the "Diplomatick Act."

Captain Elliot had been for months in the United States, observing the mounting sentiment for annexation there. He had hurried back to Galveston early in December and started toward Washington-on-the-Brazos to learn the intentions of Mr. Jones's government. His steamer lay grounded on sand bars between Galveston and Houston a week, but at least he did not fall through the hatch and break his ribs, as he once had done en route to the seat of the Texan Government. On December 21 he was closeted with the President and his Acting Secretary of State. After further conferences Elliot wrote Aberdeen:

Unlike most other public Men in the Southern parts of the American Confederacy or here, Mr. Jones is remarkably cautious and reserved, and with a moderate degree of the skill and firmness of his predecessor he will probably be able to controul affairs very materially with much less appearances of direct interposition than General Houston, and with less stormy opposition than General Houston's heats and rather free expression of his antipathies were apt to produce. . . .

I believe Mr. Jones will be guided by a just appreciation that the only course which can be safe or successful is the direct . . . he is not at all likely to make shipwreck of the fair and liberal consideration with which Her Majesty's Government in particular, will regard the necessities of his position at home, by any unworthiness either in his representations, or his reserve.

In private life he is a worthy and friendly man, of a plainness of speech, and simplicity of manner which help the feeling of confidence, and I certainly know no one in Texas, now eligible for the station he fills, of sounder judgment, more experienced in the Affairs of the Country, or generally better fitted for it.

Elliot reported that the President believed a majority of intelligent Texans preferred independence, but under all the circumstances, "it ought to be no matter of surprise there should be a very general feeling in favour of annexation to the United States." For the present

this Government can only watch the turn of events, and above all things carefully abstain from any course likely to persuade the people that they are secretly working against annexation. It may be depended upon, however [Elliot believed], that they would neither advance one step to meet or encourage it. The policy . . . will be to let all further advances and proposals come from the United States, reserving their own right to reject or accept them. . . .

He does not doubt [Elliott hopefully judged] if it were in the power of this Government to declare to the people of Texas that such a proposal [peace with Mexico] was before them, He and his friends would have strength enough to turn them aside from any further thought of annexation. He also expressed the hope . . . that Her Majesty's and the French Governments would lose no time in placing their Representatives here in a situation to conclude definitely at any propitious moment, so that everything [interposition with Mexico] may be irrevocably completed before disturbing movements can come back from the United States.

If Lord Aberdeen could be convinced there was hope, Elliot might yet block annexation. His last instructions from the Foreign Office had indicated that Aberdeen was no longer disposed to let his agents intervene in Texas-Mexican relations. If Elliot could only get new instructions that untied his hands . . .

In Texas, Brazorians did not propose to wait for news from the Potomac or the Thames. They were sure that Jones, like Houston, opposed annexation, and two hundred of them gathered on December 21 to declare themselves on the subject. Ammon Underwood, Jones's old friend and former landlord, "done all in my power to change the objectionable portions of them"; he was "convinced that your own discrimination, your own knowledge of the people, as well as their future happiness and the glory of the achievement, will secure all your eminent abilities and energies in its favor"; but the other 199 doubted it, and so informed Congress.

For six weeks the Texas Congress ignored annexation; then for two weeks it talked of little else. The Senate foreign-relations committee, after considering resolutions from citizens in mass meetings assembled, called on the President for all correspondence on annexation, especially that with the Chargé of the United States.

After a study of the documents the committee reported that the "time has not yet arrived when action on the part of the Government of Texas would be either appropriate or availing," but added that annexation had been "already emphatically *willed* by the *people* of both countries."

The senators believed that the United States legally acquired Texas when she bought from Napoleon the land west of the Mississippi, and that the reannexation of the Republic would rectify the "mutilated purchase of Louisiana." They also were sure that Texas would be more prosperous and contented as one of the United States than pursuing "the imaginary glory" of independence, burdened with debt—and with slavery inviting "the misplaced philanthropy of the world."

Texans had wanted annexation since 1836; when the United States opened wide the door they would respond "without waiting for the new-born discoveries of those who pretend to be the peculiar keepers of their best interests." Annexation would solve every Texan problem. Its defeat would curtail immigration from the United States and bring into Texas monarchical Europeans who would so alter Texan institutions as perhaps to bring on a war in which the "American union itself would perish."

"Texas," the Texan Senate declared "would form an iron band which would hold the Union together." That was not an opinion widely held north of Red River at that moment.

The report was unanimously adopted and ordered printed for the information of the voters, along with the diplomatic correspondence "which explains the attitude of His Excellency" in regard to this "all-absorbing question." The senators, the President regretted to see, were "going it blind" again. Two days later they rejected the nominations (submitted by Houston) of General Terrell as Chargé to France and Major Reily to the United States; both were suspected of opposing annexation. The *Telegraph* said Terrell received only five votes, Reily four.

In the House, the committee on the state of the Republic also wrote an opinion on annexation. Much as Texans wanted it, the report declared, they were not indifferent to the terms upon which they would "surrender all their rights as a separate, free, sovereign and independent government. . . ."

The United States acquired Texas along with Louisiana; she had had no more right to abandon Texas in 1819 than she would have "now to cede Louisiana or Arkansas, a part of the same purchase, with all their inhabitants, without their consent." The relinquishment of Texas in 1819 was "a *nullity* and totally void."

"Let Texas demand . . . that Texas be restored to the Union without further unnecessary delay." If the "same unworthy councils which undertook to exchange this fertile country for the barren sands and fetid everglades of Florida . . . still resist, successfully, our restoration to the Union from which we were so unjustly expelled," the committee proposed that the President of Texas negotiate treaties to admit European goods duty-free in return for reciprocal treatment of Texas cotton and sugar. The President would also negotiate with the United States for the cession to Texas of a port of entry on the Mississippi through which Texas goods could move without the payment of United States duties. And he would reopen peace negotiations with Mexico.

The House committee was trying to fashion an alternative— but it was using sledge hammers instead of surgical instruments. Why couldn't the gentlemen leave annexation and its alternative to the President? He knew better than they how to manage this business. In view of the Senate's published declaration, this House proposal would frighten no one.

As the problems thickened about President Jones, and as Congress showed, day after day, a disposition to make more difficult, if not impossible, the Jones plan of alternatives, he received a letter from ex-President Houston, who was

without one care about the affairs of Government, and only intent upon domestic happiness and prosperity. In great part, this arises from the assurance that you will administer the affairs of Government with equal ability and capacity with which they have been conducted for the last three years, and I hope you will receive from the Representatives of the people, a more cordial and honest support than any accorded to me. . . .

On the last day of the session, the fourth effort to elect Jones's campaign manager, M. P. Norton, to a district judgeship succeeded. The House that day declined, 7 to 16, to table a resolution of thanks to Speaker Lewis but, for want of a quorum, was unable to pass it. The Senate tabled the treaties with the Hanse towns and reduced the appropriation for the diplomatic corps of the Republic to barely enough to support two chargés in the whole wide world.

During the sitting of Congress, which seemed to President Jones longer than it actually was, he was facing vexatious problems on which he neither sought nor wanted legislative help.

His Cabinet was incomplete. Ebenezer Allen was Attorney General and W. B. Ochiltree Secretary of the Treasury, but Dr. Hill resigned as Secretary of War and Marine, and the Secretaryship of State remained vacant. Jones asked Allen to look

after foreign relations temporarily. Ashbel Smith, whom the
President considered the second-best Texan diplomat, would be
Secretary of State when he got home from London. There was
no hurry about filling the Secretaryship of War and Marine.
Chief Clerk Hamilton looked after the non-existent army and
the inactive navy.

Handicapped as he was, President Jones handled public busi-
ness in strict conformity with accepted canons. Her Britannic
Majesty's Chargé, who had had years of experience, confided to
Aberdeen that

official intercourse whether personal or by correspondence cannot
be conducted on terms of more care, or safety, or considerateness
toward the proper Officers in communication with them; or at the
same time in a manner more honourably mindful of that dignity and
character which it is their duty to uphold.

At Washington City, Raymond was sitting in the Texan Legation, watching Congress—and parrying questions about Texas
and the attitude of the Jones administration. Good Charlie Raymond knew what to say; he was telling statesmen that when the
United States decided what it wanted to do about annexation,
"then it will be time for our Government to declare its disposition and mark its course."

Poor Major Reily, Houston's nominee to succeed Van Zandt
as Chargé to the United States, tarried two months in Kentucky,
awaiting senatorial confirmation of his appointment; then, he
wrote Jones, he

received assurances of my rejection . . . resolved to come home and
die decently . . . with my diplomatic head clean off. . . . All I
can say about annexation is simply this. It is very much like the
Millerite doctrine of the end of the world. It may be to-day—it may
be next session—it may not be until the saints of the present day are
dead. . . .

General Terrell, unaware that his nomination, too, had been
rejected by the Texas Senate, arrived in London in January after
a tedious forty-day voyage. Lord Aberdeen received him with
great kindness and "without any ceremony" and "entered, without preface and with evident concern, upon the affairs of Texas."
Britain, Terrell found, was prepared to go "to any length" to

prevent annexation, and Elliot would receive fresh instructions to that effect; and, he added to Jones,

if Texas is not blind to her own interests she may during the next three years—yes, my dear Doctor, during your present term of service, she may become one of the most prosperous little communities on the face of the globe. I pray Heaven in its mercy, and our rulers in their wisdom, to avert the evil of annexation. . . .

During the sitting of Congress, General Duff Green, Tyler's ambassador-at-large, hurried back to Texas to "stand behind Major Donelson's chair"—and to lobby for a dazzling project. The scheme was to conquer California and northern Mexico for Texas with the aid of United States Indians. "Before the 'espousals' are perfected," British Consul Kennedy commented, he "desired that the bride should bring a still more ample dowry." All he needed was charters for two corporations from the Texan Congress, and he was offering Anson Jones stock in exchange for his blessing. When the President declined to bless the enterprise, Green—so the Cabinet and other government officers certified—

grossly insulted your Excellency, the President of this Republic, by threats that should you, as Executive, not sign and approve certain bills which he already had, or intended to introduce into Congress, he would call a convention of the people and revolutionize the country.

When the President ordered Allen to give Consul Green "a passport out of the limits of the Republic," that injured and misunderstood public servant explained that in making his public threats "Nothing was farther from my intention than to offer the slightest disrespect to the President, or to resort to any improper measure." Captain Elliot remarked to Jones, "If he and Mr. Calhoun do not blow up annexation, it is fire-proof, that's all."

Jones let the matter drop. His chief concern that season was not General Green's schemes, nor annexation, nor whether Congress would enact the Jones legislative program. His thoughts were centered on a bedroom at the plantation where Mary soon would go into labor. She was a robust and sensible woman, but the duties that fell to her in getting the Barrington place ready, the anxieties of the campaign, and the vicarious woes of the presidency had made this pregnancy a difficult one. That her husband was involved in delicate matters of epochal significance at the very time she was incapacitated to share his worries or even give him the small attentions that would make his problems seem simpler increased her nervousness. And her nervousness increased his apprehensions for her. As a physician, he knew she was in no imminent danger; but as a husband, he was worried.

The baby—a girl named Sarah—was born "about 5 minutes before 11 o'Clock at night," January 8. The President remained close to Barrington several days; then, when he knew that mother and child were doing nicely, he took a room in town for the remainder of the congressional season to catch up with his work and to observe the currents of public opinion.

Colonel James Morgan, Texan representative of Samuel Swarthwout and other New York speculators and tireless promoter, wrote from the seat of government on January 22:

I have been here ever since the inauguration of Pres^t Jones and of course a pretty steady lobby member. I have also been placed in a situation to understand what is going on and what is in embryo. . . . Col. M. & Prest. J. has not only to occupy the same room but the same bed! . . . What I don't know of what is going on here nobody need try to find out! . . . As *I* am known to be decidedly opposed to annexation, the President is *suspected* also the more so from his known partiality to Capt *Elliot* Her M^s Chargé. Now, no One Can know Capt Elliot without being partial to him; and as the Capt and your Humble servant are on very Social terms it may not be surprising that things do "look yellow to the jaundiced eye." . . .

Well then let me tell you that if the present Congress of the U. S. does not agree to annex us an acknowledgment of our Independence by Mexico is certain—Great B. will inforce it—, and if we do once get that acknowledgment we will never be annexed! . . .

Capt Elliot has left for Galveston—Mr. Donelson . . . leaves to-day for N. O. . . . Mon Saligny is at Galveston. A large Majority of the Citizens of Galveston are opposed to annexation: but fully ¾ths of the people of the Republic are in favor of it—yet will be satisfied with Independ gov. . . .

The Texan Congress adjourned February 3. Two days later President Jones appointed Ashbel Smith, M.D., Secretary of

State, and Congressman William G. Cooke, Secretary of War and Marine. Cooke had asked the President to dismiss acting Secretary M. C. Hamilton "for indecorous language": Jones was accommodating him—and giving him the job.

Smith had not yet returned home, but he had reached Boston on December 21 and written Jones that he would start for Texas as soon as he recovered from seasickness. Before Smith could begin his new duties the Texans knew that annexation resolutions had passed one house of the United States Congress and the other house was debating them. At the end of February, President Jones received a note that William M. Gwin, M.D., formerly M.C., had scribbled him from Washington City on January 25:

> Milton Brown's Texas resolutions have just passed the House of Representatives. . . . This is glory enough for one day. No one doubts here now but that Texas will be annexed this session.

The newspapers of the Republic did not share Gwin's jubilation. The *Civilian* at Galveston was declaring that under the Brown resolutions Texas would surrender everything and get "nothing in return" but the dubious honor of statehood and a growing threat to her labor system from abolitionists. At Washington-on-the-Brazos, W. D. Miller—no longer secretary to the President but publisher of the *National Register* and official printer to the Texan Government—declared the proposal threw Texas into the "grave of insignificance and infamy," reduced her to "a state of imbecile and hopeless dependence," where she would remain until American politicians found new ways to make political capital of the issue.

In London, Chargé Terrell discovered that the temperature of the Foreign Office had cooled. The craggy countenance of the Earl of Aberdeen wore "a sarcastic sneer" when he called on February 8 to negotiate a new trade treaty. It was obvious, "both from his looks and his manner, that something had gone wrong." England had no intention of making another treaty with "a nation that had been for some time endeavoring to subvert the one already existing," His Lordship told the Texan; "I have just been informed . . . that your new President, Mr. Jones, is secretly in favor of annexation and is doing all he can privately to

forward the measure, while the Texas newspapers are holding out
to the world that he is opposed to it."

Terrell "replied mildly, but with firmness," that

Dr. Jones was decidedly in favor of annexation; that as Secretary of
State he had labored faithfully to accomplish the measure, as had all
the members of the then Administration, except myself; that . . .
when Dr. Jones's name was placed before the people as a candidate
for the Presidency, the opposition press, knowing that a very large
majority of the people of the Republic were in favor of annexation,
labored to produce the impression that he was opposed to that
measure; that he was in favor of what was denounced as British
influence, and even of the abolition of slavery, and all this to defeat
his election. . . . yet, I could assure him that he was not doing
anything at present, either openly or secretly, to favor annexation.
That . . . I knew from the time of the rejection of the treaty of
annexation by the Senate of the United States, he had concluded
Texas must work out her own independence; but he hoped for the
cooperation of England, France, and the United States. . . .

The Earl appeared to be satisfied with these statements and opinions. He became cheerful, free, and communicative. . . .

A week after the Texan Congress adjourned in February, Ashbel Smith belatedly arrived at Washington-on-the-Brazos to begin his duties as President Jones's Secretary of State. As they
canvassed every facet of the complex and fast-changing diplomatic situation Smith told the President of an interview he had
had with the Mexican Consul General in New Orleans en route
home. The meeting was almost farcical in its anonymity but not
in the information Smith gleaned from it.

We met singularly, by arrangement . . . in Col. Forstall's office.
No other person than Señor Arrangoiz was at any moment present
at the interview—no introduction of any kind—neither his name or
quality nor mine was pronounced—he had been personally described
to me. Entering the office alone, I found sitting there alone a gentleman of quite fair complexion—we commenced talking—the interview lasted long—the range of topics and views was wide and comprehensive. I left satisfied that Mexico would make peace on the
basis of independence.

Why, Smith wanted to know, had Jones not authorized him
to execute the "Diplomatick Act"? In retrospect it seemed to

him he could have had the whole thing "completed at a single sitting" and that the Texans would have approved it "with shouts of Joy."

"It was hardly fair to deprive you of the honor of negotiating a treaty in London," the President replied, "but the negotiation shall take place here, and you as Secretary of State shall conduct it for Texas." The negotiation the President had in mind, however, was for something less disadvantageous to Texas than the "Diplomatick Act." He and Smith agreed upon the strategy of alternatives.

While the Secretary was familiarizing himself with the routine and the problems of his new office, Citizen Sam Houston hitched Saxe Weimar, his saddle horse, outside Smith's door and strode in, booted and spurred, riding whip in hand, thinking and speaking in the third person.

Saxe Weimar is at the door, saddled [the ex-President declaimed to the man who came as near as any man to being his confidential friend]. I have come to leave Houston's last words with you. If the Congress of the United States shall not by the fourth of March pass some measures of annexation which Texas can with honor accede to, Houston will take the stump against annexation for all time to come.

Then he embraced Smith, Indian-fashion, and without another word or a pause for reply he strode through the door, mounted Saxe Weimar, and was on his way.

A few days later Secretary Smith was at Galveston laying a plan before the British Chargé. Captain Elliot had planned to set at rest "rumors of undue influence on the part of Her Majesty's Government" by leaving the Republic for ten months—until December, 1845; but after listening to the new Secretary of State he decided to remain at his post. President Jones's government was seeking to get its alternative to annexation on Texan terms. Mr. Secretary Smith explained what His Excellency wanted and hoped Captain Elliot would arrange:

1st   That Mexico should at once propose the acknowledgment of the complete Independence of Texas.

2nd   That Texas upon her part would in that case stipulate in the treaty never to annex herself, or to become subject to any country whatever.

3rd   That the question of limits, and indemnity . . . should be the subject of Negotiation . . . [maybe] arbitration. . . .

Elliot transmitted the proposal to London on March 6, with a warning that overt European opposition to annexation would insure its success. The sound policy was for England simply to facilitate direct agreement between Mexico and Texas, as Jones and Smith suggested.

In Washington City annexation was moving along. At the end of February, Texas knew that the House of Representatives in January had voted, 120 to 98, to admit Texas as a state. She was to keep her debts and public lands, and there was to be no slavery north of 36° 30'. Boundaries were to be adjusted by the United States. Not for another month would Texas know whether the Senate had agreed. Many believed that no annexation resolutions could pass that body.

While the House was debating, thirty-five senators soberly considered if, and how, they could gracefully reverse the votes they had given against annexation last June. After listening for weeks to McDuffie of South Carolina and Benton of Missouri denounce each other's motives in the Texas business, the Senate decided to await a report of its foreign-relations committee on whatever resolutions the House might pass and turned to other items on the calendar.

A waggish senator dubbed the Texas resolutions Lazarus and wondered when the stone would be rolled away from the tomb. Not until February 4 did it move, but even then Lazarus did not come forth. The Senate committee recommended non-concurrence in the House resolution in a report so long and so involved that the *Globe* estimated that ten days of concentrated study were required to understand what, if anything, it meant.

During the three-week Senate debate the air was full of oratory and the galleries packed, but few senators listened. Many of them were busy writing out speeches to explain to voters back home why the admission of Texas was reprehensible in June and desirable in February; they had no time to listen to expositions of that same theme by their colleagues. Almost every senator had some change of terms to propose; many were troubled over the constitutionality of conferring statehood on a foreign nation by resolution; a few die-hard Whigs threatened to filibuster annexation to death.

At a night session, February 27, with lobbies jammed with representatives and galleries crowded with spectators, the Senate argument ended. A substitute proposal was lost by a tie vote. Then the Senate, 27 to 25, approved resolutions which would bring Texas into the Union upon her acceptance of this action of Congress, or by treaty, at the option of the President of the United States. The guns on Capitol Hill were booming a premature salute to the twenty-eighth state as senators started home that evening.

There was still a chance that the House might delay accepting the Senate stipulation authorizing the President to negotiate a new treaty if he preferred, but at a single sitting next day the House agreed to everything, 132 to 76. The sun was setting as the final vote was taken. "The deed," the New York *Tribune* commented, "was done in darkness, as was meet." Again that night the guns on Capitol Hill saluted the unborn state of Texas as clerks prepared the joint resolutions for President Tyler to sign the next morning.

Poor Tyler was fidgeting in the White House, his term almost expiring, while the legislators quibbled over the method of admitting Texas. He was not stickling over method; he only wanted action before he became a private citizen again. He had three days of official life left when he wrote his name on the joint resolution. Should he leave annexation to Mr. Polk, or should he take the step which, he had believed for nearly four years, would "throw so bright a lustre around us"?

Exactly eight years ago—March 3, 1837—this Texas business had begun when President Jackson paused, as he was leaving the the White House forever, to send the first United States Chargé to Texas. For seventy-two hours Tyler hesitated, then on the night of March 3 he wrote Chargé Donelson to proceed at once to Texas to get "speedy and prompt" acceptance of annexation.

The steamer *New York* reached Galveston on March 20 with unofficial news of the annexation resolution.

XXXIII

ALTERNATIVES

ON MARCH 24, Captain Charles Elliot and Count Alphonse de Saligny paced the Galveston wharf as they waited impatiently for Her Majesty's warship *Electra* to dock. For four days—ever since the *New York* had brought news of the passage of the annexation resolutions—they had haunted the wharf, peering through the captain's binoculars for a British or a French flag in the Gulf; now the *Electra* was creeping in. They hoped she carried dispatches from the Foreign Office.

All around them knots of Texans were discussing the annexation as if it had already been consummated and suspiciously eying these foreigners who were conversing earnestly in unintelligible French. Men just landed from New Orleans were answering questions—piecing out the meager details they knew with conjectures. Everybody seemed sure that Texas would be in the Union before the end of the year, and importers were wondering if they should not hold up shipments from the States until Texan tariff ceased to operate.

At last the *Electra* docked and her captain stepped ashore, saluted Her Britannic Majesty's Chargé, and handed him a leather dispatch pouch that had been two months and a day on its way from London. Elliot and Saligny hurried to the British Legation, where Elliot opened the bag and with practiced eye skimmed through twenty-five hundred words of diplomatic verbiage to find what he could do. Aberdeen at last knew that Mexico was willing to grant independence under British and French guarantees, and he was authorizing Elliot to "immediately confer unreservedly" with Saligny and "lose no time" in presenting the offer and getting from the Texan Government "a full and frank explanation" of its intentions.

Saligny had identical orders. Elliot had been conferring unreservedly with him for weeks. They knew exactly what they wanted to do; now they had authority to do it.

All Texas knew the United States had "opened wide the door," but the government would remain in official ignorance of it until it received authenticated documents stamped with a great seal. A messenger from Washington City was moving overland by way of the Red River toward the Texan capital; Donelson "was expected every hour" at Galveston on his way there. Elliot and Saligny must do their work before President Jones officially knew of the annexation offer.

At sunup next morning they were dashing toward the Brazos to execute the greatest diplomatic coup of their careers. They must get His Excellency's promise "neither to assemble Congress, nor to entertain any Negotiations for Annexation" until Mexico acknowledged Texan independence. They knew the United States had acted; they knew Mexico was ready to act; they must contrive delay in Texas. Congress must not be assembled; it was "by far the least respectable or trustworthy" Elliot had ever seen, already "deeply committed" to annexation.

President Jones had been little in his office since the Congress adjourned. He rode into town whenever the mail arrived, read his letters, and returned home as soon as he could. During the campaign he had refused to mingle with the people because he was negotiating matters that could not be publicly discussed; now he was even deeper into those matters, and much conversation would be unwise. His private secretary knew where to find him if he was needed at the office, and he knew how to judge whether he was needed. Mr. Secretary Smith could parry the inquiries of visiting politicians and editors.

February 17 the President's ox teams began hauling heavy furniture and trunks from Cooke's plantation house to Barrington. He visited Independence to buy "fruit and ornamental Trees & other things," then planted them around his new house. March 1, the day President Tyler was officially approving the annexation resolutions, the President of Texas

took Capt. Gratz to Barrington and commenced laying off & making Garden then had heavy rain. Went to town & transacted business in Executive Office.

The next day began the tenth year of Texan independence. President Jones was "in town all day"—hiring another Negro boy to help with his moving, receiving ceremonially a gift of a Buffalo robe from his Indian friend, Ramon Castro, and listening to Lieutenant C. B. Snow recite a patriotic poem of his own composition commemorating a decade of Texan independence. Then, until the sixth, he was at Barrington, getting the family settled, hiring the Reverend Mr. Tryon's girl Susan as housemaid at seventy-two dollars for the year, and supervising the last work on the chimneys. His health was bad; an attack of "swelled throat and fever," which had been epidemic in February, laid him up for eight days.

Mon. 17th   Went to town & transacted business in Ex. Office. Dr. Smith came home with me in my buggy.

Tues. 18th   Went to town wrote letters for Mr. Tryon &c &c Moved to the new office in 2d Story of Mr. Ross' Store.

Wed & Thurs. 19th & 20th   Staid at Home & assisted in ploughing   Mr. Campbell commenced building Office Stables & negro quarters on the 20th.

Tues. 25.   Mr. & Mrs: Pierpont arrived.

Wed 26 & Th. 27th   Sick at home.

At noon on March 27 loafers on Washington's Main Street watched two dust-covered foreigners gallop up to Mr. Ross's grocery, dismount, and race up the stairs, saddlebags in hands. The man they wanted to see was not there. Across the street they hurried to the Department of State where, luckily, the Honorable Ashbel Smith, M.D., K.S.J., sat at the pine table that served as his desk. He dismissed the clerks, sent a porter to Barrington with a note to His Excellency the President, and closed the door.

There was "full and frank" discussion with Elliot and Saligny. Smith would play their game, but he was uneasy about the perplexities the turn of events would give the President.

The next morning His Excellency dragged himself from bed and rode to town. His lips were parched and his hands trembled, as he gave concentrated attention to the business at hand. He was about to get those alternatives for which he had worked four years—and get them simultaneously.

At long last the strings were being concentrated in the square, blunt-fingered, surgical hands of Anson Jones, M.D., as he sat in a makeshift office over a store in the dilapidated town where the Texans had first asserted their independence, listening to a plan to preserve independence forever. If he felt any elation, no hint of it showed on his impassive fever-flushed face or in his heavy-lidded hazel eyes. He made no predictions. His concern was only to hammer this alternative into tangible and usable shape.

When Elliot, then Saligny, began verbosely to urge "every argument that presented itself," His Excellency stopped them with a weary gesture. He knew all they had to say; he could say it better than they could. He was as willing as they for Mexico to offer recognition, but the captain and the count would please bear in mind that in this business he "was but the agent of the people." He conceived of himself as an honest broker, trying to get the best possible offers; he wanted the bidding to go as high as possible. Then his people could take the best proposal.

Would His Excellency accept their good offices to get from Mexico immediate, final acknowledgment of Texan independence? Would he, indeed! He was the man who had suggested it three long years ago; but while England and France dilly-dallied, Texan sentiment had gone very far in the other direction. It might be "in vain to resist the tide." He did not want to convoke Congress immediately to consider annexation.

But [Elliot reported to Aberdeen] it was not till the President had consulted his Cabinet twice . . . and requested us to meet them once, and urge our own views, that we were enabled to dispose him to agree to the arrangement. . . .

The arrangement was brief and simple. Texas accepted the intervention; but the "advanced condition of circumstances" and "the difficulties and risks" to which Texas was exposed required that she speedily be furnished "decisive proof that Mexico was at once ready to acknowledge the independence of this Republic, without other condition than the stipulation to maintain the same." The President agreed to delay action on annexation for ninety days, but he made it of record that Texas could choose annexation rather than accept the Mexican treaty, "without any breach of faith."

By one o'clock March 29 the papers were signed and sealed in triplicate. Elliot was to proceed to Mexico and Smith to Europe—and the whole negotiation was to be known only to the governments concerned with it.

The President wrote in his diary: "Frid. 28th   Went to town, to see Capt. Elliot & M de Saligny. Sat 29th   they left."

He counted it a good day's work. Mexico earlier had conditioned Texan recognition on European guarantees. Now England and France had agreed to obtain Mexican recognition of Texas without involvements—and Texans were free to accept annexation if they preferred it. The alternatives would be clearcut, honorable, and equally attractive.

That day W. D. Miller's leading editorial in the *Texas National Register* was captioned "Are We Annexed?"

The earnest friends and advocates of annexation, in disappointment, must answer No! [Miller wrote] . . . The time fixed by political forecast for the annexation to be effected, and the day prescribed by pious augury for the destruction of the world, have both passed by, leaving the speculator and the religionist equally confounded at *some unaccountable mistake in their respective predictions.*

At Bastrop, General Burleson's home town, the Honorable and Reverend R. E. B. Baylor interrupted district court to announce that annexation had been offered, and recessed for celebration. "We felt something like the children of Israel," one of the participants said, "when Jehovah flung back the Red Sea betwixt them and their foes. Judge Baylor, Baptist preacher though he was, made a full hand with the boys." He considered no man drunk on such a day "as long as he could pronounce the word Epsom."

Time was on the side of the Europeans. Four days after President Tyler instructed Major Donelson to hurry to Texas, the new President wrote him to wait for further orders. March 10 the new, but almost identical, instructions were forwarded. Not until March 24, the day Elliot and Saligny started to see President Jones, did Donelson leave the United States.

When he learned in Galveston that the Europeans had preceded him, he "put off in a hurry after them." Ten miles from Washington-on-the-Brazos he met these friendly foreigners on their way back to the coast. They could not tell him anything "exactly"; they "supposed" President Jones was waiting for the good news Donelson was bringing. Apparently they had done nothing, Donelson reported to his Secretary of State; "if they made a communication to this government . . . it is a secret between them and the President."

The major hurried to the Department of State. Mr. Secretary Smith was busy packing his papers and was singularly uncommunicative. Then he sought the President—and learned that Smith was on leave of absence and that Attorney General Allen was charged with foreign relations. Before he left town, Allen, too, was given leave of absence. It was all very mystifying—perhaps "some settled scheme of delay."

President Jones was cordial and attentive but told the major he had not yet determined what he should do. Annexation was a most grave subject, not to be acted upon hastily, he explained to the Chargé, who was there to get a prompt, decisive, and affirmative answer. He had "a decided opinion but would dwell awhile upon it, until aided by his cabinet," two members of which were on leave. The matter was indeed most grave—and the President's problem was to contrive a delay of three months; to take no action, to say nothing, that would weight the scales in favor of the alternative Donelson was presenting—or the one Jones could not yet mention.

Fever seized the President again that day. He took a room at the hotel and lay abed four days before he could travel the four miles to Barrington. There he slowly recovered. The alternatives he long had sought were almost in his hand. The United States was eager "to plight the troth." Mexico was equally eager to prevent the wedding. In less than ninety days everything would be ready to present to the people. Until then his lips were sealed. Months ago he had told Donelson that the annexation proposal "would be received with welcome and fairly and promptly submitted to the people." He had assured Elliot and Saligny that peace with Mexico would be welcomed and presented, fairly and promptly, to the people.

Frankness [Jones held] is a quality I very much admire, but I did not esteem it the province of Texas to read other nations a homily on the subject, by affording exclusive examples of it to them. She . . . stood in need of all the advantages which . . . a prudent and discreet silence on the part of her Chief Executive Officer could give her. . . . If jealousy of European powers had been the efficient cause of the immense change of sentiment in the United States [he reasoned] . . . it might be well to keep this jealousy alive a little longer. The old proverb, "There is many a slip," etc., might apply.

Annexation resolutions had passed the United States Senate by a vote of 27 to 25. If one senator had changed his vote, the measure would have been killed by a tie. Annexation could not take place until the new United States Congress (which would not assemble until December) approved all the details. The new Congress could decline to admit Texas into the Union even after Texas had accepted the invitation. Anti-Texas sentiment was not dead; it might increase before Congress finally acted. Texas needed an alternative to keep interest alive in the United States. She might even prefer to accept the alternative.

President Jones's problem now was to make the delay he had promised seem reasonable, without disclosing the reason for it. He could profess uncertainty whether to call Congress or a convention, or both—since the whole matter was extra-constitutional. He had faith in himself as a negotiator and he was sure he could get more for Texas under a treaty than the resolutions offered. He could, and did, quibble over the terms offered. Polk and Donelson did not want a treaty; they wanted immediate acceptance of the joint resolutions.

If Mexico agreed to the terms Jones had outlined, and Jones insisted on negotiations with the United States, he might play these alternatives against each other. But there was one great hazard: a fund of $100,000—more than the total budget of the Republic—earmarked for a special United States commission to Texas. Could Jones checkmate the almost house-to-house canvass of the Texans that United States agents could undertake? He might—with the aid of strategically placed Texan leaders who understood what he was aiming at; but he could not enlist aid without violating his pledge of secrecy. It was grave, most grave.

No hint of what he wanted came from him. He was spending most of his time at Barrington, alleviating his anxiety with farm

work. Two of his Cabinet, also pledged to secrecy, made a few
halting efforts, but they could not say enough to make a convincing story. Allen, who preferred independence, and Ochiltree,
who wanted annexation, were traveling about, reassuring the
people that all was well. Cooke of War and Marine did not
"trouble his head about the matter."

Ashbel Smith was on his way to London and Paris. If the
Mexican alternative should be taken, Texas needed to be represented there by her number-one diplomat; if annexation should
be embraced, there would have to be ceremonial leave-taking
and assurances that the government of the expiring Republic
appreciated the exertions of those powers to keep her alive.
Smith was the man to do either.

Raymond still sat in the Texan Legation at Washington City,
waiting for the new Chargé to arrive. Jones had appointed
David S. Kaufman, chairman of the foreign-relations committee
of the Senate, who was shrewd enough to understand the Jones
strategy without having it diagrammed for him; but the President
would need Kaufman more in the special session of Congress,
if he called one, than at Washington the next few months. Kaufman delayed his departure till summer.

George Wilkins Kendall of the New Orleans *Picayune*,
alarmed by the "unpleasant" and "unexpected" apathy of the
Texan press toward the glorious news of annexation, hurried
to Texas in April to investigate. Since 1841, when he had
marched toward Santa Fé with Lamar's men—and landed in
a Mexican prison with them—he had considered himself a sort
of guardian of Texas, and he had made the *Picayune* the best
source of information on the Republic.

With a Hungarian count and "an English pleasure traveller"
Kendall reached Washington-on-the-Brazos after

swimming, digging and floundering from Houston . . . two days
of the time completely weather and water bound. With our horses
we could get along well enough . . . but the Count's lameness . . .
induced us to purchase a wagon at Houston, and it is not altogether
so simple a matter to swim a vehicle of that particular description,
neither is it so easy to dray it through the deep, heavy, black mud
of the prairies. Our English companion . . . thinks the roads of
Texas in a highly uneducated state. . . .

And Kendall wondered if the Texan President was making good use of what education he had.

Kendall was there, "coat off, and sleeves rolled up," to work for annexation and expose British machinations. He found,

Sitting upon the same log upon the banks of the Brazos . . . as many men as the log would hold: it was a shady spot, the spot where that old log slumbered, and there in diplomatic conclave might have been seen Anson Jones, Sam Houston, Capt. Elliot, the Count de Saligny, and Major A. J. Donelson—perhaps not all at one and the same time, but one time and another all felt the log. And I was there too, watching every movement, and especially watching Elliot, a long ways the smartest man in the crowd.

The *Picayune* editor suggested that the next time the President of Texas contemplated an intrigue with foreigners he should remember:

> A chiel's amang ye takin' notes,
> An' faith he'll prent 'em.

On his way out of Texas, Smith reported to Jones that he found

everywhere, very great, *very intense* feeling . . . an immense majority of the citizens are in favor of . . . annexation as presented in the resolutions . . . they will continue to be so, in preference to independence, though recognized in the most liberal manner by Mexico . . . [and] should it be suspected that the matter was to be deferred till the European powers can in any wise be heard from or consulted, especially England . . . an attempt will be made . . . to plunge the country into a revolution. The plan has been matured. . . . When it is known I am going to Europe . . . *I feel convinced that public opinion will be inflamed beyond control.*

Should he continue toward Europe? If he could with honor resign the mission, he would do so; he was ready to join the annexationists and thought the President was too. Jones noted on the back of that letter:

Dr. Smith does not clearly understand the object of his mission— which is simply to explain to European Governments our true position on the annexation question.

The voters of Texas were as ignorant as European governments as to the "true position" of President Jones. A Brenham mass meeting, April 11, declared his "doubtful" attitude "places the question in a precarious situation" and demanded, if he did not act soon, that county mass meetings ratify the joint resolutions and form a state government. Secretary Ochiltree found at Galveston "deep and intense feeling . . . but nothing I would call excitement. (Hunt, of course, is absent.)"

General Memucan Hunt, an accomplished rabble rouser, was going to and fro in the land, doing what he could to spread alarm —and to confront President Jones with alternatives he did not want. He attended the Brenham meeting and told Attorney General Allen of the plan of "some of the most influential men in the lower country, to take forcible possession of the Custom House at Galveston; and even stronger & more violent measures. . . ." Hunt was convincing the people who listened to him that the President and his Cabinet "have been and are now secretly opposed to annexation"; and that "it would be impossible for Great Britain & Mexico to offer any terms, no matter how favorable, that Texas would accept."

At Washington-on-the-Brazos, Hunt met Archibald Yell, former Governor of Arkansas, special agent of the United States to work up annexation sentiment. "I have never," declared Hunt, who was an expert judge of propagandists, "made the acquaintance of a gentleman . . . with whom I was more pleased. . . ."

At Houston the annexation rally on San Jacinto Day overflowed the Presbyterian Church and moved to the courthouse. Judge Norton, who had been on both sides of the question, presided. Three speakers opposed annexation; three others, including Secretary Ochiltree, spoke for it; and the meeting demanded prompt acceptance of the annexation proposal.

At another Houston rally Senator William Lawrence planned to sway the multitude against annexation.

He had, however [Francis R. Lubbock wrote], steamed up too high for the occasion, and though an admirable speaker, upon taking the platform, he gazed vacantly at the crowd, and in a moment more measured his full length upon the floor. Dr. Francis Moore, the chairman, who was an ardent annexationist and a very ready man, pointed with his *one arm* at the prostrate man, and said most emphatically, in a loud tone: "Gentlemen, Colonel Lawrence has the floor." This settled the question, and the gathering, with much merriment, left the hall.

Old Ayes and Noes Pilsbury presided at the Brazoria rally, and Congressman Tod Robinson delivered the oration. Everybody of importance was there—and most of them made speeches, all "red hot for annexation, with or without the consent of the Jones administration." The Brazoria resolutions were sent by messenger to Galveston, where James Love got up a meeting that endorsed them.

At Shelbyville in East Texas, O. M. Roberts, Isaac Van Zandt, and Kaufman were able to insert into the resolutions demanding immediate annexation an expression of "utmost confidence in the President" and skepticism that "he would attempt to blast or defer the hopes of a confiding people."

One after another twenty counties spoke, all for annexation. The highest vote recorded against it was at Nacogdoches, where three citizens said they preferred independence.

There is but little doubt [thought Mrs. James F. Perry, sister of Stephen F. Austin and a former patient of Dr. Jones], but that Pres' Jones is opposed. . . . one hundred such men as Jones & Houston could not humbug the people of Texas out of annexation. . . . No proposition that England France and Mexico could make us would have any influence on our actions now. . . .

Kendall of the *Picayune,* watching things in Texas, announced in an extra: "Captain Elliot and Mr. Saligny between them, have poured the 'leprous distilment into the porches' of President Jones's ear by the quart"—and a good many Texans believed it. Had Jones sold out to Britain? Captain Elliot was his confidential friend, the godfather of his second son. Elliot had hurried to Washington-on-the-Brazos, spent a day with the President, then dashed away on a secret mission. Kendall

dogged him to Galveston, and when in every grocery and bowling alley he proclaimed that he was going to Charleston, in the British Frigate *Eurydice,* I suspected that he was going to the City of Mexico, to prevent annexation if in his power. I was right, came out in the *Picayune* with the mysterious movements of the "Man with the White Hat". . . .

Latent anti-British feeling, coupled with vague fears that England, if she got paramount control in Texas, would abolish slavery and maybe do worse things, produced all sorts of rumors. President Jones became overnight a hated man. He was burned in effigy. There was talk of deposing him, of lynching him. A solemn promise prevented his explaining what he was about. It probably would not have helped much if he had been free to talk.

If only Elliot could fetch back that Mexican treaty in time for it to be considered on its merits! As he waited, waited, he called Congress to meet on June 16; then he called a convention to meet at Austin on July 4 to consider annexation "and any other proposition" which might be made "concerning the nationality of the Republic."

The President of Texas moved silently among the trivia of daily existence as he waited for Elliot to return, sharing his thoughts with no one. He "paid Rev. Mr. Tryon $36. hire for Girl Susan Six months," bought three thousand bricks for $30, and a trundle bed for $20. He ate potatoes, cucumbers, and squash from his own garden and built two shelves in the closet under the staircase.

Official and unofficial agents of the United States swarmed through Texas, whipping up annexation frenzy. Donelson concentrated first on ex-President Houston. He emerged from his first conference with the Old Chief "under a full conviction that if the adoption of our proposal depended upon his vote, it would be lost." But Houston began to waver. Andrew Jackson pleaded with him; President Polk found a job for a Houston protégé and said he hoped the Hero of San Jacinto would represent Texas in the Senate. There was a pleasant rumor that Houston would soon be President of the United States—and there was no doubt that the Texans had made up their minds in favor of annexation. Houston had come, if not to open advocacy, at least to acquiescence, when he left for the United States to visit Old Hickory before the meeting of the Texan Congress.

But Anson Jones could not leave Texas; and, having charted a course, he was less quick to give it up. He did not admit even to himself that he preferred continued independence to annexation, but the very fact that he was saying nothing when everybody else was shouting annexation was evidence enough to his constituents.

"You know," Senator Pilsbury had written one of Jones's old neighbors in Brazoria, "he can look up chimney and into the pot at the same moment." Jones himself had written to the Secretary of the Texas Legation at Washington City: "I am satisfied we shall do very well in either event . . . and therefore keep 'cool as a cucumber' & 'calm as a May morning.' "

Anson Jones, throughout his life, was a singularly isolated man. In the annexation matter his isolation was almost complete. He could (but did not) say, as Houston had on another occasion: "I consulted none; held no councils. . . . If I err, the blame is mine." He did not attempt to influence a single member of the Congress, or the convention, or even of his Cabinet—nor did he disclose to his closest political associates his own preference. His strategy in 1845 was one he had determined upon in 1842. With less than his usual acuteness Jones failed to observe how fundamentally the situation had changed. Long after it was clear to everyone else that the Texans did not desire an alternative to annexation, even though it would get better terms from the United States, Jones—with the stubbornness of a solitary man—persisted on the course he had started.

Ashbel Smith looked

with admiration on the sublime calmness of Mr. Jones, who pursued the unruffled tenor of duty amidst threats, denunciations and falsehoods . . . amidst insidious plots to betray him into fatal measures and to overturn his administration.

One acute danger arose from the combined activity of United States agents and naval officers and Texan leaders disaffected with Jones. Duff Green was still in Texas, still eager for conquest; Archibald Yell and ex-Postmaster General Wicliffe had come to block British intrigues; and Commodore Stockton, U.S.N., was at Galveston with the *Princeton, St. Mary's, Saratoga,* and *Porpoise.* On the northern and eastern borders of Texas, United States troops were concentrated—all ready to pounce on Mexico if she made a move.

The age-old dream of adventurous Texans to march into Mexico came to life again. Why not occupy the Rio Grande Valley with Texan volunteers to make certain Mexico would not encroach upon the territory of Texas? There were rumors that

Mexico was moving troops to the border. Commodore Stockton consulted Major General Sidney Sherman of the Texas Militia and ex-President Lamar; then Sherman and the commodore's secretary laid the plan before President Jones. The last three days of May they conferred at Washington-on-the-Brazos. His Excellency's answer was No.

I see not one single motive for Annexation [he told the eager warriors] if it is not for security and protection, or if we are *to do our own fighting,* and I tell you plainly that I will not be made the scape goat in such an affair. . . . The United States Government must take all the responsibility, and all the expense and all the labour of hostile movements upon Mexico. . . . Somebody else must break up the state of peace. It shall not be me.

While pro-annexation, anti-Jones sentiment mounted in Texas, Elliot waited in Mexico for the treaty. Cuevas, the Foreign Minister, months before had expressed his willingness to make peace with Texas; when a draft was presented he agreed to sign "tomorrow." Elliot, as he waited three weeks, added the word *mañana* to his vocabulary. The chairman of a Mexican congressional committee was preparing a report upon the question of Texas—a report that started with the conduct of the Duke of Alva in the Low Countries and proceeded leisurely toward the circumstances of the battle of San Jacinto nearly three centuries later. The Mexican Congress and Cabinet survived the reading of the report, and on May 19 the arrangement with Texas was as complete as Mexico could make it.

Unlike the treaty that Santa Anna had signed at Velasco in 1836, this one could not be repudiated by Mexico—it had been approved in advance—and it contained all that was essential for the permanent independence of Texas. When Elliot handed it to him on June 4, President Jones promptly proclaimed it. France and England were not signatories, but they would see that it was carried out in good faith. It was peace without strings—and with strong backing.

On June 4 the President wrote in his diary:

Issued proclamation of Peace with Mexico. Same day rec⁴ proposals of peace from the Comanche Chief Santa Anna the last enemy which Texas had. Accepted them. Now my country for the first time in ten years is actually *at peace with* ALL *the World.*

Now at long last Anson Jones was "enabled to declare to the people of Texas the actual state of their affairs with respect to Mexico, to the end that they may direct and dispose them as they shall judge best for the honor and permanent interests of the Republic." He was offering them "the alternatives of peace with the world and Independence, or annexation and its contingencies."

He believed it was a notable achievement. He was oblivious of the frenzy against him, and against the treaty with Mexico, that had seized the Texans. It was, he said, only a "fever, and like all fevers . . . must run its course for good or for evil." Texans wanted no alternative; they wanted annexation. While that sentiment was solidifying, Jones had perforce been silent. Now that he could speak it was too late. Those who listened professed to detect sinister intrigue in what he said and what he failed to say. The physician had been too intent on compounding a prescription to observe that his patient had developed an allergy to the medicine he was preparing. What he had brewed might have been what she needed three years ago or last year. Now it was valueless—worse than valueless, because the patient believed it was a lethal potion.

The Congress which reassembled on June 16 was composed of "avowed, determined, irreconcilable, foes to the Administration . . . and inefficient, lukewarm, indifferent supporters, or rather apologists. . . ." Secretary Allen predicted the damage they would do would "depend upon the moderation of the Opposition. . . . little justice is likely to be accorded to the Executive. . . ."

President Jones knew now that the storm was up. "I felt its *blasts* all around me. Demagogues, emissaries, factionists, disorganizers, and personal and political enemies, all, all united against me. . . ."

Kaufman was there. He had written the President: "It will be my duty and pleasure on all and every occasion to put you right before the people; and I really believe that, when your whole course of policy is laid before them, they will award you the meed of an honest and patriotic statesman."

John S. (Rip) Ford, even before the President's message was read, moved to accept annexation. His Excellency did not appear before Congress; he sent his message by his private secretary.

A great crisis, he told them, as if they did not know it, had arisen since the adjournment of the regular session. He now had the pleasure to present the long-sought alternatives. Congress would consider annexation and the Senate would advise him upon the Mexican treaty. A convention on July 4 would ratify, on the part of the people, whatever action Texas in its wisdom should take.

The alternative of Annexation or Independence [he pointed out], will thus be placed before the people of Texas, and their free, sovereign and unbiased voice, will determine the all-important issue, and . . . the Executive . . . will give immediate and full effect to the expression of their will.

His situation has . . . been one of great delicacy and embarrassment. Questions of much difficulty have been presented for his determination, upon which the fate and welfare of the country depended, and without precedent or constitutional guide for his governance, he has been obliged to assume in consequence, great and severe responsibilities. He trusts, however, that Congress will approve the course he has adopted, and by their enlightened counsels, relieve and direct him in the course hereafter to be pursued. . . .

He wanted the Senate to receive the treaty but take no final action upon it. They would leave the alternative open. Then the President could say to Donelson: "You see how it is. Mexico is willing to grant peace if Texas declines annexation. The terms of the first two sections of your joint resolutions are not generous and they are vague. The third section authorizes annexation by a treaty. Ask President Polk to act under that section of the resolutions. Negotiation of a treaty will give both countries time to be certain what they want. It will enable Texas to stipulate clearly what arrangements she thinks preferable to assured independence. It will enable the United States to decide, without hurry or pressure, if she ought to grant what Texas wants. This is too grave a matter to be decided in hot haste. My term runs until December 1847; Mr. Polk's until March 1849. We are reasonable men and want to do the best thing for our constituents. Let this fever die down in both countries; let us negotiate; then let our constitutional advisers and our constituents consider calmly what is best."

That was the alternative within an alternative that President Jones wanted. The Senate and the House unanimously approved the annexation resolution. In secret session the Senate unanimously rejected the Mexican treaty, then lifted the injunction of secrecy. The President's strategy was ruined. "The Senate," he commented sadly, "are so much afraid of the people, they dare not do right."

The houses agreed on a tribute to Andrew Jackson, a vote of thanks to ex-President Tyler, appreciation for their presiding officers; but as to the President of the Republic of Texas, they were silent until the last day. Then General McLeod in the House declared "the course of the Executive in relation to the question of annexation . . . unpatriotic and unwise" and recommended that the convention end Jones's tenure "that he may not be enabled to throw further obstacles in the way of this great measure, and ultimately effect its defeat."

In the Senate, James K. McCreary, M.D., moved a vote of no confidence: "the President in thus *arbitrarily* exercising the powers of negotiating a treaty has done an official act unworthy of the Executive of Texas, and degrading to the country, and has set at defiance the known and express will of the people, and therefore justly deserves the censure of this body." Then he moved to table his own motion, and when that failed he withdrew it—but it was not expunged from the official record.

While the censure was under discussion a committee called to ask the President if he had anything else to communicate. His Excellency replied that he "had nothing more" to lay before the Congress.

XXXIV

MR. JONES'S TEXAS

THE President of the Republic whose Congress had just voted its extinction had no time immediately to contemplate the sorry ending of his four-year labor for alternatives. Charles Raymond, Secretary of the Texas Legation, and Captain J. G. Tod, T.N., had just arrived from the capital of the United States with news that officials there feared some intrigue in Texas might defeat annexation. With Chargé Donelson, the President "laughed and joked a good deal about the excitement on the Potomac." "President Jones has always been open and candid," Donelson declared, and added that the only "trouble and difficulty" could come from the United States. Everyone seemed happy at Washington-on-the-Brazos.

But on July 4, when His Excellency "started for Houston with Mrs. Jones, Child & Servant," he had time to examine what had happened against the background of what he had planned. He had conceived it his duty, as agent of the people, to force the bidding high by exciting British-American rivalry. That he should be suspected of complicity in British intrigue amazed him. Elliot and Saligny, even Donelson, could testify there was no intrigue—only a dutiful, skillful performance of public trust.

He had done his duty, and if it were to do over again, he would do the same thing. There was no sense, the moment annexation was offered Texas, "to kick away the ladder by which she had ascended to it"; no gentleman could have said to Elliot and Saligny at that juncture, "We want no more of your good offices."

How easy it would have been for another man, he bitterly reflected, to have silenced all clamor by leading the annexation excitement. It would have been a violation of national faith and of a personal pledge, and it might have defeated annexation; but it would have insured momentary popularity. His inconvenient conscience had not let him consider that course, and he was reaping the reward of duty well done. The storm of popular excitement, he reflected, having no other object to beat upon, was spending its fury and breaking its waves against him.

During those six days after Congress adjourned at Washington-on-the-Brazos, delegates to the convention were converging on Austin to complete annexation without another thought of peace with Mexico. On the evening of July 3 an informal committee of delegates worked until near midnight drafting an ordinance assenting to annexation.

Next morning at eight the convention officially assembled in the old capitol—a schoolhouse since 1842—and unanimously elected Thomas J. Rusk president. "Our duties," he declared, "are plain and easy . . . to enter the great American Confederacy with becoming dignity and self-respect." Baptist Judge Baylor nominated Methodist Chauncey Richardson to "address the throne of grace in a fervent and appropriate prayer" and "for several minutes after he closed, the whole assembly seemed to be absorbed in silent devotion." An indigenous flavor was given proceedings when the delegate from Béxar asked for an interpreter. With only Richard Bache of Galveston dissenting, the ordinance accepting annexation was adopted immediately and without debate.

Through fifty-six hot July and August days the delegates worked away at a constitution for the new state—and at intervals considered informally what they should do about President Jones.

Rusk had come to the convention convinced that the President's negotiation with Mexico would "be productive of nothing but his own disgrace and hasten our action upon the question of annexation." J. Pinckney Henderson, leader among the delegates, feared "the President is not as *anxious* as some of us are to see the measure consummated, but . . . will carry out the wishes of the people. . . . If," he sagely added, "the President is opposed to our wishes, this is a bad time to excite him or punish him . . . rather let us *coax* him on."

General McLeod had suggested in Congress that the convention relieve His Excellency of all connection with the government, and there were delegates, led by President Rusk, eager to oust the President. Discussed first in hotel lobbies and on street corners, it soon became an absorbing, unofficial project.

The President and his family traveled on July 4, not toward Austin but to Houston, where Mrs. Woodruff was fatally ill. After he saw that nothing could be done for her and while they waited for her to die, the President sought semi-scientific relaxation with Dr. A. Crane, a gifted phrenologist recently arrived in the Republic.

Professor Crane [the *Morning Star* reported] has literally had his hands full. . . . He has examined the knots, bumps, and protuberances upon some dozens of heads, including the President's . . . and has caused quite a sensation among those who entertain a due regard for the maxim "know thyself."

On July 9 they buried Mrs. Jones's mother, and the President "took charge of four of Mrs. Woodruff's children & started for home." At Barrington a letter awaited him from Judge Ochiltree, Secretary of the Treasury, who was a delegate to the convention:

. . . come to Austin *with the Government at the earliest possible date*. This Convention is mighty to do mischief. . . . Your enemies are actively, busily at work to undermine you. . . .

He would go to Austin, but not at once. There were things for him to do at home and in his office in Washington.

The *Texas National Register* stated the case for President Jones in an editorial on July 10:

Because the President of the Republic thinks it perhaps unbecoming on the first intelligence of the passage of the annexation bill to go into paroxism of rapture, eat whole roast oxen, drink beer by the barrel, and burn barrels of tar, he is opposed to annexation.

Because his cabinet officers think it unbecoming to fling up their caps and strain their lungs for Polk, Dallas, Oregon, Texas, and *annexation*, they are opposed to annexation.

Because his minister to England does not think it becoming to damn John Bull and British influence, he is opposed to annexation.

Because the President accepts the offered intervention of England and France to move Mexico to the acknowledgment of Texian Independence, an intervention which Lamar offered five millions of money for, and which Houston himself repeatedly solicited, he is opposed to annexation.

Because he procured that recognition from Mexico, he is opposed to annexation. Because if terms are to be had, he takes measures to secure them; because he gives to the people the honor of a choice between unquestioned independence and annexation; because in the event of annexation, he avoids the possibility of a war; because he thinks the opponents of annexation entitled as citizens of a free country, to some consideration; because he esteems it the duty of the President, not to take the lead in popular excitements, but rather to look out that those excitements are no prejudice to the country;—as the ship never more needs a skillful helmsman, than when running directly before the gale with a full head of canvass,—for such reasons he is denounced by a great portion of the press, alarmed and alarmists, at home and abroad, as a traitor to the cause of annexation and of the country.

For a month, while the convention wondered what schemes of iniquity the President might be up to, he remained at Barrington, only occasionally visiting the executive office. On July 12 he notified President Polk officially that the convention had accepted annexation and sent the letter by General Besancon, U.S.A. Four days later Chargé Donelson called to take formal leave of what was left of the government to which he had been accredited, then the major went on to Austin "as a private citizen" to coach members of the convention on their duties.

After sitting two weeks in convention, Secretary Ochiltree came to Barrington to urge the President to hurry to Austin. The President's gray horse started for Austin next day, but its rider was Ochiltree, not Jones. His Excellency remained at Barrington to watch his field hands harvest tobacco, potatoes, and fodder, and to supervise the finishing of the slave quarters and his office in the yard. His only presidential acts were to send a new Secretary of the Texan Legation to the United States and to confer with his Secretary of War and Marine.

Ochiltree had come down personally to urge him to hurry to Austin; he declined. His neighbor and former host, James L. Farquhar, wrote from Austin after Ochiltree's return that there was "considerable excitement"; he was certain that if His Excellency did not come "we will get into confusion." Still he lingered at Barrington, waiting for the convention's fever to run its course.

It would be awkward to take a hand in the squabble without violating his notions of presidential dignity. He would wait still awhile.

August first Major Crumpler came to Barrington, direct from Austin, with a letter from Colonel Van Irion, Washington County delegate:

Excuse me for interrupting you for a moment, and for this imposition upon your patience. . . . the intentions of the Convention . . . [are] to destroy and abolish the present existing Government, and to establish in its stead *one* of a provisional character. . . . Nothing definite as yet has been done. . . . They have been waiting your expected arrival . . . though whether you come or not, the attempt will be made. . . .

Major Crumpler added details. Rusk was in back of the movement, and a majority, with maybe six to spare, was committed to ousting the President from office. He lingered still at Barrington. Colonel D. E. Twiggs with his regiment of United States dragoons was daily expected at Washington from San Augustine on his way toward the Rio Grande. It was the President's duty to remain there to receive him. His Excellency served tea to the officers at Barrington on Saturday afternoon.

Monday morning came another note from Secretary Ochiltree:

We have been anxiously expecting you. . . . I find the opinion gaining ground, that on the passage of the Constitution by the Convention it will operate as a *supersedeas* of the present Government. . . . If you were now here, your presence would do much to allay the feeling which a few persons are most industriously endeavoring to get up. . . . men . . . from whom I little expected such a course. . . . I hope this scrawl will meet you on the road up.

The President's bags were already packed, and that day, with his private secretary, his Secretary of State, and the Treasurer of the Republic, he started for Austin. Of his Cabinet, only Cooke, Secretary of War and Marine, was left behind.

As he rode His Excellency pondered how men who would not listen to reason, who would not be governed by the canons of propriety, had bungled all the plans he had made. He had, with infinite finesse, obtained alternatives and presented them to Congress, in the hope that both would go before the convention. But these feverish Texans would not judge dispassionately the alternatives—or the man who had contrived them. They were rushing in such pell-mell haste that they might actually overshoot their objective. Like boys chasing a butterfly, they were about to "crush it in their imprudent and impatient grasp."

At Austin on August 16 he went directly to the room Colonel Thomas William Ward had been holding for him since the convention opened. As soon as Delegate Richard Bache heard he was in town he moved that a committee be sent to "consult with him concerning the transfer of the government, by the Convention, from an independent republic, to a Republican State Government." The long-discussed scheme was at last out in the open. Under the rules of the convention it could not be discussed until next day, but in every bar and lobby that evening men speculated on the date of the eviction of President Jones.

The convention hall was crowded at eight-thirty on August 16. A tall, one-armed man with a pugnacious nose and a shock of prematurely white hair had the floor. He was Francis Moore, Jr., M.D., veteran editor of the *Telegraph,* veteran legislator of the Republic, veteran annexationist, and inveterate opponent of every President Texas had ever had.

I know [he began] the object in view is to establish a Provisional Government to supplant the present. And I am unwilling thus to call upon the President immediately upon his arrival after a tedious journey, indisposed and fatigued as I believe he is.

I believe every motive of policy should induce the people to retain the present form of government and the nationality of Texas, until . . . we shall have the final assurance of merging our nationality with the great Union of North America. If we rashly and indiscreetly part with our existence as a nation . . . we throw off the treaty-making power and cut off all our treaties now established . . . placing ourselves at the beck and under the control of our enemies in the United States . . . we show ourselves so humble, so submissive, as to . . . crawl *sub jugo,* as a conquered country, into the American Union. . . . our revenue will be cut off; our nation instead of commanding the respect of other nations will merely excite their pity. If our enemies in the United States succeed . . . we shall have then to depend upon the treaty making power. If we retain our government and President, we can then immediately form a new treaty.

Bache explained lamely that he only wanted to show "the respect which I thought due from this body to the President . . . a matter of courtesy that the President should be consulted upon this subject. It has been in agitation some time." The Bache proposal was tabled, and on Isaac Van Zandt's motion Messrs. Hemphill and Hogg were appointed "a committee to wait upon His Excellency the President, and invite him to a seat with the President of the Convention."

He came and sat silently beside Rusk. There was not much that he and Rusk could converse about, and he was not invited to address the convention. "Visited the Convention," only that, he wrote in his diary that night.

General Morehouse was writing from Austin:

The enemies of the President are willing to sacrifice any and all, so as to reach the administration . . . they have 27 members that will vote right or otherwise against the administration. And there being such a number of anxious and meritorious expectants to be made Governor they *might* possibly forsake all party creed and religion to effect their object. In the streets Dr. Miller—Davis—Baylor—Henderson are spoken of as candidates. . . . If such a d——ble thing should take place. . . . The President's appearance at this time I am in hopes will put an end to this matter. But only God can tell how matters will go.

Two days later the convention declined to evict the President. On August 23, when General Cazneau made a final effort to oust the President, he could muster only sixteen votes.

Anson Jones retained his office, but the convention prescribed in detail his duty for the remainder of his tenure. He would submit the Constitution and ordinance of annexation to the people; after canvassing the returns he would notify the President of the United States of the results; he would proclaim an election for the third Monday in December to fill state offices, fix a date for the assembling of the Legislature, and finally he would deliver to the Governor all public records and properties. "From this time," the President wrote, "I had no further material control . . . my duties . . . became merely ministerial."

On August 28, President Rusk exhorted the delegates to do all they could

to make this constitution as acceptable to the people as possible, in order that it may appear . . . that the vile slanders . . . that we are a band of disorganizers, is false and foul.

I trust . . . the angry passions . . . will be hushed, that all sectional feelings and jealousies and the strife of personal ambition will cease and . . . [Texans will be] united as a band of brothers. . . .

When the convention adjourned that day President Jones, in his room at Colonel Ward's, dutifully proclaimed October 13 as the day on which citizens of the Republic would express their "opinions for and against annexation" and approve or reject the new Constitution. There could be no referendum on peace with Mexico.

The Convention adjourned on yesterday [Dr. Johnson wrote his wife] and most of them are gone. Genl Rusk is here on a big spree & has been for two days. I believe they made a pretty good constitution & did nothing very wrong. They left the Govt. as it is.

The President waited until the highways were clear of delegates, then rode slowly to Barrington. Things were going well there, if not at Austin. His new barn and stables were finished, six acres of his fine Cuban tobacco had been cut and yielded fine leaf, the corn was ready to gather, and his plantation office was ready for occupancy.

The election on October 13 was a halfhearted one, there being no vocal opposition either to annexation or the Constitution. Only about six thousand voters (half the number who voted in 1844) went to the polls, and only twenty of the thirty-six counties reported results. On November 10 President Jones proclaimed the Constitution adopted and set December 15 for the first state election. The *Texas National Register* pointed out that the Legislature would select two United States senators and urged the voters to

call upon every man who solicits their suffrage and know for whom he would cast his vote for senators. Instruct your representatives through the ballot box; designate the men of your choice. . . .

President Jones believed that a reaction in his favor had set in and that he might be chosen a United States senator. The *Northern Standard* had nominated him and the *Register* was joking about the suspicions against him. Ashbel Smith returned from his European mission in October and spent two days at Barrington. The *Register* reported:

A grave individual in this neighborhood of lively imagination shakes his head and wonders if they have divided the gold for which they bartered away Texas to Great Britain.

Hamilton Stuart of the Galveston *Civilian,* who had not always been a political friend, wrote the President:

. . . I . . . guess your views . . . simply by supposing how a sensible man would think and act under the circumstances. . . .
. . . As high as was the station you filled, I did not envy it at the time when the *denouement* approached—embarrassed and hurried as it was—of the delicate measures in which you had labored with so much caution and skill for the last three years. A clamorous pack have rushed in to devour the fruits of your labors, but an enlightened public opinion will yet do you justice, both in Texas and the United States.

General Houston, back home from the United States and ready to accept a senatorship, "arrived at Barrington dined & Staid the day," as did General Terrell, recently returned from London. After they had gone President Jones went to Austin for three weeks, to see that the government houses had been repaired and the departments were functioning. He had returned the government there in October and sent Mr. Campbell ahead to make the buildings weather-tight. A presidential salute greeted him as he rode into town. It was very pleasant.

At Austin and along the road men were asking him if he would represent Texas in the Senate. Other men were asking Allen, Terrell, and Ochiltree as they traveled about if Jones would serve. It was pretty certain that Houston would have one place. The other might go to Jones or to Rusk. Ochiltree wrote from Austin:

I left Rusk at Crockett in *one grand spree.* I have never seen him so perfectly outrageous; he seemed to have hydrophobia, and was snapping and snarling like any cur. Gen. Houston, yourself, and my humble self came in for no small . . . abuse. . . . If there be "truth in wine" he is most deadly hostile. . . .

From Nacogdoches Terrell wrote:

The people, many of them . . . are already becoming ashamed of the course they pursued toward the Government a few months ago. [And later from Houston] Old Sam is here. We had a long and confidential interview. . . . it is his opinion that Rusk will not suffer his name to be run when the crisis comes. . . . My opinion is that the old dragon would like for your name to be associated with his. I remarked that I believed a great many of the people were becoming sensible of the injustice that had been done you in the late excitement. . . . he heartily concurred, and expressed the belief that these things would eventually be of service rather than an injury to you.

Before Christmas the President's drooping spirits were rising. He wrote on December 20 to Jesse Grimes, who had asked if he would be a candidate: "I place myself at the disposition of those with whom I have heretofore acted & shall most cheerfully abide their determination."

To Moses Johnson, manager of his presidential campaign, he wrote more fully:

There is one respect in which I could be of more service to Texas in the Senate than any other person. The verbal promises made by Mr. Polk of what the U. S. would do for this country in the event of annexation were made to *me only* by Gov. Yell who was sent here for that express purpose. It is of *infinite importance* to this country that those pledges should be fulfilled. I alone know of them, & if I should be at the City of Washington, there could be no *misunderstanding* . . . & no backing out. . . . The Boundary question is one in this category—— The improvement of our bays & harbors & the expenditure of moneys for the protection of our coast, building fortifications &c &c is another.

Four days later he added:

I believe there is no quarrel between me & Houston, if there be I do not know of it, *certes* there is no cause. . . . My conduct must certainly have insured his entire approbation & (however vain it may be considered in me) of every honest & intelligent man whose preju-

dices have not usurped the place of his reason. He has declared
himself unequivocally. . . . Certainly "the great Chief does not
speak to his *red* (headed) child with a forked tongue." Western
brings a *rumor* that Noesy [Pilsbury] will be a candidate for the
Senate—— I rather think it is for the House of Reps & if he should
be elected it ought to be called the House of *Rips*.

Pilsbury put him in mind of the recent Congress, and that reminded him of General McLeod, who started the movement to
depose him from the presidency. "Sat Night Dec. 27th & 28th,"
he wrote in his diary, "Had a very queer dream about H.
McL——d ship towns rivers cedar plains Law Books, &c
&c &c apparently lasting two days."

From the Treasurer's office in Austin, Moses Johnson wrote
the President on New Year's eve:

. . . I am certain . . . that with the aid of all of your cabinet &
those who of right ought to aid you, you can succeed without doubt.
. . . Col. Cooke . . . thinks you are sure of the Bexar & part if not
all of the Gonzales vote & . . . I have heard that the [Galveston]
Civilian will sustain you. . . . What a glorious political achievement
over the noisy pigmy politicians to have Genl. H & yourself succeed
& then your Cabinet all provided for by the favor of the President
of the U.S.
If they will all unite & use their utmost exertions I believe success
is as certain as if the Almighty had decreed it, but without such
united effort we are all half whipped for the success of Genl. H. is
but half a victory. . . .

That New Year's Eve the President recorded a hope that was
non-political.

I trust truth will ultimately prevail & posterity judge me correctly.
. . . I had a difficult task to perform to secure success to this great
measure by exciting the rivalry and jealousy of the three greatest
powers in the world & at the same time so to act as to affect my
object and to maintain the perfect good faith of Texas towards all
these powers. The people were & are impatient, they have been so
ground down by years of adversity, poverty & war, & they look to but
one object, escape from the manifold evils of the past. . . . The cry
has been & is Annexation at once at any price & at any Sacrifice. But
I have been unwilling to break the national faith, in order to gratify

this unfortunate impatience. Like *"Curtius"* I have had no alternative but to leap into the Gulf. . . .

The first Governor would be J. Pinckney Henderson, chosen in December by a seven-to-one majority over Dr. J. B. Miller. Less than ten thousand votes were cast—a fourth less than in the last presidential election. The President had only one remaining ministerial act to perform: to proclaim the date for convening the first Legislature as soon as he received official news that the Congress of the United States had admitted Texas into the Union.

On January 7 he "started for Houston & Galveston with 20 bales Tobacco" from his experimental field at Barrington and two days later "arrived at Houston, put up at the Old Capitol." There in the Old Capitol

Tuesd. Morning (13th) at day light Capt. Tod bearer of dispatches arrived at Houston and delivered to me the letter of Mr. Polk and the official copy of the act admitting Texas into the Union   Capt. Chas Elliot arrived at the same time. Issued my Proclamation [convening the Legislature on February 16] & started expresses to Eastern & Northern Texas. In the afternoon started on board Steam Boat in company with Capt⁸ Tod & Elliot for Galveston.

Captain Elliot was making his final communication to the head of the nation to which he had been accredited. He assured President Jones of his "perfect satisfaction" with the manner in which he had fulfilled all promises and that M. de Saligny also was satisfied; but "uttered the bitterest complaints against Gen. Sam. Houston." To Lord Aberdeen the British Chargé wrote:

General Houston ever since I have known him, has always been more emphatic in the expression of his determined opposition against Annexation than the present President, and more sanguine in his avowed belief that the people of this Country would never sacrifice their independence if it's acknowledgment could be secured from Mexico. Speaking of Mr. Jones I believe that he went as far as he could, to secure a wiser and more honorable turn than affairs had taken. . . . If General Houston has said some of the things which have been imputed to him . . . respecting his public transactions ["coquetting"] with Great Britain and France, I am concerned for him, and . . . there has been no public and direct refutation of reports. . . .

From farewells with Captain Elliot, the President turned to conferences with Colonel Daingerfield, just returned from his mission to Europe. One by one all his foreign agents had come back home on the eve of the extinction of the Republic. Daingerfield was the last to return—and the only one to bring the archives of his legation with him. The President ordered the collector of customs at Galveston to continue his work until February 16, then with Colonel Daingerfield started to Barrington to rest a few days before ending his administration decently and in order.

There he found a letter from Governor-elect Henderson, declining to appoint General Terrell to the Supreme Court. That, Jones noted on it, "closed our correspondence." A few days later W. D. Miller showed him a letter from the Governor-elect: "Should Rusk not be a candidate," he said, "I would like to see the President elected but I really think there will be no probability. . . . I should not and shall not interfere. . . ."

On February 1 the President, Colonel Daingerfield, and Secretary of State Allen entered the capital; again Major Beall, U.S.A., fired a presidential salute—the last one Anson Jones would ever receive. He wanted to be much alone the next few days, more alone than he could be at a hotel. He had a bed placed in the executive office and took his meals at Colonel Ward's.

My dear [he wrote Mary the day the Legislature convened] Gen. Rusk is a candidate . . . he will be elected. . . . I feel no regret at this result, & know you will not. . . . Gen. Burleson was chosen President pro tem. of the Senate. . . .

Please present my kindest regards to Mrs. Allen. Tell her the Colonel is very well but extremely busy. Both of us behave like *Gentlemen* & keep our words *pretty well,* not all together teetotallers but duly temperate in all things. . . .

The weather is fine & people appear in good humor with themselves and each other. Candidates are busy all over town. . . . There will be many a long face in a few days.

He was not much interrupted as he wrote out his valedictory. Everybody wanted to see the Governor, not the man who was on his way out. As he watched from his window the preparations about the capitol—building a platform beside the door of Representative Hall, decorating the homely façade of the old building with flags, erecting a new flagpole beside the old one that, since 1839, had flown the flag of his Republic—then looked toward President Hill and saw cannon mounted there, the drama of the occasion came poignantly over him.

He tore into shreds the address he had prepared, "rather a so so affair," unworthy of the occasion and of him, and with that gift of language that came to him occasionally in moments of great significance he wrote another valedictory which so accurately captured what he felt that he did not need to refer to his manuscript as he delivered it.

At noon on February 19, Their Excellencies, the President and the Governor-elect, attended by joint committees of the two houses and marshaled by the United States Army officers, took their places on the flag-draped platform. Behind them on the gallery were the legislators, before them a "goodly number" of citizens—"about half the number that attended the Inauguration last winter."

"After being introduced, seated &c., a prayer, rich with fervor of the Christian patriot, was made by the Hon. R. E. B. Baylor. The President then arose," advanced to the lectern, and spoke:

The great measure of annexation, so earnestly desired by the people of Texas, is happily consummated. The present occasion . . . [is] the most extraordinary in the annals of the world, and one which marks a bright triumph in the history of republican institutions. . . .

I, as President of the Republic, with my officers, am now present to surrender into the hands of those whom the people have chosen, the power and the authority which we have some time held. This surrender is made with the most perfect cheerfulness. . . . I lay down the honors and the cares of the Presidency with infinitely more of personal gratification than I assumed them. . . . Whatever injustice may have been done me in moments of excitement . . . the public mind will settle down into proper conclusions . . . my fellow-citizens will then judge me rightly. At least, I have the approbation of my own conscience—a reward in itself above all price, and repose upon the assured belief that history and posterity will do me no wrong. . . .

The lone star of Texas, which ten years since arose amid clouds over fields of carnage, and obscurely shone for a while, has culminated, and, following an inscrutable destiny, has passed on and become fixed forever in that glorious constellation which all freemen and lovers of freedom in the world must reverence and adore—the American Union. . . . Blending its rays with its sister stars long may it continue to shine, and may a gracious Heaven smile upon this consummation of the wishes of the two Republics, now joined together in one. "May the Union be perpetual, and may it be the means of conferring benefits and blessings upon the people of all the States," is my ardent prayer.

The final act in this great drama is now performed. The Republic of Texas is no more.

In the silence that followed his peroration the President stepped forward to lower, with his own hands, the banner of his Republic. The weather-beaten pole broke in two as the flag came down for the last time.

Then the brass cannon on President Hill boomed a salute to the newest American state. The United States flag ascended its new flagstaff, and the crowd cheered as it faced toward the future—all but the man who until that moment was President of the Republic. As Governor Henderson delivered his brief, businesslike address, Anson Jones sat with his eyes fixed on the broken flagpole.

XXXV

MISSION ACCOMPLISHED

ANSON JONES, cotton and tobacco grower, sat in his plantation office four miles from Washington-on-the-Brazos on a December morning in 1856, rereading a letter that took his mind back over eleven drab years.

His Barrington plantation where he had spent those years was small—only three hundred acres, worked by five slaves and several hired hands—but it was a model of neatness and efficiency. The doctor's seeds were scientifically bred; his fields were picked over three times each season; his cotton brought a premium in Galveston and a larger premium in New York, where he occasionally marketed it. His corn and tobacco—with which he began experimenting more than a decade ago—were good, too, and even the thrifty Germans who were moving into the county had no better vegetables, fruits, flowers, and shrubs.

Barrington was his. He had created it; it was his demesne. He took pride in what he had wrought there in a decade, and his thrifty nature approved the balance sheet of his plantation account books. He was as successful a planter as, in the days of his poverty, he had dreamed of becoming. Barrington was not an Orozimbo or an Eagle Island, but it was his. Here his children were growing up, sturdy healthy children, and better read than the neighbors'. The doctor had seen to that. One room of the house was the schoolroom, where the doctor's sister Mary, who had kept his house in Brazoria, heard their lessons every day; and they had access to his office in the yard, which held nearly a thousand books.

Samuel, born during the senatorship, was fifteen now, a strong, alert lad interested in scientific things, already capable of managing the plantation. Charles, born on election day while Jones was Secretary of State and named for the British Chargé, was a student; had had a term at St. Paul's College. Sarah—"Sissy"—

child of the presidency, was her mother over again: quiet, capable, responsible. Then there was Anson—not Anson Junior, but Cromwell Anson, named in honor of the doctor's most notable ancestor. Anson had been born at Barrington. He was the lively one, seven years old now, full of mischief and curiosity and boundless energy. Barrington was theirs too. He and Mary had created it for them.

To own a comfortable plantation house where he could dispense Southern hospitality once had seemed to him an ultimate; now that he had it, it gave him little pleasure. His friends of other days lived in distant parts of this bustling state and seldom visited somnolent Washington—which was not on the way to anywhere else.

All around him were planters and farmers doing almost as well as he—immigrants from Germany or the States, who never aspired to be gentlemen and were interested only in raising cotton and corn. When they came to dinner or sat on the veranda the doctor found them mentally and spiritually earthy. They had not helped create this Texas that was making them prosperous; they were not even interested in hearing how it had been done. They respected the doctor as a farmer; they were glad to have him as neighbor when there was sickness. But none of the things they found in him to admire were the things he wanted to be admired for. They did not understand him, would never understand him.

There was, in truth, little human companionship for him in the neighborhood, or in all Texas. For a decade he had been withdrawing into his home—and into himself. He attended to daily chores, then retired to his office in the yard to read, to remember, to think.

Around the walls were his books—medical books, scientific books, history, philosophy; mostly English, some French, a few Latin, one or two in Greek. It was the sort of library a country gentleman should have, but he had not assembled it merely to decorate his walls. He read to escape the tedium of an uneventful life—and to escape recollections that recurrently tormented him.

In the corner by his desk were great cabinets of his correspondence; on the shelf above, his diaries and memorandum books. During the last ten years he had reread many times every letter in that file; studied in the light of what he now knew the endorsement he had written when the letter was received, and added notes. Those letters contained the true history of Texas. It was his duty to share it with others. Methodically, painfully, he had forced himself to copy the material in duplicate; he had been "impelled, yet dreaded" to do it; six hundred manuscript pages he laboriously copied out, then said "with entire and perfect confidence, 'The *Past,* at least is secure.' " That was four years ago. The bulky bundles were there; he had completed his part of the work. Someday he would publish that record, but not yet. He had toyed with taking it to New York and Philadelphia to be printed, but always decided to wait. There was no hurry about it. It would be done at the proper time, perhaps by someone else.

The next shelf contained the manuscript volumes of his genealogy that, seven years ago, had seemed important. Months of research in New England established the fact that his people had been in America since 1660 and that he was a descendant of the Cromwells. Filed with the genealogical charts was a deed to two acres of barren Massachusetts soil, sentimentally more precious than the forty-four square miles of Texas he owned—because there his people had lived when America was young.

The silver top of his humidor bore the Cromwell arms, as did all the plate and flat silver of the Barrington establishment. He could not eat a bite without recalling that he was a Cromwell; that his people had created the British Commonwealth, had helped found America; and that in that tradition he had done his part to create this new corner of the Anglo-American world. He knew that, even if other men had forgotten.

Other papers in the file recorded him a founder of St. Paul's parish at Washington, heaviest contributor to the fund to build the church the bishop said was the handsomest in Texas. Bishop Freeman had confirmed Mrs. Jones and baptized the children on his first episcopal visitation while he was a house guest at Barrington. The doctor was a warden of St. Paul's but not a communicant. He respected religion and read his Bible, but he found little solace in it. For a time church and chores connected with it had filled the void in his life that fraternal activity once filled.

He had been a trustee of St. Paul's College at Anderson—the town named for Kenneth L. Anderson, his Vice-President, who died there in 1845. He had contributed heavily to that college, helped draft its charter, had sent his sons there. He had even made an appeal for its support at the Triennial Convention of the church in New York, but support did not come. He had allied himself with a small and unpopular sect that the unecclesiastical Texans confused with the Catholics. The college withered and died. It was regrettable—but the doctor had seen so many things he was connected with wither and die. . . .

The stream of Texan politics had flowed on without him for a decade. In February 1844 he had told his friends that if he should accept any office after annexation it would be United States senator, "but," he sagely added, "it is too soon to 'count chickens' . . . the eggs may all be addled." When Jesse Grimes and other friends suggested him for the Senate in 1846 he was willing, but widespread misunderstanding of his role in annexation had addled the eggs. The first state Legislature declined even to give him a vote of thanks for services as President and sent Houston and Rusk to Washington. Houston's election, he then thought, was attributable to his masterful ambiguity on annexation; Rusk's, to his inexplicable personal popularity.

Maybe each would be satisfied with a single term—maybe he would succeed one of them when the Texans understood as clearly as he did that Anson Jones was the Architect of Annexation. Miller, Houston's secretary, wrote him confidentially in 1847 that if the general should decide not to return to the Senate he and Rusk wanted the doctor to take his place. Jones had taken that for what it was worth; neither he nor Houston, nor anybody else, believed Houston would decline re-election—and his term had twelve months to run. He tried hard not to count chickens, but Miller's hint lifted the senatorship from the subconscious to the conscious. Was any Texan better fitted for the senatorship? Did any know so much about verbal commitments as yet unfilled in connection with annexation? And on the basis of past services to Texas, did any man better deserve the honor? Jones could think of no one.

As he was beginning to meditate on these things the war of the ex-presidents began in the United States and spilled over into Texas. John C. Calhoun began it when he asserted that he was Architect and Chief Engineer of Annexation. John Tyler claimed that role for himself. Houston claimed it for Andrew Jackson, suggested that Houston, too, had played a major role in the business, and asked Jones to set the record straight. The doctor had little else to do. "I have enlisted for the 'duration of the War' & shall . . . not solicit a discharge," he wrote Ashbel Smith.

In his library at Barrington he relived the whole struggle for annexation, refreshing his memory from his files and his diary, finding in the documents things he had not before noticed, filling in the gaps with recollections already a little warped. Before the end of 1847 he completed his *History of Annexation,* which appeared serially in the Galveston *Civilian,* then in pamphlet form. Houston had asked him to write, but he was not prepared for what he wrote. He demonstrated that neither Calhoun, nor Tyler, nor Jackson, nor Houston was the indispensable man in annexation. Jones was the man.

As he thought back over their long and close connection it became clear to him that Houston was a villain, had always been a villain. He had been the enemy of Stephen F. Austin. He had mismanaged the San Jacinto campaign; he had not wanted to fight, and during the battle was incapacitated by an overdose of opium either to command or to understand what was going on. His first administration was a failure—except for Jones's skillful diplomacy. He had helped wreck Lamar's administration for no higher motive than to demonstrate that only Old Sam could govern Texas. His second administration had been a fairly good one—but Jones, not Houston, had made it that.

And how had Houston rewarded him? He had tried to get him out of the race for the presidency; failing that, he had tried secretly to defeat him and elect Burleson; then, when Jones refused to be pushed aside, Houston had tried to ruin his administration. And now Houston was appropriating to himself credit for all Jones's achievements. There was nothing, absolutely nothing, in Houston's career that Jones could approve.

With the monomania of a depressed and isolated man, he evolved a straw man who lacked the virtues of Sam Houston but had all his vices plus a good many Jones invented for him. This caricature of Houston was senator from Texas, determined, apparently forever, to misrepresent Texas at Washington. The shadow of Houston had always fallen between Jones and everything he wanted. In the past he had ignored that shadow and pressed on toward what he wanted; he might do that again. Houston was untrue to Jones, untrue to Texas, untrue to the whole South.

When Houston voted to exclude slavery from the Oregon Territory, Jones published Houston's order to accept the Diplomatick Act—the "Vermilion Edict" that would have made annexation forever impossible if Jones had not been resolute enough to disobey it. Houston "regretted" that a former assistant should try to "inculpate" him or claim merit for disobedience and promised at a later time to attend to A. Jones.

The doctor called his son Sam Houston Jones to him and informed him that henceforth his name was Samuel Edward Jones and made note of it in his diary. No descendant of Cromwell would bear the name of that "traitor."

For four years the doctor thought of little but Sam Houston and his villainies. He ignored passing events to fill his diary with the record of Houston's perfidy and faithlessness. In 1849 neighbors asked him to run against old Timothy (Ayes and Noes) Pilsbury for Congress. Pilsbury, too, was a rascal, but an insignificant one. He declined. Only a great crisis could call him from his plantation; and when he went to Washington it would be to the Senate.

One day in 1849 they carried him unconscious into the house, his left arm limp and purple. His horse had thrown him. He recovered, but the arm did not, and none of the books in his library told him what to do for it. That arm was useless and a constant source of pain, but the injury lifted him temporarily out of the past. No Texas physician could suggest a cure. He went to Philadelphia and New York. Dr. McClellan was dead, but maybe his friend Dr. Wiltbank, or his old college mate Gross, greatest surgeon of the period, could help him. Orthodox medical science gave him no relief: cold-water cure, electricity, iodine colchicum, a new variety of German leeches—everything was tried but amputation. He had gloves, which he was never to appear in public again without, made to conceal his withered and discolored hand, but he found nothing to assuage the pain.

Preoccupation with his insoluble medical problem diverted his mind from the past, even from contemporary politics, and he began while in the States to evolve large industrial plans. For a time he could even joke about his senatorial aspirations. When he heard that Rusk was "dangerously ill" he pronounced him only dangerously drunk and playfully wrote Mary: "If he dies, please have me appointed to the Senate." Senator Houston left his card at the doctor's Philadelphia hotel; when the doctor visited Washington he left cards for both the Texas senators.

He was in the States when the Compromise of 1850 was agreed upon—"everything for the North & Nothing for the South," with Houston, of course, voting for every item. It was thoroughly bad, but it gave Texas ten million dollars to pay off claims against the late Republic. When he returned home he asked for $1,000 for property lost in 1836, $8,978.06 salary as President from the date of annexation to the end of the three years for which he had been elected, $3,600 additional pay as Minister in 1838–39. He had not pressed these claims while Texas was poor; now she had money and he wanted his part of it. The Legislature thought otherwise.

A statesman in retirement could not keep his name out of the papers. The Philadelphia *Herald* in 1851 suggested ex-President Jones for the vice-presidency of the United States next year, and other papers reprinted the story. It was very pleasant, however improbable. Houston was angling for the presidency, and if Jones were taken up as Vice-President it would "take the wind out of" the Houston boom. That gave him some satisfaction.

After the elections of 1852, which called neither Jones from his plantation nor Houston to the White House (but did not involve Old Sam Jacinto's seat in the Senate), the doctor slipped back into the old groove of retrospection for a couple of years; for a time the misrepresentations of Polk and Tyler and Donelson and others placed Houston in a secondary role in his thoughts. When he had set that record straight he faced about to the present.

In 1853 he invented a "gravito-magnetic" device about which for a time he was as enthusiastic as his old preceptor Hull had ever been about his truss. He planned to perfect it at Franklin Institute, interest Samuel F. B. Morse in it, and maybe go to Europe to market it. And he had a dozen other irons in the fire— steamship lines, railroads, mining, manufacturing, trading. His concentration on large economic schemes, a renewed interest in the Odd Fellows, his election as delegate to the Triennial Convention of the Episcopal Church almost rejuvenated him. How could he have spent so much time reliving the past when there were so many things to do in the present?

He sailed from Galveston in August 1853 aboard the *Persever-ance,* went by way of Mobile, Montgomery, and Charleston to Baltimore, where he visited with the Grand Sire of the Odd Fellows. In Philadelphia he "attended Theatre to witness the performance of the 'Lone Star or Texian Bravo.' " After visiting relatives and capitalists in New York and buying a summer place sixteen miles from the city, he returned to Philadelphia to sit once more among the Odd Fellows in the Grand Lodge of the United States.

How much like his old self he was beginning to feel—attending Grand Lodge, visiting his alma mater and medical colleagues, sitting for portraits. He saw Mme. Anna Thillon in the *Bohemian Girl,* met Mr. Barnum, and heard Ole Bull and Adelina Patti, then was off to New York for church and railroad business, more concerts and plays. He "prepared Bye laws & regulations" for the stockholders' of Atlantic & Pacific Rail Road, paid a thousand-dollar assessment on his stock, and returned to Texas by way of the Ohio and Mississippi.

On December 4 he was back in Galveston to organize the Grand Encampment of Texas I.O.O.F. and install its officers. Regrettably the $384.50 regalia he had bought in Philadelphia had not arrived, and the affair lacked pomp and majesty. Then he boarded the *Eclipse* for Houston. The skies were overcast and the roads muddy as he jogged toward Barrington. He knew he was back in Texas.

His slave boy Willis drove him to Austin to lobby for his enterprises. For almost a year the railroad business was hopeful enough to buoy his already sagging spirits; the others failed more promptly. His strange bedfellows in the Atlantic & Pacific venture included Robert J. Walker, Mr. Polk's Secretary of the Treasury, and Thomas Jefferson Green of Texas Rail Road, Navigation, and Banking memory.

Corporate finance was strange to him—and more disreputable

than politics. Before the end of 1854 he "lost all confidence" in his associates, resigned from the board of directors, and charged his expenses and investments to experience.

As his hopes of an industrial fortune withered and died his withered arm became increasingly troublesome. Morphine no longer dulled the pain that periodically racked it. He was a physically broken man, increasingly aware of his infirmities and of the needs of his growing family. He renounced business, as he had already renounced politics. He thought for a time of moving to Galveston but decided against it. He would henceforth make Barrington his world. It would give him security if not affluence.

But it was no use for him to forswear politics. He had been too long accustomed to meditate upon it to give it up, and the very leisure farming gave him made it inevitable that he should ponder it more and more—but for variety he turned to new issues. When the Kansas-Nebraska Act was passed by Congress early in 1854, Senator Houston lined up with the Yankees. Jones, for the moment, held his peace, but privately he marked it down as another evidence of Houston's treachery.

Later that year the Know-Nothing party entered Texas. It was, Jones thought objectively, an anti-foreign, anti-Catholic, un-American movement—and Sam Houston had joined it. Jones might have interrupted his leisure to combat it in any event, but with Houston connected with it, it became his solemn duty. In June 1855 a state convention of the new party met secretly at Washington-on-the-Brazos under the chairmanship of Judge R. E. B. Baylor and nominated gubernatorial and congressional candidates. That was getting too close to home. The doctor promptly sent the *Ranger,* the local newspaper, the first of "upwards of fifty" articles against this new menace to American principles. "For more than a year and a half," he recalled, "I 'slept in armor,' and did not lay down my arms until treason to the Union and the Constitution was prostrated in the dust."

Houston declared that George Washington and Andrew Jackson, if living, would join the new party, as Houston himself was doing. Jones knew not what those departed worthies would have done and was not surprised at what Houston was doing; but he knew what Jones would do.

He had not been among the "distinguished Democrats" who

addressed in person the gathering at Austin in November to celebrate the defeat of Know-Nothingism in the state elections, but
his blessing was read at the meeting. He continued to grind out
newspaper articles, and on July 29 of the following year he spoke
more than two hours to his fellow citizens in mass meeting at
Washington, reviewing the whole sorry plight of the Union. Ostensibly he was talking in support of the national Democratic
ticket and against "the most active and unscrupulous party ever
organized . . . led on too by men hitherto the most influential";
actually he was pointing out Sam Houston's contribution to national confusion, although he never spoke his name.

I came here to-day [he concluded] as I went to Columbia in 1835,
to take counsel with my fellow-citizens in the impending crisis of our
national affairs. My voice, I know, must soon be hushed in the grave,
towards which we are all hastening; but feeble as it is, I have felt
it incumbent on me to raise it once more, and perhaps for the last
time, in behalf of Texas. . . . I shall sleep quietly to-night. . . .

He slept well that night and succeeding nights. The old thrill
of telling a friendly audience of voters what it wanted to hear
was tonic to him. The crisis to call him from retirement was here.
The more he thought of Houston, the oftener he saw his own
name in the papers; every time he remembered his ovation at
that Washington mass meeting, the clearer it seemed to him that
he must go to the Senate.

On that crisp December morning in 1856 he held in his
withered, gloved hand a letter that invested with hope all the
vague yearnings of the drab, frustrated years. He read it through
again, as he had many times in the two weeks since it came. It
was from W. B. Stout of Clarksville. He wanted to know if the
doctor would be good enough to suffer his name to go before the
Legislature for the senatorship.

With elastic step and shoulders squared he strode across the
room to sharpen a new quill and open a fresh quire of paper.
Composition never came so easy as it did that morning. His pen
moved swiftly, surely, across the sheets, as if transcribing passages indelibly fixed in his memory. When his pen at last stopped
he read what it had written: a thirty-five-hundred-word essay
which distilled the solitary ruminations of a decade.

The Texans, he wrote Stout, would not, could not, return to the Senate the man who had deliberately and completely

betrayed, in quick succession, his own State . . . the Southern people . . . the principles of the Democracy. . . .

You and I, my dear sir, have a right to speak plainly . . . we have, both of us . . . fought his battles . . . and received not a few wounds in his defense. It was my fortune to co-operate with him longer and more closely than . . . any other man. . . . My own deliberate conviction is . . . he has been a . . . curse to the country, and brought upon it very many more and greater evils than benefits. . . . The South . . . must rid herself of her traitors . . . demagogues.

I should distrust my own abilities . . . [but] if . . . I should be selected for so distinguished position, I should accept it with feelings of pride and gratitude, and discharge its duties . . . with an eye single to the best interests of Texas and the Union. . . . I have made it an invariable rule *never* to seek office, or to decline it when there appeared to me a necessity for my accepting public trust. In 1846 . . . I retired to my farm with the expectation of remaining there the remainder of my life. Recent events "like a fire-bell in the night alarmed me" . . . circumstances . . . no longer permit me to decline a call of my fellow-citizens to serve them, should such a call be made upon me. . . .

He made a copy of the letter, then rode into town to mail it. His air was that of a man of affairs concerned with important business—but not too preoccupied to chat with the postmaster and storekeepers and the farmers around the square. The atmosphere was crisp and stimulating, and the universe was friendly. How could he have ever doubted that life had purpose, or that justice must triumph? He began training his boys to manage the plantation and showed Charles how to find things in his files. He might soon be spending much of his time away from Barrington.

During the hot months of 1857 Senator Houston was riding from county seat to county seat, asking Texans to elect him Governor. When he came to Washington County he was not a guest at Barrington, nor did the doctor hear his speech. Houston had no chance against the Democratic organization that battled for Hardin R. Runnels—and a state Legislature pledged to retire the Old Hero to private life. That defeat—the only one Houston ever received at the polls—meant he was no longer a contender for the senatorship. Before election day Thomas J. Rusk died, a suicide. The new Legislature would send two new Texas senators to Washington.

Jones did not travel among the people or write to legislators. He was technically not even a candidate; he said to everybody who inquired that he never sought office, but he would accept if the people called him. He had letters from associates of the forties, which he answered promptly with copies of his letter to Judge Stout. On rainy days he read and reread the letters on which his hope fed. Cousin Oliver Jones was working for him in Austin County, and Judge Stout in northern Texas. Ashbel Smith no doubt was doing the same at Houston and Galveston and Uncle Jesse Grimes in middle Texas—neither had written, but surely he could count on them.

The *Texas Ranger* at Washington published everything he gave the editor; he wrote not of the senatorship, but upon the issues of the day and phases of Texas history that newcomers to the state should be apprised of. Every week or two that journal had a pro-Jones editorial which was copied in other papers.

On August 29 the doctor read with satisfaction the *Ranger's* magnificent two-column review of his career. For senator, the *Ranger* had a

preference, for a gentleman, who, although no office hunter, and notwithstanding his worth and qualifications cannot be excelled, has been shamefully overlooked by the press, and for no other reason, as we conceive, but for his commendable modesty. That man is the Hon. ANSON JONES, and we here give some of the many reasons which actuate us in the selection we have made from a number of worthy and well-qualified gentlemen who have been named by their friends in connection with the office.

Jones had been a Texan twenty-four years, the article continued; he had been a leader of the independence struggle, an outstanding congressman, ablest diplomat at Washington (so Calhoun said) in 1838–39, senator and *de facto* Vice-President of the Republic during part of Lamar's administration, Secretary of State, and, for the last two years of the Houston regime, *de facto* President. Twenty-one numbered paragraphs enumerated the achievements of his brief presidency. "Another has claimed the credit of them (as is his wont), but they belong to Anson Jones, and to him alone," the *Ranger* declared.

And what has been his reward?
Rudely thrust aside in 1846, when he had . . . saved the country. . . . Traduced and wounded, he retired to private life, where he has quietly remained ever since.

It is due to Anson Jones to send him to the Senate—due to his talents, to his faithfulness, to his services. . . . If his claims are ignored by our Legislature . . . the stain of ingratitude will be fixed, deep and indelible, upon the fair escutcheon of our gallant and proud young State, which "all great Ocean's water" can never wash out.

That, the doctor thought, stated the case comprehensively and presented his claims. The *Ranger* was not quite accurate in saying that the Texan press had overlooked him. The *Telegraph*, although it was supporting E. M. Pease for senator, very decently conceded that

if the choice of the Legislature should fall upon the Ex-President, our State will have in him a representative in the Senate chamber who will reflect great credit upon its choice, who will well represent her interests, and always defend her cause.

And wasn't the *Item* at Huntsville, Houston's home town, supporting him? He particularly liked its editorial on the ingratitude of republics:

What will become of the saying that "Republics are ungrateful," if an ex-President and an ex-Governor are sent from Texas to the United States Senate? Already an ex-President has been there, and an ex-Chief Justice; should Anson Jones and J. Pinckney Henderson be chosen by the next Legislature, what a grand position will Texas occupy before the world! . . . We should not be at all surprised if both were chosen.

The Galveston *Civilian* opposed him, of course, as it always had; and DeMorse's *Northern Standard* admitted no pro-Jones articles to its columns. That was all right. Newspaper scribblers did not determine elections. Hadn't most Texas papers supported Burleson in 1844? It seemed to the doctor that nothing more needed to be done. It was generally known that he was willing to re-enter the service of Texas, and his special claims had been

well stated in a few papers. Texan legislators—except members
of that first Legislature who declined to thank him—were not
fools. They surely, in this crisis, would be guided by "considerations of public interest," and, other things being equal, they
would do the honorable thing by an old, faithful, too-long-neg-
lected public servant.

The doctor arrived at Austin by stagecoach on Sunday, October 25, a full week before the new Legislature convened. He settled himself in a comfortable room with a fireplace in the Smith
Hotel. There were newer inns, but Smith's was the old Bullock
House, and he felt at home there. He and it belonged to the same
epoch.

He looked about town (mentioning casually that he would be
there a week or two) and made a few courtesy calls before legislators and lobbyists congested the place. First, of course, the ex-
President paid his respects to the present chief executive of Texas,
E. M. Pease, who had been his lawyer two decades ago.

That amenity done, the doctor strolled along streets whose
names were familiar but from which the landmarks had been removed. A brick-and-stone building with a smart cast-iron front
stood where his log-cabin office had been. The makeshift capitol
of the Republic and the flimsy President's house were gone. A
pretentious domed State House now crowned Seat of Empire
hill, and the governor occupied a commodious colonnaded mansion nearby. But the cottage he had built for Mary seventeen
years ago still stood, and the French Embassy, and a few other
familiar houses. They recalled faces and incidents of the era
when he played a purposeful part in affairs—as he was about to
do again.

Tuesday he took time to report to Mary:

As yet there is no crowd—but one member has arrived—Mr
Everett. The Supreme Court is in session, but this does not bring
many here. . . . In the course of the week, however, the town will
be full of people. . . .

The question about U. S. Senator stands just as I told you I
thought it was, before leaving home—nothing further will be known
for a week or two, at least. . . .

I may be too busy to write again soon. . . . I can say nothing
definite, now, about the time of my returning home.

The busyness he anticipated was answering inquiries of legislators when they called to make certain he would not decline the
senatorship and to verify the soundness of his views. He had
copies of his articles and letters to show them that would answer
every question to their complete satisfaction—if too many of
them were not briefless young lawyers.

He invited none of them to his room, but the door was always
open. It was their duty to seek him out, not his to buttonhole
them like a candidate for precinct office. As he sat by his fire
waiting, waiting, he thought through all that had been done to
bring him to the eve of a new career, and he pronounced it good.
He had not volunteered; he had been asked if he would serve
Texas as her senator. He had waited two weeks to reply, with
dignity and restraint, that the crisis would not permit him to
decline. The legislators knew that from the newspapers; they also
knew, or could easily learn, where they could talk over national
problems with him.

General Henderson, Judge Hemphill, Judge Scurry, Colonel
Potter, Colonel Oldham, General Hamilton, Judge Franklin,
Governor Pease, and all the other hopefuls could electioneer and
pass around cigars if they thought it appropriate. Jones would let
the electors, like the office itself, seek the man. He sat alone in
his room, arranging and rearranging his clippings and papers
with suppressed excitement. It would be pleasant to have a few
visitors, but actually, he reasoned, men as well informed as legislators of Texas ought to be did not need to ask Anson Jones what
he had done for Texas or what his principles were. Maybe,
surely, that was the reason they did not call to see him.

The day before the voting the Austin *State Gazette* published
a very sensible communication from a citizen who "deemed it
not inappropriate" to suggest Anson Jones as the logical successor to Houston, and to point out that the general, "jealous of
Jones' intellect and business capacity . . . has publicly defamed
and slandered him . . . which, by-the-by, is one of the best evidences that we have of Jones' purity." That was the only move
made at the capital in his behalf.

The representatives of the people did not seek him out. Enter-
tainment was better elsewhere, and in other hotel rooms and in
chambers of the capitol the senatorship was decided. To the men

of that Legislature Dr. Jones was a puttery, puffy-faced old man with a withered arm, who belonged to another epoch.

On the afternoon of November 8 they quickly agreed J. Pinckney Henderson should succeed Rusk and began balloting on Houston's successor.

Gen. Henderson [the doctor thought] . . . is a statesman of some ability, and patriotic. But . . . objectionable to *me,* on account of his . . . views . . . and habits . . . which are those of a gamester and a sot.

For ten and a half hours—until one-thirty in the morning—the legislators balloted behind closed doors. Chief Justice John Hemphill was chosen to take Houston's place at Washington.

Anson Jones got not a single vote.

When someone thought to tell him he packed his bags and started, unnoticed, toward Barrington.

I only aimed to declare by my presence . . . that I was ready and willing to respond . . . to any questions the Representatives of the people . . . might deem proper to ask. . . .

My MISSION . . . was *accomplished;* the *duty* . . . fully *performed.* . . . I was not in the least disappointed.

Weary with physical and spiritual weariness that could never be assuaged, he moved in a sort of daze toward the place he had called home. That Legislature in a single day had invalidated everything he hoped for, everything he was, everything he had.

Now he was plodding back to face the matter-of-fact comments of those stolid German neighbors; to cope with Mary's brave, tearless assurances that it really didn't matter, that they really hadn't wanted to go to Washington; to be reminded in everything he heard, everything he saw, that he had failed.

He had failed before, but never in Texas; not in twenty-four years had he failed. His numbed brain recalled that when a man failed he always moved on, made a new start. That was it: move on, start over again; that was what he would do.

He would leave Barrington with all its chattels and slaves— and all its associations. He would move to Galveston—Galveston held no memories for him. He would practice medicine once more. His children could attend city schools. He and Mary would attend the theater and concerts and make new friends among recent settlers, to whom the Republic of Texas seemed as remote and as irrelevant as Greece and Rome.

After a quick sale of the plantation for a fourth less than its value, and a cheerless Christmas, Mary watched from the front door of Barrington as the doctor started through rain and muddy roads to the coast.

EPILOGUE

ON THE fifth day of January 1858 the bayou boat brought to the city of Houston a weary, prematurely aged passenger. At Galveston he announced that he would begin the practice of medicine, had rented a house, and deposited with his bankers a bulky manuscript upon which he had labored for almost a decade. "I merely mention this," he wrote his wife, "for your information, in case of any accident to myself."

As he shuffled off the boat the hustle and bustle of Houston jarred his taut nerves. Avoiding traffic as well as he could, he plodded first to the post office—where he extended a gloved hand for a single letter addressed in a familiar script—then to the corner of Main and Texas streets to enter the sprawling, porticoed building that stood there. It was the house he knew best in all Texas. In recent years it had become to him a sort of symbol.

Two decades earlier, when this city was only a promoter's dream and Texas and he were young, he had first crossed the threshold of that house when it was the capitol of the new Republic. There he served as congressman. There he was commissioned a diplomat. There he had convinced himself that "somehow or other the destiny of Texas was interwoven with my own." The building had undergone vicissitudes during subsequent years, as he himself had. Now it was a hotel, called, in token of its former grandeur, the Old Capitol. Thornton Thatcher had recently "leased and thoroughly repaired and renovated" the old wooden building and was promising "those who may favor him with their calls that no efforts shall be spared to make their stay agreeable." If he could rest a day or two in physical comfort there, perhaps the memories that tormented his tired brain would leave him. Then he might find courage to resume his journey—and to begin, in his sixtieth year, a new career.

Mr. Thatcher gave him the room he wanted, and he followed the host down a familiar hallway. At last alone in his room, he broke the seal of his letter and read what his wife had written from their plantation:

> I feel confident this little trip will be of service to you . . . being among more congenial spirits . . . will have a good affect at least I hope so. . . .
> Cromwell . . . said yesterday to me that it did not appear right to come in the room & not see Pa laying on the lounge. I often find myself thinking if not saying the same thing. . . . I trust we will soon be together again. . . .
> Blot out the past, forget you were ever engaged in the promotion of the best interests of Texas & above all, try to forget her ingratitude toward you—I pray god you will do this. . . .
> Do let me hear. . . . I feel so anxious. . . .

Blot out the past? Forget?

This city, this building, the very room in which he sat were peopled with ghosts—figures more real to him than the men he passed in the lobby. The Whartons, who persuaded him to become a Texan; his partner, Berryman; his cousin Ira; his confidant, Anderson, who had been his Vice-President—and a host of others whose faces he could not clearly see—these were the congenial spirits that surrounded him as he read. Dead, all of them; dead like the Republic of Texas.

After a while he roused himself to find a pen and write:

> DEAR MARY . . . for fear of accident or delay I write you today. . . . I may not reach Washington until Friday night—or even later. . . .

He posted the letter, then resumed his meditations. He was mentally living through a quarter century, remembering how once he had believed the star of Texas and his own star were indissolubly linked together. The destiny of Texas was now, and for twelve years had been, in the keeping of other men. His own star had waned. For a few days he had made himself say he could begin a new career as a physician, but in his heart he knew it could not be. He was old and tired and unspeakably weary.

In the miserable isolation of Barrington he wanted "to spend the remainder of his days in more social life." A week in Galveston and Houston convinced him that every person he met would open a new wound. Here was the *Telegraph* telling the world, "We are glad to see him looking none the worse because he had not as many friends in the legislature as he ought to have had on a recent occasion."

Twelve years ago this month he lodged in this very house. There he received official news that Texas had been admitted into the Union. There, with his own quill, he had convoked the first state Legislature.

That had been the culmination of annexation. He was the Architect of Annexation. In ways that only he now remembered, he had consummated that measure. It was not Houston, nor Rusk, nor Henderson, nor Hemphill; it was he. That first Legislature denied him even a paltry vote of thanks. The present one had ignored his very existence. Still, they said he looked none the worse. . . . What could a man do, where could he turn, to escape his enemies and avoid the commiseration of his friends?

Four days he brooded; then the gloom lifted. There were still things for him to do—if not for Texas, for his own little family. He would try again. He made a round of calls, and friends thought him cheerful and full of plans; but when he crossed the threshold of the Old Capitol that evening the pall settled upon him again.

In other years he had walked that corridor with Grayson and Collinsworth and Childress and Rusk—all dead now, and by their own hands.

To a friend who sat with him that night he said, "My public career . . . began in this house, and I have been thinking it might close here."

They found Anson Jones next morning with a bullet through his head.

Before the year ended, his widow sent a bulky manuscript to a New York publisher with this note:

As these pages will pass through the Press so, too, will . . . pain, pleasure, & regret, pass through my heart. . . . I give them just as they were left by him, without note or comment. In [them] . . . may traced the resignation of a heart too sensitive to battle success-fully with the bitter sorrows with which his eventful and varied life was strewed. Wounded, deeply wounded, yet amidst accumulated sorrows, forbearing, trustful and uncomplaining to the last. How far the merits of this Work may be perceived or appreciated becomes not me to judge.

I only deem it, my most sacred duty,—one I owe to his memory, to his orphan children,—to myself, and the *Truth of History*, to submit these Records to the Public. They must judge.

NOTES

(Page numbers are in roman type, line numbers in italic.)

1, *3.* Anson Jones, "Private Memoirs," *Memoranda and Official Correspondence Relating to the Republic of Texas*, p. 8 (hereafter cited as *Memoranda*). All quotations in this chapter from Jones are taken from *Memoranda* unless otherwise indicated.

10. A. A. Parker, *A Trip to the West and Texas*, p. 181; George W. Erath, *Memoirs*, p. 15.

16. Mary Austin Holley, *Texas* (1836), pp. 31–32; Eugene C. Barker (ed.), *Austin Papers*, II, 1109 (hereafter cited as *AP*).

29. Memoranda, p. 9.

I. THIRTEENTH CHILD

3, *8. Memoranda*, p. 1, gives this date and adds "another record says 1799."

16. Parke Godwin, *Biography of William Cullen Bryant*, I, 145–146.

30. Jones, MS Memorandum Book VII, p. 29, AJP.

4, *3.* Flatware engraved with the crest is in San Jacinto Museum of History and in Jones's plantation house, Barrington, in Washington State Park.

23. Memoranda, p. 3.

5, *4.* M. M. Bagg, *Pioneers of Utica*, p. 355.

6, *31.* Bagg, *Pioneers*, p. 355.

7, *32.* M. M. Bagg, *Founders of the Oneida County Medical Society*, pp. 8–10.

37. MS Minutes, Oneida County Medical Society, September 5, 1820. Statute on licensing of physicians is in *Laws of New York* (1806), Ch. 138.

9, *7.* Edith Stow Haworth to Mattie Austin Hatcher, May 4, 1927, typescript in Dallas Historical Society; for DeZeng see *Appleton's Cyclopaedia of American Biography*, II, 163. Jones mentions neither Stow nor Miss DeZeng but says DeZeng aided him financially after he left Bainbridge (*Memoranda*, p. 6).

31. Memoranda, pp. 5–6.

10, *4.* He "subsequently paid every dollar" (*Memoranda*, p. 6).

15. Memoranda, p. 6.

19. Completion of the Erie Canal, 1825, made New York the principal port.

30. Frederick P. Henry (ed.), *Standard History of the Medical Profession of Philadelphia*, p. 149.

11, *15.* Where and what Jones taught is not of record. Neither the *Annual Reports of the Controllers of the Public Schools* (1819–1832) nor any Philadelphia *Directory*, 1822–1824, lists him.

19. Lowry's MS Consular Letters, 1810–1827, contain no mention of Jones.

36. William Spence Robertson, *Rise of the Spanish American Republics as Told in the Lives of their Liberators*, Chs. ii, vii. David G. Burnet, ad interim President of Texas in 1836, as a youth joined the 1806 expedition of Miranda and "under his orders . . . the first gun was fired in behalf of Spanish American independence" (A. M. Hobby in *Texas Almanac, 1873*, p. 158).

12, *25.* William Duane, *A Visit to Colombia in the Years 1822 & 1823*, p. 79.

28. E. M. Lowry to Secretary of State, February 1, 1826, Consular Letters, LaGuayra, 1810–1827. Consul Lowry died January 24, 1826.

II. BROTHERLY LOVE IN PHILADELPHIA

13, *3. Desilver's Philadelphia Directory, 1828/1833.*

22. After the college moved from Canonsburg to Washington it was known as Washington and Jefferson College.

28. James W. Holland, *The Jefferson Medical College of Philadelphia from 1825 to 1908*, p. 1.

31. George M. Gould, *Jefferson Medical College, 1826–1904, a History*, I, 45.

14, *4.* J. T. Scharf and Thompson Westcott, *History of Philadelphia*, I, 546; H. M. Lippincott, *Early Philadelphia: Its People, Life, and Progress*, p. 120.

11. Holland, *Jefferson Medical College*, p. 2.

12. Samuel D. Gross, *Autobiography*, I, 27.

15, *17.* Gross, *Autobiography,* I, 27–29. Jones's only reference to his alma mater is: "In the winter of 1826–'7 I attended a full course of lectures in Jefferson Medical College, and in March, 1827, received the degree of Doctor of Medicine in that institution" *(Memoranda,* p. 7). Neither his diploma nor any letters regarding the college are in the Jones Papers.

   23. Gould, *History,* I, 45. His medical education cost Jones a total of $95.00: $5.00 for his 1820 license, $90.00 for his lectures and diploma.

   26. Records of the Dean's Office.

   29. Holland, *Jefferson Medical College,* p. 2.

16, *11.* *Centennial of Harmony Lodge (1892),* pp. 2–3.

18, *2.* *Journal of the Proceedings of the Right Worthy Grand Lodge,* pp. 62–135.

   5. Ibid.

   15. He resigned from Harmony Lodge in November, 1832 *(Centennial,* p. 4).

   16. A. G. Hull to Jones, October 13, 1832, Jones Papers. Hereafter cited as AJP.

III. NADIR

19, *1. Desilver's Philadelphia Directory* for 1831 and 1833 and *New Orleans Directory* for 1832 list Spear as a resident merchant.

   10. Memoranda, p. 7.

   12. Dr. John Wilbank of Philadelphia reminded Jones in 1833 of his "sacrificing as you did a lucrative practice in this agreeable city." He signs: "Your friend and servant as well as intended father in *law* if not in medicine." (Wilbank to Jones, September 24, 1833, AJP).

   17. Hull to Jones, October 13, 1832, AJP.

   29. New Orleans *Emporium,* November 9, 1832.

20, *3.* J. M. Mason, "Early Medical Education in the Far South," *Annals of Medical History,* IV (1932), 67–68.

   35. Theodore Clapp, *Autobiographical Sketches and Recollections,* pp. 117–151.

21, *10. Louisiana Advertiser,* November 10, 1832; *The Courier,* November 12, 1832; *Emporium,* November 9, 1932.

   27. J. M. Mason, "Early Medical Education in the Far South," *Annals of Medical History,* IV (1932), 64–79.

   36. Michel's New Orleans Annual and Commercial Register, 1833, p. 112. *Registre du Comité Medical de La Nlle Orléans, 1816–1851* lists A. H. Jones, admitted December

10, 1832, but identifies him as "natif de Claremont, âge 28 ans." Advertisement of Dental Institute, *Emporium*, November 5, 1832: Fee was $5.00 a year; "Itinerant Dentists will not be employed."

22, *9. Memoranda*, pp. 7–8.

32. Ibid., p. 8.

23, *8.* Twelve bales of buffalo hides consigned to J. W. Breedlove (*Courier de la Louisiana*, October 1, 1833).

18. Barclay to Jones, June 8, 1833, AJP.

24, *5. Memoranda*, p. 9.

7. Erath, *Memoirs*, p. 14.

9. No. 10744, filed August 8, 1833; tried February 28, 1834; neither the defendants nor their attorneys, McCaleb and Gray, appeared; judgment $445.72 and costs. Records of First Judicial District Court, New Orleans.

14. New Orleans *Bee*, October 14, 1833; *Courier de la Louisiana*, October 15, 1833.

IV. MR. AUSTIN'S TEXAS

25, *10.* Eugene C. Barker, *Life of Stephen Fuller Austin*, p. 24. Hereafter cited as *Life*.

17. Padillo's Report, December 27, 1819, in Eugene C. Barker (ed.), *Readings in Texas History* (hereafter cited as *Readings*), p. 42.

28. Moses Austin to J. E. B. Austin, April 8, 1821, *AP*, I, 385.

26, *6.* Jefferson to Hugh Nelson, March 12, 1820, *Writings of Thomas Jefferson* (Library Edition, 1903), XV, 238.

27. Jonas Harrison to Stephen F. Austin, December 8, 1832, *AP*, II, 900.

27, *4.* Moses Austin to J. E. B. Austin, March 28, 1821, *AP*, I, 385.

14. Maria Austin to Stephen F. Austin, June 8, 1821, *AP*, I, 395. Moses Austin died June 10.

36. Maria Austin to Stephen F. Austin, December 15, 1821; Joseph Hawkins to Austin, February 6, 1822, *AP*, I, 450, 476.

28, *14.* Austin to the colonists, June 5, 1824, *AP*, I, 815.

23. Barker, *Life*, p. 72.

27. Austin to J. E. B. Austin, May 20, 1823, *AP*, I, 644–645.

29, *19.* Barker, *Life*, p. 149. *Abstract of Original Titles in the General Land Office* (Houston, 1838) lists grants made by Austin and other empresarios.

21. Eugene C. Barker, *Mexico and Texas, 1821–1835*, p. 21.

30, *1.* Barker, *Life,* pp. 296–328 analyzes the law and its effects.

   17. Barker, *Mexico and Texas,* p 28, quotes from Luís Pérez Verdía, *Compendio de la Historia de México,* an outline of this turbulent decade.

   30. Frank W. Johnson, *A History of Texas and Texans,* I, 178–211.

31, *6.* *Life of Sam Houston: The Only Authentic Memoir,* p. 69. A campaign biography attributed to Charles Edwards Lester, apparently dictated by Houston.

   10. Eugene C. Barker, *The Father of Texas,* p. 137.

   12. Edna Rowe, "The Disturbances at Anahuac in 1832," *Quarterly* of the Texas State Historical Association, VI (1903), 265–299. This journal and its successor, *Southwestern Historical Quarterly,* are cited hereafter as *SWHQ.*

   19. Mary Fisher Parmenter *et al., The Life of George Fisher,* traces his incredible career.

32, *29.* *Texas Almanac for 1859,* pp. 32–33; Charles A. Gulick (ed.), *The Papers of Mirabeau Buonaparte Lamar,* I, 142–143 (hereafter cited as *LP*). These and other significant papers are available in Ernest Wallace and David Vigness, *Documents of Texas History* (1963).

33, *12.* Rupert N. Richardson, *Texas the Lone Star State* (1943 ed.), p. 98, quoting an 1832 letter to S. M. Williams.

   30. Richardson, *Texas,* p. 104.

   38. Mexía to John Austin, July 16, 1832; Mary Austin Holley, *Texas* (1833), p. 155.

34, *5.* Richardson, *Texas,* p. 101.

   25. H. P. N Gammel (ed.), Journal of the Convention, *Laws of Texas,* I, 475–503.

   30. Barker, *Life,* pp. 407–409.

35, *3.* June 30, 1828. Barker, *Mexico and Texas,* p. 4.

   19. John Henry Brown, *History of Texas,* I, 229–230.

36, *15.* Barker, *Life,* pp. 430–459.

   20. Richardson, *Texas,* 111.

   26. *Memoranda,* p. 100.

V. FIVE THOUSAND A YEAR

37, *3.* *Memoranda,* p. 8.

   8. *Constitutional Advocate and Texas Public Advertiser,* Brazoria, September 5, 1832; clipping from an unidentified Brazoria paper, May 20, 1833, in *AP.*

11. *Biographical Directory of Texas Conventions and Congresses, 1832–1845*, p. 46 (hereafter cited as *Biographical Directory*). John Austin's headrights were dated July 21 and August 24, 1824 (Lester G. Bugbee, "The Old Three Hundred," *SWHQ*, I (1897), 110).

16. Austin to Carr, March 4, 1829, *AP*, II, 179.

23. [Fiske], *A Visit to Texas*, pp. 21–22.

38, *20.* Mattie Austin Hatcher, *Letters of an Early American Traveller, Mary Austin Holley*, pp. 113–117. Letter dated December, 1831.

24. Parker, *Trip*, p. 219.

26. Hatcher, *Letters*, p. 114.

31. J. Villasana Haggard, "Epidemic Cholera in Texas, 1833–1834," *SWHQ*, XL (1937), 222.

35. Perry to Austin, October 26, 1833, *AP*, II, 1009; Arciniega to Secretary of State, August 12, 1833, cited in *SWHQ*, XL (1937), 224.

37. *Memoranda*, p. 104.

39, *1.* Holley, *Texas* (1836), pp. 110–111.

17. The *Advocate* apparently began publication November 23, 1833, and was discontinued the following March (Joe B. Frantz, "Newspapers of the Republic of Texas," MS, p. 18; [Ike Moore (ed.)], *Texas Newspapers, 1813–1939*, p. 29; Eugene C. Barker, "Notes on Early Texas Newspapers," SWHQ, XXI [1917], 139).

25. William Ransom Hogan, *The Texas Republic*, p. 259.

28. *Advocate* extra, March 27, 1834.

39. *Ibid.* William Austin, John's brother, established the hotel. Smith was assisted by Mrs. Stephenson.

40, *3.* *Advocate*, February 22, 1834.

5. *Ibid.*, March 27, 1834.

8. Hogan, *Texas Republic*, 102.

14, 17. Hogan, "Social and Economic History of Texas," MS, Ch. III.

20. *Advocate*, February 22, 1834.

22. Hatcher, *Letters*, p. 51.

41, *23.* Mrs. A. H. Mohle, MS sketch of Mrs. Anson Jones. Hereafter cited as Mohle MS.

35. *Memoranda*, p. 10.

42, *10.* Abner J. Strobel, *Old Plantations and Their Owners of Brazoria County, Texas, passim.*

43, *23.* Barker, *Life*, p. 460.

29. *Ibid.*, p. 464; Almonte, "Report," *SWHQ*, XXVIII (1925), 177–222.

35. Printed card, November 22, 1834, *LP*, I, 175–177.

44, 1. *Advocate*, February 22, 1834.

19. *AP*, II, 1074; *LP*, I, 201.

24. Strobel, *Old Plantations*, p. 40, says the arm remained stiff and Wharton learned to write with his left hand.

28. *Memoranda*, p. 10.

45, 1. Barker, *Life*, p. 469.

5. *AP*, III, 23–24, lists the voters.

24. Mohle MS. Adele B. Looscan in SWHQ, X (1906), 172–180, reprinted in Mattie Lloyd Wooten, *Women Tell the Story of the Southwest*, pp. 222–227.

30. *Republican*, March 14, June 6, 20, 1835.

46, 9. Records of County Clerk, Angleton.

12. *Republican*, March 14, May 9, 1835. Dr. Jones's bill for calls at Peach Point plantation, February to November, 1835, was $173.00 (Perry Papers).

VI. AN ANXIOUS OBSERVER

47, 8. William C. Binkley (ed.), *Official Correspondence of the Texas Revolution*, I, xxiii–xxxviii, graphically describes these confusions.

24. *Memoranda*, p. 11.

48, 5. Barker, *Life*, p. 474.

30. For details see *Histories* by Yoakum, Wooten, Brown, Wortham; briefer treatments are in Richardson, *Texas*, Gambrell, *Pictorial History*, and Binkley, *Texas Revolution*.

49, 6. *AP*, III, 99; *Texas State Gazette*, November 16, 1850. A draft in *LP*, I, 222, lists ninety-nine signers.

15. *Memoranda*, p. 105; Diary, May 6, 1852, AJP.

20. James K. Greer (contrib.), "Journal of Ammon Underwood," *SWHQ*, XXXII (1928), 137.

24. Richardson, *Texas*, p. 118.

34. Gail Borden, Jr., quoted in Barker, *Life*, p. 479.

50, 37. *AP*, III, 116–119.

51, 3. Barker, *Readings*, p. 213.

52, 7. Barker, "The Texan Declaration of Causes for Taking up Arms against Mexico," *SWHQ*, XV (1912), 173–185.

11. *Texas Almanac, 1858* (p. 97) and *Biographical Directory* (pp. 19–20) list delegates.

24. *Memoranda*, p. 12.

32. H. H. Bancroft, *History of Mexico,* V, 33n; Wilfrid H. Callcott, *Church and State in Mexico,* p. 56.

53, *5.* H. J. Offut to Austin, February 15, 1836. *AP,* III, 315.

16. Memoranda, pp. 12–13.

31. Ibid., p. 13.

54, *5.* Biographical sketches in *DAB* and *Handbook of Texas.*

24. Ruthven, *Proceedings,* I, 7; James D. Carter, *Masonry in Texas,* pp. 211–291; S. W. Geiser in Dallas *News,* April 9, 1933, for the 1828 petition.

55, *14. Memoranda,* pp. 13–14.

21. Ibid., p. 14. Written in 1849 or 1850.

24. Ruthven, *Proceedings,* I, 7. The lodge reconvened at Houston in 1837. Jones, as Grand Master, chartered it as Holland Lodge No. 1, Grand Lodge of Texas.

VII. 1836

56, *27.* John Henry Brown, *Life and Times of Henry Smith,* pp. 188–194.

57, *3. Ibid.,* p. 196.

12. John Henry Brown, *Life and Times of Henry Smith,* pp. 188–205, has documents and sympathetic treatment of Smith. Ralph W. Steen, "Analysis of the Work of the General Council," *SWHQ,* XL (1937), 309 *et seq.*

58, *15.* Urrea's diary is translated in Carlos E. Castañeda (ed.), *Mexican Side of the Texas Revolution,* pp. 204–283. Ruby Cumby Smith, "James W. Fannin Jr. in the Texas Revolution," *SWHQ,* XXIII (1919), 79 ff.

21. Amelia W. Williams, "A Critical Study of the Siege of the Alamo," *SWHQ,* XXXVI–XXXVII (1932–1934). Lon Tinkle, *13 Days to Glory* (1958), and Walter Lord, *A Time to Stand* (1961), won the Summerfield G. Roberts Award for best interpretation of the character of early Texans.

28. Louis Wiltz Kemp, *Signers of the Texas Declaration of Independence,* pp. 26–28. Jones got two votes at Brazoria, two at Chocolate Bayou, one at Columbia.

59, *20.* Ruthven, *Proceedings,* I, 5–7.

35. Kemp, *Signers,* pp. v–xxiv; Richardson, "Framing the Constitution of the Republic of Texas," *SWHQ,* XXXI (1928), 191–220; James K. Greer, "The Committee on the Texas Declaration of Independence," *SWHQ,* XXX–XXXI (1927–1928).

60, *14.* Andrew Jackson Houston, *Texas Independence,* pp. 135–136.

17. Millard to Thomas B. Huling, February 22, 1836, Huling Papers.

30. Houston's version in A. J. Houston, *Texas Independence,* pp. 157–160.

34. Marquis James, *The Raven,* p. 233, quoting W. Fairfax Gray.

38. Bexar First Class, File 330, Zavalla No. 477, General Land Office. His claim for a league and *labor* (4,605 acres) was approved, then voided, and finally allowed after Jones filed suit for it.

61, *3.* Sam Houston Dixon and Louis Wiltz Kemp, *The Heroes of San Jacinto,* p. 67.

26. Barker, "The San Jacinto Campaign," *SWHQ,* IV (1901), 237–345, evaluates all available primary, and some secondary, sources.

38. Kuykendall, whom Barker thought "apparently free from prejudice," wrote this twenty or more years after 1836 (*SWHQ,* IV (1901), 302).

62, *5.* Order from the Adjutant General to Millard, April 2, 1836, *Memoranda,* pp. 130–131.

15. *Narrative of Robert Hancock Hunter,* p. 18. Jones wrote that the reprieve was brought by Colonel William G. Cooke (*Memoranda,* p. 131).

18. Kuykendall's statement, quoted in Barker, "San Jacinto Campaign," *SWHQ,* IV (1901), 301.

63, *8.* Mohle MS.

23. N. D. Labadie, "San Jacinto Campaign," *Texas Almanac for 1859,* pp. 44–61.

35. Henry Millard to Thomas B. Huling, April 1, 1836, Huling Papers.

37. Labadie, "San Jacinto Campaign," *Texas Almanac for 1859,* p. 45; Barker, "San Jacinto Campaign," *SWHQ,* IV (1901), 330.

38. J. H. Kuykendall, quoted in Barker, "San Jacinto Campaign," *SWHQ,* IV (1901), 301.

64, *9.* *Memoranda,* p. 15.

16. Dixon and Kemp, *Heroes,* pp. 65–69.

20. Labadie, "San Jacinto Campaign," *Texas Almanac for 1859,* p. 45.

28. Barker, "San Jacinto Campaign," *SWHQ,* IV (1901), 330.

65, *9.* John J. Linn, *Reminiscences of Fifty Years in Texas,* p. 252.

15. *Memoranda,* p. 16.

24. *Ibid*. Characterization of Perry in Houston's Senate speech, February 28, 1859, quoted from *Congressional Globe, 1859*, pp. 1433–1439, in Dixon and Kemp, *Heroes*, p. 51. Rusk's statement is in his letter to Louis P. Cook, May 5, 1843, quoted in *Heroes*, p. 52.

26. Unsigned, undated note in Houston's hand, Washington D. Miller Papers. Jones wrote, August 24, 1855, that during the battle Houston was "stupefied and stultified with opium" (Sidney Sherman, *Defense*, p. 23).

37. *Memoranda*, p. 16.

66, 3. *Ibid.*, p. 16; Sherman, *Defense*, p. 23.

22. Dixon and Kemp, *Heroes*, p. 90.

25. There was no agreement among veterans on this and many other points. Jones thought, nearly twenty years later: "Gen. Houston intended to cross the *Neches* (not the Sabine) before fighting. At Donohoe's he was *compelled* by the unanimous sense of the entire army to deflect from the road and go to Harrisburg from which resulted the victory" (Sherman, *Defense*, p. 23).

30. Labadie, "San Jacinto Campaign," *Texas Almanac for 1859*, p. 48.

67, 2. A. J. Houston, *Texas Independence*, p. 213.

7. *Ibid.*, p. 216; Labadie, "San Jacinto Campaign," *Texas Almanac for 1859*, p. 49. La Bahía (pronounced *Laberdie* by Anglo-Texans) was the official name of the town until 1829, when the Congress of Coahuila y Texas changed it to Goliad—anagram of (H)idalgo, who led the 1810 Mexican revolt against Spain (*Handbook of Texas*, I, 699). Long after 1836 it was commonly referred to by its earlier name, but later Texans unconsciously edited the battle cry to "Remember Goliad." "After such a speech, but d——d few will be taken prisoners—that I know," remarked Alexander Somervell (Labadie, "San Jacinto Campaign," *Texas Almanac for 1859*, p. 49).

18. *Memoranda*, pp. 16–17.

68, 3. Labadie, "San Jacinto Campaign," *Texas Almanac for 1859*, p. 49.

36. Henry Stuart Foote, *Texas and the Texans*, II, 296–305.

69, 10. Herbert Gambrell, *Mirabeau Buonaparte Lamar*, pp. 82–84; Philip Graham, *Life and Poems of Mirabeau B. Lamar*, p. 36.

24. Neill, former commander at the Alamo, was chief of artillery.

He was given a pension for life during Jones's presidency. Dixon and Kemp, *Heroes,* p. 73.

70, *1.* Mosely Baker, quoted in Barker, "The San Jacinto Campaign," *SWHQ,* IV (1901), 284–285.

27. Texas Almanac for 1859, p. 54.

71, *13, 29.* Hunter, *Narrative,* pp. 23, 24.

72, *2.* A. J. Houston, *Texas Independence,* p. 241. The official report says 783 Texans were in the battle, but lists 845 names. Muster rolls show 863. Dixon and Kemp, *Heroes,* p. 31, lists 918 names, including 13 duplicates. Cf. William C. Binkley, "Activities of the Texan Revolutionary Army after San Jacinto," *Journal of Southern History,* VI (1940), 339.

24. Labadie, "San Jacinto Campaign," *Texas Almanac for 1859,* p. 54.

33. "The Private Journal of Juan Nepomuceno Almonte, February 1–April 16, 1836," SWHQ, XLVIII (1944), 10–32.

73, *2, 30. Texas Almanac for 1859,* pp. 56–57, 60.

74, *10.* Foote, *Texas,* II, 312.

25. Hunter, *Narrative,* pp. 25–26.

34. A. J. Houston, *Texas Independence,* pp. 234–235.

37. The only known draft signed by Houston is in the Hall of State, Dallas. It was addressed to the *Louisiana Advertiser,* New Orleans, and was found among the corporate papers of the Dallas *Morning News* shortly before the Texas Centennial celebrations of 1936. The publisher of the *News* presented it to the Dallas Historical Society in 1940. Frank X. Tolbert's *The Day of San Jacinto* received the Summerfield G. Roberts Award for 1959.

75, *10.* Hunter, *Narrative,* pp. 24–25.

21. Labadie, "San Jacinto Campaign," *Texas Almanac for 1859,* p. 61.

26. Hunter, *Narrative,* p. 26.

34. Mohle MS.

76, *10.* A. J. Houston, *Texas Independence,* p. 237.

16. Amelia W. Williams and Eugene C. Barker (eds.), *The Writings of Sam Houston,* I, 399 n (hereafter cited as *WSH*). *Biographical Directory* (p. 179) says he was accidentally wounded in the leg en route from Galveston to San Jacinto and died in Zavala's house April 26 or 27 "from loss of blood and general weakness."

24. Biographical Directory of Texan Conventions and Con-

gresses, p. [8], lists members of Burnet's Cabinet with dates of their tenure in most cases.

27. *Memoranda,* p. 17. Jones was "paid as surgeon from 10 April to 10 May 1836." Burnet certified on November 21, 1836, "that Dr. Jones was appointed Apothecary General by the government ad interim" (Comptroller's Military Service Records, No. 6006). Burnet refers to Jones as Apothecary General on May 20, 1836 (*Official Correspondence,* II, 698).

34. "IMPORTANT FROM TEXAS. By packet steamer Nashville from New Orleans, which arrived on Tuesday [June 14] evening, we have received various documents . . . among them the original copies of the 'Private Journal of the Mexican Campaign and Its Progress,' by Almonte, together with a 'General Order Book,' both contained in two folio manuscripts" (New York *Herald,* June 16, 1836). Publication of the translation began June 22 under the heading *Singular Disclosure.* "The original, in the Spanish language, is now in our possession. It was picked up on the battle ground of San Jacinto by Dr. Anson Jones and was sent to us via Galveston Island on the 12th of May last. The journal has been seen and examined by Mr. [George C.] Childress, the diplomatic representative from Texas, who left this city a few days ago for Washington" (Quoted in "The Private Journal of Juan Nepomuceno Almonte, February 1–April 16, 1836" [introduction by Samuel E. Asbury], *SWHQ,* XLVIII [1944], 11–12).

38. He got his money on May 22 (*Official Correspondence,* II, 698).

77, 9. New Orleans *Bee,* May 23, 1836, gives a two-paragraph account of General Houston's arrival on the *Flora,* and published his report of the battle the next day.

12. C. T. Neu, "The case of the Brig *Pocket,*" *SWHQ,* XII (1909), 276–295. Poor Jerry Brown "got into personal difficulties, was relieved of duty, and was succeeded in command by H. L. Thompson in April, 1838" (*Handbook of Texas,* I, 225).

VIII. BRAZORIA

78, 10. Hall to Smith, January 28, 1836, *Official Correspondence,* I, 355–361, for invoices of typical shipments from New Orleans.

79, 4. Carlos E. Castañeda (trans.), *The Mexican Side of the Texas*

Revolution, pp. 241–243. The diary was published at Victoria, Mexico, in 1838.

34. E. Morehouse, "Account of His Military Movements in March and April, 1836" (undated), *LP,* III, 272–274.

80, *7. Memoranda,* p. 130. Dr. Jones had been curator of the Graham estate since November 1, 1835 (*Texas Republican,* February 14, 1835).

18. Fifteen years later Jones was still claiming $1,000 "for Property injured, used and destroyed at Brazoria by the Army in March and April, 1836" (Spoliation Claim No. 53, August 1851).

22. Ewing to Jones, October 28, 1836, and Jones's endorsement thereon, *Memoranda,* p. 131. Jones had been paid for services from April 10 to May 20, and received $1,782.66 pay as surgeon and Apothecary General for the period ending October 6, 1836. Congressman Rusk presented Jones's claim for services as Apothecary General from October 6, 1836, to May 7, 1837, $1,465. 33 1/3. President Houston approved a joint resolution granting him that amount, plus $210 "for the rent of a store house from 1st July 1836 to the 1st day of February, 1837" (*House Journal,* 2d Cong., reg. sess., 250; Gammel, *Laws of Texas,* I, 1401). On December 14, 1837, while he was a congressman, he received 1,280 acres for having served in the Army from May 10, 1836, to May 10, 1837 (Atascosa County File, Bexar Donation Certificate No. 4, General Land Office).

81, *28.* Binkley, *Journal of Southern History,* VI (1940), 340, shows that of the 2,503 men in the army in July and August, 1836, 1,831 had arrived after San Jacinto, and 39 of the 53 captains were newcomers.

35. Rusk to M. B. Lamar, June 1, 1836, *LP,* I, 395.

82, *3.* Corinne Montgomery, *Texas and her Presidents,* p. 9. Bache, a 42-year-old newcomer from Philadelphia, had served in the United States Navy (*Biographical Directory,* p. 47).

18. Foote, *Texas,* II, 335–344, gives a long-winded but spirited account of the Velasco incident.

33. See *LP,* I, 417–418, for Lamar's account, written July 17, 1836, to Burnet. Yoakum, *History,* II, 183–188, gives Felix Huston's version.

39. P. H. Bell to Lamar, September 6, 1836, *LP,* I, 446–447.

83, *2.* McKinney to Rusk, May 19, 1836. Rusk Papers.

16. Official Correspondence, II, 670–671.

19. Zavala to Burnet, undated, endorsed "Received this letter on 22 April at post of Galveston" (*Official Correspondence,* II, 642).

26. *Official Correspondence,* II, 744.

28. Kemp, *Signers,* p. 379.

32. *Official Correspondence,* II, 883–884.

38. Richardson, "Framing the Constitution," *SWHQ,* XXXI (1928), 214–217.

84, *25.* *WSH,* I, 446.

85, *6.* Millard to Huling, August 2 and 21, 1836, Huling Papers.

12. Houston to Guy M. Bryan, November 12, 1852; Yoakum, *History,* II, 193–194.

19. E. Andrews to Austin, September 8, 1836; *AP,* III, 430.

IX. A MAMMOTH SCHEME

86, *20.* Strobel, *Old Plantations,* p. 23.

23. Ira Jones's estate consisted of land worth $112.00 and claims for pay and land which "could only be obtained by suit" (Probate Minutes, Brazoria County, D, 100).

87, *2.* *Memoranda,* p. 17.

9. Louis W. Kemp, "The Capitol(?) at Columbia," *SWHQ,* XLVIII (1944), 3–9.

20. Cf. *Biographical Directory,* pp. 23–24, and Dixon and Kemp, *Heroes, passim.*

88, *3, 12.* *Telegraph,* February 3, 10, 1837.

89, *12.* Andrew Forest Muir, "Railroad Enterprise in Texas, 1836–1841," *SWHQ,* XLVII (1944), 339–345; S. G. Reed, *A History of Texas Railroads,* pp. 10–22; C. S. Potts, *Railroad Transportation in Texas,* pp. 24–25; William M. Gouge, *The Fiscal History of Texas,* pp. 60–61. Hogan, *Texas Republic,* pp. 97–99. For Austin's withdrawal see George L. Hammeken, "Recollections of Stephen F. Austin," *SWHQ,* XX (1917), 378; Thomas W. Streeter, *Bibliography of Texas, 1795–1845, Part I; Texas Imprints,* I, 168.

36. *House Journal,* First Congress, First Session, pp. 247, 260–262; MS Senate Journal, afternoon sessions, December 13, 14, 1836; *WSH,* VI, 87–88; Green, *Reply,* pp. 57–61.

90, *14.* For Galveston, see Gammel, *Laws of Texas,* I, 1130–1131; Frederic Leclerc, *Texas and Its Revolution,* p. 43. For Houston, see E. W. Winkler, "The Seat of Government," *SWHQ,* X (1907), 167–171; Gambrell, "Founders of the

Society," *Proceedings* of the Philosophical Society of Texas, [I] (1937), 7–17.

19. Memoranda, pp. 18–19.

23. Green to Archer, quoted in *Memoranda,* p. 288.

28. Reed, *Texas Railroads,* p. 10.

91, *10.* Charter, Gammel, *Laws,* I, 1188–1192.

92, *9. Memoranda,* pp. 288–289.

27. Quoted by Muir, "Railroad Enterprise in Texas, 1836–1841," *SWHQ,* XLVII (1944), 343.

94, *7.* This Franklin letter was reprinted in the *Democrat* and perhaps other pro-Jones newspapers during the presidential campaign of 1844.

X. THE CITY OF HOUSTON

95, *7.* Congress convened at Columbia October 3, 1836, and within a month was seeking a new site. November 30 Houston was selected, effective April 1, 1837 (Winkler, *SWHQ,* X [1907], 156–171).

17. Telegraph, August 30, 1836.

23. John Henry Brown, *Indian Wars and Pioneers,* p. 357.

96, *2.* Mohle MS.

13. [City of Houston]. *History of Texas . . . Houston and Galveston* (1892), p. 263.

97, *8. Houston and Galveston in the Years 1837–1838* (anonymous), pp. 19–25.

18. Z. N. Morrell, *Flowers and Fruits from the Wilderness,* p. 66.

22. Hogan, "The Theatre in the Republic of Texas," *Southwest Review,* XIX (1934), 383.

29. "Extracts from the Diary of W. Y. Allen, 1838–1839," *SWHQ,* XVII (1913), 44.

98, *8. Telegraph and Texas Register,* May 2, 1837.

27. Telegraph, May 16, 1837.

36. [Edward Stiff], *A New History of Texas,* p. 95.

99, *11.* Quoted by S. W. Geiser, "Audubon in Texas," *Southwest Review,* XVI (1930), 126–127.

24. Stiff says that in 1838 "there were not more than forty women among some thousand of men." Max Freund (ed.), *Gustav Dresel's Houston Journal,* p. 131, collates estimates of population, 1837–1839.

38. Mohle MS.

100, *33.* Inventory of Hugh McCrory estate, Probate Records, Harris County, A, 296–297; deed for Lot 6, Block 54, March 10,

1837, is in AJP. B. H. Carroll, Jr., *Standard History of Houston,* p. 39. Sketch of Hugh McCrory, MS in L. W. Kemp Papers. *Telegraph,* December 23, 1837, carried notice that John Woodward [Woodruff] and Mary Mc-Crary [McCrory] would administer the estate of James McCrary [Hugh McCrory].

XI. MR. JONES OF B.

101, 7. *House Journal,* 2d Cong., called sess., October 5, 1837, p. 30. Later that year Russell was elected to succeed Wharton in the Senate.

103, 4. Gouge, *Fiscal History,* p. 63, quoting *House Journal,* 1st Cong., May 5, 1837. *Senate Journal,* 2d Cong., adj. sess., 8, shows the protocol was still followed.

22. *House Journal,* September 30, 1837, 19.

37. Cf. roster of First and Second Congresses, *Biographical Directory,* pp. 23–26.

104, 11. *House Journal, passim.* The *Telegraph* published the *Journal* serially.

31. *House Journal,* September 25–November 4, 1837, 11, 103, 122.

105, 6. *Telegraph,* December 2, 1837, has text of Jones's speech.

13. Diary, June 1, 1852, *Memoranda,* p. 106.

14. Collinsworth had resigned and died before the Supreme Court held its first session in January, 1840 (James W. Dallam, *Opinions of the Supreme Court of Texas, 1840 to 1844,* p. 1).

27. *Telegraph,* July 29, 1837, quoted by Muir, "Railroad Enterprise in Texas, 1836–1841," *SWHQ,* XLVII (1944), 342.

32. Gouge, *Fiscal History,* pp. 227–229.

106, 13. Green, *Reply,* p. 61.

21. *SWHQ,* XLVII (1944), 344.

30. Green, *Reply,* p. 59.

107, 7. *Memoranda,* pp. 105–106.

13. Gouge, *Fiscal History,* pp. 137–141.

23. *Telegraph,* November 18, 1837.

35. *House Journal,* April 17, 18, 19, 24; November 23; December 1, 12, 13, 1837; April 17, 1838.

108, 8. Muir, "Railroad Enterprise in Texas, 1836–1841," *SWHQ,* XLVII (1944).

11. Memorial, June 1837, endorsed in Jones's handwriting: "Drawn up and presented by Anson Jones. The result was

the incorporation of the Soc. prayed for," Dienst Collection.

26. *Senate Journal,* 1st Cong., 2d sess., June 10, 1837, 48; *House Journal,* June 10, 12, 1837, pp. 146, 147.

34. Gammel, *Laws,* I, 1381, 1421; *Senate Journal,* 2d Cong., 58, 91; *House Journal,* 215, 229, 282, 287.

109, 24. See W. Eugene Hollon and Ruth Butler (eds.), *William Bollaert's Texas,* p. 300, for conditions in 1844.

110, 4. The Legislature repealed the 1837 act in 1848, leaving medical practice unregulated until 1873. Gammel, *Laws,* III, 21; VII, 526. Pat Ireland Nixon, *A History of the Texas Medical Association,* 48, 54.

110, 38. *House Journal,* 2d Cong., November 20, 1837, p. 143; December 8, 1837, p. 238; May 11, 1838, p. 109; May 1, 1838, p. 66; May 11, 1838, p. 110; Diary, July 28, 1838.

111, 26. Delightful contemporary accounts of Texas are Max Freund (ed.), *Gustav Dresel's Houston Journal;* Andrew Forest Muir (ed.), *Texas in 1837;* Willis W. Pratt (ed.), *Galveston Island: Journal of Francis Sheridan, 1839–1840.*

XII. GUIDE, PHILOSOPHER, FRIEND

112, 25. Ruthven, *Proceedings,* I, 7–8.

32. Philip Graham, "Mirabeau B. Lamar's First Trip to Texas," *Southwest Review,* XXI (1936), 376.

39. *Telegraph,* January 13, 1838.

113, 13. *Proceedings* of the Philosophical Society of Texas (edited S. W. Geiser), 1937, [I], 6–21.

25. The Memorial of December 5, 1837, with facsimiles of signatures of the charter members, in *The Philosophical Society of Texas* (anonymous), pp. 2–3; MS Minute Book, San Jacinto Museum of History.

114, 3. Sadie R. McLean, "The Second Congress of the Republic of Texas," MS, p. 68.

8. *Ibid.*

27. *Memoranda,* pp. 19–20.

115, 10. *House Journal,* October 23, 1837, p. 39.

22. *Ibid.,* October 23, p. 74, October 25, 1837, p. 87.

116, 13. *WSH,* II, 98.

21. McLean MS, p. 5.

29. *House Journal,* called sess., September 30, 1837, *et passim.*

117, 10. *Telegraph,* May 16, 1837.

118, 32. "Minutes of the Convention . . . December 20, 1837,"

Ruthven, *Proceedings*, I, 9–10 (reprinted with a correction in J. C. Kidd, *History of Holland Lodge*, pp. 19–20) ; James D. Carter, *Masonry in Texas . . . to 1846*, pp.312–320.

119, *16.* Ruthven, *Proceedings*, I, 20–24.

XIII. ANNEXATION?

120, *6.* George P. Garrison, "The First Stage of the Movement for the Annexation of Texas," *American Historical Review*, X (1904), 74.

20. George P. Garrison (ed.), *Diplomatic Correspondence of the Republic of Texas*, I, 80. Cited hereafter as *TDC*.

27. Biographical Directory, p. [8].

121, *8.* Jackson to the House, December 22, 1836. *H.R. Exec. Doc. 15*, 24th Cong., 2 sess., 1.

38. TDC, I, 89–91, 125–126, 137, 155.

122, *8. Ibid.*, pp. 157–158, 190.

36. Ibid., p. 184.

123, *9.* Dated March 5, 1837 (*TDC*, I, 201).

11. Sketch of LaBranche in Alcee Fortier, *Louisiana*, II, 20–21.

13. Wharton's letter of credence as Minister probably arrived after he had left Washington. It is undated but endorsed April 10 (*TDC*, I, 203).

27. TDC, I, 207.

29. Ibid., p. 209.

124, *3.* Lt. J. W. Taylor's report, April 21, 1839.

7. Alex Dienst, "The Navy of the Republic of Texas," *SWHQ*, XII (1909), 273–274.

124, *39.* Jim Dan Hill, *The Texas Navy*, pp. 74–80.

125, *20.* W. Fairfax Gray, *From Virginia to Texas*, p. 219.

126, *1. TDC*, I, 237.

13. Ibid., pp. 231, 244. LaBranche's letter of credence, dated July 21, 1837, was presented October 26.

18. Ibid., p. 246.

127, *5.* Louis J. Wortham, *History of Texas*, IV, 11–15, quoting *H.R.Doc. 45*, 25th Cong., 1st sess., 11–13. Not in *TDC*.

35. Hunt to Forsyth, September 12, 1837, Wortham, *History*, IV, 17–23.

128, *6. TDC*, I, 273 (Grayson), 286 (Hunt).

9. House Journal, 2d Cong., called sess., September 28, 1837.

20. Ibid., October 26, 1837, p. 71.

26. Ibid., November 9 (misprinted October 24), p. 109.

31. Ibid., December 15, 1837, p. 273.

37. *Telegraph*, April 21, 28, May 9, 12, 1838, *fide* Schmitz, *Texas Statecraft*, p. 62.

129, 30. *House Journal*, 2d Cong., adj. sess., 32.

39. *Ibid.*, May 1, 2, 1838, 69, 73.

131, 13. *Memoranda*, pp. 132–133; *WSH*, II, 246. Dated June 12, 1838.

21. Linn, *Reminiscences*, pp. 272–273.

132, 2. Introduction to Diary for 1838, 3–4 (daily entries begin July 28), abridged in *Memoranda*, pp. 21, 27.

5. *WSH*, II, 255–256. Irion ordered payment of $4,500 for his outfit July 14 (Connor [ed.], *Texas Treasury Papers*, I, 117–118).

13. Diary, July, 1838, AJP.

35. *Ibid.*, July 20–22, 1838.

XIV. THE THREAD

133, 13. He almost got through New Orleans "without any notice." The *Courier*, July 25 gave him two lines of type: "The Honorable Anson Jones, Minister Plenipotentiary to the United States, arrived on the Columbia." The *Bee*, July 26, merely listed among the passengers "Jones," without Christian name, occupation, or destination.

20. Diary, July 25–28, 1838.

24. The indignity was still rankling Jones in 1852, when he added this note to his Diary for 1838.

134, 12. Diary, July 29, 1838.

18. *Telegraph*, May 19, 23, 26, 1838.

135, 12. Diary, August 9, 1838.

18. Diary, August 11, 1838.

136, 10. Diary, August 22, 1838.

16. *Ibid.*, August 23, 1838.

30. *WSH*, II, 105.

137, 11. *TDC*, I, 329–330.

38. July 12, 1838 (*TDC*, I, 338–341).

138, 36. Diary, August 26, October 2, 1838.

139, 3. Melvin Ryder Collection, National Writers Club, New York.

11. Diary, August 28, 1838.

23. For Johnathan Elliot, see *Appleton's Cyclopaedia of American Biography*, II, 331. His *Code*, first published in 1827, was expanded in the second edition (1834) to include rules of etiquette.

140, 4. Diary, August 29 to September 2, 1838.

14. *Ibid.*, September 4, 1838.

141, *14. Ibid.*, September 4–23, 1838.
   18. Ibid., September 26–31, 1838.
142, *5. Ibid.*, August 30, October 8, 1838.
   18. Ibid., October 9, 1838.
143, *4.* The President spoke longer but said nothing more (*TDC*, I, 347).
   22. Diary, October 9, 1838.
   25. Ibid., October 3, 1838.
   29. Ibid., October 10, 1838; *TDC*, I, 347–348.
144, *12.* Diary, October 11, 1838. For Monroe Edwards see Webb and Carroll, *Handbook of Texas*, I, 547.
   32. TDC, I, 348.
145, *20.* H.R. *Exec. Doc. No. 2*, 25th Cong., 3d sess., 1838, 33.
146, *21. TDC*, III, 856–860.
   27. Proclamation, July 4, 1838, *WSH*, II, 260–261.
   35. H. H. Bancroft,*History of Mexico,*V,186–205. Significance of the Pastry War to Texas was that Santa Anna, having lost a leg, became again a national hero, returned to the presidency, and resumed harassment of Texas in 1842.
147, *17. Memoranda*, pp. 133–135.
   23. Ibid., p. 137.
148, *5.* November 29, 1838 (*TDC*, I, 354).

XV. JEANNETTE

149, *5. Appleton's Cyclopaedia of American Biography*, VI, 107.
   17. Diary, November 30, 1838. Nathaniel Amory to James H. Starr, November 29, 1840, describes Jeannette Thruston (Starr Papers).
150, *2.* Diary, October 23, 1838.
   5. Ibid., November 22, 1838.
   11. Ibid., December 1, 1838. He first wrote "Poor old Adams," then deleted "old."
151, *13. Ibid.,* November 30, 1838.
   24. Mrs. E. F. Ellet, *Court Circles of the Republic*, p. 245.
152, *9.* Diary, November 18, 1838.
   18. DAB, IX, 346–347.
   29. Wortham, *History*, IV, 31, says that Hughes "apparently entertained for a while the idea of casting his lot with the new republic," but cites no evidence.
153, *12. Memoranda*, p. 149. Dated April 24, 1839.
   41. Ibid., p. 150. Same date.
154, *14.* Hughes to Jones, June 10, 1839, enclosing Hughes to Palm-

erston and Palmerston to Hughes, same date, *Memoranda*, pp. 151–152.

29. Henderson to Jones, June 20, 1839, *Memoranda*, p. 146.

155, *11.* Dated Stockholm, March 24, 1840, received by Jones July 5, *Memoranda*, p. 155. Hughes, unhappy at having had no official recognition of what he had done for Texas, is having sent to the "archives of your new and noble republic" a complete account with supporting documents. He wanted Rumigny to be officially thanked and suggested a Texas town be named for him. What reward Hughes should receive, he does not suggest. Jones was chairman of the Senate foreign relations committee when he received this letter, but apparently recommended nothing. In 1844 Hughes suggested this again; Jones tried "but have not been seconded by Gen. Houston" (*Memoranda*, p. 378).

26. *TDC*, I, 362.

156, *2. LP*, II, 319.

23. M. A. Bryan to James F. Perry, February 11, 1839, Perry Papers.

27. Diary, February 7, 1839.

35. *Ibid.*, January 8, 1839.

157, *9. Ibid., passim.* Mareschal wrote his government on December 2, 1838, that "Mr. Jones, who like nearly all his compatriots, was born in the United States, can hardly be considered a foreign agent, except as a matter of form." Austria, Haus- Hof-, under Staatsarchiv, Wien, Staatskenzlei, Nordamerika, Berichte, 1838, fasz.3, ff. 122–128 v., *fide* Thomas P. Martin.

26. Bryan to Perry, February 11, 1839, Perry Papers.

31. Diary (November 29, 1838, AJP) mentions these as "already added to our family" three days before Congress convened. Neither Jones nor Bryan identifies the other boarders.

158, *6.* Diary, January 8, 9, February 19, 1839.

13. Ellet, *Court Circles*, p. 249; Diary, January 1, 1839.

15. Diary, January 23, 1839.

24. *Ibid.*, January 1, 2, 3.

26. *Ibid.*, March 12, 1839.

36. Amory to Starr, November 29, 1840, Starr Papers.

XVI. MR. LAMAR'S TEXAS

160, *9.* Biographical sketches in *Handbook of Texas, passim*; Walace

Hawkins, *The Case of John C. Watrous*; William Preston Johnston, *The Life of General Albert Sidney Johnston*; for Dunlap, *WSH*, I, 432 n.; for Hunt, *WSH*, I, 525 n.

39. Jones to Bee, January 21, 1839, *TDC*, I, 358.

161, *3.* Bryan arrived February 1, while Minister Jones was visiting Philadelphia (Bryan to Perry, February 2; Diary, February 2; Diary, February 4). Sketch of M. A. Bryan in *Handbook of Texas*, I, 233–234.

15. TDC, I, 376. Bryan had read of Dunlap's appointment in a New Orleans paper on his way to Washington. Bryan to Perry, March 4, 1839. Perry Papers.

161, *18.* President Lamar, on February 23, expected Dunlap to "leave in a few days for the city of Washington" (*LP*, II, 466).

23. Dunlap to Lamar, February 23, 1839, *LP*, II, 466–467. Commission issued March 13, instructions March 14 (*TDC*, I, 367–378).

162, *2.* Diary, February 9, March 25, 26, 30, 1839.

6. Jones to Webb, March 19. *TDC*, I, 379.

15, 32. Diary, April 5–12, 1839.

163, *8. Ibid.*, April 13, 1839. Jones later drew a line through "though it is of a very equivocal kind" and omitted the words from *Memoranda*, p. 33.

12. Ibid., April 18, 1839. He revised but did not change the meaning of the last sentence for publication in *Memoranda*, p. 33.

20. Ibid., April 25, 1839.

23. Treat to James Morgan, June 8, 1839, Morgan Papers; Schmitz, *Texas Statecraft*, p. 98.

28. Diary, May 2, 1839.

32. Ibid., May 4, 1839.

164, *11.* Webb to Jones, March 14, 1839, AJP. Not in *TDC* or *Memoranda*.

33. Memoranda, pp. 142–143.

165, *9. TDC*, I, 386.

27. LP, II, 573.

36. Diary, May 8; inventory of clothing, May 13, 1839, AJP.

166, *5. Ibid.*, May 9–25, 1839. He later struck out "the degradation of human nature." All entries between April 15 and May 24 are omitted from *Memoranda*, p. 33.

7. Bryan to Perry, February 26, 1839, Perry Papers.

XVII. LIKE CERTAIN FEVERS

167, *9. LP*, II, 578. "Capt. Oliver Mate Mr. Young Cabin passen-

gers Messrs. Williams Hyde Hamet Bryan Carey and Self.
Forward five sailors cook & Steward" (Diary, May 26,
1839).

27. Houston *Morning Star*, April 19, May 3, 1839. Lamar did
well by the Robertses, father and son, if not by the daughter. Willis and Samuel got a total of five appointments
during the three-year administration. Olivia was his "dear
friend" who was "recurrently bursting into a more ardent
feeling" (Graham, *Life and Poems of Lamar*, 11).

168, 5. *Memoranda*, p. 294.

14. George Bancroft published the first volume of his ten-
volume *History of the United States* in 1834, the second
in 1837. Critics thought it an extended Fourth of July
oration (J. F. Jameson, *History of Historical Writing in
America*, p. 100).

23. Diary, April 4, 1839.

31. Edwin Waller to Lamar, May 9, 1839, *LP*, II, 568.

169, 2. *Memoranda*, p. 22.

17. Diary, June 21, 1839. Commodore Ribaud was returning to
France after the Pastry War. Customs Collector Roberts
gave him a letter of introduction to President Lamar and,
with Texan generosity, dubbed him Admiral (*LP*, V,
296).

22. Diary, June 22, 1839.

170, 5. *Ibid.*, June 24, 1839.

9. *Ibid.*, June 29, 1839.

171, 23. Complete text, *Memoranda*, pp. 291–295.

33. Ruthven, *Proceedings*, I, 47; Diary, June 30–July 7, 1839.

37. Diary, July 20–August 2, 1839.

172, 12. *Telegraph*, August 7, 1839, quoting Brazoria *Courier*.

26. Diary, August 3, 5, 1839.

173, 4. *Ibid.*, August 14, 15, 17, 20, 21, 1839.

8. E. T. Miller, *Financial History of Texas*, pp. 70, 391.

19. *LP*, III, 58.

27. *Ibid.*, p. 6.

174, 3. *LP*, III, 66.

8. *Ibid.*

17. Diary, September 2, 1839; *Biographical Directory*, p. 28.

24. *LP*, III, 97.

29. *Biographical Directory*, pp. 27–30, for personnel of Third
and Fourth Congresses.

33. "My friends, in their zeal and devotion, had *pledged* me to
serve if elected, and I was compelled to redeem their

pledges" (Note in *Memoranda*, p. 33, appended to Diary
entry for July 20, 1839).

175, *12. Morning Star,* April 17, 19, 1839.

    17. Ibid., June 8, 1839.

    25. LP, III, 11.

    31. Telegraph, July 31, 1839.

176, *8.* Diary, September 9, 12, 1839.

    14. Diary, September 13–19, 1839. He ends this meditation
with: "What will become of the gold button gentry of
the Army & Navy—poor fellows, you have a sad fate before you—for to go or stay is death or at least starvation."

    17. Ibid., September 24, October 3, 10, 1839. Five to seven
deaths occurred daily for several weeks (Hogan, *Texas
Republic,* p. 229; *Memoranda,* p. 22).

    26. Diary, October 3–22, November 1, 1839.

XVIII. CITY OF AUSTIN

177, *23.* A. W. Terrell, "The City of Austin from 1839 to 1865,"
SWHQ, XIV (1910), 114.

    30. Winkler, "Seat of Government," *SWHQ,* X (1907), 235.

178, *3. Senate Journal,* 4th Cong., November 12, 1839, 7.

    9. Mohle MS; *LP,* III, 11.

    15. "Diary of W. Y. Allen," *SWHQ,* XVII (1913), 59–60.

    30. Telegraph, December 11, 1839.

    34. Graham, *Lamar,* p. 58; *Senate Journal,* 4th Cong., Decem-
ber 12, 1839, 127.

179, *6. Senate Journal,* 4th Cong., November 12, 1839, 6.

    13. List of Property Loaned, August 12, 1839, Domestic Cor-
respondence.

    25. Diary, November 6, 1839.

    33. Ibid., September 16, 1839.

    37. Senate Journal, 4th Cong., 176.

180, *9.* Diary No. 2, flyleaf, lists lots and prices. Total investment
was $7,785 for 19 lots, price of one not recorded. Earlier
he had bought a share of Galveston City Company stock
for $840 (Diary, September 28, 1839). As a statesman he
disapproved of the Galveston and Austin projects but now
that they were going concerns, he put his money into them.

    27. Austin *City Gazette,* October 30, 1839; Winkler, "Seat of
Government," *SWHQ,* X (1907), 234–240.

    36. Ibid.

181, *3.* "Diary of W. Y. Allen," October 14, 1839, *SWHQ,* XVII
(1913), 60.

10. Diary, November 8, 1839.

13. George L. Crocket, *Two Centuries in East Texas*, pp. 233–235.

20. Austin *City Gazette*, November 13, 1839; *Brazoria Courier*, December 3, 1839; Diary, November 11, 1839.

182, *26.* Austin *City Gazette*, November 27, 1839. Lamar clipped this article and filed it (*LP*, III, 193–196). Cf. James, *The Raven*, pp. 310–311, for another interpretation of Jones's participation in the Houston dinner.

XIX. SOME COURTLY LANGUAGE

183, *6.* Diary, November 21, 1839.

8. *Memoranda*, p. 35.

21. Diary, December 10, 1839; also in *Memoranda*, p. 36.

29. Winkler (ed.), *Secret Journals*, November 25, 1939, p. 142.

184, *2.* *Ibid.*, February 3, 1840, p. 178; Diary, April 9, 1839.

5. Winkler, *Secret Journals*, December 10, 1839, p. 147, January 4, 1840, p. 168. Jones and five others voted aye, six voted nay. Vice President Burnet broke the tie with an affirmative vote.

31. Paris was the scene of their courtship and honeymoon, but for the wedding they crossed the Channel to be married in St. George's Chapel, London. Mattie Lloyd Wooten (ed.), *Women Tell the Story of the Southwest*, 179; *DAB*, VIII, 526; Crocket, *Two Centuries*, pp. 288–291.

185, *1.* *Biographical Directory*, p. 10; *TDC*, I, 23.

31. Diary, April 9, 1839.

186, *2.* Diary, April 25, 1839.

3. Anson Jones was Mr. Jones of Ba; his adopted cousin, Oliver Jones, was Mr. Jones of A. in the *Senate Journal*.

8. Winkler, *Secret Journals*, pp. 162–165.

19. *Ibid.*

26. Schmitz, *Texan Statecraft*, p. 107.

187, *11.* Winkler, *Secret Journal*, p. 166. Four senators voted to table the resolution, but it passed without a record vote.

16. Diary, December 19, 20, 1839.

21. *Morning Star*, December 27, 1839, describes these importations.

27. Diary, February 4, August 3, 1840. Lot No. 1, Division B (Deed Records, Travis County). For the teamster episode see *TDC*, III, 1323; John Nathan Craven, *James Harper Starr*, pp. 67–68.

188, *15.* Harriet Smither (ed.), *Journals of the Fourth Congress*, December 17, 1839, I, 148.

32. Ibid., December 14, 1839, I, 137.
189, *3. Ibid.*
    9. Gouge, *Fiscal History,* p. 105.
    29. Ibid., pp. 103–104.
190, *21.* Ruthven, *Proceedings,* I, 46–51.
191, *19.* Diary, February 20, 1840.
192, *6. Morning Star,* December 31, 1839.
    15. Austin *City Gazette,* January 15, 1840.
    17. Telegraph, December 11, 1839.
    20. Memoranda, p. 22.
    26. Diary, January 19, 1840.
    30. Ibid., January 20, 1840.
    33. Ibid., January 11, 1840.
    38. No law authorized payment of her claim, dated April 12, 1836, and it was rejected (*Journals,* I, 208).
193, *3.* Smither, *Journals,* I, 231, 237.
    7. Mrs. A. B. Looscan, "Oliver Jones and his Wife," *SWHQ,* X (1906), 178.
    11. Diary, January 30, 1840.
    29. Diary, February 9, 15, March 1, 1840.
    39. Ibid., March 7, 12, 1840.
194, *6. Ibid.,* March 13, 22, 1840; Yoakum, *History,* II, 298–299.
    13. Diary, April 6, 19, 27, 1840.
    30. Clipping from *Greenfield* [Missouri] *Vedetta,* February 2, 1908, Dienst Collection.
    36. The Jones-McCrory license is in Texas Memorial Museum, Austin (Austin *Statesman,* August 28, 1944).
195, *21. Memoranda,* pp. 20–21.
    31. Diary No. 3.

XX. NOT BY MY VOTE

196, *21.* Austin *City Gazette,* October 21, 1840.
197, *1.* Diary, November 3, 1840.
    6. Ibid., November 23, 1840.
    22. Ibid., October 17, 18, 1840.
    25. Ibid., November 3, 1840. He later deleted the derogatory words.
    36. LP, III, 451.
198, *1.* Diary, November 7, 1840.
    5. Ibid., November 20, 1840.
    8. Memoranda, p. 37.

19. Memoranda, p. 23; Austin *City Gazette,* December 23, 1840.

27. Winkler, *Secret Journals,* pp. 197–198, 221; Diary, January 27–29, 1841.

37. House Journal, 5th Cong., January 12, 1841, p. 293.

199, *11.* Gouge, *Fiscal History,* p. 106, quoting committee report and Speaker Kaufman's summary of achievements of the session.

14. Ibid.

33. Winkler, *Secret Journals,* pp. 193, 194, 201.

37. Ibid., p. 201.

200, *11. Ibid.,* p. 200; *WSH,* II, 366.

16. Winkler, *Secret Journals,* p. 188.

34. Memoranda, pp. 158–159.

201, *2.* Austin *City Gazette,* January 13, 1841.

29. Diary No. 3, Business Data, February 2, 1841.

33. Pay and mileage received February 5, $896.00 (Diary No. 3).

202, *14. Ibid.,* February 26, 1841.

XXI. FAREWELL TO POLITICS

203, *15.* Diary, December 3, 1839.

17. Ibid., April 17, 1839.

30. Ibid., January 1, 1840. On New Year's Day, 1840, he was dejected. "If it were not for appearing to yield too easily to adverse circumstances, I would resign my Seat in the Senate today," he wrote.

204, *14. Ibid.,* November 23, 1839.

25. Austin *City Gazette,* January 15, 1840.

27. Diary, April 17, 1839.

30. Ibid., December 14, 1839.

39. Ibid., April 17, 1839.

205, *7. Sentinel,* February 26, 1840.

8. Ibid., March 4, 1840.

13. LP, June 15, 1840, V, 430.

19. Austin *City Gazette,* February 26, 1840.

206, *2. LP,* III, 366–367.

8. Ibid., p. 372.

19. See *WSH,* II. Probably his longest silent period.

26. Austin *City Gazette,* September 9, 1840. A week earlier Jones had presided over a dinner for General Felix (Long Shanks) Huston (*Ibid.,* September 2).

207, *19.* Huling Papers.
   23. Jewett to James H. Starr, July 15, 1841, Starr Papers.
   25. LP, III, 507.
208, *1.* Diary, April 11, 1841.
   7. Ibid., April 14–29, 1841.
   14. Austin *City Gazette,* May 26, 1841.
   33. Ibid., June 2, 1841.
   36. Ibid., May 26, 1841.
   40. Ibid., May 19, 1841.
209, *1. Ibid.,* May 19, 1841.
   15. Diary, June 4 to August 14, 1841.
   27. Ibid. Samples of the letters are in *Memoranda,* pp. 160–166.
   37. Much correspondence on the Santa Fe expedition is in *LP,*
        II, III.
210, *9. Memoranda,* p. 169.
   16. Ibid.
   27. Ibid., pp. 163–164.
211, *14. Ibid.,* pp. 160–161.
   19. Ibid., p. 162; Diary, August 16, 1841.
   27. Memoranda, p. 23. Ledger in Ammon Underwood Papers.
   39. Morning Star, August 19, 1841.
212, *5.* Houston received 7,915 votes, Burnet 3,616 (Thrall, *History,*
        p. 318).
   8. Sentinel, August 26, 1841.
   10. Morning Star, August 19, 1841.
   14. LP, III, 506.
   19. San Augustine *Red-Lander,* August 12, 1841.
   22. Austin *City Gazette,* October 6, 1841; Thrall, *History,* p.
        318.

XXII. WITHOUT MONEY, WITHOUT CREDIT . . .

213, *12.* Houston to "My fair country women and my country men,"
        November 25, 1841, *WSH,* II, 394.
   25. Memoranda, pp. 167–168; *WSH,* II, 390–391.
214, *8, 16.* To Mrs. Jones, November 10, 1841, AJP.
   24. Ibid., November 19, 1841.
215, *2.* Maurice G. Fulton (ed.), *Diary and Letters of Josiah Gregg,*
        I, 108.
   8. To Mrs. Jones, December 7–8, 1841, AJP.
   12. Memoranda, p. 168.
   19. Ibid., p. 23. Written in 1850.
   29. To Mrs. Jones, December 13, 1841, AJP.
   38. House Journal, 6th Cong., December 13, 1841, p. 137.

216. *20.* Josiah Gregg, *Diary*, I, 108.

29. *House Journal*, 6th Cong., December 13, 1841, p. 137.

217, *4.* Gregg, *Diary*, I, 110; *Telegraph*, December 22, 1841; *Senate Journal*, 6th Cong., 115.

23. Teulon to Jones, October 7, 1841, *Memoranda*, pp. 106–107.

218, *8.* *Handbook of Texas*, I, 820.

16. *Ibid.*, II, 725–726.

26. To James Morgan, December 22, 1841, Morgan Papers.

29. Winkler, *Secret Journals*, p. 212.

219, *6.* *Handbook of Texas*, I, 453; Ralph Bayard, *Lone Star Vanguard*, pp. 162, 306.

28. *The Red-Lander*, August 24, 1844, reported that Vice President Burleson had broken twenty tie votes in the Senate—nineteen against Houstonian measures, one for the President's program.

38. *LP*, II, 459; To Mrs. Jones, January 3, 1842, AJP.

220, *10.* To Mrs. Jones, January 3, 1842, AJP.

14. *Ibid.*, December 19, 1841, AJP.

21. *Morning Star*, January 22, 1842.

29. To Mrs. Jones, November 10, 1841, AJP.

221, *24.* Gouge, *Fiscal History*, p. 110. On the same page Gouge quotes the *Gazette*, September 1, 1841, "as we cannot trust ourselves to tell so important a story in our own words."

222, *12.* Gouge, *Fiscal History*, p. 111.

21. *Senate Journal*, 6th Cong., November 2, 1841, p. 5.

25. *House Journal*, November 3, 1841, p. 8.

36. Gouge, p. 269, guesses it was about $4,381,004.64 on September 30, 1841.

39. Gouge, *Fiscal History*, pp. 115, 269.

223, *4.* *Journals of the Sixth Congress*, III, October 1, 1841, p. 315.

14. *House Journal*, November 22, 1841, p. 60.

24. *House Journal*, November 22, 1841, p. 59, November 30, 1841, p. 94; Gammel, *Laws*, II, 684–686.

224, *2.* *House Journal*, December 3, 1841, p. 87.

14. *WSH*, II, 399–408.

19. To Mrs. Jones, December 21, 1841, AJP.

28. *Ibid.*

34. *Memoranda*, p. 120.

225, *24.* *Memoranda*, pp. 120–125.

28. *House Journal*, 59; Yoakum, *History*, II, 431.

31. *Memoranda*, p. 24.

38. Gammel, *Laws*, II, 728.

226, *5. Ibid.*, p. 750.
  14. To Mrs. Jones, January 3, 1842, AJP.
  18. Memoranda, pp. 24–25.
  20. To Mrs. Jones, December 21, 1841, AJP.
  25. Memoranda, pp. 23–24.

XXIII. SECRETARY OF STATE

227, *6. House Journal,* 6th Cong., January 11, 1842, p. 361.
  21. Handbook of Texas, II, 860; *WSH,* II, 478.
228, *13.* Jones, *Letters Relating to the History of Annexation,* p. 5.
    Hereafter cited as *Letters* (1852).
  28. Daily Bulletin, December 13, 15, 1841, *fide* Schmitz, *Texan
    Statecraft,* p. 171.
  38. By the same margin the House failed to impeach Burnet
    and Chalmers (*House Journal,* 99–110, 175–182).
229, *13.* AJP.
  17. Telegraph, January 19, 1842.
  28. House Journal, January 11, 1842, p. 363.
  37. House Journal, January 31, 1842, pp. 434–436; *WSH,* II,
    462–465.
230, *20. LP,* IV, 28.
  36. LP, IV, 1–2.
231, *14. Memoranda,* p. 55.
232, *6.* T. M. Marshall, "Diplomatic Relations of Texas and the
    United States, 1839–1843," *SWHQ,* XV (1912), 278.
  9. Ibid.
  22. Biographical Directory, pp. 157–158; *Handbook of Texas,*
    II, 459; Diary, January 26, 1842; Schmitz, *Texan State-
    craft,* p. 177.
233. *4. Memoranda,* p. 177.
  25. Jones to McIntosh, January 20, 1842, *TDC,* III, 1355.
    Probably the most adroit diplomatic letter Jones ever
    wrote. He later wrote: "I deemed it most expedient to
    treat on the matter with *his* Government, with whom I
    adjusted the same without *condemning my own Govern-
    ment*" (*Memoranda,* p. 177). Saligny did not return
    until April.
234, *16. House Journal,* 6th Cong., December 3, 1842, p. 86.
  18. Hamilton is said to have "had a fiery temper, but he had
    also a sweetness of disposition" (*DAB,* VII, 187–188).
  33. TDC, III, 944.

235, *19.* Winkler, *Secret Journals,* pp. 221–224. Mary Katherine Chase, *Négociations de la République du Texas en Europe, 1837–1845,* pp. 105–111.

  26. Gammel, *Laws,* II, 880–888.

  35. Arthur Ikin brought the treaties and was commissioned Texas consul for London. In 1841 he published his *Texas: Its History, Topography, Agriculture, Commerce, and General Statistics,* to encourage emigration and trade (*Handbook of Texas,* I, 874). The first two treaties were ratified January 26, 1841. The slave treaty was brought by A. T. Burnley, loan agent for Texas since 1837 and owner of slave plantations in Mississippi and Texas (*Handbook of Texas,* I, 254). The third treaty was approved without a record vote (Winkler, *Secret Journals,* p. 218).

236, *4. TDC,* III, 1352.

  21. Chase, *Négociations,* p. 123. WSH, II, 115. *Handbook of Texas,* II, 110. *TDC,* III, 1375.

  27. There is no adequate biography of Ashbel Smith, but see *Handbook of Texas,* II, 620–621; sketch by Chauncey D. Leake in Smith's *Yellow Fever in Galveston,* pp. 1–11; Pat Ireland Nixon, *The Medical Story of Early Texas, passim;* and Nixon, *History of the Texas Medical Association, 1853–1953.*

  34. TDC, III, 1356.

XXIV. MR. HOUSTON'S TEXAS

237, *2.* Hyde to Damon Coats, February 9, 1842, Adriance Papers.

  6. Huling to Thomas H. Espy, February 6, 1842, Huling Papers.

  13. Houston to Jones, February 5, 1842, *Memoranda,* p. 170.

  14. J. M. Ogden to Damon Coats, February 9, 1842, Adriance Papers.

  21. Diary, February 9–14, 1842.

  25. Memoranda, p. 168.

238, *7.* Johnson, *History,* p. 474; Bancroft, *North Mexican States and Texas,* II, 347–348.

  25. Memoranda, p. 171.

  29. Houston to Jones, *Ibid.,* p. 172.

239, *17. Ibid.,* p. 190.

  26. LP, IV Pt. 1, p. 2; *Memoranda,* pp. 190–191. Thomas F. McKinney delivered Jones's reply to Lamar.

240, *17. TDC*, III, 949.

26. Memoranda, p. 200.

241, *11. TDC*, III, 1357.

20. Diary No. 3, Expense a/c for 1842, March 16, 1842.

32. John Henry Brown, *History*, II, 211–215.

242, *3. WSH*, IV, 193.

5. Diary, March 10, 1842.

22. WSH, II, 499–508.

28. Memoranda, p. 172.

38. WSH, II, 500–502.

243, *7. Memoranda*, p. 172.

18. WSH, II, 503–506.

31. Brown, *History*, II, 215–216; *WSH*, II, 509–510.

34. Diary, March 15, 1842; Expense a/c, March 16, 1842.

244, *2. WSH*, II, 492.

7. Niles' Register, LXII, 49–50.

33. WSH, II, 513–527. Joseph Eve, United States chargé, thought "Houston has brag[g]ed higher than San Ta Ana" (Joseph Milton Nance (ed.), "A Letter Book of Joseph Eve, United States Chargé d' Affaires to Texas," *SWHQ*, XLIII [1939], 486).

36. Diary, March 21, 1842.

245, *8. WSH*, II, 529–530.

22. Ibid., pp. 538–539.

31. Memoranda, pp. 172–173.

35. Ibid., p. 178.

246, *11.* Diary, March 26, 1842; *WSH*, II, 536–538.

24. WSH, III, 16–17.

33. TDC, III, 952.

36. WSH, III, 15.

247, *6. WSH*, III, 22.

14. Ibid.

17. WSH, III, 23–26.

38. Journals of the Sixth Congress, July 12, 1842, III, 48.

248, *3. LP*, IV, Pt. 1, p. 5.

17. WSH, III, 23–26.

24. Memoranda, pp. 171–172.

36. Ibid., p. 187.

39. Ibid., Memoranda, p. 192.

249, *30.* Saligny to Guizot, April 23, 1842, quoted in Chase, *Négociations*, pp. 122–123.

35. Ibid.

250, *12. WSH*, IV, 91.

    16. Diary, May 17, 1842.

    22. TDC, I, 563.

    26. WSH, III, 58.

    39. Ibid., p. 66.

251, *9.* Diary, June 9–14, 1842. Contract, never consummated, is in Public Debt Papers, Texas State Library.

    22. Diary, June 20, 1842.

    33, 37. Memoranda, pp. 189–190.

252, *11.* Smither, *Journals of the Sixth Congress*, III, 1, 2, 97.

    25. Ibid., III, 112.

    28. Ibid., p. 121.

    37. Ibid., p. 124; *Memoranda*, p. 193.

253. *10.* Smither, *Journals* (Sixth), III, 124.

    14. Ibid., p. 158.

    21. Morning Star, July 9, 1842. Smither, *Journals* (Sixth), III, 144.

    32. Smither, *Journals* (Sixth), III, 125–127, 149.

    38. Ibid., p. 151.

254, *35.* July 24, 1842, issues of *Civilian* and *Gazette*, quoted in Smither, *Journals* (Sixth), III, 160–161.

255, *5.* Smither, *Journals* (Sixth), III, 62.

    10. Memoranda, p. 193.

    17. Ibid., p. 179.

    31. WSH, III, 126–127.

    36. Diary, July 22, 1842.

256, *5.* Smither, *Journals* (Sixth), III, 168–175.

    15. Memoranda, pp. 193–194.

    33. Ibid., pp. 186–187.

257, *24. WSH*, III, 137–138.

    29. Memoranda, pp. 185–186.

258, *3. TDC*, I, 571–572.

    9. Diary, August 31–September 10, 1842.

    11. WSH, IV, 136–143.

    15. Ibid., IV, 136.

    22. Ibid., III, 135.

    26. Ibid., p. 127.

    39. TDC, I, 578.

259, *17. Ibid.*, III, 1009–1011.

    26. Winkler (ed.), "The Bexar and Dawson Prisoners," *SWHQ*, XIII (1910), 294.

    35. Nixon, *Medical Story*, p. 255; Rena Maverick Green, *Samuel Maverick, Texan: 1803–1870*, pp. 164–168.

260, *10. LP,* IV, Pt. 1, 35–37; "Woll's Report," *SWHQ,* LVIII (1955), 523–552.

19. WSH, III, 170.

26. Yoakum, *History,* II, 363–367; Brown, *History,* II, 222–232.

36. See T. J. Green, *Journal of the Texian Expedition against Mier,* for details.

261, *2.* Diary, September 23, 1842.

13. Memoranda, pp. 196–197; *WSH,* III, 160–161.

24. Memoranda, p. 197.

XXV. WASHINGTON-ON-THE-BRAZOS

262, *6.* Wallis and Hill (eds.), *Sixty Years on the Brazos,* p. 96 (hereafter cited as Wallis, *Sixty Years).*

17. "Diary of Adolphus Sterne," *SWHQ,* XXXIII (1929), 77.

19. Frank Brown, "Old Washington," MS, p. 10.

263, *3.* Georgina Burleson (comp.), *Life and Writings of Rufus C. Burleson,* pp. 670, 696; W. L. McCalla, *Adventures in Texas,* p. 79.

6. See town advertisements in *Telegraph* and other papers for 1842.

17. George W. Bonnell, *Topographical Description of Texas,* p. 41.

26. Wallis, *Sixty Years,* p. 41.

31. Ibid., p. 67.

264, *8. Red-Lander,* October 20, 1842.

15. E. D. Adams (ed.), *British Diplomatic Correspondence Concerning the Republic of Texas, 1838–1846,* p. 127 (hereafter cited as *BDC).* This letter, dated November 15, 1842, is also in *SWHQ,* XVI (1912), 77.

18. Houston lectured Congress, January 8, 1844: "Washington is the constitutional seat of government, . . . was so regarded by the convention at the date of the formation and adoption of the constitution. None other was known or named. . . . here the constitution was framed and other acts done, recognizing it as the seat of government" *(WSH,* III, 514).

21. WSH, III, 155.

27. Wallis, *Sixty Years,* p. 96.

33. Ibid.

265, *6. BDC,* p. 127; also in *SWHQ,* XVI (1912), 77–78.

16. Wallis, *Sixty Years,* pp. 156–157.

23. *TDC*, III, 1404.

28. Diary, October 29–December 2, 1842; R. L. Biesele, *History of German Settlements in Texas, 1831–1861*, pp. 66 ff.

37. *WSH*, III, 179.

266, 2. Diary, November 14–24, 1842; *House Journal*, 7th Cong., called sess., November 14–24, 1842, 3–7.

6. *Senate Journal*, November 14–30, 1842, 3–8. Quorum November 30.

11. *WSH*, III, 199–200.

20. *House Journal*, November 24, 1842, 9.

27. Diary, November 24–December 15, 1842.

39. *WSH*, III, 204.

267, 16. *Ibid.*, pp. 203–216.

29. *House Journal*, December 2, 1842, 16–28. For Cazneau see *Biographical Directory*, p. 64; *Handbook of Texas*, I, 318.

268, 2. *House Journal*, December 3–15, 1842, 30–66.

16. *Senate Journal*, December 2–15, 1842, 9–23.

26. Diary, December 15–17, 1842.

38. *Senate Journal*, December 16, 1842–January 14, 1843, 23–136. For Jack see *Biographical Directory*, p. 111; *Handbook of Texas*, I, 899–900.

269, 5. *House Journal*, December 16, 1842–January 16, 1843, 67–285.

21. *Morning Star*, December 22, 1842.

270, 16. *House Journal*, January 14, 1843, 247–248; December 15, 1842, 70.

21. *House Journal*, January 14, 16, 1843, 246, 278; *Senate Journal*, January 9, 11, 1843, 88, 91, 95, 100. Divorce was by act of Congress only during the Republic. The Gilmores and twenty-nine other unhappy couples were included in a divorce bill which the Senate passed, then voted, 7–6, to table (*Senate Journal*, January 14, 1843, 125–126).

271, 6. *Senate Journal*, January 16, 1843, 120–136; *House Journal*, January 16, 1843, 254–285; Winkler, *Secret Journal*, 276–278.

12. *WSH*, IV, 164.

19. *WSH*, III, 299.

22. Jones to Norton, January 15, 1843, M. P. Norton Papers.

31. Diary No. 3, Moneys Received for the Year 1842.

XXVI. ARMISTICE

273, *20. TDC*, I, 614–618.

    26. Ibid., III, 1267–1268, 1399–1403; Schmitz, *Texan State-craft*, p. 184.

274, *5. TDC*, III, 1534–1538.

    21. WSH, III, 310. The Order of San Jacinto was reconstituted by the Sons of the Republic of Texas in 1941 (*SRT Yearbook, 1962*, p. 66).

    30. Diary, January 24, 1843.

    39. Ibid., January 31, 1843.

275, *28. TDC*, II, 123–124.

    39. Ibid., pp. 217–218; *Handbook of Texas*, II, 361.

276, *5. WSH*, IV, 174.

    16. TDC, II, 130, 132–138; *Memoranda*, p. 211; *WSH*, IV, 66.

    29. Memoranda, p. 215.

    37. Ibid., p. 219.

277, *11.* Diary, April 2, 3, 4, 1843.

    23. For Elliot see *Dictionary of National Biography*, XVII, 251; *Handbook of Texas*, I, 556. Clagette Blake, *Charles Elliot, R.N., 1801–1875*, has portrait.

    31. Memoranda, pp. 207–209.

278, *24. WSH*, IV, 184–186.

    30. BDC, pp. 172–178.

279, *13. WSH*, IV, 183, 206.

    22. Ibid., III, 351–353.

    38. Ibid., III, 329–331.

280, *8. Ibid.*, III, 369, 354–376; C. W. Raines, "The Alamo Monument," *SWHQ*, VI (1903), 300–310.

    18. Wallis, *Sixty Years*, pp. 96–97.

281, *11. Ibid.*, pp. 97–99.

    29. Diary, April 10, 12, 1843.

    36. WSH, III, 364.

282, *4.* Diary, April 24–May 15, 1843; Jones to Mrs. Jones, May 3, 1843, AJP.

    10. Diary, May 6, 1843.

    19. To Mrs. Jones, May 6, 1843, AJP.

    28. TDC, II, 164–170.

    34. Memoranda, pp. 222–223.

283, *9.* Murphy to Upshur, June 5, 1843, cited in G. L. Rives, *United States and Mexico, 1821–1848*, I, 559.

    22. TDC, III, 1090–1091.

    38. WSH, III, 409–410.

284. *13.* Murphy to Legare, July 6, 1843, quoted in Rives, *United States and Mexico,* I, 560.

31. TDC, II, 195.

XXVII. AN UNCERTAIN DIE

285, *5. Memoranda,* p. 224.

20. LP, IV, Pt. 1, 20.

286, *5. Memoranda,* p. 225.

20. Jones to Smith, July 9, 1843, *Memoranda,* p. 227. On November 1, Jones bought a printing press at Houston for $410 (Diary No. 3, Cash Expended 1843). The paper, a weekly, was published during the last five months of 1843 (Ike Moore [ed.], *Texas Newspapers, 1813–1939,* p. 108).

30. Spirit of Missions, October, 1843, quoted in DuBose Murphy, *Short History of the Protestant Episcopal Church in Texas,* p. 14.

287, *2. Handbook of Texas,* II, 632–633.

8. Memoranda, pp. 231–233.

17. Memoranda, pp. 233–236.

21. Ibid., p. 242.

29. WSH, III, 422–424; *Memoranda,* pp. 241–242.

36. Biographical sketches in *Handbook of Texas.*

288, *14.* Jones to Miller, August 17, 1843, Washington D. Miller Papers.

32. Diary, August 4 to September 7, 1843.

289, *11. Memoranda,* pp. 253–255.

18. Ibid.

28. WSH, III, 422.

36. Diary, September 22, 1843.

290, *3.* Yoakum, *History,* II, 415.

6. Diary, October 2, 1843.

11. Cramayel, who disapproved of all he saw and heard in Texas, was temporarily replacing Saligny (Chase, *Négociationes,* pp. 122, 124–137; *TDC,* III, 1427).

23. Memoranda, pp. 258–259.

36. Diary, October 20–November 1, 1843.

291, *3.* Diary No. 3, Cash Expended 1843, October 30–November 6.

23. Memoranda, pp. 263–265.

292, *4. Ibid.,* pp. 261–263.

9. Diary, November 10, 11, 1843.

28. TDC, II, 207–210.

293, *2. Ibid.,* pp. 221–224.

    17. Memoranda, pp. 259, 261.

    31. Ibid., p. 261.

294, *4.* S. H. Everitt to Jones, November 19, 1842. This East Texas physician who served with Jones in the Texas Senate had just returned from the United States, where he found "that Texas, in the Northern States, stands as low in the grade of nations as it is possible a nation can be and exist" (*Memoranda,* p. 270).

    15. WSH, III, 448.

    24. Ibid., p. 456.

295. *9. Memoranda,* pp. 265–267.

    20. Ibid.

    24. Ibid. By 1845 he had convinced himself that his opponents were "speculators, and 'war dogs' . . . as well as the personal enemies of Gen. Houston generally. I probably lost more than I gained by my association with him."

296, *13. Morning Star,* November 16, 1843.

    33. News, November 28, 1843. For Lamar's influence on the *News,* see Sam Acheson, *35,000 Days in Texas,* pp. 16–19.

297, *3. Handbook of Texas,* II, 289.

    6. Memoranda, p. 273.

    28. House Journal, December 13, 1843, 13.

    33. Henry F. Gillette to Smith, December 14, 1843, Ashbel Smith Papers.

    34. A visiting English woman described the statesmen "seated on candle boxes and sugar casks . . . each . . . whittling away without interruption" (Houstoun, *Texas and the Gulf of Mexico,* II, 171).

298, *8. WSH,* III, 459–474.

    37. Ibid.

299, *2.* Diary, December 17, 1843.

    22. TDC, II, 232.

    34. Senate Journal, December 18, 1843, p. 18.

300, *22. WSH,* III, 484–491.

301, *9.* For Dr. January and the other physician-congressmen see Nixon, *Medical Story,* p. 372 *et passim.*

    15. Diary, December 21–28, 1843. He moved into the Cook place December 27.

    32. Morning Star, November 12, 1843.

302, *2. Memoranda,* p. 275.

    4. Ibid., p. 279.

    8. Ibid., pp. 281–282.

33. Ibid.

36. December 27, 1843, Norton Papers.

303, *10. House Journal,* December 18, 19, 22, 1843, 39, 44, 65.

20. Ibid., December 29, 30, 1843, 87, 98. Tiana Rogers Gentry, whom Houston married in a Cherokee ceremony in 1830, bore him no children (Llerena Friend, *Sam Houston,* p. 28). The legend, never substantiated, that Houston was the father of many red-headed Indians in the Territory, still circulates.

29. Diary No. 3, Cash Received 1843 in Exchequer Money.

304, *20.* Diary, December 31, 1843.

XXVIII. THE ABSORBING QUESTION

305, *16.* Jones to Norton, January 15, 1844 (misdated 1843), Norton Papers.

306, *10. Ibid.,* January 18, 1844.

37. WSH, III, 502.

307, *5. Telegraph,* January 10, 1844.

28. WSH, III, 513–517.

36. Jones to Norton, January 21, 1844, Norton Papers.

308, *7. Memoranda,* p. 301.

12. Ibid., p. 303.

18. Rives, *United States and Mexico,* I, 583, quoting Upshur to Murphy, January 16, 1844.

24. TDC, II, 239.

309, *17.* Winkler, *Secret Journals,* pp. 294–298. *House Journal,* February 5, 1844, 440.

310, *8. TDC,* II, 248.

30. WSH, IV, 238–239.

311, *36. House Journal,* February 5, 1844, 410–440; *Senate Journal,* February 5, 1844, 237–245; Winkler, *Secret Journals,* February 5, 1844, 301–302.

312, *8. WSH,* IV, 253.

16. Memoranda, p. 307.

23. Ibid.

28. Ibid.

35. Ibid., pp. 308–309.

313, *2. Memoranda,* pp. 308–309.

16. Ibid., pp. 309–310. Power was the largest importer of British goods in Texas (William M. Morgan, *Trinity Protestant Episcopal Church, Galveston,* p. 19).

29. Memoranda, pp. 310–311.

38. Ibid., pp. 311–312.

314, *2. Ibid.*

20. *Ibid.,* pp. 312–314. Jones's endorsement: "I disapprove the publication, and shall persuade Mr. Manson not to make it. Note, 1845.—It was never published."

34. Memoranda, pp. 299–300.

315, *2.* Diary, January 3 to November 9, 1844, shows he hired eight Negroes, let Houston hire his William for $16.00 a month, and employed Major J. Chenoweth to manage his farm. Mr. Campbell commenced building his Barrington house January 29.

12. January 21, 1844, Norton Papers. Jones had bought from Mary Kesler at Houston "a certain negro boy slave for life named Solomon about 50 yrs. & of dark complexion on October 25, 1843" (Washington County Deeds, F, 222). Henry F. Gillette wrote Ashbel Smith, February 21, 1844: "George has . . . given Eliza to Dr. Anson Jones for this year" (Ashbel Smith Papers).

18. Diary, January 24, 1844.

27. "The United States having invited that negotiation will be a guaranty of their honor that no evil shall result to Texas from accepting the invitation" (Justin H. Smith, *Annexation of Texas* [1941 ed.], p. 165, quoting *Senate Document No. 349,* 28th Cong., 1st sess., 4).

33. WHS, IV, 259.

316, *8.* Jackson to Houston, January 18, 23, 1844. Houston Williams Collection, quoted in Marquis James, *Andrew Jackson: Portrait of a President,* pp. 476–477; also in his *The Raven,* pp. 345–346.

27. WSH, IV, 260–265.

317, *42.* Norton Papers.

318, *6. Memoranda,* p. 322.

22. Morning Star, February 27.

27. Telegraph, February 28, 1844.

319, *8. Northern Standard,* February 24, 1844.

19. TDC, II, 259–260.

29. Ibid., p. 261.

320, *8. Memoranda,* p. 323. The letter, marked "private," is misdated February 27.

XXIX. SECRET, DARK AND DILIGENT

321, *18.* H. A. Wise, *Seven Decades of the Union,* pp. 222–225; Lyon G. Tyler, *Letters and Times of the Tylers,* II, 294.

See Charles M. Wiltse, *John C. Calhoun, Sectionalist,*
pp. 161–163, for another version.
27. *TDC,* II, 263. March 20, 1844.
322, 4. *TDC,* II, 265.
25. *Memoranda,* pp. 333–335.
36. Murphy to Tyler, March 10, 1844, quoted in J. S. Reeves,
American Diplomacy under Tyler and Polk, p. 147 (hereafter cited as Reeves, *Diplomacy*).
323, 8. *Ibid.,* p. 129.
19. *TDC,* II, 269–273.
24. *Ibid.*
324, 6. *WSH,* IV, 301.
10. J. D. Richardson (comp.), *Messages and Papers of the
Presidents,* IV, 307.
26. Tyler, *The Tylers,* II, 331.
325, 18. Quoted in *Northern Standard,* March 9, 1844.
27. *Memoranda,* pp. 328–329.
326, 3. Norton Papers.
24. *Memoranda,* pp. 331–333.
327, 5. Jones to Norton, April 13, 1844, Norton Papers.
15. *Memoranda,* p. 335.
26. *Ibid.,* p. 336.
31. *Ibid.,* p. 337.
328, 6. *Morning Star,* April 6, 1844.
26. April 7, 1844, *BDC,* pp. 304–308; *SWHQ,* XVIII (1914),
104–108.
33. *Ibid.*
329, 3. See Greer, *Colonel Jack Hays,* pp. 92–113, for border incidents.
13. *Memoranda,* p. 338.
28. *WSH,* IV, 297.
330, 5. *Memoranda,* pp. 338–339.
9. *Ibid.,* p. 341.
27. *Ibid.,* pp. 339–340.
32. *Ibid.*
36. *Ibid.,* p. 342.
38. *WSH,* IV, 303.
331, 21. *WSH,* IV, 309–311; *TDC,* II, 274–276.
36. *Memoranda,* p. 347. *WSH,* IV, 308.
332, 2. Jones to Norton, May 2, 1844, Norton Papers.
15. *Memoranda,* p. 349.
33. Jones to Miller, May 3, 1844, Washington D. Miller Papers.
39. *Memoranda,* p. 349.

333, *5. Ibid.*, p. 350.
   23. Ibid., pp. 350–351.
   30. WSH, IV, 320–325.
   36. Ibid., pp. 318–319.
334, *10. Memoranda*, p. 352.
   14. Ibid.
   21. Jones to Norton, May 16, 1844, Norton Papers.
335, *3. WSH*, IV, 325–327.
   9. Ibid., pp. 327–328.
   18. Ibid., p. 328.
   20. Memoranda, pp. 352–353.
   34. Ibid., pp. 355–356.
   36. Ibid., p. 355.
336, *13.* May 15, 1844, Washington D. Miller Papers.
   36. Evans to Jones, June 9, 1844, AJP.
337, *7.* Snively to Jones, May 20, 1844, AJP.
   24. Memoranda, pp. 353–354.

XXX. WARY AS FOXES

339, *4.* Norton Papers.
   6. Northern Standard, February 3, 17, March 2, 9, 1844.
   11. Telegraph, June 3, 1844.
   15. Ashbel Smith Papers. Another correspondent wrote Smith, July 11, that Burleson's election seemed certain; his want of education increased his popularity.
   18. Jones to Norton, June 6, 1844, Norton Papers.
   19. June 8, 1844, Norton Papers.
   35. Memoranda, pp. 360–361.
340, *13. Memoranda*, p. 362.
   28. Ibid., pp. 362–363.
341, *4. Ibid.*, pp. 363–364.
   21. Ibid., p. 368.
   30. Ibid., pp. 365–366.
   35. Ibid.
342, *9. Ibid.*, p. 366.
   19. James Reily to Norton, June 23, 1844, Norton Papers.
   31. Jackson to Lewis, April 8, 1844, quoted in Smith, *Annexation*, p. 264.
   37. Ibid.
343, *8.* J. Q. Adams, *Memoirs*, XII, 49, quoted in Smith, *Annexation*, p. 280.
   15. Murphy to Houston, July 3, 1844, Yoakum, *History*, II, 432.
   19. Callcott, *Santa Anna*, pp. 190–191.

344, *10, 15. Memoranda,* pp. 371–374;*WSH,* IV, 338–340.
   24. July 9, 1844, Norton Papers.
345, *8. Vindicator,* undated broadside.
   12. July 21, 1844, Norton Papers.
346, *11.* To Norton, July 11, 1844, Norton Papers.
347, *26. WSH,* IV, 354–356.
348, *13.* Reily to Starr, August 5, 1844, Starr Papers.
   20. Vindicator, July 27, 1844, quoted in *Memoranda,* p. 159.
   26. Vindicator, August 17, 1844.
   31. Ibid.
349, *5. Memoranda,* p. 284.
   25. TDC, II, 293–295.
350, *5. Memoranda,* p. 281.
   8. TDC, II, 296.
   16. August 25, 1844, Norton Papers.
   18. Bee, September 9, 1844.
   35. Vindicator, August 17, 1844, in *Memoranda,* p. 284.
351, *7. Red-Lander,* July 20, 1844.
   16. Intelligencer, July 11, 1844.
   35. Northern Standard, August 21, 1844.
   37. The anti-Jones press died hard. Nearly two months after the election Editor Charles DeMorse soliloquized: "When we saw the incumbent President . . . speaking in favor of his successor . . . When we have seen his legal Cabinet advisor, Terrell, uniformly the uncompromising opponent of annexation . . . When we see Col. Reily, another English policy man . . . making skyscraping speeches in favor of Doct. Jones. Finally, barefaced as it is, when so soon as the result of that election was known, Mr. Attorney Gen. Terrell is sent Minister to England, and Mr. Reily Minister to U. S., and our able and indefatigable Charge d'Affaires, Mr. Van Zandt . . . recalled. This, fellow-citizens, is the raising of the first curtain in that political farce, in which Pres. Houston is the stage manager, Doct. Jones the prompter and you are the dupes. If before the election Messrs. Terrell and Reily were observed . . . dusting the scenes, their assiduity have won their promotion" (*Northern Standard,* November 20, 1844).
352, *13. Telegraph,* September 25, 1844, for incomplete returns by counties. Thrall, *History,* p. 340, gives total vote as 12,752: Jones 7,037, Burleson 5,668. A joint session of the 9th Senate and House canvassed the votes December 5. Official returns tallied 6,443 for Jones; 5,054 for

Burleson; 38 scattering. Votes "informally returned" were 550 for Jones, 640 for Burleson, 9 scattering (*House Journal,* December 5, 1844, p. 20).

XXXI. INTERLUDE

353, *24.* Diary No. 1, July, 1838–January, 1839, fly leaf.
354, *11.* Estimated population, 1831, 20,000; votes polled in the last election of the Republic of Texas indicate a population of 125,000 (*Handbook of Texas,* I, 321).

   36. William B. Ochiltree to Jones, September 24, 1844, *Memoranda,* p. 385.

355, *17. Memoranda,* pp. 383–384. Endorsement: " 'An honest man's the noblest work of God.'—A.J."

   26. Ibid., pp. 386–387.
   29. Ibid., p. 390.
   37. Ibid., pp. 391–392.

356, *9. Memoranda,* pp. 392–393.

   26. Winchell to Jones, November 16, 1844; *Memoranda,* 401–404.

357, *23. TDC,* III, 1154.

   26. Ibid., p. 1155.

358, *6.* Houston to Mrs. Houston, September 28, 1844, *WSH,* IV, 373.

   27. WSH, IV, 371–372.
   34. Memoranda, pp. 371–373.

360, *4.* Jones, *Letters* (1852), pp. 20–21; also in *WSH,* IV, 372.

   23. Memoranda, p. 389.
   31. Biographical Directory, [p. 8]; sketches in *Handbook of Texas.*

361, *4. DAB,* VII, 540–542.

   10. Memoranda, pp. 385–386, 387–388.
   16. Ibid., p. 398.
   30. Ibid., pp. 398–399.
   37. BDC, p. 377.

362, *9. Telegraph,* December 18, 1844; *TDC,* I, 43.

   18. Reeves, *Diplomacy,* p. 181.
   32. BDC, p. 436.

363, *16. Memoranda,* pp. 404–405.

   25. Terrell to Miller, November 26, 1844, Washington D. Miller Papers.
   36. Smith, *Annexation,* pp. 297–321.
   39. Ibid., p. 321.

XXXII. THE PRESIDENT

365, *12.* Richardson, *Messages,* III, 2195–2198.

    29. Callcott, *Santa Anna,* p. 214.

366, *14. BDC,* p. 405.

    28. Con DeWitt Catterton, "Political Campaigns," MS, *passim.*

367, *13. Biographical Directory,* pp. 160–161, 152.

    31. House Journal, 9th Cong., 1st sess., December 3, 1844, 5–6.

368, *3.* Memoirs of John S. Ford, MS, 297–298.

    23. Biographical Directory, p. 154; *Biographical Directory of the American Congress,* pp. 1774–1927, 1413; *Senate Journal,* December 4, 1844, 8.

    32. Biographical Directory, pp. 128–129.

369, *10. WSH,* IV, 392–398.

369, *36.* Corinne Montgomery informed citizens of the United States: "The four men who, in turn, have been called to the highest place in the Land of the Lone Star, are as diverse as men can well be in mind and lineament, but they are agreed on three points—in their strong love for Texas—in a devout faith in the glories of her future destiny—and in the extraordinary littleness of their faith in each other.

    "Dr. Anson Jones . . . promises to imitate closely the moderate non-committalism of his predecessor . . . He is a plain, practical New Englander, ready for a speculation, either in his public or private capacity, so that it be safe and decorous; but he will run no disagreeable risk . . . will take care not to venture beyond his depth for friend or foe . . . will make no personal sacrifices . . . Jones will be a miniature edition of Houston in water colors, as Houston himself is an imperfect copy of General Jackson—without disrespect to the old hero be it said—done in chalks.

    "Of the four Presidents of Texas, Jones is the least favored by nature. He is of inferior stature, and wanting in beauty of expression. He has not the forcible diction of Burnet, the persuasive grace of Houston, or the noble sincerity of Lamar; but he is courteous, self-possessed, discriminating, and well educated. There is a spice of petty malevolence in some of his papers, as Secretary of State, but he imputes these blots to Houston. A short time will prove him" (*The United States Magazine and Democratic Review,* XVI [1845], 282, 291). She substantially repeats this in her *Texas and Her Presidents,* published in New York in 1845. Corinne (sometimes Cora) Montgomery was the pseudonym of Jane McManus. She first came to Texas in 1832 but spent much time in the United States. She married General William L. Cazneau, Lamar's devoted partisan, and it was meeting again with Lamar in Washington in 1845 that inspired her to write "The Presidents of Texas," published with a full-page portrait of Lamar. Lamar returned the compliment by dedicating his *Verse Memorials* (New York, W. P. Fetridge and Company, 1857) to her. (Graham, *Life and Poems of Mirabeau B. Lamar,* pp. 69, 91; *Handbook of Texas,* II, 122).

370, *4. House Journal,* December 6, 1844, 23; *Senate Journal,* December 6, 1844, 19.

30. WSH, IV, 401–405.

371, *10. House Journal,* December 9, 27–30.

372, *10. Ibid.*

16. Jones, *Letters* (1852), p. 11.

30. J. K. Holland, "Reminiscences of Austin and Old Washington," *SWHQ,* I (1897), 90.

373, *11. House Journal,* December 4–16, 1844, 7–57; *Senate Journal,* December 4–16, 1844, 7–38.

19. Memoranda, p. 385.

26. House Journal, December 18, 1844, 73.

374, *4. Senate Journal,* December 18, 1844, 45–54.

16. Ibid., January 7, 1845, 118–119.

22. House Journal, January 9, 1845, 181–183.

32. House Journal, December, 1844, 7–124; *Senate Journal,* December, 1844, 3–100.

375, *12. House Journal,* January 30, 1845, 354–356.

18. Senator George A. Pattillo of Jasper presented the petition of R. E. B. Baylor and others for the incorporation of San Jacinto University on December 28, 1844. A week later he proposed to change the name to Milam University, and the next day, as the senators were ready to vote, he moved that institution bear the name of the soldier-preacher-judge who had drafted the petition (*Senate Journal,* 9th Cong., December 28, 1844, p. 78, January 3, 7, 8, 1845, pp. 78, 105, 115, 125; *House Journal,* January 25, p. 299. Gammel, *Laws,* II, 1130–1133). The legendary and undocumented story of the naming of the institution is in Carroll, *A History of Texas*

Baptists, pp. 229–230: Baylor and William M. Tryon, a committee of the Texas Baptist Education Society, drafted the charter. Each insisted that the institution be named for the other. The deadlock was broken when Kenneth L. Anderson, Vice President of the Republic and presiding officer of the Senate, agreed with Tryon that it should be called Baylor. Baylor became first president of the trustees and first professor of law, continuing to serve as district judge and volunteer evangelist. He died in 1873 and was buried on the Baylor campus at Independence (Carroll, *History of Texas Baptists,* p. 906).

376, 23. BDC, p. 397.

377, 6. *Ibid.,* pp. 397–398.

22. *Memoranda,* pp. 410–411; *House Journal,* December 30, 120.

378, 12. *Senate Journal,* January 22, 1845, 180–197.

22. Winkler, *Secret Journals,* January 24, 1845, 311; *Telegraph,* February 5, 1845.

379, 6. *House Journal,* January 30, 1845, 338–342.

23. *Memoranda,* p. 409.

31. *House Journal,* February 3, 1845, 379–395; *Senate Journal,* February 3, 283–296; Winkler, *Secret Journals,* 311–312.

380, 15. BDC, p. 408.

22. *Memoranda,* pp. 408–409.

32. *Ibid.,* p. 421.

381, 7. *TDC,* III, 1170–1172; *Memoranda,* pp. 415–416.

14. BDC, p. 380.

23. *Memoranda,* p. 413.

31. Green to Allen, January 1, 1845, Home Letters Nos. 45, 135; Elliot to Jones, January 14, 1845, and endorsement, *Memoranda,* pp. 413–414.

382, 37. James Morgan Papers.

383, 3. Diary, February 5, 1845.

16. *Memoranda,* pp. 418–419.

28. *Civilian,* February 12, 1845; *National Register,* February 22, 1845.

384, 20. *Memoranda,* pp. 422–424.

37. Ashbel Smith, *Reminiscences,* pp. 65–66.

385, 10. *Ibid.,* pp. 64–65.

25. *Ibid.,* p. 70.

386, 9. BDC, p. 455.

14. Smith, *Annexation,* p. 332, citing *Congressional Globe.* Rives, *United States and Mexico,* I, 690, says the vote was 118 to 101 but does not cite his source.

387, *7.* See Smith, *Annexation,* pp. 333–347, for details. He quotes the New York *Tribune* of March 1, 1845.

18. Ibid.

37. Morning Star, March 23, 1845; *BDC,* p. 460.

XXXIII. ALTERNATIVES

388, *30.* Aberdeen to Elliot, January 23; received March 22, 1845, *BDC,* pp. 428–433.

389, *38.* Diary, March 1, 1845.

390, *21.* Diary, March 17–27, 1845.

391, *28. BDC,* pp. 462–472.

392, *21.* March 29, 1845.

30. Noah Smithwick, *Evolution of a State,* p. 282.

393, *6.* Donelson to Buchanan, March 28, April 1, 1845, Annie Middleton, "Donelson's Mission to Texas in Behalf of Annexation," *SWHQ,* XXIV (1921), 266, 270.

19. E. I. McCormac, *James K. Polk,* pp. 352–355.

394, *7.* Jones, *Letters* (1852), pp. 11–12.

395, *6.* Smith, *Reminiscences,* p. 81.

39. New Orleans *Picayune,* April 26, 1845, quoted in Hogan, *Texas Republic,* pp. 55–56.

396, *8.* Fayette Copeland, *Kendall of the Picayune,* p. 122.

29. Galveston, April 9, 1845, *Memoranda,* pp. 446–449.

36. Ibid.

397, *8. Memoranda,* p. 450.

25. Hunt to Rusk, Henderson, and Anderson, April 18, 1845, Rusk Papers.

398, *3.* F. R. Lubbock, *Six Decades in Texas,* p. 166.

10. Ibid.

18. Ibid., pp. 165–167.

24. Emily Perry to Stephen F. Perry, April 27, 1845, Perry Papers.

38. Copeland, *Kendall,* pp. 132–139.

399, *5.* On February 9, 1850, he remembered that "in the town of San Augustine, I was burned in effigy, or came very near that honor, as well as in many other parts of Texas" (Memorandum Book 5, Mrs. Beatty Oldham Collection). A few anti-Jones newspapers modified their hostility after the "glorious news" of the joint resolution came. The *Northern Standard,* April 9, 1845, said the time had come to "let the British Lion go howling to other lands, 'seeking whom he may devour'." By April 23 the editor had come the full circle: "We have never in any conversation with the President heard him utter one word against Annexation or against the resolutions of the American Congress . . . . the President will cordially cooperate." After counselling, May 7, against "rash or summary measures," the paper hailed Jones's calling elections for the Convention "a noble act" and called on the President's opponents to "with noble unanimity act in concert with him. . . . The President has nobly thrown himself in the breach and said to the boldest, 'Come on. I will be true to my station and will lead the van' " (*Northern Standard*, May 14, 1845).

13. Smith, *Reminiscences*, pp. 72–79; Lubbock, *Six Decades*, pp. 165–167.

20. Diary, May 6–30, 1845.

34. Smith, *Annexation*, p. 439; McCormac, *Polk*, pp. 355–358.

400, *3.* Pilsbury, to J. H. Polly, January 5, 1845 (misdated 1844), Domestic Correspondence, Texas State Archives.

25. Smith, *Reminiscences*, p. 67.

401, *3.* Smith, *Annexation*, pp. 446–448.

5. Diary for May, 1845: "Wed. Thurs. & Friday 28.29 & 30th in town, on business with Gen. Sherman and Doct. Wright of the Princeton." Only that.

13. Elliot to Bankhead, June 11, 1845, quoting Jones's "own words as nearly as I can remember them" (*BDC*, pp. 501–502). Jones endorsed a letter from Ebenezer Allen, June 5, 1845: "I will not manufacture a war to please Mr. Polk. Commodore Stockton, through Dr. Wright, and Gen. Sherman have received an emphatic No. The United States, I believe, have a good enough cause of war against Mexico. Let their Congress determine. It is not my business to do so" (*Memoranda*, p. 468).

26. Smith, *Annexation*, pp. 423–431.

402. *6.* Proclamation in Jones, *Letters* (1852), pp. 21–22.

10. Elliot quoting Jones, *BDC*, p. 501.

30. May 4, 1845, with Jones's endorsement, *Memoranda*, pp. 459–461.

35. *Memoranda*, p. 456.

37. *House Journal*, June 16, 1845, 5.

403, *19.* *Senate Journal*, June 17, 1845, 7–8.

404, *5.* "I advised my friends in the Senate not to reject or adopt the preliminary treaty with Mexico, but to suspend action, and let it go to the Convention for decision. This would have a favorable effect on our relations with the United States, and be just as regards Mexico" (Jones's endorsement on notification of rejection of the treaty, June 21, 1845, *Memoranda,* pp. 472–473). Donelson had written Calhoun, April 24: "Genl Houston brought all his influence to bear against our proposals, and in favor of resorting to negotiation" (*Correspondence of John C. Calhoun,* p. 1031).

22. *House, Senate, Journals,* June 16–28, 1845.

XXXIV. MR. JONES'S TEXAS

405, *11.* Tod to James Buchanan, June 1–11, 1845, quoted in McCormac, *Polk,* pp. 369–70; John G. Tod, Letterbook and Journal, August, 1844–January, 1846.

14. Diary, July 4, 1845.

26. Jones, *Letters* (1848), p. 24.

406, *25.* William F. Weeks (reporter), *Debates of the Texas Convention, 1845,* pp. 5–9.

31. Thomas J. Rusk to George D. Phillips, June 13, 1845, Rusk to John R. Stanford, same date, Rusk Papers.

36. Henderson to Memucan Hunt, May 8, 1845, Rusk Papers.

407, *13.* Houston *Morning Star,* July 12, 1845.

16. Diary, July 9, 1845.

21. July 8, 1845, *Memoranda,* p. 477. Charles F. Taylor contested Ochiltree's election but was not seated (Taylor to Starr, July 5, Rusk to Starr, July 11, 1845, Starr Papers).

23. He was occupied principally with getting the Woodruff children settled, cutting tobacco, and gathering sweet potatoes for the table. Diary, July 11 to 16, 1845.

408, *34.* Diary, June 19–31, 1845. William D. Lee was commissioned secretary of the legation at Washington. William G. Cooke was still secretary of war and marine, still unconcerned about annexation except as it affected his department.

38. *Memoranda,* p. 479.

409, *13.* Diary, August 8, 9, 1845.

30. *Memoranda,* p. 483. Donelson, apprehensive that eviction of the Jones administration might defeat annexation, wrote Henderson and perhaps other delegates, pointing out that the President had done "substantially all that the most zealous friends of the proposals could have done . . . his conduct created no real obstacle" (Donelson to Henderson, June 30, 1845). To Buchanan he wrote, the same day, that Jones "is not so bad a man as many that are abusing him" (George P. Hammond (comp.), *New Spain and the Anglo-American West*, II, 95–100).

34. Diary, August 11, 1845; *Texas National Register,* August 14, 1845.

410, *7. Memoranda,* p. 44.

14. Debates of the Texas Convention, 1845, p. 570.

411, *2. Debates,* pp. 585–586.

6. Ibid., p. 586.

10. Ibid.

25. E. Morehouse to Thomas G. Western, Domestic Correspondence.

38. Jones, *Letters* (1852), p. 17.

412, *8. Debates,* pp. 758–759. John S. Ford declared: "A body of men better qualified . . ., actuated by purer motives and more exalted patri[o]tism never met and never separated" (Ford, MS, p. 391).

18. August 29, 1845, Moses Johnson Papers.

24. Diary, August 31: "Started for home. Wed. Sep. 3ᵈ Arrived at home." September 25: "Went to town, ordered the removal of Offices & Archives to Austin. Offices to be closed on the 4th"; *Texas National Register,* October 2, 1845.

29. So Elliot reported Jones as guessing, January 18, 1846 (*BDC,* p. 583), but a later official compilation showed 9,578 votes cast, 7,853 for Henderson. In 1844, 12,752 votes were cast (*Memoranda,* p. 620). Oral voting, rather than ballots, was used in the 1845 election.

413, *9.* Diary, October 6; *Texas National Register,* October 9, 1845.

20. Memoranda, p. 502.

24. Diary, October 26, 27, 1845.

29. Diary, November 2–26, 1845.

414, *3. Memoranda,* p. 506.

15. Ibid., p. 507.

33. December 18, 1845, Moses Johnson Papers.

415, *6.* December 22, 1845, Johnson Papers.

26. December 31, 1845, Johnson Papers.

416, *2.* Diary, January 1, 1846 (redated "December 31, Retrospect") ; *Memoranda,* p. 42.

20. Diary, January 7, 14, 1846; *Memoranda,* p. 508.

38. BDC, p. 590.

417, *10.* Diary, January 15–25, 1846.

13. Memoranda, p. 509.

17. Henderson to Miller, January 26, 1846, Washington D. Miller Papers.

24. Diary, February 1, 1846; Frank Brown, "Annals," p. 6.

35. February 16, 1846, AJP.

418, *18.* To Mrs. Jones, February 19, 1846, AJP.

419, *11.* Austin *Democrat,* extra, February 20, 1846, quoted in Jones, *Letters* (1852), pp. 25–27.

14. Jacob DeCordova, *Texas: Her Resources and Her Public Men,* p. 144. After the inauguration Jones wrote his wife that his Valedictory was longer than his Inaugural "and a rather better piece of composition, perhaps. My friends think well of it. . . . I never felt better, or happier than I have to-day. I was indeed relieved from a vast and distressing burthen." He attended the inaugural ball, then finished the letter: "I returned home about 3 O'Clock last night, pretty badly 'dog bit'—not so badly hurt however as His Excellency the Governor who fell about 2 O'Clock" (AJP).

XXXV. MISSION ACCOMPLISHED

420, *11.* "My Cotton arrived in Newyork about ten days since. . . . Mr. Brower sold my cotton at 12¾ cents which . . . is much better than to have sold at home . . ." (Jones to Mrs. Jones, August 30, September 10, 1850, AJP).

20. Orizimbo (Dr. Phelps's) and Eagle Island (Wharton's) were the plantations Jones knew best in Brazoria County (Stroebel, *Old Plantations,* pp. 21, 23–28).

421, *20.* His already large library was increased by 360 volumes, at a cost of $600.00 in 1852 (Catalogue of Miscellaneous Books from Dr. W. J. A. Birkley, November 25, 1852, AJP). "Sister Mary left for the North, after a visit of six & a quarter years. . . . paid her expenses home" (Plantation Memorandum Book No. 12, June 3, 1856).

422. *7.* Jones to Miller, October 16, 1852, Washington D. Miller Papers.

33. DuBose Murphy, *Short History of the Protestant Episcopal Church in Texas,* pp. 22, 31; Diary, December 3, 7, 1848.

423, *3.* St. Paul's College opened in 1852, closed in 1856. Chartered in 1853, it enrolled sixty pupils, including three of college grade the next year (Murphy, *Short History,* 34).

5. Bishop Freeman estimated there were two hundred Episcopalians in Texas in 1847 (Murphy, *Short History,* 18).

25. Miller to Jones, March 8, 1847, *Memoranda,* p. 514. Houston was reelected for a six-year term, December 15, 1847 (Wooten, *Comprehensive History,* II, 19).

424, *4.* Houston to Jones, October 18, 1847, *Memoranda,* p. 515; *WSH,* V, 19.

425. *10. WSH,* V, 28–29.

12. Note, 1849, *Memoranda,* p. 254.

36. Ashbel Smith to Jones, July 9, 1850, AJP; Jones to Mrs. Jones, July 7, November 12, 28, 1850, AJP.

426, *6.* Jones to Mrs. Jones, December 23, 1850, February 9, 1851, AJP.

17. August 21, 1851, he thought the State owed him $31,003.02 —for salary as President to the end of his term, loss of exchange on salary as minister to the U.S., salary as acting Vice President, 1841 (all with interest at 8 per cent), $1,000 for property damage at Brazoria, 1836, and $10,000 for negotiating the One Million Loan with M. Bourgeoise d'Orvanne in 1842. He reasoned that the presidential "Office & its emoluments were vested in me for three years by the election of 1844, & although the Republic had a right to dispense with my services, it could not justly, legally or equitably deprive me of my individual & vested rights. This would be 'common law,' common sense & common justice." He added: "I am willing to cancel all claims upon the State of Texas on condition that the amount of depreciation of the money in which I have been paid for services rendered & supplies furnished the late Republic of Texas be made up to me. Or, I am willing said claims should be referred by the Legislature to any court . . . I am further willing to contribute any amount I may receive from the government to Educational Purposes within the State of Texas" (MS Memorandum Book 5, for 1849–1857, Mrs. Beatty Oldham Collection, pp. 9–11).

17. His claim, disallowed by the auditorial board, the public debt committee of the House, and district court in Travis county (Austin), went on appeal to the Supreme Court of Texas. Mr. Justice Royal T. Wheeler handed down the decision in 1855. He held that the people have a right to change their form of government and that an officer deprived of office by such change "has no claim against the new government for salary or indemnity for the loss of office" and that obviously "there can be no such thing as emoluments of office where there is no office . . .; the law of contracts has no application to the case." Jones, he added, "may have a claim on the generosity or sense of justice of the new government. But it can give no legal right which can be enforced against it" (Anson Jones v. Shaw & Swisher, Auditorial Board, 15 Tex. 577–581 [Tex. Sup. Ct., 1855]. See Jones to Mrs. Jones, December 7, 1853, AJP).

24. *Spirit of the Times,* Philadelphia, February 15, 1851, published a letter from Washington, signed Tecumseh: "General Cass is most named for President, in connection with Dr. Anson Jones, ex-President of Texas, or Speaker Cobb of Georgia, for Vice-President." Jones is described as "most emphatically a Northern man with Southern principles of the true union and compromise stamp. I doubt not his name will be presented." Jones thought that would "make a certain old gentleman of our acquaintance *rave* considerably" and guessed he had as good a chance as anyone for the second office (Jones to Mrs. Jones, February 21, 1851, AJP).

35. Jones to Mrs. Jones, September 19, October 27, November 2, 1853, AJP. In Philadelphia he consulted Dr. Birkley and A. F. Porter, who, after he obtained "the secret and all information in connection with it," backed out.

38. Jones to Mrs. Jones, December 7, 1853, AJP. "Had the Legislature properly seconded my views . . . the welfare of Texas would have received, as I think, a new and important impulse in the right direction. . . ." (*Memoranda,* p. 108).

427, 2. He was a petitioner for a charter for Star Lodge No. 22 at Washington in 1851; became Grand Master of Texas in 1852; was representative to the Grand Lodge of the United States in 1853 (Walker, *Odd Fellowship,* pp. 160–175).

5. *Memoranda,* pp. 106–112; MS Memoranda Books No. 9 and No. 10, AJP.

23. See AJP, beginning with Jones to Mrs. Jones, August 13, 1854, for details.

428, 3. *Memoranda,* p. 111; Jones to Mrs. Jones, November 6, 1853, AJP.

428, 33. *Memoranda,* p. 542.

429, 17. *Memoranda,* pp. 544–573, has the full text from *The Ranger,* August 23, 1856. He attributed the two-thirds majority given Democratic candidates partly to the speech.

31. Stout's letter, dated November 17, 1856, is not in *Memoranda* or AJP.

430, 23. Jones to Stout, December 6, 1856, *Memoranda,* pp. 574–580. Note also his "Endorsement on copy retained," *ibid.,* pp. 580–582.

431, 4. Friend, *Sam Houston,* pp. 248–254. In the 1857 election, Houston received 28,678 votes, Runnels 32,552. Six days before election day, Senator Rusk took his own life (*Handbook of Texas,* II, 517).

432, 12. See *Memoranda,* pp. 596–603, for full text.

21. *Memoranda,* pp. 604–605, quotes *The Ranger's* quotation from the *Telegraph.*

31. *Memoranda,* p. 625.

433, 12. Bullock House, built in 1839, was Austin's first and most famous hotel. It became Swisher's Hotel in 1852 and Smith's in 1858 (*Handbook of Texas,* I, 244).

17. Pease, like Jones a New Englander, arrived in Texas in 1835 and "fired a shot in the first skirmish of the Texas Revolution" at Gonzales. He read law, first under Don Carlos Barret at Mina, then under John A. Wharton at Brazoria. He became Wharton's partner in one of the great law firms of the Republic. After service in the House and Senate, he was elected governor in 1853 and 1855 (*Handbook of Texas,* II, 351–352). His Austin home, Woodlawn, where he lived the remainder of his life, was and still is one of the showplaces of the capital (Dorothy Kendall Bracken and Maurine Whorton Redway, *Early Texas Homes,* pp. 60–61).

27. A. W. Terrell, "The City of Austin from 1839 to 1860," *SWHQ,* XIV (1910), 113–128.

32. Jo Everett was a new representative from Rusk County (*Members of the Legislature of the State of Texas, 1846–1939,* p. 29).

39. Jones to Mrs. Jones, October 27, 1857, AJP. A long, cheerful letter.

434, 9. *Southern Intelligencer,* December 9, 1857, commented: "we have never heard of his [Jones] conversing with a single member upon the subject."

20. Sketches of the candidates in *Handbook of Texas, passim.*

35. The letter, signed "F." and dated Washington Co., October 25, appeared in the *State Gazette* November 7, 1857 (*Memoranda,* pp. 625–626).

435, *9.* Jones's comment, October 21, 1857, on an editorial in the *Huntsville Item* favoring Jones and Henderson for the Senatorship (*Memoranda,* p. 625).

13. In caucus, November 7, Jones had five votes, but was dropped from the next ballot. Hemphill received a majority on the twenty-second ballot; Jones's name was not in nomination in the Legislature (*Texas Sentinel,* November 14, 1857; Galveston *News,* November 17, 1857). Jones disapproved more of Hemphill than of Henderson. He wrote November 13: "A South Carolina birth, a negro wife and family, and a life of public and notorious licentiousness and *incest* . . . have outweighed, in the opinion of the present Legislature of the State, all higher considerations, and by the aid of intriguing lawyers, selfish aspirants, and demagogues, been rewarded with a U.S. Senatorship" (*Memoranda,* pp. 640–641). For Hemphill's career, see *Handbook of Texas,* I, 795; Lynch, *Bench and Bar of Texas,* pp. 69–73.

20. Jones to J. G. Tod, November 16, 1857; *Memoranda,* pp. 642–643. He says also, with brave and tattered dignity, "I had determined to leave when I did, before I received the tidings of that casualty. . . . The election of some other than myself I very plainly saw as a foregone conclusion. . . ."

24. Final entries in Plantation Memorandum Book No. 12 (written in a cramped and trembling hand) : "Fri. [October] 23ᵈ Started for Austin, arrived Sun. 25ᵗʰ. Started home Thurs. November 5ᵗʰ arrived Fri. night 6ᵗʰ. 9ᵗʰ Frost & Ice. 10ᵗʰ Frost. Mon: 16ᵗʰ Rain & cold continually. 17ᵗʰ clear & cold, finished hauling fodder. . . . [in a firmer hand]: Fri. [December] 11ᵗʰ Went to town & made Deed to James P. Flewellen for "Barrington." . . . Sat. [12th] Mr Henderson completed the Ginning of my Cotton which Ends the Work on the plantation of Barrington."

436, *5.* "On Saturday last I contracted to sell out a part of my property in this county" (Jones to H. Stuart, November 25, 1857; *Memoranda,* p. 645). He sold 465 acres to James P. Flewellen, November 23, for $8,324.50, and an additional 18½ acres to him for $146.67 on December 17. Interest on deferred payments, ten per cent (Deed Records, Washington County, Book Q, under dates February 15 and February 22, 1858).

7. Samuel and Charles, the older boys, had been sent to stay
with Mrs. Jones's brother. "Your Pa will leave here on
Wednesday night next for Galveston . . . & will not return
until after we move so I wish you & Charley to be home,
by the first. . . ." (Mrs. Jones to Samuel and Charles Jones,
December 20, 1857). Jones arrived at Hockley, December 28, "in time to be left by the cars, which I saw in the
distance. We found the roads in horrid condition; & the
whole country is covered with water. . . . The Stage *bogged*
down, *with the horses,* once, & it took five yoke of oxen to
pull it out. I got a little wet. . . ." (Jones to Mrs. Jones,
December 29, 1857, AJP).

EPILOGUE

437, 7. Jones to Mrs. Jones, January 1, 1858. "I think you may look
for me on Wednesday night next, weather permitting."
He signed the letter "Ever Affectionately Thine, Anson
Jones," with rubric. The house he rented from Richard
Doswell was on Tremont street "close to where Col. [Wil-
liam T.] Austin lives & next door to Mr. Lynn's (the
English consul) . . . the price is $35. per month . . . com-
pletely furnished, from top to bottom, & also the kitchen
. . . So you had *best sell* all the furniture & c" (Jones to
Mrs. Jones, January 3, 1858, AJP).

22. *Memoranda,* p. 9.

28. Card in Tri-Weekly *Telegraph,* January 8, 1858.

438, 15. Mrs. Jones to "My Ever Dear Husband," December 31,
1857, AJP. Endorsed by Mrs. Jones. "My last two letters
to Dr. Jones, neither of which were filed by him as was
his Custom."

28. Jones to Mrs. Jones, Tuesday afternoon, January 5, 1858,
AJP. He added: "I am in tolerable health only. . . . I
need not enlarge."

439, 5. Tri-Weekly *Telegraph,* January 1, 1858.

26. The suicide of Peter W. Grayson and James Collinsworth
while candidates for the presidency in 1838 so shocked
Jones that he wrote a long paragraph in his diary when
he learned of it in New Orleans, July 29 (*Memoranda,*
p. 28). Grayson died at Bean's Station, Tennessee, July 9;
James Collinsworth, chief justice of Texas, drowned himself in Galveston Bay later the same month. George C.
Childress, author of the Texas Declaration of Independ-

ence, disemboweled himself with a Bowie knife in a Galveston boarding house, October 6, 1841. Rusk, who had succeeded Collinsworth as chief justice and had gone with Houston to the United States Senate, took his own life at Nacogdoches, July 29, 1857, thus creating a vacancy Jones yearned to fill (Sketches in *Handbook of Texas,* in WSH, and in Kemp, *The Signers of the Texas Declaration of Independence*).

31. Tri-Weekly *Telegraph* extra, Saturday, January 9, 1858. "SHOCKING AFFAIR! *Suicide of Ex-president Anson Jones.*" Dr. Jones

. . . was found lying across his bed this morning at half past 8 o'clock with a discharged pistol in his hand and his brains blown out. . . . He had apparently been drinking perhaps more freely than was his wont, and was observed to be in low spirits.

A friend of his, Mr. W. D. Smith, observing this, made it in his way to be with him as much as possible while he might remain in the city.

The evening after his arrival [Wednesday] in conversation with Mr. Smith, he made this remark:

"I have been having some very serious thoughts today. My public career, as you are aware, began in this house and I have been thinking that perhaps it might close here." . . . Mr. Smith turned the conversation with some light remark. Subsequently during the last two days, he talked, as Mr. Smith was with him, a good deal of his past life, expressing a satisfaction with his public career, and observing there was nothing in it he could desire to change.

Yesterday he appeared to be almost entirely recovered from his depression, and was out calling during the morning upon several of his friends in this city. He spoke of leaving for home on this morning's train and appeared to be as cheerful as usual. At night Mr. Smith spent an hour or so with him before bed time. During the time he was there Dr. Jones again alluded to the fact that he had begun his public career in that house and he might yet close it there. The remark was received as before, and little thought of it. When he retired, a negro, one of the servants of the house, was, at his request, sent to his room to stay with him. The negro says that at about 12 or 1 o'clock Dr. Jones waked him up and gave him some directions about the room. At about three o'clock he awoke him again and sent him for a glass of spirits. The negro was unable to get any. He then told him to leave the room, as he didn't want him any more. This was the last that was known of him last night.

At about the hour above mentioned, Mr. Smith went to call for him and finding the door locked and getting no response, he had the door broken open, when Dr. Jones was found as above described. No one had heard the report of the pistol in the night, though persons were sleeping in rooms nearby. It is supposed that, brooding over some troubles, in a moment of depression, he lost control of himself and committed the fatal act.

Thus has fallen another great man of Texas by his own hand. We well remember a conversation with Dr. Jones soon after the death of the lamented Rusk upon that sad event. How little did we imagine that the next of the men whom the Republic of Texas had delighted to honor, that would go, would be Dr. Jones . . . Peace to his ashes!

Presumably written by E. H. Cushing, who became editor of the *Telegraph* in 1856. He came to Texas in 1850, after graduating from Dartmouth College (E. B. Cushing, "Edward Hopkins Cushing," *SWHQ,* XXV [1922], 262).

On January 11 the *Telegraph* gave the coroner's verdict adding:

There was found in his room the following memoranda on a slip of paper: "Deposited Jan. 1st. 58 with E. B. Nichols and Co., R. and D. G. Mills, acceptance for $5,192.50. J. P. Flewellin's note for $1,132.50. Deposited in Bank 2 vols. Manuscript History of Texas. Anson Jones." This was all the memoranda found about the deceased.

The *Telegraph* reported the funeral on January 13: The mortal remains of Anson Jones, Ex-President of the Republic of Texas, were buried with appropriate honors yesterday in this city . . .

At 2 o'clock P.M. the Masonic Fraternity assembled in their Lodge Room where the body had been deposited for two days past, and marched in procession, preceded by the Washington Light Guards, to the Court House. Arrived there, a beautiful and touching eulogy was delivered by the Hon. Ashbel Smith . . . Seldom has it been our lot to listen to so good an eulogy, never to a better . . .

After the eulogy the procession was again formed in the following order, under the command of E. F. Gray, Esq., Marshall:

Music

Washington Light Guards with arms reversed

Milam Rifles

Independent Order of Odd Fellows

Masonic Fraternity

Pall Bearers

The Hearse

Pall Bearers

Mayor and City Council

Citizens

The Procession marched to the Masonic Cemetery, where the burial rites of the Odd Fellow and Masonic fraternities were performed, of which bodies he was the first Grand Master of their Lodges in the State. The body having been deposited in the vault, the Washington Light Guard fired three volleys over it.

The inclemency of the weather and the muddy condition of the streets prevented many from attending upon the ceremonies who would otherwise have been present. Considering the discomforts mentioned, the turnout was very large.

The same issue of the *Telegraph* reported that Ashbel Smith, who officiated, had been defeated for the state senatorship in a special election January 11, two days before the funeral.

Receipt of "H. G. Pannell & Co., Wholesale and Retail Dealer in All Kinds of Furniture for coffin and trimmings, $40., burial expenses, $5., case for coffin, $5. Recd. payment by Thornton Thatcher" (AJP).

Later the body was placed in the Episcopal Cemetery, Galveston, under a "Marble slab covered with appropriate inscription" (Galveston *News,* July 6, 1858). Still later it was moved to Glenwood Cemetery, Houston (*Handbook of Texas,* I, 923). The inscription:

In Memory of

ANSON JONES

Last President of the late Republic of Texas; Projector and Consummator of her Annexation to the Confederacy of North American States; First Grand Master and

Implementer of Ancient York Masonry in Texas; The
Revered of Senates and the Light of Cabinets.!

The echo of his words linger in the Councils of his
Country, alone unheard by ears deaf to the claims of
merit, dull to the voice of Honor, and dead to the call of
Justice;
To him the Sand
To Thee the Marble!
Born 20th of Jan. 1798
Migrated October 1833
Departed 9 of Jan. 1858

Let him rest in peace
Safe in the hand of one Disposing Power,
Or in the natal or the mortal hour.

At Austin on January 14, 1858, the same senators who
had declined to vote for Jones in November unanimously
resolved that "the long public service, and in high stations, of the deceased, will justly live in the history of the
Country," agreed to "wear the usual badge of mourning
for thirty days," and adjourned for the day (AJP). A
few days later the senators and representatives created
twenty-three new counties. Section 16 of the Act specifies
the boundaries of "the county of Jones, (named in honor
of Ex-President Anson Jones). The county seat thereof
shall be called Anson." Approved February 1, 1858
(Gammel, *Laws*, IV, 966).

Shortly after Jones's death, Jacob DeCordova's *Texas:
Her Resources and Her Public Men*, published in Philadelphia in 1858, reached Texas. In his sketch of the
"Life of Anson Jones, M.D." (pp. 138–140), written the
year before, DeCordova makes this ironic statement:

This [Jones's contentment in retirement] is a beautiful
lesson to the over ambitious man: let him contemplate it,
and receive from it the benefits it is calculated to impart;
let him so run the race which is before him, that, at its
close, he too may be able to retire, with a mind and heart
at rest with himself and all the world, to the repose and
quietude of a private life, and be content therewith.

The next year, the Galveston *News*, never a partisan of
Jones, published in its *Texas Almanac for 1860*, pp. 149–
157, a detailed and appreciative "Memoir of Ex-Presi-

dent Jones," said to have been written by "his friend, ex-President Burnet" (Thrall, *Pictorial History,* 576–577). The friendship apparently developed after both men left public office.

440, *9.* Dated September 7, 1858. Nearly half a century later Mrs. Jones added in a trembling hand: "Someone will be able to burn this. *I can't.* 1904" (AJP). She was the first president of the Daughters of the Republic of Texas, 1891–1908, and became a life member of the Texas State Historical Association when it was organized in 1897. She never married again, and lived on until December 31, 1907 (death notice, *SWHQ,* XI (1908), 243).

Publication of the book was a vexatious matter; internal evidence indicates that it was not proofread. Mrs. Jones wrote that in the fall of 1858 she placed the manuscript with Ebenezer Allen and Dr. Ashbel Smith, who had served together in the Jones Cabinet. Smith took it to New York to arrange for its publication within three months. D. Appleton and Company estimated the cost of 1,000 500-page books at $500 or $600. Mrs. Jones deposited $1,000 and Smith wrote Appleton to proceed. Delays "under various pretenses" followed. Allen filed suit against Appleton late in 1860, and Appleton shipped the books about the time the suit was filed. "I of course was instructed by Allen not to receive them. I have learned that the boxes or some of them were broken open during the war and books taken by anyone who felt curious enough to read them. Allen died in the summer of 1862. Some three years since I made an unsuccessful effort to settle the matter." Appleton claimed $1,744.50 (Mary Jones to Louis A. Rottenstein, undated, AJP).

The successor firm to D. Appleton and Company has no records of this matter. The managing director of Appleton-Century writes that "many papers were destroyed in a fire in the D. Appleton offices or warehouse around 1900" (Charles Duell to Herbert Gambrell, November 29, 1963). A search of the federal and state court records in Galveston has failed to locate data on the suit (James Noel, U.S. District Judge, to Herbert Gambrell, January 24, 1964). But there is a sequel.

Seventy years the cache of *Memoranda* remained unknown to book dealers and Texana collectors, first in a warehouse, then in the attic of a Galveston home. The few copies that came on the market brought high prices. Then, in 1929, a clerk in a Houston store learned of them and paid $500 for the lot—585 copies. A feature article in a Sunday newspaper brought eighty-eight buyers the next day, and Texana collectors and dealers quickly depleted the stock. The profit on *Memoranda* enabled the man to open his own bookstore and in 1931 he began publishing limited editions of Texana. Logically and gratefully he named his publishing venture the Anson Jones Press (Herbert Fletcher to Herbert Gambrell, October 27, 1963).

Wide dissemination of Jones's *Memoranda,* the publication of Texana items by the Anson Jones Press, and renewed interest in the history of the Republic stimulated by plans for a statewide celebration of the Centennial of Independence in 1936, put the name of the last president of Texas into circulation again after nearly a century of oblivion.

Controversy as to whether a statue of Jones should be erected with public funds in the town and county named for him stimulated greater curiosity about the man and his role in Texas history.

While the first edition of this book was in press, the American Medical Association was celebrating its hundredth birthday by dramatizing the career of a pioneer physician in each of the forty-eight states. Anson Jones was selected to represent the founders of the profession in Texas and his career was presented in a nation-wide radio broadcast on April 26, 1947.

Since 1956 the Texas Medical Association has made an annual Anson Jones Award "for distinguished, accurate, lay, medical reporting." And belatedly the name of Anson Jones has been added to the list of early Texans whose names are being given to public school buildings throughout the state.

Maybe the wistful hope he expressed in his valedictory as President in 1846 is being fulfilled a century later: "the public mind will settle down into proper conclusions. . . . [and I] repose upon the assured belief that history and posterity will do me no wrong."

BIBLIOGRAPHY

UNPUBLISHED SOURCES

The unpublished materials cited most frequently in this study are located in the following depositories, for which the indicated symbols will be used in citations:

TSA, Texas State Archives, Austin.
SJMH, San Jacinto Museum of History, Houston.
UTLA, University of Texas Library Archives, Austin.
RL, Rosenberg Library, Galveston.

PUBLIC AND ORGANIZATIONAL RECORDS

Brazoria County. Probate Minutes. Records of the County Clerk, Angleton.
Comité Medical de la Nlle Orléans. Registre, 1816–1851. Tulane Medical Library, New Orleans.
Comptroller's (Texas) Military Service Records. TSA.
Consular Letters (Texas, 1836–1846). National Archives, Washington.
Consular Letters (La Guayra, Venezuela, 1810–1817).
Domestic Correspondence. TSA.
Executive Record Books. TSA.
Galveston County. Probate and Deed Records. Galveston.
General Land Office (Texas). File 330, Zavalla No. 477.
———. Atascosa County File.
Grand Lodge IOOF. Minutes, Miscellaneous Papers. Philadelphia.
Grand Lodge, AF & AM. Records of the Secretary. Philadelphia.
Harris County. Probate Records. Houston.
Home Letters. Republic of Texas, Department of State Letter Book II (1842–1845, 15; 1842–1847, 16), TSA.
Louisiana First Judicial District Court. Register of Suits Filed. New Orleans.
Masonic Grand Lodge of Texas. Miscellaneous Papers. Waco.
Miscellaneous Papers, Texas Collection. Baylor University, Waco.
Oneida County Medical Society. Minutes. Utica, New York.
Public Debt Papers. TSA.
Spoliation Claims. TSA.
Washington County. Deed Records. Brenham, Texas.

PRIVATE PAPERS

Adriance (John) Papers. UTLA.
Austin Papers. UTLA.
Bollaert (William) Papers. Ayer Collection, Newberry Library, Chicago.
Briscoe (Andrew) Papers. SJMH.
Brown, Frank. "Annals of Travis County"; "Old Washington." UTLA.
Bryan (Moses Austin) Papers. UTLA.
Buchanan (James) Papers. Historical Society of Pennsylvania, Philadelphia.
Burnet (David G.) Papers. RL.
Dienst (Alex) Collection, UTLA.
Ford (John S.) Papers. UTLA.
Franklin (Benjamin C.) Papers. UTLA.
Gray (W. Fairfax) Papers. UTLA.
Huling (Thomas B.) Papers. UTLA.
Johnson (Moses) Papers. UTLA.
Jones, Anson. Diaries. Anson Jones Papers. UTLA.
Jones, Anson. Memorandum Book No. 5 (including Plantation Memorandum Book No. 12). Collection of Mrs. Beatty Oldham, Houston.
Jones, Anson. Memorandum Books. Anson Jones Papers. UTLA.
Jones (Anson) Papers. UTLA.
Kemp (L. W.) Papers. UTLA.
Lockhart (John W.) Papers. RL.
Miller (Washington D.) Papers. TSA.
Mohle, Mrs. A. H., Sketch of Mrs. Anson Jones. UTLA.
Morgan (James) Papers. RL.
Norton (M. P.) Papers. TSA.
Oldham (Mrs. Beatty) Collection. Houston.
Perry (James F.) Papers. UTLA.
Philosophical Society of Texas. Constitution. SJMH.
Roberts (Oran M.) Papers. UTLA.
Ryder (Melvin) Collection. National Writers Club, New York.
Rusk (Thomas J.) Papers. UTLA.
Smith (Ashbel) Papers. UTLA.
Smyth (George W.) Papers. UTLA.
Starr (James H.) Papers. UTLA.
Tod (J. G.) Letterbook. UTLA.
Underwood (Ammon) Papers. Private Possession, Columbia, Texas.
William (Samuel M.) Papers. RL.

THESES

Catterton, Con DeWitt. "Political Campaigns of the Republic of Texas of 1841 and 1844" (1935). UTLA.
Clark, Imogene Wood. "Anson Jones after the Annexation of Texas" (1938). UTLA.

Covington, Nina. "The Presidential Campaigns of the Republic of Texas 1836 and 1838" (1929). UTLA.
Frantz, Joe B. "Newspapers of the Republic of Texas" (1940). UTLA.
Hogan, William Ransom. "Social and Economic History of Texas" (1942). UTLA.
McLean, Sadie R. "The Second Congress of the Republic of Texas" (1929). UTLA.
Rodney, Imogene Burleson. "Early Political Career of Anson Jones" (1939). UTLA.
Smither, Harriet. "The Diplomatic Service of Ashbel Smith to the Republic of Texas" (1922). UTLA.
Yarborough, Yancy Parker. "The Life and Career of Edward Burleson, 1798–1851" (1936). UTLA.

PUBLISHED SOURCES

NEWSPAPERS

Advocate of the People's Rights (Brazoria), 1834.
Bee (New Orleans), 1832–1845.
Benjamin Levy's Prices Current (New Orleans), 1832.
Brazos Courier (Brazoria), 1839–1840.
Bulletin (Matagorda), 1837–1839.
City Gazette (Austin), 1839–1842.
Civilian and Galveston Gazette (Galveston), 1838–1858.
Constitutional Advocate and Texas Public Advertiser (Brazoria), 1832, 1833.
Courier de la Louisiana (New Orleans), 1832.
Daily News (Galveston), 1842–1858.
Emporium (New Orleans), 1832.
Intelligencer (La Grange), 1844–1846.
Louisiana Advertiser (New Orleans), 1832.
Morning News (Dallas), 1933.
Morning Star (Houston), 1839–1846.
National Banner (Houston), 1838.
National Register (Washington), 1844–1846.
National Vindicator (Washington), 1843–1844.
Northern Standard (Clarksville), 1842–1857.
Ranger (Washington), 1849–1851.
Red-Lander (San Augustine), 1841–1847.
State Gazette (Austin), 1850, 1857.
Statesman (Austin), 1944.
Telegraph and Texas Register (Houston), 1835–1858. (Before 1837 at San Felipe de Austin and Columbia).
Texas Republican (Brazoria), 1834–1836.
Texas Sentinel (sometimes *Centinel*, Austin), 1840–1841.

Tri-Weekly Telegraph (issued by *Telegraph and Texas Register*, Houston), 1858.
Weekly Picayune (New Orleans), 1844–1845.

BOOKS AND ARTICLES

The following symbols are used in the Notes to indicate these frequently cited works:

AP, The Austin Papers.
DAB, Dictionary of American Biography.
LP, Papers of Mirabeau Buonaparte Lamar.
SWHQ, Southwestern Historical Quarterly.
WSH, Writings of Sam Houston.

Abstract of the Original Titles of Record in the General Land Office, An. Houston, National Banner Office (Niles & Co., Printers), 1838.
Acheson, Sam. *35,000 Days in Texas: A History of the Dallas News and Its Forebears.* New York, Macmillan Company, 1938.
Adams, Charles Francis (ed.). *Memoirs of John Quincy Adams, Comprising Portions of his Diary from 1795 to 1848.* 12 vols. Philadelphia, J. B. Lippincott and Company, 1874–1877.
Adams, Ephriam Douglass (ed.). *British Diplomatic Correspondence Concerning the Republic of Texas, 1838–1846.* Austin, Texas State Historical Association, 1917. (Reprinted from *Southwestern Historical Quarterly*, XV–XXI).
———. *British Interests and Activities in Texas, 1838–1846.* Baltimore, Johns Hopkins University Press, 1910.
Adams, Randolph G. "Abel P. Upshur," in Samuel Flagg Bemis (ed.), *The American Secretaries of State and Their Diplomacy*, V, 61–124. New York, Alfred A. Knopf, 1928.
Allen, W. Y. "Extracts from the Diary of W. Y. Allen, 1838–1839" (ed. W. S. Red), *SWHQ,* XVII (1913), 43–60.
Appleton's Cyclopaedia of American Biography. 6 vols. New York, D. Appleton and Company, 1894.
Almonte, Juan Nepomuceno. "The Private Journal of Juan Nepomuceno Almonte, February 1–April 16, 1836" (ed. Samuel E. Asbury), *SWHQ,* XLVIII (1944), 10–32.
Anonymous. *History of Texas . . . Houston and Galveston.* See [Houston, City of].
———. *Houston and Galveston in the Years 1837–1838.* See *Houston and Galveston in the Years 1837–1838.*
———. *Philosophical Society of Texas, The.* [Dallas, n.p., 1936].
Austin Papers. See Barker, Eugene C. (ed.).
Bagg, M. M. *Founders of the Oneida County Medical Society.* Utica, New York, Curtis & Childs, 1881.
———. *Pioneers of Utica.* Utica, Curtis & Childs, 1877.

Baker, D. W. C. *A Texas Scrap-Book*. New York, A. S. Barnes and Company, 1875.

Bancroft, Hubert Howe. *History of Mexico*, V (*Works*, XIII). San Francisco, A. L. Bancroft and Company, 1885.

———. *History of the North Mexican States and Texas*, II (*Works*, XVI). San Francisco, A. L. Bancroft and Company, 1889.

———. *History of Texas and the North Mexican States*, II. San Francisco, The History Company, 1890. (Identical with the above except for title and Preface. A special printing sold by subscription in Texas, apparently.)

Barker, Eugene C. "The San Jacinto Campaign," *SWHQ*, IV (1901), 237–345.

———. "The Texan Declaration of Causes for Taking up Arms against Mexico," *SWHQ*, XV (1912), 173–185.

———. "Branch Tanner Archer," *Dictionary of American Biography*, I (1928), 338.

———. "Land Speculation as a Cause of the Texas Revolution," *SWHQ*, X (1906), 76–95.

———. "Notes on Early Texas Newspapers," *SWHQ*, XXI (1917), 127–144.

———. *The Father of Texas*. Indianapolis, Bobbs-Merrill Company, 1935.

———. *The Life of Stephen F. Austin, Founder of Texas, 1793–1836*. Nashville and Dallas, Cokesbury Press, 1925; second edition, Austin, Texas State Historical Association, 1949.

———. *Mexico and Texas, 1821–1835*. Dallas, P. L. Turner Company, 1928.

——— (ed.). *The Austin Papers*. 3 vols. Washington, Government Printing Office, 1924, 1928, Austin, University of Texas Press, 1927.

——— (ed.). *Readings in Texas History*. Dallas, Southwest Press, 1929. (Some printings have the title *Texas History for High Schools and Colleges*.)

Bayard, Ralph. *Lone Star Vanguard: The Catholic Re-Occupation of Texas (1838–1848)*. St. Louis, Vincentian Press, 1945.

Bemis, Samuel Flagg (ed.). *The American Secretaries of State and Their Diplomacy*. 10 vols. New York, Alfred A. Knopf, 1927–1929.

Benson, C. C. "Albert Sidney Johnston," *Dictionary of American Biography*, X, 136.

Biesele, Rudolph L. *The History of the German Settlements in Texas, 1831–1861*. Austin, Von Boeckmann-Jones Company, [c. 1930].

———. "Prince Solm's Trip to Texas, 1844–1845," *SWHQ*, XL (1936), 1–25.

Binkley, William C. *The Texas Revolution*. Baton Rouge, Louisiana State University Press, 1952.

———. "Activities of the Texan Revolutionary Army after San Jacinto," *Journal of Southern History*, VI (1940), 331–346.

———. *The Expansionist Movement in Texas, 1836–1850*. Berkeley, University of California Press, 1925.

————. "The Last Stage of Texan Military Operations against Mexico, 1843," *SWHQ*, XXII (1919), 260–271.

———— (ed.). *Official Correspondence of the Texan Revolution.* 2 vols. New York, D. Appleton-Century Company, 1936.

Biographical Directory of the American Congresses, 1774–1927. Washington, Government Printing Office, 1927.

Biographical Directory of the Texas Conventions and Congresses. [Austin, n.p., 1941].

Bollaert's Texas. See Hollon, W. Eugene (ed.).

Bonnell, George W. *Topographical Description of Texas. To Which is Added an Account of the Indian Tribes.* Austin, Clark, Wing & Brown, 1840. (Although Texas then had no copyright procedures, this book bears this statement: "Copy-right secured in the Republic of Texas and in the United States . . . . Cruger & Bonnell, public printers, Austin.")

Blake, Clagette. *Charles Elliot, R. N., 1801–1875.* London, Cleaver-Hume Press, 1960.

[Bowen, Daniel]. *History of Philadelphia . . . to the Year 1839.* Philadelphia, Daniel Bowen, 1839.

Bracken, Dorothy Kendall, and Maurine Whorton Redway. *Early Texas Homes.* Dallas, Southern Methodist University Press, 1956.

Brooks, Elizabeth. *Prominent Women of Texas.* Akron, Werner Company, 1896.

Brown, John Henry. *History of Texas.* 2 vols. St. Louis, L. E. Daniel, 1892.

————. *Indian Wars and Pioneers of Texas.* Austin, L. E. Daniel, n.d.

————. *The Life and Times of Henry Smith, the First American Governor of Texas.* Dallas, A. D. Aldridge and Company, 1887.

Burleson, Georgiana J. (comp.). *The Life and Writings of Rufus C. Burleson.* Waco, privately printed, 1901.

Callcott, Wilfrid H. *Church and State in Mexico.* Durham, Duke University Press, 1926.

————. *Santa Anna: The Story of an Enigma Who Once Was Mexico.* Norman, University of Oklahoma Press, 1936.

Carroll, B. H., Jr. *Standard History of Houston.* Knoxville, Tennessee, H. W. Crew & Co., 1912.

Carroll, J. M. *A History of Texas Baptists.* Dallas, Baptist Standard Publishing Co., 1923.

Carter, James D. *Masonry in Texas . . . to 1846.* Waco, Grand Lodge of Texas, 1955.

Castañeda, Carlos Eduardo. *The Fight for Freedom (Our Catholic Heritage in Texas, VI).* Austin, Von Boeckmann-Jones Company, 1950.

———— (trans.). "Statistical Report on Texas by Juan N. Almonte," *SWHQ*, XXVIII (1925), 177–222.

———— (ed., trans.). *The Mexican Side of the Texas Revolution.* (By Santa Anna, Caro, Filisola, Urrea, Tornel.) Dallas, P. L. Turner Company, 1928.

Chase, Mary Katherine. *Négociations de la République du Texas en Europe, 1837–1845.* Paris, Librairie Ancienne Honoré Champion, 1932.

Chitwood, Oliver Perry. *John Tyler, Champion of the Old South.* New York, D. Appleton-Century Company, 1939.

Christian, Asa Kyrus. *Mirabeau Buonaparte Lamar.* Austin, Texas State Historical Association, 1922 (reprinted from *SWHQ*, XXIII–XXIV).

Clapp, Theodore. *Autobiographical Sketches and Recollections . . .* Boston, Phillips, Sampson & Company, 1857.

[Coleman, R. M.]. *Houston Displayed, or Who Won the Battle of San Jacinto.* Velasco, n.p., 1837.

Connor, Seymour V. (ed.). *Texas Treasury Papers.* Austin, Texas State Library, 1955.

Copeland, Fayette. *Kendall of the Picayune.* Norman, University of Oklahoma Press, 1943. (Texas Institute of Letters Award book, 1944)

Crane, William Carey. *The Life and Select Literary Remains of Sam Houston.* Philadelphia, J. B. Lippincott and Company, 1884.

Crocket, George L. *Two Centuries in East Texas.* Dallas, Southwest Press, 1932.

Curlee, Abigail. "Robert Mills," *Dictionary of American Biography,* XIII, 13.

Craven, John Nathan. *James Harper Starr: Financier of the Republic of Texas.* Austin, Daughters of the Republic of Texas, 1950.

Dallam, James W. (comp.). *Opinions of the Supreme Court of Texas from 1840 to 1844, inclusive.* St. Louis, Gilbert Book Company, 1883.

Debates of the Texas Convention (William F. Weeks, reporter). Houston, J. W. Cruger, 1846.

DeCordova, Jacob. *Texas: Her Resources and Her Public Men.* Philadelphia, E. Crozet, 1858.

Desilver's Philadelphia Directory and Stranger's Guide. Philadelphia, 1828–1833.

Dewees, William B. *Letters from an Early Settler of Texas.* Louisville, New Albany Tribune Print, 1852.

Dienst, Alex. "The Navy of the Republic of Texas," *SWHQ,* XII–XIII (1908–1910).

Diplomatic Correspondence of the Republic of Texas. See Garrison, George P. (ed.).

Dixon, Sam Houston, and Louis Wiltz Kemp. *The Heroes of San Jacinto.* Houston, Anson Jones Press, 1932.

Dobie, J. Frank. *The Flavor of Texas.* Dallas, Dealey and Lowe, 1936.

———. *Guide to Life and Literature of the Southwest.* Austin, University of Texas Press, 1943; another edition, Dallas, Southern Methodist University Press, 1952.

Duane, Colonel William. *A Visit to Colombia in the Years 1822 & 1823.* Philadelphia, T. H. Palmer, 1826.

Duniway, Clyde Augustus. "Daniel Webster," in Bemis (ed.), *The American Secretaries of State and Their Diplomacy,* V, 30–66. New York, Alfred A. Knopf, 1928.

Eby, Frederick (comp.). *Education in Texas: Source Materials.* Austin, University of Texas Bulletin, 1918.

Edwards, Herbert Rook. "Diplomatic Relations between France and the Republic of Texas," *SWHQ,* XX (1917), 209–241, 341–357.

Ellet, Mrs. E. F. *Court Circles of the Republic.* Hartford, Connecticut, Hartford Publishing Co., 1870.

Erath, George W. *Memoirs.* Austin, Texas State Historical Association, 1923 (reprinted from *SWHQ,* XXVI–XXVII [1922–1924]).

[Fiske]. *A Visit to Texas.* New York, Van Nostrand and Dwight, 1836.

Folsom, Charles J. *Mexico in 1842 . . . Texas and Yucatan . . . the Santa Fe Expedition.* New York, privately printed, 1842.

Foote, Henry Stuart. *Texas and the Texans.* 2 vols. Philadelphia, Thomas Cowperthwait and Company, 1841.

Fortier, Alcee. *Louisiana: Comprising Sketches of Parishes, Towns, Events, Institutions, and Persons.* 2 vols. N.p., Century Historical Association, 1914.

Freund, Max (trans., ed.). *Gustav Dresel's Houston Journal.* Austin, University of Texas Press, 1954.

Friend, Llerena. *Sam Houston, the Great Designer.* Austin, University of Texas Press, 1954. (Summerfield G. Roberts Prize book, 1955)

Fulton, Maurice G. (ed.). *Diary and Letters of Josiah Gregg.* 2 vols. Norman, University of Oklahoma Press, 1944.

Gambrell, Herbert. "Founders of the Society," *Proceedings* of the Philosophical Society of Texas, [I] (1937), 7–17.

——. *Mirabeau Buonaparte Lamar: Troubadour and Crusader.* Dallas, Southwest Press, 1934.

—— and Virginia Gambrell. *A Pictorial History of Texas.* New York, E. P. Dutton and Co., 1960. (Summerfield G. Roberts Award book)

Gammel, H. P. N. (comp.). *Laws of Texas.* Vols. I, II. Austin, Gammel Book Co., 1898.

Garrison, George P. *Westward Extension.* New York, Harper & Brother, 1906.

——. "The First Stage of the Movement for the Annexation of Texas," *American Historical Review,* X (1904), 72–96.

—— (ed.). *Diplomatic Correspondence of the Republic of Texas.* 3 vols. Washington, Government Printing Office, 1908–1911.

Geiser, Samuel Wood. "Audubon in Texas," *Southwest Review,* XVI (1930), 378.

—— (ed.). *Proceedings,* Philosophical Society of Texas, I (1937), 3–21.

Godwin, Parke. *A Biography of William Cullen Bryant.* 2 vols. New York, D. Appleton and Company, 1883.

Goebel, Julius Jr. *The Recognition Policy of the United States.* New York, Columbia University Press, 1915.

Gouge, William M. *The Fiscal History of Texas.* Philadelphia, Lippincott, Grambo and Company, 1852.

Gould, George M. *Jefferson Medical College of Philadelphia, 1826–1904. a History.* New York, Lewis Publishing Company, 1904.

Graham, Philip (ed.). "Mirabeau B. Lamar's First Trip to Texas," *Southwest Review,* XXI (1936), 369–389.

————. *Life and Poems of Mirabeau B. Lamar.* Chapel Hill, University of North Carolina Press, 1938.

Gray, W. Fairfax. *From Virginia to Texas, 1835: Diary of Col. Wm. F. Gray . . . 1835–36 and . . . 1837.* Houston, Gray, Dillay and Company, 1909.

Green, Thomas Jefferson. *Reply to the Speech of Gen. Sam Houston Delivered in the U.S. Senate Aug. 1, 1854.* Washington, privately printed, 1855.

Green, Beulah Gale (ed.). *Narrative of Robert Hancock Hunter.* Austin, privately printed, 1936.

Green, Rena Maverick. *Samuel Maverick, Texan: 1803–1870.* San Antonio, n.p., 1952.

Gregg, Josiah. *Diary and Letters . . .* (ed. Maurice G. Fulton). 2 vols. Norman, University of Oklahoma Press, 1944.

Greer, James Kimmins. "The Committee on the Texas Declaration of Independence," *SWHQ,* XXX, XXXI (1927–1928).

————. (ed.). "Journal of Ammon Underwood," *SWHQ,* XXXII (1928), 124–151.

————. *Colonel Jack Hays, Texas Frontier Leader and California Builder.* New York, E. P. Dutton and Company, 1952.

Gross, Samuel D. *Autobiography.* 2 vols. Philadelphia, G. Barrie, 1887.

Gulick, Charles A. Jr. and others (eds.). *The Papers of Mirabeau Buonaparte Lamar.* 6 vols. Austin, Texas Library and Historical Commission, 1920–1927.

Haggard, J. Villasana. "Epidemic Cholera in Texas, 1833–1834," *SWHQ,* XL (1937), 216–230.

Hamilton, R. G. de R. "James Pinckney Henderson," *Dictionary of American Biography,* VIII, 526.

Hammekin, George L. "Recollections of Stephen F. Austin," *SWHQ,* XX (1917), 369–380.

Hammond, George P. (comp.), *New Spain and the Anglo-American West.* 2 vols. Los Angeles, privately printed, 1932.

Handbook of Texas (Walter Prescott Webb and H. Bailey Carroll, eds.). 2 vols. Austin, Texas State Historical Association, 1952.

Hatcher, Mattie Austin (ed.). *Letters of an Early American Traveller, Mary Austin Holley.* Dallas, Southwest Press, 1933.

Hawkins, Walace. *The Case of John C. Watrous.* Dallas, Southern Methodist University Press, 1950.

Henry, Frederick P. (ed.). *Standard History of the Medical Profession of Philadelphia.* Chicago, Goodspeed, 1897.

Hill, Jim Dan. *The Texas Navy in Forgotten Battles and Shirtsleeve Diplomacy.* Chicago, University of Chicago Press, 1937.

Hogan, William Ransom. *The Texas Republic: A Social and Economic History.* Norman, University of Oklahoma Press, 1946.

————. "The Theatre in the Republic of Texas," *Southwest Review,* XIX (1934), 374–401.

Holland, J. K. "Reminiscences of Austin and Old Washington," *SWHQ,*
I (1897), 92–95.

Holland, James W. *The Jefferson Medical College of Philadelphia from
1825 to 1908.* Philadelphia, (reprint from *Founders' Week Memorial
Volume*), 1908.

Holley, Mary Austin. *Texas: Observations, Historical, Geographical, and
Descriptive, in a series of letters . . . 1831.* Baltimore, Armstrong and
Plaskitt, 1833. (Reprinted, with biographical introduction, in Mattie
Austin Hatcher, *Letters of an Early American Traveller . . . 1935*).

Holley, Mary Austin. *Texas.* Lexington, J. Clarke and Company, 1836.

Hollon, W. Eugene, and Ruth Lapham (eds.). *William Bollaert's Texas.*
Norman, University of Oklahoma Press, 1956.

Houston, Andrew Jackson. *Texas Independence.* Houston, Anson Jones
Press, 1938.

Houston and Galveston in the Years 1837–1838. (Inedited reprint of eight
anonymous articles in *Hesperian or Western Monthly,* Columbus, Ohio,
1838). Houston, Union National Bank, 1926. Text of the complete
series of twenty-five articles, published serially in *Hesperion* (beginning September, 1838, and concluding April, 1839), carefully edited
by Andrew Forest Muir, is in *Texas in 1837* (Austin, University of
Texas Press, 1958).

[Houston, City of]. *History of Texas . . . Houston and Galveston.* Chicago,
Lewis Publishing Company, 1895.

[Houston, Sam]. *The Life of Sam Houston: The Only Authentic Memoir
of Him Ever Published.* New York, J. C. Derby, 1855.

Houstoun, Mrs. [M. C. F.]. *Texas and the Gulf of Mexico; or Yachting in
the New World.* 2 vols. London, John Murray, 1844.

Howard, William E. *The Romance of Texas Money.* Dallas, privately
printed, 1946.

Hunter, Robert Hancock. *Narrative of Robert Hancock Hunter.* Austin,
privately printed, 1936.

James, Marquis. *The Raven: A Biography of Sam Houston.* Indianapolis,
Bobbs Merrill Company, 1929. (Pulitzer Prize biography).

Jameson, J. Franklin (ed.). *Correspondence of John C. Calhoun.* Washington, Government Printing Office, 1900.

———. *History of Historical Writing in America.* New York, James F.
Carr, 1961.

Jefferson, Thomas. *Writings of Thomas Jefferson,* XV. Washington, Thomas
Jefferson Memorial Association, 1903–1904.

Johnson, Allen, and others (eds.). *Dictionary of American Biography.* 20
vols. New York, Charles Scribner's Sons, 1928–1936.

Johnson, Frank W. *A History of Texas and Texans* (edited and extended
by Eugene C. Barker and E. W. Winkler). 5 vols. Chicago, American
Historical Society, 1914.

Johnston, William Preston. *The Life of General Albert Sidney Johnston.*
New York, D. Appleton and Company, 1878.

Jones, Anson. *Memoranda and Official Correspondence Relating to the Republic of Texas, Its History and Annexation, Including a Brief Autobiography of the Author.* New York, D. Appleton and Company, 1859.

——. *Letters Relating to the History of Annexation.* Galveston, Civilian Office, 1848.

——. The same, with Appendix. Philadelphia, n.p., 1852.

Kemp, Louis Wiltz. *The Signers of the Texas Declaration of Independence.* Houston, Anson Jones Press, 1944.

——. "The Capitol (?) at Columbia," *SWHQ,* XLVIII (1944), 3–9.

Kendall, George Wilkins. *Narrative of the Texan Santa Fé Expedition.* 2 vols. New York, Harper & Brothers, 1844.

Kennedy, William. *Texas: The Rise, Progress and Prospects of the Republic of Texas.* 2 vols. London, R. Hastings, 1841.

Kidd, J. C. *History of Holland Lodge.* Houston, n.p., 1920.

Kuykendall, J. H. "Reminiscences of Early Texans," *SWHQ,* VI, VII (1903–1904).

Labadie, N. D. "Narrative of the Anahuac, or Opening Campaign of the Texas Revolution" and "San Jacinto Campaign," *Texas Almanac for 1859,* pp. 30–40, 40–64.

Lamar, Mirabeau Buonaparte, Papers. See Gulick, Charles A., Jr. (ed.).

Leake, Chauncey D. (ed.). *Yellow Fever in Galveston . . . 1839. by Ashbel Smith.* Austin, University of Texas Press, 1951.

Leclerc, Frederic. *Texas and Its Revolution* (James L. Shepherd III, trans.). Houston, Anson Jones Press, 1950.

Lord, Walter. *A Time to Stand.* New York, Harper & Brothers, 1961. (Summerfield G. Roberts Award, 1962)

Linn, John J. *Reminiscences of Fifty Years in Texas.* New York, D. and J. Sadlier and Company, 1883.

Lippincott, H. M. *Early Philadelphia: Its People, Life and Progress.* Philadelphia, J. B. Lippincott Company, 1917.

Lockhart, John Washington. *Sixty Years on the Brazos.* (See Wallis and Hill [eds.]).

Looscan, Mrs. Adele B. "Sketch of the Life of Oliver Jones and his wife Rebecca Jones," *SWHQ,* X (1906), 172–180.

——. "Genealogical and Historical Register of the First General Officers of the Daughters of the Republic of Texas Elected in 1891," *SWHQ,* V (1902), 347–351.

Lubbock, Francis R. *Six Decades in Texas.* Austin, B. C. Jones and Company, 1900.

Lynch, James D. *Bench and Bar of Texas.* St. Louis, Nixon-Jones Printing Company, 1885.

Maillard, N. Doran. *The History of the Republic of Texas.* London, Smith, Elder and Company, 1842.

Marshall, Thomas Maitland. "Diplomatic Relations of Texas and the United States, 1839–1843," *SWQH,* XV (1912), 277–293.

516 BIBLIOGRAPHY

Mason, J. M. "Early Medical Education in the Far South," *Annals of Medical History,* IV (1932), 64–79.

[Masons]. *The Centennial of Harmony Lodge No. 52, A.F. & A.M. of Pennsylvania.* Philadelphia, n.p., 1892.

McCalla, W. L. *Adventures in Texas.* Philadelphia, privately printed, 1841.

McCormac, Eugene Irving. *James K. Polk: a Political Biography.* Berkeley, University of California Press, 1922.

McKitrick, Reuben. *The Public Land System of Texas, 1823–1910.* Madison, Bulletin (No. 905) of the University of Wisconsin, 1918.

Members of the Legislature of the State of Texas, 1846–1939. Austin, n.p., 1939.

Michel's New Orleans Annual and Commercial Register. New Orleans, 1833.

Middleton, Annie. "Donelson's Mission to Texas in Behalf of Annexation," *SWHQ,* XXIV (1921), 279–291.

———. "The Texas Convention of 1845," *SWHQ,* XXV (1921), 26–62.

Miller, E. T. *Financial History of Texas.* Austin, University of Texas Bulletin, 1916.

Montgomery, Corinne. "The Presidents of Texas," *United States Magazine and Democratic Review,* XVI (1845), 282–291.

———. *Texas and Her Presidents.* New York, E. Winchester, New World Press, 1845.

[Moore, Ike (ed.)]. *Texas Newspapers, 1813–1939.* Houston, San Jacinto Museum of History Association, 1941.

Morgan, William M. *Trinity Protestant Episcopal Church, Galveston, Texas, 1841–1953.* Houston and Galveston, Anson Jones Press, 1954.

Morrell, Z. N. *Flowers and Fruits from the Wilderness.* Boston, Gould and Lincoln, 1872.

Muir, Andrew Forest. "Railroad Enterprise in Texas, 1836–1841," *SWHQ,* XLVII (1944), 339–345.

——— (ed.). *Texas in 1837.* Austin, University of Texas Press, 1958. (See *Houston and Galveston in the Years 1837–1838.*)

Murphy, DuBose. *A Short History of the Protestant Episcopal Church in Texas.* Dallas, Turner Company, 1935.

Nance, Joseph Milton (ed.). "A Letter Book of Joseph Eve, United States Chargé d'Affaires to Texas," *SWHQ,* XLIII–XLIV (1939–1941).

———. *After San Jacinto: The Texas-Mexican Frontier, 1836–1841.* Austin, University of Texas Press, 1963.

Neu, C. T. "The Case of the Brig *Pocket,*" *SWHQ,* XII (1909), 276–295.

———. "The Annexation of Texas," in *New Spain and the Anglo-American West,* II, 71–102. Los Angeles, privately printed, 1932.

———. *New Spain and the Anglo-American West,* Vol. II. Los Angeles, privately printed, 1932.

New Orleans Directory. New Orleans, n.p., 1832.

Newsom, W. L. "Postal System of the Republic of Texas," *SWHQ,* XX (1916), 103–131.

[New York.]. *Laws of New York.* Albany, State Printer, 1806.

Nixon, Pat Ireland. *The Medical Story of Early Texas, 1819–1853.* San Antonio, Mollie Bennett Lupe Memorial Fund, 1947.

———. *A History of the Texas Medical Association, 1853–1953.* Austin, University of Texas Press, 1953.

Norwood, William F. *Medical Education in the United States before the Civil War.* Philadelphia, University of Pennsylvania Press, 1944.

[Odd Fellows]. *Journal of the Proceedings of the Right Worthy Grand Lodge of the Independent Order of Odd Fellows in the State of Pennsylvania, commencing Dec. 1823 and ending March 1847.* Philadelphia, n.p., 1847.

Official Correspondence. See Binkley, William C. (ed.). *Official Correspondence of the Texan Revolution.*

Parker, A. A. *Trip to the West and Texas.* Concord, William White, 1836.

Parmenter, Mary Fisher, and others. *The Life of George Fisher.* Jacksonville, Florida, H. and W. B. Drew Company, 1959.

Peareson, P. E. "Reminiscences of Judge Edwin Waller," *SWHQ,* IV (1900), 33–53.

Philadelphia Directory and Register. Philadelphia, McCarty and Davis, 1822, 1823.

Philadelphia Index or Directory. Philadelphia, 1823.

Philadelphia, World's Medical Center. n.p., n.d.

Philosophical Society of Texas, The. [Dallas, n.p., 1936].

Philosophical Society of Texas, *Proceedings* (S. W. Geiser [ed.]), I (1937), 3–21.

Potts, Charles Shirley. *Railroad Transportation in Texas.* Austin, University of Texas Bulletin, 1909.

Quaife, Milo Milton (ed.). *The Diary of James K. Polk.* 4 vols. Chicago, A. C. McClurg and Company, 1910.

Rather, Ethel Zivley. "Recognition of the Republic of Texas by the United States," *SWHQ,* XIII (1910), 155–256.

Red, George Plunckett. *The Medicine Man in Texas.* Houston, Standard Printing and Lithographing Company, 1930.

Red, William S. (ed.). "Allen's Reminiscences of Texas, 1838–1842," *SWHQ,* XVII (1914), 287–304.

Reed, S. G. *A History of the Texas Railroads and of Transportation.* Houston, St. Clair Publishing Company, 1941.

Reeves, Jesse S. *American Diplomacy under Tyler and Polk.* Baltimore, Johns Hopkins University Press, 1907.

Richardson, James D. (comp.). *Messages and Papers of the Presidents,* IV. Washington, Government Printing Office, 1896.

Richardson, Rupert Norval. "Framing the Constitution of the Republic of Texas," *SWHQ,* XXXI (1928), 191–220.

———. *Texas the Lone Star State.* New York, Prentice-Hall, 1943. Revised edition, 1958.

Rives, George L. *The United States and Mexico, 1821–1848.* 2 vols. New York, Charles Scribner's Sons, 1913.

Robertson, William Spencer. *Rise of the Spanish American Republics as Told in the Lives of Their Liberators.* New York, D. Appleton and Company, 1918.

Rowe, Edna. "The Disturbances at Anahuac in 1832," *SWHQ,* VI (1903), 265–299.

Ruthven, A. S. *Proceedings of the Grand Lodge of Texas, Ancient, Free and Accepted Masons, 1837–1855.* 2 vols. Galveston, Richardson and Company, 1857–1860.

Scharf, J. Thomas, and Thompson Westcott. *History of Philadelphia.* 3 vols. Philadelphia, L. H. Everts & Co., 1884.

Schmitz, Joseph William. *Texan Statecraft, 1836–1845.* San Antonio, Naylor Company, 1941.

———. *Thus They Lived.* San Antonio, Naylor Company, 1935.

[Sherman, Sidney]. *Defense of Gen. Sidney Sherman against the charges made by Gen. Sam Houston in his speech delivered in the United States Senate, February 28th, 1859.* Galveston, News Book and Job Office, 1859. (Reprinted by Smallwood, Dealey & Baker, Houston, 1885, for the Sherman heirs after Crane's *Life and Select Literary Remains of Sam Houston* appeared in 1884.)

Siegel, Stanley. *A Political History of the Texas Republic, 1836–1845.* Austin, University of Texas Press, 1956.

Sioussat, St. George L. "John C. Calhoun," in Bemis (ed.), *The American Secretaries of State,* V. New York, Alfred A. Knopf, 1928.

Smith, Ashbel. *Yellow Fever in Galveston, Republic of Texas, 1839* (biographical introduction of Chauncey D. Leake). Austin, University of Texas Press, 1951.

———. *Reminiscences of the Texas Republic.* Galveston, Historical Society of Galveston, 1876.

[Smith, Henry]. "Reminiscences of Henry Smith," *SWHQ,* XIV (1910), 24–73.

Smith, Justin H. *The Annexation of Texas* (corrected edition). New York, Barnes and Noble, 1941.

———. *The War with Mexico.* 2 vols. New York, Macmillan Company, 1919.

Smith, Ruby Cumby. "James W. Fannin Jr. in the Texas Revolution," *SWHQ,* XXIII (1919–1920), 79, 284.

Smither, Harriet. "English Abolitionism and the Annexation of Texas," *SWHQ,* XXXII (1929), 193–205.

Smither, Harriet (ed.). *Journals of the Fourth Congress of the Republic of Texas.* 3 vols. Austin, Texas Library and Historical Commission, 1929.

———. *Journals of the Sixth Congress of the Republic of Texas.* 3 vols. Austin, Texas Library and Historical Commission, 1940–1945.

Smithwick, Noah. *The Evolution of a State, or Recollections of Old Texas Days.* Austin, Gammel Book Company, 1900.

Solms-Braunfels, Carl. *Texas, 1844–1845.* Houston, Anson Jones Press, 1936.

Sons of the Republic of Texas. *Yearbook 1962.* Houston, privately printed, 1962.

Steen, Ralph W. "Analysis of the Work of the General Council of Texas, 1835–1836," *SWHQ*, XL, XLI, XLII (1937–1939).

[Stiff, Edward]. *A New History of Texas.* Cincinnati, George Conclin, 1847.

Streeter, Thomas W. *Bibliography of Texas, 1795–1845, Part I, Texas Imprints,* 2 vols; *Part II, Mexican Imprints; Part III, United States and European Imprints,* 2 vols. Cambridge, Harvard University Press, 1955, 1956, 1960. (Streeter's comments on the listings contain invaluable sidelights on the history of the period and many of the personalities.)

Strobel, Abner J. *The Old Plantations and Their Owners of Brazoria County, Texas.* Houston, Union National Bank, 1930.

Terrell, Alex. W. "The City of Austin from 1839 to 1865," *SWHQ*, XIV (1910), 113–128.

Texas Almanac for 1858; for 1859; for 1860. Galveston, W. and D. Richardson, [1857, 1858, 1859].

Texas in 1837 (ed. Andrew Forest Muir). Austin, University of Texas Press, 1958.

Texas Indian Papers (ed. Dorman H. Winfrey), I (1825–1843), II (1843–1845). Austin, Texas State Library, 1959, 1960.

Texas Newspapers (ed. Ike Moore). Houston, San Jacinto Museum of History Association, 1941.

Texas, Republic of. *Journals* of the House of Representatives and the Senate, First through Ninth Congresses.

———. *Opinions of the Supreme Court from 1840 to 1844 inclusive* (comp. James W. Dallam). St. Louis, Gilbert Book Company, 1883.

Texas, State of. Weeks, William F. (reporter). *Debates of the Texas Convention.* Houston, J. W. Cruger, 1846.

Texas, Supreme Court. 15 *Tex.,* 577–581, 1855.

Texas Treasury Papers (ed. Seymour V. Connor), I (1836–1840). Austin, Texas State Library, 1955.

Thomas, A. O. "Money of the Republic of Texas," *The Numismatist,* LVIII, 775–800.

Thrall, Homer S. *A Pictorial History of Texas.* St. Louis, N. D. Thompson and Company, 1879.

Tinkle, Lon. *13 Days to Glory.* New York, McGraw-Hill Book Company, 1958. (Summerfield G. Roberts and Carr P. Collins awards, 1959.)

Tolbert, Frank X. *The Day of San Jacinto.* New York, McGraw-Hill Book Company, 1959. (Summerfield G. Roberts Award, 1960.)

Tyler, Lyon G. *Letters and Times of the Tylers.* 3 vols. Richmond, Whittet and Shepperson, 1884–1896.

Wallace, Ernest, and David Vigness (eds.). *Documents of Texas History.* Austin, Steck Company, 1963 (an earlier edition, covering the years 1528–1846, published by Texas Technological College Library, Lubbock, 1960).

United States Congress. *H.R. Executive Document 35,* 24th Congress, 2d Session; *H.R. Executive Document 2,* 25th Congress, 3d Session.

Walker, W. H. *Odd Fellowship in America and in Texas.* Dallas, privately published, 1911.

Wallis, Jonnie L., and L. L. Hill (eds.). *Sixty Years on the Brazos: The Life and Letters of Dr. John Washington Lockhart, 1824–1900.* Los Angeles, privately published, 1930.

Webb, Walter Prescott. "William H. Wharton," *Dictionary of American Biography,* XX, 35.

———. "The Last Treaty of the Republic of Texas," *SWHQ,* XXV (1922), 151–173.

Webb, Walter Prescott, and H. Bailey Carroll (eds.). *The Handbook of Texas.* 2 vols. Austin, Texas State Historical Association, 1952.

Weeks, William F. (reporter). *Debates of the Texas Convention.* Houston, J. W. Cruger, 1846.

West, Elizabeth Howard. "Southern Opposition to the Annexation of Texas," *SWHQ,* XVIII (1914), 74–82.

Whiteley, Emily Stone. "Christopher Hughes," *Dictionary of American Biography,* IX, 346.

Williams, Amelia W. "A Critical Study of the Siege of the Alamo and the Personnel of Its Defenders," *SWHQ,* XXXVI–XXXVII (1932–1934).

Williams, Amelia W., and Eugene C. Barker (eds.). *The Writings of Sam Houston.* 8 vols. Austin, University of Texas Press, 1938–1943.

Wiltse, Charles M. *John C. Calhoun, Sectionalist, 1840–1850.* Indianapolis, Bobbs-Merrill Company, 1951.

Winfrey, Dorman H. (ed.). *Texas Indian Papers,* I, II. Austin, Texas State Library, 1959–1960.

Winkler, Ernest W. "The Seat of Government of Texas," *SWHQ,* X (1906), 167–171.

———. "The Bexar and Dawson Prisoners," *SWHQ,* XIII (1910), 294.

——— (ed.). *Secret Journals of the Senate, Republic of Texas, 1836–1845.* Austin, Texas Library and Historical Commission, 1911.

Wise, Henry A. *Seven Decades of the Union.* Philadelphia, J. B. Lippincott and Company, 1872.

Wooten, Dudley G. (ed.). *A Comprehensive History of Texas.* 2 vols. Dallas, William G. Scarff, 1898.

Wooten, Mattie Lloyd (ed.). *Women Tell the Story of the Southwest.* San Antonio, Naylor Company, 1940.

Worley, J. L. "The Diplomatic Relations of England and the Republic of Texas," *SWHQ,* IX (1905), 1–40.

Wortham, Louis J. *A History of Texas.* 5 vols. Fort Worth, Wortham-Molyneaux Company, 1924.

WSH. See Williams, Amelia W., and Eugene C. Barker. *The Writings of Sam Houston.*

Yoakum, Henderson. *History of Texas.* 2 vols. New York, Redfield, 1855. (Reprinted, without notes, in Wooten, *Comprehensive History,* I, 1898).

ACKNOWLEDGMENTS

In the processes of preparing this book friends have helped me above and beyond the line of duty, especially these: Mrs. Clayton S. Scott, who gave me first access to the Anson Jones Papers; Miss Winnie Allen, who had them photostated for my use; Samuel Asbury; Eugene C. Barker; A. P. Brogan; T. Wood Clarke, M.D.; James A. Creighton; Frederic Duncalf; W. Neil Franklin; Louis Wiltz Kemp; Samuel Wood Geiser; Milton R. Gutsch; William Ransom Hogan; John H. McGinnis; Thomas P. Martin; J. Lloyd Mecham; Pat Ireland Nixon, M.D.; C. P. Patterson; Thad W. Riker; Henry Nash Smith; Harriet Smither; Lon Tinkle; Laura Underwood; and Walter Prescott Webb. Virginia Gambrell's critical judgment and collaboration amounted to joint authorship. To them and to the staff members of the historical depositories cited in the Bibliography, I am grateful.

The Notes, which are an addition to this new edition, and the Bibliography, which has been basically revised, cite significant works published since 1947, as well as those that appeared earlier. The Bibliography is, in effect, a selective checklist of published materials dealing with Texas between the years 1821 and 1858; it may be useful to collectors and librarians.

As in the preparation of the earlier edition, the staff members of the Dallas Historical Society in the Hall of State, the Eugene C. Barker Texas History Center of the University of Texas, the Fondren Library of Southern Methodist University, and the Archives of the Texas State Library have been most helpful.

HERBERT GAMBRELL

INDEX